THE DOMINION OF WAR

Mexico City, September 14, 1847. The entrance of the U.S. Army under Winfield Scott.

THE
DOMINION
OF WAR

Empire and Conflict in America, 1500–2000

Fred Anderson
and
Andrew Cayton

Atlantic Books
London

For Samuel DeJohn Anderson
and for Elizabeth Renanne Cayton and
Hannah Kupiec Cayton, with love.

First published in the United States of America by Viking,
A member of the Penguin Group (USA) Inc.

Published in Great Britain in hardback by Atlantic Books, an imprint of Grove Atlantic Limited.

Grateful acknowledgement is made to the following for permission to reproduce photographs:

p. ii: Lithograph by Adolphe Jean-Baptiste Bayot, 1851, after a painting by Carl Nebel, courtesy of the Special Collections Division, University of Texas at Arlington Libraries, Arlington, Texas; *pp. 14, 19, 20*: courtesy of the Robert Dechert Collection, Annenberg Rare Book and Manuscript Library, University of Pennsylvania, Philadelphia; *p. 79*: courtesy of the Historical Society of Pennsylvania (HSP), Philadelphia; *p. 105*: courtesy of the Washington/Custis/Lee Collection, Washington and Lee University, Lexington, Virginia; *p. 108*: courtesy of the Mount Vernon Ladies' Association; *p. 161*: courtesy of the Maryland Commission on Artistic Property of the Maryland Archives, MSA SC 4680-10-0079; *p. 214* Portrait of Andrew Jackson courtesy of the Addison Gallery of American Art, gift of The Alfred and Margaret Caspary Foundation in Memory of Thomas Cochran; Portrait of Rachel Jackson courtesy of The Hermitage: Home of President Andrew Jackson, Nashville, TN; *pp. 235, 296, 297, 341*: courtesy of the Library of Congress; *p. 253*: courtesy of the Georgetown University Art Collection; *p. 278*: courtesy of the Ohio Historical Society; *pp. 319, 320*: courtesy of The General Douglas MacArthur Foundation; *p. 390*: courtesy of the U.S. Army Signal Corps; *p. 404*: courtesy of the Harry S. Truman Library; *p. 413*: Photographer, SrA Rodney Kerns, courtesy of the Defense Visual information Center.

Maps drawn by Mark Stein Studios: pp. 11, 69, 89, 121, 165, 230, 258, 277, 299, 331, 388, 402

1 3 5 7 9 8 6 4 2

A CIP catalogue record for this book is available from the British Library.

1 903809 73 8

Printed in Great Britain by MPG Books Ltd, Bodmin, Cornwall

Atlantic Books
An imprint of Grove Atlantic Ltd
Ormond House
26–27 Boswell Street
London
WC1N 3JZ

CONTENTS

LIST OF ILLUSTRATIONS

The Vietnam War Memorial at sunrise

Brian G. Green/National Geographic, ngs0_7802/Getty Images

Introduction

The Mall in Washington, D.C., is a good deal less inviting in January than in April, when the cherry trees around the Tidal Basin burst into bloom and tourists loiter in the sun. But because the ways in which the Mall and its monuments give meaning to the events of American history are clearest in the winter—and because the story we have to tell is in many ways a wintry tale—it may not be amiss for us to begin on the Mall with the trees bare and the skies gray, walking down the path that leads from the Lincoln Memorial to the Vietnam War Memorial. In spring, the transition between the two would be muted by the trees and plantings of Constitution Gardens. In winter, the contrast is stark and unmistakable.

Behind us, the majesty of the Lincoln Memorial leaves no doubt about the importance of the sixteenth president and the Union that he, more than anyone else, preserved. The steps that visitors must climb to enter the monument prepare them for what they find within: an immense, melancholy statue of the Great Emancipator, bracketed by the Gettysburg Address and the Second Inaugural Address—majestic phrases that explain the meaning of the greatest blood sacrifice in American history. But the Vietnam Memorial makes no such unmistakable statement. We do not climb to meet this monument or even look up; we merely walk along a gradually descending path beside a polished granite wall. The only words inscribed on the stone are the names of 58,000 American women and men who gave their lives between 1959 and 1975, in the longest war the United States has ever fought.

As we walk, the black wall seems to rise beside us, as if thrust from the earth by the columns of names that lengthen on its face. The roll of the dead begins almost imperceptibly at ground level, then rises inexorably—waist height, shoulder height, head height, higher—until at the monument's center the names of the dead hang over us with an almost unbearable weight of sadness. Here we are left to draw our own conclusions by a monument that does not presume to instruct us on the meaning of the deaths to which it bears witness. And here, at the turning of the path where the twin walls join, we pause, as so many do, to look back.

Because it is winter, the colonnade of Lincoln's Greek temple looms white through the screen of trunks and bare branches, and it is suddenly clear that the narrowing V of the wall has been sited precisely to direct our gaze upward to the Memorial and to the hillside crosses of Arlington National Cemetery beyond. Turning again and looking up the path, it also becomes apparent that the oblique angle at which the walls join is not merely the product of Maya Lin's superb aesthetic sense: the black arrow of the wall ahead points directly toward the marble shaft of the Washington Monument.

Here, surrounded by wars laid up in stone, the questions press in on us. Why this location, half in seclusion apart from the center of the Mall? Why this orientation, directing our attention toward the two great monuments that define the Mall's long axis? Why, for that matter, should the Korean War Memorial—less powerful emotionally but still evocative in its depiction of a rifle squad moving out, laden with combat gear—have been located in the counterpart space on the opposite flank of the Lincoln Memorial? And why, finally, do the facing halves of the new World War II monument bestride the Mall at the head of the Reflecting Pool, claiming a place as central as Washington's obelisk and Lincoln's Doric shrine?

Silent though their stones may be, the monuments on the Mall speak unmistakably to Americans about the relationships between, and the relative importance of, five wars—the Revolution, the Civil War, the Korean Conflict, the Vietnam War, and World War II. Even stronger implicit messages can be discerned in the *absence* of monuments commemorating other conflicts: the War of 1812, the Mexican-American War, the Spanish-American War, World War I, numerous military interventions in the Caribbean and beyond, and three dozen or more Indian wars by which the citizens of the Republic appropriated lands that native peoples had called home for a thousand generations. All these messages are rooted in a commonly accepted "grand narrative" of American history, a story so familiar that the meanings of the memorials can be deciphered by almost any citizen who has had the benefit of a public school education.[1]

As everyone knows, wars have often punctuated the history of the United States and not infrequently have produced generals who become presidents. Nor have generals like Washington, Jackson, Grant, and Eisenhower been the only veterans to whom Americans have looked for political leadership. Even men who rose to only modest rank—Captain Harry Truman, Lieutenant John Kennedy, Lieutenant Commander Richard Nixon, and Lieutenant Jimmy Carter, for example—drew attention to their service records when they were candidates for the nation's highest office. Previous military service, of course, has never been a prerequisite for election; but whether the man is Thomas Jefferson or William Jefferson Clinton, presidential candidates who have never worn their nation's uniform have always been subject to the charge that they are unfit to act as commander in chief of the armed forces.

Of course a concentration on past wars is not enough to make Washington's memorials distinctive, any more than the tendency of successful generals to become political leaders is uniquely American. Every capital city in Europe and the Americas commemorates the glories and sacrifices of military conflict, and one needs to look no further than Cromwell, Napoleon, and de Gaulle to find notable examples of generals who have gone on to govern nations. But while the martial cast of their nation's capital is commonplace, Americans' reactions to it are not; nor has their willingness to elect former generals to the presidency made them immune to ambivalence about their wars, especially those wars that expanded the geographical domain of the United States. The rhetoric that justified the founding of the United States made inescapable connections between empire and tyranny. Perhaps for that reason, American historians have generally approached the imperial dimension of the nation's history obliquely, treating occurrences of jingoism like the war fevers of 1812, 1846, and 1898 as unfortunate exceptions to the antimilitarist rule of republicanism. No American Napoleon conquered this continent, no jackbooted legions subdued it; the United States grew by settlement. Apart from the regrettable Indian wars, the great movement west consisted of the essentially benign inclusion of ever-larger territorial realms into democracy's dominion, freedom's sphere. Or so Americans, for the most part, believe.

With great justification, Americans also think of the United States as a refuge from tyranny, where those willing to bear the burdens of work and the obligations of citizenship can share equally in the blessings of liberty. Since Americans believe themselves to be a peace-loving people, it is an article of faith that their wars have been forced upon them by those who would destroy their freedom. Thus since the autumn of 2001 Americans have remembered New York on September 11 as they have remembered Pearl Harbor since December 7, 1941—and as earlier generations remembered the explosion of the *Maine,* the bombardment of Fort Sumter, and the first shot fired at Lexington—as a moment in which an enemy of liberty showed his barbarous hand and thereby justified the response of a free people, terrible in its wrath. So Americans tend to believe that by winning wars, they make the world a better, safer, freer place. George Washington himself articulated this faith just one week before he took command of the Continental Army. On June 26, 1775, en route from Philadelphia to the army's headquarters in Cambridge, Massachusetts, he paused to reassure the Provincial Congress of New York that in taking up arms against the British empire, Americans were acting defensively, within limits and with a clear purpose in mind. "When we assumed the soldier," he said, "we did not lay aside the Citizen, & we shall most sincerely rejoice with you in that happy Hour, when the Establishment of American Liberty on the most firm, & solid Foundations, shall enable us to return to our private Stations in the bosom of a free, peaceful & happy Country."[2] Americans do not fight, therefore, except to fulfill a solemn obligation to defend their own—or others'—liberty.

This is the argument that the monuments on the Mall sustain in marble and granite and bronze. This why they make three great wars for freedom—the Revolution, the Civil War, and World War II—the central, defining moments of American history. And this is why there are no more important words on the Mall than those inscribed inside the Lincoln Memorial. The Gettysburg Address, composed in November 1863 to give meaning to the torrents of blood spilled in and around a small Pennsylvania town in early July, also gave meaning to the ordeal of the Union. There, in fewer than three hundred words, Abraham Lincoln made the Civil War something much nobler than a struggle by one part of a riven nation to bend another part to its will. It was a test of the capacity of human beings for self-government, the supreme trial of a revolutionary United States "conceived in Liberty, and dedicated to the proposition that all men are created equal." And at the heart of America's agonies, Lincoln explained sixteen months later in his Second Inaugural Address, was the need to expiate the great sin of slavery, to cleanse the Republic of the stain it had borne since birth.

It is impossible to imagine a more powerful conception of the nation's history than this. Because Americans so clearly identify liberty and equality as the core values of the Republic, they necessarily make the inception of those values in the Revolution, the extension of liberty's promise to all Americans, and the defense of liberty beyond America's borders central elements in their collective story. It is not, therefore, the size of the sacrifice but the transcendence of the ideals that motivated it to which the Washington, Lincoln, and World War II memorials speak. Counting the cost in human lives would only blur our sense of the significance of the great wars for freedom that they commemorate.

If Korea and Vietnam make it only to the margins of the Mall, it is hardly surprising that the War of 1812, the Mexican-American War, the Spanish-American War, and the many wars against North American Indians are altogether missing from it. Less central to the grand scheme, they caused fewer deaths, created fewer heroes, and engaged smaller proportions of the population as soldiers and sailors. Controversial in their day, they seem in retrospect wars less to defend American liberty than to extend American power. They are, indeed, hard to see as anything but wars for empire. Yet these wars, too, are part of America's story.

While we acknowledge that the creation and preservation of the United States are events central to the history of North America, we also maintain that the Revolution and Civil War cannot be fully understood unless they are seen together with those other, less well remembered wars waged against native peoples, Mexicans, and the agents of European empires. Indeed, we maintain that the American Revolution and the Civil War can best be understood as unanticipated consequences of decisive victories in the great imperial wars—the Seven Years' War and the Mexican-American War—that preceded each by a little more than a decade. In both cases, the acquisition of vast territories created severe, protracted, and ultimately violent debates over sovereignty and citizenship. Those bitter postwar disputes over the empire's future led to civil wars and ultimately to revolutions that altered the fundamental meanings of rights and citizenship, and redefined the bases of imperial governance.

In the following pages we construct a history of North America that emphasizes wars and their effects and stresses the centrality of imperial ambitions to the development of the United States. It therefore stands in contrast to a set of popular notions about the shape of American history, which taken together comprise a grand narrative so deeply embedded in American culture that they persist despite the long-running efforts of professional historians to correct or revise them. This story might be diagramed to look like a great suspension bridge, in which Jamestown and Plymouth serve as anchor points for a chronicle of institutional growth and population expansion that rises to its first peak in the Revolution and the establishment of the federal Constitution. From there the narrative cables descend as post-Revolutionary political tensions diminish during the early national era, only to rise again as sectional conflicts grow between North and South, to reach a second peak in the Civil War. This great climax, the crisis of the Union, settles the all-important issues of citizenship, freedom, and nationhood that the Revolution had left unresolved. From Appomattox and the Thirteenth, Fourteenth, and Fifteenth Amendments, the story descends once more, as Americans work out the implications of citizenship and equality before the law, to the twentieth century: the American Century, in which the United States finally fulfills its destiny in the world as a whole. Before assuming global leadership, however, the nation and its ideals must pass through a third great trial. Hence the Second World War stands as the last great pylon and the Cold War as the long descent of the cables to the present day.

Like a suspension bridge, this popular understanding of America's story offers a robust, serviceable, and aesthetically pleasing structure, a design arguably central to maintaining political community in a vast, chronically fragmented nation. But just as there are other means than bridges to cross bodies of water, there are other ways to tell the American story. Ours begins with the proposition that war itself has been an engine of change in North America for the past five centuries and indeed has largely defined that history's meaning. America's wars, however, have not been uniform in either their character or their consequences, and the story as we tell it depends on recognizing that wars can have very different implications and consequences depending (among other factors) on whether they are localized conflicts between nonstate groups, large-scale contests between empires, revolutionary wars, wars by which a triumphant empire consolidates control over its conquests, or wars of foreign intervention. Making such distinctions allows us to examine the interrelationships and interactions between wars and to explore the ways that one conflict has connected to another—and another, and another—over time.

At least from the middle of the eighteenth century to the present, American wars have either expressed a certain kind of imperial ambition or have resulted directly from successes in previous imperial conflicts. "Imperialism" is, of course, a loaded term, full of negative connotations. We suggest, however, that it can most productively be understood in the sense of the progressive extension of a polity's, or a people's, *dominion* over the lands or lives of others, as a means of imposing what the builders of empires understand as order and peace on dangerous or unstable peripheral regions. To found a narrative of American development on the concept of dominion is to forgo the exceptionalist traditions of American culture—those durable notions that the United States is essentially not like other nations but rather an example for them to emulate, a "shining city on a hill"—in favor of a perspective more like the one from which historians routinely survey long periods of European, African, or Asian history. Indeed, because throughout recorded history "empire has been a way of life for most of the peoples of the world, either as conqueror or conquered,"[3] the story we outline makes the long-term pattern of America's development look broadly similar to those of other large, successful nations.

Emphasizing the imperial elements in American history thus serves several purposes. It enables us to depict the continuities between the growth of Britain's American colonies and the revolutionary United States in the eighteenth century, the territorial expansion of United States in the nineteenth century, and the propagation of American power throughout the Western Hemisphere and the world in the twentieth. By offering an alternative story of American development, it serves the heuristic function of providing a different view of familiar episodes and personalities. Most of all, it illuminates the expansion of territorial domain and the extension of economic and political sway as features of the American experience so central to the nation's approach to the world that Americans may be more apt to see them as parts of the natural order than as products of specific, contingent historical circumstances. In that sense, the utility of such an approach may be to make it easier for Americans to perceive aspects of their nation's behavior that may seem natural or innocuous when viewed from within but that seem both intentional and troubling to those who view the United States from without.

More than anything else, ours is a story of power—or, more precisely, a story of how power has been acquired, defined, used, contested, and lost in North America. It describes a past, and implies a present, in which human beings exercise far less control over events than they think they do: a past in which the unintended consequences of a persistent quest for power are often the most important of all. To tell this tale, we divide a half millennium of North American history into four major periods: an *Age of Contact* (the 1500s), an *Age of Colonization and Conflict* (c. 1600–1750), an *Age of Empires and Revolutions* (c. 1750–1900), and an *Age of Intervention* (1900 to the present).

In describing the Age of Contact, we trace the consequences of the sixteenth-century collision between radically different systems of war, trade, and empire that had previously arisen in Europe and the Americas. In general, European expansion and the intrusion of various competing European groups throughout the Atlantic and Caribbean basins had tremendously disruptive effects for Europe and the Americas alike. The specific experiences of Spanish colonizers in this era also had effects that lasted well beyond it, as other Europeans began to imagine their own imperial destinies in the New World.

In the Age of Colonization and Conflict, Europeans from England, France, and the Low Countries sought to realize those dreams by establishing colonies in North America. Perhaps the most striking unanticipated result of these colonizing enterprises was the intensification of warfare among competing native groups. These tremendously destructive conflicts reflected larger patterns of cultural and diplomatic exchange by means of trade and war that the Europeans did not fully understand but nonetheless sought to exploit to their own advantage. By the beginning of the eighteenth century, interactions between Indian and European peoples resulted in the emergence of a diplomatic and political system that reflected a balance of power in which native groups played a balancing role. Indian diplomats playing one European power off against another helped to stabilize relations between competing empires until the middle of the century.

The vast conflict known in Europe as the Seven Years' War (1756–63; its North American phase, 1754–60, is sometimes called the French and Indian War) ended this period of relative stability, introducing our third epoch, the Age of Empires and Revolutions. Unlike the three previous wars between Britain and France, this one ended in a decisive victory, as a result of which the North American empire of France ceased to exist and Spain (France's ally in the final year of the war) was compelled to surrender its imperial claims east of the Mississippi River. This left Britain (in theory, at least) the proprietor of the eastern half of North America; it also marked a turning point in Native Americans' power to exert decisive influence over outcomes on the continent.

After 1763, dominion in North America, however hotly resisted, was exercised in the east by Great Britain and in the west and southwest by Spain. Both powers attempted in the postwar period to define the terms of membership in their empires in ways that would be acceptable to a wide range of peoples, including metropolitan Britons and Spaniards, Anglo-American and French colonists, and American Indians. The defeated Spanish succeeded best in reforming their empire, which survived for more than a half-century thereafter. The victorious British, by contrast, failed, so alienating their colonists by attempted reforms that just a dozen years after the Peace of Paris that ended the Seven Years' War, the thirteen North American colonies took up arms against the empire. In their efforts to mount resistance to a sovereign king in Parliament in the decade before war broke out, colonial leaders used arguments that stressed what had usually been called the rights of Englishmen, stressing the centrality of political freedom and the protection of property and other rights. Because the colonists were a chronically divided lot, however, the leaders of the resistance movement took care to couch their explanations and appeals in universalistic language: as defenses of natural rights, not merely the liberties of Englishmen.

The War for American Independence (1775–83) shattered the British empire and made those universalized ideas the foundation of American political identity. It took another dozen years after the end of the war in 1783, however, to produce the complex of agreements and understandings we call the Revolutionary Settlement, which became the basis of a new, successful, and aggressive American empire, the United States. In our scheme, therefore, imperial and republican elements *together* formed the basis of revolutionary political culture, and the American Revolution appears as a violent, institutionally creative phase lasting from 1775 to 1789 within a four-decade-long process that extended from 1754 to 1800, in which a monarchical empire expanded into the trans-Appalachian west, disintegrated, then was succeeded by an imperial republic capable of exerting control over the interior of the continent.

With the election of Thomas Jefferson as president, bands of white American citizens on the marches of the Republic defined the political community as a brotherhood of white Protestant men like themselves. Finding no place in their new world for native peoples, these borderers treated suddenly vulnerable Indians as racially different peoples to be removed—or exterminated. In the War of 1812, Americans conjoined defiance of British efforts to dictate their commercial and diplomatic policy with a war of conquest, by which they intended to secure control of eastern North America. Though the Americans failed to conquer Canada, they effectively destroyed the power of American Indians east of the Mississippi River, thereby consolidating the United States' claim to the region from the Great Lakes to the Gulf of Mexico. The conquest of the Southwest, begun by Andrew Jackson in his campaigns against the Creeks in 1813–14 and continued in 1818 when he invaded and occupied Florida, came to

completion in 1819 with the annexation of Florida and the subsequent removal of most Indians to lands west of the Mississippi.

As important as these aspects of the War of 1812 were, the war's most
significant legacy proved to be a distinctively American just-war ideology.
Unlike the members of the Revolutionary generation, who justified taking
up arms to defend a fragile liberty against Britain's seemingly unlimited
sovereign power, proponents of war argued that offensive warfare—against
the British in Canada, the Creeks in Alabama, and the Spanish in Florida—
was justified because conquest would liberate the oppressed and expand the
sphere of freedom. It was a justification Americans applied again in their
next imperial war—and indeed in every subsequent war in the Republic's
history.

Great Britain and the United States ceased to compete militarily after
1815, leaving Mexico, which declared its independence from Spain in 1821,
as the last remaining obstacle to the dominion of the United States in North
America. Mexico's creole elite, staunch defenders of a conservative social
order, were as capable of resenting metropolitan interference in the early
nineteenth century as the leaders of Britain's North American colonies had
been in the latter decades of the eighteenth, but their fears of political radicalism and racial warfare inhibited the growth of a viable revolutionary
movement. When the Mexican elite finally agreed to declare Mexico's independence, therefore, it was not to defend the rights of individuals but rather
to preserve the prerogatives of their class, the power of the Roman Catholic
Church, and the stability of the social order. The Mexican leaders' fears of
revolution and racial war, along with the rich geographic diversity of their
nation, inhibited the emergence of an American-style revolutionary settlement and created a fertile field for caudillos, violence, and local rebellions.
One of the latter, on the remote northeastern fringe of Mexico, created the
Republic of Texas in 1836. A decade later, the United States annexed Texas,
provoking a war with Mexico in 1846. Within two years American soldiers
overwhelmed Mexican resistance, seized the national capital, and forced a
peace, the Treaty of Guadalupe Hidalgo (1848), that deprived Mexico of
fully half its territory.

As in the aftermath of the Seven Years' War, the accession of vast
amounts of territory created a furious debate that shredded the political fabric of the victorious empire. Then it had taken twelve years for the imperial
community to collapse in civil war; it now took thirteen. Adding the lands
from the Rockies to the Pacific coast to what Americans thought of as the
empire of liberty made the question of slavery's expansion into the con-

quests inescapable. The Revolutionary Settlement broke down as Northern and Southern Americans came to see each other as potential tyrants intent on subjugation. Thus in April 1861, Southerners and Northerners went to war to make the American empire safe for their own, mutually exclusive, notions of liberty, convinced that no alternative remained but an appeal to the god of battles. Mexican liberals and conservatives, meanwhile, were already locked in a civil war that lasted for years. In both countries, imperial war had begotten revolutionary wars that ultimately redefined the nature of citizenship and the relationship between federal and local authority in ways no one could have imagined before the imperial war began.

In short, revolution had once again emerged as an unanticipated consequence of an imperial war, and once again it created a new political synthesis. In the United States and Mexico alike, new revolutionary settlements were predicated on the supremacy (in theory, if not in daily practice) of the national government, the uniformity (in theory, if not in fact) of citizens' rights, and the permanence of the state. The second Revolutionary Settlement in the United States was completed in 1877 with the congressional compromise that led to the election of Rutherford B. Hayes to the presidency and the withdrawal of the last federal troops from the "reconstructed" South. In Mexico, a settlement was worked out during the presidency of Porfirio Díaz in the 1870s and 1880s.

The last act of the Age of Empires and Revolutions was the subjugation of Indian resistance west of the Mississippi River by elements of the U.S. Army, a process completed a little more than two decades after the Civil War by the confinement of native groups to reservations throughout the West. Meanwhile, the industrial transformation of the American economy and the rise of corporate capitalism, trends accelerated by the Civil War, produced an American governing elite that had less interest in territorial acquisition than in the expansion of economic dominion, in the United States and beyond its borders. This metamorphosis did not mean that Americans ceased to debate the relationship between the exercise of coercive national power and the commitment to universal freedom; the terms of the debate, however, shifted.

Just how far they moved became evident with the Spanish-American War in 1898: an imperial war with a decisive victory that resulted not in a third American Revolution but rather in an alteration of long-established patterns of conquest and incorporation. Previous imperial adventures had opened vast, thinly populated regions to Anglo-American colonization in the certainty that the territories carved from them would be populated by white settlers who would eventually lead them into the Union as states. Victory in 1898, however, yielded conquests comparatively poorer in land than in population; and those millions of conquered Cubans and Filipinos were not only overwhelmingly nonwhite but Catholic, or even Muslim, in religion. When Filipino insurgents, resisting American liberation between 1899 and 1902, killed or wounded more than 4,000 U.S. soldiers and demonstrated what the true costs of an overseas empire could be, American leaders embraced an alternative imperial policy—interventionism—that allowed them to exercise power beyond the borders of the United States but that did not require yet another revolutionary reconstruction of American political culture.

Elements of continuity nonetheless remained strong as the Age of Empires and Revolutions gave way to the Age of Intervention. Americans continued to fight wars according to the just-war ideology first worked out in the War of 1812—the notion that to be justified wars must either protect or expand the sphere of liberty—and that they have applied, in one form or another, ever since. As an imperial republic, the United States remained dedicated to using force not only to impose stability on disorderly peripheral regions but to create the conditions for liberty as Americans understood them—free markets, the protection of property rights, and the rule of law— in temporary protectorates. Having established the pattern of intervention in defense of freedom (and by creating American hegemony) in Cuba and the Philippines, the United States intervened militarily in Mexico and throughout the Caribbean basin, then perfected the practice by intervening in Europe in 1917 to defend democracy and expand freedom's sphere.

World War I, however, laid bare the terrible costs of modern war. Most Americans found them bearable for the comparatively short time needed to subdue the German imperialists in Europe, but had no interest in perpetuating them as an open-ended commitment to liberating Asians or South Americans or Russians from their various oppressive regimes. Moreover, the emergence of the Soviet Union as the revolutionary and imperial successor to tsarist Russia put the United States on the ideological defensive for the first time in its history. A republic that had regarded itself as the very embodiment of liberal revolutionary principles in the nineteenth century became a leading proponent of the status quo. In the 1920s and 1930s, Americans turned to celebrating their history as a series of sacrifices made by Americans in the defense of liberty, an essentially conservative reading of their past that nonetheless left them prepared, when confronted with the crisis of Pearl Harbor, to revive the commitment of the United States to the military liberation of peoples beyond the seas.

World War II, construed as a struggle against various tyrannies—German Nazism and Italian fascism in Europe, Japanese militarism in the Pacific and Far East—catapulted the United States to a position of global leadership from which, this time, it did not retreat. American opposition to communist regimes in China, the Soviet Union, and elsewhere during nearly a half century of cold war was, in that sense, a continuation of the defense of freedom conducted with such striking success in 1941–45. The limits of this commitment, made evident in Vietnam between 1968 and 1973, in effect confirmed the terms on which Americans were still willing to support foreign interventions; for it was only the palpable disconnection between the public justification of that war (the defense of freedom in South Vietnam) and its prosecution that finally convinced a majority of the American people that the war was no longer worth the sacrifice of lives and treasure.

In sum, then, the version of American history in the following pages emphasizes contingency, proposes an unfamiliar set of turning points and phases of development, suggests that war and imperialism have powerfully influenced American development from the seventeenth century through the present day, and recasts familiar triumphs as tragedies. It identifies imperialism and republicanism as inseparable twin influences in the creation and growth of political culture in the United States. It denies that chauvinist demands for imperial wars in 1812, 1846, and 1898 were somehow exceptions to an otherwise pacific history in which Americans make war only when they have been driven to it by the need to preserve their threatened liberties. It implies that the great American military interventions of the twentieth and early twenty-first centuries have been as much efforts to establish and preserve hemispheric—and ultimately, global—hegemony as they were efforts to defend ideals of freedom against the designs of would-be tyrants. Finally, it argues that the defining moments of American political culture and nationhood, the Revolution and the Civil War, can be understood as the unintended consequences of vaunting imperial ambitions.

We have chosen to make our case for this broad argument in the form of a narrative constructed, as concretely as possible, around the lives of eight men: Samuel de Champlain, William Penn, George Washington, Andrew Jackson, Antonio López de Santa Anna, Ulysses S. Grant, Douglas MacArthur, and Colin Powell. We have adopted this approach in order to explore both the ways in which larger patterns have constrained and structured the lives of human beings and the ways in which the decisions and actions of individuals have inflected the direction of historical change. We have avoided theoretical statements and generalizations that might tend to overdetermine the narrative or to diminish the ambiguity, unpredictability, and messiness of the lives and events we try to describe. By embedding the argument in our narrative—by making it, in effect, the plot—while allowing the actions of our characters to drive the story's development, we have tried to avoid depending on normative or ahistorical definitions of empire and liberty and to steer clear of prescriptive judgments. This approach, we hope, offers sufficient scope to explore tensions between larger patterns of development and contingent events, to seek out the intersections between private and public life, and to describe historical processes as compounded of social forces and individual choices. North America's historical trajectory thus appears, in the pages that follow, not merely to be the product of demographic, economic, and political forces but the result of the interaction of those great structural factors with an array of unpredictable, emotional elements—ambition, greed, fear, courage, hatred, idealism, and various other human correlates of war, and life—in contexts that provide ample room for accident, unintended outcomes, and chance.[4]

In this way, we intend the story of Samuel de Champlain to illustrate how the larger European search for profits in trade with natives led to the transformation of warfare and the destruction of whole Indian nations, and also to show the ironic consequences, in Champlain's own life, of dealing with native people who had interests of their own to pursue. William Penn's story demonstrates how a colony founded on principles of peaceful coexistence could succeed beyond anyone's expectations yet still create crushing losses for its founder, while engendering the population growth and territorial expansion that ultimately brought on a horrifying, decisive imperial war. George Washington's long quest to impose an imperial order on the North American interior suggests the continuities that link the British empire and its American successor. Yet Washington, too, finally found himself left behind by changes in the political culture he helped to transform; like Penn, he proved most useful as a symbol of values that his countrymen liked less to live by than to celebrate, and to claim as their own.

Through the career of Andrew Jackson, we trace the emergence of a populist, nationalist empire whose white male citizens defined liberty as the province of people like themselves. Because they saw the United States as a bastion of freedom, they could not fathom why people unlike themselves detested it; why (for example) Indians so stubbornly resisted assimilation or why Mexicans understood Americans and their values as a threat their own well-being and to good order generally. We use the career of Antonio López de Santa Anna to explore the similar, yet hardly parallel, ways in which the tensions between liberty and power, consent and coercion, influenced the development of the United States and Mexico in the first half of the nineteenth century. Ultimately these contradictory pressures exploded in an imperial war over possession of the southwestern quarter of North America in 1846–48 and in bloody civil wars both north and south of the Rio Grande not long after. Those conflicts dominated the lives of Ulysses S. Grant and his contemporaries, giving powerful impetus to North America's trajectory of development in the later nineteenth century.

The life of Douglas MacArthur, who was five years old when Grant died and whose career in the U.S. Army spanned more than half a century, allows us to observe the metamorphosis of a nineteenth-century republican empire that had asserted its control over central North America in the name of liberty into a twentieth-century global power capable of intervening on behalf of freedom all over the planet. Finally, Colin Powell's career as an army officer and public servant suggests the continuity of dilemmas fostered by America's long historical trajectory that remain unresolved.

We chose subjects whose lives either overlapped in time or came close to doing so and who were involved in as many aspects of our story as possible. Thus we picked Douglas MacArthur rather than (say) Dwight Eisenhower not only because of the importance of MacArthur's own career but because his father participated in the Civil War, the subjugation of the Plains Indians, and the suppression of the Philippine Insurrection. We chose U. S. Grant because his career was framed by Mexico, because he sent tens of thousands of men to their deaths even as he doubted the justice of war, and because his Northern, middle-class male sensibility contrasted sharply with the Southern patriarchal world of Andrew Jackson. Antonio López de Santa Anna offered us a chance to highlight the divergent histories of North Americans as well as resistance to the imperial ambitions of the United States. Questions of personal identity, particularly with regard to notions of masculinity and race, run throughout the lives of all eight figures. The studied self-control of Champlain, Penn, Washington, and Powell contrasts sharply with the kinds of emotion that shaped the lives of the passionate Jackson, the domestic Grant, the opportunistic Santa Anna, and the ambitious MacArthur. Imperialism thus manifests itself in both public and private forms: men who exercised power to impose order on the world at large were no less driven by the need to master or release emotional energies within the smaller worlds of family and household.

This book attempts to narrate the ambiguous and ironic relationship between war and freedom in the making of North America and in the creation of the United States as an actor on the world stage. It does not devote much attention to battles or to military history at the operational level; rather, it investigates wars as defining moments in the construction of cultural and territorial borders, in North America and beyond. It argues that wars—not only as fought but also as contemplated, criticized, defended, and remembered—have furnished crucial occasions for Americans to debate who they are and to express what they hope their nation represents. It maintains, finally, that the quest for liberty and the pursuit of power together have created an American historical dialectic catalyzed and made dynamic by war.

The Dominion of War, in short, attempts to describe anew certain fundamental patterns of development and important sources of change over the *longue durée* of North America's past, and thus to renarrate a tale we may too easily assume we know, with a significance we may too readily believe we understand. It tells of a continent's shaping and a nation's growth: a chronicle that begins in war, and ends—with us.

CHAPTER ONE

Champlain's Legacy: The Transformation of Seventeenth-Century North America

He was awake now, but could not shake the dream from his mind. He had stood with his companions at the foot of a mountain, on a narrow shore, by a lake of sparkling beauty. Yet there was only horror in what he beheld: everywhere before him men struggled in the water, gasping for breath, dying. To the others he had said, We must save them. *But they replied,* Let them die. They are Iroquois, our enemies. They are worth nothing. *And so, one by one, they drowned.*[1]

T he man who woke from this nightmare was Samuel de Champlain, and the lake by which he slept we now call by his name. It was July 29, 1609. He and two French musketeers were accompanying sixty Montagnais, Huron, and Algonquin warriors on an expedition against the Mohawks, easternmost of the Five Nations of the Iroquois. The Frenchmen, the first Europeans to see the lake and the country around it, were also among the first Europeans ever to join an Indian war party as combatants. Before nightfall on the following day, Champlain's new allies discovered that his dream had been a prophetic vision. What they could not know was that their victory over the Mohawks marked a turning point in North American history.

No more a seer than his allies, Champlain, too, failed to grasp the significance of the battle he helped win. He had, after all, come to North America to trade and perhaps to save some souls, not to fight in local wars. In pursuing those ostensibly benign goals, however, Champlain came to understand that the goodwill of his trading partners depended on his will-ingness to join them against their enemies. The more he learned about In-dians, in short, the more he found himself pressed to participate in their wars.

In deciding to become an active ally, Champlain responded to the exi-gencies of the moment. But when he placed his weapons and his skills at the disposal of his allies, he inaugurated a pattern of interaction among French and Indian peoples that persisted for a century and a half. Champlain thus played both a symbolic and a causal role in changing the cultural and polit-ical landscape of eastern North America. For the previous century, Euro-pean contacts had altered but not transformed native patterns of war and trade. Now, however, the creation of colonies in North America intensified the long-standing competition among native groups and made the Indians' wars more violent and uncontrollable than they had ever been before.

These terrible transformations did not occur solely because a lone Frenchman decided to enlist himself and his matchlock musket in the ser-vice of an Indian war party. Nevertheless, because Champlain's career in North America spanned the transition between the sixteenth-century Age of Contact and the Age of Colonization and Conflict that followed, his story casts a powerful light on the unintended consequences of European-Indian interactions. In pursuing his dreams of trade and conversion, Champlain helped bring an old order to a violent end and made himself midwife to the nightmarish birth of a new era.

"I Wished to Help Them Against Their Enemies"

When Champlain dreamed of men drowning before his eyes in the summer of 1609, he was about forty years of age—old for war—and far from home. A circuitous route had led him from the town of his birth, Brouage, in the province of Saintonge, north of Bordeaux, to the spot where he slept, deep in the American forest.

We know nothing of his education, although it is clear that growing up in a port town had given him a chance both to learn how to sail small ves-sels and how to make excellent, accurate harbor charts. The interminable civil wars of his homeland had also given him, as a young man, the skills of a soldier. During the Franco-Spanish struggle known as the Eighth War of Religion (or the War of the Three Henrys, 1585–98), he served as a cavalry quartermaster in the army of Henri de Navarre. Such a post would ordinarily have kept him out of the line of fire, yet late in 1594, at about age twenty-four, he took part in the storming of Fort Crozat, outside Brest. That act earned him a reputation for bravery; the battle secured northwestern France for Navarre, a Protestant who had lately converted to Catholicism in order to reunite a kingdom long riven by religious bloodshed. By 1598 Navarre had triumphed over his enemies and ascended the throne that he occupied as His Most Christian Majesty, Henri IV. With that, the brave young quartermaster who had taken to calling himself Samuel *de* Champlain (thereby granting himself a *noblesse* to which he had no particle of a claim), found himself out of a job.

He was not unemployed for long. His uncle commanded a merchant ship, the *Saint-Julien,* lately contracted to repatriate Spanish soldiers to Cadiz; he gave Champlain a berth as a junior officer on the voyage. At Cadiz his uncle hired out the *Saint-Julien,* "a staunch ship and a good sailer," once more—this time to sail with the *flota,* or annual convoy, that carried European goods to New Spain to exchange for the silver, cacao, and other riches of the Indies that it would bear home to Spain. Thus Champlain first crossed the Atlantic in 1599, beginning a fascination with the New World that led him back again and again. By 1635, when he died at Quebec, the *habitation* he founded in 1608, he had made the voyage at least a dozen times.[2]

Champlain did not return with the *flota;* instead, he lingered two years in the West Indies and Mexico. This sojourn fired his imagination and changed his life. New Spain—Mexico—in particular impressed him: "A more beautiful country," he thought, "could not be seen or desired." It was a rich country, too: a land of "fine forests" and "plains stretching as far as the eye can reach, covered with immense droves of cattle," its mines poured silver worth millions of pesos annually into the Spanish royal treasury. New Spain also charmed him with its natural wonders—exotic trees (including the guava, whose miraculous fruit had flesh that could stop diarrhea in two hours and skin that cured constipation "straightaway"), such amazing animals as the iguana and the jaguar, and birds of every description and hue. Most of all, the monumental scale and architecture of "the beautiful city of Mexico" captivated him. Here was a place "superbly constructed of splendid temples, palaces and fine houses," with "streets extremely well laid out" and lined with "handsome shops . . . full of all sorts of very rich merchandise"— a city, truly, that symbolized the power and wealth of the Spanish Indies.[3]

Only the natives disappointed him. Those not yet subjected to the king of Spain worshiped the moon, practiced cannibalism, and were "deprived of the light of reason." Those whom the Spanish did control, on the other hand, had been so extensively persecuted, tortured, enslaved, and slain in the course of being subdued that "the mere account of it arouses compassion for them." They were Christians, of a sort; but they attended Mass less for the love of God than for fear of the beatings that priests inflicted on absentees. Doubtless as a result, Champlain found Mexico's Indians to be "of a very melancholy disposition," notwithstanding the "quick intelligence" that enabled them to "understand in a short time whatever is shown to them" and a remarkable fortitude in enduring "whatever ill-treatment or abuse is bestowed upon them."[4]

Champlain understood in a general way the historical events that had made New Spain into the land he so admired. He knew, for example, that it had been less than a century since Castilian conquerors had transformed the Valley of Mexico from the seat of the Aztec state into one of the principal bastions of Spain's globe-girdling empire. Like literate sixteenth-century Europeans generally, he also understood the decisive victory that Hernán Cortés and the conquistadors had achieved as proof that the Spanish were the greatest empire-builders since antiquity. What neither he nor any of his contemporaries understood, however, was the extraordinary degree to which Spain's triumph had depended upon the interplay between Aztec and Castilian ways of war and expectations about empire. Indeed, what had happened in Mexico during the years of the conquest, 1519–21, not only shaped the world Champlain described eighty years later but profoundly influenced the interactions between European colonizers and American peoples for centuries to come.

From a modest start in the Valley of Mexico during the fourteenth century, the Aztecs had built an imperial state and a large standing army on the foundation of a religious system that required human sacrifice and a political system geared to war and the exaction of tribute. By the beginning of the sixteenth century, the Aztecs, governing from the great metropolis Tenochtitlán, exercised hegemony over perhaps 12 million people across central Mexico, sustaining their power by extorting food, precious metals, textiles, and labor from subject peoples. Perpetual warfare set the bounds of this empire, for two reasons. The Aztec economy (even to the extent of provisioning Tenochtitlán's population of 200,000) depended on a steady supply of tribute, which could only be maintained by fear of military retribution; and the Aztec religious system demanded the blood of human beings to maintain the balance of the cosmos and insure that the sun would rise each day. By 1500 approximately 50,000 prisoners of war had to be taken annually to serve as sacrificial victims.

Cortés was a thirty-four-year-old lawyer discontented with the slow pace of his advancement in Cuba when he landed on the coast of Mexico, essentially as a freebooter, in 1519. Operating in defiance of his superior, Cuba's governor, he brought with him about five hundred soldiers, fourteen small cannon, a handful of horses, and little real idea of what he might encounter. Once this tiny force of would-be conquistadors demonstrated the military advantages of crossbows, gunpowder weapons, horses, and steel to the peoples they encountered near the coast, it was not particularly difficult for the Indians to see them as potentially useful allies against their Aztec enemy. Cortés, a brilliant practitioner of realpolitik, understood this well enough to ally himself with, first, the Cempoalans, and later (after initial clashes in which he and his armored men held their ground against massed formations of archers and slingsmen hurling stones) with the warlike Tlaxcalans. It was thus not merely a few hundred intrepid Castilians who conquered Tenochtitlán in 1521 but a few hundred Castilians in the company of perhaps 200,000 Indian allies. The conquest, as we now know, was effected less by technological and tactical superiority than by the support of these native warriors; it was ultimately secured by the devastating effects of the smallpox that the Spanish inadvertently introduced in the course of their invasion. Cortés and his men, however, concluded that the collapse of the Aztecs represented God's will and lost no time in inserting themselves in the place of the empire's previous rulers. Thus they were able to compensate themselves for the trouble of conquering Mexico by continuing to collect tribute through the existing system and to repay God for his help by instituting Christianity as the state religion.[5]

The benefits of escaping Aztec hegemony appealed so powerfully to the Indians who allied themselves with Cortés that they failed to see the consequences of alliance until the devastations of epidemic disease made it impossible for them to resist Spanish control. Meanwhile Cortés and the governors who succeeded him continued to use Indian labor to extract the silver that funded their conversion of the Aztecs' hegemonic empire into a territorial one, New Spain. The prolonged collapse of Mexico's Indian population eventually slowed and, after about a century, ceased; intermarriage between Spanish creoles and Indians produced the mestizo population that gradually increased until it finally predominated, stabilizing both the labor supply and cultural relations.

By the 1550s, Spanish rule was secure in central Mexico and the means of conquest were thoroughly understood; indeed, another conquistador, Francisco Pizarro, effectively replicated them in western South America by taking over the Inca Empire, a feat of even greater audacity than that of Cortés. Having twice seen the face of success, the Spanish sought to repeat this pattern of conquest in subsequent efforts at colonization and imperial organization. Even in areas less well suited to the process than Mexico had been, would-be conquistadors sought alliance with indigenous peoples as a first step toward their subjugation, the collection of tribute, and an enforced conversion to Christianity. This was the case with Spain's first colony on the mainland to the north of Mexico, Saint Augustine. There, however, the attempt produced results substantially different from Spain's spectacular triumphs in Mexico and Peru.

Because the Spanish crown expended the wealth of conquered peoples largely to create a centralized empire, settlement expanded from Mexico according to strategic decisions made in Madrid. Imperial authorities quite reasonably assigned first priority to defending the treasure fleets that carried American bullion to the metropolis. Hence the decision to establish Saint Augustine in 1565 represented an attempt to secure the Atlantic coast of Florida against the Huguenot (French Protestant) buccaneers who had previously founded a base there to prey on the deep-laden galleons that sailed annually through the Bahama Channel.

In Florida, as in Mexico, the Spanish invaders first allied themselves with local Indians (the Timucua) who had earlier tried to draw the French into their wars with neighboring peoples but who now feared French domination. The more numerous Spaniards and their Timucuan allies defeated the French, whereupon the Spanish slaughtered most of the Frenchmen as heretics, sending the few survivors home to tell the tale. The Spanish governor, Pedro Menéndez de Avilés, then followed the well-established pattern of establishing fortified settlements, sending out missionaries (paid from the military budget) to convert the Indians, and collecting the tribute necessary to make the enterprise self-sustaining. But Florida was not Mexico, and the path to Saint Augustine's survival led through three perilous decades of uncertainty.

In the first place, the absence of gold and silver made Saint Augustine itself a poor colony, hence—from the perspective of the royal treasury—an expensive outpost of empire. Economizing where it could, the crown refused to assign a large permanent garrison and made no concerted effort to encourage civilian settlement. Second, the dispersed Indian peoples of the region lacked the preexisting political organization that had facilitated conquest in Mexico and Peru and were unaccustomed to paying tribute. When the Spaniards tried to exact it by force, the Indians resisted, driving the

Spanish soldiers, missionaries, and settlers back from the seven bases they had established in 1565–67 to Saint Augustine itself. The fort saved them, for the Indians, lacking artillery to batter down its walls, could hope only to starve out the defenders. Because the garrison could be resupplied by sea, the starvation siege failed, and the Spanish managed to hang on to their last precarious foothold on the Florida coast.[6]

But there is a difference between maintaining a beleaguered military outpost and planting a viable colony, and for nearly three decades the fate of Saint Augustine hung in the balance. It was only at the end of the sixteenth century, at about the time Champlain was visiting the Indies, that conversions occurred near the fort among "rival tribes [who] saw security advantages in being allied with the Spanish." Spanish officials now claimed "overlordship by arranging peace between tribes," while missionary friars who proved adept at mediating disputes in native communities forged ties with the leaders of dominant factions. Thereafter the colonization of Florida depended on establishing missions among native groups willing to receive them (thirty-six missions were operating by 1675) while maintaining a garrison and small Spanish population at and around the fort of Saint Augustine.

This was hardly conquest on the model of Mexico or Peru. When the bishop of Santiago de Cuba visited Saint Augustine more than a century after its establishment, he found just 1,500 Spanish settlers but confirmed more than 13,000 Indian converts. Since the Spanish garrison supported Christian Indians in conflicts with their unconverted neighbors and since the settlers remained few and clustered in a comparatively small region, the colony may be said to have taken root only after the local Guale, Timucua, and Apalachee Indians succeeded in defining the conditions of occupancy and the Spaniards had acquiesced in the modus vivendi thus created. Spanish authorities in Seville or Madrid had no accurate idea of what had happened, and Saint Augustine's colonists no doubt thought, because tensions had subsided, that God had at last favored their enterprise. But the Guales, Timucuas, and Apalachees who had integrated the Spanish into their own system of warfare, alliance, and trade knew better. If the Spanish remained in Florida and evangelized among its native peoples, it was because they did so on terms that their Indian hosts found acceptable.[7]

Champlain spent the rest of his life learning his own version of this lesson about the limits of European power in North America. Returning to France in 1601, he wrote (and lavishly illustrated) an account of his travels in the Caribbean and New Spain and set about securing himself a position on another transatlantic voyage. His interest, like that of most previous

French explorers, centered on the northern reaches of North America, far from Spain's dominions. For seventy years—ever since Jacques Cartier's voyages of exploration between 1534 and 1541—French cartographers had understood the Saint Lawrence River as an avenue to the heart of the continent, and European fishermen and whalers had long used the shores of the Gulf of Saint Lawrence to make seasonal camps for drying cod and rendering oil from whale carcasses. Those camps had become the scene of lively exchanges between the fishermen and native peoples. One of the items the fishermen brought home in the 1580s had particularly interested French merchants: the pelts of beaver, whose undercoat provided fur ideally suited to making felt for the big, fanciful hats that were the rage of European fashion.

Northern Europe's waning beaver populations meant that these pelts commanded premium prices, but the French wars of religion (civil wars largely driven by Spain's imperial ambitions and fueled by silver from its American mines) had so disrupted commercial life that the great merchants were unable to exploit North American fur supplies systematically. Only Breton and Basque fishermen-traders carried on a modest fur trade by calling in during the summers at Tadoussac, a small, deep harbor at the confluence of the Saguenay and Saint Lawrence rivers. There an Algonquian-speaking people whom the French called the Montagnais controlled access to the northern interior by the Saguenay and provided pelts they had gained both by hunting and by trading with groups further inland. They traded on terms uncommonly favorable to themselves. By the last years of the sixteenth century, Montagnais middlemen routinely withheld pelts each summer until enough ships arrived at Tadoussac that they could play one buyer off against the rest, acquiring the best trade goods at the lowest cost.[8]

With the conclusion of the wars of religion and Henri IV's consolidation of power in a newly unified kingdom, the king saw the utility of reestablishing French claims to North America as a means of countering Spanish power in Europe. He easily understood that the profits of a well-organized monopoly on the fur trade could be used to reward his courtiers and other supporters, who in turn could create permanent settlements in North America at no direct cost to the crown. In 1599, therefore, Henri awarded a ten-year monopoly to an old comrade in arms, Commander Aymar de Chaste, and his partners Pierre de Chauvin de Tonnetuit and François Gravé du Pont. They built a trading post at Tadoussac in 1600 only to find that, monopoly or no, Breton and Basque fisherman-traders kept coming there, too, while the Montagnais went on withholding furs to force the Europeans to compete for them. In the hope of locating an alternative to Tadoussac and perhaps of finding trading partners less sophisticated than the Montagnais, Gravé du Pont outfitted the little fleet of three vessels that sailed from Honfleur in March 1603 with Samuel de Champlain aboard.[9]

This voyage carried Champlain up the Saint Lawrence to the site of Quebec and beyond as high as the Lachine rapids above Montreal, the limit of navigability for seagoing vessels. He carefully noted the qualities of the land he observed ("The farther we went," he wrote, "the finer was the country"), but the place that made the strongest specific impression on him was Tadoussac, because that was where he first encountered large numbers of the people whom he and his companions called *les sauvages*.[10] There, in late May and early June, he witnessed an extraordinary assembly of Indians—Montagnais and their allies, Etchemins (Malecites) and Algonquins, a thousand in all—as they celebrated a recent victory over their Mohawk enemies. With great care he described their feasting, orations, songs, display of enemy scalps, and dancing (he especially admired the Algonquins' victory dance, which began when "all the women and girls" suddenly "stripped themselves stark naked"). The ceremonies, he noted, concluded with a ritual in which each Montagnais warrior "took what seemed proper to him, such as [wampum], tomahawks, swords, kettles" and gave them to one or more warriors from among his people's allies, so that "every one had a present," which they "carried away . . . to their lodges."[11]

Champlain and his companions returned to Tadoussac early in August and found the Montagnais, Malecites, and Algonquins again engaged in feasting and dancing as they prepared for a new expedition against the Mohawks.[12] War, Champlain concluded, was perpetual among *les sauvages,* and the alliances that enabled groups like the Montagnais to contend against their enemies were cemented and continually renewed by the kinds of rituals and gift-giving he had witnessed. These were his first insights into the culture and society of the native peoples alongside whom he spent most of his remaining years.

Champlain's view of the Indians and their potential reflected the ethnocentrism of his age. He found it possible to admire them for their bravery in war, their physical qualities ("they are agile, and the women are well shapen"), their personalities (they "are to a man of a very cheerful disposition"), and even their technology ("In the winter . . . they make a kind of racket twice or thrice as big as ours in France, which they fasten to their feet, and so walk on the snow without sinking"). But he dismissed their religion as mere superstition, based on a faith in prophetic dreams that were in fact "visions of the Devil." In the absence of sound morals, Indian society was lawless, families ties were weak, and individuals were "given to revenge." In their personal dealings, he thought, they were "great liars, a people in whom it is not well to put confidence, except for good reason, and standing on your guard." And yet, for all that, he found that the Montagnais did profess belief in a Creator—a strong enough hint at monotheism that he ventured to offer a thumbnail sketch of Christian doctrine to Anadabijou, one of their chiefs. When "the said Sagamore told me that he approved what I said," Champlain concluded that with the right instruction "they would speedily be brought to be good Christians, if we were to inhabit their lands, which most of them desire."[13]

This mixture of observation, analysis, and wishful thinking suggests that Champlain was beginning to envision a future Canada colonized by French people of good character, trading with *les sauvages,* spreading the gospel among them, bringing them peace, and saving their souls. The colony of New France would enrich his sovereign (and, *s'il plaît à Dieu,* his servant Champlain), adding to his power as New Spain enhanced the power of the Spanish king; but it would do so with none of the debilitating effects that Spanish repression had on the Indians of Mexico. Champlain did not yet imagine that Anadabijou's approval of Christian principles might have been an attempt to make polite conversation with a talkative guest or that the Indians might expect something more than catechetical instruction in return for allowing the French "to inhabit their lands."

Champlain's old skills as a maker of harbor charts, his emerging talents as a practical ethnographer, scribe, and publicist, and his ability to lead exploring parties procured him a role in the next stage of exploration, which began in the spring of 1604. Champlain suggested to Pierre de Gua, sieur de Monts (a Protestant merchant from Saintonge the king appointed to lead the fur monopoly following the death of Aymar de Chaste), that the best site for a permanent trading post might lie somewhere on the Atlantic coast, away from Tadoussac's highly developed commerce. With this in mind, de Monts organized an expedition to explore Acadia (modern Nova Scotia) and the coast of Norumbega (New Brunswick and New England). Champlain went along as geographer, returning to France only in the autumn of 1607.

Three summers of exploration, mapping, and trading gave Champlain unparalleled knowledge of the coastline from the Bay of Fundy to Cape Cod and greatly expanded his experience in dealing with Indians. Above all, these years taught him the importance of maintaining friendly relations with the Indians who permitted the French to set up *habitations* on their lands. Generosity in trade and loyalty to one's native hosts, he found, were

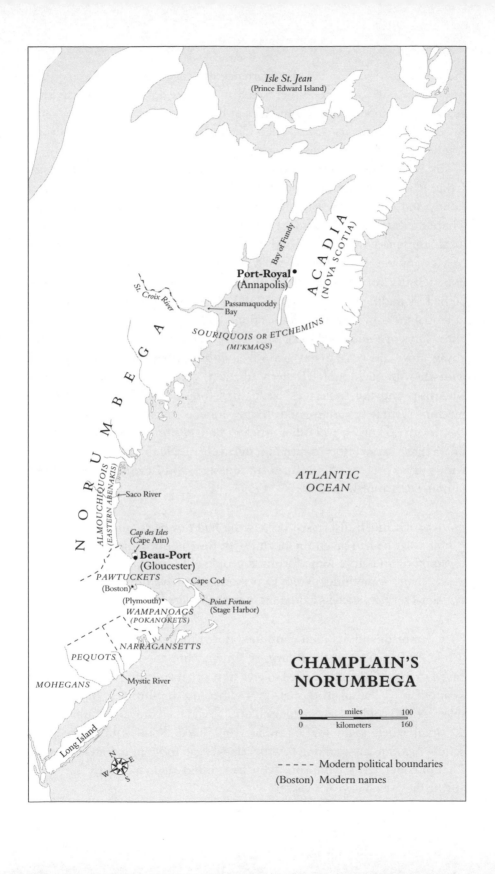

Isle St. Jean
(Prince Edward Island)

Bay of Fundy

A C A D I A
(NOVA SCOTIA)

Port-Royal •
(Annapolis)

St. Croix River

Passamaquoddy
Bay

SOURIQUOIS OR ETCHEMINS
(MI'KMAQS)

N O R U M B E G A

ALMOUCHIQUOIS
(EASTERN ABENAKIS)

Saco River

Cap des Isles
(Cape Ann)

Beau-Port
(Gloucester)

PAWTUCKETS
(Boston) •

Cape Cod

(Plymouth) •
Point Fortune
(Stage Harbor)

WAMPANOAGS
(POKANOKETS)

ATLANTIC
OCEAN

NARRAGANSETTS

PEQUOTS

MOHEGANS   Mystic River

Long Island

**CHAMPLAIN'S
NORUMBEGA**

0   miles   100
0   kilometers   160

N
W   E
S

- - - - - Modern political boundaries

(Boston) Modern names

the twin keys to success. Yet his experience also suggested that the very qualities essential to forging commercial alliances were apt to make those Indians who had previously been enemies of his allies into enemies of his own. A story that threads its way through Champlain's account of his sojourn in Acadia and Norumbega illustrates this point.[14]

In 1605, after spending a miserable winter on an island in the Saint Croix River near Passamaquoddy Bay, de Monts's men crossed the Bay of Fundy and built a new *habitation,* Port-Royal, on the Acadian peninsula. There they established friendly relations with Membertou, the chief of the local Souriquois (Mi'kmaq) band while taking pains to retain the goodwill of Messamouet, the sachem of the Mi'kmaqs who had lived near the abandoned Saint Croix settlement.[15] Both sachems understood the advantages to be had by trading with the French, and Messamouet in particular saw the potential for using this new connection as a means of expanding his influence. Thus in September 1606, Messamouet accompanied Champlain on a voyage down the coast to the Saco River with the intention of making peace with the Almouchiquois (Eastern Abenaki) sachem, Onemechin.[16] The Mi'kmaqs and the Eastern Abenakis had long been enemies, and Onemechin accurately interpreted Messamouet's lavish diplomatic gift— "kettles, axes, knives, and other articles" he had previously obtained from the French—as an effort to turn him into a client. He therefore reciprocated with a paltry present of "Indian corn, squashes, and Brazilian beans." Messamouet, Champlain wrote,

> departed much displeased because he had not been suitably repaid for what he had given them, and with the intention of making war upon them before long; for these people give only with the idea of receiving something, except to persons who have done them some signal service, such as aiding them in their wars.[17]

Champlain and his men continued down the coast to the Island Cape (Cape Ann), where to their surprise Onemechin soon appeared. He behaved strangely when they tried to give him a coat as a gift. He "presented it to another" (Champlain thought it was because he found it "uncomfortable . . . [and] could not adapt himself to it"[18]) and then drew Quiouhamenec, the local chief, aside for a private conference. Soon Quiouhamenec's band—Algonquian-speaking Pawtuckets—began to act in threatening ways. This disconcerted Champlain, who had found them perfectly agreeable during the previous year's visit.[19]

The voyage thereafter became increasingly unpleasant. Calling in at a handsome harbor they named Beau-port (Gloucester) on September 30, the French found themselves forced to draw their weapons and make a hasty exit when the Pawtuckets seemed to be preparing an attack. Two weeks later, at Port Fortuné (Stage Harbor), they were less lucky. The local Wampanoag warriors launched a surprise assault on a group of Frenchmen baking bread, killing four and severely wounding a fifth.[20] When Champlain tried to retaliate, he suffered several more casualties without killing any warriors or taking a single prisoner. He returned to Port-Royal with "four or five" men whose wounds festered with such a "stench" that the rest of the crew "could scarcely bear it."[21]

This abrupt reversal of fortune in dealing with the Indians left Champlain frustrated and puzzled. Had they thought it to their advantage, Messamouet and Membertou might have explained to him that all this mischief could be attributed to Onemechin, sachem of the Saco Abenakis, and his evident intention to persist in hostility toward the Mi'kmaqs—and thus to their ally, Champlain. Soon it came to war. During the winter of 1606–07, a warrior from Onemechin's band killed Panonias, a Malecite ally of the Mi'kmaqs who had acted as an interpreter on Champlain's exploring voyage of 1605. On June 20, 1607, Membertou led about 400 Mi'kmaq and Malecite warriors in a flotilla of canoes from Acadia to Abenaki country on the Saco. Champlain did not accompany them on the raid but noted that they returned on August 10 after killing twenty Abenakis, including Onemechin and another chief.[22]

Membertou's raid confirmed Champlain's belief that an extravagant desire for revenge motivated *les sauvages* in their dealings with one another. "This whole war," he wrote, "was solely on account of Panonias, one of our Indian friends, who . . . had been killed at Norumbega by the said Onemechin's . . . people." He did not yet understand the degree to which what had happened depended on French, not Indian, designs. The Mi'kmaqs' attack was unusually effective because two years of trade with the French had brought quantities of edged weapons—hatchets, knives, swords, arrowheads—into their possession. Wittingly or no, by their presence in Acadia as traders, the French had tipped the balance of power along the coast of Norumbega in favor of the Mi'kmaqs, to whom they had become not just neighbors and friends but also arms-suppliers and, perforce, allies.

Champlain understood little of this when he sailed for France in the fall of 1607. Uppermost in his mind was what he would advise the sieur de Monts (who had previously returned to France) concerning the future

"Carte Geographique de la Nouvelle France," published with Champlain's account, *Voyages Made to the Great River Saint Lawrence,* in 1613, was in part based on his 1607 map of Acadia and Norumbega.

activities of the company, that and the completion of a magnificent map of Acadia and Norumbega, based on his own detailed observations. But though Indians and their world no longer preoccupied Champlain as he returned to France, his next venture in America put them squarely before him, with effects even more dramatic, unforeseeable, and far-reaching than his experience thus far could have led him to expect.

By now he knew that Acadia and Norumbega were rich in fish and timber and might even yield copper; but insofar as the company's future profits lay in furs, its success would depend on locating a trading post further inland on the Saint Lawrence. There, closer to the source of prime beaver pelts, Champlain could make direct contact with interior peoples and outflank the small-time independent traders who infested Tadoussac.[23] De Monts agreed, named Champlain his lieutenant, and outfitted another fleet of three ships to return in 1608. One would make further explorations in Acadia; another would trade at Tadoussac; the third, *Le Don de Dieu,* would carry Champlain and the supplies he needed to establish a year-round trading post at a spot the Indians called Quebec, the Narrows. He had identified it on his voyage of 1603 as a good anchorage, with a defensible location for a fort on the north shore, where the "soil[, if it] were tilled . . . would be as good as ours" in France.[24] On July 3, he and his crew began to build the *habitation* there that in time became the capital of New France.

Champlain came to Quebec to stay, and—once he had beaten down a small mutiny among his workmen, gotten a crop of winter wheat and rye into the ground before frost, and survived the first terrible winter—he had every reason to believe he could. Two French boys, who had spent the winter with the local Montagnais band in order to learn their language, had become fluent enough to act as interpreters. The Montagnais themselves had embraced their new neighbors because Champlain's fortified trading post offered them shelter when their enemies attacked and held stocks of food to help them through times of scarcity.[25] Eager now to begin making a profit for his employers, Champlain engaged Montagnais guides to conduct him up the Saint Lawrence in June 1609. He hoped to contact the Algonquins who lived upriver, some of whom had visited Quebec the previous year; most of all, he wanted to establish relations with the Hurons who lived even further west, beside a great freshwater sea.

Before Champlain had traveled a dozen leagues up the Saint Lawrence, he met perhaps three hundred Hurons and Algonquins who were coming to Quebec to make his acquaintance.[26] Following an exchange of speeches and presents, the leader of the Algonquins, Iroquet, and the Huron chief, Ochasteguin, offered Champlain a proposition that he could not refuse. "Some ten moons ago," they reminded him, not long after his arrival at Quebec,

> Iroquet's son had come to see me, when I had given him a kind reception, and had told him that . . . I wished to help them against their enemies. With these they had long been at war, on account of many cruelties practised against their tribe under colour of friendship. They said that, having ever since desired friendship, they had asked all the Indians I saw on the river's bank to come to meet us for the purpose of making an alliance with us. Since these had never seen Christians, this fact also moved them to come and see us; that I might do with them and their companions whatever I liked; that they had no children with them, but only men skilled in war and full of courage, who knew the country and the rivers in the land of the

Iroquois. And that they now besought me to return to our settlement, for them to see our houses, and that three days later we should
all set off on the war-path together.[27]

Champlain assured them that he personally would join them on the expedition "for their greater satisfaction, and that they could see that I had no
other intention than to make war," for he feared that "evil reports [had
been] made to them"—probably by the crafty Montagnais—suggesting that
the French could not be trusted to keep their promises. Then, he wrote, "I
said no more, awaiting an opportunity of showing them by results more
than [words what] they could expect of me."[28]

They returned to Quebec for several days of feasting, gift-giving, and
oratory before departing on June 28 for the River of the Iroquois (now the
Richelieu). This offered the quickest route to the Mohawk country and also
the one likeliest to yield contact with enemy warriors prepared to do battle.
At the river's mouth, however, the majority of the Indians rethought their
priorities. "The result of which," Champlain wrote, "was that only a part of
them decided to come with me, whilst the rest went back to their own
country with . . . the goods they had bartered."[29] Champlain and two other
Frenchmen armed with matchlock muskets therefore joined just sixty or so
warriors—Montagnais, Huron, and Algonquin—to paddle upstream in
twenty-four canoes toward "a very large lake, filled with beautiful islands,"
that no Christian had yet seen.[30]

Champlain observed the Indians' behavior ever more closely as they
neared the "large, beautiful region near the lake, where . . . their enemies
lived,"[31] setting down the first detailed European description of a native
military campaign in the northeastern woodlands. He admired much of
what they did. They traveled during the day, he noted, in three divisions: "a
troop of scouts" ahead, to look for signs of the enemy; the main body, "always under arms," in the middle; and behind them a third "troop for hunting, scattered in various directions" but always taking care not to betray the
expedition's presence.[32] At night, the Indians made camp by constructing
bark huts or wigwams near the shore and felling trees to make a barricade
on the land side, all "so quickly that after less than two hours' work, five
hundred of their enemies would have had difficulty in driving them out."
After sending scouts to make sure that no enemy war parties were within
"two or three leagues," they cooked a meal and retired for the night without
posting guards. This lackadaisical practice, so unlike the care with which
they organized their movement by water, struck Champlain as folly. He

tried to persuade them to "have men posted to listen and see whether they might perceive anything, and not live as they were doing like silly creatures." The Indians laughed him off. Having worked hard all day long, they said, they needed their sleep.[33]

Champlain's companions were casual about security because they knew, more or less, where to find their foes and what to expect from them when they met. All casualness vanished when they judged that they were within three days' travel of the Mohawk settlements. At that point, he noted, "they proceed stealthily at night, all in a body, except the scouts. In the day time they retire into the thick of the woods, where they rest without any straggling, or making a noise, or making a fire even for the purpose of cooking." They also ceased to hunt, eating only "baked Indian meal . . . which becomes like porridge" when "steeped in water."[34] During the daytime encampments the leaders also prepared their warriors for battle. "The chiefs take sticks a foot long," Champlain wrote,

> one for each man, indicating by other ones, a little larger, their chiefs. Then they go into the woods and clear off a place of five or six feet square, where the chief, as sergeant-major, arranges all these sticks into an order as he sees fit. Then he calls his companions, and they come all armed, and he demonstrates to them the rank and order that they will observe when they are fighting with their enemies. All this the savages regard attentively, remarking the figure that their chief has made with the sticks. Afterward they retire from there, and put themselves in order, according to what they have seen of the said sticks. Then they mix one amongst another, and again returning to their order two or three times, they go back to their huts without need of a sergeant to maintain their ranks. . . . Such is the rule they maintain in their warfare.[35]

At each encampment the Indians also consulted "their *Pilotois* or *Ostemoy,* who are the people who play the part of wizards," asking them what portents of the future they had seen in their visions or dreams.[36] These "superstitious ceremonies," Champlain believed, were as foolish as their refusal to post guards, for they could only detract from the vigilance, "courage, and good hope" with which soldiers should approach battle. For this reason he was irritated when the Indians pestered him to tell "whether I had had dreams and had seen their enemies"—and more than a little disconcerted when, during his midday sleep on July 29, he dreamed vividly of "our enemies, the Iroquois, drowning before our eyes." His companions, however, rejoiced. "This [dream] gave them such confidence that they no longer had any doubt as to the good fortune awaiting them."[37]

They met the enemy that night near the promontory of Ticonderoga, at the head of the lake. It was a Mohawk war party of about 200; like the invaders, they had been traveling under cover of darkness. Neither side expected to meet the other on the water, and for a time all was shouting and confusion. Then, according to Champlain, "We drew out into the lake and the Iroquois landed and arranged all their canoes near one another. Then they began to fell trees . . . and they barricaded themselves well." The Montagnais and their allies lay offshore "within bowshot" of the Mohawks, sending warriors in two canoes to parley, and arrange a battle for the following morning. For the remainder of the night, the two groups hurled insults across the water in a way unsurprising to Champlain, who recognized it as behavior "such as is usual at the siege of a city" in Europe. Before dawn they debarked into a meadow a few hundred yards from the Mohawk fort and made ready for battle.[38]

Champlain and his countrymen donned helmets and light armor, loaded their muskets, lit the slow-burning match cord that would ignite the charges when they pulled the triggers, and waited as the Indians drew themselves up in battle order. Champlain watched the Iroquois warriors—"in appearance strong, robust men"—issue from the barricade clad in wooden armor, armed with bows and flint-tipped arrows. They "came slowly to meet us with a gravity and calm which I admired," he noted. "Our Indians likewise advanced in similar order, and told me that those who had the three big plumes were the chiefs . . . ; and I was to do what I could to kill them." As they advanced, Champlain's fellow musketeers, along with several Indians, slipped off into the trees at the verge of the meadow and took up firing positions.[39]

Champlain hung back, trailing the advancing warriors until they halted within bowshot of the Mohawks. Then

> Our Indians began to call me with great cries: and gave me passage by opening in two parts. And I put myself at their head, marching some twenty paces ahead, until I was within some thirty paces of the enemy, where immediately they saw me. I halted. . . . Just as I saw them making ready to draw their bows on us, I laid my cheek to the arquebus [musket] and aimed straight at one of the three chiefs, and with the shot two of them fell to the ground. One of their companions was also wounded, who died some time later. I had put four

This engraving, "The Defeat of the Iroquois at Lake Champlain," followed a sketch (now lost) that Champlain provided, but added elements, notably the depiction of the Indian warriors as naked, which followed the artistic conventions of the day. In fact warriors on both sides wore wooden plate armor or at least carried shields like those depicted in the next illustration.

balls in my arquebus. Then our people, seeing this shot so favorable for them, commenced to utter such great cries that one could not have heard it thunder, while the arrows flew thick on both sides. The Iroquois were astonished that two men should have been killed so quickly, even though they were armored with wooden plates bound together with cotton cord, which were proof against their arrows. This gave them great apprehension. As I was reloading, one of my companions fired a shot from the woods, which astonished them once again so much that, seeing their chiefs dead, they lost courage and took to flight, abandoning the field and their fort, fleeing into the depths of the wood, where we pursued them, and where I killed still more. Our Indians also killed several and took ten or twelve prisoners. The rest fled with the wounded. Among our Indians fifteen or sixteen were wounded by arrows, but these soon recovered.[40]

To Champlain's chagrin, his allies showed no inclination to annihilate their fleeing foes. He could not understand such a lack of initiative; letting slip a matchless opportunity to kill or capture the entire enemy party, they stopped to collect the armor and shields and weapons the Mohawks had

Early-seventeenth-century Huron dress. These engravings show native costumes similar to those worn by the Algonquins, Montagnais, and Iroquois that Champlain encountered. A and C show warriors equipped for raids; E depicts a warrior in armor made of wooden panels bound together with cotton cord.

dropped as they fled, feasting on the provisions they found within the barricade and dancing to celebrate their victory. Three hours later, with the surviving Mohawks miles away and safe, Champlain's allies returned to their canoes and paddled northward, toward home.

That evening they stopped, thirty miles down the lake, for one more ceremony. Choosing a prisoner, the Montagnais kindled a fire and bade him sing his death song. Then they stripped and tortured him, applying brands to his back, fingertips, and genitals, ripping out his fingernails, scalping him and pouring hot pitch into the wound, and slicing open his arms to get at the sinews, which they twisted around sticks and ripped out. Champlain, aghast at the sight, nonetheless found the man's fortitude astonishing: "he bore it so firmly that sometimes one would have said he felt scarcely any pain." When offered a burning stick to apply to the victim, he refused: Christians, he told them, "do not commit such cruelties"; when they killed, Christians "killed people outright." Eventually, despite their protests, he seized his musket and "with one shot caused [the victim] to escape all the tortures he would have suffered." The Indians then dismembered and disemboweled the corpse, scattering its parts, though "they kept the scalp, which they had flayed, as they did with of all the others whom they had killed in their attack." When they continued the next morning, the Frenchman understood that the rest of the prisoners would meet the same fate when their captors brought them home.[41]

If Champlain had no qualms about participating in a battle, the captive's death clearly disturbed him; the more so, perhaps, because he understood that he would have to witness the torture of many prisoners if he hoped to maintain friendly relations with his allies. He had gone too far down that path now to turn back. The Hurons and Algonquins "were all much pleased at what had taken place in the war, and because I had gone with them willingly. So we all separated with great protestations of mutual friendship, and they asked me if I would not go to their country, and aid them continually like a brother. I promised them I would."[42] He also accepted the gift of a scalp and "a pair of shields belonging to their enemies . . . to show to the king. And to please them I promised to do so."[43] Finally, when he returned to Quebec, several Algonquins who had left the expedition at the mouth of the Richelieu paid him a visit to express their regret at not having taken part in the fighting. To make amends they presented him "some furs in consideration of the fact that I had been there and had helped their friends."[44]

Champlain sailed for France in September to make his report to the king and the sieur de Monts. Not by nature a reflective man, he nonetheless understood that he had crossed a significant threshold: military alliance, he knew, was the key that would open amicable trade relations with the Indians of the interior. In his report to de Monts, Champlain described the favorable "prospects for the future in view of the promises of the natives called Ochatequins," or Hurons. These "good Iroquois" had agreed to allow him "to complete the exploration of the great river Saint Lawrence, on condition we carried out the promise to assist them in their wars" against "the other Iroquois [of the Five Nations], who are their enemies . . . farther south."[45] He had risked his own life, and deprived several Mohawks of theirs, for the sake of securing a steady supply of beaver pelts. That was a long step beyond the diplomatic and commercial alliance he had forged with Membertou and Messamouet, who had not insisted that he actually join them in attacking their enemies. But the potential rewards of an alliance sealed with blood, he now knew, were vastly greater.

In a variation on the theme Cortés had sounded in Mexico a century before, Champlain had moved from observing Indians to trading with them and from trading to participating in their wars as an ally. He went to war again with more decisive results in the coming year, when he returned to Canada in time to join another war party of Montagnais and Algonquins. Upon his arrival at Quebec, a group of Montagnais warriors "importuned me with questions as to whether I should fail in what I had promised them. I reassured them and made them fresh promises, asking them whether they had found me false in the past. They rejoiced greatly," he observed, "when I repeated my promises to them." Yet still they pressed him:

> "There are many Basques and Mistigoches (for so they call the Normans and the people of Saint Malo) who say that they will accompany us on the war-path. . . . Do they speak the truth?" I said that they did not, and that . . . what they said was merely in order to obtain possession of the Indians' goods.[46]

The success of the previous year had raised the stakes. Even if Champlain had seen this as a reason for caution, however, he could not decline to take part in a new expedition, for his prospects of profit now depended on meeting the Indians' expectations.

Champlain accordingly arranged a trade fair and took part in preparatory ceremonies at Trois Rivières, on the Saint Lawrence downriver from its confluence with the Richelieu, just before the expedition. Expectations high, he sailed from Quebec with "four pinnaces [schooners] loaded with merchandise for bartering furs with among others the Ochateguins [Hurons], who were to . . . bring along as many as 400 men to go on the war-path."[47] This time, however, the path proved unexpectedly short.

On June 19, 1610, Champlain was at the rendezvous point, an island at the mouth of the Richelieu where he expected to meet another 200 Algonquin warriors, when messengers from a scouting party brought word that a force of about a hundred Mohawks had been discovered nearby. Champlain and ten musketeers joined the warriors, who now rushed to attack the Mohawks, whom they found trapped within a defensive barricade. In a bloody assault the allies killed virtually everyone in the fort, many by point-blank musket fire: the French "hardly missed a shot, and fired two or three bullets each time, and for the most part had [their] arquebuses resting on the . . . barricade" as they aimed into the crowded enclosure. In the end, only fifteen Mohawks survived to be taken captive. All save a single warrior, whom the Montagnais gave to Champlain and who later escaped, died under torture.[48]

Thus intercultural exchanges that began with mutual observation and trade in 1603 progressed to military alliance and victory in 1609 and culminated, the following year, in a massacre. And yet for all the slaughter it produced, Champlain's alliance-building did not yield the profits he had anticipated. The wound he sustained in the battle—an arrow split his ear and lodged in his neck—was scarcely dressed before he realized that "other pinnaces" had followed his expedition upriver. These vessels belonged to interlopers—the Mistigoches (Normans and Malouines) whom he had earlier denounced—who had already begun to trade with Champlain's allies. When the expected party of Algonquins arrived, too late to participate in the fighting, the Mistigoches "carried off the better part" of their pelts, he wrote. "It was doing [the interlopers] a great favour to search out for them strange tribes, in order that they might later on carry off the whole profit without running any risk or hazard."[49]

Champlain's venture thus came to a bitter end in 1610, and worse followed. Not long after he returned to Quebec he learned of the assassination of King Henri IV and the accession to the throne of the nine year-old Louis XIII, developments that called into question not just the welfare of the kingdom but the future of the sieur de Monts and his associates in the fur trade. Despite all their work, the trade had not yet begun to pay off; hence Champlain's continuing quest to establish contact with interior peoples who lived close to the supply of furs and beyond the reach of competitors. As long as Henri lived, the associates could hope at least to retain their monopoly by virtue of de Monts's position at court. Henri's murder changed everything for Champlain and de Monts; they were compelled to spend years talking up Canada and trying to enlist as business partners those courtiers who controlled access to the young king—a process as frustrating as the effort to create an exclusive trading partnership with Indians near the source of the best pelts. Champlain returned to Canada to govern Quebec and trade for furs as best he could until 1615, when he opened a new phase in Canada's history by introducing missionaries and forged an alliance directly with the Hurons by taking part in yet another expedition against the Iroquois.

War and Trade in the Age of Contact

Champlain was only one of many western Europeans who ventured across the Atlantic in the sixteenth and seventeenth centuries, a period of extended interaction among peoples who had previously known little or nothing of each other. From the Bight of Benin to the harbor of Havana, from Hudson's Bay to the Bay of Biscay, millions were affected, directly or indirectly, in the exchange of goods, animals, plants, people, and pathogens. The peoples of the Atlantic rim shared the same fundamental human needs for food, sex, security, and transcendence, but they participated in cultures that expressed those needs, and societies and economies that organized the pursuit of them, in strikingly different ways. Systems of war and trade, for example, were as old as human societies in Europe, the Americas, and Africa but were conducted according to different rules and served different ends on the continents where they had arisen.

Champlain's experiences illustrate the consequences of the convergence of these systems during the Age of Contact. Although he understood participation as an ally in wars among Native Americans as a means to the end of gaining advantage in the fur trade, Champlain's actions in 1609 and 1610 must be seen as part of a long-running interaction between European and North American patterns of trade and war. In the sixteenth century, that prolonged encounter catalyzed a Military Revolution that transformed the European state system. Over the course of the seventeenth and eighteenth centuries, it reshaped the world.

Champlain's formative experiences as a soldier in France's Eighth War of Religion were, in a very real sense, the product of Spain's ability to extract riches from the mines of Mexico and Peru. The European warfare system was already in flux from the introduction of gunpowder weapons and the Reformation's loosening of restraints on wars within Christendom when torrents of American bullion flooded into Spain's treasury in the aftermath of Cortés's and Pizarro's conquests. This extraordinary influx of wealth produced a period of extraordinarily destructive and expensive warfare, driven largely by Spain's ambition to dominate Europe and determination to defend the Catholic faith. As Holy Roman Emperor from 1519 to 1556, Charles V (King Charles I of Spain) used the treasure of the Indies to build the greatest army in Europe. Under Charles and his son Philip II, Spain fought France five times; supported a seven-decade-long war in the Netherlands in an attempt to keep Dutch Protestants from asserting their independence from Rome and Madrid; sent an Armada against England; conducted land campaigns against Muslim states in North Africa; and fought the Mediterranean naval war against the Ottomans that climaxed at the Battle of Lepanto (1571). Meanwhile wars eddied everywhere on the edges of the Spanish vortex, fueled by the silver that circulated throughout western Europe as a consequence of Spain's vast military expenditures.[50]

Yet the American silver that sustained the worst warfare and the worst inflation that Europe had ever seen did not enable that continent's princes to win decisive victories. With two minor exceptions—the war of the Schmalkaldic League (1546–47) and the war of Ostia (1557)—every European conflict of the sixteenth century proved to be prolonged, prodigiously expensive, and indecisive. These great wars introduced new weaponry (the arquebus, the pistol, the long pike, improved and more mobile artillery), new tactics and formations (the Spanish Square and the cavalry caracole, the regiment and the division), new styles of fortification (the artillery-resistant *trace italienne*), and vastly enlarged standing armies. Such innovations, however, balanced the advantages of offense and defense so closely that every war became a war of attrition: belligerents fought until they exhausted their resources, then negotiated treaties of peace in order to recover financially and rebuild their armed forces. Intensive developments in recruiting, logistics, and administration strained the financial capacities of governments to the limit, inducing monarchs to claim ever larger powers while inflicting ever more widespread misery and death.[51]

The sixteenth century's indecisive land warfare promoted another trend, too, of vast consequence for the future of the world: a great expansion of Europe's navies. Spain's celebrated attack on England with the Armada of 1588 represented the first attempt to break through to victory in the Netherlands revolt—a deadlocked land war—by sending a fleet to sweep the English from the Channel and disable them from further aiding the Protestant Dutch.[52] The Armada, of course, did not succeed, and the Anglo-Spanish War of 1588–1604 ended as indecisively as most other sixteenth-century conflicts. The destruction of his Armada, however, so concentrated the gloomy mind of Spain's King Philip II that its "defeat . . . was not so much the end as the beginning of the Spanish navy."[53] England, France, and the Dutch responded with a naval arms race that lasted a century, produced major improvements in ship and armaments design, and gave their fleets the capacity to operate over oceanic distances. By the dawn of the eighteenth century, European navies could project force around the world and thus sustain imperial competition on a global scale.

By the time Champlain leveled his musket at the Mohawk warriors, then, Europe's rulers were groping their way toward a realization that seems axiomatic today: that "war is merely the continuation of policy by other means."[54] Wars were only the most violent phases of a perpetual competition for dominance among rulers who knew that money was the sinews of war and who believed that the supply of wealth in the world equaled the amount of treasure—gold and silver—in existence. Because commercial competition among states amounted, in effect, to the zero-sum game of gaining this wealth, early modern statesmen instinctively understood trade as the continuation of war by other means.[55]

But warfare and trade as practiced in North America at the beginning of the Age of Contact had little to do with the practices and assumptions that were becoming normative in Europe.[56] Most aboriginal groups north of Mexico, east of the Rockies, and south of central Canada—the region of maize cultivation—regarded war and trade (not, as the Europeans thought, war and peace) as opposite conditions in relations between groups. War and trade, in fact, were so different that they tended to come under the control of different sets of leaders.[57] The affairs of ordinary life and diplomacy were typically arranged by "civil chiefs"—older men whose talents in conciliation, negotiation, and oratory tended to sustain understanding and cooperation between groups. The destructive, emotional, and supremely antisocial activities of warfare, on the other hand, were the province of young, impulsive, vigorous men, led by "war chiefs." Unlike European countries, in which monarchs and parliaments claimed an indivisible supreme power and decided whether their nations would wage war or pursue peace, in North America among native peoples, the idea of a single sovereign universally responsible for policy was unknown.

Anthropologists identify the prevalent form of aboriginal conflict east of the Rockies as "mourning war." Mourning wars resembled feuds (which is what Champlain took them for) insofar as one group compensated for deaths it had suffered by exacting corresponding lives from the enemy group held responsible for the killing. But mourning wars differed crucially from feuds in that they also controlled population losses by producing captives who could be adopted to replace the dead.[58] Mourning wars might go on indefinitely at varying levels of activity and indeed were virtually perpetual among inveterate enemies. The principal goal, however, was not so much the destruction of an enemy's population as the support of one's own.

North American military encounters in the Age of Contact tended to occur in one of two ritualized forms, raids or pitched battles. Raids aimed at securing women and children as captives for adoption, or at capturing enemy warriors for ritual torture and execution, which served as a means of acquiring their spiritual power. Pitched battles were much larger affairs that occurred less frequently because they required the participation of men from several villages or of allies from other nations. What Champlain witnessed at Ticonderoga on July 30, 1609, was intended to be just this sort of battle, in which ranks of armored men first showered insults, then arrows, on each other. Had he and his two compatriots not intervened by firing their muskets into the Mohawk ranks and turning the fight into a rout, combat would doubtless have continued with further exchanges of arrows. Since the sharp but brittle flint arrowheads could not easily penetrate wooden armor, few men would likely have died in the battle. Massed confrontations might also evolve into single combat between champions representing each side, in a kind of lethal sporting event. Whatever form pitched battles took, however, the wholesale destruction of enemies was never the goal. The point of a battle was to demonstrate martial skills and to capture what enemies could be taken or, failing that, to acquire the trophies, such as scalps or heads, by which a warrior could appropriate the spiritual power of his adversary.[59]

Peace was typically established by diplomatic rituals that instituted trading relations between groups; indeed, trade was so much a part of the definition of peace that "the absence of trading relationships could easily lead to a presumption of hostility."[60] Trade differed from war in every way. Trade emphasized sociability: based on ideals of reciprocity and traditionally conceived of as mutual gift-giving, exchanges built connections both within and between groups. Trade was therefore fundamentally *anti*competitive, since its ultimate goal was not to gain wealth but to create mutual obligations and alliances of advantage to all. The most significant items—for example, tobacco, shell beads, and crystals—were sacred in character and could not be traded without endowing the exchanges themselves with spiritual power.[61] Men controlled long-distance trade between groups, but women as well as men participated in local exchanges of goods and food. Because of the need to maintain balance, recall past connections, and sustain mutual trust between groups, trade relations could never be entrusted to impulsive leaders. Only men who had survived their warrior youth and lived long enough to achieve self-control, learn the difficult arts of conciliation, and acquire the wisdom of age could act as civil chiefs.[62]

The reciprocity and cooperativeness of trade relations did not necessarily imply equality between the partners. Indeed, the privileged access of one trading partner to a desirable commodity implied a fundamental *in*equality in most alliances. Even before the beginnings of European contact, it seems clear that Indian groups able to obtain such spiritually powerful items as wampum used them strategically to enhance their own position vis-à-vis other groups. Of such imbalances of power as well as the mutual need for security were alliances made. With a massive increase in the availability of

European manufactures at trading posts like Quebec, trade goods became crucial to the construction and maintenance of alliances. This was especially the case when the available items—initially, anything made of iron, steel, or brass, later guns and ammunition—could be used to increase the military capacity of one's group.

The onset of colonization radically destabilized Indian practices of war and trade. Intimations of these changes can be seen in Champlain's encounters with natives along the New England coast in 1606. When the Mi'kmaq (Souriquois) sachem Messamouet tried to establish trading relations with the Eastern Abenaki (Almouchiquois) chief, Onemechin, his extravagant gift of metallic goods announced his connection to a new, powerful ally. This left Onemechin to choose between two clear alternatives. On one hand, he could opt for peaceful relations with the Mi'kmaq and an open channel to French trade goods through Messamouet. This would increase his power in dealing with other bands in his area but subordinate him to Messamouet, who could ultimately control his access to the Europeans' goods. On the other hand, he could reject Messamouet's proposed alliance. If he did that, the best he could do in the short run would be to try to eliminate the French ally whose presence had destabilized the accustomed balance of power. That was, in fact, the course he chose. In doing so, he effectively made active warfare inevitable between his band and the Mi'kmaqs.

But war, when it came, was of a different sort than Onemechin had known. Ordinarily, the killing of a single man—in this case, the Malecite (Etchemin) go-between Panonias, an ally of the Mi'kmaqs—would have occasioned retribution, but it would have been a retaliation roughly proportional to the injury suffered. When Messamouet and Membertou's bands struck back in the summer of 1607, however, they did so with what must have seemed exceptional fury. While Champlain was not a witness and therefore did not describe precisely what took place, the likeliest scenario is that when the Mi'kmaqs and Abenakis organized themselves for a pitched battle, the metallic weapons that the Mi'kmaq warriors had acquired from the French gave them a destructive power far greater than that of their foes.

To take twenty lives, including those of two chiefs, was much more than a simple retaliation for Panonias's death. It was an unmistakable attempt to use superior force to subordinate the Abenakis, a goal that Messamouet's earlier diplomatic approach had failed to achieve. Under normal conditions, no group would risk striking such a blow because it would invite retaliation in kind; only a people emboldened by access to superior weapons would have tried it. That peace between the Mi'kmaqs and the Abenakis was eventually negotiated by a French mediator—Champlain's ship carpenter Champdoré, who remained in Acadia—suggests that the Saco Abenakis were at last compelled to make peace (and thus to enter into trade with the Mi'kmaqs) on an unequal footing, just as Messamouet had intended.[63]

The results were even more dramatic and far-reaching in 1609 and 1610, when Champlain agreed to join his Montagnais, Algonquin, and Huron partners in expeditions against their Iroquois enemies. He understood, of course, almost nothing of the source of enmity between the groups; it seems to have grown up as a result of the disappearance, fifty to sixty years earlier, of the Iroquoian peoples who had inhabited the Saint Lawrence Valley from Quebec to Lake Ontario. Five Nations Iroquois warriors ranging northward from their homeland to hunt in the vacated region had collided with Montagnais, Algonquins, and Hurons who were entering the area from the east and west.[64] The seasonal trade with the French at Tadoussac had given the Montagnais and their allies some degree of advantage over the Five Nations in this shadowy half-century of struggle. Champlain's establishment of a trading post and *habitation* at Quebec, however, and his willingness to use terrifying gunpowder weapons on behalf of his Montagnais, Algonquin, and Huron friends, fell on the Five Nations like a thunderbolt.

The defeat of the Mohawks at Ticonderoga in 1609 and even more the annihilation of the Mohawk war party in the valley of the Richelieu in the following year effectively threw the Five Nations back from their northern hunting grounds and cut them off from access to French trade goods, unless, of course, they were prepared to subordinate themselves to the Montagnais. A whole generation passed before the Iroquois began to regain the ground they had lost to the Montagnais, Hurons, and Algonquins as a consequence of their alliance with Champlain. In the meantime, the old practice of great war parties and pitched battles vanished, a casualty of the French muskets and steel arrowheads that rendered wooden armor useless and massed formations suicidal. Raids—less governable, because they represented war at the level of the village rather than any larger unit—now became the main mode of military operations.

How the Mohawks recovered, and the revival of the Five Nations fortunes generally, was a story that also began, by sheer coincidence, in 1609. On September 13, as Champlain was sailing for France to report to the sieur de Monts, Henry Hudson was guiding his stout little sixty-ton ship, the *Half Moon,* past the isle of Manhattan, heading north up a broad estuary that he hoped would lead him to the Pacific. Hudson, an English navigator, had been hired by the Amsterdam chamber of the Dutch East India Company to sail to Asia by way of the Barents Sea. When icebergs and fog blocked his way, he prudently avoided a mutiny by heading west and south to seek a warmer passage. What he found on the North American coast at 41° north latitude was not a route to the Orient but a river navigable for more than a hundred and fifty miles inland whose banks were peopled by natives of varying degrees of friendliness. The most cordial were those who lived near the height of navigation at the site of the modern city of Albany.

These were the Mahicans, an Algonquian-speaking people, and from about the nineteenth through the twenty-third of September, they entertained Hudson and traded eagerly with the *Half Moon*'s crew. So amiable were relations that at the end of his stay Captain Hudson repaid the Mahicans' hospitality by inviting "the chiefe men of the Countrey" on board and giving them "so much Wine and *Aqua vitae,* that they were all merrie"—one of them, indeed, to the point of unconsciousness. The contrast between Hudson's introduction of one powerful European commodity and Champlain's demonstration of another could hardly have been stronger; only time showed that in their own ways they were equally deadly.[65]

Whatever impression their hangovers may have left with the Mahican chiefs, Hudson's reports to the Amsterdam chamber impressed the merchants sufficiently that several petitioned the States General for the right to build a fort and engage in the fur trade on the upper reaches of Hudson's river. In 1614, Fort Nassau, a tiny blockhouse on an island, staffed by ten to a dozen traders, opened for business. With interruptions, trade continued on or near the site of Albany until the larger, more permanent post, Fort Orange, was established on the west bank, ten years later.[66]

The establishment of trade with the Dutch did not work to the immediate benefit of the Mohawks.[67] Far from it: the decade and a half that followed 1609–10 was a time of decline for the Mohawks and indeed the Five Nations of the Iroquois as a whole, for they found themselves increasingly disadvantaged in their competition with the Saint Lawrence Valley's Indians; their ability to acquire Dutch trade goods depended on the goodwill of the Mahicans, who occupied the territory along the Hudson. The Dutch States General's grant of a monopoly of the Indian trade to the Dutch West India Company in 1621 and the subsequent establishment of Fort Orange as a company post in 1624 brought the affairs of the Mohawks to a crisis. Interested in dealing with Indians as close as possible to source of peltry, the Dutch began to extend their diplomatic and trading connections northward. The Mohawks could not ignore these overtures to their mortal enemies—peoples who already enjoyed privileged access to trade goods and edged weapons on the Saint Lawrence—so in 1622 they approached Champlain with proposals for peace. A formal treaty, deeply gratifying to the French leader, followed in 1624.

Peace with the French was but a prelude to war with the Mahicans, whom Mohawk war parties attacked soon after the treaty had been concluded. The Dutch urged the Mahicans to fight to the death and promised to aid them against the Iroquois, whom they saw as interlopers and troublemakers. Unfortunately, the musketeers of Fort Orange proved far less competent military allies to the Mahicans than Champlain and his fellow gunmen had to the Montagnais. By late 1628, the Mahicans had abandoned their bottomland villages around Fort Orange for the less dangerous uplands and mountains east of the Hudson.[68]

The subjugation of the Mahican people was no welcome development to the Dutch, nor, in a more complicated way, was it immediately favorable for the Iroquois, victors though they were. That the Mohawks now commanded the routes of access to Fort Orange of course forced the Dutch to open a direct trade with them; moreover, the Dutch could now deal with the Algonquins, Hurons, and Montagnais only on Mohawk sufferance. Fewer partners meant smaller profits for the West India Company, and a set of trading ties limited to a group whose lands lay well to the south of the prime beaver country. Meanwhile, the Mohawk attacks on the Mahicans were less the product of a well-considered policy than of the freelance efforts of war chiefs and warriors, evidently undertaken without respect to the wishes of the Iroquois civil chiefs who had negotiated peace with Champlain in 1624. The success of the Mohawks in driving out the Mahicans, in other words, bespoke both a weakening of traditional controls on warlike behavior and an intention on the part of the war chiefs to dominate commercial relations with the Dutch.

It made perfect sense for the war chiefs to want to do so. Like Beowulf, "lord and lavisher of rings,"[69] the most successful Indian leaders were not only the bravest and most skillful but the most generous ones. By the 1620s in eastern North America, the most desirable gifts to distribute to one's followers were items of European manufacture. The logic of aggression was thus straightforward, but it held a terrible peril. If war chiefs usurped the policy-making functions of civil chiefs, the old ways of conciliation that had made trade the antithesis of war might be corrupted. If indeed warfare became primarily a means to achieve material ends, there might be no limit to the extent or duration of war's violence. The degree to which this was understood in seventeenth-century Iroquoia is impossible to determine, but in retrospect nothing could be more clear than that by seizing control of the area around Fort Orange, the Mohawks had entered a new, supremely hazardous phase of their history.

"Wherefore Now Consider What You Wish to Do"

No one knew better than Samuel de Champlain that Indians controlled the destiny of European settlers and settlements in North America. Without their tolerance for colonization and their cooperation in trade, virtually all European dreams of empire were doomed to fail. To survive, Champlain and colonists like him had to steer a course through uncharted seas of intercultural diplomacy. Ultimately, their success depended on choices made by Indian leaders in America and by financiers and government officials in Europe, groups whose agendas and intentions could fluctuate with chaotic unpredictability.

Champlain, therefore, worried about the Mohawks' new relationship with the Dutch. By 1628, New France had been at peace with the Iroquois league for four years, but he had enough experience with Indians to know that the peace was as fragile as the powers of civil chiefs to control young men were limited. Mohawk warriors might at any time resume their raids against the *habitants* and Indians of the Saint Lawrence Valley. By this point he had given two decades of his life to the colony—long enough to know how much its survival remained in doubt. The resumption of war between Champlain's native allies and the Iroquois would only make things worse, especially if the Dutch sold substantial quantities of weapons to the Five Nations.

This distressed him because he had worked so hard against the odds to make New France a stable and profitable colony. He had striven to create closer ties with the fur-rich Hurons far to the west, but the Normans and Malouines and Basques had continued to poach on the trade from Tadoussac, thereby keeping the company's profits so small as to discourage investors. As a result, the company remained seriously undercapitalized and Quebec's population had not risen above seventy to eighty *habitants*. Moreover, New France had yet to become agriculturally self-sustaining, which gave Champlain considerable anxiety as he contemplated his colony's vulnerability to attack.

Things had begun to look up, it was true, after the 1624 peace agreement with the Iroquois, when an extraordinary cleric, Cardinal Richelieu, came to dominate the politics of the French court. Richelieu took a keen interest in Canada, which he perceived not only as a trading venture but as an engine for expanding French influence internationally. In 1627, the cardinal sponsored the formation of the Compagnie de la Nouvelle-France (known, because of the number of courtiers, clerics, and merchants who held stock in it, as the Company of One Hundred Associates) to colonize, trade with, and evangelize in Canada. In return for the right to grant lands in the Saint Lawrence Valley and a monopoly on every economic activity in the colony except fishing, the company agreed to settle 4,000 colonists in Canada over the coming fifteen years and to pay the expenses of a new Jesuit initiative to convert the Indians. The first four hundred colonists left France in May 1628 aboard a convoy of five ships. Neither the settlers nor their ships, however, reached Quebec.

Unfortunately for Champlain's hopes, Richelieu's Catholic zeal had also stimulated an armed revolt by France's Protestants in 1625. England supported the rebels and declared war on France in 1626, but the Huguenots' hope of success faded two years later when the military incompetence of the Duke of Buckingham left them trapped in La Rochelle, besieged by a massive army under Richelieu's direct command. Hoping to distract the French by attacking their interests elsewhere (and to reap a tidy profit in the process), an English merchant long based in Dieppe, Gervase Kirke, obtained a letter of marque from King Charles I authorizing him to launch a privateering expedition against Quebec. Ships under the command of his French-born sons, David, Thomas, and Louis, were therefore waiting to pick off the Hundred Associates' convoy as it sailed up the Saint Lawrence with the colonists and supplies that Champlain desperately needed. By that time they had already seized all the shipping and trade goods they had found at Tadoussac and offered the booty to the Montagnais in return for furs. The Montagnais, always in search of new trading partners, were only too happy to oblige.[70]

David Kirke paused long enough from harvesting profits at Tadoussac to dispatch several small vessels upriver as far as Cape Tourmente, twenty miles below Quebec, the spot where, the Montagnais informed him, the colony pastured its cattle. Kirke's men herded the animals into the barn, barred its doors, and burned it to the ground. Then they sent Champlain an exquisitely courteous note from Kirke, inviting him to capitulate. "I know," the letter read, that when you are distressed for want of food, I shall more easily obtain what I desire—which is, to take your settlement. And in order to prevent any ship arriving, I am determined to remain [at Tadoussac] until the season of navigation has closed, so that no ship may come to revictual you. Wherefore now consider what you wish to do: whether you are willing to surrender the settlement or not; for, sooner or later, with God's help, I must have it.[71]

Champlain, well-versed in the etiquette of European siege warfare, declined with equal politesse. The barn, he wrote, had been only a little thatched hut (*une petite chaumière*), while the immolated cattle were but "a few beasts dead which in no way diminish what we depend on for our living." In view of Quebec's supplies of "grain, Indian corn, pease, and beans, not to mention what this country produces," surrender would be unthinkable: "honour demands that we fight to the death." Therefore, he concluded, "We are now waiting from hour to hour to receive you, and resist . . . the claims you are making on these places."[72]

It was all bravado. The barn had been no mere *chaumière* but a big stable in the Norman style, sixty feet long and twenty wide. The beasts had been Quebec's entire cattle herd. Despite Champlain's warnings to investors who saw little utility in sending farmers to a trading colony, New France had not yet begun to produce much food of its own. Because only a few acres had been brought under cultivation so far—most of them by hand hoeing, since oxen were first used to plough in the spring of 1628—the colonists still relied on provision shipments from France. Unfortunately, the supply ship for the present year had been in the convoy Kirke seized. Thus when Kirke's ultimatum arrived, the total stock of gunpowder in Quebec's Fort Saint-Louis amounted to fifty pounds, and the storehouse held only "four or five barrels of quite poor biscuit, which was not much, and some peas and beans, . . . without any other commodities."[73] Champlain immediately cut the ration of peas to seven ounces a day, hoping that the English would leave in time for relief vessels to arrive before winter.

Unfortunately, Kirke made good on his threat to wait until ice made navigation on the Saint Lawrence impossible, and no supply ship came. As bad as that was, however, it did not necessarily doom the colony. If the local Montagnais and Algonquins could supply them with eels and moose, the *habitants* could pass the winter without starving. But that fall, in return for the exorbitant price of a hundred beaver pelts, the Montagnais traded only twelve hundred eels to the French. In the winter, only one chief, Chomina, offered to have his hunters provide moose, and they brought in only "a small number for so many persons."[74] By May 1629, the French were surviving on roots grubbed up in the woods. Champlain began to contemplate abandoning the colony.

The heart of Quebec's problem lay not in the absence of food—in fact, the eel run had been heavy that fall and moose remained plentiful all winter—but rather in the unwillingness of the Indians to trade. That, in turn, stemmed from an incident that had taken place in October 1627, when "some savages" murdered two French cowherds driving cattle from the meadows of Cape Tourmente to Quebec. The Montagnais maintained that the killers had been Iroquois raiders or perhaps renegade Algonquins from upriver, but Champlain knew perfectly well they had done it themselves. He therefore ordered one suspect to be imprisoned and took three hostages, promising to release them only when the Indians turned over the criminals.[75]

The Montagnais would probably have been willing to make payments in reparation for the killings had Champlain made his demands in that form, but to turn the killers over to him for trial and execution, as he required, was entirely alien to Montagnais notions of justice. By the same token, they understood the taking of a prisoner and hostages as grave provocations. So long as Champlain held them captive, Indian relations remained poised on a knife-edge of hostility. Thus when Kirke's raiding party showed up at Cape Tourmente, the Montagnais not only made no effort to resist the landing but sent messengers to tell Champlain that *French* ships had appeared downriver. Moreover, Champlain soon learned that the "perfidious and treacherous" Montagnais had actually cooperated in the destruction of the cattle: a visit to Cape Tourmente revealed that "some six cows" had escaped burning, "but these the savages had killed."[76]

In spite of everything, Champlain held the prisoner all winter, insisting that the Montagnais turn over his accomplices. In June, with the colonists entirely out of preserved food and living mainly on groundnuts and roots, Champlain finally gave up and offered to turn the prisoner over to Chomina, the only chief who had maintained relations with the French. He hoped vaguely that the other local leaders would see this as a sign of favor and recognize Chomina as their spokesman. But in fact the colony was entirely at the mercy of the Montagnais:

We had to let [the criminal] go or live in continual alarm and apprehension with those savages, who would not have been disposed to render help in our necessity. Indeed, seeing us feeble, and weak in

number and left without help, they might have made an attack upon
us, or on those who went to look for roots in the woods.[77]

If the English came back, Champlain knew, he would have no hope of holding out without the support of the Indians. But in fact it was already too late.

The Kirke brothers returned with three ships mounting twenty-two
cannon and carrying a hundred and fifty armed men on the morning of July
19. On the heights above Quebec, Fort Saint-Louis had seven cannon,
about fifty cannonballs, and forty pounds of gunpowder. The small arms in
the arsenal totaled nineteen muskets, ten halberds, and a dozen pikes. The
colony's defense force consisted of eighty malnourished men, women, and
children. Champlain, seeing the hopelessness of his position, sat down to
draw up terms for the colony's surrender.

It was a bloodless conquest and—apart from the trade goods and furs
that the company lost—an easy peace. Champlain, the other company officers, and several priests were given passage home. The colonists, traders,
and interpreters remained, retained their property, and went to work for a
new set of masters, who immediately reprovisioned the colony and began to
exploit its commercial potential. That fall the Kirkes sent home furs valued
at nearly thirty thousand pounds sterling. The following year they exported
the highest number of beaver pelts ever, thirty thousand in all, worth
seventy-five thousand pounds.[78]

The Kirkes found little but profit in the conquest of Quebec; Champlain felt nothing but pain. He had done everything humanly possible to
sustain the colony, and failed. He had warned the company, year after year,
that the lack of agricultural self-sufficiency made the colony vulnerable to
seizure by an opportunistic, commercially minded enemy like England. By
closing the Saint Lawrence to the supply vessels without which the
colonists could neither eat nor supply the trade goods necessary for good
Indian relations, the Kirkes had given Champlain the bitter gift of vindicated prophecy. Yet if he was fully honest with himself, he must also have
realized that the damage he had done to relations with the Montagnais had
been the critical factor in the loss of the colony. There was simply no way
that a group of French traders, farmers, and missionaries located deep in the
interior of North America could survive in the absence of an amicable (or at
least mutually profitable) relationship with the natives. Ultimately, the fate
of New France lay in the hands of *les sauvages*.

Despite the humiliation of losing the colony, Champlain spent the next
three years in France working to revive interest in Canada and its future, and

he went back as soon as he could after England returned the colony at the Treaty of Saint-Germain-en-Laye (1632). He planned to strengthen New France from the inside out. Whereas Quebec before the conquest had been a morally lax and religiously heterodox place, the spiritual life of the colony was now to be given into the hands of the Society of Jesus, an order noted no less for its zeal than its rigor. Equally important were the efforts he made to place relations with the Montagnais on a new footing. Immediately after arriving in May 1633, he limited the trade in alcohol, which the English had used to boost the volume of furs brought in to trade; promised that he would protect them from their enemies, the Iroquois, whose raids had been increasing in severity and frequency; and made a diplomatic speech in which he promised the Montagnais chief Capitanal that "Our sons shall wed your daughters and henceforth we shall be one people."[79] All this, he hoped, would reassure the Indians of his friendship and ensure that the French would never again be compelled to deliver Quebec into the hands of an invader.

Events soon proved the frailty of these hopes. When Iroquois raiders killed two *habitants* near Quebec in early June, Champlain realized that the Five Nations, now armed by the Dutch, posed a grave threat to the French themselves. When a delegation of Hurons appealed for arms and aid not long after, Champlain conceived a bold plan that would not only deal with the Iroquois but bind the northern Indians once more to the French. He wrote to Richelieu asking that 120 soldiers be permanently stationed in New France. He would place those troops at the head of a grand alliance of Huron, Algonquin, and Montagnais warriors and lead them on an expedition through the heart of Iroquoia.

It was an audacious strategy for reversing the rising power of the Iroquois and restoring France's influence with its traditional Indian allies. Given that gunpowder arms were not yet in widespread use even among the Mohawks, it was by no means an irrational gambit. Given the unlikelihood that a man of Champlain's age—sixty-three—could actually lead such a campaign, it was also, obviously, a chimera. When the cardinal did not reply to his request for troops, Champlain did not renew it.[80] Instead, he contented himself with refurbishing Fort Saint-Louis and building fortified trading posts at strategic locations along the Saint Lawrence from Richelieu Island above Quebec to the Lachine rapids above Montreal. Even if he could not annihilate the Iroquois, these new posts unmistakably pledged his support for the peoples who cooperated with the French—peoples who, as Champlain now knew better than perhaps anyone else, controlled the destiny of the colony to which he had dedicated his life.

In October 1635, Champlain suffered a severe stroke. He clung to life until Christmas Day, when his chaplain administered the last rites; then he slipped quietly into eternity. The next spring, when the Hurons arrived at Quebec with the winter's pelts for trade, they also brought a great gift of wampum to console the French. It was a fitting memorial for the man who, more than anyone else, had set the course of intercultural cooperation that New France followed for the next century and a quarter. That policy of accommodation and mutual reliance, Champlain's most significant legacy, preserved the colony until the Seven Years' War—that is, until its rulers once again lost control of the Saint Lawrence to an English invader and repeated the fateful mistake of imagining that a colony dependent on amicable relations with *les sauvages* could compel them to conform to French cultural norms.

The Beaver Wars and the Imperial Iroquois

Death spared Champlain the knowledge of the darker legacies his choices bequeathed to North America's peoples. As we have seen, his dealings with the Montagnais, Algonquins, and Hurons had tipped the balance of power in the northeastern woodlands against the Five Nations of the Iroquois, who suffered heavy losses until they secured a European trading partner of their own in the Dutch. Despite Champlain's deepening concern with the Iroquois in his last years, he knew too little of their culture to grasp how great the peril of aggression would be once the Five Nations had access to large supplies of Dutch arms or how catastrophic the coming readjustment in the balance of power among Indian peoples would be. He did not live to understand that the Dutch alliance would allow the Iroquois to become the most formidable military power in eastern North America.

Champlain had known, of course, of the ferocity of Iroquois warriors. It is doubtful, however, that he grasped the cultural wellspring of the Five Nations' aggressiveness toward other native peoples. Since pre-Contact times—probably from the mid-fifteenth century—Iroquois religious life had centered on a ideal of peace among the Five Nations, maintained by elaborate condolence rituals and shared beliefs. This gospel had gathered the Mohawks, Oneidas, Onondagas, Cayugas, and Senecas into a spiritual alliance, the Great League of Peace and Power, and for all practical purposes had eliminated mourning wars among them. Killings that might otherwise have led to war would be "covered up" by the ceremonial presentation of gifts to the bereaved, and a council of chiefs from every clan in the League met annually to perform the rites necessary to maintain harmony among the nations. Unfortunately for the peoples who lived within raiding distance of Iroquoia, however, these peaceable beliefs had a strongly evangelical dimension. Because Deganawidah, the originator of the faith, had taught that all nations were to be brought together in the common peace, the Iroquois were obligated to offer alliance to all who would accept the gospel. Peoples who refused the invitation to sit down with the Iroquois beneath the Tree of the Great Peace could be conquered and compelled to do so.[81]

The lure of Dutch arms and religious incentives to aggression combined explosively with a third factor: epidemic disease. Before the close and continuous contact with the Dutch that began in 1628, the Mohawks and other Iroquois nations had been largely insulated from such deadly maladies as measles, influenza, diphtheria, plague, and—most fearsome of all—smallpox. With the end of that isolation, however, those diseases struck repeatedly and with devastating effect. Smallpox blazed through Iroquoia first, when an epidemic ravaged the whole of the Great Lakes basin in the 1630s; perhaps half of those infected died. Though those who survived the terrible onslaught of the disease were immune to the smallpox virus thereafter, they lacked defenses against other pathogens. During the half-century that followed the first smallpox outbreak, at least six more epidemics swept through Iroquoia in a succession of horrors that reduced the population of the Five Nations by half within a generation. Ultimately 75 percent or more of the Iroquois perished.[82]

Apart from traditional cures—purging, fasting, and sweats that hardly improved the chances for survival of victims who were already suffering extreme physiological stress—Iroquois culture offered only one way to support populations suffering such losses: war. The peace that the Five Nations had negotiated with Champlain and the French-allied Indians in 1624 collapsed as warriors raided northward in quest of captives to adopt and beaver pelts to trade for Dutch weapons. For their part, the Fort Orange traders learned that despite the Iroquois' own lack of fur supplies, they could be counted on to bring in thousands (soon tens of thousands) of pelts a year, taken as plunder in expeditions against northern peoples who traded with the French.

Among the Five Nations, warfare became an instrument of commerce and survival, for it furnished the means to acquire the furs the Dutch demanded in return for the weapons that the Iroquois needed if they were to supply the captives necessary to replace the dead. Dutch scruples about selling guns and ammunition to natives vanished when Mohawk warriors began to offer beaver pelts worth 240 guilders in return for a musket and a pound of powder. With the beginnings of the Dutch firearms trade to the Iroquois in the 1640s, the Five Nations became the most feared Indians in the Northeast.[83]

What followed was, in proportion to the populations involved, the most widespread and destructive warfare in North American history. Because they occurred principally among native peoples, these conflicts barely rate a mention in most American history textbooks; they do not, indeed, have a consistent name. Early chroniclers called them the Wars of the Iroquois; historians now refer to them most often as the Beaver Wars because one of the principal objects of Iroquois raiding was to acquire pelts for trade. The motives of the Five Nations were in fact far more complex than that name would imply. More than a means to acquire weapons, the raids that gained so many pelts were a desperate attempt to support dwindling populations.[84]

Between the 1640s and 1667, Five Nations warriors made war on no fewer than fifty-one other native peoples,[85] conquering and depopulating large areas of the Great Lakes basin and the Ohio River Valley. In 1649–51, Iroquois warriors annihilated, scattered, or absorbed the Hurons, Petuns, and Neutrals living in an arc north and west of Lake Ontario and also the Algonquins of the Ottawa River Valley. By 1657, they had visited the same fate on the Eries, south of the lake whose name (and little more) witnesses that they once existed; simultaneously they attacked the Susquehannocks, a powerful Iroquoian people who lived in the Susquehanna Valley. These groups were particularly inviting targets because most were linguistically and culturally related to the Five Nations. But the demand for captives was so great that the Iroquois attacked virtually any group they could reach, including the French, among whom they killed or captured nearly 300 colonists before 1666. They could surely have extirpated New France altogether had they chosen to try.[86]

That they did not suggests that the Iroquois saw greater utility in allowing trading posts like those that Champlain built at Lachine and Richelieu Island to remain in operation as lures to attract western Indians with canoe-loads of furs. At least until the end of the 1650s, the Five Nations retained the ability to make war or peace with the French as it suited them: one truce they observed with the French between 1653 and 1658 seems mainly to have been intended to allow them to carry on raids more effectively against "virtually every Indian people in the Northeast." By 1661–62, Iroquois raiders were attacking "Abenakis [in] New England, Algonquians [in] the

Subarctic, Siouans [on] the Upper Mississippi, and various Indians near Virginia, as well as enemies closer to home."[87]

The need for captives sustained the Beaver Wars, while the demand for furs to trade for Dutch muskets and ammunition extended them further and further afield. These factors also limited the capacity of the Iroquois to carry on the fight. The perpetual influx of captives diminished Iroquois cultural coherence. Though the captors could control the external behavior of adoptees, they remained unable to effect permanent changes in religious identity and similarly deep-seated beliefs. Meanwhile, Iroquois military successes produced not only corpses and captives, but refugees—thousands of whom fled to the protection of more distant nations or coalesced into multiethnic villages and coalitions. Such displaced groups as the Wyandots (as the remnants of the Huron people were known) and the threatened Algonquian- and Siouan-speaking nations of the interior, eventually established communities in the region west of Lake Michigan and south of Lake Superior. There they forged an alliance with the French as a means of acquiring the weapons and other trade goods they needed to survive. Then, with French encouragement, they gradually reestablished themselves on lands that Iroquois attacks had emptied.

The depopulation of vast stretches of eastern North America; the destruction of thousands of native lives; the disappearance of whole cultural groups, some of which we know only by name, if that: these, too, were Champlain's legacy. Had he lived to see the devastation take place, he could scarcely have understood that such vast consequences could follow from his desire to trade with *les sauvages,* to bring the light of the gospel among them, and to increase the power and wealth of his king and nation. Ultimately, the willingness of Champlain's successors to follow his example in seeking alliance with the peoples of the interior served to restabilize, across the whole of the northeastern woodlands, the balance of power that the Iroquois-Dutch partnership had profoundly disordered. It also permanently marked the character of relations between the French and Indians.

No European colonizer was ever more successful than the French in dealing with the Indians on terms that Indians found acceptable. Such successes depended on French willingness to comply with their allies' expectations, especially by marrying into Indian families, mediating disputes among Indian groups, and engaging in continuous diplomacy, evangelization, and trade. By assuming the role of Father as understood by the Algonquian-speaking Indians who made up the bulk of France's allies—that is, by acting as a reconciler of individuals and groups in conflict, a giver of

gifts and sponsor of rituals that could compensate for injuries and losses and
thus avoid further resort to violence—French imperial representatives gave
their native allies a center of connection and direction they had never had
before. These activities contributed to a heavy drain on the French treasury
and made New France a fabulously unprofitable colonizing venture. Yet
they also created what has been called a "middle ground": the geographical
region west of Lake Michigan that became the homeland of the refugee
peoples fleeing the Iroquois and also a metaphorical cultural zone that depended not on the dominance of Europeans over Indians, but on cooperation between them on terms acceptable to both. On the basis of this
Franco-Indian alliance and the cultural accommodation that sustained it,
the native peoples of the interior managed increasingly well to resist Iroquois attacks.[88]

The Beaver Wars began tapering off in 1665, when the Seneca, Cayuga,
Onondaga, and Oneida nations made peace with the French. They finally
concluded in 1667 when the Mohawks—always the best-armed, and always
the most closely tied to the Dutch—joined in the peace. The precipitating
cause of the treaties of 1665 and 1667 was England's conquest of New
Netherland, which occurred as a consequence of a European commercial
conflict, the Second Anglo-Dutch War (1664–67). The abrupt transformation of the old Dutch colony into New York marked the beginning of a major, protracted, and profoundly important change in the fortunes of the
Iroquois League.

The Anomalous English Empire

Even as the Beaver Wars raged throughout the Northeast and the Great
Lakes basin, the new English settlements along the eastern seaboard were
flourishing without becoming enthusiastic participants, on the French
model, in indigenous systems of trade and war. Indeed, the most distinctive
feature of the English effort to build an empire in North America was their
comparative reluctance to forge military alliances with native groups. Between 1607 and the late 1640s, England's colonies in North America remained restricted to the littoral of the Chesapeake Bay, where tobacco
growing came to dominate economic life, and to areas around Massachusetts Bay and Long Island Sound, which lacked a dominant staple and thus
developed a more diverse economy based on farming, fishing, shipbuilding,
and seaborne commerce. In neither region did colonists seek out close ties

to Indians, much less to create alliances like the ones that Champlain built up in New France. The result was an anomalous empire, built more in opposition to than cooperation with native peoples.

Disease offers a partial explanation. Terrible epidemics devastated native populations in the areas of English settlement between 1616 and 1618, about a decade after the first settlers arrived in Virginia, two years before the Pilgrims landed at Plymouth, and a decade before the Great Migration brought thousands of Puritans to New England. As much as 75 percent of the Indian population of southern New England had died off before the *Mayflower* dropped anchor. In such a context it becomes possible to see the celebrated receptiveness of the Pokanoket chief Massasoit to the Pilgrims as less a sign of friendliness than desperation, for his remnant band badly needed an ally to help them resist domination by their western neighbors, the Narragansetts, who had yet to suffer from epidemic disease.[89] It is also possible to understand why, especially in New England, settlers regarded Indians as relatively inconsequential.

Important as these early epidemics were in explaining the relative lack of English interest in developing ties with the Indians, an even greater source of indifference came from attitudes and expectations developed in Ireland, England's first colony. There the distinctive model of the English "plantation" had emerged in the previous century, along with the attitudes that accompanied colonization. The colonial plantations of Ireland were, quite literally, small transplantations of English society onto Irish soil, in enclaves created by driving out or destroying the native population. Sixteenth- and seventeenth-century Ireland proved a notoriously refractory domain, and the Irish were so much given to resistance and rebellion that English rule could be enforced only by repeated military interventions. Indeed, after more than a century of English colonization, the Irish were truly subjugated only in 1649–50 when Oliver Cromwell led the New Model Army in a brutal campaign of reconquest following a great rebellion, then followed up by confiscating millions of acres of land and expelling, deporting, or enslaving tens of thousands of natives.[90]

Understanding the attempt to replicate English society on lands cleared of their previous inhabitants as the model for colonization helps to explain aggressive behavior in England's earliest American settlements that is otherwise hard to fathom. Small in numbers and weak as they were, the colonists of Roanoke in 1585 (one of England's earliest attempts at permanent settlement, in what is now North Carolina), preferred extorting food from the local Algonquian Indians over seeking to make friends with them. The

Indians promptly withdrew from the region, leaving the colonists no choice but to abandon the colony. When Jamestown was founded two decades later, the settlers were once again less interested in trading for food with the numerous and powerful Powhatan confederacy than in simply taking it by force. Jamestown barely survived the resulting war. Unlike Champlain's eager search for an alliance with the natives, early English settlers were too much in the thrall of Ireland's example to conceive of accommodation as an approach to colonization.

Following initial attempts by the Indians to mount a military resistance— the Virginia Indian War of 1622–24, New England's Pequot War in 1636–37, and the Second Virginia Indian War of 1644–46—peace between English and native groups came to depend upon the willingness of Indians to sell or cede lands to the colonists. The thirty years' peace that followed the conclusion of these early conflicts depended explicitly on these land transfers, which to a substantial degree presumed the physical separation of indigenous and colonizing peoples. Because New England and the tobacco colonies of the Chesapeake (unlike Spanish, French, and Dutch settlements) rapidly developed substantial farming populations, and most of all because their stocks of cattle, pigs, and other domestic animals grew at a geometric rate, an insatiable hunger for land became a defining feature of English colonization.[91]

From the very earliest phases of settlement, then, English colonizers followed a path that led more toward apartheid than cultural engagement with native peoples.[92] Physical separation and land cessions produced more than a generation of peaceful coexistence between the English colonists and their Indian neighbors, but the founding of new colonies in the 1660s, 1670s, and 1680s, together with the mushrooming growth of human and livestock populations among the colonizers, generated demands for land that Indians could no longer satisfy without surrendering their autonomy wholesale. The renewal of Indian resistance in turn produced a new round of wars: Metacom's (King Philip's) War of 1675–76 in New England and the simultaneous Susquehannock War in the Chesapeake, which in turn triggered the Virginia insurrection of 1676, Bacon's Rebellion. These intensely destructive conflicts succeeded in excluding Indians from or subjugating them within the limits of English settlements. Apart from a paltry fur trade and some limited missionary activity in the Indian "praying towns" of Massachusetts, there was comparatively little close, continuing, and cooperative interaction between native and English groups, nothing even remotely comparable to the rate of intercultural exchange in New France and New Netherland.

Anglo-Indian warfare in the seventeenth century in part reflected the patterns of intercultural conflict in Ireland, but it also grew out of the colonists' ignorance of native cultures and martial skills, which a closer relationship with Indians might have fostered. Lacking the woodcraft to engage Indian warriors directly, the English had little choice but to attack Indian population centers and to destroy food supplies instead. "Battles" like the destruction of the Pequots' Mystic River fort on May 23, 1637, in which an English force set fire to a stockade filled with women, children, and old men, became the preferred English mode of combat. The early success of such tactics helped overcome an already weak set of English cultural proscriptions against the indiscriminate killing of "savage" or "heathen" enemies. It also stunted the willingness and the ability of the English to learn Indian tactics and techniques of mobile warfare.

Moreover, Anglo-American colonists seldom distinguished carefully among different Indian peoples, so in times of war they tended to attack all Indians, including those who had previously been friendly. Since success in wars against the natives opened up access to lands to which the English could claim by right of conquest, there was little practical advantage in developing cooperative ties with or intimate knowledge of Indian nations. Even in wartime, when the English desperately needed scouts and warriors to help their militiamen locate the enemy and avoid ambush, the colonists tended to prefer recruiting Indian auxiliaries from subjugated groups to trying to work out alliances with independent peoples.[93]

The logic of intercultural alliance encouraged French and Spanish colonizers to try to understand the variety of Indian peoples and cultures, and both proved more willing than the English to adopt the tactics of the native groups with whom they dealt directly. The French in particular proved amenable to Indian influences. After the crown took direct control of New France in the reign of Louis XIV and assigned responsibility for the colony to the Ministry of Marine, the task of defense passed to a cadre of professional soldiers, the Troupes de la Marine, who learned techniques of raid and surprise from the Indians and practiced them with a skill second only to native warriors. To a more modest degree, even the militiamen of New France—ordinary colonists who could be called out to defend the colony—understood and employed Indian-style tactics. Together with the assiduous maintenance of alliances, the successful adaptations of Canadians to Indian warmaking enabled New France to withstand Anglo-American assaults in the imperial wars of the first half of the eighteenth century and to keep the expansionist New Englanders mainly on the defensive.[94]

These very different approaches to intercultural relations influenced not only the ability of Europeans to exploit Indians but also Indian modes of resistance and cultural interaction. This manifested itself most notably in that pan-Indian movements seldom or never appeared among peoples who lacked sustained contact with the English; native groups, it seems, learned best what they had in common from dealing with colonizers who took few pains to distinguish one Indian from another. The earliest known attempt to organize a general resistance to English colonization occurred in the aftermath of the Pequot War, when in 1642 the Narragansett sachem Miantonomi—a former ally whose faith in the English was shattered when he witnessed the massacre of the Pequots at the Mystic River fort—crossed the sound to Long Island to implore the Montauks to join his people and other nations in a general alliance against the English:

> For so are we all Indians as the English are, and say brother to one another; so must we be one as they are, otherwise we shall all be gone shortly. . . . [For] these English having gotten our land, they with scythes cut down the grass, and with axes fell the trees; their cows and horses eat the grass, and their hogs spoil our clam banks, and we shall all be starved.[95]

Miantonomi's proposal—to kill the English but keep their livestock to eat until the deer came back—did not win over the Montauk leaders, and Miantonomi indeed died at the hands of another Indian chief, the Mohegan sachem Uncas, the following year. Similarly, in 1676 the Wampanoag leader Metacom (King Philip) tried to create a generalized Indian resistance among New England's various peoples. He succeeded in attracting support from Pocassets, Nipmucks, Narragansetts, and Indians from the Connecticut Valley and brought devastation to the frontiers of three colonies as a result. The refusal of the Mohawks to join in attacking the New Englanders, however, and their decision to pursue their self-interest by attacking the Wampanoags instead, brought about the disintegration of Metacom's coalition and ultimately caused his defeat.

That the Mohawks cooperated with the English against the Wampanoags in 1676 indicated both a shift in the balance of power and an adjustment of English attitudes toward Indian alliances that had begun in the mid-1660s. Although the fundamental pattern of English intrusion, Indian resistance, and Indian exclusion persisted through the nineteenth century, England's conquest of New Netherland in 1664 added an element of complexity to the picture, as the English effectively inherited a connection to the Iroquois League from the Dutch. This alliance, the Covenant Chain, proved enormously important for the development of the British empire in North America in the eighteenth century. It grew out of series of commercial wars between England and the Dutch Republic and the terrible disruptions that the Beaver Wars visited upon the Five Nations.

The Covenant Chain and the Origins of Iroquois Neutrality

England's emergence from the chaos of civil war allowed Parliament to respond to the intrusion of Dutch traders into England's overseas commerce in the 1650s. The first Anglo-Dutch War, 1652–54, stemmed from a law, the Navigation Act, by which Parliament forbade goods to be carried to England except in English and English colonial vessels; it was specifically aimed at the Dutch, whose merchant marine, the largest in the world, had previously carried most of England's overseas trade. This war was almost wholly naval, and successful for England in that it produced several notable victories and created a secure basis for the growth of England's own merchant marine.[96] The prospect of a new commercial war between England and the Dutch United Provinces following the Restoration prompted King Charles II to order a preemptive naval strike against the colony of New Netherland in 1664. Apart from the brief English occupation of Quebec in 1629–33 and the Dutch takeover of a tiny Swedish colony on Delaware Bay in 1655, this was the first direct confrontation between European colonizers on the North American mainland and the first removal of one colonial power by another. Conquest came easily to the English because a decade of Indian warfare in the lower Hudson Valley—the Esopus wars—had gravely weakened the Dutch colony.

Given the success of the Dutch at exploiting the Indian trade at Fort Orange, it may seem surprising that New Netherland ultimately fell victim to the effects of an Indian war. The Esopus wars, however, can be explained by New Netherland's having grown into a colony with two very different halves. Upriver, the Fort Orange traders had continued to cultivate relations with the Mohawks and other Indians in return for pelts; they had farmed only minimally, in the immediate vicinity of the fort. Downriver, the Dutch had passed through a brief initial phase of trading at New Amsterdam, then, after the upriver traders monopolized the fur supply, settled down to exploit the agricultural potential of the lower Hudson Valley and western Long Island.

By the 1650s, the downriver settlements were replicating the English pattern of expansion in human and livestock populations, and they did so in an atmosphere already poisoned by Governor Willem Kieft's efforts, beginning in 1640, to exact tribute from the natives of the lower Hudson Valley. When these bands resisted, Kieft provided muskets to the Mohawks in return for their promise to act as his allies in punishing the river Indians. Following a fierce Mohawk attack on one group in 1643, Kieft ordered the massacre of refugees who sought shelter at Pavonia, across the Hudson from New Amsterdam, and the enslavement of those who somehow escaped the slaughter. Raids and counterraids festered for five years in a conflict that rendered life increasingly miserable for the downriver Dutch and left their Indian neighbors with a thousand or more deaths to mourn.[97]

In 1645 the Dutch population of New Netherland had fallen below a thousand, and the river Indians finally forced Kieft to agree to a peace on their terms. Peace lasted only seven years, but it did provide a respite during which immigration resumed, the Dutch population grew, and farming and livestock-rearing became the economic mainstays of life along the lower Hudson. This worried the Indians, who watched the growth and bided their time until Kieft's successor as governor, Pieter Stuyvesant, took the colony's troops on an expedition to conquer New Netherland's tiny competitor, New Sweden. In mid-September 1655, the river Indians took advantage of this opportunity to launch attacks everywhere from Esopus, a hundred miles up the Hudson, to New Amsterdam itself. Fighting tapered off over the winter, only to resume three years later when settlers tried to reoccupy the deserted boweries of Esopus. It flared again in 1659, 1661, and 1663. Only in 1664, after repeatedly burning crops and villages and appealing (with limited success) to the Mohawks for help, did Stuyvesant succeed in restoring peace. By that time his colony was in such disarray that there was no question of mounting a defense when a tiny four-frigate English fleet appeared off Manhattan, carrying an expeditionary force of about three hundred soldiers. Stuyvesant surrendered the colony on September 8, 1664.[98]

New Netherland's transformation into New York undermined the ability of the Iroquois to continue the Beaver Wars, most obviously because it cut the Iroquois off from Dutch arms and ammunition just as the French-allied Indians of the middle ground were becoming increasingly well-armed, well-organized, and aggressive. Under Charles II, English foreign policy was strongly pro-French, and Westminster discountenanced the kind of unrestricted arms trade that would have allowed the Iroquois to attack New France or its allies. Finally, in 1665, the French government, having taken over direct control of Canada, sent a full army regiment, more than a thousand strong, to the colony in the company of its first governor-general, Daniel de Rémy de Courcelle. The Carignan-Salières Regiment instantly increased the population of New France by more than a third and altered the balance of power on the frontier. The forts that the French now established on the Richelieu River–Lake Champlain corridor made it impossible for the Iroquois raiders to move freely into and out of Canada or attack at will. To demonstrate the new military might of the French, the regiment mounted an invasion of the Mohawk country in 1666 and burned four fortified towns.[99]

By this point the four western Iroquois nations had already made their peace with the French, leaving only the Mohawks to carry on the fight. Yet the Beaver Wars had exhausted them, massive adoptions had brought a great many Catholic converts and other Francophile Indians into their villages, the French had shown themselves capable of striking with great force into their heartland, and the English were uninterested in helping them to retaliate or even defend themselves. Reluctant as they were to accept peace, the Mohawks had no choice. They negotiated an end to hostilities with France and its allied peoples in 1667.

The peace settlements of 1664–67 brought a fifteen-year-long cessation in a conflict that dated from Champlain's day and created a whole new range of challenges for the Five Nations. French traders and missionaries now penetrated Iroquoia for the first time, sparking factionalism and secession as Catholic converts rejected traditionalist values in favor of those preached by the Jesuit fathers. In the mid-1670s, unrest in the Mohawk villages and a rising sense of anxiety over French influence generally had reached such a pitch that the English governor of New York, Sir Edmund Andros—a client of the Duke of York, later King James II—found it possible to forge the alliance that came to be known as the Covenant Chain. Although its immediate purposes were limited, the Covenant Chain became the foundation for all subsequent Anglo-Iroquois diplomacy, opening a new era in English approaches to Indian relations as a whole.

Andros had two pressing concerns: he hoped to enlist Iroquois aid against Metacom's Wampanoags and the other Indians who were devastating the New England frontier; he also needed their help in subduing the Susquehannocks who were simultaneously attacking colonists in the northern Chesapeake. He had a third, long-term goal as well: to assert crown authority over Anglo-Indian relations and manage intercultural diplomacy with a coherence and strategic direction that the colonies, as inveterate competitors for advantage, could never attain on their own. The Iroquois had motives of their own for establishing the alliance. Together with the revival of a profitable (and more stable) fur trade at Albany, the Covenant Chain gave Anglophile and traditionalist factions the leverage they needed to expel Jesuit missionaries from Iroquois villages, a first step in the spiritual renewal of the Great League of Peace and Power. Beginning in about 1684, Iroquois warriors renewed the Beaver Wars, raiding the Indian allies of New France, bringing home captives for adoption as well as pelts to exchange for muskets, powder, and lead at Albany.

Meanwhile, Charles II died, and Andros's patron, the Duke of York, ascended the English throne as King James II. James assigned the indefatigable governor the task of organizing a new supercolony, the Dominion of New England, that would incorporate all the provinces north of Maryland. It was a scheme intended to impose a magisterial imperial design on the squabbling, diverse colonies of English America. But so severe was opposition in England to the Roman Catholic James and his absolutist ambitions that Parliament overthrew him in the Glorious Revolution of 1688, in favor of his Protestant daughter, Mary, and her Dutch husband, William of Orange. Counterpart rebellions against James's officeholders broke out in Massachusetts and New York in 1689. As a consequence, Andros and his would-be imperial proconsuls found themselves in jail, awaiting deportation to England.

Regime change in New York and Massachusetts abruptly altered the strategic position of the Iroquois in their confrontation with the French. Two years earlier, during the summer of 1687, the governor-general of New France, the marquis de Denonville, had retaliated for the Five Nations' raids by leading more than 2,700 regulars, militiamen, and Indian allies in a massive attack on Iroquoia. While conceived on a vastly larger scale, Denonville's invasion put into effect Champlain's invasion plans of 1633 and brought great destruction to the Five Nations. They fought back with raids against French trading posts and the farming settlements of the Saint Lawrence Valley and enjoyed enough success by 1688 to force a cease-fire.

This truce might well have grown into a restoration of peace had not the Glorious Revolution suddenly changed the direction of diplomacy in Europe and America alike. England's new ruler, William III, quickly brought his kingdom into an anti-French coalition, the League of Augsburg, which commenced hostilities against Louis XIV's France in May 1689. When news of the European war arrived in the summer, Iroquois leaders sensed the potential for great gains against New France. In August the Five Nations abandoned the previous year's armistice and destroyed the farming settlement of Lachine, at the very back door of Montreal.[100]

The Five Nations decided to involve themselves in what Europeans knew as the War of the League of Augsburg and the English colonists called King William's War because they expected their Covenant Chain allies to give them the military aid that would become the basis for a renaissance of Iroquois power. They could not have made a worse miscalculation. Two Anglo-American attempts to invade Canada, in 1690 and 1691, foundered on shoals of disorganization and political factionalism in the English colonies, but not before both had brought the Five Nations into violent confrontation with their Catholic kinsmen, who had moved to missions on the Saint Lawrence in the late 1660s and early 1670s. The English proved useless to the Iroquois when the French and their allies struck Iroquoia with devastating raids. As early as 1691, the Mohawks had lost half or more of the warriors they had been able to field before the war.[101]

By 1694 the League was suffering so badly that neutralist factions in each of the Five Nations sought to make peace. They failed, and the comte de Frontenac, Denonville's successor as governor-general of New France, mobilized his middle-ground allies for new attacks. In the summer of 1696, Frontenac himself led a new invasion of the Iroquois heartland, burning crops and villages and leaving famine in his wake. Even after the Peace of Ryswick ended the War of the League of Augsburg in 1697, the French refused to cease their assaults. By 1700, between a quarter and a half of all Iroquois warriors and at least a quarter of the prewar population of Iroquoia had perished.[102]

Defeat compelled the loosely coordinated League to operate in a more coherent way as a political confederacy, and it cost the Anglophile and neutralist factions their ability to dominate Iroquois diplomacy. The result, a new influence for Francophile voices in the Great Council and their successful maneuvering for power among the confederacy's leaders, finally permitted the Five Nations to conclude simultaneous treaties at Albany and Montreal in 1701. At Montreal the Iroquois spokesmen promised to remain neutral in future wars between the French and British crowns; in return the French promised to allow free access to hunting grounds above the Great Lakes and the right to trade at the new emporium they had established in the west, Fort Detroit. At Albany the League's diplomats granted the Five Nations' claim to the Great Lakes—a claim they had asserted on the basis of their conquests in the earlier Beaver Wars—to the English crown. By 1701 that claim had become the merest fiction, but by ceding it the Iroquois reaffirmed their relationship to the English through the Covenant Chain and placed themselves under the theoretical protection of the English monarchy.

The Grand Settlement of 1701 succeeded in its initial purpose of saving the League from annihilation. In the end, however, it did much more, for in the 1710s it became the basis of a coherent policy of Iroquois neutrality. Having suffered severely in the renewal of the Beaver Wars, then having faced extinction in King William's War and its aftermath, the Five Nations now knew better than to put their trust in an exclusive alliance with either France or Britain. Henceforth the League's best hope of survival depended on its ability to maneuver between two European empires in chronic conflict.[103]

Transformation

Eastern North America in the first year of the eighteenth century differed radically from its condition on July 30, 1609, when Samuel de Champlain leveled his overcharged arquebus at the Mohawk warriors who stood ready to fight another kind of battle. On that day, from Newfoundland to Florida, a few hundred European colonists eked out existences, as traders or fishermen or farmers, at the sufferance of native peoples who numbered more than a million. By September 1701, when the Iroquois concluded the Grand Settlement, a quarter-million Europeans lived east of the Mississippi and native populations were diminishing under the pressure of epidemics and war. In Champlain's day, Indian people eagerly embraced European trade goods in order to increase their own power; a century later, natives who had come to rely on those manufactures lived and worked within the embrace of an Atlantic economy. If in retrospect the implications of these trajectories seem unmistakable, however, it would be a mistake to imagine that contemporaries understood the future as one in which native peoples were somehow doomed to vanish from the scene.

Quite the contrary. At the beginning of the eighteenth century, nothing could have been clearer than the power of native peoples to determine historical outcomes in North America. Indians controlled the fur supply and access to land. They dictated the terms on which Europeans could travel more than a few miles beyond their settlements. Most of all, Indians wielded military power vastly disproportionate to their numbers: a few hundred warriors could disrupt the life of whole colonies at will. The destruction of Schenectady, New York; Salmon Falls, New Hampshire; and two towns in Maine in the winter and spring of 1690 left no doubt that Indians were deadly foes—if anything, deadlier than ever.

In this sense, the final installment of Champlain's legacy was made payable a half-century after his death. The cooperative intercultural relations he established had transformed the Indians' world into a violent, disease-ridden, dangerous place. New France needed Indian allies to survive in this unstable world, for if the Indians withheld their cooperation, as they had in 1628–29, the colony was doomed. As a result, authorities in New France at the beginning of the eighteenth century attended so assiduously to the interests of their native allies that along a 2,800-mile arc from the Gulf of Saint Lawrence to the mouth of the Mississippi, Indians were acting as allies of the French, *not* against other Indians but against the English enemies of His Most Christian Majesty.

Against this Franco-Indian coalition the northern English colonies had only the battered Five Nations, bound by a Covenant Chain that effectively allowed the Iroquois to stipulate the terms and the price of their cooperation. For the next half-century the stability of North America and the welfare of its peoples reflected the creativity of Indians and colonists who accepted their places in a world structured by interactions between competing empires and learned how to exploit the needs of those imperial states to their own benefit. The fate of the Iroquois League, like that of other native groups in buffer zones between imperial spheres of influence, depended upon their ability to play empire off against empire in a diplomatic system that allowed Indians to control the balance of power. At the same time, a new Anglo-American colony, Pennsylvania—dedicated to principles that foreswore coercion and violence in dealing with Indian groups—became central to the functioning of that intricately balanced system. The founder of Pennsylvania, indeed, attempted to invert Champlain's approach to intercultural relations and make his colony a kind of laboratory to test the proposition that an empire could rest secure on relationships that were not ultimately predicated on war.

CHAPTER TWO

Penn's Bargain: The Paradoxes of Peaceable Imperialism

O ne of the few images of a figure from the seventeenth century still familiar today is that of a rotund Quaker in a broad-brimmed hat standing at the center of a group of Indians and colonists. William Penn beams at a richly robed chief and spreads his arms in what looks like a benign embrace of natives and Englishmen alike. Examined more closely, however, his right hand can be seen to point to a map held by one of his associates while his left inclines toward the bolt of cloth that two kneeling servants present to the chief. Other natives, including women and children, intently observe this offer of yard goods for real estate, while in the left foreground servants lounge beside a stack of unopened chests. On the right, counterbalancing the material riches the chests imply, an Indian mother sits, oblivious to everything but the baby she nurses. Her older children—a girl wearing a bracelet and necklace, and a boy with a quiver of arrows—seem far more interested in the bargain being struck between the Quaker and the chief.

In this tranquil scene, only the boy carries arms, and those are toys. A warrior sitting at the feet of the chief has cast aside his arrows and bow, holding instead the long stem of a peace pipe. Three half-finished European houses rise as a sunlit backdrop, contrasting with the dark Indian huts that huddle beneath an immense elm. Light pours in from behind Penn and his fellow Quakers, flooding the features of the Indians in the central group; behind them on the right, other natives linger in the forest gloom, waiting to be drawn into the light that the artist associates with the Quaker and his offering.

At six feet by nearly nine feet in size, *William Penn's Treaty with the Indians* was an imposing canvas when first exhibited at the Royal Academy of the

William Penn's Treaty with the Indians, by Benjamin West, 1772.
Courtesy of the Pennsylvania Academy of the Fine Arts, Philadelphia.
The Joseph Harrison, Jr., Collection (gift of Mrs. Sarah Harrison).

Arts in May 1772. Its most impressive impact was felt later, in myriad re-
productions that made it one of the most widely recognized images of the
day. Its creator was Benjamin West, a Pennsylvanian who had come to Eu-
rope to study in 1760 and whose star was rising fast among British artists.
He had painted the picture on commission from William Penn's son,
Thomas, who approached him after seeing his first great historical scene,
The Death of General Wolfe, in 1771. That painting had made West rich; *Penn's
Treaty* made him eminent.[1]

The Penns hoped the painting would help to counter the efforts of their
critics in the Pennsylvania Assembly, who had long sought to have the
crown revoke the family's charter and place the colony under direct royal
rule. West cast the history of the province in a light that supported the
Penns' legitimacy as owners of Pennsylvania's best lands and disposers of its
highest offices. Here was the founder in the act of creating an orderly,
benevolent society, one that, thanks to his pacifism and honest dealings with
the Indians, enjoyed uninterrupted peace for nearly three-quarters of a century after the date of the treaty, 1682. In depicting this first transaction between the proprietor and the Indians, the picture communicated no hint
that by 1772 the children of William Penn were no longer in any meaningful

sense Quakers, much less pacifists; no sign that in negotiating with the Indians over the previous forty years they had aimed less at fair dealing than
the expropriation of tribal lands; no indication that from 1755 through 1758
and again in 1763 and 1764 Pennsylvania had been the scene of brutal frontier warfare between whites and Indians. West painted his picture to sustain
a myth, and he did it brilliantly.

Curiously for a man who had dedicated years of his life to separating the
heirs of William Penn from their province, Benjamin Franklin, the most famous American in London and the agent the Pennsylvania Assembly had
sent to lobby the crown and Parliament to end the Penns' proprietorship,
was on excellent terms with the artist.[2] Their association was, however, a
wholly understandable one, for both were Britons who shared the accident
of an American birth, men attached by affection and interest to what they
believed was the greatest empire since Rome. Among the many things on
which the two would have agreed was that the artist's two great history
paintings, though superficially quite different, were really about the same
thing. *The Death of General Wolfe*, an allegory of empire, assembled not only
high-ranking English officers but a Scottish Highlander, an American
ranger, a British enlisted man, and a Mohawk warrior to hear the hero of
Quebec utter his dying words at the very moment of conquest. *Penn's Treaty*,
although a peaceful scene, was equally an apotheosis of empire. "The great
object I had in view in forming that composition," West later explained,
"was to express savages brought into harmony and peace by justice and
benevolence, by not withholding from them what was their reight [*sic*], and
giving to them what they were in want of, as well as a wish to give by that art
a conquest made over native people without sward or Dagder [sword or
dagger]."[3] Conquest might be either glorious and violent or peaceful and
benevolent, but the result was the same: the extension of a civilizing British
dominion in North America.

To Benjamin West, William Penn was the most successful imperialist of
all. He and Franklin wholeheartedly agreed that the cultural strategies Penn
pioneered in 1682—peace, fair trade, and liberality in dealing with Indians
on terms that Indians found acceptable—remained valuable not just because they were humane but because they offered the most efficient means
to extend Britain's sway. Though the actual moment in 1682 when Penn secured peaceful relations with the Indians of the Delaware Valley differed
from the mythological event that West imagined, inseverable cords of empire nevertheless bound the real treaty to its allegorical representation.
Penn's accommodationist approach decisively shaped life in his province

and influenced North American development generally, by allowing territorial expansion and rapid population growth in the very center of Britain's mainland colonies to proceed without war. It was not until the middle of the eighteenth century that it became clear how the elements of Penn's imperial success story had created the conditions for its own catastrophic collapse.

"A Sufferer for Truth's Sake"

That England's most famous pacifist was the son of one of England's most notable fighting admirals is not the least of the ironies in William Penn's life. Without his father's influence, however, it is hard to imagine that pacifism and the rejection of coercive social relations would ever have become so central to his life. Even more importantly, it was his father's naval career and connections that enabled Penn to obtain the proprietorship of Pennsylvania. Warfare, then, formed the indispensable context for the creation of the only American colony ever to be founded on the ideal of peace and the principles of brotherly love.

William Penn was twelve when he took his first real measure of the father whose name he shared. Since his son's birth on October 14, 1644, William Penn had frequently been at sea or away from home on navy business. In 1656 he retired from active service and moved his family from England to the manor of Macroom, in County Cork, part of the estate that had been bestowed on him about three years before for faithful service to Oliver Cromwell, England's Lord Protector.[4] The occasion of Penn's retirement was the failure of the "Western Design," Cromwell's ambitious attempt to secure the island of Hispaniola as an English foothold in the heart of the Spanish Caribbean, a base from which to seize the wealth of the Spanish Main. Although he was naval commander on the expedition, Penn had not, in fact, been responsible for its failure. The five weeks he spent in the Tower of London at Cromwell's order on his return, however, persuaded him that he would be happiest with the Irish Sea between himself and the Lord Protector.[5] Safe in the south of Ireland, Penn nursed his resentments, improved his estates, and got to know young William.

The hearty, hard-drinking admiral and his introspective son spent a good deal of time in each other's company, not all of it pleasant. Most likely, it was in this period that William Penn began to evolve what became two of his defining, seemingly inconsistent, characteristics: a deeply antiauthoritarian personality and a tendency to insist that others defer to him. The

younger William had also begun to show a propensity for religious experience entirely lacking in his father.[6] His conversion to Quakerism did not
come until he was twenty-three, but he first heard the preacher whose
words later converted him, the "Public Friend" Thomas Loe, during this
time. Loe stressed the operation of the Inner Light, or God's direct revela-
tion to the believer of his presence and grace, a message that appealed to a
"solitary & Spirituall" boy as he struggled to cope with a formidable, authoritarian father.[7]

Not every moment of his four years at Macroom were spent in spiritual
seeking and emotional turmoil; the younger William also found time to enjoy the country life and learn how to comport himself as a gentleman. He
grasped something of estate management from watching his father inspect
rent rolls and deal with tenants; learned to shoot, fence, and ride to the
hounds; and in general experienced life near the top of an English colony's
social hierarchy. There is no evidence that he ever questioned the rightness
of his family's position in the colonial ruling elite. Indeed, he seems to have
loved it.[8]

The death of Oliver Cromwell in September 1658 and subsequent
movements to restore both Parliament and monarchy revived William
Penn's career. Chosen as member of Parliament for the borough of Wey-
mouth, the admiral went back to England in time to join his fellow MPs in
inviting Charles II to return from exile and assume the throne. He accompanied the fleet that escorted the king home from the Continent in May
1660 and strode down the gangway of the *Royal Charles* at Dover as a knight
as well as an admiral. Soon he was appointed commissioner of the Admi-
ralty, where he served under Lord High Admiral James, the Duke of York
and the king's younger brother.[9]

Sir William lost no time in grooming his sixteen-year-old son for a career at court. The first step, enrollment at Oxford University, was easily accomplished. Controlling young William, however, was another matter. In
October 1661, during his second year of study at Christ Church, one of Oxford's more extravagantly Anglican colleges, William experienced some sort
of religious conversion, what he later described as "an opening to joy."
Thereafter he refused to don the surplice, the white outer gown that priests
wore in leading worship, which the college required its students to wear
when attending chapel. Because the Puritans, anathema at Christ Church,
had long derided the surplice as a popish bauble, Penn's rebellion struck
college and university authorities as unmistakable evidence of retrograde religious and political beliefs.[10] Despite fines from the dean and harassment

by tutors and fellow students, William steadfastly refused to conform. He finally made himself such a nuisance that the university expelled him in March 1662.

His father, furious, initially responded by "whipping, beating, & turning [him] out of Dores."[11] Given William's temperament and spiritual trajectory, such "bitter usage" probably only increased his fervor, but the admiral's fury soon subsided. When a series of draconian acts in Parliament crowded the prisons with conscientious believers and Nonconformist clergymen, the elder Penn bundled him off to France, where he could study without risking imprisonment. There, safe in the company of a respectable tutor and a companion of impeccable pedigree (Robert Spencer, later the Earl of Sunderland), William could grow up a little, polish his manners, and improve his French; with luck, he might even develop a vice or two to take the edge off his adolescent religiosity and make him a gentleman fit to be presented at court. Or so a father could hope.

Penn's two years in France, from the summer of 1662 through the summer of 1664, were as important to his later development as his years in Ireland had been. In the Paris of Louis XIV, Racine, and Molière, Penn grew perhaps even more worldly than his father wished; as one of the admiral's subordinates noted, the younger Penn brought back not only excellent fencing skills and fluent French but "a great deal of the French garb, and [an] affected manner of speech and gait."[12] But in fact he spent less time in Paris and at the royal court, Fontainebleau, than at the Académie Protestante de Saumur in southern France, where he studied with the Huguenot moralist Moïse Amyraut, his nation's greatest advocate of toleration. Amyraut's academy introduced Penn to rigorous theological disputation, a vision of a just society based on freedom of conscience, and a notion that it was the believer's obligation to apply in the world the principles of his faith: to live, not just advocate, the gospel of Jesus Christ. Penn's time in France thus equipped him to function in later years as a religious controversialist and advocate of toleration who could at the same time match the most sophisticated Stuart courtiers in manners and wit. At the time of his return to England, however, William probably experienced it all as a conflict between his outward appearance as a gentleman and his inner spiritual longings. His father, looking less deeply into his son's soul, liked what he saw on the highly polished surface well enough to send him off to Lincoln's Inn, the oldest and most distinguished of London's Inns of Court, to make a lawyer of him.

The admiral, meanwhile, returned to the sea for the last great military adventure of his life. In 1665 England and Holland, which had been raiding

each other's colonies and commerce for two years, formally declared war.
England's first move was to engage the Dutch fleet in the Battle of Lowestoft, on June 3. The Duke of York commanded the English fleet of 150
ships; the real direction of the fighting, however, rested with the commanders of the fleet's three squadrons, one of whom was Sir William Penn, captain of the duke's flagship, the *Royal Charles*. England's victory at Lowestoft
was, arguably, a high point in the life of the man who in time ascended the
throne as King James II.[13]

William dutifully spent the war in Lincoln's Inn in preparation for taking over the administration of the family's Irish estates. The admiral intended William's legal education to make him an able administrator and
defender of the family's interests, and William (to all appearances a dutiful
son, at last) returned to Ireland in 1666 to perform those roles.[14] There,
however, he reencountered Thomas Loe. As they had a decade earlier, the
words of the Quaker evangelist stirred his soul; he began to attend meetings
and in due course he experienced "convincement." In September 1667 he
was arrested along with eighteen others at a Quaker meeting in Cork. He
employed his legal skills to get them released from prison, but could not
keep the news of his arrest from reaching his father. The admiral summoned him back to England to answer for his actions.[15]

Sir William was, predictably, furious. But his rage once again evoked
more resistance in William, who began to act as a Public Friend, preaching,
debating, and publishing pamphlets to propagate the Quaker message. In-
temperately so: his third tract, "The Sandy Foundation Shaken," landed
him in the Tower of London on the charge that he had denied both the doctrine of the Trinity and the divinity of Christ. He remained there for eight
months before publishing a recantation, "Innocency with Her Open Face,
Presented by Way of Apology for the Book Entitled, The Sandy Foundation
Shaken." "I conclude Christ to be God," he wrote; "I sincerely own, and
unfeignedly believe . . . in one holy, just, merciful, almighty and eternal
God, who is the Father of all things."[16] His views on Trinitarianism remained obscure, but he received his discharge anyway, at the end of July. Sir
William lost no time in packing him off to Ireland.

This rustication had two purposes: to get him as far from London and
publicity as possible and to use his legal skills to increase the yield of the
family's rents. Sir William had grown infirm with gout and other maladies
and longed to retire to his Irish estates, but he could not afford to do so until they produced an income of £1,000 a year.[17] His son welcomed this new
exile as an opportunity to continue as "a sufferer for Truth's sake" while he

repaired his family's fortunes, twin goals of spiritual advancement and material aggrandizement of the sort he pursued, without any sense of contradiction, for the rest of his life. To accomplish the former he preached and traveled, wrote and sought the release of Friends imprisoned for conscience' sake. To achieve the latter, he hired a secretary: a poor Quaker schoolmaster named Philip Ford, to whom he promised an annual salary of £40 plus expenses.

To serve God at first hand and Mammon through an underpaid employee proved a fateful choice, but in 1669–70 Penn found it only a liberating one, for it relieved him of his most onerous responsibilities for managing the estates. He soon fell into the habit of signing Ford's accounts without pausing to inspect them. Years passed before he learned that Ford routinely used the Penn family's cash balance to make investments on his own account, a practice that enabled him to prosper while his master's fortunes languished. Meanwhile, Penn also became accustomed to borrowing money from Ford to meet current expenses. When he was finally forced to enter debtors' prison in 1707, it was because he could not clear his obligations to the heirs of Philip Ford.[18]

Penn was spared the consequences of trusting his steward for more than three decades; meanwhile, it was thanks to Ford's efficiency that he was able to spend late 1669 and the first half of 1670 working wholeheartedly for the Society of Friends. He might have gone on much longer in that way had not Sir William, in collapsing health, called him home in the summer of 1670 in order to set the family's affairs in order. William reached his father's bedside only a week before his death. The admiral remained lucid long enough to bring about a deathbed reconciliation and to write a letter to the king, begging royal indulgence for his troublesome son. Then he died, on September 16, 1670, freeing William, at last, from the restraints that paternal disapproval and financial dependency had imposed. From that day on, William Penn—lawyer, gentleman, religious controversialist, Public Friend—heeded his conscience, gave rein to his ambitions, and followed the promptings of the Inner Light.[19]

Penn now came into his own, joining England's leading Friend, George Fox, in the long campaign to control Quakerism's anarchic impulses and make it an institutionalized, orderly sect. In 1672 he paused to marry a Quaker heiress, Gulielma Springett. Marriage brought Penn fatherhood, domestic happiness, and financial stability: Gulielma bore him seven children over the twenty-two years before she died (whereupon he remarried and fathered seven more), and her great dowry enabled him to finance an aristocratic style of living and go on making generous contributions to the Society of Friends. The result was a decade-long spiritual flowering, during which Penn wrote and spoke on freedom of conscience, lobbying influential members of the court and Parliament in the hope of making religious toleration the law of the realm.

In a dozen important pamphlets written during this period, Penn argued for "an absolute individual freedom of belief or conscience and an equal freedom of worship" premised on the complete separation of Church and State.[20] Penn insisted that the repression of dissent was not only ethically wrong but had negative economic consequences; freedom of conscience, on the other hand, produced prosperity. For proof, he argued, one needed to look no further than the Netherlands, where the tolerant, ingenious Dutch had taken some of the least promising terrain in Europe and built upon it a trading nation of vast wealth, England's greatest commercial and naval competitor.

According to Penn, a good ruler should act as an impartial arbitrator among those who adhered to various faiths; the king who governed best was one who through respect for "all religious interests" made a "concord of discords."[21] By the same token, Parliament should promote moral behavior by basing laws on Christian precepts, which would not only safeguard property rights and protect persons but also suppress those vices (such as drunkenness, sexual license, and profaneness) that deprived men of their reason. Such legal restraints on vice were the counterpart of toleration since the free exercise of conscience would increase the rationality of men and make them better, more productive members of the commonwealth. If toleration became the foundation of English public life, the Quaker testimonies—Friends' refusal to take oaths and doff their hats to social superiors, their witness against war and the bearing of arms, and their substitution of the loving, leveling "thee" for the formal, hierarchical "you" in all forms of address—would inspire others to seek the Inner Light. It was a magnificent vision, and Penn pursued it with a convert's zeal. The only problem was that it refused to come true.

Instead, political conditions in Britain deteriorated sharply. Penn had believed that his natural allies in Parliament were the Whigs, an alliance of factions skeptical of the crown's prerogative powers and dedicated to the idea of a Protestant dynasty on the throne. To Penn's horror, however, the parliamentary elections of 1679 returned a strongly antipapist Whig majority in the House of Commons, and they lost no time in undertaking a campaign to exclude the Catholic Duke of York, James, from the succession.

The Exclusion Crisis distressed Penn on many levels. His connections to the court ran largely through James, who had stood by his father's side at the Battle of Lowestoft and remained fond of the admiral to his death. Penn's conversations with the duke had convinced him that he "was against all persecution for the sake of Religion" and that "he was for doing to others, as he would have others do unto him; & he thought it would be happy for the world if all were of that minde."[22] It was bad enough that the Whigs opposed the accession to the throne of a man whose tolerationist principles were so sound; what made it intolerable for Penn was his fear that the Exclusion Crisis would pitch England headlong into another civil war. King Charles was growing increasingly antipathetic to all religious dissenters because most of them backed the Whigs, while by his forceful assertions of the prerogative and his prorogations of the House of Commons he seemed to be preparing to govern without Parliament. Passions among the Whigs, meanwhile, were running so high that the pacifist Penn could find no principled grounds for supporting them. By the end of 1679 he had "resolved to withdraw himself from all manner of [political] meddling, since things to him appeared violent and irreconcilable."[23]

Penn withdrew from politics without losing his desire to free the world of religious persecution. He therefore he began casting about for some means of realizing his vision outside of England. Three episodes—his father's retreat to Ireland in 1656, his education in France, and his Irish exile of 1669–70—suggested the value of removal from England's controversy and struggle. A new retreat might offer the key to realizing the goal of a tolerant society. Perhaps he could still show England a way out of its mire of persecution and rancor.

"I Desire to Winn and Gain Your Love & Freindship"

In his own lackadaisical fashion, Charles II had promoted colonization in North America more consistently than any English monarch since his grandfather James I. He had good reasons to do so. Under heavy obligations to the powerful men who had supported him during his exile, he had few resources with which to reward them. A major exception was his power to grant the right to found colonies on North American lands claimed by the crown. The institutional form of such grants was the proprietorship, a feudal relic that conferred not only rights in land but also delegated the crown's authority to create and administer governments to men designated as "Lords

Proprietary." In this manner, by 1680 Charles had given away virtually everything along the eastern seaboard that was his to grant except for two regions: the lands that lay west of what is now New Jersey and north of Maryland and those that separated what is now North and South Carolina from the Spanish colony of Florida. William Penn now fixed on the northern tract as the site for a colony in which his fellow Quakers might find a refuge, where ideals of toleration might serve as the foundation of all government, and from which he might earn enough profit to fill his depleted personal coffers.[24]

To realize his scheme, Penn exploited an unpaid debt. King Charles had borrowed monies on the order of £11,000 from Penn's father during the 1660s and neglected to pay it back; with interest, the sum now due came to approximately £16,000. Penn offered to cancel the debt in exchange for the grant of a proprietary colony across the Delaware River from New Jersey.[25] Amazingly, Charles agreed. On March 4, 1681, the Privy Council issued a charter to "give and grant unto the said William Penn, his heirs and assigns, all that tract or part of land in America" between 40 degrees and 43 degrees north latitude, from the Delaware River westward 5 degrees of longitude. The colony, to be called Pennsylvania, would incorporate 45,000 square miles of land, an area considerably larger than Ireland and Wales combined.[26]

Personal considerations clearly played a part in the decision to grant Penn so vast a domain. The Duke of York supported Penn's application, as did the Earl of Sunderland, who had been Penn's traveling companion in France back in 1662–64 and was now one of His Majesty's principal secretaries of state. The king, moreover, thought it likely that Pennsylvania would become a magnet for dissenters, thus perhaps freeing the realm of thousands of the Whigs he detested. The most significant factor in Charles's decision, however, was undoubtedly the practical advantage this grant offered: to create Pennsylvania was to extend English settlement into the center of eastern North America at no greater expense than the cost of the parchment and ink for its charter. By assuming the right to obtain lands within the bounds of the province from the native inhabitants and to dispose of them thereafter by sale, Penn accepted the responsibility for—and the expense of—clearing Indian titles, organizing and administering a government, erecting courts, enforcing laws, finding colonists to settle the land, and every other tedious, costly task associated with founding a colony. To a monarch as indolent as Charles II, Penn's willingness to perform so many beneficial functions at his own expense was a bargain indeed.

Penn recognized that he had been given an incomparable opportunity "to serve God, to honor the king, and to make his own profit."[27] The form of the grant—he was to hold the land "in free and common socage"—gave him virtually exclusive administrative and legal authority over the colony in return for payment of a nominal rent to the crown (two beaver pelts per year) and one-fifth of all the precious metals discovered in the province. He could institute any form of government and create any kind of society he wished.

Penn's intention to use his powers as proprietor to create a utopian scheme of government was hardly novel. Like the proprietors of other colonies—the Lords Baltimore in Maryland, the Earl of Shaftesbury and his fellow Carolina proprietors, and the Duke of York—Penn believed he could project his vision on North America as if it were a blank screen. He approached the creation of Pennsylvania's government with uncommon care and a determination to forestall unanticipated results. Drawing on several models, including a radical plan already in place for the Quaker colony of West Jersey, Penn strongly asserted his power to shape Pennsylvania's Frame of Government. The province was to have a bicameral legislature, in which the upper house (or Council) could check the democratic tendencies of the lower (the Assembly). Assemblymen could consent to taxation but could not initiate bills or even set their own dates of adjournment, for those were powers reserved to the proprietor. Radical though it was, Penn's design was far from democratic. While he had faith that liberty of conscience would produce a peaceable, industrious, orderly society, he also believed that even Quakers needed the kind of loving guidance he was prepared to supply.[28]

The indispensable requirement for any society, of course, is people, and even before he drafted the Frame of Government, Penn began to publicize his colony. He published two tracts, a ten-page pamphlet entitled "Some Account of the Province of Pennsylvania in America" and a two-page broadsheet, "A Brief Account of the Province of Pennsylvania," before the end of 1681; both were speedily translated into German and Dutch for publication in Europe, as virtually all of Penn's subsequent promotional tracts were.[29] He was necessarily vague in describing a province he had not yet seen but strong in his insistence that it would offer opportunities for the kind of sturdy, independent country life that was growing rare in an England "effeminated by a lazy and luxurious living."[30] Land would be cheap; even indentured servants would receive fifty acres when they completed their terms.[31] Colonists could expect to work hard and to endure *"present inconveniences"* until their labors produced *"future ease and plenty."*[32]

"Some Account of the Province of Pennsylvania" was so persuasive that between July 14 (when land sales began) and the end of October 1681, Penn sold more than 300,000 acres. By 1685 the total had surpassed 700,000, and before he died it exceeded a million. His pamphlets carefully avoided any mention of Quakerism or even religious toleration to minimize the radical vision that was, in fact, behind the enterprise.[33] Word of Pennsylvania's opportunities therefore circulated among Quakers by word of mouth and the advocacy of Public Friends; consequently Quaker tradesmen, shopkeepers, and farmers made up the great majority of the so-called First Purchasers. About half of them actually went to Pennsylvania; the rest resold their land to later immigrants. Both for this reason and because of his persistent publicity for the colony in the Low Countries, western Germany, and the poorer parts of Britain (notably lowland Scotland, northern Ireland, and Wales), Quakers predominated among colonists in Pennsylvania for only a brief period and only so long as settlement remained closely tied to Philadelphia.

That was fine with Penn. He had never intended that the colony be settled solely by Quakers. At the level of principle, Pennsylvania had to be a refuge for all peoples who desired to escape persecution and live in peace. At the level of practicality, there simply were not enough Quakers to make Pennsylvania financially viable, and Penn's colony-related expenses were approaching £6,000 a year.[34] On the other hand, it was crucial that members of the Society of Friend be the colony's leaders. He took pains, therefore, to foster close connections among the Quakers who made the largest purchases of land, those who made up the Free Society of Traders (the commercial syndicate chartered to function as an import-export agency and direct the economic development of the colony), and those who held the colony's government offices. If Pennsylvania was to be both a peaceful and an orderly society, its public and economic life should rest safe in the hands of an elite closely allied with the proprietor.[35]

Penn's extraordinary intention to deal with Indians fairly, generously, and—uniquely—to refrain from coercion by arms or the threat of violence reflected his distinctive combination of idealism and pragmatism. Without Indian cooperation, he had no hope of acquiring enough territory to produce the capital he needed to support his "holy experiment." Since he had begun selling lots to the First Purchasers in July 1681, before a formal treaty had been made with the Indians, it was imperative that he put Indian relations on a stable footing as soon as possible. Above all, he knew that he had to keep the natives from misconstruing the intentions of the colonists who would soon begin flooding into southeastern Pennsylvania.

Because he himself could not immediately come, he wrote the Indians a letter, which he asked his cousin, the deputy governor William Markham, to deliver, along with a substantial gift of trade goods, as a diplomatic communiqué. Penn explained that while his king had given him "a great Province" in the Indians' country, he wished to inhabit it only with their "Love and Consent, that we may always live together as Neighbours and freinds." He was "very Sensible of the unkindness and Injustice" that European settlers had too often shown toward native people and knew their bad behavior had caused "great Grudgeings and Animosities, sometimes to the shedding of blood." But, he assured them, he was "not such a Man" as those who had done harm; rather,

I desire to Winn and gain your Love & freindship by a kind, just and peaceable life; and the People I send are of the same mind, & shall in all things behave themselv[e]s accordingly; and if in any thing any shall offend you or your People, you shall have full and Speedy Satisfaction for the same by an equall number of honest men on both sides that by no means you may have just Occasion of being offended against them; [and] I shall shortly come to you my selfe. . . . [I]n the mean time I have sent my Commissioners to treat with you about land & a firm league of peace. [L]ett me desire you to be kind to them and the People, and receive thes[e] Presents and Tokens which I have sent you, as a Testimony of my Good will to you, and my resolution to live Justly peaceably and friendly with you.[36]

As a kind of first installment on these promises, Penn had already set out twenty conditions, or "Concessions," by which those who purchased property from him were expected to abide. Five of these pertained to colonists' conduct toward Indians, stressing equality of treatment and the protection of native interests. All commercial transactions, including those between Indians and planters, were to take place in the public market, where inspectors could certify weights and measures to prevent fraud, so "that the natives may not be abused or provoked." If any colonist should "affront or wrong" an Indian, the same penalties and laws would apply as if the affronted or wronged party had been a planter. If on the other hand an Indian wronged a colonist, the injured party had no right to take the law into his own hands; he could only make a

complaint to the governor or his deputy. The governor in turn would negotiate a settlement "with the king of the said Indian, that all reasonable satisfaction
be made to the said injured planter." Indians were to have the same rights "to
the improvement of their ground and providing sustenance for their families"
as the planters. Most unusual of all was the provision Penn mentioned in his
letter to the Indians: disputes between natives and colonists were to be settled
by arbitration—"ended," as he put it, "by twelve men, that is, by six planters
and six natives; that so we may live friendly together and, as much as in us lies,
prevent all occasions of heart burnings and mischiefs."[37]

No other colonial proprietor in America took so much care to establish
standards for the fair treatment of natives, but of course no other proprietor
had tried to create a colony without a militia, either. Penn's province, *by design,* would be a place in which the Indians were better-armed and militarily more competent than the colonists. In such a circumstance, equality,
equity, and justice formed the only reasonable, prudent basis for Anglo-
Indian relations.[38]

"Much Time in Councel"

Penn arrived in his province on October 29, 1682, and immediately set
about organizing the government, distributing lands, laying out Philadelphia, and establishing relations with the neighboring colonies of New York,
New Jersey, and Maryland. Like the local Lenni-Lenape (or Unami, or
Delaware) people with whom he met that winter at the traditional council
spot of Shackamaxon, upriver from Philadelphia, Penn was eager to reach
an agreement regarding land. Reassuring the natives that his intentions
were as peaceable as the two thousand or so migrants who had already arrived in the region, he moved quickly to add to the earlier purchases by the
deputy governor, William Markham, which included the land on which
Philadelphia was being built.[39]

Penn desperately needed more land to sell to new settlers—his cash-
flow problems were now acute—but he knew or sensed enough about
Delaware culture not to rush the negotiations. He took instruction in the
Delaware language, intent on being able to listen and learn as well as to inform the Indians of his needs. It is clear from his description of one of his
early meetings with the Delawares that he was a quick study. He explained
how a "councillor," speaking "in the Name of his King," delayed a discussion of the specific terms of sale in order to explain "the Indian custom,

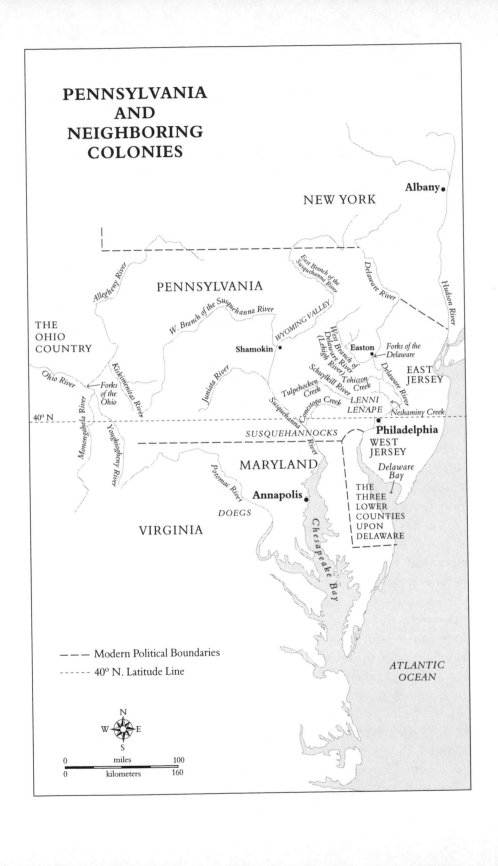

PENNSYLVANIA AND NEIGHBORING COLONIES

NEW YORK

Albany•

THE OHIO COUNTRY

PENNSYLVANIA

Allegheny River

East Branch of the Susquehanna River

Delaware River

Hudson River

W. Branch of the Susquehanna River

WYOMING VALLEY

West Branch of Delaware River (Lehigh River)

Shamokin•

Easton

Forks of the Delaware

Ohio River

Kiskiminitas River

Forks of the Ohio

Juniata River

Schuylkill River

Tohiccon Creek

Delaware River

EAST JERSEY

Tulpehocken Creek

Conestoga Creek

LENNI LENAPE

Monongahela River

Youghiogheny River

40° N

Susquehanna River

SUSQUEHANNOCKS

Neshaminy Creek

Philadelphia

WEST JERSEY

Potomac River

MARYLAND

Delaware Bay

Annapolis•

THE THREE LOWER COUNTIES UPON DELAWARE

DOEGS

VIRGINIA

Chesapeake Bay

ATLANTIC OCEAN

— — — Modern Political Boundaries

- - - - - 40° N. Latitude Line

N
W   E
S

0   miles   100
0   kilometers   160

to . . . take up much time in councel before they are resolv'd." Penn was impressed both with the speaker and the Indians who attended the conference:

> Dureing the time that this Person spoak, not a man among them was observ'd to whisper, nor smile[:] the old grave, the young reverend in their deportment. [T]hey speak little, but fervently & with eligance. I have never seen more naturall sagacity considering them without the help (I was goeing to say the spoil) of Tradition, and he will deserve the name of wise that outwitts them in any treaty about a thing they understand.[40]

The care and sensitivity with which Penn approached Indian diplomacy may have come more naturally to him than to other Europeans because he was accustomed to the solemnity and gravity with which Friends spoke in a meeting for worship, where the silence could only be broken when a member responded to the promptings of the Inner Light. Similarly, the Quaker insistence on speaking the truth without the coercive rituals of oath-swearing would have served as a natural point of entry in a cross-cultural dialogue. Penn also enjoyed a singular advantage in knowing enough Delaware that he could at least follow the drift of an Indian speech without a translator's constant interruptions. Yet if Penn thought that he understood everything that was going on in his meetings with the Delawares, he was wrong. In fact, the Delawares had pressing needs that made his friendship more valuable to them than he knew.

The Susquehannock War had recently transformed the regional balance of power in ways extremely threatening to the Delawares. Historically, theirs had been a decentralized society of villagers, loosely associated in three regional defensive groupings—the Unami, the Munsee, and the Unalatchigo—in the Schuykill and Delaware river drainages.[41] Since the 1630s and early 1640s, they had been subordinated allies of the Susquehannocks, a powerful group of Iroquoian-speakers who lived in the Susquehanna drainage, further to the west.[42] This tributary relationship had done much to shield them from attacks by the Five Nations Iroquois during the Beaver Wars. But the Susquehannocks, weakened by conflict with the League, had also come under attack by Marylanders and Virginians in the 1675–76 frontier war that triggered Bacon's Rebellion. At that point, Sir Edmund Andros, the governor of New York, had invited the Mohawks to attack both Metacom's Wampanoags in the east and the Susquehannocks to the south to take pressure off the New Englanders and Virginians. Mohawk intervention tipped the scales in the colonists' favor and helped bring an end to both wars.

The League Iroquois benefited greatly from making war on the Wampanoags and the Susquehannocks: by showing their commitment to the new Covenant Chain alliance with Andros and the English, they gained access to arms and ammunition and supported their populations with new supplies of captives. The Susquehannocks, by contrast, suffered terribly. In February and March of 1677, under intense pressure from every side, the Susquehannocks gathered with the Delawares at Shackamaxon and, in effect, decided to split themselves in two. Most would migrate northward to live as "adopted" clients of the Mohawks; the rest would live among the Delawares.[43] Emptied of its human population, the lower Susquehanna Valley would become a Delaware hunting ground.

Under these circumstances, the Delawares urgently needed a new ally to take the place of the Susquehannocks. In their meetings with Penn, therefore, the Delaware chiefs took pains to determine that he was his own man, subservient to neither the governor of New York nor the proprietor of Maryland. They also needed to discover what kinds of trade goods he could supply. In this, too, they were encouraged, for notwithstanding his own nonviolent convictions, Penn was perfectly willing to provide firearms and ammunition in quantity. By the very first land purchases, which William Markham had negotiated in 1681, the proprietor had already transferred seventy muskets, fifteen pistols, 170 pounds of gunpowder, and more than 200 pounds of bar lead and shot to the Delawares. A great deal more might be made to flow from that same source.[44]

The lands that Penn desired were extensive, amounting at first to more than 450 square miles and ultimately to about three times that area. But even the larger zone did not extend significantly above the falls of the Delaware, nor did the proposed purchases touch on the now essentially vacant lands of the Susquehanna Valley. That region of ample game supplies and fields formerly planted by the Susquehannocks remained one to which any native villagers displaced from the lower Delaware Valley could easily move. Thus there was no immediate reason for the Indians to feel that selling the territory Penn requested in any way threatened their livelihoods. Moreover, Penn showed himself to be willing, in a way most English purchasers were not, to respect Indian notions of property rights by making repeated purchases of tracts from all groups that had a claim to them and by allowing the Indian sellers to reserve rights to hunt on and move freely through lands he had purchased.[45]

All this reassured the Indians and created the basis of a relationship that could be understood from the very beginning as mutually beneficial. Following the initial meeting at Shackamaxon, therefore, transfers of land proceeded expeditiously. By the middle of 1684 Penn had acquired rights to roughly thirty miles of riverfront property both upstream and down from Philadelphia, in blocks extending back fifteen to twenty miles into the interior. He needed every square foot of it. He was more hard-pressed financially than ever now that he was actually in America and dealing with natives who drove hard bargains (in August 1683 he was already grumbling that "that w[hi]ch would have bought twenty miles" of land the year before was "not buying now two"). The future of his Holy Experiment depended on selling as much land as possible to settlers, and soon. However much potential colonists might appreciate freedom of conscience, Pennsylvania's future would rest on its ability to offer them titles to farmland at modest cost.

What ultimately proved most reassuring to the Delawares was what must initially have been hardest for them to grasp: Penn's pacifism. The absence of a militia made his province by far the least threatening to Indian people of any in colonial America; effectively it guaranteed that even if individual colonists dealt dishonorably or violently with individual natives, the province itself would never be able to coerce them by force of arms. By renouncing organized violence at the same time that he made no attempt to deny Indians the weapons they needed for hunting and self-defense, Penn in effect offered the Indians of his province a virtually ironclad guarantee of their own security.

As a result, Pennsylvania became as much a place of refuge for Indians displaced by American wars as it was an asylum for Europeans fleeing the war, famine, and persecution of the Old World. The well-known migrations into southeastern Pennsylvania of Scotch-Irish emigrants and Palatine Germans from the upper Rhine Valley were in fact preceded by earlier inmigrations of Indian villagers who resettled the lower Susquehanna drainage. The major groups among these included Susquehannocks, who moved back from Iroquoia under the supervision of Seneca chiefs and established villages near the mouth of Conestoga Creek (where they were henceforth known as the "Conestoga Indians"); Unami Delawares from the region around Philadelphia; Conoys and Nanticokes displaced from Maryland; Tuscaroras from what is now North Carolina; Tutelos from Virginia; and Shawnees, a people driven from their Kentucky homeland by Iroquois raiders, who regathered on the Susquehanna after wanderings that had taken some to the Illinois country, others to what are now South Carolina and Georgia, and still others to Maryland.[46]

Many of these peoples, like the returning Susquehannocks at Conestoga Creek, acknowledged a tributary connection to the Five Nations; Iroquois influence, as a result, was strong on the Susquehanna. The Delawares and the Shawnees, by contrast, used direct connections with Penn to preserve themselves from Iroquois domination for another two generations. Yet however their formal affiliations might play out, the benefits to all the Susquehanna groups were similar: thanks to Penn's policies, all of them were able to lead more independent and secure lives than had been possible since before the nightmare years of the Beaver Wars. Such was the benefit of trading with Penn's province and accepting the protection of a proprietor who had forgone the prerogative of coercion.

Penn and his province gained incalculable advantages from friendly relations with the Indians. The economic benefits were clear to Philadelphia's merchants, who gained access to beaver pelts and to the deerskins that were becoming an increasingly important component of the fur trade. Most important of all were the strategic and diplomatic benefits that the relationship afforded to the province as a whole. The well-armed Indian allies who lived on the colony's western and northern frontiers provided Pennsylvania with what amounted to a shield against attack: a level of security unmatched elsewhere in colonial North America. This in turn enabled Penn to realize his pacifist's dream of being able to dispense with a militia and reduced the role of the state to the administration of justice and the provision of such minimally essential services as the registration of deeds. The absence of war on Pennsylvania's frontiers for nearly three-quarters of a century came to pass not because Pennsylvanians learned to live by the Golden Rule as their proprietor hoped they would, but because the Indians protected the Euro-American settlements of the lower Delaware Valley as a by-product of defending themselves.

Crisis and Recovery

Penn had intended to bring his family to the colony and then remain to govern it directly, but he found one insuperable obstacle to doing so: Charles Calvert, the third Lord Baltimore, proprietor of Maryland. Because Pennsylvania's southern boundary overlapped substantially with Maryland's northern border, Baltimore feared that the new colony would diminish the lands and population of his province.[47] Pennsylvania's spectacular population growth only exacerbated his anxieties. By early 1684, after fewer than three years of settlement, Pennsylvania already boasted more than seven thousand English, Irish, Dutch, and German inhabitants, 40 percent of whom lived in Philadelphia, the third-largest settlement in British America. Baltimore therefore set sail for London in May 1684 to challenge his upstart neighbor's claim before the Privy Council. When Penn learned of his rival's departure some weeks later, he made haste to follow, determined to protect his family's fortune as well as his dream of a truly tolerant society.[48]

At one level the feud between Baltimore and Penn testified to the ego-strength of grandees mutually determined to allow nothing to slip from their grasp; at another, it revealed the costs and benefits of the Stuart kings' approach to empire-building in North America. To grant whole provinces to proprietors was to take advantage of individual initiative and to mobilize private capital in achieving public goals. It also invited—indeed, guaranteed—competition between powerful men that was capable of causing political disruption at home and creating conflicts between colonies abroad. When Penn returned to England in October 1684, his old ally in the struggle for toleration, James, Duke of York, was thinking about ways to minimize this destructive competitiveness. In cooperation with the loyal retainers like Sir Edmund Andros whom James would use to implement the scheme, he was planning to make his own colony of New York a base from which to extend royal control over all of the North American provinces. The duke was not yet in a position to begin doing so, however, because England was still wracked by political crises provoked by the prospect that he, a Catholic, would succeed to the throne upon the death of his brother.

Whatever else Penn thought when he disembarked at Worthing, Sussex, on October 6, 1684, he knew he had not arrived in the Peaceable Kingdom. The king, he discovered when he went to court a few days later, had grown "sowr & Stern." He seemed "Resolv[e]d to hold the rains of pow[e]r with Stiffer hand, then heretofore, especially over those that were observed to be State or church dissenters: conceiving that the opposition w[hi]ch made the government uneasy, came from that sort of people, & ther[e]fore they should either bow or break."[49] In the midst of plots to ensure that his successor would be a Protestant rather than his Catholic brother James, the king ordered several Whig leaders imprisoned in the Tower of London, then had them judicially murdered. Dissenters of every stripe, including Friends, were rotting in jail for refusing to take oaths affirming their allegiance. Under these unpromising circumstances, England's most conspicuous Quaker had to wait until Charles's death, in early 1685, to gain ground in his controversy with Lord Baltimore.[50]

The accession of the Duke of York to the throne as King James II was the opening Penn needed. James liked Penn better than Baltimore and appreciated the Quaker's advocacy of religious toleration, a policy that James intended to use to undermine the Church of England. Ever sensitive to royal preferences, the Privy Council rendered an initial judgment in Penn's favor. "[F]or Avoiding Further Differences," the Lords Councillors recommended that the territory comprising the modern state of Delaware (and thus Philadelphia's access to the Atlantic Ocean) go to Penn.[51] It was a triumph, and a mark of Penn's standing at court. And yet he did not return to his province, despite the fierce political dissension that had sprung up there after his departure.[52] Massachusetts's charter had been revoked late in the previous year, and the king was planning to revamp the northern colonies into a more efficient, coherent, and autocratic empire. Would James's regard for Penn prompt him to exempt Pennsylvania from his general program of reform? Because there was no way to know, Penn dared not leave England until the issue had been resolved.[53]

Meanwhile he became caught up again in his old dream of bringing religious toleration to England. The king solicited his advice on toleration and in the spring of 1686 demonstrated his regard for Penn directly by issuing a general amnesty for Quakers imprisoned because they had refused to take the Oath of Allegiance or pay tithes to the Church of England. More than 1,200 Friends were released, and the king followed with annual Declarations of Indulgence in 1687 and 1688 to protect them from further prosecution. Penn was suddenly England's most notable Dissenter, closer to the center of power than ever before and enjoying what was in many ways the most exciting time of his life. He undertook at least one diplomatic mission as James's personal emissary to the court of William of Orange, wrote tracts advising Dissenters to practice political moderation, and resumed his traveling ministry as a Public Friend.[54]

And yet all the while, despite the growing prosperity and population of his province, he was realizing no income from it. Quitrents were minimal, land sales had leveled off, and returns from his neglected Irish estates fell steadily.[55] Penn, never attentive to his financial affairs, was sliding deeper and deeper into debt to his steward, Philip Ford. Desperate for money, he entered "a series of contractual agreements, in which [he] kept renewing his obligations to Ford on increasingly stringent terms."[56] Ultimately, he leased Pennsylvania itself to Ford and his heirs for a term of 5,000 years, to cover

his current debt of £6,000.[57] These agreements gave Penn the right to recover his property if he paid the amount due, but he never had cash enough
to do it.

Matters rested uneasily between Ford and Penn in 1687; in 1688, with
the Glorious Revolution, they gave way to more intense, intractable anxieties. The overthrow of James II exposed Penn to charges of treason and
forced him to move about to avoid arrest. Brought before the Privy Council for questioning in December and forced to post a heavy bond for good
behavior, Penn became a fugitive from justice on February 27, 1689, when
the council issued a warrant for his arrest on suspicion of high treason. Between the issuance of the warrant and the end of the year, Penn went underground, moving from place to place to avoid being taken up. Meanwhile,
his income dried up entirely. The Irish rents evaporated as that Catholic isle
rebelled in support of James. The new governor whom Penn had deputized
in July 1688 to administer Pennsylvania, an old Cromwellian soldier named
John Blackwell, so alienated the Quaker leaders in the legislature that government fell into deadlock and all proprietary revenues vanished beneath a
wave of passive resistance. After thirteen embattled months, Blackwell resigned and the upper house took control of provincial administration.
Thomas Lloyd, the Quaker merchant who had led the opposition as president of the Council, became Pennsylvania's de facto governor.[58]

Penn could do nothing about it. The new king, William III, took an
army to Ireland in June 1689 to suppress the rebellion; when he left, those
deemed risks to public safety were ordered arrested. In August Penn found
himself once more in the Tower of London. He was released on bail after a
month and bound over for trial at the court of King's Bench in the Michael-
mas (autumn) session. Fearing that he would be beheaded and his estates
would be seized by the crown, Penn made a secret agreement with Philip
Ford, conveying the ownership of the province to him. Ford in turn assigned it in trust to a third party, further to insulate the proprietorship from
forfeiture. Penn then made a new will that made no mention of the agreement.[59]

Penn's case never went to trial. A hearing was held in November 1690,
with the consequence that he was released, only to be proclaimed for treason
again on February 5, 1691.[60] Although he longed to return to Pennsylvania
and indeed published a plan for opening new settlements on the Susquehanna during this time, the crown's unwillingness to release him from suspicion disabled him from doing so. Once again he went underground, in

effect vanishing from sight for the next three years; rumor had it that he took refuge in France. Wherever he was, Penn's existence now became a misery of powerlessness and poverty, lived out in the shadows. He tried from time to time to communicate with the Council of Pennsylvania by letter but in effect lost all influence there. In October 1691 the Privy Council recommended that the crown assume direct responsibility for governing Penn's province, assigning the governorship as an additional duty to the governor of New York, an Anglican army officer named Benjamin Fletcher.

The result for Pennsylvania was deepening division and drift. When William III took England to war with France as a part of the League of Augsburg, Governor Fletcher, a good soldier, took no account of the Quaker colonists' pacifism and tried to make Pennsylvanians contribute to the war effort. He immediately encountered the same passive resistance that had driven Governor Blackwell to distraction. Thanks to the Privy Council's addition of the three Lower Counties (modern Delaware) to Pennsylvania in 1685, Fletcher was not without allies in the Assembly, for the decidedly unpacifist Swedes, Finns, Dutch, and Anglicans who inhabited the western shore of Delaware Bay supported him in the hope that he would build coastal fortifications to protect them from French privateers. Nevertheless the legislature's Quaker majority refused to cooperate with the governor at any level.[61] All Penn could do about any of it was to send letters that alternately begged and threatened, which accordingly either were ignored or contributed to the growth of antiproprietary sentiment.

The crown's long cat-and-mouse game with Penn finally ended through the intercession of friends at court, who late in 1693 persuaded Queen Mary (in the absence of King William, who was on the Continent fighting Louis XIV) to lift the cloud of suspicion that had hung over him for five years. With political rehabilitation came an offer to return Pennsylvania to his control, provided that he rule it directly and make the province cooperate in the war effort. Penn agreed to go to Pennsylvania and, despite his pacifist scruples, to see to it that the colony would contribute either a company of infantry or the equivalent in annual monetary support. The crown therefore restored proprietary status to him in August 1694. Yet he did not return to his province for another five years.

Personal, financial, and political concerns all conspired to delay him. Penn's wife, Gulielma, always frail, died in February 1694. Ill-suited to a life as a widower, he fell in love before the year was out with a woman twenty years his junior and embarked on a courtship that culminated in their marriage on March 5, 1696. She was Hannah Callowhill, and, like Gulielma, had not only a firm Quaker faith to commend her but a substantial dowry: her father, Thomas, was a leading merchant and linendraper in Bristol.[62] Despite the relief that came with Hannah's dowry, Penn still faced huge financial pressures. He now owed Philip Ford £10,657, and Ford (now technically, if secretly, the owner of Pennsylvania) insisted that Penn pay the debt before he would return the title of the colony to him. After protracted negotiations, Ford finally agreed to let Penn *rent* Pennsylvania for £630 a year.[63] At least now, in the spring of 1697, Penn's path was clear: if he was ever to salvage his family's fortunes, it would have to be in Pennsylvania.[64]

But he could not simply go there and ask the legislature to provide revenue for himself and his family until the War of the League of Augsburg had ended. His agreement to make Pennsylvania contribute symbolic support for the war effort contradicted the Peace Testimony, and he knew that he could be called to account for it. No argument he could make would persuade the Quakers in the Assembly, much less the weighty Friends of the Philadelphia Monthly Meeting, that he had acted properly.[65] If he hoped to reestablish his political influence it could only be done in time of peace, when the possibility of being disciplined by the Meeting for a breach of testimony could be avoided.

For all these reasons it was early September 1699 before Penn, his pregnant wife, and his teenage daughter sailed for Pennsylvania. Fifteen years had passed since he had seen his province, ten since he had lost it, five since the queen had restored it, and two and a half since he had recovered it from Ford; yet he had every intention of setting Pennsylvania—somehow—to rights and salvaging his fortune. Then, he believed, he could spend the rest of his life at his manor of Pennsbury, outside Philadelphia, a haven of peace.

"A Land of Freedom & Flourishing"

The Pennsylvania to which Penn returned on December 3, 1699, was prospering economically and booming demographically. Despite King William's War (as the colonists called the War of the League of Augsburg), the provincial population had grown to 18,000 and was expanding rapidly. High levels of immigration from England, Germany, Ireland, and nearby colonies (especially New York and Maryland) had moderated the recession that accompanied the war, for the newcomers needed to be outfitted and provisioned

William Penn as he appeared at approximately the
time of his second voyage to Pennsylvania.
A sketch by Francis Place.

as well as provided with land to farm. With the return of peace, Philadelphia's merchants resumed the export of provisions, barrel staves, and livestock to the West Indies; wheat- and cattle-growers in the Delaware Valley
quickly became the most commercially oriented farmers in the northern
colonies. Meanwhile the demand for shipping created the foundation for a
vigorous, diversified urban economy of artisans and shopkeepers; when
Penn arrived, Philadelphia's population of approximately 5,000 made it the
second-largest city in English North America, trailing only Boston.[66]

All this growth had done little to benefit the proprietor.[67] No effective
political mechanism had been in place to sustain his political interests during fifteen years of absence, and distrust of this distant yet potentially powerful figure had become the dominant factor in Pennsylvania's politics. To
Penn the colony looked almost ungovernable. Worst of all was the colonists'
evident ingratitude. They lived in a province that guaranteed freedom of
conscience, offered plentiful opportunities for economic advancement, required no military service, and levied next to no taxes; yet none of them, so
far as he could see, had any sense of obligation toward the man who had
made it all possible. They were too self-interested to cooperate willingly
with Penn and for all their prosperity too stingy to compensate him for the

tens of thousands of pounds he had laid out as a consequence of what he believed had been wholly altruistic motives.

Penn's most pressing requirement, of course, was to make money, and
he set about doing so as soon as he arrived. Two things were necessary. One
was to induce the legislature to grant him an annual income; the other was
to acquire more lands from the Indians for sale to new immigrants. The former proved by far the more frustrating. Two successive legislatures not only
refused to cooperate but were more and more riven by factionalism.[68] The
leader of the legislature's Anglican party began an extremely effective letter-
writing campaign to the Privy Council and to allies in the House of Lords
aimed at annulling the Pennsylvania charter. By September 1701 Penn realized that unless he went to London to defend the charter in person, he
would in all likelihood lose his province altogether.[69] When he announced
his plans to return to England, however, he found but little sympathy for his
plight among the Quakers who dominated the Assembly. Instead, they quite
calculatingly took advantage of his distress to propose alterations in the
Frame of Government that transformed the Council from an upper house
of the legislature into a board of advisers to the governor, gave the Assembly
powers more nearly like those of Parliament—the right to elect its own officers and the power to impeach proprietary officials, for example—and
transferred property disputes from the jurisdiction of the proprietor to the
ordinary civil court system.

These proposed changes to the Frame galled Penn, who believed he had
already conceded too much to the Assembly.[70] He knew that they would effectively create a unicameral legislature, weaken the governor to near-
impotence, and dismantle what remained of the proprietor's power to
influence legislation in the province. Hate the changes as he did, however,
he agreed to them before departing for England because he feared that if he
lost control of the colony, such measures would provide important safe-
guards for Pennsylvania's Quakers against the aggressions of royal governors. Finally, in a codicil to the new Frame of Government—now known as
the Charter of Privileges—Penn permitted the Lower Counties to separate
themselves from the jurisdiction of the Upper (Quaker-dominated) Counties and form a legislature of their own. The only remaining link between
the two would be a common governor. Penn had in effect given up any pretext of controlling his colony.[71]

He had not, however, given up the hope that the colony could be made
profitable, so before leaving he instructed James Logan, who was to stay behind as secretary of the province, to

Use thy utmost Endeavours . . . to receive all that is due to me. Gett
in Quittrents, Sell Lands, according to my Instructions. . . . Look
carefully after all fines forfeitures Escheats Deodands and Strayes
that shall belong to me as Proprietor or chief Governour. Gett in the
Taxes and Friends Subscriptions and use thy utmost Diligence in
making Remittances to me. . . .[72]

Penn must have known that the quitrents over the two decades of Pennsylvania's existence had barely covered the costs of collection and that even if
Secretary Logan managed to lay hands on them, every deodand and es-
cheated estate in the colony would yield only negligible returns, but he was
desperate for every penny. His greatest hope centered on the Susquehanna
Valley. Five years earlier, after buying out New York's dubious claim to the
region, he had publicized his intention to colonize it.[73] Responses then had
been enthusiastic, and only Penn's inability to travel to Pennsylvania and
acquire the land from the Indians had stopped him. Now he remained optimistic about a new surge of land sales.[74]

Accordingly, in 1700 he set about acquiring the entire valley. He began,
as was his custom, by approaching the peoples who occupied the land he
wished to purchase. On September 13 he received a deed from the Susquehannocks living at Conestoga Creek to "all the said River Susquehanna and
all the islands therein and all the lands situate lying and being upon both
sides of the said river and next adjoining to the same extending to the utmost confines of the lands, which are or formerly were the right of the
people or nation called the Susquehanna Indians."[75] The following April,
sachems from the valley, representing the Conestoga Susquehannocks,
Shawnees, and Conoys, traveled to Philadelphia to ratify the cession. The
agreement was also a treaty of peace, articulating principles for dispute settlement under proprietary authority, establishing a supervised system of
trade to protect the Indian groups from exploitation, and extending to the
Indians "the full & free priviledges & Immunities of all the said Laws as any
other Inhabitant" of Pennsylvania. The Indians understood this last provision, in tandem with oral promises made at the time of the agreement, as a
guarantee that all the territory west of the river would be permanently reserved for their use.[76]

In addition to the eleven sachems from the Susquehanna who set their
marks to the agreement, one Iroquois chief—identified as "AHOOKASSONGH
Brother to the Emperor"—was also present, evidently representing the
League as an observer. At that moment the Iroquois were in no position to do

more than witness the proceedings: having been pushed to the point of collapse by the French and their allies during King William's War and after, the Five Nations were preparing to negotiate treaties with the French at Montreal and the English at Albany in a desperate effort to maintain their independence. Penn, unaware that the League was tottering on the brink, was delighted at the possibility of opening direct trade with the Iroquois; thus after the conference he asked the Delawares to carry a wampum belt and a message of friendship to the League Council on his behalf. But the Delawares, seeing little advantage in helping the Iroquois rebuild their strength, neglected to carry Penn's belt and message to Onondaga until 1712.[77]

The proprietor obviously understood the Indian trade as a source of income, and he also fully appreciated its necessity in preventing wars between natives and colonists. He knew that trade nurtured relationships and facilitated the exchange of information, enabling colonists to reassure Indians of their peaceful intentions and allowing the Indians to remind the province's authorities of their obligations under previous agreements. Above all, he grasped the importance of his personal participation to the ongoing process of building trust and cooperation. To acquaint himself with conditions among the Indians on the Susquehanna, therefore, Penn visited the region after the conclusion of the treaty, lodging with Indians along the way—the only colonial proprietor ever to do so. He found that the valley was home to roughly a thousand warriors (a number that implied a local population on the order of five thousand) who were engaged in a war against the distant "Carolina Indians." He deplored that conflict and tried to persuade his hosts that they should end it; yet he also took satisfaction in the knowledge that, despite their superior military capability, no Indian group had ever threatened to attack the far more vulnerable colonists of eastern Pennsylvania.[78] Indeed, the Delawares joined the Indians of the Susquehanna in requesting a final conference with Penn in October when they learned that his departure for England was imminent. Their purpose, they said, was to reiterate the agreements "that he and We have solemnly made for us and our Posterity," which otherwise might be forgotten.[79] Penn reassured them: he would never forget.

Nor did he return to make good on his promises. Not long after that meeting, on November 3, 1701, Penn and his family sailed for England. Arriving home on the eve of the War of the Spanish Succession, he spent the rest of his life staving off attacks from an unexpected (if not unpredictable) quarter, the family of Philip Ford (Ford had died at the beginning of 1702). Penn realized that if probated, Ford's estate would show the massive debts, secured by the entire province of Pennsylvania, that he owed his former steward. He therefore begged Ford's widow and executrix, Bridget, to give him time to make good on the debts. She agreed.[80] But no matter where Penn turned, he could not raise money; indeed, he continued to spend more than he brought in.

Hannah was pregnant with the Penns' fifth child when the Fords finally lost patience and probated Philip's estate in October 1705. Three years of lawsuits and countersuits followed, with the result that Penn was arrested for debt and confined from January to October 1708 in debtors' prison. Ultimately, he and the Fords settled out of court for a payment of £7,600, a sum that Penn borrowed (of course) from nine wealthy Friends, including his father-in-law. Lacking any other asset, the proprietor mortgaged the province to them as security for the loan.[81]

Early in 1709, Penn, now sixty-four years old, sent his wife and their five surviving children, the oldest of whom was now nine, to live with her father and mother. He sold the family's country house to help cover his debts and moved into lodgings in London, where he intended to pursue the measure that would restore his financial independence: the sale of Pennsylvania's government to the crown for £20,000. The province had become, in Penn's view, no more than the cause of "a Sorrow, that if not Supported by a Superiour hand, might have overwhelm'd me long agoe": a place that for its inhabitants had "prov'd a Land of Freedom & flourishing," but which for him was "the cause of Grief Trouble & Poverty."[82]

Penn was in the midst of negotiations with the crown in April 1712 when he suffered the first of a series of strokes. The one that finally incapacitated him came in October while he was writing to James Logan, pleading for him to send money and "deliver me from my present thraldom . . . for it is my excessive expences upon Pennsylvania that sunck me so low, & nothing else, my expences yearly in England ever fal[l]ing short of my yearly income."[83] Exactly four weeks earlier the crown had finally settled on a price (£12,000) for the province, but Penn never received a penny. He lived on in increasingly frail health for another five years, losing first the ability to write, then the capacity to speak intelligibly, then the ability to walk unaided, and finally the ability to recognize friends and relatives. He died in his sleep on July 30, 1718.[84]

Although his efforts had given him little but years of frustration and ultimately left him a broken man, William Penn died as the most successful agent of imperial expansion that England had yet produced. In 1700, Philadelphia's customhouse annually yielded revenues to the Exchequer that exceeded

£8,000; yet the expenses of provincial administration and Indian diplomacy were still borne almost entirely by the proprietor. By 1720 the city's population stood at 10,000 (close behind Boston, which it soon surpassed), its annual imports were doubling with each decade, and its shipbuilding industry was turning out vessels to carry the province's grain to markets from the West Indies to the Iberian Peninsula and the Mediterranean.

With Pennsylvania's large family sizes and favorable mortality regime, natural increase alone would have driven demographic growth at a rate sufficient to double the population with each passing generation, and immigration fueled even more explosive expansion. Germans from the Rhineland and Scots from the Lowlands and Ulster poured into the colony after the War of the Spanish Succession (Queen Anne's War), boosting the average decadal growth rate to nearly 150 percent. Pennsylvania's Euro-American population shot upward from 18,000 in 1700 to more than 120,000 by the end of 1750.[85] By any measure except the ones that mattered most to Penn, his province was a tremendous success story.

Pennsylvania attracted so many people because it had the unshakable reputation of being "the best poor man's country on earth."[86] In practice, that meant that the province offered good land at reasonable prices; farms five to six times the size of those in Europe were available on terms that allowed ordinary farm families to own the land they lived on rather than merely lease it. Crop yields were high—initially as much as three times those possible on the long-farmed soils of western Europe. Moreover, like the rest of British North America, Pennsylvania was chronically short of workers, which pushed wages to levels far higher than those common in western Europe. Entrepreneurs recruited servants in England, Scotland, Ireland, and the western German states and shipped them to masters who eagerly purchased their services under multiyear indentures; thus the demand for labor as much as the availability of land stimulated and sustained immigration. Finally, peace itself provided an immense incentive for Europeans to immigrate. Of all the places one could live in the Atlantic world, Pennsylvania was the one least likely to suffer the horrors of war.

Penn's great contribution was to create the conditions in which a dynamic society could flourish—and then not to interfere with its development. Penn the provider of land, the facilitator of migration, the publicist, the guarantor of toleration, the agent of peaceable relations with the Indians: at all these explicitly noncoercive roles he excelled, and they enabled his colony to thrive even though they brought him precious little power or financial reward. When Penn acted most explicitly as proprietor—as lawgiver,

exacter of revenues, and would-be moral guide—he failed most spectacularly, exacerbating the feral quality of colony's political life and building
support for the antiproprietary party, which he hated. His colonists loved
him best when he was least present in their lives, least insistent that they
owed him some duty or compensation or respect. It was therefore only
when he was dead that William Penn fulfilled his final role as the symbol of
a society founded on benevolence and tolerance, revered at a safe distance
by a people who in practice preferred the individualist pursuit of happiness
to the collective achievement of the founder's ideals.[87]

The Violent Genesis of a Long Peace

The hallmark of intercultural relations in Pennsylvania from the early 1680s
until about three decades after Penn's death was a system that allowed colonial and native societies to develop along parallel paths.[88] So long as large
farm families could replicate their independent lives from generation to
generation by buying the land they needed, they had no wish to acquire it
by the far more dangerous and costly means of conquest. So long as the Indians had access to the European trade goods they needed to lead the lives
that they wanted; so long as they had weapons to defend themselves against
their enemies; so long as the colonists' demands for land did not become so
extravagant as to deprive them of the territory they needed to hunt, fish, and
farm as they wished: while these conditions were met, peace could endure.

That peace *could* endure, of course, did not mean that it was somehow
inevitable. The long containment of conflict and violence in Pennsylvania
depended also on the activities of go-betweens, mediators sufficiently well-
versed in the languages and cultures of both Indian and European people
that they could defuse potentially explosive conflicts as they arose. The
most important mediator present from the beginning was the Swedish fur
trader Lars Pärsson (Lasse) Cocke, who demonstrated his cultural versatil-
ity in another way by becoming a naturalized British subject and changing
his name to Laurence Cox. A succession of traders like Jacques and James
Le Tort (father and son); the brothers Peter and Michael Bizaillon; Martin
Chartier; and Conrad Weiser followed him, while on the Indian side many
others appeared: some as obscure as Shawydoohungh (Indian Harry) and
others as prominent as Shickellamy, Scarouady, and Pisquetomen. By minimizing the destructive effects of such perennial frictions as theft, fraud,
rape, and murder, the mediators became the indispensable political sausage-

makers of the Pennsylvania frontier.[89] Had it not been for their efforts, war would almost surely have broken out in 1728 and again in 1743; it is unimaginable that peace would have endured in Pennsylvania until 1755 without them.[90]

Ironically, the third factor that helped preserve peace in Pennsylvania until the middle of the eighteenth century was the bloodletting that afflicted the peoples all around it. We have seen how in the mid-1670s Metacom's War (King Philip's War) destroyed most of the Algonquian groups in southern New England, deprived the survivors of virtually all their remaining lands, and pushed the one group that could not be conquered, the Abenakis, into the French alliance that visited raids and kidnappings on the Massachusetts, New Hampshire, and Maine frontiers for another half-century.[91] Meanwhile, the Susquehannock War of 1675–76 eliminated the Susquehannocks as a military threat to Euro-American colonization in the Chesapeake Bay area. With the return of peace, smaller nations like the Doegs were confined to reserves, just as remnant Algonquian bands were in New England following Metacom's War. Those who escaped confinement, like the Conoys of the Potomac Valley, migrated northward to seek shelter on the Susquehanna, strengthening Penn's alliance system there.[92]

Wars simultaneously afflicted the southeastern quadrant of North America. Slavery, the defining characteristic of South Carolina from its beginning in the 1660s, became the first engine to drive intercultural trade in the region.[93] Just as the French and Dutch had done in the quest for pelts, early Carolina traders armed friendly Indian groups with muskets in return for the Indians' agreement to raid other nations for captives. These were typically sold in turn to West Indian planters, who worked them to death alongside the African slaves who grew and processed their sugar. Because the English demand for human chattel was apparently insatiable, Indian slave raiders themselves soon became targets for enslavement. The Shawnees, for example, moved east from the Mississippi Valley during the Beaver Wars and settled in the Savannah region; they conducted captive-taking expeditions against other Indians during the 1680s, only to find that they themselves were the targets of raids by Catawbas from the Piedmont. This threat, more than any other, compelled the Shawnees to migrate northward to the Susquehanna, where they, too, added numbers and defensive strength to Pennsylvania's Indian shield. Two other groups proved to be the South Carolina slave merchants' greatest suppliers of slaves. The Yamassees, a people who abandoned Spanish Florida for South Carolina in order to avoid being evangelized by Catholic priests, enthusiastically raided the Christian Indians of the Florida missions.

The Creeks of the Apalachicola, Chattahoochee, and Flint valleys (the principal drainages of what are now western Georgia and eastern Alabama) hunted
for captives as far west as the Mississippi Valley.[94]

The Indians in Pennsylvania's orbit had the means to defend themselves
against these depredations, but most groups in the Southeast did not. The
1680s and 1690s, therefore, saw the same kind of devastation in that region
as the Beaver Wars brought to the Great Lakes basin four decades earlier.
Queen Anne's War (the War of the Spanish Succession, 1702–13) unleashed
the worst destruction of all.

Early in the war, British agents in South Carolina armed the Yamassees
and Creeks and encouraged them to attack the Spanish in Florida as part of a
larger imperial strategy. In practice, however, the Yamassee and Creek raiders
concerned themselves less with imperial goals than with gaining slaves for
sale in Charleston. They ripped through poorly-defended mission villages
throughout Florida, killing perhaps 3,000 people and enslaving 10,000 more,
80 percent of the peninsula's Indian population. In 1711, near the end of the
war, a clash between the Iroquoian-speaking Tuscaroras of North Carolina
and a German immigrant group whose members had unwisely tried to settle
on their lands offered the pretext for another massive slaving expedition.

In this harrowing episode, the Tuscarora War, a handful of South Carolina provincial soldiers joined hundreds of Yamassee, Creek, Catawba, and
Cherokee warriors to attack and destroy the Tuscarora homeland. About
1,400 Tuscaroras were killed, and a thousand enslaved. The remainder,
about 2,500 in all, escaped to take refuge with the Iroquois of New York.
The League welcomed the Tuscaroras as reinforcements and brothers, formally adopting them in 1726 and transforming the confederacy into the Six
Nations of the Iroquois.[95]

The end of Queen Anne's War brought no more than a brief respite to
the Southeast. In 1715, the Yamassees found themselves deeply indebted to
Carolina traders and threatened with enslavement themselves. In response,
they joined with the Creeks and Catawbas to hunt down and kill the slave
traders wherever they could find them. With its frontier aflame, South Carolina appealed to the Iroquois League and the Cherokees, offering arms and
huge diplomatic gifts in return for help. Ordinarily adversaries, the Iroquois
and the Cherokees laid aside their differences long enough to join in attacking their enemies the Yamassees, Catawbas, and Creeks in the horrific conflict known as the Yamassee War (1715–18). As in the Tuscarora War, ethnic
cleansing followed wholesale slaughter and enslavement. The remnants of
the Catawbas were confined to a small reservation; the minority of Ya-

massees who escaped death or enslavement fled to Florida; the Creeks removed westward into Alabama. By one estimate, five-sixths of the Indians
in South Carolina perished or were driven out as a result of the Yamassee
War. Those who survived were either subordinated and confined within reserves or remained, like the Cherokees, on the extreme margins of the
province. The Carolinas were now wide open for settlement by Euro-
Americans and their slaves, Indian and African alike.[96]

In the midst of so much suffering, the comparative security of the
Delawares, Shawnees, and other Indian groups in alliance with Pennsylvania stood out all the more strongly. The devastations of war in neighboring
regions gave a huge impetus to the maintenance of peace within Penn's
colony. The trade that Pennsylvania's Indians enjoyed was absolutely essential to their ability to defend themselves. By the 1720s, nothing could have
been clearer than that any people who wished to defend its autonomy
needed a European ally and arms-supplier to do so. In every clash between
colonists and natives, from Metacom's War to the destruction of the Yamassees, what weighed decisively in favor of the English colonies was not
the martial skill of the militia—which was mostly negligible—but rather
that the colonists had the ability to replenish exhausted stocks of arms, ammunition, and food while the Indians—except for those who had a European ally to supply them—did not.

The subordination or destruction of so many peoples effectively recon-
figured native power in eastern North America and—paradoxically—made
it possible for a new period of stability to emerge in intercultural relations.[97]
By the mid-1720s, each of the three European empires influenced a fairly
well defined zone of interaction with native peoples. The smallest lay in the
southeast and belonged to Spain. Despite the blows suffered in Queen
Anne's War, the Spanish managed to retain Florida through an alliance system with the Yamassees and other surviving Indians. Spanish influence extended from the southern frontier of Georgia across the Florida peninsula
and along the Gulf coast as far west as the present site of Pensacola. A
French zone, based principally on Indian alliances, reached from the Gulf of
Saint Lawrence to the Great Lakes, down the Mississippi Valley to New Orleans, and east along the Gulf coast to Mobile Bay, where it met the Spanish. A thickening band of expansive agricultural settlements from New
England to coastal Georgia defined the British imperial zone. With the exception of the Delawares and the other groups allied with Pennsylvania, by
the late 1720s, no large Indian groups remained unsubordinated within the
settled regions of the British colonies.

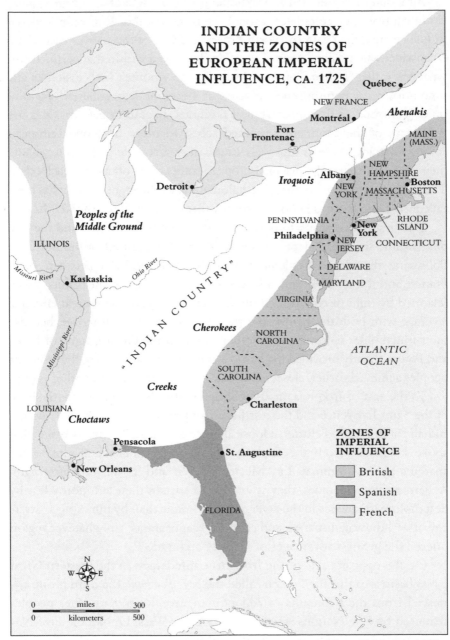

INDIAN COUNTRY AND THE ZONES OF EUROPEAN IMPERIAL INFLUENCE, CA. 1725

Québec

NEW FRANCE

Abenakis

Montréal

Fort Frontenac

MAINE (MASS.)

NEW HAMPSHIRE

Albany

Iroquois

NEW YORK

Boston

MASSACHUSETTS

Detroit

Peoples of the Middle Ground

PENNSYLVANIA

New York

RHODE ISLAND

Philadelphia

NEW JERSEY

CONNECTICUT

ILLINOIS

Ohio River

DELAWARE

Missouri River

Kaskaskia

MARYLAND

VIRGINIA

Mississippi River

"INDIAN COUNTRY"

Cherokees

NORTH CAROLINA

ATLANTIC OCEAN

SOUTH CAROLINA

Creeks

Charleston

LOUISIANA

Choctaws

Pensacola

St. Augustine

New Orleans

ZONES OF IMPERIAL INFLUENCE

British

Spanish

French

FLORIDA

N
W E
S

| 0 | miles | 300 |
| 0 | kilometers | 500 |

After "Eastern North America in the eighteenth-century imperial world," in Daniel K. Richter, *Facing East from Indian Country: A Native History of Early America* (Cambridge, Mass.: Harvard University Press, 2001), 165.

Although these imperial zones should not be thought of as continuous areas of control, they completed a rough, elongated oval of European imperial influence encircling eastern North America. Most of the natives east of the Mississippi who retained control over their lives lived within that perimeter, in what was called "Indian Country." Inside Indian Country, six "clusters of autonomous local communities... acted as more or less coherent political units."[98] Insofar as their geographical positions, migration patterns, and the waterways of the continent permitted access to more than one European colony for trade, these groups were in the most favorable position to pursue their own self-interest by playing European competitors off against each other. The Indians' virtuosity in this great diplomatic game brought on what has been called the Long Peace, a period of stability that lasted until the mid-1750s.

The first native group to practice balance-of-power politics and the one that became the most adept at using it was the Six Nations of the Iroquois. Following the Grand Settlement of 1701, their position between New France and New York and assertions of control over the Ohio Valley (claimed by right of conquest in the Beaver Wars) gave them great effective leverage with both the British and the French empires. Moreover, because their much older cultural and religious union in the Great League of Peace and Power already provided the basis for a political confederacy, the Iroquois peoples achieved earlier, closer coordination in policy than any other group.

To the east of Iroquoia, in an oblong territory between the south shore of the Saint Lawrence and the northern frontier of New England, lived the Indians of the second cluster: a loose alliance of culturally similar bands that spoke languages from the Eastern and Western Abenaki groups. They shared a history dominated by Metacom's War and its vengeful aftermath. As seminomadic peoples, they were able to sustain their autonomy less by deft diplomatic moves in the style of the Iroquois than by pursuing a "strategy of withdrawal, dispersal, and cautious reappearance" in whatever region offered the greatest advantages of security and trade.[99]

On the opposite side of the Iroquois confederacy, in the western Great Lakes basin area that the French called the *pays d'en haut,* the third group coalesced from the fragments of Algonquian, Iroquoian, and other peoples shattered by Five Nations attacks in the Beaver Wars. Unlike the Five Nations and the Abenakis, these groups did not even share closely allied languages, only a common history of flight, fragmentation, and destruction. Many of the groups that finally found shelter from the Iroquois in the area south of Lake Superior and west of Lake Michigan had been historic enemies, and all had reason to be mutually distrustful. The French, understanding these refugees as potential allies, began in the 1680s to cultivate their complex "Middle Ground" alliance with them. French arms and supplies and direction made it possible for the Indians of the *pays d'en haut* to take their revenge on the Iroquois in the 1690s and were the crucial element in forcing their old enemies into a posture of neutrality after 1700.[100]

Just as the three northern clusters were products of the Beaver Wars and Metacom's War, the three groups in the southern half of Indian Country coalesced in the aftermath of the Yamasee War. The northernmost of these, the Cherokees, were Iroquoian-speakers who lived on the western edge of South Carolina in three village groupings that extended from the Piedmont (the Lower Towns) across the valleys of the Great Smoky Mountains (the Middle Towns) into the Tennessee Valley beyond (the Overhill Towns). Wary of the Carolinians after the Yamassee War, they sought trade connections with the Virginians—thus practicing play-off politics between English colonies that they rightly understood to be competitors—and to a certain extent with the French in upper Louisiana.[101]

The Cherokees feared the two other groups in the Southeast, both Muskogean-speakers far better situated geographically to play empires off against each other. The easternmost were the Creeks, whose complex balancing act counterpoised the French of Louisiana against the Spanish of Florida against the English of Carolina. After the falloff in the Indian slave trade, they found a new commercial resource in the white-tailed deer that had multiplied astronomically after native populations collapsed throughout the Southeast. Fully half of the million deerskins that passed through Charleston annually at midcentury were harvested by Creek hunters. Their economic influence and dexterity in maneuvering between all three European powers made them the most influential, powerful group in the Southeast.[102]

Creek power tended to move their western neighbors, the Choctaws of the lower Mississippi Valley, into a closer alliance with the French of Louisiana. The Choctaws in that sense resembled the Indians of the *pays d'en haut,* although they also had enough access to the Spanish of western Florida and the English of Carolina and Georgia to pose a threat, and thus to keep the French from behaving in an imperious manner. France's approach to Indian relations was in that sense as much a product of Indian power as of French perceptiveness concerning Indian cultures. Military attacks (or the threat of them) were always the ultimate teaching tools the Indians possessed in demonstrating that Europeans trading and living among them did so on sufferance. The Choctaws taught the French one such lesson, suddenly and unmistakably, by assaulting their posts at Mobile and Natchez in 1747.[103]

All six groups prospered and grew during the Long Peace because no one of them—and none of the European empires—could gain the upper hand. Their leaders understood that they needed to accommodate themselves to the Europeans' demands for land, furs and hides, military allies, evangelization, and so on. They knew that an exclusive alliance with any of the empires was dangerous and that dependency in trade or diplomacy had all too often proved the prelude to outright subordination and confinement on reservations. Those chiefs also presided over societies they could only lead by persuasion and in which competing leaders could rise as they acquired followings. The autonomy that balance-of-power diplomacy gave the six clusters of peoples in Indian Country was thus never so much the result of a systematic policy as a product of the factiousness of native peoples living in decentralized societies. Factionalization proved to be an adaptive feature in intercultural politics during the Long Peace because of the multiplicity of connections it fostered. The bewildering complexity of Indian societies and politics kept the representatives of European empires constantly searching for a key to unlock their mysteries and in the process only multiplied the connections that tended to hold the empires' own domineering ambitions in check.[104]

Ironically, when this system broke down in catastrophic warfare at midcentury, it was a consequence of two developments in the heretofore peaceful province of William Penn. First was a shift in the practice of pacific imperialism by the last and greatest of Penn's stewards, James Logan. The second—and decisive—change was that Penn's heirs finally succeeded in making Pennsylvania what it had never been for their father, a paying proposition.

"Govern'd by Their Interest"

While he lived, William Penn had always made it a point to deal with his king and his God directly, but where the matters of the world were concerned—at least the humdrum details of financial management and the administration of government—he preferred to use intermediaries. The man who had remained in Pennsylvania to act as his personal representative and to fill the powerful office of secretary of the province, James Logan, was the ablest of the stewards who passed through the proprietor's employ between 1669 and the end of his life. Penn had hired him as casually as he did all the others: like Philip Ford, Logan was an impecunious former schoolmaster with abundant talents for commerce but no capital with which to begin a merchant's career. As with Ford, the paltry compensation that Penn offered compelled Logan to embark on a second career in trade merely to live comfortably. Logan's ambitions, however, were never merely material. A gifted linguist with a scientific bent, he came to be known on both sides of the Atlantic for his accomplishments as a botanist, classical scholar, and mathematician.[105]

Logan brilliantly defended the proprietor's interests during his first eight years of service as secretary of the province, but he had to rely on fees rather than salary for his compensation and never enjoyed a reliable income. In 1709, fed up with his pinched and precarious circumstances, he sailed to England to demand that Penn compensate him for a decade of service, during which he had ably defended the proprietor's interests against assaults by antiproprietary politicians in the Assembly. Penn, who appreciated his service, made a lump-sum payment of £1,000 and promised him a higher income in the future. Logan invested the money carefully (he bought the rights to about 8,000 acres of Pennsylvania land from First Purchasers who had decided not to emigrate) and returned to Philadelphia in 1711. He intended to work only another couple of years for Penn while he accumulated the capital he would need to launch a full-time career as a merchant.[106]

Soon after he reached Philadelphia, he discovered that the prospects for profit were uncommonly favorable in what he called "the skin trade." The Tuscarora War was undermining Charleston's dominant position as a supplier of deer hides, and English buyers were clamoring for more. Logan quickly forged connections with the Susquehanna Valley traders—James LeTort, Peter Bizaillon, John and Edmund Cartlidge, and others—whom he had previously employed as go-betweens in Indian diplomacy. These men were in a position to use their knowledge of the Shawnees, Delawares, and other peoples of the valley to exploit opportunities that lay to the west of Pennsylvania. From the west branch of the Susquehanna, portage paths gave access to creeks that flowed into the Allegheny and therefore to the Ohio, a vast domain emptied of human occupants during the Beaver Wars and now home to the largest concentration of deer and other game in North America. Logan provided guns, ammunition, rum, and other goods to his traders, who in turn sold them on credit to the Indian hunters who harvested the hides and brought them back to Logan's trading post on the Susquehanna tributary of Conestoga Creek. Logan could effectively control the traders by either extending credit in trade goods or withholding it; the traders disciplined the Indian hunters by the same means. It was the classic strategy of the fur trade, and Logan brought it to something like perfection.

By 1715 Logan had built (at proprietary expense) a road passable to wheeled traffic from his trading house to Philadelphia and was hauling out hides at such a rate that the long, swaybacked covered wagons he used on the route came to be known as Conestogas. That year he shipped hides worth £1,000 to England. By 1717, when profits climbed to new heights as a result of the Yamassee War, he effectively monopolized the skin trade in the province. It was "a nauseous drudgery," he complained, to deal with such commodities and men as the trade required. But the profits were splendid and produced the capital that Logan now used to make himself one of the richest men in British America.[107]

He made his fortune by combining the Indian trade with land speculation. He had already completed, at proprietary expense, the survey of 60,000 acres on the east side of the Susquehanna.[108] When settlers arrived in the last half of the 1710s, they found that the most farmable lands in the Susquehanna tract could not be purchased directly from the proprietary land office at the modest official rate but rather were available only by private purchase from James Logan, who—having previously bought up the best plots at the official rate—was prepared to sell them for whatever price the market would bear. In this way Logan quintupled his net worth in less than a decade. By 1720 he was almost certainly the richest, as well as the most influential, man in the province.[109]

Logan's idea was to make a profit while promoting settlement in an orderly way that would allow colonists and Indians to live side by side with as little friction as possible. Thus, for example, when the area around Conestoga Creek became a focus of settlement and the farmers' cattle began to stray into native cornfields, Logan created an Indian preserve, Conestoga Manor, from proprietary lands, and ordered the Indians' fields to be securely fenced at the proprietor's expense. Logan's dedication to maintaining order was very real, for he understood how easily colonists could enrage Indians by encroaching on their lands. He also believed that the costs of maintaining order justly fell to the proprietor along with the costs of government generally.

Penn's death, therefore, opened a new phase in the history of his province's settlement frontier. All proprietary activity ceased until his estate was probated and the legal ownership of the province determined. Those proved hugely complicated tasks. Because Penn had been at the point of selling the rights to the government of Pennsylvania to the crown at the time of his stroke in 1712, his last will had assigned responsibility for completing that transaction to two aristocratic trustees who enjoyed good connections at court. With the death of Queen Anne in 1714 and Penn's own demise in 1718, the transfer fell into a kind of legal limbo that left it utterly unclear to whom—the trustees? Penn's widow? his eldest male heir?—the government of the province properly belonged.

Penn's will, moreover, designated certain parcels of land in Pennsylvania to his children by Gulielma Springett while assigning the bulk of the lands and the rights of proprietorship to his children by Hannah Callowhill. But could the proprietorship be divided? Was the will even a valid instrument? If not, Penn's eldest (and dissolute, irresponsible) son by Gulielma, William Jr., would inherit the entire estate. William promptly complicated matters by trying to exercise the functions of the proprietor without reference to the will; he complicated them further by dying in 1720. At that point *his* eldest son, Springett Penn, moved immediately to assert his rights as sole proprietor. The case, now tangled beyond recognition, was consigned to the Court of Chancery, where it disappeared under a mountain of pleadings and counterpleadings. The case remained unresolved for another seven years. Hannah herself did not live to see the case settled; she died, worn out with grief and worry, in the spring of 1727.

The chancery decision, rendered in July of that year, assigned the entire proprietorship to the sons of Hannah Penn, but that judgment, in the time-honored way of actions in chancery, did not resolve the issue. It was not until 1731, thirteen years after the death of William Penn and nearly twenty after he had lost the capacity to exercise his proprietary powers competently, that the children (and grandchildren) from the first marriage renounced their claim to the proprietorship in return for a cash payment from the children of the second marriage.[110] Without this out-of-court settlement, another set of suits would in all likelihood have kept the ownership of the province tied up in chancery for at least another decade.

The effects of this Dickensian legal nightmare reached far into the backwoods of Penn's province. The Palatine Germans and Scotch-Irish who flooded into Pennsylvania after Queen Anne's War found that no new lands could be surveyed and no new treaties with the Indians could be concluded until the courts had identified the legitimate proprietor.[111] The 60,000 acres Logan had surveyed east of the Susquehanna were soon sold and settled. Thereafter, most would-be landholders, unable to buy property legally, simply located a patch of promising ground, cleared it, and began to farm with no great concern for who—proprietor or Indians—actually owned it. James Logan could do nothing but write with increasing desperation to Penn's heirs, pleading for someone to come and take charge. "The Palatines crowd in upon us and the Irish yet faster," he warned; something had to be done to protect the province from the "Settlem[en]t of those vast numbers of poor but presumptuous People."[112] The numbers of families living on farms they did not legally own complicated the routine functions of government, for property tax evasion was routine among squatters who had every reason not to draw attention to their locations, and quitrents became almost impossible to collect. Logan worried most of all that the rising tensions between natives and colonists over land rights would erupt in war.

In the summer of 1727, enough settlers had spilled across the Susquehanna that Captain Civility, a Conestoga chief, found it necessary to remind Logan that Penn had promised, a quarter century earlier, that no "Christians or white people" would be allowed to settle west of the river.[113] In May 1728, a potent combination of rumors of Indian conspiracy and the murder of three Indians by settlers in the Schuylkill Valley very nearly started a war, and set Logan and his go-betweens scrambling to avert further violence.[114] Their success in organizing the peace conference that restored amicable relations was largely a matter of good fortune. In the absence of an organized militia, a breakdown in negotiations would necessarily have led to a bloodbath. Logan put it as plainly as he could to Penn's heirs, begging them to settle the unrest among the natives with another treaty. If one of you does not come soon, he wrote in 1729, "we may expect a war that would run this province in the extremest confusion, none being worse fitted for it."[115]

The previous decade of uncertainty had convinced Logan that without a proprietor to negotiate treaties with the Delawares and other Indians, the best hope of securing Pennsylvania's frontier lay with the Iroquois League, which had so often proved willing to police native groups the English could not control. As early as 1721 Logan arranged for Governor Sir William Keith to cooperate with Virginia's governor, Alexander Spotswood, in dividing responsibility for Indian relations. Virginia would manage everything to the east and south of a line that followed the Potomac to its headwaters then ran southwestward along the ridge of the Appalachians; Pennsylvania would act in concert with other northern colonies already allied with the Iroquois to handle Indian affairs to the north and west of the line.[116]

Not long after, the Iroquois sent a delegation to Conestoga, where they asked to treat with the Pennsylvanians about matters of trade. In June 1721, therefore, Logan and Keith traveled to Conestoga to treat with the Seneca orator Ghesaont and several other League chiefs. Keith merely informed them of the agreement he had reached with Spotswood, promised further cooperation between the Pennsylvanians and the League, and left. Logan, however, remained to speak at greater length of trade and land. The Iroquois, he learned, were distressed with the terms of trade at Albany, where goods were expensive and the traders had begun dealing directly with the French at Montreal, cutting the Iroquois out of their previous position as middlemen. As an Indian trader, Logan was of course extremely interested in this item of information. In his capacity as proprietary agent, he also took pains to explain that his master, William Penn, had purchased the Susquehanna Valley from its present inhabitants at a treaty, witnessed by the Iroquois representative Ahookassongh, in 1701; any ancient Iroquois claims to the Susquehanna were therefore unlikely to be entertained. But the message that Logan carried away for himself was more compelling.[117]

Logan's conversations with Ghesaont and the other chiefs convinced him that if properly cultivated by representatives of the empire and not merely left to the management of Albany's notoriously self-interested fur merchants, the Iroquois might indeed be used to maintain order along the whole British colonial frontier north of the Carolinas. This would have a double benefit: for Pennsylvania, the Iroquois could control Indian groups on the Susquehanna that the province could not otherwise discipline; for the empire, League diplomats could be used to counter French influence in the west, which had been growing ever since the establishment of New Orleans and Detroit at the beginning of the century.[118] If along the way to stabilizing the frontier and improving the position of the British empire vis-à-vis the French it became possible for James Logan to capture all or part of the Indian trade that had centered at Albany, so much the better.

With all this in mind, Logan urged Governor Keith to take up the cause of Pennsylvania-Iroquois relations at a great council in Albany in the summer of 1722. Logan himself could not attend, but he coached Keith well before he left; and at the treaty conference attended by a full representation of the League and the governors of Virginia and New York, Keith proposed that the Covenant Chain be extended to include all of Britain's colonies. With the acceptance of that proposal, the colonial authorities recognized the Iroquois as sole spokesmen for a variety of other peoples, including the Conestogas and other Susquehanna bands. The Great Treaty of 1722 thus took a long step toward defining Six Nations as a kind of suzerain, empowered not only to speak on behalf of other native peoples but to dispose of the very lands on which they lived.[119]

A half-dozen years passed before the League Council at Onondaga appointed an Oneida chief, Shickellamy (The Enlightener), to represent the Six Nations' interests on the Susquehanna to the government of Pennsylvania. He arrived in time to witness the 1728 Philadelphia peace conference that barely averted war. Logan and Keith lost no time in recognizing Shickellamy as official spokesman for the Susquehanna Indians, a move that allowed Logan henceforth to deal with the various Susquehanna groups through him and thus avoid the complexity of negotiating with multiple chiefs, as Penn had always done. Soon non-Iroquois spokesmen, such as Captain Civility of the Conestogas and the Delaware king, Sassoonan, faded into inconsequence.[120]

Once it became clear that Logan and the other English authorities had given the Iroquois the upper hand, the Shawnees, Delawares, and others on whose lands the white settlers were pressing began to abandon eastern Pennsylvania. To maintain their autonomy, many Delawares withdrew from the region north of Philadelphia and relocated to Shamokin at the Forks of the Susquehanna; others, along with a great many Shawnees, migrated further west to the Ohio country. Some of the traders who had made their homes at Conestoga followed them. The easier access to game in their new homes on the Ohio meant that the numbers of hides harvested rose and the migrants prospered, notwithstanding the transportation costs that the traders (who now assumed responsibility for packing the skins back to Philadelphia) folded into the prices they charged for trade goods. The greater distance between themselves and the Euro-Americans also increased the cultural independence of the migrants and made it easier for them to resist acculturation and conversion to Christianity. As the attractions of life on the Ohio became clear, the westward shift accelerated. By the mid-1740s, most of Pennsylvania's Delawares and Shawnees were living west of the Alleghenies.[121]

Meanwhile, James Logan, the most important man in the fastest-growing British colony in North America, was systematically rethinking the foundations of imperial control. Britain's future in North America depended, Logan concluded, on its ability to exploit the new Iroquois alliance. In the summer of 1731 he prepared an overview of the empire for the British prime minister, Sir Robert Walpole; he titled it "Of the State of the British Plantations in America: A Memorial." It was a remarkable document, for it outlined an imperial vision nurtured in North America itself, a vision that blended metropolitan concerns with perspectives rooted in the experiences of provincial officials and Indian traders. Logan's analysis reflected the realities of power as the most perceptive of North America's Britons understood them.[122]

Of all the European powers, he observed, Britain undoubtedly had the strongest claim to North America and also had the largest and most vigorous population; incalculable amounts of wealth and strength could be gained from the colonies. Yet the French, despite considerable disadvantages in population and resources, claimed in America "a Countrey nearly Equal to all Europe in Extent, while the English bounded by [the] Appalachian Hills have comparatively only a Skirt along the Shoar."[123] The secret of French success centered on their alliances with Indians from the Saint Lawrence to the Great Lakes to the Mississippi, which enabled them to move and trade at will throughout the interior. Through commerce, military support, evangelism, and intermarriage, the French had made themselves "Masters of almost all the Indians on the Eastern part of the main." The English, by contrast, remained divided, weak, and dependent on only one potentially formidable ally, "the 5 or 6 Nations" of the Iroquois. Even that strategic relationship was under threat, for the French were trying simultaneously to attract the League by offering favorable terms of trade and to intimidate it by building a fort and trading post on Lake Champlain, at Crown Point.[124]

Logan explained for Walpole the conviction that Champlain and Penn had shared: good relations with the Indians depended on trade, for while "the generality" of natives "never forget [an] ill turn nor remember a good one; yet they may be Govern'd by their Interest."[125] There was no time to lose in cultivating the Iroquois, who alone had the potential to establish control over the Delawares, Shawnees, and other Indians who had removed to the Ohio Valley. Eventually the British would need to acquire the Ohio's "Excellent Lands" for interior farming colonies into which the population of the seaboard provinces could expand. "Under the present State of Affairs," however, "it would be altogether in Vain to Attempt" such settlements, for the French and their allies would be sure to attack the colonists as soon as they appeared. If the region were not to be altogether lost, therefore, it was imperative to trade on generous terms with the Iroquois, opening fortified trading posts on their territories as the French had done at Detroit and elsewhere. An excellent location for such a post would be on the south shore of Lake Erie.[126]

Beyond these sensible measures, Logan argued, the crown should do everything in its power to promote union and cooperation among colonies that were as a rule much too weak and divided to stand up against the French and their Indian allies. Those who might object that a united British America would grow restive and seek independence were merely indulging "their Political Speculations without any just foundation." There was "no Danger of any Revolution of that kind, while the Colonies are treated with Tenderness and Humanity and not Considered only as Slavishly Subservient to the Interest of the Countrey they came from."[127]

The real danger was not civil war within the empire but a clash with the other imperial powers in North America. France and Spain together might profit greatly by such a venture, especially if they combined their naval strength to seize Britain's ill-defended, maladministered, and immensely rich West Indian sugar islands. "To conclude," he wrote,

> tho' the American Plantations are of such Importance to Britain, that the Loss of any of them to another Power especially to France might be its own ruin, from the hints given in this Paper . . . it will appear in what Condition they are at present to defend themselves and how growing the Danger is of their being lost without different Measures. In case of a War the Allies of Britain may think themselves less [obliged?] to yield [her] any Assistance [in America], and yet there it is manifestly the Interest of France to begin it.[128]

Logan was a Quaker, although (he confessed) a less rigorous one than Penn had been.[129] He, like Penn, believed that England's imperium was essentially benevolent and deserved to expand. Where he differed most from Penn was in his acceptance of military defense as a part of the enterprise of empire. He was fully aware of the connections between expansion, trade, and war. Given his perspective, based in the expansive and dynamic center of Britain's American colonies, it would be hard to imagine his missing those connections or imagining that Pennsylvania would be spared in the event of a new clash between Britain and the Bourbon powers. The only solution, therefore, was by fostering a colonial union and cultivating ties with the one most eligible Indian ally, to erect a defense so strong that the French and Spanish would not dare attack. This notion of peace through strength was a long way from William Penn's vision. There can be no doubt, however, that it resulted directly from the forces that Penn's success had unleashed.

But then, Penn's own children had also moved a considerable distance from his ideals. William Penn Jr. had died an Anglican. The sons from Penn's second marriage—John, Thomas, and Richard—had never felt a religious fervor like their father's, and their commitment to Quaker values was fading. What remained of their father's convictions, particularly after the death of their mother, was the faith that Pennsylvania could make the family rich. Thus when the thirty-year-old Thomas Penn finally arrived in Philadelphia in August 1732 to represent his family's interests and to straighten out the extraordinary tangle of proprietary affairs, he lost no time in making his intentions clear to James Logan. Logan in turn explained that Penn had arrived just in time to take advantage of a great opportunity, for chiefs from the Oneida, Cayuga, and Seneca peoples had lately come to Philadelphia to speak about trade on behalf of the Six Nations.

With some coaching from Logan, Penn offered the chiefs somewhat more than they had expected. As the representative of the proprietary family, he recognized the Six Nations as speaking for all the other Indians in alliance with Pennsylvania: the Delawares, Shawnees, Conestogas, and the rest. In return he hoped that the Iroquois would be as uncles to them, responsible for directing, controlling, disciplining them in the interest of peace and good order. At the end of the conference Penn declared that the new council fire that had been kindled would now be kept alight at Philadelphia, where the Iroquois would be free to resort to it at any time without having to use New York as an intermediary.[130]

The Iroquois, no doubt wondering what strings might be attached to such a privileged relationship with Pennsylvania, took the matter under advisement for four years before returning to accept it. By this agreement the Six Nations formally accepted the role as Pennsylvania's frontier police force that Logan had been urging for the last fifteen years.[131] Logan intended this phenomenal grant of authority to cement an alliance with the Iroquois that would render Pennsylvania secure against frontier war and attacks by the French and their allies; Thomas Penn quite clearly understood it primarily as a means to obtain land for his family to sell. He therefore ordered Logan to arrange new land cessions in eastern Pennsylvania and to open the proprietary land office for the first time in a decade and a half.[132] Logan complied and managed in short order to browbeat Sasoonan, the Delaware king, into ceding a broad swath of land in the Tulpehocken Valley. But not all of the Delaware chiefs were so pliable or cowed by the threat of Iroquois power. The most defiant of all was Nutimus, who refused to sell the hunting grounds north of Philadelphia that his band claimed.[133] This act of resistance led directly to the most notorious—and fateful—land swindle of the eighteenth century, the Walking Purchase of 1737.

In response, Thomas Penn and James Logan produced what they maintained was a copy of an "ancient deed," dating from 1686, by which the Delawares had ceded lands ostensibly at the Forks of the Delaware—the confluence of the Lehigh and Delaware rivers—to the extent that a man could walk in a day and a half. The time had come, they said, to carry out this walk. The "ancient deed" was in fact a copy of a document recording a transaction that had long ago taken place further to the south, but the description of the location was vague enough that Logan could maintain that it pertained to land between Neshaminy Creek and the Delaware River: that is, the territory that Nutimus had refused to sell. The new arrangement with the Six Nations, as strong-arm operators and real estate brokers in the service of Pennsylvania, meant that Logan and Penn needed only to have Iroquois agreement to stage the walk and determine the size of the cession.

The Delawares, deprived of the ability to speak for themselves, were reduced to the status of resentful spectators when the "walk" took place in the fall of 1737. The proprietors had ordered a track cleared through the woods and had recruited three specially trained young men who ran for twelve hours on September 19, and for another six on the following day. Only one of the three lasted through the whole race. When he finished at noon on September 20 he had completed somewhat more than the equivalent of two marathons: fifty-five miles along a track that described a total cession in excess of 1,200 square miles, or three-quarters of a million acres.[134]

It was, of course, a flagrant fraud, one that was much protested by the Delawares thereafter. The Penns, of course, were deaf to their protests. At first Nutimus and many of his followers simply refused to move away, but the connivance of the Six Nations in the dispossession kept the fraud from becoming a *casus belli*. To make an end of the Delawares' resistance, the Iroquois reaffirmed the cession by a solemn treaty conference at Easton, Pennsylvania, in 1742. At that meeting the Onondaga orator Canasatego castigated Nutimus for remaining on his land then ordered the remaining Delawares at the Forks to depart immediately to Shamokin or Wyoming in the Susquehanna Valley.[135] The Delawares complied but never doubted that while the Six Nations had abused them as the servants of the Penns, they had never been conquered. The Delawares knew; they remembered; and they looked forward to the day they would take their revenge.

Penn's Bargain

When Richard, John, and Thomas Penn took over the administration of their father's province, Pennsylvania finally became a consistent producer of revenue for the family. James Logan disliked their grasping ways but never failed to facilitate them: whereas the Penn family had realized an average of £400 annually from land sales between 1701 and 1730, they earned an average of £7,150 a year between 1731 and 1760, an eighteenfold increase. Logan was hardly in a position to despise them for their greed. He had himself done magnificently and had never been excessively scrupulous about how he made his fortune. But in the end his real commitment and what kept him on the job as Thomas Penn's adviser in matters of Indian diplomacy long after he could have retired in comfort was his conviction that the Iroquois offered the only possible security for the unarmed province. As bad as the consequences might be for the Delawares, Shawnees, Conestogas, Conoys, and others once allied with Pennsylvania, the threat that France posed to the province and to the British empire in America worried Logan infinitely more. In the end, Logan did not hesitate to sacrifice the interests of Pennsylvania's native peoples on the altar of empire.

This ironic turn of affairs occurred because Pennsylvania had been so tremendously successful in expanding the population and geographical extent of the British empire in America. By emphasizing the voluntarist aspects of life in his province, minimizing the coercive powers of the state, promoting religious toleration, and offering the prospect of peace, William Penn had created a province where something like the pursuit of happiness really seemed to be possible. But the very real bargain that the founder offered—affordable land, personal liberty, security, peace—could not be indefinitely sustained because it was, at bottom, too good to be true. A colonizing population that doubled every eighteen years simply overwhelmed the possibility that native peoples and colonists could continue to develop side by side in peaceful parallel societies under the same imperial umbrella. James Logan was perhaps the first person in Pennsylvania to understand that and to accept it as the necessary price of empire.[136]

The impact of this new imperial approach on Pennsylvania's Indians was direct, immediate, and ultimately tragic. In the short run, however, it seemed as if it might actually offer a kind of liberation. By the late 1740s, enough Delawares, Shawnees, and others had relocated to the Ohio to become the seventh population cluster in Indian Country capable of practicing play-off politics between European empires. It was not immediately clear to the immigrants to the Ohio country that their position, squarely between the French and the British, and their attempts to live independently of the Europeans and the Iroquois alike would bring on the clash of empires that Logan had foretold in his "Memorial." This great conflict, the Seven Years' War, ended the Long Peace of the eighteenth century and altered the whole landscape of empire in North America. That it was an event of catastrophic consequences for the Indians and brought to a close the two-and-a-half-century-long era during which native peoples played a determining role in American historical development was not the least of its tragedies. Only then, in the bloody dawn of the Age of Empires and Revolutions, was it revealed that Penn's bargain had, however unwittingly, been a deal with the devil.

CHAPTER THREE

Washington's Apprenticeship: Imperial Victory and Collapse

John Adams—brilliant, stout, prickly, fretful, and short—was perhaps the hardest-working delegate at the Second Continental Congress, a man so busy that it took him more than two weeks after the assembly convened on May 10, 1775, to write to his beloved wife, Abigail, back in Massachusetts. His first letter home was brief and general. "Our Business is more extensive . . . and hazardous" than at the First Congress, he reported, but "our Unanimity will not be less."[1] Only his second letter, written on the twenty-ninth, carried the personal and political news that Abigail craved. "The military Spirit that runs through the Continent," he wrote, "is truly amazing." Two thousand volunteer troops turned out daily in Philadelphia for training; their officers included three of the Pennsylvania delegates. Yet it was the martial character of a delegate from Virginia that most impressed Adams: "Col[one]l Washington appears at Congress in his Uniform and, by his great Experience and Abilities in military Matters, is of much service to Us."[2]

It seemed clear to many of the delegates that George Washington, a man of few words, had put on the blue-and-buff uniform of the Fairfax Independent Company in order to make a public statement.[3] Adams, who saw the necessity of bringing the southern colonies into the struggle, believed that Washington was announcing his willingness to lead the colonies' military forces (currently made up entirely of New Englanders) against the British army that occupied Boston. Seizing on that assumption, he worked tirelessly to see that Congress offered Washington the command of the Continental Army on June 15. Washington's perseverance in that position throughout the Revolutionary War has led historians to infer that by wear-

George Washington in his uniform as
colonel of the First Virginia Regiment, 1772.
A portrait by Charles Willson Peale.

ing the uniform Washington was actively campaigning for the appointment.[4] It would be easy enough to take the next step and conclude that in
seeking the generalship he had already embraced the cause of independence, and was prepared to risk his life and fortune to achieve it. But was
that in fact what he was trying to communicate?

We cannot know, for Washington—characteristically—never explained
his motives. A hint of what the act of donning a uniform meant to him, however, can be found in the only previous occasion on which we know he wore
one after his resignation as colonel of the First Virginia Regiment in 1758. In
May 1772, when the Philadelphia artist Charles Willson Peale came to Mount
Vernon to paint Washington's portrait, he dressed in his old colonel's regimentals as a means of commemorating his service in the Seven Years' War.
Peale gave the picture a wooded background to suggest the western Pennsylvania landscape through which Washington had marched as a division
commander on General John Forbes's expedition against Fort Duquesne
in 1758. So that there could be no mistake about the setting, Peale painted
a folded sheet of paper bearing the words "Order of March" in Washington's

waistcoat pocket. Moreover, in addition to the gorget at his throat, the sword at his side, and the officer's fusee at his back, Washington chose to include a fourth military accouterment in the picture: a faded red sash. Such sashes were panels of heavy silk mesh, ten to twelve feet long and perhaps three feet wide, that officers wore into battle. They did not do so merely to look dashing: should the wearer be wounded, his men could unfurl the silk into a litter and use it to carry him from the field. The sash that Washington wore in the painting had belonged to General Edward Braddock, who gave it to him as a memento after suffering a mortal wound at the Battle of the Monongahela in 1755. Unless Washington pointed them out, Peale would not have known that the sash bore the stains of Braddock's blood.[5]

Washington had never before sat for a portrait, and for all he knew would never do so again.[6] Thus it seems fair to conclude that the uniform and other elements recalling his service in the Seven Years' War were important enough to him that he wished to make them part of what might be the only permanent record of his appearance. In 1772 Washington chose to be portrayed as a soldier of the crown, a veteran of the imperial war that had broken French power in North America and transferred sovereignty over the eastern half of the continent to Great Britain. In 1775 he wore the newer uniform of a volunteer company whose members had pledged themselves "to defend to the utmost of our Power, the legal prerogatives of our Sovereign King George the third, and the just Rights & Privileges of our Country, our Posterity & ourselves upon the Principles of the British Constitution."[7] Washington was no more prepared than his fellow delegates in the Continental Congress to abjure allegiance to King George III. It took more than a year of bloodshed and violence to convince a majority in Congress that all hope of reconciliation was dead and that they had no alternative but to declare Independence.

Because most modern Americans are accustomed to thinking about the beginnings of the Revolutionary War in terms of the Independence that followed rather than the war for empire that had preceded it, they find the ambivalence and confusion of 1775 hard to imagine. Yet for Washington and other colonials of his generation, the Seven Years' War—what they called "the late French War" or "the French and Indian War"—had been a world-shaping event. Since 1763 they had been trying to cope with the unforeseen consequences of decisive victory over France, trying to define a set of political relationships within the empire in which all Britons, whether born in the United Kingdom or America, were partners. They did not yet understand that the Seven Years' War had marked the beginning of a epochal divide in North American history, the onset of what we have called the Age of Empires and Revolutions. In late May of 1775 they certainly did not know that the fighting begun in Massachusetts the previous month would develop into a truly revolutionary war and continue the vast transformation that the Seven Years' War had begun.

George Washington, a loyal subject of the crown when he put his uniform to attend the sessions of the Continental Congress, was at the center of all these astonishing developments. An advocate of empire long before he became a the hero of a revolution, his youthful enthusiasms and blunders had been central to the origins of the Seven Years' War. His revolutionary transformation paralleled that of a republic not yet born: the American nation that eventually claimed him as its Father.

Surveyor, Speculator, Soldier, Spy: The Rise of George Washington

The greatest influence that Washington's own father, Augustine (Gus), had on his son was to die in 1743, when George was eleven years of age. Gus, not quite fifty at his passing, had been a younger son and the third in a line of successful planters, all of whom had met their Maker at roughly the same age. Early death was commonplace in the Chesapeake, but its repetition over three generations kept the ambitious Washingtons from rising higher than the second rank of the provincial gentry.[8] Most of Gus's property went to his oldest son, Lawrence, who was twenty-five when his father died, fourteen years older than his half-brother George. George's far smaller portion—Ferry Farm on the Rappahannock, with 260 acres of indifferent soil and ten slaves plus half interest in Deep Run, an undeveloped tract of 4,360 acres—promised a station far below his father's. Until he was twenty-one, moreover, his property remained under the control of his formidable mother, Mary Ball Washington.[9]

Gus died before he could do much to shape his son's character. The authoritarian and possessive Mary did more—much more, it seems, than George wished. By the age of fourteen he was trying to escape, begging to go to sea as a midshipman in the Royal Navy. She forbade it in terms that implied her determination to keep him under her thumb as long as she possessed a thumb, and that suggested no force on earth would ever budge her from Ferry Farm. Not long after, George developed an interest in surveying that took him increasingly away from his mother, to Mount Vernon, the Potomac plantation where Lawrence lived.[10]

Lawrence Washington, c. 1740.
This portrait, by an anonymous artist, shows him as
he appeared at the time of his appointment as
captain in the American Regiment,
before the siege of Cartagena.

Lawrence took a paternal interest in the lad, who reciprocated by making a hero of his brother. The older Washington was everything that the shy, gawky, haphazardly educated boy longed to be. An English public-school education had given him the easy, polished manner of a gentleman. Lawrence had lately built on the foundation inherited from his father by marrying into the powerful Fairfax clan, whose great house, Belvoir, lay just upriver from Mount Vernon.[11] Lawrence encouraged George to become a surveyor and made it clear why—apart from the excuse to absent himself from Ferry Farm—it made sense for him to study the art of laying out plats with a circumferentor and a two-pole chain.[12] Although no training could have been a more symbolically apt prelude to a life dedicated to defining and defending territorial, political, and cultural boundaries, Washington's early pursuit of surveying was simply a pragmatic and prudent response to the circumstances of his life and his region.

The prosperity, indeed the rule, of Virginia's gentry depended on speculating in land. A provincial economy based on slavery and tobacco, a crop that impoverished the soil, made territorial expansion imperative for Virginia's elite. Because plantable ground was an inelastic resource whereas the supply of slaves was as elastic as the ability to reproduce, the great planters could all too easily foresee the day when their descendants, seated on worn land, might be bankrupted by feeding and housing their all-too-fertile, underemployed slaves. Virginia had to grow or die.

Flexible inheritance strategies could solve part of the problem. As Gus Washington's case implies, planters often wrote wills that stipulated that their estates *not* go (as a strict application of the principle of primogeniture required) exclusively to the eldest son. Planters who harbored dynastic ambitions did indeed take care to pass along the lion's share of their lands to their eldest sons, for social and economic status correlated directly to the number of cultivated acres one owned. But it was equally important to the long-run welfare of family lines that younger sons be given surplus slaves and undeveloped land—such as George's ten slaves and his half of the Deep Run tract—on which to found their own plantations.

Planters seeking properties for younger sons created a steady demand for "unimproved"—that is, forested—land. That demand, growing along with Virginia's population, motivated the province's wealthiest gentlemen to secure vastly larger, more remote tracts. As crown lands, Virginia's unallocated territories to the south and west of the Rappahannock could be sold or granted only by authority of the governor and Council.[13] Gentlemen with money and political connections could pick up forty or fifty or even a hundred thousand acres of forest for pennies per acre, provided that they agreed to "seat" families on those tracts within a reasonable period of time. They could then resell land at a tidy profit merely by waiting for expanding population to drive up demand. Even greater advantages could be achieved with a modest additional investment—the building of a small house, the loan of tools and seed—that allowed properties to be rented out to backwoods farmers in return for a share of the crops they grew. As the tenants felled trees and planted new fields, they "improved" the land and increased its value. Tenants might eventually buy the farms in which they had invested so much labor; if they did not, their leases could be terminated and the land sold off at premium prices.

This system conferred advantages that went beyond profit. Great planters who owned speculative holdings were able to seat their younger sons, sons-in-law, and other kinsmen on the best of those lands, designating them as agents for the sale or rental of the remainder. The wealthiest local residents therefore controlled access to land, virtually insuring the deference of smaller planters. When new county governments were created, the governor and Council allocated the key positions—justice of the peace, militia commander, sheriff, county surveyor—to the sons and other agents of the big speculators, confirming their social status and cementing their institutional power to rule. The election of prominent local landholders to the House of Burgesses followed as naturally as night followed day. Land speculation thus freed Virginia's aristocrats from complete dependence on tobacco for their income even as it enabled them to replicate the social and political hierarchies of the Tidewater on the frontier. However unrefined and even democratic they may have appeared to those who passed along their rutted roads, Virginia's backcountry counties were never outside the control of gentry figures.[14]

Surveyors sustained this system, both as land scouts working for the great speculators and as public officials entrusted with establishing the legal boundaries of all purchases and grants. Because no title could be registered without an official survey, they formed the third leg of the tripod—speculator, agent, and surveyor—on which the land system of Virginia rested. Even more significant for the surveyors themselves was the lucrative official schedule of fees for their services. Surveyors seldom failed to collect what their clients owed: official plats and descriptions alone could make land titles legal, so would-be owners had every reason to pay surveyors promptly. Such reliable access to cash gave the men with the circumferentors capital to purchase tracts for themselves. In this way surveyors frequently acquired speculative holdings of ten or even twenty thousand acres: tracts that while far smaller than those of the grandees were sizable enough to make a successful surveyor a man of consequence.[15]

Lawrence Washington wanted his brother to learn surveying because of opportunities close to home. His wife's second cousin, Lord Thomas Fairfax, sixth Baron Cameron, was sole proprietor of the Northern Neck, the peninsula between the Rappahannock and the Potomac rivers.[16] By the time Lord Fairfax came to control the proprietorship, the lower reaches of the Northern Neck had long since been divided into the tobacco plantations that provided livelihoods for prosperous gentry, such as the Washingtons. Because the quitrents to which he was entitled were not only modest but notoriously hard to collect, Fairfax's only hope of realizing a truly lordly income from the grant required the sale of new lands, and that in turn depended on having the Privy Council recognize the bounds of his grant as extending well inland. Fortunately for his lordship, the Privy Council obliged in 1745, issuing a decision that construed the original grant, made in

1649, as including all the lands that lay between the Rappahannock and the Potomac from their mouths to their headwaters. That ruling assigned Lord Fairfax a domain of more than 5 million acres, an area as big as Wales. He in turn entrusted the surveying and sale of tracts to his cousin and agent, Colonel William Fairfax, the master of Belvoir, and the father-in-law of Lawrence Washington.[17]

Lawrence thus saw surveying as a respectable, socially useful occupation that had every prospect of opening the door to far greater wealth than George's modest inheritance provided. Lawrence also knew that no matter how able George might prove in setting metes and bounds, his ultimate success depended on developing a close personal connection with the Fairfax family. Lawrence accordingly introduced George to his father-in-law and eventually to the eccentric bachelor baron himself, the only British nobleman to make his home in the North American colonies. Both Fairfaxes saw in the boy something they liked.

In March 1748 Colonel William Fairfax invited the sixteen-year-old George to accompany his own twenty-four-year-old son (and assistant agent) George William on a springtime expedition to survey tracts in the northern Shenandoah Valley. This journey, on which Washington assisted a more experienced surveyor, afforded him two important opportunities. The first and most immediately important was the chance to prove himself trustworthy and competent within sight of a patron whose support he would need if he were to rise in the world. Second, his month-long trip beyond the Blue Ridge allowed him to glimpse a western world that fired his imagination and that soon became the focus of his dreams.

George sufficiently demonstrated his skills as a surveyor that George William Fairfax commended him to his father, who in turn began to use young Washington's services extensively. In 1749 Lord Fairfax himself saw to it that Washington was appointed as county surveyor in the new county of Culpeper at the foot of the Blue Ridge, even though he was only seventeen. It was George's first public office and the first step on his long, determined climb to the top of the Virginia elite. He worked hard for his patrons: by the spring of 1751 he had run nearly 200 surveys on proprietary lands west of the Blue Ridge.[18]

The ties that Washington cultivated with the Fairfax family gave him the contacts he needed to advance in a social system structured by patronage. A young man's intelligence and ambition mattered little if he had no patron to vouchsafe his qualities within the small circle of men who controlled access to public offices and significant economic opportunities. Thanks to the

Fairfax connection, while still in his teens Washington forged ties with eminent planters—Richard Corbin, Virginia's receiver general; John Robinson, its treasurer; Landon Carter, a rising power in the House of Burgesses;
and others—who sponsored his ascent.[19]

Washington absorbed the attitudes of the class to which he aspired without criticism if not without anxiety. He keenly felt his lack of formal education and strove all the harder to make up for it by copying out lists of
aphorisms on polite behavior (an activity by which he intended to polish
both manners and penmanship), by reading popular works of literature for
clues to the mysterious codes of genteel conversation, by interrogating
Lawrence and his other older half-brother, Augustine, and by carefully observing the manners and behavior of the Fairfaxes and other provincial aristocrats. Instinctively understanding that speech is merely the small change
of silence, he began to cultivate the reserved, formal manner that later ob-
servers cited as evidence of his dignity and imperturbable self-assurance.[20]

Yet Washington also knew that a refined, reserved personal style was not
enough to win him respect and power. His tenuous and dependent position
made the need to prove himself worthy all the more urgent. That meant
finding a way to serve the public interest with the steadfast selflessness that
his contemporaries called "virtue" and understood, above all, as the quality
that defined a gentleman.[21] Lawrence, as always, offered the model: he had
served as a captain in the regiment that Virginia sent to take part in the siege
of Cartagena in 1740. The siege was a fiasco, with a mortality rate that exceeded 80 percent, but by his faithful service and survival Lawrence had
shown himself worthy of the public trust. Soon after his return he was
elected as a member of the House of Burgesses and appointed adjutant general of the provincial militia.

Exalted notions of a gentleman's attributes, then, influenced Washington's efforts to build his own character as strongly as the desire for wealth
and lands shaped his economic activities. Those ambitions, compounded by
the anxieties he felt about his own less-than-secure claim to gentility, increased his readiness to look down on the manifestly ungenteel people he
encountered while surveying. Thus on his first trip west, Washington
showed little interest in a group of Indian warriors he met "coming from
War with only one Scalp," describing them only in terms of their drinking
and "comicle" dancing.[22] He had no more understanding for a party of German backwoods settlers who seemed "to be as Ignorant a Set of People as
the Indians."[23] On another surveying expedition, he described a family in
whose cabin he had taken shelter as something less even than savages. They

slept together, he wrote, "before the fire upon a Little Hay Straw Fodder or bairskin . . . Man Wife and Children like a Parcel of Dogs or Catts." "Nothing," he wrote, "would make it [such rude company] pass of[f] tolerably but a good Reward[.]"[24]

Washington's scorn for Indians and frontier folk was hardly unusual in eighteenth-century British America, where the most unfavorable depictions of backcountry life invariably came from those with the most elevated notions of their own gentility.[25] Indeed, Washington's adolescent disdain for Indians and backwoodsmen demonstrated the degree to which he had internalized the values of the Fairfaxes and their class. He was never drawn to the country beyond the Blue Ridge by some romantic desire to gaze on unexplored vistas. Although he was certainly capable of admiring nature—as, for example, the "beautiful groves of Sugar [maple] Trees" he saw on the Shenandoah in March 1748, when he "spent the best part of the Day in admiring the Trees & richness of the Land"—what he most appreciated was how nature might be put to use.[26] The "richness of the Land" impressed the novice surveyor and gentleman because he was learning how it could be transformed into riches of a more tangible sort.

By the time Washington began his career as a land speculator in late 1750 by purchasing a thousand acres he had surveyed along a Shenandoah tributary called Bullskin Run, he had fully embraced the expansionist values, attitudes, and behaviors of the Virginia gentry.[27] No less than Lawrence or Colonel William Fairfax, Washington understood the imperial enterprise as a civilizing mission. Though speculators, agents, and surveyors worked togther to create profit for themselves, they also believed that they were investing energy and undertaking financial risks to bring order, law, and security to a chaotic zone whose inhabitants—barbarians, or nearly so—desperately needed the good government that the gentry alone could provide. Gentry expansionism was in that sense an explicitly future-oriented enterprise and not only because distant lands purchased for a pittance gained value when populations grew and the demand for farms increased. It also looked ahead to the continuing replication of Virginia's social order and thus the extension of English law, institutions, and civilization—and all the blessings (including slavery) that accompanied them.

Washington and his mentors claimed no manifest destiny to establish English dominion over the continent of North America. Yet they also acknowledged neither a legal nor a practical westward limit to their colony's expansion. The charter of Virginia, issued in 1609 before anyone in England had a notion of North America's true size, stipulated no western boundary but the Pacific Ocean and sketched a northern border that angled off on a northwesterly axis vaguely parallel to the Potomac until it struck the Great Lakes—or, arguably, the Bering Strait. Even with the Northern Neck proprietorship, where a clear western limit did exist, Virginians looked beyond, planning future acquisitions even further west, notwithstanding the enormous amounts of land nearer home that remained to be surveyed and settled.

The reflexive quality of gentry expansionism explains why in 1744 Virginia's delegates had eagerly gone to Lancaster, Pennsylvania, to negotiate a treaty with representatives of the Iroquois League: they hoped to acquire lands for settlement beyond the western boundary of the Fairfax proprietary lands and indeed beyond the Alleghenies, in the Ohio River Valley. At this point the leaders of the Six Nations had been working hand in glove with Thomas Penn and James Logan for eight years and fully appreciated the benefits they enjoyed as a result of the English authorities' willingness to recognize them as spokesmen for the Delawares, Shawnees, and other peoples they claimed as clients. Canasatego and the other League chiefs came to Lancaster as confident negotiators, ready to assert sovereignty over several southern Indian peoples, to secure Virginia's recognition of their warriors' right to pass freely through the province to raid the Cherokees and Catawbas of South Carolina, and (not coincidentally) to collect a substantial diplomatic gift. In return, the Iroquois spokesmen were prepared to cede all of the League's remaining claims within the limits of Pennsylvania, Maryland, and Virginia.[28]

It is clear in retrospect that the Six Nations' diplomats at Lancaster believed that Virginia's bounds extended no further west than the Shenandoah Valley and that they had no intention of surrendering any of the League's claims beyond the Alleghenies. But the Virginia delegates, for obvious reasons, chose to interpret the Iroquois cession as encompassing all the trans-Allegheny lands that fell within the vast zone defined by the 1609 charter. The following year, the House of Burgesses bestowed 300 square miles of territory at the confluence of the Allegheny and Monongahela rivers on a syndicate of Northern Neck gentlemen, including Lawrence Washington, who had formed the Ohio Company. If they fulfilled their obligations to seat settlers on the land, another grant of nearly 500 square miles was to be added; more and larger grants would inevitably follow. Confident of Virginia's expansion into the Ohio Valley, they were positioning themselves to dominate a realm that might one day dwarf even that of Lord Thomas Fairfax.[29]

George Washington was only thirteen when the Ohio Company was

formed and therefore not a stockholder; but because Lawrence was a founding member, George's anticipated career as a surveyor made him fit into the
Ohio scheme like a cog into a gearwheel. (Indeed, in 1749 or 1750, when he
set himself up as an independent surveyor, George volunteered to locate the
sites of way stations on the route to the Forks of the Ohio on the company's
behalf.)[30] Lawrence's death in 1752 propelled George to greater participation in the development of the West. Although not yet a member of the
Ohio Company—his sister-in-law, not he, inherited Lawrence's share—he
had a family interest to protect. That private concern in turn created the opportunity he longed for: to serve the interests of his province and prove
himself a public-spirited gentleman worthy of membership in Virginia's
elite. All he had to do was to accept an offer that Virginia's lieutenant governor made in the fall of 1753.

Because Governor Lord Albemarle had not the slightest desire ever to set
foot in Virginia, he assigned the office of lieutenant governor, in 1751, to an
ambitious Scottish merchant and midlevel imperial bureaucrat, Robert Dinwiddie. By 1752 Dinwiddie had acquired a share in the Ohio Company and
with it a keen interest in promoting colonization beyond the Alleghenies.
Both as a representative of the crown and as a man with investments to defend, Dinwiddie looked with concern on reports that the French had begun
to build forts on Lake Erie and the Allegheny River. It seemed obvious that
they intended to assert direct control over the entire Ohio Valley, ground that
he knew was rightfully Virginia's and now (at least in part) his own.

Dinwiddie reported these French "encroachments" to his superiors in
London, where ministers sympathetic to his views authorized him to take
vigorous measures, including the construction of his own forts and—if
necessary—the use of force, to preserve the integrity of His Majesty's dominions. Because the ministers' instructions also forbade him to act as an
aggressor, Dinwiddie decided in the fall of 1753 that he must first send a letter to the French commander on the Allegheny, demanding that he leave
British territory forthwith. If the French refused, he he would begin a fort-
building program of his own to secure Virginia's claims to the upper Ohio
Valley. Should the French then choose to contest those claims, Dinwiddie
regarded his instructions as authorizing him to take military measures
against them.[31]

Washington was the obvious choice to carry this message to the French.
At twenty-one he was old enough to hold positions of public trust—the
Council had recently made him adjutant general of the militia of the
province south of the James River, with the rank of major—yet young and

strong enough to undertake an arduous journey. His eagerness to serve the province was evident and genuine, and he relished a chance to see the Ohio country. That he spoke neither French nor any Indian language, had little formal education, knew nothing of native cultures, and utterly lacked diplomatic experience were not obstacles. Indeed, his evident *lack* of qualifications commended him for a job that Dinwiddie publicly described as "express Messenger." Because he looked so much like an errand boy, he was all the better suited to fulfill the governor's private instructions to gather information about "the Numbers & Force of the French on the Ohio, & the adjacent Country."[32] Washington's role as courier, in other words, furnished a cover for his more critical task of gathering intelligence on a potential enemy. He would be not only the governor's emissary but his spy.

Between his departure on November 1, 1753, and his return to Williamsburg from a cold, wet, and dangerous journey in mid-January 1754, Washington traversed more than 500 miles by horse, foot, canoe, and raft, delivered Dinwiddie's letter, secured the French reply, and gathered the first reliable intelligence the British had about the situation west of the Alleghenies. The picture was far from encouraging.

The French, Washington reported, had constructed three forts along waterways from Presque Isle on the southeast shore of Lake Erie to the confluence of the Rivière aux Bœufs and the Allegheny at Venango. He had found the regional commandant at the middle post, Fort Le Bœuf. Captain Jacques Legardeur de Saint-Pierre had received him with impeccable politesse but showed no disposition to make the "peaceable departure" that Dinwiddie's letter demanded. Washington had, moreover, seen unmistakable evidence of French intentions to move downriver with the spring freshets to the Forks of the Ohio. He and his companions had counted more than 200 canoes and bateaux on the banks of the Rivière aux Bœufs and its tributary creeks. Many more under construction, lay nearby.[33]

Indian relations also looked unpromising, but Washington knew too little of Indian cultures to realize just how shaky they were. Most of the natives living along in the upper Ohio and its tributaries were Delawares, Shawnees, and Mingo Senecas, all of them, the English thought, subordinates of the Iroquois League, governed by headmen whom the Great Council at Onondaga had appointed as its regents. Near the Forks of the Ohio, Washington met two of these regents, the Seneca Tanaghrisson (the "Half King" who was supposed to speak for the Delawares) and the Oneida Scarouady (Onondaga's spokesman for the Shawnees). Both chiefs assured him that they would join Virginia in demanding that the French leave the territory, but when the time came to travel from the Forks to the French posts, only Tanaghrisson and three Mingo warriors accompanied Washington's party.

Washington failed to understand that no matter what Tanaghrisson had told them, the French interpreted his escort's puny size and lack of diversity as evidence that the Delawares and Shawnees were uninterested in following the Half King's lead to support the British.[34] Even Washington could understand, however, that if Virginia did not establish a powerful presence at the Forks of the Ohio before the French, in the spring or early summer of 1754, an alliance with the region's Indians would be stillborn. Dinwiddie concurred. He moved immediately to send a small expedition to construct a fort at the Forks and asked the House of Burgesses to authorize a regiment of volunteers to secure command of the Ohio.

Washington let it be known that he would gladly accept an appointment in the force that was to be raised. The command of the regiment would obviously have to go to an experienced officer, but the post of lieutenant colonel, or second in command, was one for which he felt qualified. By March 20, 1754, thanks to Fairfax's influence and Dinwiddie's goodwill, he had his wish, and his commission.

It was a moment of fulfillment. A decade after his father's death left him a boy with limited prospects, Washington had grown into a young gentleman with skills and patrons and lands and an office in which he could demonstrate his capacity for public service and earn the reputation he coveted. Everything suggested that he stood at the threshold of even greater accomplishments: military glory and a place of leadership in colonizing a new western realm. He threw himself into recruiting, equipping, training, and supplying his regiment's soldiers, hiring or impressing the wagons and horses necessary for an expedition to the Ohio, making ready to march at the earliest possible moment. With the self-confidence of the truly ignorant, he pressed relentlessly on, driven by a ferocious determination to prove himself.[35]

On April 18 Washington was camped with about 160 men at Winchester in the Shenandoah Valley, eager to march for the Forks of the Ohio, where an advanced detachment was building the stockade he expected to defend against the French. Four days later, at the Ohio Company's fortified storehouse on the upper Potomac, where he was awaiting more troops, he was surprised to see the officer who was supposed to be building the fort at the Forks ride up. The French, he now learned, had arrived on April 17, a thousand strong with eighteen pieces of artillery. Unable to resist this overwhelming force, Virginia's construction crew had surrendered their recently completed fort.[36]

Lieutenant Colonel Washington listened carefully, made the necessary reports to his superiors, and ordered his men to make ready to march for the Forks. With only the foggiest notion of what he could do and no idea of where it would lead, George Washington committed himself to the imperial mission that defined the rest of his life and opened a new epoch in North American history.

The Collision of Empires

Something clearly began early in the morning of May 28, 1754, when forty men under Washington's command attacked a detachment of Canadian militiamen who were escorting an officer of the *Troupes de la Marine* on a diplomatic mission: an effort to find the Virginians and urge them to leave the Ohio country in peace. The killing of Ensign Joseph Coulon de Villiers de Jumonville and twelve of his men brought severe retaliation a month later when Jumonville's older brother led a French and Indian force against the Virginia regiment at its hastily constructed palisade, Fort Necessity. It was the first of many defeats that Washington suffered in his long career as a soldier. Yet on the day that he and the survivors of the Virginia Regiment abandoned Fort Necessity—July 4, 1754—it was far from clear that what had begun would develop into a new Anglo-French war.

The actions of the young Washington, eager to prove himself and bold to the point of foolhardiness, sparked a cataclysm long in the making. In the early 1750s, the lands that lay between the Forks of the Ohio and the Mississippi became the focus of the hopes and fears of groups that included Indians in the region, colonists from Quebec to Savannah, and government ministers at Whitehall and Versailles. Both the French and British governments believed that the 1748 Treaty of Aix-la-Chapelle had created little more than an armistice in the interminable conflict between their nations. Each imperial administration construed its own intrusion into the Ohio country as a defensive measure necessitated by the aggressions of the other. Neither they nor the North American colonists, however, understood that the most important reason behind the Anglo-French confrontation was the striving of Indian peoples on the upper Ohio for independence.

The Delawares, Shawnees, Mingo Senecas, and other Indians who lived in the Allegheny and Ohio valleys numbered more than 2,500 by the middle of the 1740s.[37] Having fled westward to escape the growing numbers of land-hungry Pennsylvanians, they had every reason to think that their location between the French and British empires would make it possible to pursue strategies similar to those of the Abenakis, the Iroquois League, the Algonquians of the *pays d'en haut*, the Cherokees, the Creeks, and the Choctaws. They would play off one imperial power against another to ensure their access to trade goods, stimulate the giving of diplomatic gifts, and, by the creation of judicious counterbalancing alliances with both European powers, free themselves from Iroquois domination.

The Indians of the Ohio Valley were more determinedly independent-minded than Europeans, or the Iroquois for that matter, supposed. The Mingos, as the westernmost branch of the Seneca people were known, were of course Iroquois, but the League Council at Onondaga regarded them as hunters temporarily absent from their homeland who had no more right to speak for themselves than the Delawares or the Shawnees. In truth, however, the Mingos were the most independent-minded subgroup of the Seneca nation. Largely descendants of Eries, Neutrals, Monongahelas, and other peoples destroyed in the Beaver Wars, they saw their return to the Ohio country as an opportunity to reestablish communities on ancestral ground. They were far more ready to follow their own counsel than Onondaga's directives.[38]

A number of Pennsylvania traders, eager to compete for the skins and pelts that the Ohio Indians could furnish, had followed the Delawares and Shawnees west. The traders' presence helped sustain the Indians' dream of independent life. The most important was an irrepressible Irishman, George Croghan, who began trading west of the Alleghenies in the early 1740s in competition against James Logan's long-established network. Croghan and his associates succeeded in establishing a successful trading post at Logstown on the Ohio below the Forks, then extended their trading network west down the Ohio and northwestward to Lake Erie, where they built a post at the mouth of the Cuyahoga River in 1743. Attracted by the high quality and comparatively low prices of British goods, Indians flocked to Croghan's posts.

The weakness of the French and the larger threat to the balance of power in the interior of eastern North America posed by the Pennsylvania traders became unmistakable with the outbreak of King George's War (1744–48; the New World phase of the longer War of the Austrian Succession, 1740–48). King George's War broke the mold of previous European conflicts played out in North America when the New England colonies mounted a successful expedition against the French fortress of Louisbourg on Cape Breton Island in 1745 and seized control of the Gulf of Saint Lawrence. Sealed off from communication with Europe, Canada soon faced severe shortages of trade goods, and the government of New France was forced to curtail diplomatic gift-giving. Croghan and his associates rushed in to fill the vacuum. By 1747, he was trading with French-allied Wyandots on Lake Erie's Sandusky Bay, scarcely fifty miles south of France's great western entrepôt, Fort Detroit.[39] New France managed to maintain its Indian alliances and hence to survive the war only because the merchants of Albany saw the opportunity to gain access to Canada's fur supply and obligingly smuggled trade goods to Montreal by way of Lake Champlain. Had the New Yorkers not preferred pelts to patriotism, New France would have lost all of its Indian allies and Canada would have been left defenseless.

The relatively inexpensive British goods that Croghan and his fellow traders offered at Logstown and other western posts during the war had attenuated the Ohio Indians' ties to the French—a situation that the return of peace in 1748 did not change. Croghan merely shifted his activities from Lake Erie to a new trading post at Pickawillany on the upper Great Miami River, which was soon crowded with formerly French-allied Indians from both the *pays d'en haut* and the *pays des Illinois*. Canadian officials, linking Croghan's predatory trading behavior with Virginians' increasing interest in the Forks of the Ohio, saw nothing less than a concerted effort to drive a wedge into the heart of their empire.[40] Since 1701 the French had trusted the Iroquois League to keep English traders out of the trans-Allegheny west, and had been more than willing to recognize Iroquois claims to the Ohio Valley as a *quid pro quo*. That policy was obviously no longer viable; something had to be done before English goods (and worst of all, settlers) poured into the *pays d'en haut*.

The French responded by trying to establish diplomatic and military hegemony over the Ohio country. In 1749 the governor-general of New France put Captain Pierre-Joseph Céloron de Blainville at the head of an expedition down the Ohio River in an attempt to demonstrate the French determination to claim the region. He failed to accomplish that goal when the Indians for the most part ignored him; accordingly, in 1752 the French dispatched an Ottawa and Chippewa force from Detroit to destroy Croghan's trade emporium at Pickawillany. Yet even that dramatic act only temporarily deterred the Pennsylvanians and Virginians from meddling in the Ohio Valley.

Lacking effective commercial countermeasures, in 1753 the French began building forts from Lake Erie to the Allegheny Valley with a view to constructing a permanent trading post at the Forks of the Ohio. The goal was twofold: to exclude the English from the Ohio country and to secure the trade and allegiance of the Delawares, Shawnees, and Mingos. This was a desperate gamble, for it required the French to dismiss the Iroquois claim

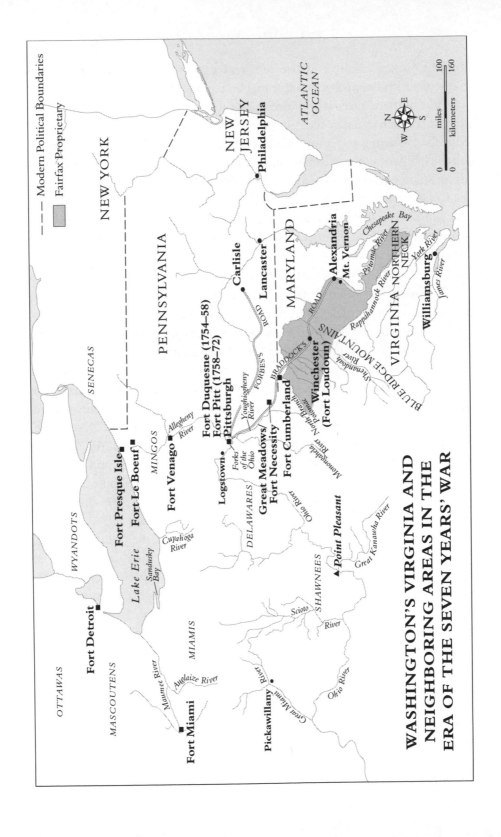

WASHINGTON'S VIRGINIA AND
NEIGHBORING AREAS IN THE
ERA OF THE SEVEN YEARS' WAR

to the Ohio as a sham and also to spend a great deal of money to sustain trade in a remote, probably unprofitable, region.[41]

All this maneuvering provided the local context for Dinwiddie's demand that the French evacuate the Allegheny-Ohio drainage in 1753, Washington's fumbling attempts to remove them in 1754, and an Atlantic world that hung on the brink of war at the beginning of 1755. The Seven Years' War was a far-flung affair, even in its origins. Without decisions in both Britain and France to dispatch regular troops to defend their colonial frontiers in 1755; without the completion of a Diplomatic Revolution that aligned Britain with Prussia (formerly the ally of France) against France and Austria (formerly the ally of Britain) at the beginning of 1756; without France's seizure of Minorca from British control in May of that year; and—most of all—without the eruption of a European war when Britain's ally Frederick the Great of Prussia invaded the Saxon territory of France's ally Austria in August: without these inter-locking, pyramiding events, the backwoods bloodshed Washington precipi-tated might have remained a merely provincial affair.[42]

Yet more unforeseeable developments were necessary to make the Eu-ropean conflict a worldwide war, notably the ascent of William Pitt to the leadership of Britain's House of Commons and his entry into a surprisingly durable political alliance with a former enemy, the Duke of Newcastle, which lasted from the summer of 1757 through the fall of 1761. The role that Washington played in the war and the impact of that the conflict had on North America and its peoples as a whole can be understood only in the context of the war's wider developments. The best way to grasp the charac-ter of the war's larger dimensions is to begin with Pitt himself.

If megalomania can be an adaptive quality in wartime political leaders, England could scarcely have produced a man more superbly equipped to lead it in the Seven Years' War than William Pitt. He was eloquent, fiercely energetic, able to recognize talent in subordinates, capable of conceiving a grand strategy by which the destruction of the French overseas empire would break the back of French power in Europe, and prepared to pursue that course with flexibility and opportunism. All of those qualities worked together because Pitt's heartfelt conviction that he was his country's savior enabled him to sound like destiny's mouthpiece. In Parliament the back-benchers believed in him and voted with him; in coffeehouses and public houses Britons hungry for imperial glory read accounts of far-flung military operations and gave him the credit for the victories gained.

So great was Pitt's identification with the war that the conflict in North America can be periodized according to his presence or absence from power. Early in the war, before he and Newcastle consolidated their alliance, Whitehall's policies centered on trying to fight the American war with American resources, under the direction of commanders in chief with virtually viceregal powers. This policy produced nothing but discord and disaster. Two stiff-necked commanders in chief—General Edward Braddock and General John Campbell, the Earl of Loudoun—so alienated the colonial governments by their peremptory demands for support that by the end of 1757 the British war effort in America had all but ground to a halt. Once the Pitt-Newcastle ministry took control of the House of Commons, however, Whitehall reversed its centralizing policy toward the colonies. In the last days of 1757 Pitt recalled the unpopular Lord Loudoun and repudiated Loudoun's insistence that colonial governments submit unconditionally to royal authority. Then, in a total reversal of course, he invited the colonists to join—voluntarily—in a grand imperial adventure.

Rather than demanding that the colonies pay for a war effort they did not direct and could not afford, Pitt promised colonial legislatures reimbursements in proportion to the monies they expended and the numbers of men they raised for the campaigns. Aware of the alienation that Loudoun had caused, he revoked the authority of the commander in chief over civilian governments and took care to phrase the crown's requirements for troops and money as requests, not commands, to the colonial assemblies. Between 1758 and 1760, policies that in effect treated the colonies as allies generated popular enthusiasm and mobilized colonial resources to a degree that would have been inconceivable in 1755–57, when the commanders in chief had tried to reduce the colonies to auxiliaries subject to imperial command. The wartime success of the British empire in North America, in other words, was directly proportional to the crown's willingness to reimburse colonial governments for their participation and inversely related to metropolitan efforts to exert direct authority over the colonies.

Something quite similar can be said for the French, who enjoyed their greatest successes early in the war when they followed the traditional Canadian policy of giving native allies free rein to attack the Anglo-American frontiers according to their own traditions of warmaking. That highly successful strategy, however, was based on what seemed a capitulation to savagery to the marquis de Montcalm, the eminently sophisticated and civilized general whom Versailles sent to direct the war effort in 1756. An episode of massacre and captive-taking at the siege of Fort Oswego in that year left Montcalm determined to turn the Indians from allies into obedient auxiliaries in the next campaign. His efforts to implement those policies and bring an end to *la guerre sauvage* in 1757 created a sense of betrayal in his allies and precipitated the so-called Massacre of Fort William Henry, in which about 500 members of the fort's surrendered garrison were killed or taken captive. Some Indian groups (mostly Catholics who lived on *reserves* in the Saint Lawrence Valley) did not abandon the French, but the great majority of France's erstwhile native allies went home disgusted at the end of the 1757 campaign, never to return. This left the Canadian militia, the colony regulars (Troupes de la Marine), and French regular forces *(Troupes de Terre)* with an impossible task: in 1758 and after, they had to defend Canada against an increasingly mobilized and enthusiastic Anglo-American enemy that outnumbered them by eighteen to one.[43]

The metropolitan French, if not the Canadians, had forgotten the lesson that Champlain learned at such cost: without Indian allies they had no hope of defending New France. Their success as an imperial power in North America depended on accommodation with, not dominion over, the native peoples. Once the British navy succeeded in crippling France's Atlantic fleet and preventing merchant vessels from resupplying Canada with arms, provisions, and trade goods, the cause became hopeless. By late 1758 the Indians of the Ohio country understood that the French were no longer able to maintain their western forts and made a separate peace. Anglo-American forces invaded the Canadian heartland in the following year, taking Quebec in September. When the British navy defeated the last effective French squadron on the Atlantic at the Battle of Quiberon Bay in November 1759, Versailles wrote Canada off as lost. Canada's defenders held out until the late summer of 1760 but did so in the knowledge that France's empire in North America had reached its end.[44]

The tide of successes that buoyed Britain's war effort in America from 1758 onward had its counterpart in British operations in India. After a shaky start in 1756, the army of the East India Company under a clerk turned soldier, Robert Clive, cooperated with a regiment of redcoats and the Royal Navy to sweep French troops and commercial interests from the subcontinent. Although the war in Europe continued indecisively, the successes of British operations against the French empire made Pitt fantastically popular and politically invulnerable—until King George II died in October 1760. His grandson and successor, the idealistic, dutiful, and immature George III, wanted very much to end the war and hoped to replace Pitt, whom he distrusted, with his tutor Lord Bute, whom he loved.

Pitt, however, could not be thrust from office so easily, so the war dragged on, draining the treasuries of the belligerent powers. Meanwhile,

Spain's new king, Charles III, became increasingly uneasy about its possible result. Spain, although ruled by a branch of the same family that controlled the French throne, had initially remained aloof from the war under the timid Ferdinand VI. After Charles ascended the crown in 1759, he watched Britain win victory after victory in North America and worried that if France bought a peace by surrendering its New World possessions to Britain, Spain's empire would become Pitt's next target. To insure that France would not make a separate peace, therefore, Spain offered an alliance with a secret codicil promising to enter the war against Britain in May 1762. Pitt, who learned of this plan through intercepted diplomatic correspondence, insisted on launching a preemptive war against Spain but found that neither the cabinet nor the court would support such a move. His resignation from the government in October 1761 brought on the war's final phase.

Instead of the immediate peace that George III hoped for, however, British forces in the New World responded to Spain's entry into the war in 1762 with an invasion of Cuba, taking Havana after a siege that lasted from June 8 through August 13. Both Spain and France now desperately needed to negotiate a peace, and George III and Lord Bute, who had taken over as prime minister after Pitt's resignation, finally succeeded in bringing the war to an end. The preliminary articles of the peace treaty were agreed at Paris on November 3, 1763. It was another half year before news arrived in Europe that even as the finishing touches were being put to the agreement, an improvised British expedition from India had captured Manila and taken control of the Spanish Philippines.

The Peace of Paris (February 10, 1763) confirmed the most decisive military victory the British had ever won and gave Great Britain possession of North America from the Atlantic to the Mississippi, from the Arctic to the Gulf of Mexico: a region far too vast to be controlled by the haphazard means previously employed to govern the empire. Pitt's openhanded subsidies, meanwhile, had nearly doubled the kingdom's public debt, even as his emphasis on voluntarism had convinced the American colonists that they were partners in the greatest imperial enterprise since Rome. The war left France, on the other hand, to bear a burden of humiliation greater even than its heavy public debt and created an unquenchable desire for revenge; left Spain determined to modernize and strengthen its severely shaken empire and keep control of the colonial silver on which the royal treasury depended; and left the courts of Europe to wonder if an apparently invincible Britain would seek to parlay its naval and military preeminence into hegemony over the Continent. The greatest conflict since the Thirty Years' War thus created an extremely volatile political situation in Europe, an unstable mixture that needed only a spark to ignite it.

When the explosion came, just a dozen years after the Peace of Paris, it happened once again in North America. To understand how and why that revolutionary detonation occurred as it did when it did, we must focus more closely on the specific effects of the Seven Years' War on the British colonies and especially on the experiences of George Washington. In one way or another, he applied the lessons the war taught him for the rest of his life.

Lessons Learned

Robert Dinwiddie was fond of the eager young man who carried his ultimatum to the French commander on the Allegheny in 1753 and believed strongly enough in his courage and skill to appoint Washington as lieutenant colonel of the Virginia Regiment in 1754. He had not intended for Washington to command the regiment, however; he entrusted that far graver responsibility to an older and more experienced man, the Oxford-educated mathematician and cartographer Colonel Joshua Fry. Subordinate status suited Washington well. For all his ambition, he was acutely aware of his lack of experience and expertise as a soldier, and longed to be "under the Command off [sic] an experienced Officer and a Man of Sense."[45] This was undoubtedly never more true than when Tanaghrisson, the Seneca Half King, induced him to attack the detachment of Ensign Jumonville, who (as Washington did not realize) had been sent to warn the Virginians leave the region. Tanaghrisson, rejected by the Delawares over whom he was supposed to exercise the authority of the Six Nations, desperately needed an ally to support him in ejecting the French from the newly built Fort Duquesne and regaining control over the Forks of the Ohio. It was only following the brief and confused firefight between the Virginians and the surprised Canadians on May 28, 1754, when Tanaghrisson smashed Jumonville's skull open with a hatchet and his warriors slaughtered a dozen wounded militiamen from Jumonville's escort, that Washington realized that the Half King had his own notions of how to forge an unbreakable alliance with the English. Washington realized too late that he had been Tanaghrisson's sole remaining asset in a desperate gamble to reclaim the Ohio country for the Iroquois League.[46]

Washington therefore felt his lack of experience all the more keenly when he learned on June 9 that Colonel Fry had fallen from his horse and died on the last day of May. Soon thereafter Dinwiddie, with little in the way of alternatives, promoted Washington—a man the age of a modern second lieutenant and with a great deal less training—to the rank of colonel, making him commandant of the Virginia Regiment. It was not the first time Washington had advanced by the untimely death of someone above him in the social hierarchy. It was, however, incomparably the most important to his province and to the empire he hoped to serve.[47]

Tanaghrisson soon realized that he had overestimated a man whose value as an ally was, in fact, nil. As much an innocent in war as diplomacy, Washington refused to take advice on matters in which the Half King was far more experienced than he. Thus he sited a hastily constructed fort—the only defense the Virginia regiment had against the retaliatory attack that the French were sure to mount—at the upper end of the Great Meadows, a boggy expanse of grassland beneath a wooded hill. The stockade that Washington named Fort Necessity and Tanaghrisson dismissed as "that little thing upon the Meadow"[48] was so obviously indefensible that the Half King gave up and left, along with his followers, before a powerful French and Indian force attacked on the morning of July 3, 1754. By sunset that day, Washington had lost a third of his men, killed and wounded. He might have suffered worse had not the French commander, Captain Louis Coulon de Villiers, offered him the opportunity to surrender in return for a promise to withdraw his men over the mountains and not return. Washington did not understand until months had passed that the instrument of surrender he signed (a document written in French, a language he could not read) contained a clause in which he admitted "assassinating" Ensign Jumonville.[49]

Jumonville's murder and the subsequent disaster at Fort Necessity taught Washington the first lessons he learned as a soldier of the king, an arduous five-year-long education in arms.[50] Though he learned by trial and error and as a result made terrible mistakes, he also learned never to make the same mistakes again. As with the notions of gentility he acquired by studying Lawrence and the Fairfaxes, he made his greatest strides by observing British professional officers in action, absorbing their attitudes and prejudices along with their expertise. Their missteps proved no less instructive than their successes.

Washington returned to western Pennsylvania in the summer of 1755 as an aide-de-camp to General Edward Braddock, riding beside him throughout the Battle of the Monongahela on July 9, 1755. On that terrible day, he witnessed the wounding or death of two-thirds of Braddock's 1,373-man command by an Indian force less than half its size and saw unmistakably illustrated the perils of campaigning deep in the wilderness too far from a secure base of supply and without native allies. Yet Washington never ceased to admire the general for his courage and professionalism; indeed, he kept mementos the dying Braddock gave him—his sash and pistols—for the rest of his life. Like talismans, he carried them on every subsequent campaign.

From Lord Loudoun, to whom Washington suggested in March 1757 that the Virginia Regiment be made a unit of the British army with royal commissions for its officers, he learned other lessons.[51] In Loudoun's dismissive response Washington could not have helped but sense the disdain of a man further above him in military and social rank than anyone he had ever encountered. It is impossible to imagine that Washington, who cared so much about his reputation, did not deeply feel the humiliation of learning that the commander in chief regarded him as merely another amateurish provincial officer. At any rate Washington, who had sought a commission from Braddock in 1755, never again solicited rank for himself in the British army. To be humbled one more time would have been too much to bear.

He also discovered, in the counterproductive results of Loudoun's determination to teach the colonial assemblies their duty, the folly of believing that civil authorities could be despised, coerced, or trifled with. This was a truth that did not come instinctively to Washington, who privately criticized the Burgesses and Councillors of Virginia as "Chimney Corner Politicians" too devoted to ease and too fearful of public censure to support their own province's regiment adequately.[52] His conviction that no military end could be accomplished without the support of civilian authority became the source of his greatest strength in the Revolutionary era; in the Seven Years' War lay the beginnings of that realization.

Washington's participation in the Forbes campaign of 1758, in which an Anglo-American force built forts and a military road west across Pennsylvania to eject the French from Fort Duquesne, brought him into contact with two extraordinary redcoat officers. In Colonel Henry Bouquet of the Royal American Regiment he met a man whose skills as an administrator enabled him to control and sustain thousands of soldiers, laborers, support personnel, and camp followers as they carved 150 miles of road through the woods, all the while maintaining security against French and Indian raids. Washington also saw in Bouquet's decision to allow Major James Grant to undertake a raid on Fort Duquesne without adequate support, his flaw as a commander: experience and prudence could not keep Bouquet from allowing himself to be seduced by the hope of dealing the enemy a quick, decisive blow.

That nothing worse came of Major Grant's September 14 fiasco, a smaller-scale recapitulation of Braddock's defeat, was due mostly to the overwhelming strength and superb organization of the larger force of which Bouquet's was the advance element. That in turn could be credited to General John Forbes, the expedition's commander. In Forbes, Washington saw virtually all of the positive qualities of command combined: deference to higher authority and cooperation with Pennsylvania's government, systematic attention to issues of logistics and communication and security, and (above all) patience in cultivating diplomatic relations with Indians. The latter was the key to the whole. Because Forbes never made Braddock's mistake of scorning the Indians as mere savages, it proved possible in late 1758 to detach the Delawares and other peoples on the Ohio from the French alliance by negotiation, thus forcing the abandonment of Fort Duquesne. And there was another quality to admire in Forbes, too: the moral courage of a man who, though slowly, painfully dying from what may have been stomach cancer, continued to pursue his mission with a dedication that overshadowed even Braddock's physical bravery under fire.[53]

Thanks to his ability to profit from careful observation and his relentless dedication to self-improvement, Washington came to understand very well the qualities and skills it took to administer an army regiment. By the time he resigned his commission at the end of the 1758, he knew, perhaps better than any other provincial colonel in North America, how to train, feed, house, clothe, discipline, and control a thousand men in garrisons, on patrols, and on the march. It was a vast distance to travel for a man of whom no better could have been said in the spring of 1754 than that he was ambitious, earnest, brave, and callow. This is *not* to say that by the end of the war he had perfected the virtues that later sustained him as a Revolutionary general. Especially in the crucial matter of deference to civil authority—which he initially regarded as essentially an irritant and about which he never ceased to complain—he grew a good deal further, when as a man in his forties he faced challenges far more severe than those of his twenties. Unlike most men, Washington's capacity for adaptation—his ability to learn by trial and error, observation and precept—did not atrophy as he aged. The lessons he first absorbed under the terrible pressures of war in the 1750s became the basis of truly remarkable achievements in the 1770s and beyond.

The nasty little war that Washington endured on the Virginia frontier mattered little in the grand strategy of the Seven Years' War, but it made him both a mature man and a competent military commander. It was a conflict in which he had to fight enemies accustomed to forest warfare in ways that he and his men could never be, foes so elusive that his troops almost never came to grips with them except when they found themselves trapped in ambushes or subjected to surprise attacks. At the same time Washington had to overcome the almost equally daunting obstacles that his fellow colonists erected. Until the campaign of 1758, the provincial government of Virginia never gave his regiment sufficient money or supplies to carry out its mission. Only when Pitt's promise of reimbursement freed it of the fear of bankruptcy did the House of Burgesses authorize an enlistment bounty large enough to attract adequate numbers of recruits. Before that, Washington's regiment was chronically understrength, composed of whatever vagabonds, outcasts, and rogues could be coerced into service, together with the usual quantum of adventurers and whatever impoverished men might be moved to volunteer by the promise of a modest land grant and a wage that equaled about half of what a day laborer might earn.[54] Meanwhile, the young colonel had to cope with floods of refugees driven from their homes; with anxious, angry, and recalcitrant local populations whose ideas of defense ran directly opposite his own; and with militiamen who generally responded to his appeals too late, in inadequate numbers, and without the arms and equipment they needed to perform the tasks he demanded of them.

Given all this, the unattractive features so prominent in Washington's behavior during this period—his continual complaints about lack of support, his repeated threats to resign, his efforts to go around Governor Dinwiddie to influence the Speaker of the House of Burgesses to support the regiment more generously (a tactic that finally moved Dinwiddie to break with him in 1757)—become more understandable, for they were ultimately driven by his desire to improve his regiment's miserable lot. Lack of success led him, however unwillingly, to adapt creatively to circumstances he could not escape. Knowing that the disruptions along the frontier resulted directly from raids launched from Fort Duquesne and the Indian villages of the Allegheny and upper Ohio valleys, he determined to improve the one resource he had—the regiment—by making it the most effective possible fighting force and husbanding its strength against the day he could take it west over Braddock's Road and strike at the root of the evil. To that end, he undertook an ambitious program of training and discipline for his men, exerting his authority with great rigor in the hope of making his shabby and undermanned unit the closest possible approximation of a redcoat battalion. He studied the leading military manuals of the day (especially Humphrey Bland's *Treatise of Military Discipline*), read such classics as were available in translation (Caesar's *Commentaries* was a favorite), and urged his officers to do the same. He also sought advice from officers he admired, especially Bouquet and Forbes, and strove in every way he could to build esprit de corps.[55]

Washington was reluctant to scatter his men in the forts that he located up and down the length of the Shenandoah Valley because to do so prevented him from instilling the discipline, training, and élan he thought essential for the regiment. He therefore resolved to concentrate as many men as possible at Fort Cumberland (the starting point of Braddock's Road, on the upper Potomac) and at Fort Loudoun (his headquarters at Winchester, the largest settlement in the northern Shenandoah) and to use local militiamen to garrison the outlying posts. He had a hard time doing even that. Rather than relocate to the province's strategically located forts and blockhouses, the majority of the backcountry settlers who elected not to flee the region "sought shelter in paltry forts (of their own building)" even though they were "destitute of the common supports of life."[56] These forts were generally stone houses that had been built before the war; the local militiamen had enclosed them in "small stockade" enclosures sufficient to shelter the local farmers, their families, and their animals in case of an attack.[57] Militiamen clung to these posts, inadequate as they were, because their first commitment was to defend the family members and neighbors who took shelter in them. As Washington found, to his intense frustration, they would obey his orders to turn out in order to pursue enemy attackers or garrison the larger, better supplied, and geographically vital provincial blockhouses only when they believed it was in the interests of their communities to do so.

Washington came to regard localism and the readiness of the militia to disobey him that went along with it as enemies no less pernicious than Indian war parties. He had not thought highly of the frontier settlers when he was a surveyor; now, intent on proving his own virtuous character as a servant of the crown, he responded to their parochialism by becoming even more self-consciously cosmopolitan. He became ever more convinced that military leaders must be gentlemen who, like himself, were capable of seeing beyond the interests of the locality to the greater welfare of the commonwealth and who would willingly sacrifice their fortunes and lives when called upon to do so.[58] In this context it becomes clear that his desire for a royal commission for himself and a place on the British establishment for his regiment reflected his reaction to the lack of resources at his command and the backwoodsmen's lack of deference to his authority. Until his final rebuff by Lord Loudoun in early 1757, he clung to the illusion that the uniform somehow makes the man and that a closer connection to imperial authority would enable him to overcome the resistance of the small-minded, self-interested frontiersmen and their families.

And yet despite his persistent frustration and his near-disastrous breach with Dinwiddie in the spring of 1757, Washington never carried through with his threats to resign until the Anglo-Americans had driven the French from Fort Duquesne and stabilized the Virginia-Pennsylvania frontier. In part he refrained for fear of damaging the public reputation he valued so highly. Ultimately, however, he remained with his regiment because, as the war went on, his loyalty to those whom he commanded deepened, and they responded with respect and regard for him as their leader. This motivating sense of shared identity and mission—what modern military sociologists call "unit cohesion"—gradually increased until during the campaign of 1758, Washington's regiment demonstrated such spirit, discipline, and proficiency that even regular officers and soldiers praised it. Such acceptance by the professional soldiers to whom he looked up was a matter of great moment to him and of pride for the soldiers in the regiment's ranks.[59] When he resigned his commission in December, the company officers—captains and lieutenants, who lived in closest contact with the men—wrote him a heartfelt address, thanking him for the care he had shown in teaching them to be "good Troops," lamenting "the loss of such an excellent Commander, such a sincere Friend, and so affable a Companion," and asking him to remain in command another year "to lead us on . . . in compleating the Glorious Work of extirpating our Enemies."[60] His reply, equally sincere, acknowledged "the pangs I have felt at parting with a Regiment, that has shared my toils, and experienced every hardship & danger, which I have encountered." "I thank you," he wrote, "for the love & regard you have all along shewn me. It is in this, I am rewarded. It is herein I glory."[61]

The ability to form bonds of mutual regard with subordinates suggests a capacity for empathy that had not distinguished Washington at the outset of the war, when self-regard, even vanity, was a defining characteristic in his personality. In maturing as a man and a commander, he had grown in other ways as well, most notably in his ability to appreciate the importance of Indians in fighting the war. In 1754 he had disdained them and as a consequence suffered grievously for it at Fort Necessity. In the following year he had seen the most powerful military force in North America cut to shreds as a result of Braddock's dismissive attitude toward Indian warriors. In 1756 and 1757, as his regiment and the militia garrisons up and down the frontier reeled under the blows of Shawnees and other French-allied raiders, he had come to understand that his only realistic hope of retaliation depended on persuading Cherokee, Catawba, Nottoway, and other warriors to launch raids on behalf of the Virginians. In 1758 he saw that Forbes's use of Indian diplomacy allowed him to detach the Delawares and Shawnees from the French alliance and thus take Fort Duquesne without a shot fired.

Though Washington never came to admire Indians or to see them as human beings equal in dignity and worth to himself and other Euro-Americans, he did not let the war make him an Indian-hater, as it did so many backwoods settlers. He never endorsed the view that the only good Indian was a dead one; never subscribed to the backwoodsmen's preferred solution to Indian-white relations, which came down to exclusion or genocide. Instead, Washington learned to see Indians as necessary in rendering the frontier secure and thus worth the expense it took to feed and supply them. As allies, Indians could be troublesome enough, and he always remained capable of condemning them as "insolent, . . . avaricious, and . . . dissatisfied wretches"; as enemies, however, even small numbers of them could make the frontier uninhabitable.[62] The path of intercultural accommodation, however difficult, was obviously the path of prudence.

Even as these realizations were changing his attitudes and shaping his character, the war was transforming the Shenandoah Valley, and with it Washington's views of the future of the backcountry. At the outset of the war, the valley's settlements were dispersed in open-country neighborhoods, just as those of the Virginia Tidewater and Piedmont were. The largest Shenandoah settlement, Winchester (originally known as Frederick Town), boasted barely sixty houses. Washington's decision to locate his headquarters there and concentrate as many of his troops at Fort Loudoun on the hilltop overlooking the town caused the place to grow. By the end of the war it was fully half the size of Williamsburg, the capital of Virginia, and one of the colony's larger settlements.

War made Winchester prosper. The demand for beef to feed the regiment's soldiers and fodder to feed its livestock encouraged local farmers to produce surpluses for sale on an unprecedented scale. Prosperity in turn attracted retailers to town. Merchants in Philadelphia supplied them with dry goods and provided the credit that turned the Shenandoah Valley into the southernmost outpost of the city's commercial hinterland. The population of the Shenandoah grew from about 10,000 in 1748 to about 25,000 in 1760, at which point the settlers began to push beyond it to the west and south.[63]

Washington, already a prominent landowner in the valley, watched all this happening and from it derived a notion of how frontiers should be organized. The farmers around Winchester became in his mind a model for farmers located around market towns that linked the backcountry to coastal cities and their merchants. Such settlers were eager consumers of goods produced in England and Europe, and their appetites for manufactures made them industrious in a way that more remote subsistence farmers—the localist militiamen who so often refused to respond to his orders—were not. This preference for commercial development and urbanization set Washington apart from most of his fellow planters and land speculators, who saw no advantage in promoting the growth of towns that could potentially compete with the influence of the county gentry. They did not share his perspective because, in the comfort and safety of their Tidewater plantations, they had not seen what the war had shown him: that compact settlements were not only more defensible but directly tied to the wider Atlantic world. The economic self-interest of settlers on this kind of commercial frontier could bind them to the governments and leaders of the colonies and to the empire as a whole. In the absence of those ties, the backcountry's centripetal and disorderly qualities would tend to make it indefensible and a drain on the resources of both Britain and Virginia.

Finally, the war did two more things for Washington. First, success in driving the French from Fort Duquesne enabled him to retire from the regiment with his reputation intact and, indeed, bestowed on him a deserved fame as the defender of Virginia's frontier. The freeholders of Frederick County, whose lives and properties he had done his best to defend for the previous three years, ratified his standing by electing him as their representative to the House of Burgesses. At the same time, the most eligible widow in New Kent County, Martha Custis, recognized his merits in another way by consenting to become his wife. This match, fortunate in so many ways, made him one of the larger landholders in northern Virginia and provided the material foundation to sustain his standing as a public-spirited gentleman.

Second, the war left the twenty-seven-year-old colonel with a lengthening personal history to ponder, framed by the knowledge that his life had been repeatedly spared when those of others were not. He had felt death brush his sleeve four times in five years: at Fort Necessity in 1754, when a third of his command became casualties; at the Battle of the Monongahela, when his hat and coat had been pierced by enemy bullets and two horses were killed under him; on the southwestern frontier of Virginia in 1756, when an Indian ambush had failed to trap him as he rode from fort to fort along a remote forest track; and in western Pennsylvania in November 1758, when the Second Virginia Regiment mistook the First Virginia Settlement for the enemy at dusk, unleashing volleys that killed or wounded thirty of his men before he strode bellowing between the groups to make them cease firing. In none of these encounters did he suffer so much as a scratch.

Washington was not yet a regular churchgoer or an active Freemason, but he believed that God ordered events on earth.[64] Because he, like virtually every other theist of his day, understood human history in teleological terms, he could hardly escape the conclusion that his survival served some larger purpose. More than a decade passed before events showed him what the purpose might be.

Postwar Reforms—and Crises

If the Seven Years' War has lessons to teach us today, they may well center on the degree to which a decisive victory can be more perilous for the victor than the vanquished, for there are few historical episodes that give greater occasion for reflection on the dangers of hubris in the lives of states. France and Spain, humiliated by unprecedented military losses, adapted far better to the challenges of defeat than Britain dealt with the consequences of victory. The destruction of the French empire in North America laid the foundation for an unprecedented assertion of imperial authority when a series of British ministers pursued administrative and fiscal reforms that first baffled, then angered, the king's North American subjects. Little more than a decade after 1763, the same colonists who saw the Peace of Paris as the prelude to a golden age were struggling to understand why an empire they had served and celebrated and loved seemed suddenly to have no place in it for them—except, perhaps, as slaves. The irony is as obvious as it is instructive: the unintended consequence of the greatest military triumph of the eighteenth century was the self-immolation of the triumphant empire in a revolutionary civil war.

France survived its imperial debacle. His Most Christian Majesty ceded to Britain those possessions—Canada and the interior settlements from the Great Lakes to the Gulf of Mexico—that had always been the greatest drain on the royal purse, while Britain obligingly returned the most profitable colonies, the West Indian sugar islands, to French control. The economic consequences of peace thus stopped well short of catastrophe for France, which had entered the war at the peak of its eighteenth-century prosperity and bore the wartime loss of trade so well that the values of exports and imports picked up in 1763 essentially where they had left off in 1756. The available evidence suggests that the French economy continued to grow after the war at approximately the same rate as before.[65]

Meanwhile, there was little public outcry over the war's expense because the crown had funded its prodigious military outlays principally by borrowing and then held taxes steady in the postwar period simply by continuing to borrow.[66] This policy created dire problems for the French treasury by the 1780s, but in the short run the absence of a taxpayers' revolt and the continuation of creditor confidence permitted the state to address its highest priorities: rebuilding and reforming the armed forces. Beginning in 1763, the navy constructed new ships at such a rate, and with such high standards of quality, that by 1778 it could confront the British Atlantic fleet on terms close to parity.[67] During that same period, the army raised the pay of its soldiers and greatly improved their training, discipline, housing, and medical care, invested in state-of-the-art armaments, and founded new academies to educate cadets in the arts of war. Most important, the government reformed the army's notoriously corrupt system of recruitment and gradually abolished the proprietary rights of officers, starting with the colonels who literally owned the regiments they commanded as a kind of private property.[68] With more mixed success, the king and his ministers also attempted to streamline France's civil administration and law courts and generally sought to reduce the accretions of aristocratic privilege that hampered the government's ability to raise revenues, even to function at all.[69]

The goal was to turn the tables on Britain in the next war. As the comte de Vergennes, who became foreign minister in 1774, informed the king, "It is enough to read the Treaty of Paris . . . to realize the ascendancy which England has acquired over France and to judge how much that arrogant nation savours the pleasure of having humiliated us." Therefore, he concluded, France was obligated to take revenge when the opportunity appeared, as indeed it soon did, in the breach between Britain and its colonies.[70] In this way defeat produced considerable unity of purpose in policy, while the ineptitude that commanders had shown during the war kept the military establishment's leaders from mounting an effective resistance to reform after the return of peace.

Defeat, particularly the humiliating losses of Havana and Manila, also forced Spain to rearm—something it, too, did with alacrity—and compelled it to rethink and reorganize its state system in relation to the empire. The Bourbon king Charles III came to the throne in 1759 with strong absolutist principles and soon translated them into a program of reform. With the help of vigorous ministers, Charles pursued the expansion of royal authority by increasing the number of military and civil officers who were directly beholden to the crown while undermining the old centers of privilege—the Church, the nobles who dominated municipal corporations, the merchant guilds, and other institutions—that tended to resist his initiatives. The reformers also adopted a forward-looking approach to public finance that emphasized not just the enhancement of revenues but the strengthening of the economy as a whole by improving agriculture, encouraging population growth, and fostering trade.

To defend Spain's commercial and territorial interests in the Americas, the crown extended its absolutist program to the colonies in the so-called Bourbon Reforms. Unlike the old Habsburg regime, which valued colonies principally for the silver they could produce, the Bourbon reformers understood them in mercantilist terms as an economic complement to the metropolis. Charles and his ministers therefore liberalized commerce by stages until free trade was possible throughout the empire in 1789. Simultaneously, the crown attacked long-established bastions of privilege in the colonies—the Church, monopolist merchant guilds, administrators who had purchased their offices, and Mexico City, among others—while offering new privileges to secure the loyalty of such potentially sympathetic groups as merchants in the port cities, residents of provincial towns, and creole landholders.[71]

While it may seem paradoxical that the reformers fought the ill effects of privilege by creating newly privileged groups, the imperial history of Spain in effect gave them no alternative. For more than two centuries the rules and regulations that defined relations between the New World viceroyalties and the metropolis had accumulated like barnacles on the immense, creaking Habsburg ship of state. New Spain, the viceroyalty that included Mexico and southwestern North America, had evolved a baroque system of governance in which race and place of birth determined the social and political standing of the empire's subjects and corporate institutions, each with its own obligations and specified rights or liberties, mediated social relations.[72] Spanish-American society functioned not as a collectivity of individuals but as an alliance of unequal groups, situated along a spectrum of legal privileges and customary rights. At the high end were *peninsulares*—colonists born in Iberia—and *criollos* (creoles)—colonists of pure Spanish blood born in the New World. In the middle were the *castas,* or free persons of mixed blood, of whom the most important were *mestizos,* the offspring of Spanish-Indian unions. At the bottom were purebloods of another sort, Indians (by far the most numerous group) and African slaves.[73]

Given this social and institutional complexity, the monarchy's desire to centralize control required it to encourage the growth of new centers of influence to counter the established power of dominant groups.[74] To curtail the power of the *corregidores* and *alcaldes mayores,* old-style urban magistrates who purchased their offices and regarded them as proprietary possessions, the reformers created twelve territorial intendancies (the forerunners of Mexico's modern states) governed by crown-appointed bureaucrats, the *intendentes*, and a variety of subdelegates who answered directly to them. The reformers even renewed the military power of the crown by the creation and manipulation of privilege. To encourage enlistments the Spanish government promised relief from paying tribute to the crown, offered the right to wear uniforms and medals, and granted the privilege of *fuero militar*, or trial by a special jury. Service in the army and membership in the militia effectively freed men from being treated as ordinary colonial subjects; it also integrated the army into the colonial society and polity by enabling colonists to understand it not as a metropolitan intrusion but as an extension of local and provincial authority. *Peninsulares* predominated in the highest positions of army command, but even the *peons* who stood in the ranks found that the military offered an avenue to a more cosmopolitan world and a better, more dignified life. The creole elite embraced military leadership and the direct association with royal power that it symbolized.[75]

Thus in the aftermath of the Seven Years' War the Spanish crown successfully revived its authority in the empire and laid the groundwork for a late-eighteenth-century economic boom. The population, which had grown only slowly for a century before the war, increased more rapidly, until by 1810 it had doubled its prewar level. The shock of defeat, in short, promoted an imperial renaissance that shored up metropolitan authority and bought a new, half-century-long lease on life for Spain's empire in the New World.

While France and Spain righted themselves in the wake of defeat, Britain floundered in the tide of victory. Much of what happened in the British empire can be traced to the administrative imperatives of acquiring half a continent and integrating as new subjects a hundred thousand French-speaking Catholics and about twice that many Indians, many of them former enemies. Even more pressing was the fiscal crisis that attended the near doubling of the national debt in less than a decade, an expansion that left the Exchequer with barely enough revenue to cover interest payments and the fixed costs of government. Much can be traced, too, to the psychological effects of the tremendous string of victories won between 1758 and 1762. Britain's chief ministers, accustomed to thinking of their nation as militarily invincible, adopted a peremptory style in dealing with the empire's inhabitants. Perhaps understandably, colonists found this attitude impossible to distinguish from arrogance.

The result was a series of unanticipated developments, astonishing to contemporaries in Britain and North America alike. First was the great Indian war that we still miscall Pontiac's Rebellion (1763–65), triggered by the efforts of the British commander in chief, Jeffery Amherst, to economize and reform long-standing practices in Indian trade and diplomacy. Late in the war he put a stop to diplomatic gift-giving and the subsidized Indian trade, suspended the sale of alcohol, and strictly limited the quantities of ammunition and arms supplied to Indians. Amherst wanted to reduce the profiteering and corruption of the Northern Indian Commissioner Sir William Johnson, Johnson's assistant George Croghan, and the Indian traders with whom they cooperated so closely: reasonable goals, surely, for a commander in chief who was personally honest and conscientious in the performance of his duties.

Amherst believed that his measures would not only save money and end abuses but also encourage order and industry among the Indians, since the higher prices of trade goods and the absence of debilitating rum would make them more eager and efficient hunters. What he failed to grasp was that generous diplomatic gifts and openhanded trading policies had been the very basis of comity with the Indians; in destroying this foundation he created the conditions that produced a vast insurrection. It was a war that eventually extended to virtually every native nation that had previously been allied with the French; a war that cost the redcoats at least 400 lives and the Anglo-American colonists more than 2,000 in the first year alone, reduced Britain's military presence in the West to three isolated posts, and once again emptied the frontiers of Anglo-American settlers. In the end, the Indian "rebels" ceased fighting not because British soldiers subdued them but because the French were no longer around to provide the arms, ammunition, and other supplies they needed to sustain their attacks.[76]

The Indians had never intended to destroy the English altogether, only to teach them a lesson about how to behave: not as a master but as a "father"

cast in the mold of the French original, Onontio—a figure who would me-
diate disputes, give the gifts needed to cover the dead and prevent the eruption of mourning wars, act as an ally, and superintend trade on fair terms.
Thus when the British made peace at conferences sponsored by Sir William
Johnson, they were victors only in their own minds. The Indians got back
the terms of trade they wanted, creating what they thought was a viable
middle-ground relationship with the British, who promised, in the Royal
Proclamation of 1763, to keep their settlers from encroaching on Indian
lands beyond the Appalachian crest. The British, it is true, reoccupied the
interior forts they had lost, but the garrisons they put in place were weak
and grew increasingly ghostly until the forts were abandoned, as even Fort
Pitt was in 1772. From the Indians' perspective, the treaties that ended Pontiac's War signaled a native, not a British, victory.

The Indians who rebelled against British control tried, in the only way
they knew, to maintain local autonomy and customary rights against an imperial authority heedless of local conditions and values. In that sense the
breakdown of Anglo-Indian relations following Britain's great victory predicted the future of the empire with almost eerie accuracy. In as unmistakable a way as can be imagined, the Indian uprisings showed the limited
potential of coercion as a basis for imperial control. To a degree no one in
the British ministry understood, they also discredited the redcoats as protectors in the eyes of the frontier settlers, while the prohibition of western
settlements by the Proclamation of 1763 alienated both gentry speculators
and the Indian-hating backwoodsmen who went ahead and squatted on Indian lands anyway. But British ministers, fearing insolvency at home and
looking across the Atlantic at colonies prone to the kind of localist, self-
interested behavior that Washington had deplored on the wartime frontier,
failed to see the potential for future conflict arising from their settlement of
Pontiac's War. Instead of pausing to take stock, they moved to create a program of imperial reform based on enforcing the sovereign power of the
metropolitan government. These financial and administrative measures
brought to the forefront what long had been, and long remained, the central
antagonism in Anglo-American political culture: the intractable conflict between the claims of imperial and local authority.

Defenders of local privilege usually controlled the legislatures of the
British colonies; when they did not predominate, they vigorously, vocally
opposed the exercise of executive power. Their localism arose only in part
from the three thousand miles of ocean that lay between Britain and North
America. Just as important was the colonists' tendency to understand liberty

in a *negative* sense: as the absence of metropolitan interference in the activities of local elites and the societies they dominated. This idea contradicted the *positive* definition that prevailed in Britain. There liberties were understood as concessions that a sovereign power made to its subjects: grants of specific rights like taxation by consent and trial by jury or privileges such as habeas corpus. The absence of metropolitan intervention in North America for a half-century before the Seven Years' War had encouraged the colonists to understand their aberrant sense of liberty as somehow normal. The ministers' postwar need to reform the empire decreed an end to that neglectful state of affairs. Colonial practice would be made to harmonize with metropolitan principle, and all differences would be settled in favor of the legitimate authority of the sovereign.

Since 1689 the Anglo-French wars had promoted the growth of a British "fiscal-military" state, powerful to a degree that surpassed even the absolutist dreams of James II.[77] In North America, too, the wars had increased the importance of British culture and British power, making the empire tangible to colonists in the form of scarlet uniforms, iron cannon, and the Union Jack, promoting patriotic feelings in ways that peace never could. The long process of Anglicization in the colonies, therefore, was not merely the product of Anglophilia, the rule of law, and the increasing consumption of British manufactures, but an institutional and cultural transformation driven by the relentless imperatives of imperial war.[78]

Between 1755 and 1763 war became the very lifeblood of empire and the means by which Anglo-Americans defined themselves in both territorial and ideological terms. Britons on both sides of the Atlantic had celebrated each military victory as another step in the advance of liberty and Protestantism over slavery and popery. After the war, however, Britain's efforts to limit the expansion of disorderly white settlement on Indian lands, to regularize trade, religion, and government, and to promote the empire's functioning in an economically rational, fiscally prudent, administratively enlightened fashion elicited howls of protest from colonists who had been delighted to use unlimited force to free Canadians from the grip of France and popery but who adamantly refused to submit themselves to the power of a sovereign king in Parliament. British imperial reformers, who saw the colonists as motivated solely by self-interest, failed to see that an alternative vision of empire lay behind the protests, a vision that made liberty synonymous with the absence of state intervention and defined political allegiance as an act of voluntary association. The greatest imperial victory in British history thus brought about a confrontation over the terms on which the empire would function. The fundamental issue at stake was what was eventually called citizenship.

British authority in North America disintegrated in three stages as disputes over the limits of imperial authority eroded the bonds of affection that had previously bound the empire together. The first phase, the Stamp Act crisis of 1765–66, was the most bewildering, violent, and disorderly, as tens of thousands of ordinary colonists rioted in protest against a mild tax that Parliament had tried to impose on them without their consent. The announced purpose of the tax was to pay for 10,000 royal troops to be permanently stationed in the colonies. This seemed ominous to colonists who noted that the possessions of the nearest imperial rival, Spain, lay beyond the Mississippi River, while the redcoats' miserable record in Pontiac's War suggested that the ministry did not expect to use the army as a frontier constabulary. The only plausible reason for leaving so many men in America seemed to be that they were intended to enforce laws that Parliament might pass to bring the colonies well and truly into subjection.

The wildness and wide scale of ordinary colonists' response—mobs that everywhere threatened the lives and destroyed the property of royal officials and forced the closing of ports in protest against the payment of the tax—perplexed British officials who had been confident of their ability to prevail over any colonial protests. So much violence and upheaval astonished political and cultural leaders in the colonies, too. They scrambled to reassert some measure of control over the protests and bring order out of what looked like incipient anarchy.

Scholars have attributed the violence of the Stamp Act protests to many factors, including the disordered state of the postwar colonial economies, an ideological consensus among the colonists rooted in the values of English republicanism, and the nearly universal nature of the proposed tax. The last was clearly crucial, for by touching individuals equally, irrespective of residence or occupation, the Stamp Act enabled colonists everywhere to see themselves as equally threatened. We can best appreciate those powerful influences, however, by locating them in an emotional context created by memories of shared patriotic sacrifice. Colonists could only see efforts to reform the empire and to make them pay for its troops in America as attempts to deprive them of the partnership in empire they thought they had earned.

Under pressure from British merchants who were losing vast sums as a result of the closing of American ports, Parliament repealed the counterproductive Stamp Act in March 1766. But the king and Parliament could neither ignore the unresolved problems of finance and control nor allow the colonists to dictate the shape of the postwar empire; hence the repeal was immediately preceded by a Declaratory Act in which Parliament asserted its unqualified sovereignty over the colonies. A second attempt to raise revenue from the colonies and tighten the bonds of imperial control, the Townshend Acts, followed in 1767, precipitating a second round of colonial resistance that was not resolved until 1770. Unlike the Stamp Act, which had unwarily imposed a direct tax on individuals, the Townshend Acts sought to raise revenue through customs duties charged on paper, glass, tea, and other items that the colonists commonly imported from Britain. The levy was so light and so cleverly disguised that its author, Chancellor of the Exchequer Charles Townshend, believed it would not even be perceived as a tax.

He was wrong. This time the trajectory of protest ran opposite to the seemingly anarchic opposition to the Stamp Act, largely because colonial political leaders had been so thoroughly frightened by the riots that they moved quickly to propose a nonviolent means of expressing dissent, the creation of nonimportation associations. These were agreements on the part of merchants not to import British goods until Parliament, seeing the damage that was being done to the British economy, would repeal the Townshend Acts. Crowds now were more orderly and intent more on enforcing conformity to the boycotts than on intimidating royal officials. Most of the gentlemen who organized the resistance and justified it ideologically in the public prints thought of themselves as patriotic Britons and remained fundamentally committed to the empire. Resistance began slowly, growing gradually stronger as pamphlets and newspapers explained the perils of submitting to even a mild indirect tax to which the colonists had not consented.

Nonimportation associations began to spread in 1768 after the ministry sent troops to occupy and impose order on that most fractious of colonial cities, Boston. By 1769 a remarkably effective boycott was in place in all the major ports, and imports from Britain fell by one-third from the previous year's levels. A new, more pacific administration under the leadership of Frederick, Lord North, took note. North was already in the process of settling the conflict by proposing legislation to repeal all but a single symbolic measure from the Townshend Acts—the tax on tea—in the late winter of 1770, at almost exactly the time that violence convulsed Boston in the so-called Boston Massacre.

The killing of five members of a disorderly crowd by British soldiers could easily have been used to justify an armed revolt, had Boston's patriot leaders wished to do so. Instead General Thomas Gage wisely withdrew the redcoats from Boston and the leaders of the patriot resistance cooperated with royal authorities to bring the crisis to a peaceful end in the courts. Meanwhile, the repeal of all the offensive duties but the tax on tea reassured the colonists of Parliament's fundamental reasonableness, and the non-importation associations began to fall apart. Gradually business as usual resumed within the empire. By autumn the boycotts were mostly a memory, as merchants—understandably reluctant to bankrupt themselves in defense of the right to be taxed only by consent—clutched the fig leaf of principle by abjuring the importation of tea while resuming the importation of everything else. Until late 1773, when the Tea Act precipitated a third crisis of imperial authority, tensions declined to the point that many British Americans believed a new modus vivendi might actually be emerging and with it a renewal of harmony within the empire.

An Imperialist's Progress

Like many another colonist, George Washington welcomed normalization, for during the first two phases of the imperial crisis he had been far less concerned with protesting British infringements on colonial liberties than finding his way to prosperity as a planter. The path had not been an easy one; he suffered financially in the postwar depression and went heavily into debt to his London creditors. Though he shared this fate with other Virginia planters, he found it particularly troublesome, for two reasons. In the first place, he hated depending on credit to maintain his family's style of life because he believed that independence of action was above all what defined a gentleman. In the second, he discovered that he had no knack for growing high-quality tobacco and therefore had no prospect of climbing out of debt unless he found some other way of making his plantations pay.[79] After nearly a decade of losing money, therefore, he abandoned tobacco planting for wheat farming, which seemed to promise lower labor costs and higher returns. He lost a certain amount of status by making this change, for Virginia's greatest men were "crop masters" whose tobacco commanded premium prices on the London market. But wheat farming allowed Washington to market his produce through colonial merchants and to reduce his debts to the London firms he had come to see as greedy and underhanded. He also diversified his plantation enterprises, pursuing (among other schemes) brandy-distilling, flour-milling, shad-fishing, and textile manufacture, in the double hope of achieving self-sufficiency and of producing "merchantable" commodities to sell. Most of all, he sought to salvage his fortunes by land speculation.

Close to home, he used Martha's fortune to expand his Tidewater holdings from about 5,000 acres to something like 12,000. Further afield, he became a partner in a scheme to drain the Great Dismal Swamp on the border between Virginia and North Carolina, the last large unoccupied tract below the Fall line; he invested in a second partnership, the Mississippi Company, which sought to use influence in London to acquire rights to 2.5 million acres between the Mississippi and the Wabash, in what is now southern Illinois; and he participated in efforts to revive the claims of the Ohio Company, which had fallen dormant during the Seven Years' War.[80] Most of all, he tried to capitalize on his claim to the western lands that he had the most realistic chance to acquire, the ones that were promised as a bounty in 1754 to the soldiers and officers of the Virginia Regiment.

As colonel of the regiment, Washington was entitled to claim 20,000 acres of land on the south bank of the Ohio, or 10 percent of the 200,000 acres the House of Burgesses had reserved for the veterans. He supplemented this handsome reward by buying up the land warrants of scores of his fellow veterans, eventually realizing the rights to an additional 25,000 acres.[81] From September 1767 he employed an old subordinate from the Virginia Regiment, Captain William Crawford, to identify tracts on the Ohio that he might acquire when the land grants were finally made.[82] Despite the crown's seemingly absolute prohibition in the Proclamation of 1763 on expanding white settlement beyond the Appalachians, he felt fully justified in doing so. As he explained to Crawford, "I can never look upon that Proclamation in any other light (but this I say between ourselves) than as a temporary expedient to quiet the Minds of the Indians & [therefore one that] must fall of course in a few years. . . ."[83]

In 1768 the treaties of Hard Labor (under which the Cherokees ceded their claims to certain lands south of the Ohio and west of the Appalachian ridge) and Fort Stanwix (under which the Iroquois League surrendered its claims to the whole region south of the river) seemed to bear out Washington's prophecy. In fact the Proclamation of 1763 was not revoked, only widely ignored, even by government officials; thus in late 1769 Washington persuaded Virginia's governor and Council to permit representatives of the 1754 Regiment to identify tracts in the Ohio country for future survey. Early the following August a meeting of his former officers delegated him to travel to the Ohio as a first step toward realizing their claim.[84]

Washington was delighted to oblige. In the fall he and a small party scouted lands along the river, canoeing more than 200 miles from Pittsburgh down to the confluence of the Great Kanawha, carefully examining everything along the way, and particularly looking for large contiguous stretches of fine territory.[85] By the time he returned to Mount Vernon on December 1, he had a superb notion of the value of what he had seen, and of what was at stake.

As Washington knew only too well at the time he made the trip, other speculators and syndicates also had an eye on the lands along the Ohio. A powerful and well-connected group of Pennsylvanian and London speculators called the Walpole Company seemed a particular threat: they were petitioning the Privy Council for a gargantuan grant of 20 million acres on the south bank of the Ohio with the goal of organizing an inland colony, Vandalia. The men associated with this scheme included Thomas Walpole, brother of one of the most influential politicians in England; Benjamin Franklin; the Philadelphia merchant Samuel Wharton; and the incomparable, ubiquitous George Croghan.

When Washington passed through Pittsburgh on his way home, he talked extensively with Croghan about the Vandalia project. At the time the Irishman was doing a brisk business selling tracts in the vicinity of Pittsburgh, land he had acquired in 1749 in an exceptionally dubious grant from the Iroquois League. As long as the Proclamation of 1763 remained in effect, these sales were utterly outside the law. Washington nonetheless offered to purchase 15,000 acres from him at a shilling per acre, "to be paid so soon as there can be a legal title made to the Land." He also inquired, with the utmost delicacy, about whether Croghan would consider selling his interest in the Walpole Company.[86]

Washington, prudent as ever, was trying to position himself to take advantage of what he assumed would be the inevitable migration of white farmers into a vast trans-Appalachian realm. Even before he made the trip west he had begun to talk about a scheme to canalize the Potomac and open it to navigation as high as Fort Cumberland, "whence," he wrote, "the Portage to the Waters of Ohio must commence." Such a project would make the Potomac "the Channel of conveyance of the extensive & valuable Trade of a rising Empire" that would benefit many forward-looking gentlemen.[87] Those who built the canal and collected tolls for its use would obviously profit. So would those who owned waterfront property in Alexandria, the port on the Potomac's lower reaches where goods would be transshipped to and from canal boats. Those who held lands in the upper Ohio

Valley and along the Youghiogheny-Monongahela drainage that fed it from the high ground northwest of Fort Cumberland were bound to benefit as well. The master of Mount Vernon intended to belong to all three groups.

Washington had stopped on his journey to the Ohio at Great Meadows and viewed the charred remains of Fort Necessity. Whatever emotions stirred as he did so, it was not sentimentality that prompted him to lay out thirty pistoles (£25 sterling) to buy the place in December 1770 after his return. As he had seen as early as 1754, the spot offered the best available way station between the upper Potomac and the Youghiogheny. Its 300 acres of rich hay-meadow would yield crop after crop of fodder for the draft animals that would plod past on Braddock's Road, carrying Ohio produce to the Potomac, British manufactures to Pittsburgh, and Virginia settlers to the rich farmlands Washington planned to offer for lease at the mouth of the Kanawha.

The rising empire that Washington foresaw was of course British. He understood and readily accepted that British authorities would ultimately dispose of those lands to great men like himself who had the capital needed to survey them, publicize their availability, and convey them to the new settlers. All that seemingly remained at issue was the direction that imperial authorities might take on policies to govern the inevitable expansion, once the prohibition on white settlement west of the Appalachian crest was lifted. The crown, as Washington knew, had only two alternatives. Either it could organize new interior settlements by extending the jurisdiction of existing colonies westward or it could choose to create new colonies beyond the Appalachians, on the model of the proposed Vandalia. In the former case, his claims to the bounty lands from 1754 would hold up within an enlarged Virginia; in the latter, he could best protect his interests by buying into the Walpole Company, even if that meant dealing with the likes of George Croghan. Either way, produce, goods, and settlers—an endless stream of gold—would pass through Great Meadows in transit to their destinations.

Because the British empire and imperialism structured Washington's world so completely, the logic of his political activities in the early 1770s was anything but radical. His participation in protests against the Townshend Acts—he helped draft the agreement that constituted the Virginia Non-Importation Association in May 1769, took part in relaxing it to permit more imports in June 1770, and abandoned it with relief, along with the rest of the associators, in July 1771—reflected no disposition to protest against the fact of British imperialism. His problem was not with the empire but with the current ministers of the crown. His goal was to influence, not overthrow, the political and commercial structures upon which he predicated all his plans and in which he fixed his hopes for the future.[88]

That future looked hopeful to Washington in the years of business as usual that followed Parliament's repeal of all but one of the Townshend duties. The new governor who arrived in Virginia in the fall of 1771, John Murray, fourth Earl of Dunmore, proved equally enamored of land speculation and unconcerned about those details of the Proclamation of 1763 that forbade western settlement. Washington did his best to build ties of friendship and common interest with the governor, dining or spending social evenings with him five times between late 1771 and the spring of 1773 and providing information on the Ohio country, an area in which Dunmore took an uncommonly keen interest.[89] By the spring of 1773 the two were on sufficiently good terms that Washington offered to act as his lordship's personal guide on an expedition to explore the valley during the coming summer, a proposal that Dunmore accepted.[90] In the end a family emergency prevented Washington from going: his wife's seventeen-year-old daughter, Patsy, died suddenly on June 19, and he did not wish to leave the inconsolable Martha alone for an extended time.[91]

Although Washington missed the chance to cultivate the kinds of personal bonds with the governor that might have grown out of a couple of months spent camping and canoeing along the Ohio, Dunmore proved well-disposed toward Washington's speculative schemes—so long as they did not impinge on his own. In late 1773, therefore, Washington finally secured the approval of Governor Dunmore and the Council for patenting the land grants made to the soldiers of the Virginia Regiment in 1754.[92] Even a guaranteed title to 45,000 acres of Ohio land did not put Washington's mind at ease about the future, however, for it was becoming clear to him that plans were afoot to open the valley for immediate settlement.

In early September 1773, Washington learned that Governor Dunmore, then at Pittsburgh, had promised a land grant on the Ohio below the mouth of the Scioto River to Dr. John Connolly, formerly a surgeon's mate in a Pennsylvania regiment. Washington had met Connolly on the Forbes campaign and knew him now as one of the most active speculators in Pittsburgh. By itself, Dunmore's promise was only an interesting fact, but at almost exactly the same time Washington learned that one of his former subordinates, Captain Thomas Bullitt, was surveying large tracts near the Scioto, apparently at Dunmore's direction.[93] Because the Scioto had been mentioned as the western boundary of the Vandalia colony, Washington suspected that the governor had received orders from London to distribute lands there to former provincial officers, as the Proclamation of 1763 implied might be done. If that were true, it would have an immense effect on his own plans. As he told his agent, William Crawford: "depend upon it, if it be once known that the Governor will grant Patents for these Lands, the Officers of Pennsylvania, Maryland, Carolina &c. &c., will flock there in Shoals, & every valuable spot will be taken up, contiguous to the river, on which, the Lands . . . will always be most valuable."[94]

Dunmore did indeed have plans, but not the ones Washington guessed. What the governor had seen at Pittsburgh in the summer of 1773 looked disorderly but strongly suggested opportunities for self-aggrandizement. Thanks to the crown's heroic expenditures on road-building during the war, the valleys around Pittsburgh were accessible as never before to migrants from Virginia, Maryland, Pennsylvania, and New Jersey. According to one eyewitness, Braddock's and Forbes's roads seemed "alive with Men, Women, Children, and Cattle" from all these colonies; estimates held that as many as five thousand families a year were moving to the region.[95] Dunmore believed that at Pittsburgh "and in the neighbourhood . . . I found upwards of ten thousand people settled." This was of course in flagrant violation of the proclamation, but then there was no longer a garrison at Fort Pitt to enforce imperial policy. The Indians, who maintained a "settlement immediately opposite to the town of Pittsburg on the other side of the river," were, understandably, uneasy. Pennsylvania had done little to impose control: it had appointed no magistrates, organized no militia, and made no attempt to repair or man the fort. "Upon my arrival," Dunmore reported, "the people flocked about me and beseeched me . . . to appoint magistrates and officers of militia to remove these grievous inconveniences under which they laboured."[96] Because the Penn family had never surveyed their province's western boundary, it remained unclear whether Pittsburgh lay in Westmoreland County, Pennsylvania, or Augusta County, Virginia.

These factors, in combination with Dunmore's habitual preference for action over thought, were enough to move the governor to intervene. Early in 1774 he asserted Virginia's claim to the whole of the Ohio country by commissioning Dr. Connolly and a half dozen other prominent local men as justices of the peace and ordering surveys in the area—to be carried out, as it happened, by Captain William Crawford—in preparation for issuing Virginia patents to the landholders. George Croghan, who saw more prospect for profit under Virginia's jurisdiction than under Pennsylvania's (and who indeed may have suggested the takeover to Dunmore in the first place), cast his lot with the new regime and accepted a commission as

justice of the peace. Previously indolent Pennsylvania now countered by appointing its own magistrates, who promptly ordered the arrest of officials
from Virginia. Virginia's magistrates responded in kind. By spring, the adherents of Pennsylvania were arming themselves to counter the force of the
Virginia militia, and both were preparing for what looked like an impending
civil war.[97]

To avert that conflict, Connolly and Dunmore fomented another.
Disorganized localized violence between natives and newcomers had been
common in the area since the late 1760s; now Connolly encouraged rumors
among the nervous settlers that it was all a sign of an intended Indian uprising. When in April a party of Cherokee warriors attacked three traders on
their way to the Scioto with goods intended for the Shawnees, Connolly—
now a captain of the Virginia militia as well as a justice of the peace—
blamed the Shawnees and other Ohio Indians. Militiamen took their
revenge on Shawnee and Mingo villages, massacring at least nine, and perhaps as many as forty, Indians. Anger mounted and anxieties spread on both
sides of the cultural divide as white settlers began to withdraw from exposed
farmsteads or to "fort up" in anticipation of raids. Moderate civil chiefs, especially Cornstalk of the Shawnees, tried unavailingly to restrain their
young men and restore peace. Lord Dunmore, however, was as uninterested in negotiation as the warriors. In June he ordered militia units in Virginia's western counties to prepare for an offensive on the Ohio.[98]

Dunmore wanted an Indian war for reasons that were both self-
interested and driven by what he regarded as wise policy. The proposed
colony of Vandalia, which Dunmore (like most Virginia speculators) believed was a scheme to steal Virginia's lands, had been in a state of suspended animation for two years because questions shrouding its boundaries
and the collection of quitrents had not yet been answered to the satisfaction
of the solicitor general back in England. Moreover, the Vandalia project
rested on the assumption that cessions to the crown made by the Cherokees
in the Treaty of Hard Labor and by the Iroquois League in the Treaty of Fort
Stanwix had fully cleared the Indian title to the region. But one major Indian group in the West, the Shawnees, had continued to exercise hunting
rights on the south side of the Ohio Valley, and they vehemently denied that
the Cherokee and Iroquois cessions were in any way binding on them. If
Dunmore could provoke a war and defeat the Shawnees, he could force
them to surrender to Virginia all their claims to territory in what is now
Kentucky. This would effectively turn the Ohio into the boundary between
Indian Country to the north and a vast Virginia-controlled region to the

south, open to white settlement. The province could legitimate the settlements that squatters had already established there, encourage orderly migration, and erect county governments. If Vandalia ever emerged from its embroilments with the law officers of the crown, its de jure claims could scarcely compete with Virginia's de facto control over the southern half of the Valley from Pittsburgh to the Falls of the Ohio.

A successful Indian war therefore offered inestimable benefits to the governor and his province. Lord Dunmore could claim he had prevented further violence between Indians and white settlers, make himself a hero to the land-speculating gentry of his colony, and gain a huge popular following among its ordinary colonists. That his initiative was at odds with the policy of the crown evidently did not concern him. At least it did not bother him enough to keep him from raising an army and leading them against the Shawnees in September and October of 1774.

It is clear enough that Dunmore was a gambler, willing to risk reputation and career alike on the faith that fortune favors the bold. Yet the violent expansion of Virginia's territorial control was ultimately less a bid for personal riches (though Dunmore would not have spurned them) than a means of shoring up British imperial control in the province. He needed both popular and gentry support more desperately in the summer and fall of 1774 than any Virginia governor had needed them in a century. That was because, in the spring of the previous year, Lord North's ministry had decided to save the foundering East India Company from bankruptcy by giving it a monopoly on the sale of tea in the American colonies, thus triggering the third great crisis of empire in the postwar period.

This climactic confrontation between metropolitan authorities and Anglo-American colonists arose from yet another attempt to deal with unanticipated consequences of the Seven Years' War. As we have seen, the success of the clerk-turned-conqueror Robert Clive in campaigns against the French and their Indian allies had allowed the East India Company to sweep the Compagnie des Indes from the east coast of the subcontinent by early 1761. By the end of the war, the East India Company controlled Bengal through a puppet ruler; in 1765 the Mogul emperor Shah Alam II granted the company the *diwani*, or the control of tax revenues, in Bengal, Bihar, and part of Orissa. The company expected this to produce approximately £1.5 million annually and intended to use the revenues collected to purchase tea in China, which could in turn be exported at great profit to Europe. No one fully anticipated, however, the extent to which extracting revenues from Indian peasants through the local elites would enmesh the company in the problems of governmental administration; nor did anyone fully appreciate how expensive it would be to maintain a large army to keep order and enforce the company's authority. What had looked like a bonanza turned out to be a colossal drain on the company's finances, a drain that could not be reversed by the company's assumption in 1771 of direct control over the collection of revenue. By 1773, the East India Company was bankrupt in all but name, with no asset left to sell but the 17 million pounds of tea that lay amoldering in its British warehouses.[99]

His Majesty's government could not let the East India Company fail, for to do so would have imperiled the whole commercial economy of the empire. Nor could it afford to take over direct rule of India. The solution that Britain's prime minister, Lord Frederick North, devised in 1773 was in theory an elegant one. Despite their supposed boycott of tea as a taxed commodity, American colonists drank smuggled Dutch tea in great quantities. The grant of a monopoly on the sale of tea in North America to the company seemed certain to secure a steady revenue for it at no significant cost to the Exchequer; the colonists would buy it because the company, with its vast warehoused stock, could offer tea at a price well below the level consumers were used to paying, even with the tax of three pennies a pound reckoned in. Since many merchants had quietly broken their vow to continue boycotting English tea anyway, it seemed likely to North and the cabinet that the colonists' self-interest would prevail over whatever remained of their political principles.

This was a miscalculation of the highest order. Colonists long since sensitized to the dangers of taxation without consent could only too easily perceive a devilish plot in dutied tea being offered at bargain-basement prices. The very fact of its reasonable price, indeed, seemed to many clear evidence of a conspiracy to destroy their rights as Britons. Resistance sprang up overnight in all the ports where consignees for East India tea had been designated. When the first tea ships arrived in the fall and early winter of 1773, mobs everywhere forced the consignees to resign. Everywhere, shiploads of tea were either sent back to England or impounded.

Everywhere, that is, except in radical Boston, where the singularly bad relations between patriot leaders and the royal governor were further inflamed by the East India Company's choice of consignees—the governor's sons—and the governor's refusal to bow to intimidation. The dumping of tea worth £11,000 into the harbor on the night of December 16, 1773, could not be ignored. But the measures that Parliament adopted to punish Boston—a set of Coercive Acts that among other things closed the port of

Boston and rewrote the Massachusetts charter, naming the commander in chief, General Thomas Gage, as governor of the province, and imposing a garrison that exceeded 4,000 on the town—were so draconian as to alarm colonists everywhere. Simultaneously without considering how it would be perceived in the context of the Coercive Acts, Parliament also opted to solve the long-standing problem of the West by passing the Quebec Act, creating a civil government in the new province of Quebec, granting Roman Catholic Canadians religious toleration and a full slate of legal rights, and extending Quebec's boundaries to include everything from the Great Lakes to the Ohio, as far west as the Mississippi River.

Taken together, these measures seemed so threatening that even moderates like George Washington concluded that united resistance alone could protect colonial rights and preserve a tolerable place within the empire for Americans.[100] It was the Coercive Acts that finally moved the Virginia House of Burgesses to pass a resolution on May 24, 1774, calling for a day of fasting and prayer in response to the punishment of Boston. As an act of protest, that gesture was modest enough. Washington's assumption that his own vote in favor would not offend the governor was clearly implicit in the fact that he dined with Dunmore on the twenty-fifth, breakfasted with him on the twenty-sixth, and attended a ball in honor of the arrival of Lady Dunmore on the evening of the twenty-seventh.[101]

Had Dunmore found it in himself to ignore the resolution, as Washington evidently hoped he would, it would probably have come to little. Instead he brooded on it, concluded that it was offensive to the king's majesty and Parliament's authority, and dissolved the Assembly. Incensed, the Burgesses (including Washington) adjourned to a nearby tavern and reconstituted themselves as a Convention. On May 30 they resolved "That Letters be wrote to all our Sister Colonies" recommending that an intercolonial Congress meet to coordinate "such Measures as shall be judged most effectual for the Common Rights and Liberty of British America."[102]

This call for what came to be known as the First Continental Congress was the context in which Lord Dunmore in June ordered the frontier militia to prepare to take the field; the meeting of the Congress in Philadelphia that autumn coincided exactly with active operations against the Shawnees in Dunmore's War. Intemperate as he was, the governor nonetheless had considerable insight into the priorities and psyches of both the great planters and the common folk of Virginia. He knew they were moved not only by concern at the ministry's treatment of Boston but by frustration with the ministry's unwillingness to open the interior of the continent to colonization. He believed he could count on the lure of western lands, and the visceral appeal of a war against Indians to a white population inclined to hate them anyway, to distract attention from the policies of the ministry. He evidently trusted that once the rebellious Bostonians had been taught the necessary lessons and duly subjected to British sovereignty he would be able to translate his popularity as a war leader into renewed support for the empire. He also undoubtedly hoped that the ministry would be so grateful for his having defused political resistance in Virginia that it would overlook the fact that he had launched an unauthorized campaign of conquest to do so.

Dunmore's wager that the Virginians' self-interested commitment to expanding the empire would overrule their concerns about the arbitrary exercise of power very nearly paid off. He had no trouble recruiting 2,400 provincials for his expedition even though neither the Assembly nor the crown authorized him to raise—and hence pay—a force larger than any Virginia had fielded during the Seven Years' War.[103] When 1,200 of those Virginians clashed with an outnumbered band of Shawnee and Mingo warriors at a bend in the Ohio River called Point Pleasant on October 10, 1774, the outcome was not quite the decisive victory that Dunmore later claimed. The battle in fact ended inconclusively when the Shawnees broke off contact and withdrew to their towns in the Scioto Valley, north of the Ohio; Dunmore was then able to build blockhouses to protect his supplies and concentrate his forces in the vicinity and threaten to destroy their settlements and families wholesale.

Moderate chiefs led by Cornstalk accepted an armistice and promised to attend a formal peace conference the following spring. In the interim, they agreed to withdraw from the Kentucky country in return for the Virginians' promise that they would refrain from settling on the north side of the river. The Shawnees (many of whom refused to acknowledge Cornstalk's negotiations in the first place) seem to have viewed this as at most a temporary, strategic withdrawal. Dunmore by contrast interpreted it as a permanent cession of land and the basis for a full-fledged assertion of Virginia's authority over the lands south of the Ohio.[104] Among the great planters of the province, his lordship suddenly became "as popular as a Scotsman can be."[105] When a new Virginia Convention met in Richmond in March 1775 to choose delegates to attend the Second Continental Congress (scheduled to convene in May), its members unanimously commended Dunmore "for his truly noble, wise and spirited Conduct on the late Expedition against our Indian Enemy."[106]

For these reasons it should not surprise us that Washington remained in contact with the governor through the spring of 1775, even after he had served as a delegate to the First Continental Congress and even as he was preparing to depart for Philadelphia as a delegate to the Second. His fellow delegates in the two Virginia conventions chose him for these assignments precisely because he was *not* a firebrand like Patrick Henry or an impassioned writer like Thomas Jefferson but rather a moderate man, known more for the sobriety of his views than for his readiness to make a public issue of them. From late summer 1774 through the spring of 1775, Washington continued to look for accommodation. On one hand, he believed that Parliament's measures were "not only repugnant to natural right, but subversive of the law and constitution of Great Britain itself"; on the other, he supported the campaign against the Shawnees, kept up friendly relations with the royal governor who promoted it, and nursed the hope that the king and Parliament would back down from their position in Massachusetts and restore a sensible balance in imperial governance.[107] Only in retrospect did it appear that those beliefs and actions were self-contradictory.

It took a series of events in the spring of 1775 to destroy Washington's hope that harmony could be restored without the loss of colonial rights. The first development was the rumor that Dunmore had disallowed the surveys that William Crawford had made on Washington's behalf in the Ohio country on the grounds that Crawford was not properly licensed as a Virginia surveyor. Astonished, Washington wrote to the governor on April 3 to ask if this "altogether incredible" information could possibly be accurate.[108] His Lordship's curt reply, dated April 18, did nothing to dispel his fears; on the contrary, Dunmore essentially confirmed the rumor.[109]

That the governor would casually invalidate years of effort and expense mystified Washington as much as it offended him. Was this a reprisal for his participation in the two Virginia conventions and the Continental Congress? An attempt to bully him into taking sides against his fellow planters? Or was it an effort to snatch away lands that he had already surveyed and on which he had begun to seat settlers, in order to bestow them on the governor's supporters? Washington had no way to know, but when word of a second incident arrived shortly after, he found it impossible to believe that the mercurial Scot was up to anything but mischief. Before dawn on April 21, Dunmore ordered a detachment of Royal Marines from an armed schooner, the *Magdalen,* to remove the entire stock of gunpowder, fifteen half-barrels, from the magazine at Williamsburg and carry it on board the province's station ship, HMS *Fowey.*[110]

The removal of the gunpowder would have alarmed Williamsburg's

white residents at any time. Now it raised the gravest possible anxieties, because it came at the end of a week during which rumors had flown up and
down the James River Valley that enslaved African Americans were planning an insurrection. Indeed, three slaves had already been arrested, tried,
and convicted of conspiracy. A crowd of Williamsburg whites gathered to
demand that Dunmore return the powder. Fearful that a riot might follow,
the town council tried to defuse the situation by meeting privately with the
governor and attempting to negotiate a settlement.

When the councilmen emerged, they urged the crowd to go home. The
governor, they said, had offered reassurances. He had removed the powder
only for safekeeping and would return it immediately if needed. The crowd
dispersed, the councilmen heaved sighs of relief, and quiet reigned once
more. Temporarily.

For the governor had in fact offered the councilmen more than reassurances; he had also made a threat so terrible that they had not dared to mention it in the hearing of the crowd. The next day, however, one of the
councilmen informed the Speaker of the House of Burgesses that Dunmore had said that if the Virginians were to harm any officer of the crown
in the performance of his duty, he "would declare freedom to the slaves and
reduce the City of Wmsburg to ashes."[111] The timing of the gunpowder's
removal now seemed truly sinister. The thought that the governor would
not only deprive whites of the means of defending themselves but contemplate mobilizing their slaves as a means of keeping himself in control was a
monstrosity beyond the worst nightmares of Virginia's gentry. In little more
time than it took for the news to spread from Williamsburg to the rest of the
province, Dunmore went from being the most popular governor Virginia
had ever seen to the most reviled and most feared.

Virginia's leaders—Washington among them—were still trying to
fathom precisely what this incident might mean and to decide upon a
course of action in response when news arrived that a column of British soldiers from Boston had fired on patriot militia at Lexington and Concord on
April 19. In the daylong battle that followed, seventy-three regulars and
forty-nine militiamen were killed; hundreds were wounded. News arriving
daily thereafter made it clear that thousands of militiamen from elsewhere
in New England had flooded into eastern Massachusetts on the days following the battle, trapping General Gage and his redcoats in the city.[112]
Boston was a city under siege.

Like a cymbal crash at the end of a symphonic crescendo, the news that
the king's troops had shed the blood of His Majesty's subjects in Massachu-

setts climaxed the almost intolerable tensions that had been building in Virginia. Ever since the First Continental Congress, patriot gentlemen in several counties had been creating independent militia companies, pledging, in the articles of association they signed, to defend their liberties with their lives. A half-dozen or so companies had formed by the spring of 1775, and most turned to Washington for advice on matters like training, arms, and uniforms.[113] The formation of these companies had been largely theatrical gestures, and Washington's participation, while real, was mainly ceremonial. With the gunpowder episode, however, independent companies formed in at least seven more counties. In the last days of April, several of the companies resolved to ride to Williamsburg and force the governor to return to the province's powder, still stowed aboard the *Fowey*. Dunmore replied that if any armed men approached the capital he would make a proclamation to free the slaves of the province. To make sure there was no mistaking his seriousness, he distributed weapons both to his household slaves and to several Shawnee chiefs who had been staying in Williamsburg as hostages until the peace treaty with the Ohio Indians could be concluded. It was a crisis grave enough to make many believe Virginia was on the brink of civil war. In the end, however, the Speaker of the House of Burgesses negotiated a settlement in which Dunmore gave his word that the powder would be returned. The volunteer companies that had begun to march on Williamsburg paused, reconsidered, and dispersed to their homes.[114]

With the passing of Virginia's crisis, Washington thought himself free to go to Philadelphia to help search for a solution to the much larger crisis in New England. Before he left Mount Vernon on May 4, he made sure that his trunk contained, among other clothes, the blue-and-buff uniform, cut to the specifications of the Fairfax Independent Company, that he had ordered when he agreed to lead it and the volunteer companies of Fauquier, Richmond, Spotsylvania, and Prince William counties, should they ever be required to take the field together. When he wore it to the sessions of the Continental Congress, he probably intended only to signify his solidarity with the patriot volunteers of Virginia. His fellow delegate John Adams, however, saw a larger opportunity in Washington's evident willingness to defend colonial rights by force of arms. Apart from their still-shared loyalty to the British crown and the growing conviction that a malignant faction in Parliament was bent on depriving them of their property and liberty, the colonists had little to unite them. Adams believed that appointing Virginia's most notable soldier to command the exclusively New England troops then in the field would build durable ties between colonies and regions that had never shown much in the way of mutual regard. Thus for Adams, who nominated him, and for the delegates who unanimously approved on June 15, 1775, appointing Washington commander in chief of the Continental Army (as the troops besieging Boston were henceforth known) was an essential step toward forging an effective military and political union. Without that cooperation, which would have to be sustained for God knew how long, the colonists had no hope of defending their rights against what the delegates called, as a sign of their continued loyalty to the king, the Ministerial Army. Washington understood as much; and even though, as he said, "I do not think my self equal to the Command I am honoured with," he accepted.[115]

The general, like the colonies he now served, had come a long way since 1754. Neither he nor the vast majority of his fellow colonists, however, were yet prepared to abandon the hope of reconciliation with the crown and hence the restoration of the empire. War had broken out in New England not because anyone had intended it but because both sides had concluded that the very soul of the British empire was at risk and that it was worth fighting to preserve. The colonists' willingness to take up arms to defend their vision of an empire bound together by voluntary allegiance and to protect what they understood to be Englishmen's rights was not, in that sense, radically different from the Indians' willingness in 1763 to use violence to teach the British a lesson about the proper relations between peoples who were supposed to be bound by ties of mutual respect, alliance, and trade, not by the threat of force and the expectation of submission.

This time, however, the king and his ministers could see no way to make concessions; to give any ground at all, they believed, would amount to renouncing sovereignty over the colonies. Through the previous episodes of crisis, the leaders of the resistance had mobilized ordinary colonists by publishing pamphlets and newspaper articles on the ideological issues at stake. Now it was not just lawyers and merchants and gentlemen but large numbers of artisans, farmers, shopkeepers, and laborers who had come to believe that to submit unconditionally to Parliament's sovereign power would be to exchange their liberties for enslavement. Because neither side would give ground once blood had been spilled, the result was not a mere rebellion but a full-blown British civil war.

No one in 1775 knew that revolutionary consequences would follow from the outbreak of war, any more than an observer in 1754 could have guessed that a skirmish in the woods of western Pennsylvania would precipitate a war fought around the world—much less the victory, reforms, and resistance that followed. Washington clearly did not anticipate a glorious end when, for the second time in his life, he accepted a military command for which he had not been trained and for which he was in no real sense qualified. To lead provincial troops and militiamen against the military might of the British empire was a task so daunting that his openly expressed belief that he was not equal to the command must be understood not as modesty but a plain statement of fact. It is therefore a measure of the man that George Washington accepted the challenge. His honor was at stake; and if the power he called Providence had preserved his life through campaigns and battles that had left hundreds dead and wounded in order to prepare him for some destiny still hidden from his view, he could not well decline.

CHAPTER FOUR

Washington's Mission: The Making
of an Imperial Republic

Despite his habitual future-orientation, Washington anticipated little of what lay ahead on Sunday, July 2, 1775, when he rode into Cambridge to take command of the New England troops who waited to be formed into a Continental Army. No drums beat battalions to order, no cannons boomed a salute: the welcoming ceremonies were canceled on account of rain. Besides, it was the Sabbath, and many of the officers and men billeted in the buildings at Harvard and in huts and tents on the adjacent common were attending afternoon services. The general previously in command at Cambridge, Artemas Ward, had to be summoned, along with his staff and subordinate commanders, to meet the new commander in chief at the house of the Reverend Samuel Langdon, the president of Harvard College. It was neither a ceremonious nor an auspicious occasion.[1]

Almost immediately it became apparent to Washington that the orders he now presented to the assembled generals were far from welcome. Congress had established an order of precedence in command for the Continental Army that had little to do with the system of seniority currently in force. Experienced officers had been passed over in favor of less-senior subordinates, and one lieutenant general of the Massachusetts forces had been demoted to the rank of brigadier. It seemed altogether likely that of the nine generals for whom Washington carried commissions, three would probably decline, and resentments among the others might well keep the various components of the army from functioning effectively together. Washington calmly took the matter under advisement and asked to be shown the fortifications and the British lines.[2]

George Washington in his uniform as major general and
commander in chief of the Continental Army, c. 1782.
Detail of a portrait by Charles Willson Peale.

What he saw was no more encouraging than his initial meeting with the
generals had been. The troops had dug extensive entrenchments, but the re-
doubts that should have created strongpoints along the lines were poorly
sited and far from robust in construction. There seemed to be too few men
to man the defenses adequately, tents were scarce, and no one could tell him
precisely what the state of the army's supplies was at the moment. By sunset Washington knew that weeks of work and training would be necessary
before his army would be in a state to defend itself adequately; how much
longer it would take before it could actually expel the British from their
own expertly sited fortifications in Boston and Charlestown was anyone's guess. That evening he took over General Ward's orderly book
and composed his first general orders for the army, to be issued the next
morning.

On Monday the third, twenty-one years to the day after the Battle of
Fort Necessity, George Washington rose to clear skies and warming
weather, and got to work.[3]

The Revolutionary Origins of a Republican Empire

Washington had been told to expect an army of 20,000 sturdy New England yeomen, ready to lay down their lives for their liberties. When he assumed command he already suspected that the New England forces were a good deal less numerous. Soon he learned that despite the enthusiasm for gunning down redcoats that they had shown over the past fifteen weeks, the New England troops were far from satisfactory as soldiers. Washington had no doubt that he could improve them, but he knew that to do it would be a long process. He had accomplished remarkable things with the singularly unpromising raw material of the Virginia Regiment; now he would have to apply the lessons he had learned in the last war to the needs of the present.

After the British troops in Boston, the biggest problem Washington confronted was that the 14,000 or so New Englanders under his command thought they knew what they were doing. Unlike the inhabitants of the Virginia and Pennsylvania backcountry, who were spared French and Indian attacks from the 1680s through the mid-1750s, New England's colonists had nearly a century of experience in fighting New France and its native allies. The exposure of frontier settlements to attack in the four colonial wars had led the provinces of Massachusetts, Connecticut, Rhode Island, and New Hampshire to devise a system of military recruitment capable of mobilizing thousands of volunteers annually. These provincial soldiers could be used to garrison forts on the frontiers or to act as rangers trained in "the skulking way of war," but the basic intention of the system was to create expeditionary forces large enough to strike at the root of New England's problem, Canada.

Provincials were not the same as militiamen. The militia was a compulsory institution comprised of virtually all men between the ages of sixteen and sixty that served several purposes: to promote a rudimentary familiarity with arms, provide a manpower pool from which men could be conscripted for temporary service, and act as a home guard. Provincial regiments, on the other hand, were composed of young, primarily unmarried men who volunteered to serve enlistment terms of nine months to a year in duration. Because experienced junior officers and sergeants were generally in short supply, especially at the beginnings of wars, provincial forces were notoriously expensive, inefficient, undisciplined, and ill-trained. Under some conditions they performed surprisingly well. In King George's War, for example, a expeditionary force of Yankee provincials captured the great maritime fortress of Louisbourg, and provincial ranger companies operating in Nova Scotia proved effective in fighting Indians. Usually, however, provincial battalions became proficient only toward the ends of campaigns, when their soldiers were a just few weeks from discharge. Moreover, provincial soldiers served under comparatively explicit enlistment contracts and felt remarkably free to stage mutinies or even to desert en masse if they became convinced that the terms of these agreements had been violated.

Tens of thousands of young Yankees had served as provincials in the Seven Years' War, mostly as laborers and garrison troops in support of the redcoats who did the bulk of the fighting. Inglorious as it was, provincial military service was so widespread that it touched virtually every family in the region. Veterans of the Seven Years' War led the minuteman formations and militia companies that responded to the Lexington alarm; the most experienced officers and sergeants in the army that Washington took over in July had been provincials during the previous war. These men represented the culmination of nearly a century of development in the only martial culture that British North America had produced. In a very real sense, the existence of this populist military tradition had made New England the one region capable of mounting massive armed resistance to Britain in 1775. There had been no debate in the various provinces about how to organize the forces that besieged Boston in the spring of 1775; the decision to reinstitute the provincial model of the previous wars and raise volunteers for a single campaign was instinctive and immediate.

Yet the Yankees were not good soldiers in any sense that Washington could understand. New England's provincials amounted to little more than civilians temporarily under arms, in that sense differing only in degree, not in kind, from militia. From the Battle of Lexington and Concord through the Battle of Bunker Hill they had proved themselves proficient at shooting redcoats from cover and defending entrenched positions against frontal assaults. Washington knew, however, that if he wanted an army that could stand up to British regulars in open-field battle, endure the dreadful privations of a siege, or even hold together for more than a year or two, he had to transform the raw material at hand—farm boys and apprentices and free blacks and laborers—into proficient, tough, obedient soldiers. This in turn required the proper tools, and those (as he explained, again and again, to Congress) consisted of enlistments that ran longer than a year, authority to impose the severe floggings and capital punishments that eighteenth-century armies relied upon to maintain discipline, and pay high enough to secure a cadre of officers who were, in fact, gentlemen.

Washington was especially concerned about the social standing of his officers because the New England custom was to "raise for rank": that is, the number of men a would-be officer enlisted determined whether he would serve as an ensign or lieutenant or captain. As a result, the authority of New England officers rested more on personal popularity than the expansive views on honor and virtue that Washington believed gentlemen possessed. If an officer was to serve for more than one campaign, he would have to reenlist soldiers from his unit; and that could be done only by ingratiating himself with his men, just as a would-be politician had to ingratiate himself with the electors. The eighteenth-century term for this was "to make interest" with the men, and so far as Washington was concerned, to do so destroyed discipline willy-nilly. The nub of the problem, he wrote, was that

> It takes you two or three Months to bring New men to any tolerable degree acquainted with their duty—it take a longer time to bring a People of the temper, and genius of these [New Englanders] into such a subordinate way of thinking as is necessary for a soldier— Before this is accomplished, the time approaches for their dismission, and your beginning to make Interest for their continuance for another limitted period; in the doing of which you are oblig'd to relax your discipline, in order as it were to curry favour with them, by which means the latter part of your time is employed in undoing what the first was accomplishing and instead of having Men always ready to take advantage of Circumstances, you must govern your Movements by the circumstances of your Inlistment.[4]

Washington wrote those bitter words in the winter of 1776 after he had watched thousands of his men march for home (whole battalions did so without waiting for the formality of their discharges) when their enlistments expired. Even as he wrote he was calling for temporary militia levies to patch the holes the departing provincials left in the lines around Boston and appealing for replacements to serve in the coming campaign. He knew that if he hoped to defeat the British he would have to overcome the military culture of New England itself, replacing the localized loyalties and the dangerous contractualism of the Yankee provincials with the sterner stuff of military professionalism, promoting loyalty to Congress and devotion to the

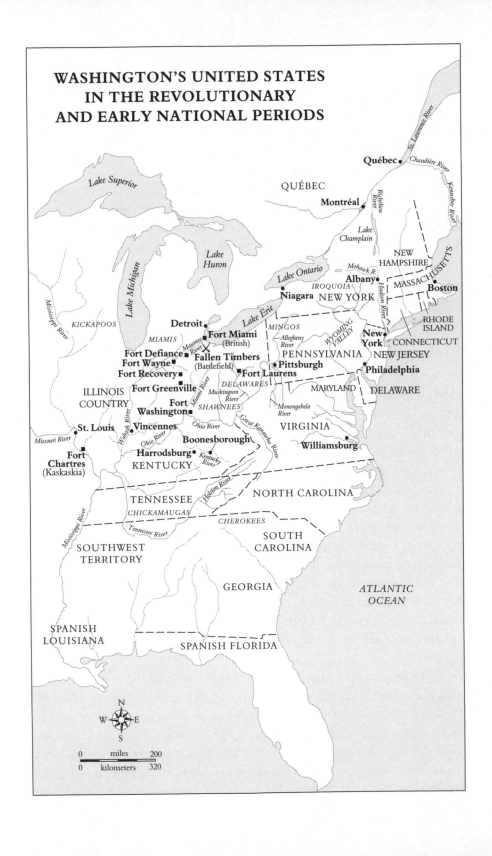

WASHINGTON'S UNITED STATES IN THE REVOLUTIONARY AND EARLY NATIONAL PERIODS

Lake Superior

QUÉBEC

Québec *Chaudière River*

Montréal

Richelieu River

Kennebec River

Lake Champlain

Lake Huron

Lake Michigan

NEW HAMPSHIRE

MASSACHUSETTS

St. Laurence River

Mississippi River

KICKAPOOS

Lake Ontario

Mohawk R.

Albany

IROQUOIA

NEW YORK

Hudson River

Boston

RHODE ISLAND

Detroit

Fort Miami (British)

MIAMIS

Maumee River

Fallen Timbers (Battlefield)

Fort Defiance

Fort Wayne

Fort Recovery

MINGOS

Allegheny River

Niagara

Lake Erie

WYOMING VALLEY

New York

CONNECTICUT

PENNSYLVANIA

NEW JERSEY

Pittsburgh

Fort Laurens

Philadelphia

DELAWARE

Fort Greenville

Miami River

DELAWARES

Muskingum River

SHAWNEES

MARYLAND

ILLINOIS COUNTRY

Fort Washington

Monongahela River

St. Louis

Wabash River

Vincennes

Ohio River

Great Kanawha River

VIRGINIA

Missouri River

Fort Chartres (Kaskaskia)

Boonesborough

Williamsburg

Harrodsburg

Kentucky River

KENTUCKY

Hudson River

NORTH CAROLINA

TENNESSEE

CHICKAMAUGAS

Mississippi River

Tennessee River

CHEROKEES

SOUTH CAROLINA

SOUTHWEST TERRITORY

GEORGIA

ATLANTIC OCEAN

SPANISH LOUISIANA

SPANISH FLORIDA

N
W E
S

```
0       miles       200
0     kilometers     320
```

"defence of the Liberties of America . . . the great and common cause in which we are all engaged."[5]

Over the previous six months, the new commander in chief had confronted issues that reappeared in one form or another throughout the war and, indeed, well beyond it as the young and fragile republic took shape. In trying to turn New England's independent-minded militiamen and provincial soldiers into an army capable of winning independence, Washington had to negotiate previously uncharted relationships between democracy and order, between national and local authority. His experience of command in the Seven Years' War had convinced him that without rigorous discipline he could never create an effective army and hence would have no hope of success against the British. At the same time, he appreciated fully that the whole justification for resisting British power by force of arms rested on the radically uncoercive idea that the only legitimate power flowed from the consent of the governed.

Throughout the war, therefore, Washington did his best to wring what concessions he could from a Congress that feared the tyrannical potential of a long-service professional army even as he sought to instill in his troops both his own sense of mission and the habits of subordination and obedience he admired in the redcoats alongside whom he had served two decades earlier. As he had on the Virginia frontier in 1756 and 1757, he tried to preserve the army, refusing to risk it unnecessarily, husbanding its strength, and as far as possible keeping it together against the day he could use it to some significant purpose. Then the hope of eliminating the enemy at Fort Duquesne had led him to keep as much as possible of the Virginia Regiment together at Forts Loudoun and Cumberland; that in turn had forced him, however reluctantly, to rely on the militia, despite its shortcomings, to defend the frontier. From 1775 through 1783 he similarly clung to the faith that as commander in chief his first responsibility was to preserve the Continental Army, even if to do so required him to use undisciplined, expensive, and unreliable militiamen in a far wider variety of roles than he would have preferred.

This was necessary in part because he intended one day to strike a powerful blow against the enemy, as he finally did at Yorktown in 1781; but Washington also understood another, more pressing reason to protect his forces. Congress, perhaps without being fully aware of the implications, had taken its first truly revolutionary step when it created the Continental Army as a *national* weapon to defend the colonists' liberties. A full year before Independence, the army represented an American union that had never before existed, that as yet had no flag, no constitution, no name. The army in that sense embodied the Revolution itself. It might be defeated many times, but as long as it continued to exist as a focus of hope for some ultimate victory, the "great and common cause" was not lost.[6]

This Fabian strategy, driven by what would today be called the need for "force protection," was more an improvisation compelled by military weakness than a product of systematic thought. Even so, Washington employed it with something like genius.[7] The creativity and resourcefulness with which he used the militia to complement the army makes this especially clear. Recognizing that militiamen would never have sufficient training and discipline to stand up against the redcoats and their Hessian auxiliaries in a formal battle, he employed them as irregulars to attack enemy outposts, harass foraging parties, and deny the British control of the countryside.[8] Doing so did not mean that he ceased to complain of the militia's indiscipline, expense, and willingness to come and go according to its own variable, localized, unpredictable needs. Yet with the possible exception of the former Quaker, General Nathanael Greene, who emerged in the last years of the war as a master of guerrilla tactics and strategic retreat, Washington understood better than any other Revolutionary leader that the army and the militia were complementary means to manage violence in pursuit of larger political ends.

Preeminent among those objectives were to defend American liberty and (from mid-1776 onward) compel Britain to recognize the independence of the United States. Washington's Fabian strategies and the Continental Army's defensive campaigns against the British main force were well suited to attaining both goals. In part this was because they invited British generals to wear their forces out in pursuit of an elusive adversary while British public opinion turned against the war and the will to continue fighting eventually eroded at Westminster and Whitehall. As important, the determination of Britain's military and political leaders to resolve the dispute by military means effectively doomed them to frustration and failure. Wherever the British armed forces went, they could—and did—bring overwhelming force to bear. Yet this policy ultimately contradicted the larger need to regain the allegiance of roughly 3 million American colonists, to win their hearts and minds. As Nathanael Greene already understood at Valley Forge in the winter of 1778, Britain's efforts to coerce civilian populations only alienated them; everywhere the redcoats went, they made enemies for the crown. "The limits of the British government in America," Greene wrote, "are their out-sentinels."[9]

By the time he became commander in chief of the British forces in America in the spring of 1778, General Sir Henry Clinton recognized the limited utility of this approach. He therefore devised a strategy by which he would use his British and Hessian regular regiments to defeat the rebel forces that held Georgia and South Carolina, then employ the army's Loyalist auxiliaries as pacification forces with a goal of reestablishing civilian government in the conquered colonies. Succeeding for a time, he ultimately failed to reckon with the determination of the armed Loyalists to settle old scores. In the end the brutality of Loyalist militiamen antagonized would-be neutrals and even moderate Tories, triggering the vicious partisan civil war that made the Carolinas a kind of hell in 1780–81. Once Nathanael Greene's brilliant campaign of harassment and retreat induced Clinton's regional commander, General Charles Cornwallis, to move his main force northward to seek victory in Virginia in May 1781, Britain no longer had sufficient forces in the Carolinas to prevent partisan forces from operating openly in the countryside. Redcoat and Loyalist garrisons eventually found themselves compelled to withdraw from their outposts; when they did, patriot militias and Continental units moved in to reclaim local control in the name of Congress.[10]

The Continentals, by contrast, never experienced insuperable problems in civil-military relations. In part this was simply because they lacked the redcoats' coercive capacities. Mostly, however, it was because Washington understood that even a half-clothed, malnourished army that did not oppress civilians was preferable to a well-provisioned army that confiscated its food and clothing at gunpoint. As a result, the impressment of supplies, wagons, and draft animals was sparingly practiced among the Americans, typically occurring only as a last resort. The army suffered so that it might remain acceptable to the society it tried to defend.

There was another face to the Revolutionary struggle, too, one less appreciated and less easily integrated into the familiar campaign-by-campaign narrative that focuses on Washington's headquarters and the major battles. This aspect of the conflict arose from the Americans' concern for the stability of their exposed frontiers: a natural worry, in view of the refugee crises that the French and their Indian allies had so often brought on by raiding exposed backcountry settlements in the colonial wars. Congress, fearing that the British and Loyalists would pick up where the French had left off as allies and organizers of the Indians, approved two initiatives in 1775 to forestall the collapse of the frontiers. Their first was aimed at securing Indian neutrality by making diplomatic overtures to reassure the various groups that the present dispute was an English "family quarrel" that in no way involved or threatened them. This overture was persuasive—initially—to groups, such as the Iroquois and the Creeks, that had suffered least in the recent past at the hands of settlers and speculators; it appealed not at all, however, to Indians who had lately been defrauded by speculators or battered by white settler incursions. Most of the Shawnees and Mingos on the Ohio, indeed, saw in the beginning of the Anglo-American war an opportunity to clear white settlers out of Kentucky and launched raids to recoup the losses they had suffered in the Virginia invasion of 1774, by then known as Lord Dunmore's War.[11]

The second initiative aimed at keeping the borderlands quiet was a two-pronged American invasion of Canada, launched in August and September 1775 from Lake Champlain and Maine's Kennebec Valley. On its face, this gambit was a resounding failure. Despite a heroic, audacious assault in a blizzard on the night of December 31–January 1, Benedict Arnold's tiny, over-taxed force failed to seize Quebec. Six months later, Continentals who had successfully occupied the Montreal district were compelled to abandon it in the face of smallpox and a powerful British counteroffensive. Yet the Canadian expedition signified more than defeat. Congress's thinking about the invasion, like its diplomatic efforts to keep the Indians neutral, reflected the quite reasonable assumption that the British now occupied the same strategic position as the French had during the colonial wars. Diplomacy was obviously worth trying to keep the Indians from tipping the balance in Britain's favor, but leaders in Congress did not trust diplomacy because at bottom they doubted that Indians would keep their promises unless agreements could be sealed with plentiful diplomatic gifts. The British manifestly held the advantage in money, trade goods, and arms, so to prevent them from arming bands of warriors and unleashing them against the northern backcountry, the safest course was to seize control of Canada. The surest way to secure American frontiers, in other words, was to expand them.

Such a strategic solution came naturally to men who were creatures of Britain's empire, whose views and perspectives had been shaped in the Seven Years' War. In that sense it is unsurprising that even in the midst of a rebellion against one empire, the Revolutionaries also acted as creators of another. Nor was there anything unpredictable in the ferocity with which they eventually lashed out at those Indians who cast their lot with the British. The most emotionally potent legacy of the Seven Years' War and Pontiac's War had been the indiscriminate hatred of Indians. In the heat of a desperate revolutionary struggle, American patriots showed little inclination

to practice restraint or even distinguish potentially friendly or neutral Indians from those who were hostile.

After the Shawnees and Mingos on the Ohio, the Cherokees were the
first to raise the hatchet against the American rebels. In May 1776, frustrated
by the lack of response on the part of the southern colonies to their complaints of settlers encroaching on their lands in what is now eastern Tennessee, the Cherokees accepted a Shawnee invitation to join them on the
warpath, secured ammunition and arms from the British, and raided frontier settlements from Virginia to Georgia. Virginia and the two Carolinas
struck back with more than 4,500 troops, devastating the Cherokee homeland. Between August and October, in loosely coordinated campaigns,
troops from the three states concentrated less on engaging warriors than on
destroying villages, burning crops in the field, and killing whatever Indians—
typically women, children, and the elderly—they could catch.

To embrace total war in this way was not new, for it merely applied on a
larger scale practices employed by colonial militias and provincial forces
since the early seventeenth century. Nor were such ferocious tactics alien to
eighteenth-century professional armies; British regulars had practiced
something like total war against Canadian civilians in the Saint Lawrence
Valley during the summer of 1759 and against Acadians, Mi'kmaqs, and
Cherokees between 1755 and 1761.[12] What set the American assaults on the
Cherokees in 1776 apart from these colonial precedents was their intent.
The goal that Virginia and the Carolinas pursued was not merely to punish
the Indians or force them to make peace but to drive them back into the interior, well beyond those regions that white settlers coveted. In the peace
conferences in 1777 at DeWitt's Corner and the Long Island of the Holston,
American negotiators demanded the cession of territory as far west as the
Tennessee River, effectively depriving the Cherokees of most of the lands
they previously occupied in the Carolinas and their hunting grounds in the
eastern third of Tennessee.[13]

In essence, the American patriots were learning to practice what we now
call ethnic cleansing, a way of making war that (then, as now) built a sense
of political and ethnic solidarity within the group that perpetrated it. Frontier whites of various groups—English, German, Scots, Scotch-Irish, and
others—who had previously differed on issues of loyalty versus resistance,
even to the point of violence, now found common ground in their shared
hatred of Indians and the British agents who stirred them up. No proof of
British malevolence could have been more convincing than the gift of thirty
packhorseloads of gunpowder and bar lead (for bullets) that Britain's

Southern Commissioner of Indian Affairs, John Stuart, made to induce the Cherokees to attack "defenceless frontier settlers." Dr. David Ramsay, the great eighteenth-century historian of Revolutionary South Carolina, believed that the present

> increased the unanimity of the inhabitants, and invigorated their opposition to Great-Britain. Several who called themselves tories in 1775 became active whigs in 1776 and cheerfully took arms in the first instance against Indians, and the second against Great-Britain as the instigator of their barbarous devastations. Before this event some well-meaning people could not see the justice or propriety of contending with their formerly protecting parent-state; but Indian cruelties, excited by royal artifices, soon extinguished all their predilection for the country of their forefathers.[14]

Beyond loss of sympathy for the crown and the extortion of very lucrative territorial cessions in the treaties of DeWitt's Corner and Long Island, two other important results emerged from the Cherokee War of 1776. First, it put an end to Cherokee opposition. Except for the Chickamaugas—a Cherokee faction that rejected the treaties, retreated to the great westward bend of the Tennessee, and raided the southern backcountry for another decade—the majority of Cherokees accepted defeat, sought to keep a safe distance from whites, and adopted the less violent forms of resistance that culminated in the Cherokee renaissance of the early nineteenth century.[15] Second, the destruction of Cherokee power intimidated other potentially hostile native groups in the South. Only when redcoat forces invaded Georgia in 1778 did the Creeks, Choctaws, and Chickasaws respond to British overtures and join the Chickamaugas in raiding the southwestern frontier.

For the time being, then, apart from Shawnee and Mingo raids against the settlements that Virginians had established in central Kentucky after Lord Dunmore's War—Harrodsburg, Saint Asaph's, and Boonesborough— the West remained quiet. The Ohio Delawares, under the influence of the moderate chief George White Eyes (Koguetagechton), did their best to follow the old play-off strategies of neutrality, though they found it increasingly hard to do so. Indian-hating frontiersmen from the western settlements of Pennsylvania were prepared to slaughter any native person they could find. They mounted an expedition in the fall of 1777 that killed several Delaware women in undefended villages; militiamen murdered the pro-American Shawnee chief Cornstalk and his son in early 1778 while they were on a diplomatic mission; a Pittsburgh mob attacked a party of Seneca diplomats at about the same time.[16] By late summer 1778 it was clear to White Eyes and his fellow chiefs that the Delawares would have to join one side or the other. Hoping that the Americans could control their settlers, they joined representatives of Congress in signing the Treaty of Pittsburgh in September.

The treaty allowed the Continental Army to build Fort Laurens, a hundred miles west of the Forks of the Ohio on the Tuscarawas River, deep in Delaware territory. The Americans' announced intent was to use this as a jumping-off point for an attack on Detroit, where the British Indian agent Henry ("Hair-buyer") Hamilton was said to be organizing western Indians for a campaign against western Pennsylvania; but in fact the fort would serve equally well as a means of dominating the Delaware heartland. When White Eyes died late in the fall of 1778 at the hand of a Virginia gunman, the tenuous alliance between the United States and the Delawares began to fall apart. Disaffected Delaware warriors attacked Fort Laurens and joined other Ohio Indians in raids against backcountry outposts; frontiersmen continued to murder Indians indiscriminately. In the summer of 1779, relations deteriorated to the point that Fort Laurens could no longer be resupplied or reinforced, and had to be abandoned.[17] By the beginning of 1780, virtually all the Indians in the eastern half of the Ohio Valley north of the river had taken up the hatchet as British allies. From then until late 1782, the region was the scene of raids and counterraids that produced some of the most brutal massacres of the Revolutionary War.

While the uncontrollable violence of Indian-hating frontiersmen destroyed the Continental Congress's attempt to gain control over the territory north of the Ohio, the new state government of Virginia pursued imperial designs with all the enthusiasm of its colonial predecessor. The Virginians' attentions focused south of the river in an attempt to extend control over lands as far as the Mississippi, in the heart of the old *pays des Illinois*. In the summer of 1777 the militia commander at Harrodsburg, George Rogers Clark, learned that the British had withdrawn their garrison from Kaskaskia, just down the Mississippi from Saint Louis. Clark, who had commanded a company in Lord Dunmore's War and settled in Kentucky shortly thereafter, conceived the idea of leading an expedition down the Ohio to induce the *habitants* of Illinois to join the American cause. That fall he made the perilous trip from Kentucky to Williamsburg to ask Governor Patrick Henry and the Virginia Council for authority to execute the plan.

Although Clark himself was an inveterate Indian-hater, the case he made turned on Indian diplomacy. "The remote situation of this town [Kaskaskia] on the back of several of the Western Nations," he observed, enables the British

> to furnish the different nations [with arms and supplies], and by presents [they] will keep up a strict friendship with the Indians; and undoubtedly will keep all the nations that lay under their influence at war with us during the present contest. . . . On the contrary, if it [Kaskaskia] was in our possession it would distress the garrison at Detroit for provisions, it would fling the command of the two great rivers [Mississippi and Ohio] into our hands, which would enable us to get supplies of goods from the Spaniards, and to carry on a trade with the Indians. . . .[18]

This geopolitical analysis made sense to Governor Henry and his supporters on the Council, one of whom was Thomas Jefferson. They believed (erroneously, as it happened) that the British at Detroit were the main cause of Kentucky's sufferings, and Clark's plan seemed to offer a means of stabilizing that region. More important, his success would confirm by right of conquest Virginia's ancient charter claims to the remote interior of North America. Their enthusiasm for his enterprise, indeed, suggests that Virginia's leaders' perspectives on the West had not altered appreciably since the time Lord Dunmore had made himself "as popular as a Scotsman [could] be" by attacking the Shawnees. Clark returned to Kentucky carrying a commission as a lieutenant colonel and orders to raise seven companies to defend Kentucky. He also carried secret orders to seize Kaskaskia and, if possible, Detroit.

The would-be conqueror of Illinois found it no easier to persuade the localist frontiersmen of western Pennsylvania, Virginia, and Kentucky to leave their private forts in 1778 than Washington had in the Shenandoah in 1756. In the end he recruited only about 175 men, a tiny but tough force that seized Kaskaskia on July 5 without firing a shot. The following month, the *habitants* of Vincennes, 180 miles to the east, voluntarily embraced Virginia's sovereignty, and Clark sent a detachment to man their fort. The Virginians held it only until the fall, when Lieutenant Colonel Henry Hamilton arrived from Detroit with a motley crew of Indians, French, and British troops, and captured the town. Clark responded by putting himself

at the head of 125 *habitants* and American volunteers and leading them overland to Vincennes on one of the most grueling winter marches in American
history. In February he surprised the fort, captured the Hair-buyer and his
men, and sent them back to Virginia as prisoners.[19]

Clark never took Detroit, nor did he realize that the raids he undertook
against the Shawnees in 1780 only drove the Indian groups on the upper
Ohio into ever-closer cooperation with the British. He did, however, retain
control of the Illinois country until the end of the war, securing with it Virginia's claim to the Far West. That he could do this had much less to do with
his own audacity than that the French and the region's Indians—
Piankashaws, Miamis, Kickapoos, Potawatomis, Illinois, and others—found
the Virginians useful in their attempts to reconstruct the familiar middle-
ground cultural landscape of the old French regime.[20]

Even as Clark formulated his plans for extending Virginia's dominion to
the Mississippi, some of the worst violence of the war convulsed the New
York frontier. Fighting there had broken out in 1777 when the flamboyant
British general John Burgoyne invaded by Lake Champlain and Lake
George in the company of warriors from three of the Six Nations of the Iroquois.[21] The presence of Mohawk, Cayuga, and Seneca warriors galvanized
thousands of New York and New England militiamen into joining with
General Horatio Gates's Continentals to defeat and capture the invaders at
the battles of Saratoga in October. The American victory, however, only encouraged warriors associated with the great Mohawk war chief Joseph Brant
to join several hundred Loyalist partisans in a devastating guerrilla campaign
against frontier settlements in northern Pennsylvania and central New York.

In the summer and fall of 1778, Brant's men cooperated with Loyalist
rangers to wipe out backwoods communities in the Wyoming Valley on the
Susquehanna and to attack German Flats and Cherry Valley along the Mohawk. In all they killed about 350 men, women, and children, then continued to terrorize smaller settlements in the region. By the middle of 1779
they had added at least a hundred more casualties to the toll.[22] In an attempt
to stem the raiding, Washington ordered General John Sullivan to march up
the Susquehanna Valley from Pennsylvania with 2,300 Continentals, rendezvous with a second Continental force of 1,400 men at the New York
border, and proceed north to the Finger Lakes district. There, in the heart of
Iroquoia, they were to pursue "the total distruction and devastation of their
settlements and the capture of as many prisoners of every age and sex as possible." Washington intended "that the country may not be merely *overrun*
but *destroyed*" in order to force the Iroquois to abandon the British and sue

for peace.[23] The prisoners were to be held as hostages to insure the future good behavior of Brant and his warriors. "Hostages," Washington observed, "are the only kind of security to be depended on" to ensure that Indians would negotiate in good faith.[24]

From August through September, Sullivan's Continentals rampaged through the homeland of the Iroquois, destroying no fewer than forty towns, "besides scattering houses." Several of these communities had more than a hundred sturdy log and frame dwellings, barns, mills, churches, and other structures built in the English style. "The quantity of Corn destroyed," Sullivan told Congress in October, "must amount to 160,000 bushels, with a vast quantity of vegetables of every kind. . . . Except [for] one Town . . . about 80 miles from Genessee, there is not a single Town left in the Country."[25] Sullivan reported only one minor engagement with the Loyalists and Brant's warriors, at Newtown (near modern Elmira) toward the end of August, in which a dozen or so of the enemy were killed and the Continentals suffered about forty casualties.

No prisoners were taken in that encounter or indeed at any other point in the campaign. Contrary to Washington's orders, those Indians who could not escape the American onslaught—mostly women, children, the elderly, and the infirm—were put to the sword and often scalped and mutilated. Sullivan and his men made no distinctions among the various kinds of Indians who inhabited the region. Towns that had been occupied by the pro-British Senecas and Cayugas and those of the neutralist Onondagas alike were laid in ashes, their crops destroyed, their orchards cut down. While this was going on, a second, smaller expedition of 600 or so Continentals and militiamen under Colonel Daniel Brodhead, operating out of Pittsburgh, moved up the Allegheny, burning Mingo and Delaware settlements with indiscriminate zeal. Brodhead's men destroyed another dozen towns, hundreds of houses, and perhaps 500 acres of cornfields. When they withdrew in early September, 200 miles of Seneca land in the Allegheny Valley was as much a smoking ruin as the upper Susquehanna drainage and the Finger Lakes district.[26]

For all the devastation they visited on the Six Nations, these incursions accomplished only half of what Congress had intended. They did effectively empty the region of Indians, who fled as refugees to the British stronghold at Niagara and did not return (hundreds starved there in the terrible winter of 1779–80). But Sullivan and Brodhead never pressed on to attack Niagara and thus could not compel the Iroquois to make peace, as the Cherokee had, with comparably vast cessions of land. Brant and his warriors refused to negotiate; instead, they raided the New York frontier with redoubled fury. In the coming two years Indians and Loyalist irregulars turned the Mohawk Valley into a charnel house.

Though Sullivan's and Brodhead's expeditions proved counterproductive, however, we should not lose sight of what Congress had *intended* to achieve: the expansion of control and hence the imposition of order by military means on a dangerous frontier. It was the same goal as that of the invasion of Quebec at the war's outset, but by 1779 it had acquired another, highly significant implication. In 1775, before Independence was declared, the Canadian expedition had been an essentially defensive strategy that had nothing to do with the forced removal of native populations. In 1779, however, the act of driving the hostile Iroquois from upstate New York enabled the United States to claim everything from the upper Mohawk Valley to Lake Ontario, Lake Erie, and the Allegheny drainage—since time out of mind the undisputed domain of the Iroquois—by right of conquest. That the Sullivan campaign happened in the same year as Clark's expedition to Illinois was probably adventitious, but the similarity in their goal of securing a claim to western lands was anything but coincidental. In both instances the political leaders who authorized the expeditions were thinking about would happen when Great Britain was finally brought to negotiate a peace. The Revolutionaries' intention was that the postwar United States would not merely be independent but would command the great waterways of the Mohawk, the Great Lakes, the Ohio, and the Mississippi, and thus control as much as possible of the continent's interior. In a truly revolutionary moment, Americans had abandoned the long-standing pattern of working through alliances, such as the Covenant Chain, to achieve expansionist ends, in favor of the simpler alternative of conquest.

Washington was surely aware of this shift in the character of imperialism, but his ability to concern himself with the shape of postwar North America remained limited while hostilities continued in 1780, 1781, and 1782. Only in 1783, while awaiting the news that the Peace of Paris had finally been signed, did he begin to reassume his old habit of looking into the future by means of looking at land. From mid-July through mid-August he escaped the boredom of his headquarters at Newburgh by making a 700-mile tour of the New York frontier, traveling north as far as Crown Point on Lake Champlain, then retracing his steps to the Mohawk, which he followed west to the portage at Wood Creek, then pressed on to Lake Oneida. Returning by way of the headwaters of the Susquehanna at Lake Otsego, he lingered to inspect the portage to the Mohawk River before making his way back to Newburgh.[27] Much of what he saw was territory devastated by Sullivan's expedition and Brant's raids, but the ravages of war impressed him less than the bright promise of the region and its waters. As he described it to a French correspondent, the chevalier de Chastellux,

> I could not help taking a more contemplative and extensive view of the vast inland navigation of these United States . . . ; and could not but be struck with the immense diffusion and importance of it; and with the goodness of that Providence which has dealt her favors to us with so profuse a hand. Would to God we may have wisdom enough to improve them. I shall not rest contented 'till I have explored the Western Country, and traversed those lines (or a great part of them) which have given bounds to a New Empire.[28]

Washington ended his tour of central New York by going into partnership with the governor of the state to buy six thousand "amazingly cheap" acres at Oriskany on the portage between the Mohawk and Wood Creek, a place sure to benefit, like the Great Meadows in Pennsylvania, from the growth in transportation links that he foresaw.[29]

Washington's resumption of his career as a land speculator marked the beginning of his transition to civilian life and his ability to act as a normal, "interested" private citizen. For eight years he had conscientiously avoided any behavior that could be construed as other than disinterested or virtuous. He established this pattern quite self-consciously in 1775 by refusing to accept any salary for serving as commander in chief, asking only that Congress reimburse him for his expenses. This gesture reflected his private conviction that virtue required the willing sacrifice of one's self-interest for the common good, and it had a public and practical purpose as well. When Washington accepted the command of an army dedicated to the defense of republican values, he knew full well that his ideologically astute contemporaries would scrutinize his every act for hints that he was following the path of Oliver Cromwell or Julius Caesar, republican generals who went on to become dictators. Any hint of self-aggrandizement, any whiff of cupidity, would lay him open to the censure of his contemporaries, and (more important in his mind) the condemnation of future generations. He therefore took as his models the Roman heroes Cato and Cincinnatus: the former, Caesar's antagonist and exemplar of classical virtue; the latter, a charismatic military leader who left his plow to command the republic's armies, then returned to his farm after defeating its enemies. As the war progressed, the distinction between the private man and the public role dissolved. Washington personified Cato; he became Cincinnatus.[30]

Every war needs heroes. This one, because its justification rested so explicitly on the defense of liberty, required heroes of an unusual sort, men who qualified not only on the familiar grounds of self-sacrifice and courage but also because they understood republicanism and embraced its ideals. Washington and the officers close to him—Greene, Henry Knox, Alexander Hamilton, and others—were indeed republicans by conviction. Yet they were never—indeed, could not have been—ideologues. Their views on military policy in particular had less to do with republican ideological prescriptions than with the practical experience of fighting a long, grueling war. In this they differed from many delegates to Congress who experienced the conflict at second hand and worried about the threat republican political writers so strongly identified with standing armies. Civilian leaders, oblivious of the localist shortcomings that were apparent to Washington and his subordinates, saw the militia as the instrument best suited to defending a free society. They preferred to imagine that the militia was what republican writers said it should be: a body of armed citizens motivated by love of liberty and the desire to defend their rights and property. As a result, Congress remained suspicious of its own army throughout the war, supporting it only to a degree the delegates deemed safe, which was to say, a level that often was barely adequate to keep the ragged, unpaid Continental soldiers from starvation.[31]

Paradoxically, Congress's suspicions and parsimony helped create a powerful sense of community within the army, nourishing a sense among officers and soldiers that they were the suffering servants of the Revolution, the true custodians of virtue. As their fellow Americans shirked their duty and pursued their self-interest, Washington's steadfast deference to Congressional authority and refusal to accept a salary provided a focus for the army's growing sense that it was something like the saving remnant in Zion. The longer the war went on, the more the Continentals tended to see themselves as a band of brothers, separated from other Americans who did not share their sufferings, more strongly bound to each other than to their own former neighbors. In this way the Continental Army became not only a symbol of the United States but the nursery of American nationalism.[32]

For this reason, too, Washington's role as commander in chief grew more important as the war dragged on from year to weary year. The man who at the end of his life was called the Father of his Country, a title previously associated only with monarchs, began that long process by becoming a father figure to thousands of Continental soldiers. They understood perfectly well that he was a strict disciplinarian who required obedience, even unto death; but they also knew him as a man who shared their sufferings, fostered their welfare, and defended their honor as his own. And they knew, most of all, that he did it in service not of a prince but of the principles they all shared.

Washington's refusal to countenance any attempt to undermine civil authority took on special significance in the context of his preeminence as both symbol of the army and its commander in chief. In March 1783, a faction of officers at the Newburgh winter encampment issued a pair of anonymous statements that hinted they might use the army to force Congress to grant officers half pay for life in compensation for wages long in arrears. Washington's sense of honor and devotion to the service were so far beyond question that if he had joined these discontented officers, the enlisted men (who had also not been paid and who had no particular reason to see that their officers receive preferential treatment) might well have been drawn into a coup d'état. But when Washington denounced these "Newburgh Addresses" as unworthy of an army that exemplified the values of self-sacrifice, the possibility of support by the common soldiers evaporated. The anonymous authors of the addresses lost their nerve, the rest of the officer corps rallied around Washington, and the first (and perhaps greatest) threat to civilian supremacy over the United States military simply collapsed.[33]

Thanks to Washington's handling of the Newburgh incident, the Continental officers' sense of their special merit did not become the basis of an American militarist tradition; neither did it vanish. Rather, it transmuted itself into the Society of the Cincinnati, which was at once a fraternal organization, a hereditary order to distinguish the male descendants of Continental officers from all other Americans, and the first veterans' lobby. In a larger sense it also became the foundation of the virtually universal support of former Continental officers for a strong national government. Only such an effective central authority, they believed, could counteract the localism that they (like Washington) saw as the chief cause of the army's sufferings during the war; only a robust national government with the power to tax could make good on its debt to them. That Washington agreed to serve as the first president-general of the Society of the Cincinnati and the presiding officer at the Constitutional Convention of 1787 was in that sense no accident. For him to abandon what he had come to regard as equally sacred commitments to the army and the United States was unthinkable.

Nothing less than a war was necessary to make a revolutionary of

George Washington. War welded together in his mind the republican values for which he fought and the military professionalism that enabled him to carry on the struggle. War burned away his political identity as a monarchist and British subject, creating in its place a new identity as a citizen of the United States. War made an Anglophile imperialist into a committed American nationalist.

War transformed the lives of thousands of other men as well. Virtually all of them saw in Washington the personification of values they had come to share. In that sense the military struggle that created the United States was a revolution, indeed. More than merely a drive for political independence, it had validated beliefs and practices that the metropolitan British had dismissed as provincial and imperfect and made them understandable as ideals of liberty and rights that had been worth fighting—and dying—for.[34] It was not the blood ties of common kinship and subjecthood but rather the blood shed by citizens in defense of liberty that sanctified the covenants of American political community. Yet nothing in this great transformation diminished the old desire to bring the interior of the continent under their government's dominion. For Washington no less than his fellow Americans, the challenge of the postwar era was to find a way to secure the values of republicanism while creating a new imperial order.

A Revolutionary Settlement and the Foundations of Empire

Washington lost no time in returning to his civilian roles and habits after he resigned his commission to Congress and rode for home on December 23, 1783. As he had promised his wife, he reached Mount Vernon in time to celebrate Christmas.[35] He was eager to return because he knew that after nearly nine years of absence his private affairs badly needed attention. When he finally examined the ledgers that his steward (and distant cousin) Lund Washington had kept in his absence, he was shaken to see the decay in his fortunes. "Much as I expected to find my own private concerns deranged," he told an English correspondent, "I [now know that I] shall realize more trouble and perplexity tha[n] I apprehended . . . in restoring them . . . to order."[36] Lund had paid scrupulous attention to maintaining Mount Vernon and its immediate surroundings, but he had repeatedly failed to collect rent from the local tenants. He had also proved far too indulgent in managing Washington's slaves, at least eighteen of whom took the ideals of liberty and equality seriously enough to run away, never to be recovered. Worst of all,

Lund entirely neglected the general's western lands, where legal tenants paid no rents for eight years and squatters took up residence at will. Some of Washington's western lands, he was shocked to learn, had actually been *sold* by squatters on the basis of fraudulent surveys and false deeds.[37]

Washington believed that his financial future depended on those lands. In the middle of the war, he said as much when he advised his younger brother, Jack, against selling land while Virginia and Continental currencies were collapsing in value. "It was ever my opinion," he wrote, "to have my property as much as possible in Lands. I have seen no cause to change this opinion; but abundant reason to confirm me in it; being persuaded that a few years [of] Peace will inundate these States with emigrants and of course enhance the price of Land, far above the comm[o]n Int[eres]t of Money."[38] He therefore resolved to travel to the Ohio country as soon as possible to collect rents, dislodge trespassers, and identify new leaseholders for the lands from which he would evict deadbeat tenants and squatters. By the time of his departure in September, he had added another purpose as well: to reconnoiter the water route likeliest to yield communication, with minimal portages, from the Potomac to the Ohio.

He did so in part at the urging of Thomas Jefferson, who had learned that northern investors were planning to improve the water route from the Hudson and the Mohawk to the Great Lakes and thence to the Allegheny. Jefferson hoped that Virginians might open workable communications with the West first, capturing trade that would otherwise enrich New Yorkers. Washington agreed. As he explained to Jefferson, he was close to realizing just such a scheme with the Maryland speculator (and later, governor) Thomas Johnson in the 1770s when the war intervened. Now, he wrote, "I am satisfied that not a moment ought to be lost in recommencing this business; for I *know* the Yorkers will delay no time to remove every obstacle in the way of the other communication, so soon as the [British-occupied] Posts at Oswego and Niagara are surrendered."[39] As he traveled to the Ohio in September of 1784, therefore, he recorded not only details of travel, the condition of his lands, and the quality of his tenants but also the character of the Potomac, the Monongahela, and other rivers as routes to the Ohio.

To Washington's regret, Indian raids on Kentucky and Ohio Valley settlements made it too dangerous to travel beyond his lands at Miller's Run, just below Pittsburgh, and he never reached his tract on the Great Kanawha. Yet, he wrote in his diary, "notwithstanding this disappointment, I am well pleased with my journey, as it has been the means of my obtaining a knowledge of the facts—coming at the temper & disposition of the Western

Inhabitants and making reflections thereon." Most of all, his trip persuaded him that "The more . . . the Navigation of the Potomack is investigated, & duely considered, the greater the advantages . . . appear."[40] The prospect of improving communications between the Tidewater and the West had once again fired Washington's imagination. The long letters he wrote to several influential men on the subject after his return signaled Washington's reemergence as a public figure.

The western journey confirmed his long-standing impressions of the backcountry and its people, whom he regarded as inveterately localist in their views, disruptive in their dealings with Indians, unreliable, self-interested, none too honest, and lazy. The essential problem, he believed, was that they had life too easy and therefore no reason to work hard. "Hitherto," Washington wrote, "the people of the Western Country[,] having had no excitements to Industry, labour very little; the luxuriency of the Soil, with very little culture, produces provisions in abundance. These suppl[y] the wants of the encreasing population." If there were a market for their produce, however, they might develop habits of diligence as a means of acquiring manufactured goods. He had seen that happen to the frontier farmers around Winchester as they developed a commercial orientation late in the Seven Years' War. The eagerness of those northern Shenandoah farmers to profit from the army's demand for beef and grain had shown Washington that even frontier folk could develop a view of the world that transcended their localities, and those who prospered had increased not only in wealth but in ambition, honesty, and punctuality in dealing with others. Inasmuch as the settlers in the trans-Appalachian interior resembled those earlier farmers around Winchester, access to eastern markets would turn their very self-interestedness to useful ends, producing the civilized behavior and values they presently lacked.

Meanwhile, by the sale of the westerners' produce abroad, the merchants of the seaboard states would "see how astonishingly our exports will be encreased; and these States benefitted in a commercial point of view." That prospect alone, he thought, "is an object of such Magnitude as to claim our closest attention." Yet it was not merely improving the character of frontier settlers and the bottom lines of merchants' balance sheets that Washington had in mind. The "much greater importance" of improved communication with the West emerged "when the subject is considered in a political point of view."[41]

The international situation concerned him most because it boded least well for the new, disorganized, decentralized United States:

> No well informed Mind need be told that the flanks and rear of . . .
> [our] territory are possessed by other powers, and formidable ones
> too—nor how necessary it is to apply the cement of interest to bind
> all parts of [the union] together, by one indissolvable band—
> particularly the Middle States with the Country immediately back of
> them. For what ties[,] let me ask, should we have upon those
> people . . . if the Spaniards on their right, or Great Britain on their
> left, . . . should envite their trade and seek alliances with them?

The situation was critical. "The Western Settlers—from my own observation—stand as it were on a pivet [pivot]—the touch of a feather would
almost incline them any way." In view of the relative ease with which communication could be developed between the Potomac—or possibly the
James—and the western rivers, it was incumbent on Virginia to "open her
Arms, & embrace the means which are necessary to establish it."

> The way is plain & the expence, comparitively speaking deserves not
> a thought, so great would be the prize. The Western Inhabitants
> would do their part towards accomplishing it. Weak as they now are,
> they would, I am perswaded, meet us half way rather than be *driven*
> into the arms of, or be in any wise dependent upon, foreigners; the
> consequence of which would be, a seperation, or a War.[42]

In other words, Washington found the prospect of opening an easy trade
between East and West compelling—and not only because land values in the
Ohio country would rise as a result. Though he readily admitted that he was
"not . . . disinterested in this matter" of land speculation, it was the future of
the republic that most concerned him.[43] The radically self-interested behavior of most Americans during the Revolutionary War had destroyed his faith
that virtue could ever be an adequate cement for a political union among the
states. Gentlemen might understand the common good and willingly sacrifice their fortunes and welfare to serve it; he himself had done so and he believed that if republican states were to survive they would always need to be
led by men of similar dedication to principle. Experience had shown him,
however, that most Americans were not great-souled patriots. Self-centered,
locally minded, ill-educated, and grasping, the common run of men could
never be trusted to act with any degree of altruism. Yet they were by no
means stupid; give them a clear path to prosperity and security for themselves and their families and they could be trusted to follow it. A republic,

whether Virginia or the United States, could survive only if it succeeded in fashioning a harness of common allegiance from its citizens' individualistic pursuits of happiness—which was to say, from their self-interest. That improved transportation links between eastern and western settlements would provide such a harness was a truth so self-evident, Washington thought, that the state should not hesitate to fund the building of canals and roads.[44]

Persuasive as this case was to James Madison and others in Washington's network of political influence, neither the bankrupt United States Congress nor the hard-pressed legislatures of Virginia and Maryland would agree to fund Washington's ambitious canalization and road-building scheme with public revenues. The most that the Virginia and Maryland legislatures were prepared to do, late in 1784, was issue charters to a joint-stock corporation, the Potomac Company, authorizing it to dig channels and build locks for navigation and to collect tolls for the use of them; connecting roads could be laid out and maintained at public expense.[45] Gratified by the willingness of the assemblies of these two states to cooperate, Washington embarked on the project with enormous enthusiasm; in the summer of 1786 he told Jefferson that his whole time was divided "between the superintendence of opening the navigations of our river & attention to my private concerns." Busy as he was, however, and "secluded from the world" as he claimed to be, he found himself increasingly frustrated by Congress's incapacity to promote the collective welfare of the United States.[46]

Given Washington's core concerns, few matters could have been more important than regulating commerce between the states and organizing western settlement in an orderly way. Congress seemed incompetent on both counts. The problem stemmed, as much as anything, from the character of Congress as an institution of government. In its first incarnation, as the Second Continental Congress, it had been essentially a military alliance improvised in 1775 to coordinate the defense of the thirteen colonies and control the violence of the war with Britain. Congress had, as a result, assumed only those powers that had been identified with royal (or executive) authority—raising and paying of armed forces, the conduct of diplomacy, borrowing money on public credit, issuing currency, and so forth—and left the sovereign functions of taxation and the administration of justice to the individual states. The Articles of Confederation (written in 1776 and adopted by Congress in 1777, but not ratified by all thirteen states until 1781) codified these arrangements, stipulating that the union was "a firm league of friendship" among the states, each of which retained full individual sovereignty in all particulars except for the powers specifically assigned to Congress.

This had worked well enough to win the war, but the states had reverted to older patterns of intramural competition in the postwar era as each pursued its own self-interest, especially in matters of commerce and finance. Lacking the power to tax, Congress could "requisition" revenue from the state governments to cover the heavy debt obligations (including the still-unpaid wages of the Continental Army) that it had contracted during the War of Independence. By the mid-1780s the imperious-sounding authority to requisition amounted to little more than a bankrupt Congress begging the states for support that they could not be compelled to provide. Repeated attempts to revise the Articles of Confederation and assign Congress a limited power of taxation came to nothing, as did efforts to expand Congress's power to regulate trade, because various states refused to ratify the proposed amendments. It was true that when neighboring states were willing to negotiate with one another, a certain amount of coordination in matters of trade and navigation could be accomplished in the absence of an effective Confederation government; the cooperation of Maryland and Virginia in the creation of the Potomac Company had proved that. But Washington knew that even if the Potomac Company succeeded in opening a commercial highway to the interior, it would never be more than a business venture. It could not by itself succeed in binding the whole of the West economically to the older settlements on the Atlantic, much less create the kind of durable political union between the interior and the seaboard states that he knew would be necessary if the United States was to endure as a nation.

Events in the last half of 1786 and early 1787 seemed to him to portend a gloomy future. In September yet another effort to draft measures that would grant Congress more regulatory power over commerce, the Annapolis Convention, failed to attract enough delegates even to begin the discussion of such concerns as the improvement of navigation on the Potomac and other rivers. This alone would have been discouraging enough, but other developments worried him even more. The unrestrained (and, to Washington, plainly wicked) growth in the volume of paper money issued by state governments; the passage of debtor-relief laws that seemed to threaten the security of property as much as the inflation of paper currency; and finally the eruption of civil unrest in Massachusetts during the winter of 1786–87: all these seemed be signs that the annals of the United States might prove to be among the shortest in the history of nations.

Massachusetts' situation in particular distressed him. In the summer of 1786 protests against taxation had broken out in the Bay State after the legislature, dominated by mercantile interests, passed a property tax that many farmers in the poorer western and central parts of the state could not pay. At first, mobs prevented county courts from meeting, hence forestalling the issuance of writs authorizing foreclosure. Confrontations grew strident: in the fall, a crowd armed with pitchforks and fowling pieces faced down a militia force in Springfield and compelled the closing of the state Supreme Court. This was a particularly worrisome event because the U.S. Arsenal in Springfield stored cannons, tons of gunpowder, and thousands of muskets, presumably a fact not lost on the protesters. Congress was barely able to muster a quorum and with a total of only eighty men in the army was incapable of defending its own arms; it had to appeal to the state government to provide a force to guard the facility. But Massachusetts had only its militia to call upon, and most of the local militiamen were marching with the protesters. In December it seemed as if a crowd might try to seize the arsenal, which was defended only by a small guard detachment; the governor hastily tried to raise troops in eastern Massachusetts to reinforce them. Then, on January 25, a force of badly armed farmers under a former Continental Army captain, Daniel Shays, tried to force an entry. Only the boldness of the guard in opening fire and the absence of discipline in the Shaysites' ranks kept the attempt from succeeding.[47]

When the troops from eastern Massachusetts under the command of Benjamin Lincoln, a former Continental general, arrived two days later, the rebels dispersed, and what came to be known as Shays's Rebellion quickly fizzled out. Despite its quick demise, however, the insurrection had far-reaching effects, for it persuaded nationalists everywhere in the United States that nothing was now more important than to reform and strengthen the authority of Congress. Although Washington deeply disliked leaving Mount Vernon, he felt compelled to accept his appointment as a delegate to the Constitutional Convention in Philadelphia the following summer because he, too, was desperate to find an antidote to the anarchic and self-interested tendencies of his countrymen. If the delegates did not succeed, he believed, it was only a matter of time before Britain would recolonize the thirteen disunited states, and the western settlers would be left to choose between Spanish and British dominion.[48]

The problems that Washington and the other fifty-four delegates to the Constitutional Convention faced in 1787 were not new, and they had always before resisted solution. All of the delegates had been born into a British imperial community united by common political values and transatlantic trade. At some level, all understood that it had been the metropolis's attempt to use its sovereign power to solve the problems of finance and control in the postwar empire that convinced many colonists to take up arms to preserve the liberties they cherished. At some level they also realized that identical issues of control and finance underlay the crisis that faced the United States. How could a diverse, geographically immense political community be held together without creating a sovereign power that would threaten the liberties and rights the Revolutionary War had been fought to preserve? Massive difficulties in political theory and scarcely less imposing practical obstacles confronted the delegates as they struggled to fashion a constitutional solution that a majority of American citizens would find acceptable.

The delegates eventually solved the most pressing theoretical problem they faced by inverting the understanding of sovereignty that had undergirded the power of the British state for more than a century. The conventional form of that doctrine, powerfully stated by John Locke in defense of the Glorious Revolution, held that when men in the state of nature created governments, they endowed them with the unlimited and indivisible power to seize property and take life. This had been the fundamental definition of sovereignty, and nothing less was necessary to create an ordered state. Because it was intolerable for people to live merely at the whim of their rulers, however, justly constituted governments ceded certain liberties back to their subjects—for example, the right to consent to taxation, the right to trial by jury, the privilege of habeas corpus, and immunity from forced testimony—to shield them from the state's overwhelming power. The great creative breakthrough that the delegates at Philadelphia made was to see that their Constitution could be constructed in a way that assigned limited powers to the national government while stipulating that the people retained sovereign power to themselves and with it the freedom to act as they pleased. The negatively defined freedom that Americans fought to secure would remain indivisible except for those aspects of it—the power to tax, administer justice, defend the nation, and so on—that they explicitly allocated to the national government to create security for themselves and their property. The powers of internal police that the colonists had come to fear in the British state could be doled out with such care and parsimony that no one would need to fear the new "federal" government that the Constitution would drape lightly over the existing jurisdictions of the states.[49]

These conceptual breakthroughs were achieved at the convention not by Washington, whose presence was largely ceremonial, but by James Madison, James Wilson, Roger Sherman, and other astute political thinkers; then they and other commentators explained, parsed, dissected, and disputed them throughout the following year in pamphlets, newspaper columns, and the debates of the state ratifying conventions. The issues in this great national debate were indeed profound, and so important for the future interpretation of the Constitution, that we may be tempted to assume they settled the fundamental problems at stake in the creation of the American republic. But the ratification of the Constitution was not so much the culmination of the Revolution as the central element in a larger set of agreements, both formal and informal, that were put in place over the next decade by which a sustainable national politics began in the United States. Like the flying buttresses that permitted Gothic cathedrals to soar to such astonishing heights, these practical agreements braced a fragile constitutional covenant and made it politically functional. By analogy to the Settlement of 1688, which made Parliament preeminent in the English constitutional system and secured the Protestant succession to the throne, the understandings and practices that buttressed the Constitution during the years of Washington's presidential administrations can be thought of as the American Revolutionary Settlement.[50]

In practice the Revolutionary Settlement was a complex compromise between nationalists and localists, whose elements can be divided into four categories. First was the Bill of Rights, ten amendments designed to guarantee that the Constitution could not be used to deprive individual citizens or the states of essential liberties. Second were those features, centering on the funding and assumption of the national debt and the creation of a national bank, that empowered the national government and chiefly benefited northern commercial interests. These occasioned the measures in the third category, concessions made to the Chesapeake planters and other southern slaveholders: the location of a national capital on the Virginia-Maryland border, astride the Potomac route to the West, and the tacit understanding that slavery would not be called into question at the national level but considered only as an aspect of property rights and left to fade away, a fate that in the 1780s seemed to lie in the not-far-distant future. The fourth category consisted of elements that organized the United States as an imperial power. These centered on the Northwest Ordinance of 1787, its implementation, and the working out of its implications for the future. The first and fourth aspects of the settlement related most directly to the rules for the exercise of military power and the projection of American power and authority into the interior of the continent.

The best-known element of the Revolutionary Settlement, the Bill of Rights, was aimed at allaying localist fears that the Constitution would create a monster of centralized state power. Unmoved by the assurances of the Federalists (that is, nationalist republicans) that a government limited to the exercise of enumerated powers could not possibly threaten the people's otherwise untouched and undivided freedom, the Anti-Federalists (localist republicans) insisted on explicit guarantees of the rights accorded to individuals as well as the reservation to the states of all powers not formally granted to the national government.[51] These protections included not only those personal freedoms familiarly invoked today and the rights enshrined in legal procedure (trial by jury, no double jeopardy, no compelled testimony, and so on) but rights articulated as restraints on the power of the United States to use its army against American citizens.

So far as the Anti-Federalists were concerned, it was not enough that the Constitution explicitly subordinated the military to civilian control by making the president commander in chief and forbidding Congress to appropriate defense funds more than two years into the future. Given the small size of the standing armed forces, the United States would necessarily rely on the militia for its defense. Citizens, the Anti-Federalists believed, should fulfill their collective obligation to defend the republic by serving in the militia; the United States must not follow the British model of imposing heavy taxes to support a large, potentially oppressive standing army.[52] A generation whose members had been exposed to the military power of the British state surely found the Third Amendment's prohibitions on quartering troops in civilian homes at least as important as the First Amendment's protections of free speech, press, and assembly. Similarly, states that had confronted redcoats employed in constabulary roles could more easily agree to Congress's power to raise and support an army with the Second Amendment to assure them that their own militias would guarantee order within their own borders and that they would have the means to defend themselves in the event that some homegrown despot gained control of the national government and sought to rule by force.

Later practice during Washington's presidential administrations confirmed what the Second and Third Amendments implied: that the United States Army would not be used to maintain public order within the states. It would instead be consistently employed only in territories administered directly by the federal government. Those territories—in effect colonies of the United States—would be administered under the provisions of the Northwest Ordinance, which after the Constitution and the Bill of Rights was the single most important element of the Revolutionary Settlement. Congress adopted the Northwest Ordinance in July 1787, even as the Constitutional Convention delegates were hammering out their draft in Philadelphia. Congress's immediate goal was to impose order on the Indian Country that lay between the Ohio River and the Great Lakes, as far west as the Mississippi and the Lake of the Woods. All three states with claims in that region—Virginia, Massachusetts, and Connecticut—had ceded them to Congress, which in turn desperately needed the revenues it could gain by selling lands there to white settlers. But the Northwest Ordinance, practical as it was, represented much more than a means of channeling dollars into an empty Treasury: it provided a robust institutional framework for the American colonization of an area far greater in extent than the original thirteen states. The first Congress under the new Constitution recognized the merits of the ordinance and adopted it as law in August 1789, virtually without alteration.

The outlines of the ordinance—its prohibition of slavery, provisions for public support of education and guarantees of legal rights (including freedom of religion) to settlers, requirements for surveying lands into six-by-six-mile townships before sale, and procedures for the formation of new states that would join the Union as equals of the original thirteen—remain familiar to modern Americans as the bedrock principles uniting new and old settlements, cemented by a common, voluntary allegiance. The differences between the incorporative logic of the ordinance and the subordinating imperial strategies of the old British empire are generally understood as evidence of the political idealism of the new United States. There is a good deal of truth to that view, for the Anglo-American settlers of the territories did indeed have the freedom to form their own state governments and the ability to achieve equality of status with all other American citizens.[53]

Yet it is important to recognize that the Northwest Ordinance made a territory's transition to statehood contingent on completing a highly specific sequence of actions aimed at moving the territory though a structured evolution into a state. No lands could be settled until the national government had formally acquired them, ordinarily by a treaty of purchase, from the resident native peoples, and rectilinear surveys had been conducted on the terrain. The ordered growth of a white settler population on lands with clear legal title would be accompanied by the graduated introduction of representative government as the population reached specified levels. It was only when the settlers had written a constitution modeled on those of the original thirteen states and when they had demonstrated their commitment to civilized republican (in practice, Protestant) forms of education, worship, and morality that the settlers of the territory would be permitted the full privileges of self-rule in a state equal in every way with the older states of the Union.[54] Thus the Northwest Ordinance established an empire capable of indefinite expansion because it was conceived as a league of self-governing republics, immune to the possibility of despotic rule from the center because (unlike the British empire) it was ultimately a voluntary association. Settlers who embraced the rules and opportunities laid out by the ordinance were never subjects; they were citizens protected by a tutelary national government until their societies could sustain the self-rule that conferred the full range of civil rights and liberties. Thus the rhetoric of freedom supported and justified the reality of federal power on which the order of the imperial periphery depended.[55]

Achieving a functional balance between federal power, local authority, and individual rights was of course crucial to achieving a durable Revolutionary Settlement; so was achieving the proper tone of political life. When Washington recited the presidential oath of office on the balcony of New York's Federal Hall, before crowds that filled Broad and Wall streets on April 30, 1789, such matters were very much in his mind. He understood the importance of setting the right precedents and achieving the proper appearances. Much has rightly been made, therefore, of the care he took to impart dignity to the national government in his first administration. In everything he did, from his habitual wearing of plain, sober, civilian suits and his practice of conferring with his cabinet officers on all important matters to his stern disapproval of political factionalism and his studied gravity on public occasions, he was aware that he was creating legacies that would long outlive him.[56] In a precisely parallel way Washington understood the critical importance of establishing the federal government's preeminence and legitimacy in the trans-Appalachian West. It was there, he believed, that the success or failure of the American experiment would be determined. Hence it was imperative not only that the national government demonstrate its efficacy to the inhabitants of the region but that it prove itself worthy of their allegiance. This was no easy task.

The government of the United States enjoyed little credibility with westerners at the outset of Washington's first administration. Congress's presence on the Ohio and the Wabash had been limited to a few forts, manned by fewer than 400 regular soldiers and a great many more undisciplined, ill-trained, poorly supplied Kentucky militiamen, whose localist and Indian-hating tendencies far outweighed their allegiance to the Confederation and their willingness to take orders from regular officers.[57] The power of the United States, such as it was, was limited to the forts and their immediate surroundings. Meanwhile, at Niagara, Detroit, Michilimackinac, and other forts on United States soil, British traders and agents supplied arms to Indian groups and encouraged the Iroquois of Canada to unite with nations living north of the Ohio in a western confederacy to oppose the United States. The Spanish cultivated relations with the southern Indians while bribing influential Kentuckians who they hoped would lead a separatist movement to bring the territory south of the Ohio River into the Spanish empire.[58] Despite it all, American settlers continued to pour down the Ohio Valley without direction or control, severely destabilizing relations with native groups that were steadily becoming better armed and more militarily formidable than ever before.[59]

Until the Treasury was properly organized and staffed, the United States government lacked the money to exert a forceful federal presence in the West. Moreover, the newly reorganized U.S. Army, although larger than before, still enlisted only about 700 men, far too few to do what Henry Knox, the new secretary of war, advocated—to "keep both [the white settlers and the Indians] in awe by a strong hand, and compel them to be moderate and just."[60] As a result, the new government had no choice but to continue supplementing the small numbers of regulars on the Ohio with large levies of Kentucky militia. The result soon became apparent when Brigadier General Josiah Harmar and 1,450 troops suffered a humiliating defeat in October 1790 near the Forks of the Maumee (modern Fort Wayne, Indiana) at the hands of Miami and Delaware warriors under Little Turtle. Harmar ordered a retreat that ended only after 150 miles at Fort Washington (modern Cincinnati), then did his best to cover up the fiasco. Washington saw through the charade and ordered the governor of the Northwest Territory (another Continental Army veteran), Major General Arthur St. Clair, to take direct command.[61]

St. Clair's expedition, in the fall of 1791, proved an even greater disaster than Harmar's. Marching from Fort Washington in the late summer, he led a force of approximately 2,000 men—600 regulars, an equal number of militia, and 800 virtually untrained volunteers who had enlisted for the campaign—slowly northward toward the Miami heartland at the headwaters of the Wabash. Poor supply, slow road-building, bad weather, and desertion kept them from reaching their destination until early November.

The 1,400 men still fit for duty were preparing to lay waste the Miami villages when a force of about 1,000 Miami, Shawnee, and Delaware warriors under Little Turtle and the Shawnee war chief Blue Jacket attacked their camp before dawn on November 4. By the time the survivors broke out of the trap and fled for their lives, nearly two-thirds of St. Clair's men—890 in all—had been killed or wounded. The Indians, who sustained about sixty casualties, could have annihilated St. Clair's entire army had they chosen to pursue it.[62]

In response to this, the greatest defeat an Indian enemy had ever inflicted on the U.S. Army (or ever would), Washington and his chief lieutenant, Secretary of War Henry Knox, took stern and vigorous measures. They reorganized the army as the Legion of the United States, secured congressional authorization to increase its strength to 5,000 men, and appointed one of the boldest of the Continental generals, Anthony Wayne, to command it. Henceforth if the United States government had to fight Indians in the Northwest, it would rely principally on regular soldiers, not militiamen. Such troops, of course, took time to recruit, train, and equip. While that was in progress, Washington's administration pursued diplomacy in an attempt to reach a peaceful, less expensive resolution.[63]

In fact, Washington and Knox greatly preferred negotiation to another military expedition because both of them believed that American settlers were fully as culpable as the western Indians in bringing bloodshed and instability to the frontier. Knox had long blamed "Whites and Savages" equally for the "deep rooted prejudices, and malignity of heart, and conduct" by which "the flames of a merciless war are . . . lighted up [and] which involve the innocent and helpless with the guilty."[64] At the end of the Revolutionary War, Washington had observed that "policy and œconomy point very strongly to the expediency of being upon good terms with the Indians, and the propriety of purchasing their Lands in preference to attempting to drive them by force of arms out of their Country." "Nothing," he had written to a committee of Congress that sought his views on Indian affairs, "is to be obtained by an Indian War but the Soil they live on and this can be had by purchase at less expence, and without that bloodshed, and those distresses which helpless Women and Children are made partakers of in all kinds of disputes with them."[65]

For a time it looked as if diplomacy would actually succeed. A treaty at Vincennes in the spring of 1792 resulted in a delegation of Potawatomis, Peorias, and Kaskasias traveling from the Wabash to Philadelphia to meet with Washington and make peace. The Indians' western confederacy began to show cracks; British influence waned. When fighting broke out between Britain and revolutionary France in 1793, however, open warfare between Britain and the United States suddenly became quite possible. British agents in the Northwest renewed the flow of arms and gifts, constructed Fort Miami at the rapids of the Maumee, and revitalized the alliance with the Miamis, the Shawnees, and the Delawares.[66]

Late in 1793, as the hope of peace ebbed, Wayne's Legion—by now better trained, supplied, and equipped than any previous force in the West— established an advanced post, Fort Recovery, on the site of St. Clair's defeat. Unlike Harmar and St. Clair, Wayne took care to construct a chain of supporting blockhouses along the road connecting Fort Washington and Fort Recovery, and in the spring of 1794 the new fort withstood heavy Indian attacks without losing the ability to bring up reinforcements and supplies. In July, Wayne led 2,000 regulars and 1,500 Kentucky militiamen to the junction of the Maumee and Auglaize rivers, fifty miles from the new British post. There the Legion built Fort Defiance and Wayne called on the Indians to make peace. When they did not respond by mid-August, he proceeded slowly, with great care, down the Maumee toward Fort Miami.

On the morning of August 20, advance elements of the legion collided with approximately a thousand Indians under Blue Jacket in a large area where thousands of trees had been felled by a violent windstorm. The Americans, surprised, took scores of casualties in short order and fell back, but this time they did not break. Wayne, bringing up his best-trained infantrymen, ordered a bayonet charge. Under pressure from a more disciplined force than any they had ever encountered before, the Indians retreated to Fort Miami, only to find that its redcoat commandant, fearful of inviting an American assault, refused to open the gates and give them shelter.

Abandoned by their indispensable ally, the warriors dispersed. The Battle of Fallen Timbers, which had by no means broken the Indians' military strength, thereupon became—retroactively—a decisive American victory. Wayne lingered in the vicinity for three days, burning native villages, cornfields, storehouses, and indeed everything his men could put a torch to outside Fort Miami's walls while the British garrison watched from within, helpless to stop the destruction. Then the legionnaires marched back to Fort Defiance, destroying Indian settlements along the river as they went. By late November, Wayne had burned and pillaged every village within reach and left the Indians to face a starving winter. The following summer he invited Little Turtle, Blue Jacket, and other native leaders of the Ohio country to Fort Greenville, thirty miles south of Fort Recovery, to discuss peace.[67]

The Treaty of Greenville, concluded on August 3, 1795, signaled an end to native resistance between the Great Lakes and the Ohio River, from Pittsburgh as far west as Cincinnati. The Indians surrendered their claims to two-thirds of the modern state of Ohio and gave up their attempt, now decades old, to prevent Anglo-American settlement north of the river. The treaty, moreover, represented much more than an act of dispossession. As the representative of President Washington and the government of the United States, General Wayne took great care at the negotiations to establish the legitimacy as well as the power of the American empire. In ways that had not been seen since the Seven Years' War, he adhered scrupulously to Indian diplomatic protocols, striving by ritual oratory and the giving of gifts to convince the Ohio Indians that the United States government was indeed a great Father on whom they could rely for protection from their enemies, including grasping land speculators and Indian-hating whites. For Wayne, as for Washington and Knox, it was not enough for the Indians to acquiesce in American rule. It was essential that they offer their willing consent and cooperation.[68]

Voluntary submission to the authority of the federal government was what Washington sought above all on the frontier, and it was crucial that it come as much from whites as from Indians. When Wayne cut roads through the forest, built and manned forts, defeated hostile warriors, and bid defiance to the British, he made the most convincing possible demonstration of the power of the new United States government. Making the interior of the continent an orderly and safe environment, however, was not something that could be indefinitely enforced by military means. White settlers and Indians had to live in peace, trusting equally in the justice and impartial protection of the United States. The orderly expansion of farming settlements, the growth of commerce, and submission to the rule of law that would follow, Washington and his fellow Federalists believed, could be trusted to produce a society in harmony with republican values. As white civilization progressed around them, Indians would gradually and inevitably lose their attachment to hunting, learn the arts of husbandry, and blend into a harmonious social order. Or so the leaders of the United States hoped; and on that hope they strove to build a new, stable imperial order in the Northwest Territory.

It was perhaps an impossible dream, but in the 1790s the Federalists still believed that great things could be accomplished under the tutelage of a benevolent national government. And in fact they managed to accomplish a surprising amount north of the Ohio River, where federal authority was unopposed and federal expenditures for military garrisons encouraged the

growth of Cincinnati and other urban centers. From those beginnings a
prosperous, smallholding, commercial-farming society eventually emerged
in Ohio, manifesting on a far larger scale the pattern of development Washington first glimpsed in the northern Shenandoah Valley at the end of the
Seven Years' War.

If this vision of empire had its roots in Washington's experience of the
prerevolutionary west, the Revolution gave it the sanction of republican values, and the Northwest Ordinance embodied it in institutional form. But
there were other ideas about the future at large in the interior of North
America in the 1790s, ideas equally imperial in implication but far less orderly in intent than the vision that Washington and his fellow Federalists
promoted. Advocates of those competing ideas could be found everywhere
in the West, but they were most clearly in the majority south of the Ohio,
where the new state of Kentucky was formed in 1792 and where the Southwest Territory (created in 1790) was following a trajectory quite unlike that
of its Northwest counterpart.

Because Kentucky had been part of Virginia before statehood, it had
never been under the direct control or authority of the United States and
the development of popular sovereignty had neither been regulated nor delayed. The Southwest Territory (whose northern third became the state of
Tennessee in 1796), lacked the kind of organized Anglo-Indian threat that
prevailed north of the Ohio and therefore attracted none of the support or
military resources that the federal government devoted to the Northwest
Territory. Both Kentucky and the Southwest Territory had been settled by
backwoods localists of the sort that Washington, Knox, and their fellow Federalists distrusted for their inveterate hatred of Indians and their reflexive
resistance to properly constituted national (and even state) authority. Slavery had been a fundamental fact of life south of the Ohio from the beginning and governed the white settlers' expectations for the future. The world
they foresaw consequently had none of the characteristics of commercial
urban development and compact farming settlement that the Federalists
sought to foster north of the Ohio. It was, rather, Virginia's society and culture writ large: a world in which the equality of white citizens rested on the
permanent subordination of slaves; where political power was configured
around patronage and exercised most decisively at the county and state
level; where manhood in the full sense meant heading a household made up
of dependents—women, children, and slaves.[69]

Americans south of the Ohio lacked none of the expansionist ambitions
of the Federalists. Indeed, their fierce antipathy to restraint on their actions

from any authority above the county (or at most the state) level proceeded in large part from their desire to appropriate Indian lands on their own schedule and to deal with Indians according to their own notions of justice and expediency. In their world, the federal government would play only the narrow roles of making public lands available for purchase cheap, and controlling Indians by confinement or (preferably) forcible removal. The direct exercise of federal power in almost any other form was unwelcome and might easily become the occasion for massive resistance.

What these southern localists hated most of all was direct taxation by the national government. That was, of course, a key feature of the federal fiscal program devised by Washington's secretary of the Treasury, Alexander Hamilton. Hamilton acquired his nationalist convictions in the Continental Army along with Washington and Knox, but he derived his understanding of public finance from English practices and institutions. In 1790 and 1791 he proposed to the new Congress an ambitious financial program that created a funded national debt and a national bank, two key features of the British fiscal-military state. From the sales of public lands and the customs duties that Congress granted, the Treasury would have been able to pay the interest on the national debt and fund the operations of the national government, but Hamilton nonetheless asked for (and in March 1791 received) an additional domestic tax on the manufacture of distilled liquors. This levy, modeled on the English excise system, was less important for the revenue it would raise than for the wealth of patronage jobs it would create for the Treasury. By appointing locally prominent figures as excise collectors in districts across the length and breadth of the republic, Hamilton would build a network of gentlemen loyal to the federal government. The excise thus would furnish a self-funding means of exerting influence, gathering political intelligence, and counteracting the predominance of localist leaders. It was a brilliant means of drawing prominent men into the national interest, one that localists accordingly mistrusted.[70]

The largest distillers in the United States were the rum manufacturers of the Atlantic port cities. They paid the excise without complaint because most were nationalists by conviction anyway and they could easily recoup the cost by raising the wholesale price on their product. Frontiersmen living west of the Appalachian crest, by contrast, found the tax oppressive and soon organized to protest it. They grew enormous amounts of corn, rye, and other grains too bulky to carry to Philadelphia or Annapolis; nor could they ship them down the Ohio and Mississippi for sale, because the Spanish authorities had closed the port of New Orleans to American commerce. The answer they had found was to brew their surplus grain as mash then distill it into whiskey, a form of alcohol that could be sold locally and was sufficiently concentrated that it could be carried on horseback to markets east of the mountains. Unlike the rum manufacturers of the seaboard cities, whiskey distillers were mainly farmers who produced modest quantities; with little money in local circulation, they simply could not afford to pay the exciseman and thus ran the risk of having their property seized for nonpayment of taxes.

Resistance to the excise was general in frontier regions from Pennsylvania to South Carolina, but some of the most visible and vocal protests occurred in the four trans-Allegheny Pennsylvania counties, largely settled by migrants from Virginia, that centered on Pittsburgh. Beginning in the summer of 1792, mass meetings of farmers petitioned against the tax. Washington found these protests particularly offensive because revenues from the excise were intended to pay for the Legion of the United States, which was being raised to defend the Ohio country. What was worse, a mob of backwoodsmen disguised as Indians attacked the house of an army officer who was prepared to offer support for John Neville, the regional supervisor of the excise. Opposition, Washington, thought, had "become too open, violent and serious to be longer winked at by Government, without prostrating it's authority."[71] He therefore issued a proclamation in September ordering "all persons . . . to refrain and desist from all unlawful combinations and proceedings whatsoever . . . tending to obstruct the operation of the laws" and calling on "all Courts, Magistrates and Officers whom it may concern . . . to exert the powers in them respectively vested" for the purposes of maintaining public order.[72]

The Pennsylvanians did not desist. They went on protesting with growing fervor in increasingly large numbers. In 1793 mobs gathered to intimidate excisemen. Such defiance was a matter of grave concern, but Washington was distracted by the growing antipathy between Hamilton and Jefferson over domestic and foreign policy, particularly concerning the question of how to respond to the French Revolution, the beheading of Louis XVI, and the outbreak of war between Britain and France. As he struggled to hold the cabinet together and steer a middle course, the two brilliant secretaries became steadily more antagonistic and promoted the formation of political parties sympathetic to their views. Finally, finding that he could not prevent Jefferson from resigning, Washington gave up and thereafter leaned on Hamilton most heavily for advice.

Meanwhile conditions in the region around Pittsburgh continued to deteriorate. By the fall of 1793 excise officers were being physically assaulted as they pursued their duties. John Neville, who as regional supervisor of the excise was the leading representative of the federal government in western Pennsylvania, took the extraordinary step of fortifying his house and arming his slaves. At public meetings radical orators flourished the rhetoric of the Revolution like a blade. Crowds of men numbering in the thousands listened then drew their own conclusions about unjust taxation, tyranny, and the obligation to take up arms in the defense of liberty.

It was in the following summer, even as Wayne's legionnaires prepared to march for the Maumee, that violence finally erupted. At dawn on July 16, Supervisor Neville found his estate, Bower Hill, surrounded by armed men. When the crowd refused to disperse, he fired a musket into its midst, mortally wounding one man. In the exchange of gunfire that followed, Neville and his slaves wounded several more members of the crowd. The mob withdrew, and Neville sent to Fort Pitt for help. The commandant came with ten soldiers to defend the place; Neville sought shelter elsewhere. The next day, 700 men returned to besiege Bower Hill. After a confused, hour-long gun battle in which four of the defenders were seriously wounded and at least two of the attackers were killed, the mob burned the place to the ground. The soldiers and Neville's slaves fled at the last minute and were made prisoner. Two weeks later, 7,000 armed men mustered at Braddock's Field, pledged to defend their rights with their lives, and threatened to sack Pittsburgh, whose wealthy merchants they identified with the Federalist commercial elite of Philadelphia and other eastern cities.[73]

When the news of what came to be called the battle of Bower Hill reached Washington a week later, he had no choice but to act. On August 7, he issued a proclamation to "command all persons, being insurgents . . . to disperse and retire peaceably to their respective abodes," ceasing their "treasonable acts" and desisting from their "dangerous proceedings."[74] Simultaneously he instructed Secretary of War Knox to alert the governors of New Jersey, Pennsylvania, Maryland, and Virginia that the president would call on them for militiamen to put down the disorders around Pittsburgh, should the insurrectionists not disperse. Washington also dispatched Attorney General William Bradford to Pittsburgh to see if a peaceful solution could be negotiated with local leaders. He was prepared to use force against the insurgents but sincerely hoped that matters might be settled short of that. He therefore authorized Bradford to use a very wide range of inducements, including the granting of a general amnesty and exemption from payment of back taxes, in return for the insurgents' submission to federal authority.[75]

Washington's decision to seek a negotiated settlement while preparing to take military measures in the event that negotiations failed precisely paralleled his attempts to reach a diplomatic settlement with the Indians of the Northwest following St. Clair's defeat. He knew war too intimately to welcome it, and he welcomed it least of all now that Wayne and the Legion were engaged in an expedition on the Maumee. Though he hoped for a decisive result in that campaign, he understood that the strength of the Indians, backed by the English, might mean a prolonged war in the West. For ideological reasons familiar to every American republican, moreover, the delicate task of suppressing civil unrest was best entrusted to militia. To use regular soldiers to discipline whites within the bounds of a state smacked too much of the occupation of Boston by British troops before the beginning of the Revolutionary War. Washington then had no real choice in the kind of military instrument he could use. If he had to put down the insurgents by force, he would have to do it with the same kind of militiamen whose shortcomings he had come to know too well in four decades of military experience. In the event that they failed or mutinied or joined the rebels, he would have no regular force to call on. Under such circumstances only a fool would have preferred coercion to negotiation, and Washington was no fool.

The president held out hope for a peaceful solution until Attorney General Bradford's report arrived with the news that moderate leaders were being intimidated by the radicals and that the radicals, having sent to Kentucky for ammunition and allies, were preparing for an armed insurrection. Convinced that he no longer had a choice, on September 9 Washington ordered the governors of New Jersey and Pennsylvania to send their quotas of militiamen to a rendezvous at Carlisle, Pennsylvania. The governors of Virginia and Maryland were instructed to dispatch theirs to Cumberland, Maryland, where they would be placed under federal command and await his instructions. On September 25, with no hope left that the radicals in western Pennsylvania would submit but with evidence that public support for suppressing the revolt was growing in the eastern settlements, Washington issued a final proclamation, elaborately explaining what he intended to do. Noting that "every form of conciliation not inconsistent with the being of the Government has been adopted, without effect," he would now use federalized militia "to reduce the refractory to a due subordination to the laws." For this reason, he warned "all persons . . . not to abet, aid, or comfort the insurgents aforesaid, as they will answer contrary at their peril."[76]

Now the president took great care to use the special-purpose army he had summoned into existence to the best possible purposes. Its men were for the most part obligated to serve only three months; they had to be properly equipped, organized, and—insofar as possible with militia—disciplined. On September 30, Washington and Alexander Hamilton (who in Knox's absence was acting as both secretary of the Treasury and secretary of war) left Philadelphia for Carlisle. That evening, on the road, they received Wayne's report on the Battle of Fallen Timbers.[77] By October 4 they were in Carlisle, where Washington personally supervised the organization of the army and settled the all-important issue of command precedence among its various officers.

These were tasks at which Washington, with so many years' experience as a commanding general, excelled. A week later he was off to Cumberland, where he performed the same functions for the Virginia and Maryland militias and conferred with the man who would command the expedition as a whole, Governor Henry "Light-Horse Harry" Lee of Virginia. After another week of organization and careful planning of the march with Lee, he traveled north to Bedford, Pennsylvania, where the two wings of the army were to join. He arrived on the nineteenth, just ahead of the final assembly of the force. Its 12,950 men far exceeded the number of Continentals Washington commanded at the siege of Yorktown. Soon they would be brought to bear on a motley collection of insurgents who, reports said, were beginning to flee in anticipation of the army's arrival. On October 20, trusting in Lee and Hamilton to use the army with care, the president issued his final orders and turned back for Philadelphia.[78]

Forty years earlier, as a young officer further out of his depth than he knew, George Washington had tried to extend the reach of the British empire across the Appalachians by military means. He had failed, of course. Yet from that failure had followed the events that brought him, at age sixty-two, to the point of projecting a new empire's power beyond those same mountains into the heart of the continent. As his coach rattled east, did he reflect on the remarkable path that connected Fort Necessity to this moment? All he wrote in his diary was that he needed "to return to Philadelphia in order to meet Congress, and to attend to the Civil duties of my Office."[79] Conscious that his constitutional role as president neither required nor authorized him to exercise direct command, he had no wish to linger with an army that had his orders and knew its mission. Besides, he was too old to lead another campaign. Winter was coming on, and he had done what he could.

Mission Accomplished?

The Whiskey Rebellion collapsed even before the militia army arrived. So many of the insurgents had fled that in the end Lee could find only twenty suspects to arrest and bring to Philadelphia for trial when the bulk of the army marched for home. Fifteen hundred militiamen stayed on in the region for another six months, causing a certain amount of disorder themselves but improving the local economy substantially as they spent freely for food, lodging, and (of course) whiskey. Back in Philadelphia, the trials dragged on for half a year. Eighteen of the prisoners were acquitted. When the other two—poor men, and said to be simpletons—were found guilty of treason, Washington pardoned them.[80]

With Wayne's victory at Fallen Timbers and the bloodless suppression of the Whiskey Rebellion, matters looked sufficiently promising that the president issued a proclamation on New Year's Day 1795 that designated Thursday, February 19, as a day of Thanksgiving for the return of domestic tranquility.[81] Diplomats in Europe were pursuing treaties that would, he hoped, stabilize the western frontier once and for all. He had sent John Jay to London early in 1794 to resolve the many differences between Great Britain and the United States on trade issues and the continued British occupation of Detroit and the other western posts. Jay's dispatches reported that agreement was reached in November; the final version of the treaty might arrive any day. Washington had been delighted to learn that, and even more pleased when Spain, worried that an Anglo-American rapprochement might herald an anti-Spanish alliance, invited the United States to send a special envoy to Madrid. On November 21, he had informed the Senate that the ambassador to Britain, Thomas Pinckney, was to proceed to Spain with a proposal that would open the Mississippi to American commerce. Thus as Washington sat in Philadelphia's Christ Church on the day of Thanksgiving, waiting out a long sermon by the Episcopal bishop of Pennsylvania on "The Reciprocal Influences of Civil and Religious Duty," he had reason to hope that the future would finally bring the United States peace abroad, prosperity at home, and stable frontiers.[82] Perhaps (though this seemed less likely) the bitter differences between Federalists and Republicans would similarly be resolved. If so, Washington's long mission would at last be accomplished, and he could retire from public life confident that the

United States, secure in its character as a republic, would go on to achieve lasting glory as an empire of liberty and order.

In fact, Jay's Treaty, when a copy came at last in March, only exacerbated political partisanship and increased the number of personal attacks on the administration by opposition politicians and newspaper editors. The United States might indeed have secured peace with Britain and stability on its frontiers, but the greatest peril of all—factionalism, the nemesis of republics throughout history—seemed increasingly likely to undermine everything that Washington had hoped to achieve. He had always tried to remain above politics as a matter of principle, and in his first administration he had largely succeeded, despite deepening divisions in public opinion over the French Revolution. After war broke out between Britain and France in 1793, the split between the Francophile followers of Thomas Jefferson, who called themselves Republicans, and the Anglophile Federalists, who looked to Alexander Hamilton for leadership, became irreconcilable. The Republican press derided Washington's policy of neutrality as the betrayal of a sister revolutionary state and a dishonorable breach of the French alliance of 1778. The concessions that Jay's Treaty now offered to Britain on seaborne commerce and neutral rights seemed to the Republicans nothing less than an abandonment of the principles of 1776 and a capitulation to British power.

As long as Alexander Hamilton remained secretary of the Treasury, the Republican press directed most of its personal attacks at him, not Washington; Hamilton's resignation at the end of January 1795, however, made Washington himself the target of Republican criticism. Despite his public display of impassivity, the president felt these attacks keenly and resolved not to serve a third term. In May 1796 he approached Hamilton, now practicing law in New York, for advice on "*my draft* of the valedictory" that he hoped to publish in the fall of the year.[83] In the pages he enclosed, Washington sounded the themes that Hamilton recast into the formal, magisterial language of the Farewell Address.

Except for a few brief remarks on his career in the service of the country, most of what Washington had written took the form of advice for the future. Americans, he said, must overcome their sectional and partisan divisions and learn to think of themselves as one people, "the Children of one common Country." They must maintain "Constitutional purity" in government, so "that our Union may be as lasting as time; for while we are encircled in one band, we shall possess the strength of a Giant and there will be none who can make us affraid." Americans, he continued, must "guard

against the Intriegues of *any* and *every* foreign Nation," remaining unentan-
gled in alliances with self-interested European nations. To maintain its independence of action, the United States must be "always prepared for War,
but never unsheath the sword except in self defence so long as Justice and
our *essential* rights, and national respectability can be preserved without it."
If the United States were able to remain at peace for even twenty years,
"such in all probability will be [the nation's] population, riches, and resources, when combined with its peculiarly happy and remote Situation
from the other quarters of the globe, as to bid defiance, in a just cause, to any
earthly power whatsoever."[84]

The advice that Washington wanted to leave his countrymen with—
"unity at home and independence abroad"[85]—distilled to its essence his
views as a man for whom republicanism and imperialism had never been
separable. The United States would become a great nation, he believed,
only if Americans resisted their fragmenting political tendencies and developed the West—what he had once described as "a vast Tract of Continent,
comprehending all the various soils and climates of the World, and abound-
ing with all the necessaries and conveniencies of life"[86]—in an orderly way.
Such a course implied wisdom and restraint, neither of which, alas, seemed
abundant in the political world he was about to leave. The new empire was
indeed in place and functioning; that was his great legacy. But if his successors allowed the character of that empire to be defined on the periphery by
the disorderly, instinctive expansionists who lived there—those like the
Whiskey Boys who despised federal authority and the Indian-hating frontiersmen who believed that any natives who could not be shouldered aside
should be killed—all his hopes for America's future would be lost.

Having pronounced his political testament in September 1796, Washington intended his last public act to be handing over power to his successor,
John Adams. Like the surrendering of his commission to the Continental
Congress in 1783, he understood this as the fulfillment of his duties as a virtuous man and servant of the republic. He also saw it in personal terms as release from an office whose burdens had become almost overwhelming. He
anticipated a happy retirement, he said, under his own "vine and fig tree." Yet
at Mount Vernon he continued to follow public events in the newspapers (he
subscribed to ten of them) and grew increasingly worried "that his final advice to the country would be ignored, and his legacy . . . abandoned."[87]

The terrible pull of the Anglo-French wars in particular bothered him,
with their potential of dividing Americans so decisively into Anglophile and

Francophile camps as to threaten domestic unrest, or worse. When the United States was drawn into an undeclared naval war with France after the XYZ Affair and it looked as if the furious divisions between Federalists and Republicans might actually break out in civil war, President Adams named him—without first directly inquiring if he would accept the appointment— as commanding general of a vastly expanded provisional army.[88] Washington accepted graciously enough, even though (as he delicately put it) the call "to exchange once more, the smooth paths of Retirement for the thorny ways of Public life" was "conducive of Sensations which can be more easily conceived than expressed."[89] His retirement had lasted fifteen months.

Washington knew that he might once more be subject to vilification or thought a hypocrite for accepting a new military post after having so publicly retired. But in the end, as always, Washington chose the side of order. He performed the duties required of him with care, thoroughness, and no public complaint. His responsibilities could largely be handled by correspondence, which he carried on at a rate only slightly less brisk than he had while president, even though he also continued to supervise the operation of his plantations, buy and sell land, and attend to his duties as president of the Potomac River Company. These were heavy responsibilities for a man who had turned sixty-seven in February 1799, but they were not ones he felt he could shirk. As he explained the month before to John Quincy Adams,

> When I offered my Valedictory Address to the People of the United States, I little thought that any event would arise in my day, that could withdraw me from the Retreat in w[hi]ch I expected to pass the remnant of a life (worn down with cares) in ruminating on past scenes, & contemplating the future granduer of this rising Empire[.] But we know little of ourselves, & much less of the designs of Providence.[90]

Throughout the rest of that year, he continued to work, write, and worry about the future—of his country, as well as his farms. In mid-November he confided in James McHenry, the secretary of war, that he had

> for sometime past, viewed the political concerns of the United States with an anxious, and painful eye. They appear to me, to be moving by hasty strides to some awful crisis; but in what they will result—that Being, who sees, foresees, and directs all things, alone can tell.[91]

He was less pessimistic and certainly less resigned about his plantations, because he could do more about them. On December 13 he wrote a brisk note
to his estate manager, James Anderson, commenting on the sad condition of
the stock pens he had observed the day before on a riding tour of his farms.
"Such a Pen as I saw yesterday at Union Farm," he chided, "would, if the
Cattle were kept in it one Week, destroy the whole of them. . . . Dogue run
Farm Pen may be in the same condition."[92] He gave Anderson no direct instruction to mind his duties and repair the pens, but then he hardly needed
to. The implied rebuke from the man whom virtually all Americans revered
as the very model of dutifulness was sufficient.

Washington may also have been brief because he was not feeling particularly well when he wrote. On his tour the previous day he had been soaked
through and chilled to the bone when a sudden turn of the weather brought
rain, sleet, and snow. On the thirteenth he was hoarse and coming down
with a cold, but "he made light of it, as he would never take anything to
carry off a cold." That evening he was "remarkably chearful" and sat with
Martha and his secretary, Tobias Lear, reading aloud passages from the
newspaper "which he thought diverting or interesting." They retired at the
usual hour. Washington, it seems, paused long enough to check the ther-
mometer one last time and finish writing his weather observations for the
day: "Mer[cury] 28 at Night." Then he lay down the pen, closed his diary,
and went off to bed.[93]

CHAPTER FIVE

Jackson's Vision: Creating a Populist Empire

I t was characteristic of George Washington that he went to meet his final enemy in a calm and orderly way. He had gone to bed with a cold on Friday, December 13, 1799. At two the next morning he wakened Martha and "& told her he was very unwell, and had had an ague." His throat was so inflamed that he could barely speak or swallow. He asked her to send for one of his farm overseers—a man who also treated the slaves when they fell sick—to come and bleed him. The doctors, who began arriving at Mount Vernon after daylight, bled him again, three more times in all, until at last "the blood ran slowly [and] appeared very thick." They applied blister compresses to his throat and legs, had him inhale steam from a teapot, administered a purgative of calomel, gave him a tartar emetic. Nothing helped.

As evening came on, Washington knew that he had not long to live and took control of his dying. He asked Martha to fetch his two extant wills and had her burn the older of the two, which had not included instructions on the freeing of his slaves. He instructed Tobias Lear, his secretary, to look after his papers and to arrange his accounts. Then he calmly ordered the doctors to surrender to the inevitable. *"I feel myself going, you had better not take any more trouble about me; but let me go off quietly; I cannot last long."* From time to time thereafter he struggled to speak, so faintly that Lear, who sat by the bed holding his hand, could barely make out the words. Late in the evening, his breath came more easily. He withdrew his hand from Lear's to touch his wrist, feeling for his pulse. Then, Lear wrote, his hand fell away and "he expired without a struggle or Sigh," sometime between ten and eleven o'clock.[1]

The passing of the great man occasioned public ceremonies throughout

North America. On December 26, soldiers, ministers, and members of Congress marched in Philadelphia in a solemn procession from Independence Hall to the New Lutheran Church on Fourth Street to hear Congressman Henry "Light-Horse Harry" Lee of Virginia eulogize Washington as "first in war—first in peace—and first in the hearts of his countrymen." He had been, as Lee wrote elsewhere, a man who "subjected his passions to his reason; and could with facility, by his habitual self-control, repress his inclinations whenever his judgment forbade their indulgence: the whole tenor of his military life evinces uniform and complete self-command."[2]

Washington was gone now, and as the citizens of the imperial republic he had led to independence looked back on his life, they also looked forward to their collective future. Nowhere were they more active than in Philadelphia, the capital of the United States in the 1790s. When Lee delivered his eulogy, at least 60,000 citizens lived in the city on the Delaware, making it one of the great entrepôts of the North Atlantic world. They knew well the sounds of construction, for everywhere they were putting up private residences and public buildings, usually of Georgian design and red brick. William Penn's century-old city remained a beacon of prosperity and tolerance for merchants, artisans, sailors, free blacks, and European immigrants. Market Street, its major east-west artery, was as dynamic as any commercial thoroughfare in the world.

The haphazard superimposition of the federal government on the bustling city reflected the half-formed quality of political power in the Republic as a whole. Presidents Washington and John Adams lived in a rented house at 190 High Street, the Senate and the House of Representatives met a couple of blocks away in the county courthouse on Chestnut Street that was dubbed Congress Hall, and the Supreme Court convened around the corner in Independence Hall.[3] Yet the improvisational character of the United States government did not obscure its authority, which seemed quite real to those men who arrived from the periphery of the Republic eager to exploit its possibilities as well as its infirmities.

Among them was Andrew Jackson of Tennessee, a brash young man who seemed out of his element in Washington's Philadelphia. Jackson had spent several months in the capital in 1796 as a member of the House of Representatives before moving the next year to the second floor of Congress Hall as one of thirty-two United States senators. Thirty years old, Jackson was six feet one inch tall and remarkably thin, with a ramrod posture, red hair, sparkling blue eyes, and little evident talent as a legislator. To the extent that his colleagues in the House and Senate noticed him at all, they thought him wild. Decades later, Thomas Jefferson remembered Senator Jackson as "a dangerous man" who could barely speak because "of the rashness of his feelings." He would "often choke with rage."[4]

The business of Congress bored Jackson, except when it involved his constituents. Then he sprang to his feet with genuine ardor. On one occasion, the congressman supported a petition from a Tennessean for the reimbursement of expenses incurred on an expedition against the Cherokees. Criticizing those who characterized the mission as belligerent, Jackson explained that the "militia acted entirely on the defensive, when twelve hundred Indians came upon them and carried their station, and threatened to carry the Seat of Government." Only when "war was waged upon the State," only when "the knife and the tomahawk were held over the heads of women and children," only when "peaceable citizens were murdered," did Tennesseans "make resistance."[5] Jackson's colleagues were unmoved; his appeal failed. He had nevertheless announced some of the most persistent themes of his career: that war was necessary in the defense of family and honor; that people, not their government, were the best judge of threats to their security and how to deal with them; and that the proper role of the United States government was to facilitate, not obstruct, local wishes.

The unhappy legislator was relieved to flee in 1798 to his wife, Rachel, and their home, near Nashville. Within a few years of the federal government's move to Washington, D.C., however, no American, in or out of the capital, was able to ignore Andrew Jackson. As the ineffective congressman became a famous general, his exploits against the Creeks and the British during and after the War of 1812 polarized his fellow citizens. To some, he was the captain of a democratic band of American brothers who saw themselves as the vanguard of American expansion. But to those who shared Washington's vision of a republican empire making an orderly progress across North America, Jackson was nothing less than darkness made visible.

"Merrit Alone Ought to Be the Road to Preferment"

The tribune of democratic imperialism was born on March 15, 1767, in the Waxhaws region on the border between the colonies of North and South Carolina. Jackson's parents were Scotch-Irish immigrants who, after arriving in Pennsylvania two years earlier, had traveled southwest down the valley of Virginia and through the foothills of the Appalachian Mountains. His father died while his mother, Elizabeth, was pregnant. Raised by his mother and his older brothers, Andrew was defiant from the beginning, a temperament fashioned by a mixture of chemistry and circumstance.[6]

The people of the Waxhaws, like border folk throughout eastern North America, valued their autonomy. Far from the political conclaves of Philadelphia, they experienced the American Revolution as an episode in an ongoing defense of family and community against an array of threatening outsiders: redcoats, Hessians, Tory irregulars, and Indian warriors. Andrew Jackson's aggressive temperament was hardly unusual in the frontier world that nurtured him. As the obscure young boy became a famous old man, telling tales of his antiauthoritarian boyhood became reflexive. One of his favorites was set in 1781: a British officer ordered the fourteen-year-old Jackson to clean his boots. He refused, so the officer slashed at him with his sword, inflicting serious cuts to his forehead and left hand. Taken prisoner, Jackson and his brother Robert fell ill. Their mother arranged for them to be exchanged; too late for Robert, who succumbed to disease, but just in time for Andrew, who took months to recover. Meanwhile, Elizabeth Jackson died of cholera she contracted while caring for two imprisoned nephews in Charleston, South Carolina.

When Great Britain recognized American independence in 1783, Andrew Jackson was a sixteen-year-old orphan who had learned to take care of himself by defying anyone who tried to control him. It was not only the British he resisted; when an American officer was "proud and haughty," Jackson told a biographer in 1843, "I immediately answered, 'that I had arrived at the age to know my rights, and although week and feeble from disease, I had the courage to defend them, and if he attempted anything of that kind I would most assuredly Send him to the other world.'"[7] Perhaps the young Jackson was not as assertive as the old Jackson remembered. No matter. These events became critical episodes in popular stories of Jackson as a democratic champion forged in the fires of frontier skirmishes in the charter war of the Republic. Liberty was never a theoretical proposition to Jackson; to the end of his life, he proudly showed the scars from his encounter with the British officer.

Describing Jackson's character as democratic barely scratches its surface: it flatters his aggression and obscures the primal quality of his rage. His was a brutish world in which freedom and violence were so inextricably intertwined that those who prospered did so less by virtue of their social connections, as Washington and Penn had done, than because they were tough enough to strike at potential enemies before they could land the first blow.

To play by the rules of British gentility was folly at best, suicide at worst. Focused on personal interests and relationships with people in his immediate
vicinity, Andrew Jackson contemplated neither the mysteries of human nature nor the dangers of democracy. He learned what he knew of moral philosophy from the British soldier Banastre Tarleton, not David Hume, and
he was always more comfortable with a pistol than a pen. The great lesson
of his youth was that survival depended on the expression of passion rather
than its restraint. Whether dueling with competitors, killing Indians, or
fighting the British, Jackson embraced violence, prospered by it, reveled in it.

After several years of desultory wandering around the Carolinas, learning the law, seducing young women, and fighting over anything and everything, Jackson migrated westward in the 1790s into the new American
settlements along the Cumberland River in what is now west-central Tennessee. The smart and ambitious Jackson was open to negotiating his future.
Uncomfortable with the power of the federal government in Philadelphia, he
championed state sovereignty and intrigued with Spanish officials in New
Orleans.

Rules and borders were in flux in Jackson's world at the turn of the
nineteenth century. No one knew exactly how to behave. The British in
Florida and the Spanish in New Orleans continued to echo the strategies of
Champlain and Penn, wooing Indians and American citizens devastated by
perpetual warfare.[8] Cherokee leaders from western North Carolina through
eastern Tennessee and northern Georgia were divided between older men
who wanted peace and younger warriors who wanted to resist the encroaching Americans with violence. Further west, the Choctaws split between supporters of the British and those of the Spanish.[9] U.S. citizens
wondered whether the United States would be able to protect them and
their interests, ensure the transfer of Indian land into private hands, and
open up the Mississippi River. Some flirted, or thought about flirting, with
the Spanish, looking for better deals than what the United States offered;
others dreamed of new, autonomous empires.

Events soon narrowed the range of possibilities. The French empire
controlled by Napoleon Bonaparte dominated Europe in the first decade of
the nineteenth century. Cajoled into returning Louisiana to France, the
Spanish watched as Napoleon, unable to occupy distant colonies and upset
by the expensive futility of efforts to prevent Haitians from establishing
their independence, sold the territory to the United States in 1803. After the
American government took control of the Mississippi River and the port
of New Orleans, the ability of the Spanish to court Americans as well as

Indians dwindled. By eliminating the Spanish and the French as significant players in the lower Mississippi Valley, the Louisiana Purchase did far more than double the size of the new republic. It stabilized Jackson's world by securing the hegemony of the United States in eastern North America.[10]

No less important was the change in the American government. The election of Thomas Jefferson as president ended Federalist efforts to direct the development of the Republic according to Washington's imperial vision. The Revolutionary Settlement that emerged from the tempestuous decade of the 1790s amounted to an agreement to respect the local autonomy of prominent white men within the parameters of the federal system created by the Constitution and implemented by the Washington administration. Reflecting a general shift of power from the core to the peripheries, politics was a contest limited to a democratic band of white brothers. In his 1801 inaugural address, Jefferson promised "a wise and frugal Government, which shall restrain men from injuring one another, shall leave them otherwise free to regulate their own pursuits of industry and improvement, and shall not take from mouth of labor the bread it has earned." The new president proclaimed the federal government "the strongest Government on earth" because "every man, at the call of the law, would fly to the standard of the law, and would meet invasions of the public order as his own personal concern."[11] The decision of individual citizens to merge public and personal interest into patriotic commitment, not armies or governments, was the true glory of the United States.

Men like Jackson, who supported Jefferson essentially because they thought he would leave them alone, applauded these words. In their view, any national government was too distant, too arrogant, and too dismissive of local interests to be trusted. State governments, on the other hand, approximated the more familiar leadership of local notables reasonably well. "In you alone," Jackson had told Tennessee's governor, John Sevier, in 1797, "is Constitutionally invested the authority and power of protecting the State in case of Invassion" as well as bringing to trial anyone who endangered his neighbors. Such power "properly belong to Each Individual State" and "never ought on any account to be Surrendered to the General Goverment or its officers." Jackson lamented that "the Executive of the Union has Ever Since the Commencement of the present Goverment, been Grasping after power." The "moment, the Sovereignty of the Individual States, is overwhelmed by the General Government, we may bid adieu to our freedom."[12]

Constitutional issues, however, rarely held Jackson's attention for long. Politics as he understood it ultimately had less to do with defining the borders of federal authority than with acquiring power and personal reputation.

Jackson embodied an emerging Southern "definition of manhood rooted in the inviolability of the household, the command of dependents, and the public prerogatives manhood conferred." If liberty was personal autonomy, it was largely reserved for a fraternity of white Protestant males who dominated others, whether they were women, slaves, and children, or Indians, Spaniards, and British. Only by first becoming "masters of small worlds" in their own families could they aspire to be masters of North America.[13]

In Tennessee, Jackson practiced law, traded thousands of acres of land, invested in a store, operated a cotton gin and a distillery, bred horses, and grew cotton and other crops. His fortunes waxed and waned. The plantation he bought outside Nashville in 1804, which he eventually called the Hermitage, became the foundation and the symbol of his importance. But wealth and connections were important only insofar as they supported his quest for independence. Jackson never acknowledged that his ability to defy efforts to exercise dominion over him rested on his exercise of dominion over others, including the 15 enslaved African Americans he owned in 1798 (a number that reached 150 in the 1830s), the American Indians he fought and later ordered removed west of the Mississippi, and the women he treated with affectionate paternalism.

The sine qua non in the construction of his all-important household was the choice of a good wife, for whom the qualifications were less love than compatibility and management skills. Jackson went about this business with his usual ardor and determination, not knowing that the decisions he and future wife impetuously made in the 1780s and 1790s would haunt them for the rest of their lives.

Twenty-one-year-old Andrew Jackson arrived in Nashville in October 1788 and took up residence in a cabin next to the blockhouse of Rachel Stockley Donelson. Eating with the Donelsons, Andrew grew particularly fond of Rachel's daughter, also named Rachel, a lively young woman of about his own age. The well-matched couple's flirting quickly earned the enmity of her husband, Lewis Robards. Rachel had married Lewis in 1785 when her family lived briefly in Kentucky. The ill-matched Robardses had fallen out almost immediately, however, amid recriminations over mutual infidelity. Rachel returned to her family in Nashville. Lewis followed her. Jackson's attention to Rachel and her attention to him, meanwhile, compounded an ugly and at least potentially violent situation. After several angry exchanges with his rival, Lewis Robards returned to Virginia, where in December 1790 he petitioned the General Assembly for permission to sue for divorce on the grounds of Rachel's desertion and adultery.

Andrew Jackson, painted by   Rachel Jackson, painted by
Samuel Lovett Waldo, c. 1819   Ralph Earl, 1826

Andrew and Rachel had long since taken matters into their own hands. A year earlier they had gone to Natchez in the Spanish territory of Mississippi, where they lived as man and wife for several months; they then returned to Nashville, where Rachel was addressed as Mrs. Jackson. Decades later, responding to political attacks, Jackson's friends claimed the couple had been married in Natchez and that Rachel's bigamy was no more than an honest mistake. More recent students of the episode suspect, however, that Andrew and Rachel were establishing her desertion and adultery to speed the case through the distant legislature. Living together without legal sanction was not the cause célèbre in 1790 that it became in 1828, when Jackson bitterly concluded that widespread public discussion of the scandal in the course of his campaign for the presidency contributed to Rachel's death, shortly after his election.

On September 27, 1793, Lewis Robards obtained a decree of divorce on the grounds that "Rachel Robards, hath deserted the plaintiff, Lewis Robards, and hath, and doth, Still live in adultery with another man." Learning this news in December, the Jacksons were officially married on January 18, 1794. In their first years together, the couple worried little about the not altogether uncommon circumstances of their courtship, concentrating instead on the more pressing challenge of establishing themselves as one of the most prominent households in the Cumberland Valley.[14]

Like hundreds of other southern Americans in the early nineteenth century, the Jacksons painstakingly constructed the lives of plantation master and mistress, particularly after he purchased the Hermitage in 1804. Unable to have children, the Jacksons became surrogate parents to the son of relatives, two nephews, and a Creek Indian boy; later, Jackson became the legal guardian of even more dependents. Rachel supervised the enslaved members of the household as well as their fictive sons while Andrew attended to the reputation of the household in the public sphere.

Though there is no doubt of their deep love for each other, there is also little doubt of the paternalistic dimension of Jackson's devotion to his wife. He was her protector as well as her lover. A visitor to the Hermitage in 1828 described the deeply religious Rachel as a "plain matron, whose whole existence was wrapped up in that of her husband." She once compared Jackson's impact on her to that of the sun on snow: he had "that Effect on my spirits when I see you returning to me againe nothing will animate or inliven me untill then." He, in turn, behaved "almost as if she were a doll." She was "wife" rather than Rachel.[15]

Public office ratified the importance of Jackson's reputation as a local patriarch. Initially, he exploited his friendships with powerful patrons to win election in successive years to the Tennessee Constitutional Convention, the U.S. House of Representatives, the U.S. Senate, and the Superior Court of Tennessee, on which he served from 1798 until 1804. None of these triumphs, however, assuaged his shame at failing to be elected major general of the state militia in 1796, a failure resulting in no small part from the doubts of Governor John Sevier, a blunt-spoken older man who was immensely popular in eastern Tennessee.

Sevier won the respect of his neighbors in battles with both Indians and Tories during the American Revolution. Having served three terms as governor, he sought the militia command himself when the post came open in 1802. He hardly expected Jackson, a thirty-five-year-old with virtually no military experience, to be a formidable opponent. Judge Jackson, however, had learned the value of patience since his defeat in 1796 and had worked hard to ingratiate himself with the militia officers who cast ballots in the election. Sevier and Jackson each received seventeen votes. Governor Archibald Roane, who had to break the deadlock, cast his lot with Jackson and issued a formal commission. To be commander in chief of the state militia was the most glittering of Tennessee's prizes. The rank conferred power as well as honor, for the victor controlled the allocation of coveted resources and rewards. Generals communicated between federal and state authorities; held the power to recognize or ignore the talents of young men; wrote the official reports of campaigns, which were often published in local newspapers; and decided where armies went and what they did. Jackson held the position until 1814, when he resigned to become a major general in the U.S. Army.[16]

In October 1803, a year after the militia election, Jackson and Sevier exchanged insults in a Knoxville street. Defending himself against Sevier's sarcasm, Jackson cited his services to Tennessee. "Services?" replied the former governor. "I know of no great service you have rendered the country, except taking a trip to Natchez with another man's wife." "Great God!" exclaimed Jackson, "do you mention her sacred name?" The two drew their pistols but were restrained by friends. Later, an exchange of notes printed in a local newspaper once more very nearly prompted a gunfight.[17] It was not the last time Jackson felt obliged to defend Rachel's honor with a pistol.

Three years later, Jackson fought a formal duel with Charles Dickinson, an impetuous twenty-seven-year-old lawyer with an unruly temper and a fondness for horses, women, and alcohol. The two men fell out initially over the payment of a forfeit from an aborted horse race. The situation deteriorated rapidly when Jackson heard that Dickinson had taken Rachel's "sacred name" into his "polluted mouth." The antagonists met on May 30, 1806, near the Red River in Logan County, Kentucky. Dickinson fired first. The bullet struck Jackson's chest, breaking two ribs and lodging near his heart. Despite shock and the loss of blood, Jackson kept his feet, took careful aim, and shot Dickinson dead.[18]

Jackson's behavior was extreme but not unusual. The young citizens of the United States, an unruly brotherhood, were both acutely sensitive to insults and excessively eager to give them. The best way to undermine a rival was to label him a coward, a liar, a deceiver, or an ineffectual protector of women and children; hence Jackson necessarily understood any slighting reference to his wife as an attack on his manhood. His rage over real and imagined ridicule of his beloved Rachel was of a piece with his desire to bring order to his local world, to control what others thought and said of him.

Because sorting out the borders of good citizenship required what amounted to a perpetual debate over character, the democratic patriarchs of the early republic sniped at each other, whispered behind each others' backs, and then (because such behavior was itself censurable) either fought to vindicate their honor or spent a great deal of time explaining themselves. Relationships formed, dissolved, and reemerged overnight; enmities might endure for days—or decades. In 1813, Jackson served as a second when his brigade major, William Carroll, fought a duel with Jesse Benton. Even though Jesse's brother, Thomas Hart Benton, was one of Jackson's protégés, honor required a break between them. Confronting each other in Nashville, Jackson, armed with a whip, charged Thomas, and Jesse shattered Jackson's left shoulder with a pistol shot. Thomas Hart Benton, who eventually rebuilt his friendship with Jackson, abandoned Tennessee for Missouri. "I am in the middle of hell," he exclaimed, "and see no alternative but to kill or be killed; for I will not crouch to Jackson; and the fact that I and my brother defeated him and his tribe . . . will for ever rankle in his bosom and make him thirst for vengeance." Organizing violence, simplifying disputes, and declaring winners, duels displayed men's characters as starkly as battles.[19]

As he grew older, Jackson learned how to use his famous temper to his advantage, and some of his legendary explosions were both premeditated and preemptive. The power of those moments rested on his hard-earned reputation as a passionate man. In a larger sense, Jackson's success in constructing and defending a small world of his own gave him the reputation and the authority to expand his imperial tendencies beyond Nashville. Equally important, he and his allies, having first defined themselves as protectors of women and children, were now able to define themselves as citizens through their aggressive protection of their communities and ultimately their nation. To make war against Indians or Spanish "dons," enemies whose supposed flaws contrasted with what Jackson took to be his own virtues and those of his fellow Americans, was to duel on a grand scale. Violent aggression against "others" allowed the relentlessly competing white men of the United States to become brothers bound together in a common cause, the defense of liberty.

Jackson and his peers considered themselves patriots because they embraced the romantic idea that the United States was a collection of men like them. Patriotism amounted to a defense of their personal honor writ large, just as national imperialism was an extension of a private desire for domination. Virtuous men did not sacrifice for the public good in the manner of Washington so much as assert themselves publicly against their enemies, within and beyond the borders of the United States. If Spaniards took an "insulting position" in the Louisiana Territory and acted in ways "degrading to our national Character," the pursuit of glory in the defense of the United States was "a laudable ambition." Merging private and public concerns, they would find "one voice" in the cause of "defending our national dignity & liberties."[20]

At times, Jackson and company seemed to be trying to persuade themselves of the compatibility of personal and public interests. Patriotism was what separated republican soldiers from the supporters of Aaron Burr, *"adventurers"* pursuing an "illegal project and enterprise." Burr, the elegant, elusive former vice president whose considerable political prospects had evaporated when he killed his longtime rival Alexander Hamilton in the most famous duel of the era, created a stir during his progress through the Ohio and Mississippi valleys in 1805 and 1806. Burr apparently planned a filibustering expedition into Spanish territory. Jackson and other western leaders flirted with Burr's enterprise because they too dreamed of acquiring land and winning fame and fortune, but when Burr was arrested in 1807 and charged with treason, they worked feverishly to separate themselves from him. Their motives, they insisted had been pure, whereas Burr's had been self-serving and corrupt: they were patriots, the antithesis of *"disappointed, unprincipled, ambitious* or *misguided individuals."*[21]

Much more convincing in conflating private and public ambitions was hostility toward Indians. As much as the rituals of a republican political culture in Philadelphia and Washington, the rituals of racial warfare—ethnic cleansing—nurtured an exclusive sense of what it meant to be an American citizen. Reassured by the presence of an enemy whose savagery legitimated their own ambitions, the angry young men of Tennessee described themselves as "inocent Citizens" and the "victims" of "the ruthless hands of Savage barbarity" incited by European agents. "[P]repare then for retaliation," Jackson ordered militia officers in April 1806 in response to reports of an attack by Creeks. Their countrymen would soon "pant for the Orders of our goverment to punish the ruthless foe, who has deprived us of our fellow Citizens of our Brothers our wifes & our children and the influence that gave it birth."[22]

Not all American males panted for revenge on Indians as Jackson and his fellow borderers did. In fact, the divergence between the designs of westerners and the plans of government officials in the new capital of Washington reflected serious divisions in American society as a whole. Members of the Jefferson and Madison administrations continued to seek alliances and to rely on commerce and education to nurture harmony. Convinced that native peoples obstructed American expansion, they nonetheless sought alternatives to war, including the granting of annuities, building schools, and sending missionaries to Christianize (hence civilize) Indian groups. To employ peaceful means was essential, because Jefferson and his followers wanted to avoid dependence on a large professional army and the attendant risk of creating an aristocratic military caste like those that went with such armies in Europe. After Jefferson's election, Congress set the size of the United States Army at 3,287 and created a military academy at West Point, New York, to train officers to function as citizen soldiers. "For a people who are free, and who mean to remain so, a well-organized and armed militia is their best security," Jefferson wrote. "Were armies to be raised whenever a speck of war is visible in our horizon, we should never have been without them."[23]

The exception that proved this Jeffersonian rule was the administration's policy toward the nations of North Africa, whose subjects had long been harassing ships in the Mediterranean. Algerians had captured two American vessels in 1785 and eleven more in 1793, holding their crews hostage and demanding the payment of ransom. Where previous governments had pursued negotiation and bribery, Jefferson responded to Algerian Pacha Yusuf Qaramanli's 1801 threat of war against the United States by ordering the USS *Enterprise* into the Mediterranean.

Jefferson intended to demonstrate that the United States would protect its commerce and defend its honor. But he did not want a full-scale war. Relying on the navy, traditionally seen by Anglo-Americans as less of a threat to liberty than an army, he imposed a temporary 2.5 percent tax on American merchants active in the Mediterranean in order to pay for their government's actions. Limited foreign war to ensure the freedom of the seas, Jefferson believed, was a risk worth taking in order to enhance the liberty of the citizens of the world as well as the United States. The episodic conflict with Algiers—the low point of which was the capture of the USS *Philadelphia* in October 1803 and the high point Stephen Decatur's subsequent foray into Tripoli harbor and burning of the *Philadelphia*—suggested that small-scale military action was acceptable if it was far away, inexpensive, and dedicated solely to removing restrictions on human beings' control over their own destinies.[24]

War with Indians in North America, on the other hand, was likely to be anything but limited or distant, and threatened to damage the liberty as well as the bodies of Americans. Indeed, Jefferson saw the dilemma of dealing with Indians as a test of the cultural as well as the territorial integrity of the United States. By insisting that Indians be given the opportunity to become American citizens, Jefferson contended that their fate was in their own hands. He genuinely hoped "to live in perpetual peace with the Indians, to cultivate an affectionate attachment from them, by everything just and liberal which we can do for them within the bounds of reason, and by giving them effectual protection against wrongs from our own people." Americans should "draw them to agriculture" so that they would give up "their extensive forests" and trade their land for goods. Then "our settlements will gradually circumscribe and approach the Indians, and they will in time either incorporate with us as citizens of the United States, or remove beyond the Mississippi." Jefferson desired "to cultivate their love," but he also presumed that Indians would recognize that they had no choice but to accept American benevolence: "our strength and their weakness is now so visible that they must see we have only to shut our hand to crush them." Should a tribe be so foolish as to "take up the hatchet," the United States government would seize their land and send them west of the Mississippi River as "an example to others, and a furtherance of our final consolidation."[25]

Jefferson eschewed violence as inconsistent with both his image of himself as a civilized man and the genius of the Republic over which he presided. He wanted Indians to offer their "affectionate attachment" to the United States. If Indians owned property, established laws, and elected officials, they could "unite" with Americans and "form one people with us, and we shall all be Americans; [they] will mix with us by marriage, [their] blood will run in our veins, and will spread with us over this great continent."[26]

Among those who tried most earnestly to implement Jefferson's vision was Benjamin Hawkins, a native of North Carolina who was a member of Washington's staff during the War for Independence and later served in the Senate. He labored among the Creeks from 1796 until his death in 1818 to achieve Jefferson's goal of making Indians into citizens. To do so, he optimistically sought to foster a revolution in gender roles: men should stop hunting and take over from farming from women. This "plan of civilization" met with its greatest success among people of mixed ancestry. Some Creeks and Cherokees took up farming, became literate in English, and owned enslaved African Americans. More difficult was the challenge of Christian conversion. Spiritual assimilation proved less attractive than economic assimilation. Faith and politics laid the foundations of cultural identity in ways that technology and material goods did not.

Cherokees were so bitterly divided over how to respond to the Americans that perhaps a thousand of them chose to migrate west of the Mississippi River. Those who remained on reserves in Georgia, North Carolina, Tennessee, and the Mississippi Territory sought to balance accommodation with the United States with the preservation of local autonomy. The creation of a National Committee in 1809 was a major step, both symbolically and institutionally, toward the formation of a Cherokee nation-state. Organized principally to prevent any further loss of land, this group defined Cherokees as citizens living within the borders of their territory who had consented to the rule of their law. They identified themselves in terms of the law and residency rather than ethnicity or family. "The Cherokee Nation was not simply a people; it was a place."[27]

But the formation of a nation was insufficient. The Cherokees had to ally with the Americans or risk being destroyed along with the Creeks. In any event, the mixed-blood Cherokee elite proved exceptional in its efforts to block American ambitions by adopting the political vocabulary of their enemies. Their success came in no small part from their integration into European culture, a trend that climaxed in the 1820s with the development of a written alphabet and the publication of a newspaper. Other Cherokees—primarily not those of mixed ancestry—dissented by upholding privately "a set of practices and beliefs that reinforced linguistic, cultural, ethical, and religious boundaries between themselves and whites."[28] Among the nativists, resistance more often took the form of separatism.

These underground currents ran even more powerfully among the Creeks. Spiritual leaders interpreted a massive December 1811 earthquake in the lower Mississippi Valley as a sign that the world was in upheaval. Determined to "make the land clear of the Americans or loose [sic] their lives," militants known as Red Sticks participated in a religious revival. Their resistance was as much to a Creek elite whose members had allied themselves with the Americans. They had long since stopped paying attention to such mixed-race leaders as Alexander McGillivray, son of a Creek-French woman and Scots trader, whose adoption of statutory law and notions of private property defined a "new order" in which resources and power were concentrated in the hands of small group of men increasingly indistinguishable from their American neighbors.[29] Hawkins claimed that the Red Sticks sought "to destroy every thing received from the Americans, all the Chiefs and their adherents who are friendly to the customs and ways of the white people." They planned "to kill any of there [sic] own People if they do not take up the war Club."[30] And they did. They murdered leaders who collaborated with the Americans and killed the cattle that represented domestic agriculture. The Creek National Council responded with assassinations of rebel leaders that provoked a full-scale civil war in 1812.

The Red Sticks' defense of their way of life reinforced American perceptions of Indians as savage and themselves as a people united in a defense of liberty rooted in religion, tradition, and race. Making war against Indians legitimized ambitious passions, controlled dangerous factionalism, and created "one sentiment" about the importance of their "attachment to the federal compact." "[A]ll must feel the injuries we have received, all must be determined to resist them," Jackson said to his fellow citizens of Nashville early in 1809; "let us . . . with one heart and hand declare to the world, that firm determination . . . to go to any length with the government of our country, in defense and support of the nation's rights and independence."[31]

Jackson therefore embraced the War of 1812 as an opportunity to defeat the British, remove Indians, and intimidate the Spanish, a chance to conclude decades of intermittent border wars. How, he demanded of the Tennessee militia, can "we, who have clamoured for war, now skulk into a corner?" At stake was not only the security of their state but the character of the United States. For this was to be "an american war," which meant that it was not about "the ballance of power among an assasin tribe of Kings and Emperors" but rather concerned the defense of the rights and reputation of men of liberty. Justified in their righteous rage, Americans would "seek some indemnity for past injuries, some security against future aggressions, by the conquest of all the British dominions upon the continent of North america." They were "*a free people compelled to reclaim by the power of their arms the rights which god has bestowed upon them.*"[32]

To American citizens who thought in such terms, the alliances between Europeans and Indians that had defined North American politics since the days of Champlain seemed both useless and wicked. Negotiation was pointless, at least where Indians were concerned. Rising to the defense of "our innocent, wifes and little babes," Tennesseans would "march into the creek nation [and] demand the perpetrators" of a recent raid "at the Point of Bayonet." Should the Creeks refuse, the Tennesseeans would "make reprisals—and lay their Towns in ashes." Jackson assured Governor Willie Blount that "the fire of the malitia is up, they burn for revenge, and now is the time to give the creeks the fatal blow, before they expect it." They would not allow Indian "blood hounds" to kill "peaceful cultivators." If "the expedition to the Creeks is not permitted by the general government the people of Tennessee will have to consider for themselves what out to be done."[33]

Jackson and others had concluded that it was time to end decades of discord in eastern North America by sorting out lines of authority and drawing clear territorial and cultural boundaries. It was time, Jackson told

Tennessee volunteers in July 1812, to follow the lead of their northern "Brothers" who were invading Canada. Before them lay West Florida, "a territory whose rivers and harbors, are indispensable to the prosperity" of Tennessee and "an asylum from which" the British encouraged "ferocious savages" to stain "our frontiers with blood." The war gave them an opportunity to extend "the boundaries of the Republic to the Gulf of Mexico" and defeat the Creeks, the Shawnees, and "the blacks at Pensacola," as well as the British. In short, "*all* our enemies should feel the force of that power, which has indulged them so long, & which they have, so long, treated with insult."[34] The War of 1812 was a significant moment in the movement from Washington's preference for orderly growth and negotiation, backed by the selective use of force when negotiation failed, to the aggressive claims of Jacksonian Democrats in the 1840s that it was the "manifest destiny" of the United States to acquire all of North America.[35]

"Conquest May Become Necessary"

The War of 1812 resulted from the convergence of the tensions that had long been growing between white Americans and Indians from the Great Lakes to the Gulf of Mexico with the tensions that were growing more rapidly between the United States and Great Britain. As much as Andrew Jackson liked to consider himself a local democratic patriarch in control of his own destiny, the war that catapulted him to international fame was the product of decisions made in London, Paris, and Washington, D.C. The bellicose rhetoric that echoed in the halls of Congress differed in tone and emphasis from the bellicosity of the borderlands, and those differences by the end of the decade made Jackson the most polarizing figure in the Republic.

Americans had good reason to be irritated with Great Britain. In the years following the War for Independence, His Majesty's governments had maintained posts south of the Great Lakes, aided and abetted Indian resistance to the expansion of the Republic, and harassed American ships on the high seas. British fears of the formidable commercial power of the United States intensified with the outbreak of the wars of the French Revolution in 1793. Neither the British nor the French wanted the Americans to supply their enemy. The Washington administration's rapprochement with Britain in the Jay Treaty infuriated the French, who provoked an undeclared "quasi-war." The conflict between the two Atlantic republics took place intermittently at sea until envoys of President John Adams reached a diplomatic resolution, the Convention of 1800, confirmed by the general European peace declared at Amiens the following year.

Three years later, hostilities resumed, and war engulfed Europe for a dozen years thereafter. Napoleon Bonaparte's multiple triumphs on the Continent encouraged him to prepare for an invasion of Britain. Only the Royal Navy kept him at bay. In 1805, the combined French and Spanish fleets ventured out of safe harbor, and in October off Cape Trafalgar the British under the command of Horatio, Lord Nelson, destroyed them. The European war was essentially a stalemate, with the British virtually unchallenged at sea and the French dominant from the Iberian Peninsula to the Elbe. Exploiting their command of the world's oceans, the British harassed American shipping and impressed American sailors, both to prevent supplies from reaching the French and to keep American merchants from expanding trade while Britain was preoccupied with war.

The Jefferson and Madison administrations employed diplomacy and experimented with economic sanctions, or "peaceable coercion" (most notably in the Embargo of 1807, a spectacular, failed attempt to halt commerce with European combatants until they stopped harassing Americans), to avoid an all-out conflict with the powerful British. By the second decade of the nineteenth century, however, more than a few Americans from the Carolinas through the Ohio Valley were fed up with British insults and alliances with Indians and were eager to fight. Rather than wondering what the United States would "gain by war," Congressman Henry Clay of Kentucky asked what the country would "lose by peace." The answers were clear: "Commerce, character, a nation's best treasure, honor!"[36]

Jackson and Clay insisted that war was a measure of last resort, a defensive action forced upon an innocent United States by a bullying Great Britain and its savage Indian allies. This argument was important to President James Madison, especially when he, reluctantly, asked Congress to declare war in June 1812. Madison, a generation older, remembered only too well the chaos of the Revolutionary War. As far from bellicosity as Jackson was from gentility, the president was a short, shy man with an extroverted wife, Dolley, who overshadowed him in public. He was also one of the most learned and thoughtful men ever to occupy the White House and well aware of the pernicious impact of war on republics throughout history. He and his countrymen needed to look no further than revolutionary France in the 1790s to find an unnerving example of a commitment to liberty compromised and destroyed by the imperial power of an army under the command of an ambitious, successful general. Madison resisted the pressure for war as long as he could. When he could no longer do so, he insisted that war had not been "declared on the part of the United States until it had been long made on them, in reality though not in name." Nevertheless, said James Monroe of Virginia (soon secretary of war and eventually Madison's successor in the White House), it was "by open and manly war only that we can get through [the crisis with Great Britain] with honor and advantage to the country. Our wrongs have been great; our cause is just; and if we are decided and firm, success is inevitable."[37]

The leading advocates of hostilities in the U.S. House of Representatives, the War Hawks, were led by John C. Calhoun of South Carolina and Henry Clay of Kentucky, men who shared Jackson's views but distrusted his judgment. Younger than Jackson, they, too, were from the margins of the Republic. They differed from the Tennessean in that they preferred to manipulate the federal political system from the center rather than the border. Clay and Calhoun wanted the United States to make war; they did not want war to make the United States.

Henry Clay was born in April 1777 in Hanover County, Virginia. Like Jackson, he lost his father at an early age; he also lost five of his seven siblings. Clay's mother remarried, and in 1792 her second husband got her son a job as a clerk in the Virginia High Court of Chancery, where his hard work and determination attracted the attention of important patrons. In 1797 Clay migrated to Lexington, Kentucky, and quickly established himself as a charismatic public speaker and an unusually effective criminal lawyer. He won election to the legislature in 1803 and 1808 and the United States Senate in 1806 and 1810. Entering the House of Representatives in 1811, he was immediately chosen Speaker, a meteoric rise even by the standards of the early republic. Thirty-five years old in 1812, Clay was an occasional duelist who loved to drink liquor, play cards, and gamble on horses. He had the ability to put people at ease. And he loved power. Few men were more at home in the halls of Congress.[38]

Born in 1782, John C. Calhoun was the grandson of Scotch-Irish who had migrated south from Virginia to South Carolina. The Calhoun family was more stable and prosperous than Jackson's, and they pointed their son in a different direction. The young Calhoun graduated from Yale College in 1804, read law at Tapping Reeve's renowned school in Litchfield, Connecticut, and was admitted to the South Carolina bar in 1807. Elected to the state legislature in 1808, he moved to Congress three years later. Like Clay, Calhoun was both a dedicated War Hawk and a man who channeled his considerable ambitions and energies into directing the federal government. The

South Carolinian valued logic and learning and was a man of iron discipline. He trained his voice for public speaking and presented himself in Congress as a man of grace and elegance who always spoke to the point. Like Clay, Calhoun rapidly became an insider, a man who defined himself as part of the national government.[39]

In explaining why the United States had to fight Great Britain, Clay and Calhoun developed what became central arguments for subsequent American wars. "If we have not rushed to the field of battle like the nations, who are led by the mad ambition of a single chief, or the averice of a corrupted court," Calhoun declared in November 1811, "it has not proceeded from a fear of war, but from our love of justice & humanity." Americans ought to resort to arms only "when it is clearly justifiable and necessary; so much so, as not to require the aid of logic to convince our reason nor the ardor of eloquence to inflame our passions." Great Britain's long train of insults had created just such a situation, and no one who treasured his liberty could indefinitely tolerate such treatment. The "manly spirit" of Southerners in particular "will not submit to be regulated by any foreign power." Explicitly eschewing "a war of conquest," Calhoun argued that to choose peace when liberty was in danger was to "mark a fearful retrograde in civilization—it would prove a dreadful declension towards barbarism." Now was the time "when the United States must support their character and station among the Nations of the Earth, or submit to the most shameful degradation" in the form of "the mad ambition, the lust of power, and commercial avarice of Great Britain." Americans, according to the Committee on Foreign Relations, "will prove to the enemy and to the World, that we have not only inherited that liberty which our Fathers gave us, but also the will & power to maintain it."[40]

Henry Clay, like his Kentucky constituents, was eager to take the war to the British and their Indian allies in Canada. Abandoning the defensive posture so important to Madison, Clay contended with characteristic exuberance that the best defense was a good offense. The fact that "[i]n making the war effective, conquest may become necessary . . . does not change the character of the war—there may be no other way of operating upon our enemy, but by taking possession of her provinces which adjoin us." Americans, Clay insisted, were a patient people coerced into action by barbarism. Clay was indignant at the mere suggestion that Canadians were "innocent" and "unoffending." "Is it not in Canada that the tomahawk of the savage has been moulded into its death-like form?" If the war took Americans beyond their borders and eventuated in the conquest of Canada, it was Britain, not the United States, that was to blame. "An honorable peace," Clay asserted, "is attainable only by an efficient war." "[A] war is offensive or defensive," agreed Calhoun, "not by the mode of carrying it on . . . but by the motive and cause which led to it. If it had its origin in ambition, avarice, or any of the like passions then it is offensive; but if, on the contrary, to repel insult, injury or oppression, it is of an opposite character, and is defensive."[41]

Clay and Calhoun were politicians trying to win an argument, and the twists and turns of their rhetoric reflect its essentially utilitarian character. Nevertheless, the notion of the War of 1812 as a just war fought to defend American liberty and American honor mattered immensely to such men as the War Hawks. Clay, who was one of the commissioners appointed to make peace with their British counterparts at Ghent in 1814, could not let go of it. Right up to the end, he and his colleagues contended that the United States had always wanted peace, denying that it had started the war with the intention of annexing Canada. Protesting far too much, they bristled at any "imputation of a spirit of conquest, or of injustice towards other nations."[42]

It was not the British but domestic critics of the war who inspired the War Hawks' most impassioned oratory. Clay and Calhoun often spoke in reaction to popular opposition to the war, which was particularly keen in New England, where commerce with Great Britain remained as important as fears of Southern domination of the national government. Since the ratification of the Constitution, many New Englanders had worried about the power that Virginia and other Southern states wielded as a result of the "three-fifths clause" of the Constitution, which apportioned representation in the House of Representatives and the Electoral College by counting each enslaved African American as three-fifths of a human being. New England Federalists tended to equate Jeffersonian Republicans with Southerners and to see the expansion of an empire of liberty as the expansion of an empire of slaveholders. The Louisiana Purchase and the admission of western states, including Kentucky, Tennessee, and Ohio, which were reliably Jeffersonian, only confirmed their suspicions. "Virginia . . . will not be content," wrote one Federalist, "without holding in hand the reins of the general government; New England will never submit to be a colony of Virginia."[43] These sentiments declined during Jefferson's first term but rebounded with the imposition of the Embargo in 1807. With good reason, New Englanders protested that they bore the brunt of the economic costs of Jefferson's effort to substitute commerce for war in dealing with Europeans.

The War of 1812 exacerbated sectional tensions. Some New England Federalists denounced the war as a blatant power play by degenerate Southerners who had lost all sense of decency. One angry minister urged "an honourable neutrality" for New England. Let "southern *Heroes* fight their own battles." During the war a minority of highly vocal Federalists advocated secession, a movement that culminated in the Hartford Convention of December 1814. While the threat of secession was never great, there was widespread discomfort in the northeastern United States. Few agreed with Thomas Dawes when he wrote in June 1812 that a legal *"rising of the New England people"* was the "one way left to save us from the yoke of Bonaparte and Virginia," but many shared the general sentiment.[44]

The War Hawks also had to deal with a revival of traditional fears about a standing army. Their commitment to a military buildup constituted a revolution among Jeffersonian Republicans. Embracing the idea of a permanent though small standing army, Clay, Calhoun, and Monroe confronted one of the basic dilemmas of Anglo-American political culture: how to defend the Republic without creating the military means for a tyrant to destroy it. Jeffersonians had always preferred the militia as "our best reliance in peace and for the first moments of war till regulars may relieve them." They believed that a republic would prosper in proportion to the degree of affection its citizens felt for it. If a nation could not depend upon its able-bodied men to rise to its defense, all was lost anyway; thus a professional army was unthinkable in a well-ordered republic. As the examples of Oliver Cromwell and Napoleon Bonaparte showed, even reformers could become tyrants when they were able to substitute coercion for persuasion.[45] For Jeffersonians, including Andrew Jackson and his friends in Tennessee, the militia *was* the people; a professional army, like a government, stood apart from them.

In their zeal for war, Clay and Calhoun dismissed such fears. In December 1811, Clay, worrying that a force of 25,000 men was "too great for peace, and . . . too small for war," understood why the idea of such a large army excited "all our republican jealousies and apprehensions." Nevertheless, the Speaker was confident that the "diffusion of political information" and the intelligence of the American people would guard against the possibility that corrupt, ambitious leaders would turn the army "against the freedom of the country." Besides, it was impossible to hide such plots in a republic like the United States, where citizens were "interested in the success of the government." In short, Americans had nothing to fear from an army that was an expression of their national strength precisely because they were so jealous of their liberties. "[W]henever the sacred rights of an American freeman are assailed, all hearts ought to unite and every arm should be braced to vindicate his cause."[46]

The arguments of Clay and Calhoun articulated what Jackson embodied: the fusion of national and individual freedom. The South Carolinian knew of "only . . . one principle to make a nation great, to produce in this country not the form but real spirit of union, and that is, to protect every citizen in the lawful pursuit of his business." Americans would "not forget the citizen in the soldier, and in obeying their officer learn to contemn their Constitution." "The national character" would acquire "energy," because war was a collective defense of "the personal rights of its citizens." Calhoun would not credit opponents of war as anything more than devotees of party. Clay went further. The "remarkable difference between administration and the opposition" was "a sacred regard for personal liberty," a sentiment sure to warm the heart of Andrew Jackson.[47]

"They Have Disappeared from the Face of the Earth"

The War of 1812 climaxed a long series of border wars provoked by competition for control of the territory whose waters drain into the Great Lakes and the Gulf of Mexico east of the Mississippi River, a final struggle to gain the power to define the cultural and political landscape of eastern North America.[48] Now the most dominant military presence in the history of eastern North America, the United States preferred conquest to accommodation. William Henry Harrison, the governor of the Indiana Territory, engaged militant Indians at Tippecanoe on the Wabash River in November 1811. The Indians withdrew after an inconclusive battle, abandoning their settlement at nearby Prophetstown and looking for protection from the British. Half a year later, Governor William Hull of Michigan Territory, too eager for glory to await a formal declaration of war, led a force of 2,000 militiamen and soldiers of the U.S. Fourth Infantry Regiment toward Detroit and a projected invasion of Lower Canada.

The cocky Americans soon tasted defeat. Outmaneuvered by Major General Sir Isaac Brock, Hull precipitously surrendered his army and the city of Detroit without a fight in August. Almost simultaneously, Indians annihilated most of the garrison retreating from Fort Dearborn, the future site of Chicago. Operations in the Niagara area also failed. Only the surprising victories of the frigates USS *Constitution* and USS *United States* over ships of the Royal Navy kept the year 1812 from being a total disaster for the Americans.

The situation reversed itself in 1813. Captain Oliver Hazard Perry led a makeshift flotilla to victory over a small British fleet on Lake Erie in

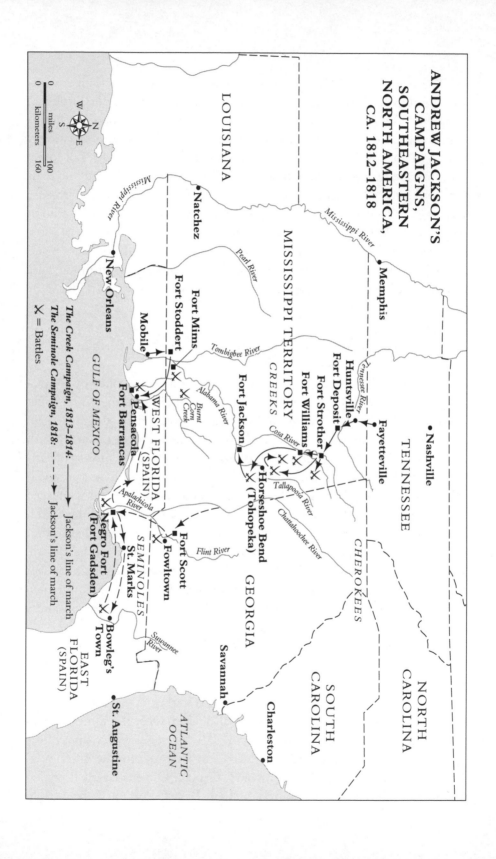

ANDREW JACKSON'S CAMPAIGNS, SOUTHEASTERN NORTH AMERICA, CA. 1812–1818

0   miles   100
0   kilometers   160

W N E S

The Creek Campaign, 1813–1814: ——— Jackson's line of march
The Seminole Campaign, 1818: – – – – Jackson's line of march
✗ = Battles

LOUISIANA

Mississippi River

Natchez

New Orleans

GULF OF MEXICO

Mobile

Fort Mims
Fort Stoddert

Tombigbee River

Pearl River

MISSISSIPPI TERRITORY

Memphis

Mississippi River

Huntsville
Fort Deposit
Fort Strother
Fort Williams

Tennessee River

Fayetteville

Nashville

TENNESSEE

NORTH CAROLINA

CHEROKEES

CREEKS

Fort Jackson

Alabama River

Burnt Corn Creek

Pensacola
Fort Barrancas

WEST FLORIDA
(SPAIN)

Apalachicola River

Negro Fort
(Fort Gadsden)

St. Marks

Fowltown

Fort Scott

Flint River

Cosa River

Horseshoe Bend
(Tohopeka)

Tallapoosa River

Chattahoochee River

GEORGIA

SEMINOLES

Bowleg's Town

Savannee River

Savannah

SOUTH CAROLINA

Charleston

St. Augustine

EAST FLORIDA
(SPAIN)

ATLANTIC OCEAN

September, thereby giving Americans effective control of the Great Lakes. Retreating into Upper Canada, the British, Canadians, and 1,000 Shawnees, Ottawas, Chippewas, Delawares, and other Indians made a last stand at the battle of Moraviantown (also known as the battle of the Thames) on October 5. They were smashed by an army of Americans and approximately 260 Delaware, Shawnee, Wyandot, and Iroquois warriors under the command of Harrison. Moraviantown was the last clear-cut victory in the north. In 1814, the U.S. Army and the British fought a series of battles along the Niagara River that resulted in the maintenance of the status quo. The Americans were unable to sustain a serious invasion of Canada.

For all practical purposes, the War of 1812 was over in the north fewer than eighteen months after it had begun. Moreover, the outcome to one degree or another seriously disappointed nearly everyone. The Indians lost all hope of holding back the Americans south of the Great Lakes; except for occasional uprisings, such as the Black Hawk War (1832), the War of 1812 put an end to Indian resistance north of the Ohio. The British, embarrassed by their defeats, fretted about containing the Americans. And the Americans failed to secure their most important objective: expansion beyond the Great Lakes into Upper Canada. In many ways, the war consolidated the political and cultural borders in place when it began.

In the south, however, the War of 1812 was as dramatic as it was decisive. The approximately 4,000 Creek Red Sticks were a formidable force. Even the perennial optimist Benjamin Hawkins complained that "the destruction of every American is the song of the day."[49] Local militia attacked a group of Red Sticks returning from Pensacola at Burnt Corn Creek in July 1813 but were driven from the field by the Indians. The Americans took refuge in a post constructed by the métis merchant Samuel Mims. In August, hundreds of Red Sticks attacked the indifferently defended stockade, killing about half of the 500 militia, civilians, métis, and Creeks gathered inside. The Fort Mims "massacre" became the rallying cry for a full assault on all Creeks. From Georgia came Major General John Floyd with 1,500 militia and Creek and Cherokee warriors, building forts and vanquishing Red Sticks in at least two major confrontations. General Ferdinand L. Claiborne moved up the Alabama River with perhaps 1,200 men in the U.S. Third Infantry Regiment and defeated militant Creeks at the Battle of Holy Ground (or Autosse) on December 23.

The most imposing of the invading American armies originated in Tennessee. Moving south under the leadership of Andrew Jackson, it burned villages and won a series of minor encounters in upper Alabama. The

climax of the campaign came on March 27, 1814, in one of the most important battles ever fought in eastern North America. Twenty-five hundred
members of the Tennessee militia joined with 500 Creeks and Cherokees to
trap a thousand Red Sticks within the impressive defenses they had constructed at Horseshoe Bend (or Tohopeka) on the Tallapoosa River. While
Jackson led an attack on the front of the Red Stick lines, General John Cof-
fee secured their rear, cutting off any hope of escape down the river. The
Americans and their Indian allies gave no quarter to the Red Sticks, most of
whom refused to surrender. At the end of the day, the victors counted some
557 bodies and estimated that they had killed another 250 warriors as they
tried to swim to safety. To a greater degree by far than the incident at Fort
Mims, the battle of Horseshoe Bend was a massacre: of the thousand Red
Sticks present, only 200 survived.[50]

Jackson called his campaign a defensive action against barbaric Indians
and renegade African Americans. "It is by waging the war in the heart of the
Enemys country," he explained in January 1814, "that effectual protection is
to be furnished to our frontiers." War was a nasty business, a responsibility
that had kept him from where he really wanted to be: home, at the Hermitage, with his wife. Jackson wanted nothing more than to return to
Rachel "on the wings of love & affection, to spend with you the rest of my
days in peacefull domestick retirement."[51] As he dealt with desertions and
disobedience among his often cantankerous troops and his own exhaustion,
he found solace in blaming the Creeks and their allies for his misfortunes.
He would not be in Alabama, he believed, had they not forced his hand.

Jackson's chilling accounts of the "*dreadfull*" "*carnage*" at Horseshoe Bend
reflect the depth of his rage at the Creeks and his understanding of the role
of war. After his men stormed the Creeks' defenses, he reported to Rachel,
"[i]t was dark before we finished killing them." The slaughter had been
necessary to persuade "those infatuated and deluded people" of the necessity of suing for peace. Redeeming "the character of Tennessee," his army
had "destroyed a confederacy of the enemy, ferocious by nature, & grown
insolent" by habit. "Barbarians, they were ignorant of the influence of civilization & of government over the human powers." Now the "fiends"
would "no longer murder our women & children, or disturb the quiet of
our borders" because "[t]hey have disappeared from the face of the Earth,"
leaving their children to exchange warfare for husbandry and the arts.
"Within a few weeks," the Tennessee militia had "annihilated the power of
a nation that had for twenty years, been the disturber of our peace." Jackson's satisfaction at the destruction of the Creeks was primal. "We have seen

the ravens & the vultures preying upon the carcases of the unburied slain. Our vengeance has been gluted."[52] Horseshoe Bend was the most decisive military encounter of Jackson's career: the climax of a life lived intimately with violence, it unleashed his passions and the fury of his men in a dance of death that continued until they had spent the last of their strength.

Jackson dictated the terms of Creek surrender without regard for his Indian allies or any past, present, or future alliances. Victory in a defensive war against barbaric aggressors required nothing less than their total destruction. Blaming the Creeks made seizing their land a righteous act by a superior people. "The hostile Creeks have forfeited all right to the Territory we have conquered" and the "friendly" Creeks should be left with only enough for farming. In Jackson's view, "the grand policy of the government ought to be, to connect the settlements of Georgia" with Tennessee and the Mississippi Territory to "form a bulwark against foreign invasion" and "influence" over the Indians. If the United States quickly populated this territory and eliminated the claims of the Cherokees and Chickasaws in Tennessee, Americans and Indians would finally live in peace. "Our national security require it and *their* security require it: the happiness and security of the whole require this salutary arrangement."[53]

Appointed a brigadier general and brevet major general in the U.S. Army in recognition of his victories, Jackson forced the Creeks to acquiesce in a massive transfer of land to the United States. Thirty-five chiefs, only one actually identified with the Red Sticks, signed the treaty of Fort Jackson on August 9, 1814. The United States acquired half of all Creek territory, a total of 23 million acres, including one-fifth of what is now the state of Georgia and three-fifths of Alabama. Fort Jackson signaled a major shift in the way in which American commissioners dealt with Indians. In the 1790s, American negotiators had worked hard to win Indian acceptance of the terms they proposed, because Indian consent mattered to the Federalists. No more. The treaty of Fort Jackson stated that they had waged "an unprovoked, inhuman, and sanguinary war" against the United States, which had defended itself "in conformity with principles of national justice and honorable warfare."[54] The devastated Creeks were forced to accept punitive terms *and* to acknowledge responsibility for their fate.

Later in 1814, a British army of 15,000 veterans of the Napoleonic wars under the command of Major General Sir Edward Michael Pakenham, a brother-in-law of the Duke of Wellington and a hero of the Peninsular Wars, arrived in the lower Mississippi Valley. Their purpose was to attack the soft underbelly of the United States and force the Republic to sue for peace.

To stop Pakenham, Jackson gathered thousands of militia from as far away as Kentucky plus creoles, free blacks, Cajuns, and Choctaws and took a stand south of New Orleans. On the morning of January 8, 1815, an over-confident Pakenham attacked Jackson's untrained but well-entrenched forces and was decisively defeated. The Americans suffered losses of 13 killed and 58 wounded; the British lost 291 dead, 1,262 wounded, and 484 prisoners. Among the fatalities was Pakenham, who lost his reputation as well as his life in North America.[55]

The Battle of New Orleans was famously unnecessary in the context of the formal war between Great Britain and the United States because a treaty of peace had been signed in Ghent, Belgium, on December 24, 1814. Nevertheless, it consolidated the transformation of eastern North America by confirming that six decades of border warfare east of the Mississippi River were at long last coming to an end. Pakenham was the agent of an anachronistic imperial order sent to make war against Americans with native allies who were in fact no longer capable of sustaining coalitions with Europeans. Jackson, the herald of a new empire, understood native peoples as at best expendable allies and at worst barbarous enemies. The multicultural character of the American army at New Orleans was a remnant of an older world swept aside by the rise of the United States in the wake of the Seven Years' War.

As the handful of Creeks and Seminoles who accompanied Pakenham's army watched the humiliated British board their ships and set sail for Europe in the spring of 1815, they must have known that things had irrevocably changed. They were running out of options, and no one was more eager to exploit their desperate situation than Andrew Jackson. When Jackson bragged that he had "defeated this Boasted army of Lord Wellingtons," he celebrated the populist triumph of the amateur over the professional, the citizen over the gentleman, the world of Nashville over the world of Philadelphia.[56] After New Orleans, he seemed as unstoppable as a force of nature.

"A Cruel & Unprovoked War Against the Citizens of the U States"

The last piece of the puzzle in southeastern North America was Florida. By the second decade of the nineteenth century, the region, claimed by Spain and dominated by British agents and merchants, was the center of resistance to the expansion of the American empire, the last bastion of defense against its exploding population. The vast majority of the roughly 3,000 Indians in

A romantic portrait of Major General
Andrew Jackson, painted by Thomas Sully,
engraved by James B. Longacre, 1820

Florida were called Seminoles after the Spanish word *cimarrón,* "wild" or
"runaway." They were mostly Creeks who had been migrating into Florida
for decades. As determined to maintain their autonomy as the residents of
the Waxhaws had been in the 1770s, they had severed connections so completely that the leader of the Creek National Council, Tustanagee Thlucco,
admitted in 1812 that while the Creeks were "all one family," the Seminoles
were "far off in a corner."[57]

Florida was also home to several thousand African Americans, many escaped from slavery. They were emboldened not only by their success but by
that of Toussaint L'Ouverture and thousands of black men and women on
the island of Haiti. Born a slave probably in 1744, Toussaint had emerged as
a leader of the revolt against French authority that erupted in the wake of
the French Revolution and a decree of general emancipation in 1794. Toussaint was an effective general and statesman and an enduring symbol of
colonial resistance to European imperialism. Despite his capture and death,
Haiti became an independent republic on December 31, 1803. As a result,
blacks in Florida were eager to liberate slaves from plantations in Georgia.

The antagonism toward Americans that they shared did not make black and native Floridians love one another: Seminoles traded in slaves, and tensions between Indians and Africans on occasion exploded into violence.

It took the threat of an American invasion to unite Seminoles, Creeks, and African Americans in opposition to the United States. Payne's War (named in honor of their most prominent leader) pitted hundreds of Seminoles and African Americans against some 150 Americans who invaded Florida in March 1812; they were followed by regular troops after the declaration of war with Great Britain. In October, from 50 to 200 Seminoles and blacks defeated about a hundred Americans under the command of Colonel David Newman. Their triumph intensified the fears of the white citizens of the United States. "Our slaves are excited to rebel," wrote one Georgian to Secretary of War James Monroe in January 1813. "St. Augustine, the whole province will be the refuge of fugitive slaves; and from thence emissaries . . . will be detached to bring about a revolt of the black population in the United States."[58] This apprehension became part of the justification for a war of conquest in Alabama and, eventually, Florida.

Following Jackson's destruction of the Creeks at the battle of Horseshoe Bend in March 1814, hundreds of Seminoles, fugitive slaves, and Red Sticks gathered at Prospect Bluff, about sixteen miles from the mouth of the Apalachicola River in the Florida panhandle. There they built what white Americans, including Jackson, labeled a "Negro Fort." Supplied by the British from Pensacola, they made the fort the headquarters of resistance to the Americans. In the summer of 1814, Colonel Edward Nicolls of the Royal Marines reported that the "Indians and blacks are very good friends and cooperate bravely together."[59]

Six months later, 2,810 people, including 250 blacks, were living on the bluff overlooking the Apalachicola. By late spring 1815, they had enclosed two acres with a fifteen-foot-high, eighteen-foot-thick parapet and ramparts mounting cannon and mortars provided by the British, all surrounded by a ten-foot-wide moat and a nearly impenetrable swamp. Formidable as the fort was, it could not withstand the British abandonment of the Indians and blacks in Florida in the aftermath of the Battle of New Orleans. Hungry residents of Prospect Bluff began leaving in search of food. In the summer of 1815, a band of "saucy and insolent" African Americans, saying "they are all free," dominated the once crowded stockade.[60]

The "Negro Fort" not only exemplified the determination of the diverse residents of Spanish Florida to maintain their autonomy; it also symbolized a multicultural world that white Americans saw as both dangerous and anachronistic. More than a strategic headquarters for raids against American settlements, the fort seemed a relic, the artifact of a traditional notion of North American empire as the dynamic product of constantly negotiated relationships among many local communities. The consolidation of the new romantic conception of the United States as an expression of a homogeneous national identity required the subjugation of all alternatives, no matter how local or peripheral. In July 1816, several hundred American and Creek warriors surrounded the Negro Fort and demanded its surrender. The fort's commander, a former Pensacola carpenter named Garzon, replied with "much abuse" that "he had been left in command of the fort by the British government, and that he would sink any American vessel that should attempt to pass it; and would blow up the fort if he could not defend it."[61] On July 27, American gunboats began a bombardment that ended with a direct hit on the magazine, causing an explosion that destroyed the fort and killed the forty or so people within its walls.

Americans no longer wondered whether they would acquire Florida but when and how they would accomplish the inevitable. The Monroe administration, which assumed office in 1817, preferred, in the tradition of Jefferson and Madison, to approach the Spanish and seek a negotiated solution. Predictably, Andrew Jackson and his fellow westerners demanded a more direct approach. Jackson urged "a permanent settlement" as soon as possible. Conquest had already made Indians "subjects" of the United States; to negotiate with them was "an absurdity." Now was the time to subjugate the renegade Seminoles and fugitive slaves who threatened the United States from enclaves beyond its borders.[62]

Jackson marched into Florida in March 1818 and attacked Saint Marks and Pensacola. Neither President Monroe nor Secretary of War Calhoun had expected their general to be so aggressive. Jackson of course made no apology for his actions. He entered Florida, he informed a stunned Spanish official, "[t]o chastise a Savage foe, who combined with a lawless band of Negro Brigands, have for some time past been carrying on a cruel & unprovoked war against the Citizens of the U States." Having destroyed villages of "Barbarians," he demanded a permanent post in Florida and Spanish support for his efforts against "these lawless & inhuman savages." The "feeble" resistance he encountered confirmed the nature of his mission as a mopping-up operation whose principal purpose was to demonstrate that the enemies of the United States could not hide and that those who aided and abetted them would feel the wrath of the Republic. The general delivered this message most dramatically by placing two British Indian traders,

Alexander Arbuthnot and Robert C. Ambrister, on trial before a court-martial for attempting "to excite the Negroes & Indians in East Florida to war against the U States." Ambrister, found guilty of fomenting Seminole raids, died before a firing squad at Saint Marks on April 29; Arbuthnot, convicted of espionage, was hanged that same day.[63]

Jackson's occupation of East Florida flustered the Monroe administration because it was engaged in delicate negotiations to acquire Florida by treaty. It outraged a Spanish government reeling from both domestic unrest and independence movements throughout its empire. But Great Britain protested only weakly. Unwilling to risk another war with the United States, Whitehall overlooked Jackson's near-summary execution of two British subjects and quietly deserted the Spanish. In October British and American diplomats concluded the Convention of 1818, extending commercial relations for a decade, resolving a dispute over American fishing rights off Canada, extending the border between Canada and the United States westward along the forty-ninth parallel from the Lake of the Woods to the Continental Divide, and agreeing to the "joint occupation" of the Oregon country from the divide to the Pacific until the permanent possession of the region could be decided. This sudden rapprochement left the Spanish minister, Don Luis de Onís, helpless to act against Jackson in Florida and hence with little option but to renew negotiations with Secretary of State John Quincy Adams. The result was the Transcontinental Treaty, signed in February 1819. In return for a U.S. agreement to assume $5 million worth of damage claims by American citizens against Spain, the Spanish ceded all lands east of the Mississippi River, agreed to a boundary running along the Sabine, Red, and Arkansas rivers as far as the Continental Divide, surrendered their claims to the Oregon country, and recognized the forty-second parallel from the divide to the Pacific as New Spain's northern border with the United States.[64]

"A Great Moral Battle for the Benefit . . . of All Mankind"

Jackson's invasion of Florida ignited a firestorm of controversy in the capital of the United States at a time when its residents were still recovering from the effects of a literal conflagration that nearly destroyed it in August 1814. A raiding force of British soldiers and Royal Marines seriously damaged the fledgling city; most damaging symbolically was the fire they set amid piles of books and furniture on the floors of the House and Senate, which gutted the Capitol building and defaced its exterior walls. Congress temporarily reconvened in the Patent Office Building, the only public structure not damaged by the British. Thereafter the House and Senate met in a temporary edifice on the present site of the Supreme Court; they did not return to quarters in the Capitol until December 1819. Construction of the building itself was not completed for more four decades.

Some Americans advocated abandoning Washington altogether in the wake of its sacking. After all, the town had few permanent residents. Members of Congress lived like "monks in a monastery" in boarding houses. Nearby Georgetown and Alexandria scarcely supplied the commercial and cultural amenities left behind in Philadelphia. And summer brought stifling heat, humidity, and disease to the banks of the Potomac. Unfinished Washington sometimes seemed like the Republic as a whole: a work in progress with an uncertain future.

Still, the sounds of rebuilding broke through the postwar gloom, promising a brighter future. The population passed 10,000. New churches, shops, and private homes graced the city's broad boulevards. Better bridges and roads, together with more regular steamboat and stagecoach service, improved connections to the outside world. In 1817, Martha Washington's granddaughter, Eliza Parke Custis Law, noted that "houses are rising in every direction; Pennsylvania Avenue is built up . . . and [there are] as many good houses on that avenue as in Boston or Philadelphia." Inside these homes the wives and daughters of Washington presided over ever more elaborate social occasions. They called on each other, planned parties, and expressed their opinions about public issues in private settings.[65]

As the seat of national power, Washington attracted ambitious people almost as easily as Philadelphia had in the 1790s. The doyenne of the city's social circles, Margaret Bayard Smith, reported that the city was "every year, more and more, the resort of strangers from every part of the Union."[66] Many arrived from the interior of North America, legislators from Tennessee, Kentucky, Ohio, Louisiana, and the new states of Alabama, Mississippi, Indiana, and Illinois. In the manner of the young Jackson, they were often brash, cocky and provincial, eager to advance the interests of their constituents on the far margins of the Republic.

Congress was at the center of Washington society. Women and men flocked to the galleries of the House and Senate to watch young legislators speak on the public stage. Later they gathered in parlors to critique performances and make or break reputations. Politicians consciously played to women with sentimental rhetoric and grand gestures, seeking approval with emotion as much as with logic. Even in the chambers of the makeshift Capitol, long orations were powerful theater presented to overflow audiences crammed into a small space.[67]

In January 1819, the main topic of conversation was the behavior of Andrew Jackson, the once obscure senator from Tennessee who had become the most formidable military figure in the Republic. Sixty-five years after the young George Washington precipitated a great imperial war over control of the Forks of the Ohio, all serious resistance to the dominion of the United States in eastern North America was at an end. Washington could have imagined neither the immensity nor the populist expansionism of this new empire. Blessed with an abundance of fertile land, a skyrocketing population, and burgeoning commerce, the United States had escaped apparently unchecked from a war with Great Britain, now the world's most formidable power.

Nevertheless, history warned that imperial republics, most notably Rome, disintegrated into chaos and civil war. Inevitably, military leaders— Caesar, Cromwell, and most recently, Bonaparte—exploited apparent anarchy to seize power in defiance of law and public opinion. George Washington had been a rare exception to this dreary pattern. Now came Andrew Jackson, a populist chieftain from the borderlands who had acted in Florida as he thought best, irrespective of the advice and orders of his civilian superiors. In 1819, while the question of the admission of Missouri to the Union focused one line of public debate on the contradiction of the enslavement of African Americans in a republic dedicated to human liberty, Jackson's seemingly uncontrollable, unconstitutional use of military power dominated another.

Jackson's exploits had made him a national celebrity. They had also earned him the full attention of Calhoun, Clay, and Secretary of the Treasury William Crawford, all of whom wanted to become president of the United States and instantly recognized the Tennessean as their most serious potential rival. Because they shared the desire to burst the bubble of Jackson's popularity, it would be naive to imagine that their attacks on Jackson were not strongly motivated by jealousy and partisanship. But it would be equally naive to imagine that their objections to Jackson's actions were solely motivated by those impulses. Indeed, when one examines the content of the debate on the general's conduct in the House of Representatives, it becomes quite clear that many thoughtful Americans were deeply worried about the role of the military in the Republic. After the War of 1812, Congress had set the size of the U.S. Army at 12,383: an 80 percent reduction in authorized strength from the height of the conflict with Great Britain but still immense by the standards of the 1780s and more than three times the size of the peace establishment during Jefferson's administration.[68] Pondering this increase in light of the military record of Andrew Jackson led speakers to consider the relationship between empire and liberty as well as the role of war in the life of the Republic.

On January 12, 1819, the Committee on Military Affairs submitted a report to the United States House of Representatives that sharply criticized Jackson for the executions of Arbuthnot and Ambrister. Representative Thomas W. Cobb, a thirty-four-year-old lawyer and Crawford ally from Georgia, immediately rose to offer an amendment. Cobb wanted both to extend the censure of Jackson to include the conquest of Saint Marks and Pensacola and to secure legislation prohibiting American officers from invading foreign territory without the consent of Congress or executing prisoners without the permission of the president. The ensuing debate consumed most of the month.

Ritually nodding to the general's achievements and offering denials of personal animus, critics denounced Jackson's disregard for—if not outright defiance of—regularly constituted authority. The future of the Republic depended upon the subordination of even heroic military officers to the will of America's elected representatives. Precisely because Jackson had "so eminently contributed to the honor and defence of the nation," Congress had a responsibility to monitor his behavior. "[T]he more elevated the station, the more exalted the character of the individual," said the House Committee on Military Affairs in urging censure, "the more necessary it is, by a seasonable, yet temperate expression of public opinion, through the Constitutional organ, to prevent the recurrence of incidents at variance with the principles of our Government and laws."[69]

Both those members who expressed concerns about constitutional authority and those who defended Jackson devoted much of their time to reviewing the history of American expansion and the Republic's dealings with Indians. His defenders argued that the Spanish and especially the British had incited the Indians and African Americans of Florida to threaten the peace and tranquility of the southern United States. Congressman Richard M. Johnson, a thirty-nine-year-old former colonel in the Kentucky militia who claimed to have killed Tecumseh at the battle of the Thames, demanded to know why Americans had to get permission from Congress "to check [the] barbarities and to punish [the] crimes" of Indians. "[W]hen a nation, either savage or civilized, . . . grossly violates the laws of nations and of humanity, retaliation, or reprisals, are always justifiable, often useful, and sometimes essentially necessary, to teach the offenders to respect the laws of humanity, and to save the effusion of blood."[70] By launching a defensive invasion of Florida, Johnson argued, General Jackson had made the entire South safe for American citizens, who properly owed him gratitude, not censure.

Jackson's critics, on the other hand, believed that he had declared war on his own. What would be the fate of the United States if generals assumed such power? "In the splendor of military achievements," warned Cobb, "[w]e become so infatuated with the man that we lose sight of principle, and we are offering him our worship, before we are aware that we have made him a god." Magnifying the danger in the case of the Seminole War was the very nature of the conflict itself. Jackson had prosecuted "an offensive war. To give it the character of a defensive war, it must appear that our country had been invaded, or was in imminent danger of invasion by the Spanish forces in East Florida, or elsewhere." Cobb concluded that any attempt to characterize the Seminole War as "a defensive war" was "an outrage upon common sense."[71]

The best answer to this charge was to prove that the Seminoles had started the war, that they were responsible for their own fate, and that Jackson had done only what they forced him to do. Thus speaker after speaker recited detailed histories of the relationship of the United States with Indians in general and the people of Florida in particular. Jackson's defenders were forced to declare that Indians at war were a sovereign people and that Europeans who helped them in their attacks were "volunteers in the service of a lawless tribe of savages, whose mode of warfare is indiscriminate massacre of all ages and sexes." Congressman John Holmes of Massachusetts concluded his defense of Jackson by shamelessly conjuring up an image of a "female form" in "some distant wilderness," who had witnessed the death of her husband and seen her children "mangled and murdered in [her] presence," before she at last succumbed "to a more lingering fate." From the grave, she told "the advocates of false humanity" that "duty and policy demand that you should punish, with instant death, every instigator of Indian barbarity, wherever he may be, and whenever he may be found." Only if you encountered a man who had lost his family could you possibly understand that "Indian warfare . . . is a war of extermination," explained John Floyd of Virginia, a native of Kentucky and a former militia general. "Have you not a family?" he asked. "Do you not love them?"[72]

Secretary of War Calhoun and Speaker of the House Clay now confronted a monster that they helped create. No one had more eagerly argued for the justice and necessity of the War of 1812 than they; no one had more directly made connections between liberty and war. Jackson embodied the logical extension of their arguments. More than a political rival, Jackson was a symbol of naked aggression, of personal liberty run rampant into violence, of a new American order in which almost anything was deemed acceptable if it could be construed as a defense of American families, American values, and American freedom. Jackson had the potential to become not so much an American king as an American emperor, a populist Bonaparte.

Calhoun weighed his ambitions against his principles and kept his doubts about Jackson private, but Clay boldly took to the floor of the House to support censure. In one of the most famous speeches of his long career, the Speaker attacked Jackson in personal as well as constitutional terms. The Seminole War, he argued, had not been a just war. A recent reading of the 1814 treaty of Fort Jackson had filled him "with the deepest mortification and regret. A more dictatorial spirit he had never seen displayed in any instrument." Not even "imperious Rome" in her wars against "barbarous nations" had indulged in "such an inexorable spirit of domination pervading a compact purporting to be a treaty of *peace,*" especially over "a wretched people, reduced to the last extremity of distress." Clay condemned the treaty as "utterly irreconcilable . . . with those noble principles of generosity and magnanimity which he hoped to see his country always exhibit, and particularly toward the miserable remnant of the aborigines." "The fault" in the Seminole War was "on our side." Unfazed by the factual inaccuracy of his position, Clay maintained that English-speaking settlers had "constantly abstained from retaliating upon the Indians the excesses practised by them toward us" and saw no reason to change now that "we are powerful and they are weak." Even when, as with Arbuthnot and Ambrister, there were good reasons to take action, it was not always "just to do what may be advantageous." The end, in other words, did not justify the means, and the means Jackson had chosen imperiled the very character and future of the Republic. Greek and Roman as well as French history bore ample witness to the danger of trusting too much to the virtue of military heroes.[73]

The Speaker who had so fervently urged war in 1812 now appealed to universal notions of decency. "We are fighting," he said, "a great moral battle for the benefit, not only of our country, but of all mankind. The eyes of the whole world are in fixed attention upon us." It was the responsibility of Americans to continue to serve as a beacon of freedom. It was their "high privilege" to transmit "unimpaired, to posterity, the fair character and the liberty of [our] country." How could they expect to fulfill their obligation if they exhibited "examples of inhumanity, and cruelty, and ambition?"[74]

These calls did not fall on deaf ears, especially in the Northeast, where doubts about slavery and militarism fueled distrust of Southerners. But scruples like the ones that Clay, Calhoun, and Cobb voiced were out of harmony with the temper of the country at large. Increasing numbers of Americans thought in terms similar to those of Jackson: assuming the rightness of an American cause and affirming a romantic vision of national greatness. The exploding population of the United States, doubling roughly every two decades; the robust and growing demand for American crops, especially cotton; the extraordinary confidence of its young and ambitious citizens: these allowed many Americans to conclude that the continued expansion of the Republic was not only inevitable but an unmitigated blessing. Ideologically as well as economically, Americans seemed to have a need for territory that neither could nor should be denied. The defense of American values and the propagation of American freedom through increasingly larger spheres offered sufficient justification for war; the United States conquered not to subjugate but to liberate territories and their peoples.

Characteristically, Jackson leapt into action as soon as he heard news of "a combination in Congress to ruin me" and rode to Washington. Arriving with great fanfare on January 23, he helped his friends organize his defense. Two weeks later, the House decisively rejected the resolutions condemning Jackson for his actions in Florida. The general celebrated his vindication with triumphal visits to New York City, Philadelphia, and Baltimore, where thousands of people who had read about him in newspapers turned out to see him in the flesh. A harsh reprimand for his behavior in Florida from a Senate committee charged with investigating the Seminole War only briefly dampened the revelries that accompanied the hero of New Orleans all the way back to Nashville.[75]

The debates over his conduct solidified Jackson's preeminence as a candidate for the presidency. He collected 40,000 more popular votes than his nearest rival, John Quincy Adams, in the four-way presidential race of 1824 but was denied the office when the election was thrown into the House of Representatives. Convinced that his defeat was the product of a "corrupt bargain" between the political insiders John Quincy Adams and Henry Clay (whom Adams appointed secretary of state), Jackson became a more formidable political force than ever. He rode the wave of his personal popularity into the White House in 1828, collecting 56 percent of the popular vote and more than twice as many electoral votes as Adams.

Andrew Jackson ceaselessly asserted the liberty of white Protestant men against all enemies, foreign and domestic. As president, he was a model of paternal benevolence in manner and tone, the battle-scarred leader who knew what was best for the members of his personal and public households. The victor of Horseshoe Bend claimed without a hint of irony that the forced exile of American Indians to lands west of the Mississippi River during his two administrations was "not only liberal, but generous. [The Indian] is unwilling to submit to the laws and the States and mingle with their population. To save him from his alternative, or perhaps utter annihilation, the General Government kindly offers him a new home, and proposes to pay the whole expense of his removal and settlement."[76]

Paternalism and the characteristic conflation of the personal and the public had always been the hallmarks of Jackson's political identity; they were never in greater evidence than in the intense uproar at the beginning of his first administration over his defense of the character of Margaret O'Neale Timberlake Eaton. At sixteen, Peggy O'Neale, the daughter of a Washington hotel owner, married John Bowie Timberlake, a naval purser. While her husband was at sea, she continued to work in the bar of her father's hotel, raised two children, and was regularly seen in public with other men, including Senator John Eaton of Tennessee. Jackson stayed with Eaton in 1823 and became fond of his friend's mistress, dismissing rumors of her multiple affairs as malicious gossip. When Timberlake died at sea in April 1828 (according to the Washington gossipmongers, he had committed suicide in despair over his wife's infidelity), Jackson urged Eaton to marry her because he would then "be in a position to defend her." The couple exchanged vows on New Year's Day, 1829. The lascivious remark that "Eaton has married his mistress, and the mistress of eleven doz. others!" summarized the tenor of Washington society's reaction to the news.[77]

Shortly before, Rachel Jackson had also died, of a broken heart, her grieving husband thought, because of the vicious accusations made during the presidential campaign of their adulterous liaison. Jackson—whose fondness for Mrs. Eaton may have had something to do with a certain similarity to Rachel (another vivacious tavernkeeper's daughter) in her youth—defiantly appointed John Eaton his secretary of war, proclaimed himself Peggy's champion, and insisted on her presence at White House functions. But the women of the capital, including the wives of Vice President John C. Calhoun and most of the members of Jackson's cabinet, were equally stubborn: they refused to call on Mrs. Eaton or include her in official social events. Soon the cabinet and indeed much of the executive branch divided itself into pro- and anti-Eaton factions, a division made permanent by the president's steadfast conviction that Mrs. Eaton was being unjustly pilloried. Eventually, in 1831, Eaton tendered his resignation from the cabinet, as did Secretary of State Martin Van Buren, and Jackson sacked the remainder with the sole exception of his pro-Eaton postmaster general. Nothing like it had ever happened in American politics before.

The president understood the Eaton affair, like the controversy over his wife's bigamy and virtually everything else in his life, as a story about men and, more specifically, about him. The decision of numerous powerful Washington wives to shun a woman they regarded as a common harlot was, in Jackson's mind, a plot by his enemies "to destroy the character of Mrs. Eaton, by the foulest and basest means, so that a deep and lasting wrong might be inflicted on her husband."[78] Ignoring the women who were, in fact, the cause of the furor, Jackson punished their bewildered spouses. Because women could not be protagonists in Jackson's world, he could no more comprehend the power that the ladies of Washington had exerted in the Eaton affair than he could credit the power that Peggy herself asserted through her sexuality.

The United States in the Age of Jackson was a far cry from what Washington hoped it would become. Jackson's many opponents denounced him as the embodiment of unrestrained populism, one of the "lawless banditti" who Washington worried would transform liberty into license and civilization into chaos. They were not entirely wrong. By the 1820s, war in the United States had become an expression of personal interest, territorial conquest, and racial hatred; the impulse to empire reflected the collective power of a brotherhood of English-speaking white men united to protect the United States and all it stood for in their minds. The defense of freedom justified it all. "As long as our Government is administered for the good of the people, and is regulated by their will . . . it will be worth defending," said Jackson in his 1829 inaugural address, "and so long as it is worth defending a patriotic militia will cover it with an impenetrable aegis. Partial injuries and occasional mortifications we may be subjected to, but a million of armed freemen, possessed of the means of war, can never be conquered by a foreign foe."[79]

Three decades after fleeing Federalist Philadelphia, Andrew Jackson presided over a nation he had conquered from the margins, not by restraining his passions but by indulging them. Now the consequences of the choices he and other Americans had made in explaining as well as fighting wars against Indians and Great Britain played out in another great war for empire, this time to the south and west, where Mexicans were striving to create their own republic even as their northern neighbors took up residence within its borders.

CHAPTER SIX

Santa Anna's Honor: Continental Counterpoint in Republican Mexico

The man who incarnated everything that Henry Clay feared Andrew Jackson would become was not an American at all but a Mexican born in Jalapa in the province of Veracruz on February 21, 1794. A son of New Spain who was president of the Republic of Mexico eleven times, Antonio López de Santa Anna dominated his nation in the second quarter of the nineteenth century to such a degree that what is commonly called the Age of Jackson in one American republic might well be called the Age of Santa Anna in the other. Both men imagined themselves as embodiments of their respective nations. Yet these two military figures, both larger-than-life Romantic figures obsessed with personal honor, diverged sharply in their understandings of political authority. Their careers show that while imperial and revolutionary wars shaped Mexico as much as they did the United States, the nations' political cultures unfolded in different contexts and produced different outcomes.

The histories of the Mexico and the United States intersected violently in the second quarter of the nineteenth century, climaxing in an imperial war that determined the fate of the southern half of the North American continent and transformed both American republics in surprising ways. The cause of that decisive conflict was a previous war, fought over the control of that region in the northeastern Mexican state of Coahuila that Americans called Texas. Emigrants from the United States declared independence in 1836 then fought a war to establish their own Lone Star Republic, whose preeminent symbol became the mission of San Antonio de Valero: the Alamo. The defense of that imposing stone structure by a doomed force of

188 Texans, who stood off 3,000 Mexican troops for twelve days in early 1836, made the Alamo an enduring icon of heroism in American culture, even as it turned the Mexican commander, Santa Anna, into an archetypal villain. To recount the Texas War of Independence and the Mexican War from the perspective of Mexico, however, is to narrate a very different story, one in which Santa Anna played a far more complex role. Viewed from the lands south and west of the Rio Grande, what Americans still tend to interpret as a fight for freedom becomes the story of a struggle to hold a nation together in the face of massive internal challenges while striving against all odds to resist the imperial ambitions of Andrew Jackson's heirs.

"For Fear that They Stood to Lose Everything in the General Disorder"

Santa Anna's parents were *criollos*. His father was a minor bureaucrat and mortgage broker who dreamed of establishing his son in commerce. Ambitious, passionate, and poorly educated, the young Santa Anna was instead "drawn to the glorious career of arms." Appointed a *caballero cadete* (gentleman cadet) in the Royal Army of New Spain in 1810, he never forgot the first sight of "shining . . . silver epaulets" on his shoulder. After service against Indians in the northern provinces, including Texas, he won promotion to lieutenant and the position of personal aide to the governor of Veracruz. The army was his "true vocation and calling," the institution where he could best display his "gentlemanly qualifications."[1]

Santa Anna came of age as an imperial officer fighting against insurgents within the borders of the viceroyalty of New Spain (and the province of Veracruz in particular) rather than enemies on its margins. He was neither a populist rebel in the mold of Jackson nor an imperial visionary like Penn. Santa Anna possessed what the young Washington craved: rank in the king's army. Frustration born of exclusion from the imperial army (and the explicit recognition of social status that accompanied it) defined Washington's early military career and helped make him, however reluctantly, into a revolutionary. Santa Anna never had that problem.

The Seven Years' War decisively influenced the world into which Santa Anna was born. In the aftermath of defeat, Spanish officials successfully revitalized their massive empire. The Bourbon Reforms increased the productivity of mines, the profitability of commerce, the security of the colonies, and the authority of the crown. *Criollos,* however, concluded that new taxes and regulations combined with attacks on such traditional institutions as the Roman Catholic Church constituted a fundamental reorganization of the relationship between colony and metropolis, an imperial revolution undertaken without their consent. *Criollo* perceptions of *peninsular* disdain bred deep resentment: the first step in the transformation of provincial shame into protonational pride.

In short, the reaction of many provincial gentlemen in New Spain to imperial reform paralleled that of their counterparts in British North America. But whereas men like George Washington were sufficiently alienated by metropolitan arrogance and intrusiveness to secede from the British empire and create a new imperial republic in its place, Mexican gentlemen with similar grievances followed an entirely different path. Why? The answer is complicated and includes the economic success of the Bourbon Reforms along with the granting of new privileges and titles to Mexican gentlemen. But ultimately what kept elite discontents from boiling over into rebellion was a general fear of social revolution led by the Indians and *castas* who outnumbered *peninsulares* and *criollos* by five to one.[2] This fundamentally reversed the ratio of whites to nonwhites in the United States, where African Americans constituted less than 20 per cent of the population and native people were generally excluded altogether. (The presence of large numbers of Germans, Scots, and Scotch-Irish slowed but did not prevent the development of a national identity among Protestant European-Americans.)

The vast majority of the close to 4 million people in New Spain were Indians, most living in communities that existed before the Spanish conquest. Organized around patriarchal kinship networks, these villages were relatively autonomous, especially those distant from the cities and mines of central Mexico. Since the Spanish could not completely subjugate the Indians, they tended to ignore them as long as they acknowledged the authority of the colonial government and the Church. Left to their own devices, villages were able to maintain preconquest religious practices and social customs or to practice a kind of religious and cultural syncretism. When Spaniards threatened this détente with higher taxes, new restrictions, or attempted interference in local affairs, Indians and *castas* generally rebelled rather than seeking redress through the cumbersome colonial legal system. Rebels were rarely punished severely, and they often succeeded in achieving limited but important local goals, such as the removal of an ineffective administrator. Hence "violence [became] a widespread way of resolving differences that, within obvious limits, was permitted by the state as a legitimate expression of grievance when the routine ways of reminding the powerful of their obligations had failed."[3]

This was not true in eastern North America, where Iroquois, Catawbas, Miamis, Osages, and others became diplomatic and military actors in the Atlantic world by trading, talking, and fighting with Europeans as well as with each other. The bases of their power disintegrated, as we have seen, with the destruction of New France and the empowerment of Britain's colonists in the Seven Years' War. That war had no such impact on native people in New Spain; indeed, it had almost no impact at all. At the end of the eighteenth century, the Spanish remained the only Europeans that Mexico's Indians had ever known, and the Spanish continued to devote themselves to exploiting mineral resources, such as silver, rather than developing internal commerce. Because the fundamental impulse in Spanish policy was to reinforce stability, not to provoke transformation, Indians in Mexico were required to do little more than render superficial obeisance to Spanish and Catholic forms. In 1800, nearly three centuries after the Castilian conquest, perhaps half of Mexico's Indians did not speak Spanish, an indication of the degree to which they remained isolated from and indifferent to life beyond their villages.[4]

Spanish dominion in Mexico, in other words, depended on maintaining a delicate balance between acknowledging local autonomy and incorporating Indians into European economic, political, and cultural structures. Occasional local rebellions over specific grievances, gentlemen agreed, were preferable to any transformation that might threaten the entire colonial edifice. Perturbed though they might be with metropolitan initiatives, few criollo leaders were willing to risk their lives and fortunes in an independence movement that might well produce an uncontrollable social revolution.

It took events in Europe, therefore, to trigger revolutionary upheaval in Mexico. In 1808, Napoleon Bonaparte invaded Spain and placed his brother Joseph on the throne. Guerrilla warfare wracked the Iberian Peninsula as the indignant people of Madrid and the provinces organized to defend their country and their king, Ferdinand VII. The residents of Mexico City and other colonial jurisdictions followed suit in refusing to recognize a Bonaparte as their monarch. When they experimented with local governments in the interregnum, they acted in the name of their deposed king and in defense of the Bourbon imperial order.

For Indians and *castas* as well as *criollos,* the monarch remained the major source of unity within the empire. People were more loyal to the person or the body of the monarch than they were to shared values or institutions. Even criollos worried that without the king, Mexican society would completely disintegrate. "I see a black cloud forming in our midst," wrote a prominent member of the Mexico City *cabildo* (town council) in September 1808. "This is *disunion*. . . . Hold on! Statesmen, clergy, nobles, monastic orders, military corps, Spaniards, Europeans, Americans, Indians, mestizos, [and] all the people who compose this fairest kingdom, now is the time for everyone to act closely together."[5] Exactly the opposite happened. A few days later, conservative elements in the capital mounted a coup to crush a movement for greater home rule.

Among the small minority of radicals who identified strongly with the most oppressed groups in Mexican society, the dream of justice and social regeneration bred talk of a revolution. Of those who did more than talk, none became more famous than the charismatic and naive priest, Miguel Hidalgo y Costilla. Born to a middling *criollo* family in 1753 in the mining region of Bajío north of Mexico City, Hidalgo was a well-educated, animated man with green eyes and, in later years, receding white hair. Ordained a priest in 1778, Hidalgo taught at the College of San Nicolás Obispo in Valladolid and became its rector in 1790. Two years later, he resigned to take up the work of a parish priest, eventually settling at the church of San Felipe Torresmochas north of Guanajuato in 1793. Hidalgo's home flourished as a local salon, full of conversation and music. In 1803, the priest relocated his extensive household, which included a mistress, children, and assorted relatives, to the parish of Dolores.[6]

Hidalgo, like other *criollos*, had a visceral resentment of Spanish arrogance. Associating the achievement of independence with the achievement of democracy and prosperity, Hidalgo and his friends expected that virtually all Mexicans would rally to their cause. They were wrong. On September 16, 1810, the same year that Santa Anna became a gentleman cadet in the Royal Army, Hidalgo, acting before officials could arrest him, publicly called for a rebellion in the name of King Ferdinand VII and the Virgin of Guadalupe, the patron saint of the cause of social justice. Attracting an immediate response from *castas* and Indians, Hidalgo demanded expanded political participation, the abolition of slavery and tributes, and the restoration of Indian land. By October, the priest was calling his movement a "Reconquest."[7]

Much as *criollo* gentlemen resented the Spanish personally, much as many desired a greater degree of democracy and equality, few were willing to join either Hidalgo or other radicals, such as Father José María Morelos, a mestizo priest who became one of Hidalgo's lieutenants. They worried about the personal consequences of social revolution, a nightmare fueled by Hildalgo's reported call for death to *peninsulares* and a brutal day and a half of rampage by Indians and *castas* at Guanajuato, the capital of Bajía. On September 28, 1810, thousands of Hidalgo's followers overwhelmed the reinforced *alhóndiga* (public granary) in the middle of town in a mere five hours. Three hundred Spaniards and *criollos* died (though not before some 2,000 rebels were killed), and the city was sacked. Guanajuato became a rallying cry for *peninsulares* and *criollos* united in defense of their privileges and their lives. Rather than support independence, as many gentlemen in British America did, *criollos,* including Santa Anna, rallied to the royal government. José María Luis Mora observed that many opposed independence "for fear that they stood to lose everything in the general disorder."[8]

The Mexican War for Independence thus played out differently from the War for Independence in the United States. Perhaps half of Hidalgo's supporters were Indians who understood the movement as a massive version of a traditional local rebellion. The typical insurgent was a married rural Indian male of about thirty years of age who had never ventured far from home.[9] For these men, nationalism, liberty, and independence were not even abstractions. They did not consider themselves either Spanish or Mexican: such an identity was utterly meaningless outside the salons of Hidalgo and his friends. The people who rallied to the priest were interested in short-term solutions to problems created by population growth, a decline in real wages, a rise in prices, and the terrible drought of 1809. Some may have hoped for intervention from their king to help them restore local religious practices and cultural customs. Very few intended to build a nation-state of citizens.

These profound misunderstandings and divisions made the War for Independence, which lasted until 1820, a ghastly conflict. *Criollo* resentment of *peninsulares* was trumped by their fear of social chaos from below. Under the command of Brigadier Felíx María Calleja del Rey and other professional soldiers, royalist troops and *criollo* militiamen smashed the initial mass rebellions. Hidalgo was captured and shot in 1811, Morelos in 1815. The insurgents' efforts to form a coherent movement for an independent nation guided by a Supreme Congress failed, in no small part because of the extraordinary diversity of the insurgents' identities, interests, and goals. Yet the very lack of central direction made the rebellion difficult to suppress; resistance actually flourished as it devolved into local rebellions and a series of guerrilla and counterguerrilla raids.[10] With guns and ammunition in short supply, much of the fighting consisted of brutal, hand-to-hand combat with knives and clubs. Perhaps 600,000 people died between 1810 and 1816, most

Agustín de Iturbide, emperor of Mexico,
painted by an unknown artist

from starvation or disease. Agriculture was ruined, industry devastated, and mining output cut in half. In 1845, per capita income in Mexico was 56 pesos, down from 116 in 1800.[11]

Calleja, who became viceroy in 1813, created flying detachments of cavalry to move quickly against rebels, whom he dismissed as "bandits." It was as a leader of one of these units in Veracruz that Antonio López de Santa Anna first made a name for himself. A brave and ruthless officer, he believed he had pacified his province in the late 1810s. But Santa Anna, like Calleja, exaggerated his success. Avoiding "conventional battlefield confrontations," insurgents "developed an effective and innovative system of irregular warfare" that "exhausted and progressively weakened the royalist army of New Spain."[12] Despite Calleja's attempts to reassert royal authority and the more conciliatory policies of his successor as viceroy, Juan Ruiz de Apodaca, which resulted in most of the insurgents laying down their arms, some rebel leaders were never apprehended. One of them in particular, Vicente Guerrero, remained active as a leader of resistance in the countryside.

"Plant[ing] the Eagle of the Mexican Empire"

Like many of his contemporaries, Santa Anna learned to treat rebellions as local events and to suppress them as quickly and ruthlessly as possible, lessons that guided his response to the Texan insurgents at the Alamo in early 1836. Santa Anna became a caudillo, a patriarchal regional leader of men who prized loyalty to each other even as they quarreled violently over status and questions of honor. In that, he resembled Jackson the Tennessee militia commander; where the two diverged was in their understanding of the source of authority.[13] Jackson craved affirmation from his peers and worked hard to obtain it in elections and duels. Santa Anna, on the other hand, wanted the imprimatur of his superiors, a regard they demonstrated typically by bestowing promotions and medals. Liberty meant the freedom to enjoy privileges reserved to the very few. By 1820, the mortgage broker's son was a consummate insider, a man to whom the anti-institutional populism of Jackson's band of democratic white brothers was anathema.

Santa Anna consciously fashioned his identity as a Romantic officer on the model of Napoleon Bonaparte. He studied the history of Greece and Rome and also Julius Caesar's account of the Gallic Wars, combed his hair from back to front in the Roman (and Napoleonic) style, and always rode a white horse. Among the honors he displayed were such royal medals as the Cross of the Royal and Distinguished Order of Isabella the Catholic. There is no reason to doubt his later assertion that he was "a very punctilious soldier" who "worked ardently and with a high degree of loyalty to fulfill the confidence and trust my commanding officer had placed in me."[14] He did not mention gaining the confidence and trust of his men as anything worth such attentive effort.

Why, then, did Santa Anna, along with so many of his contemporaries, desert the Spanish crown and become an insurgent himself? It was the first of the many abrupt turnarounds that have made Santa Anna a symbol of personal opportunism; yet here, at least, his shift in loyalty was more consistent than it first appears. Santa Anna's main goal throughout his life was to protect and preserve the privilege of liberty shared by men like him. Because he valued stability, he had no interest in fundamentally reorganizing Mexican society.[15]

Again events on the Iberian Peninsula precipitated the Mexican independence movement that Santa Anna joined. In 1820, Spanish soldiers at Cadiz mutinied after receiving orders to quash rebellions in the colonies and marched on Madrid; then the Madrid garrison mutinied as well. King Ferdinand VII, who had been ruling autocratically despite his legal status as a constitutional monarch, feared that he would be overthrown so he reestablished the liberal Constitution of 1812 and the Cortes (parliament). The liberals in the Cortes promptly attacked clerical privileges in a way that suggested even more egalitarian measures would follow, decentralized power to local communities, and allowed freedom of movement. While some Mexicans favored reform, nearly all were troubled by what these metropolitan measures, undertaken by a weak and unstable government, portended for New Spain and hence for their own future. Royalist officers in Mexico City chose the candle over the game, abandoned Spain, and created their own independence movement. The preservation of Mexico's social order mattered more than loyalty to Spain.[16]

On February 24, 1821, Colonel Agustín de Iturbide, a criollo who had fought without mercy against rebels throughout the 1810s, reached an understanding with Vicente Guerrero. With the guerrilla's support, Iturbide issued the Plan of Iguala, a document with twenty-three articles that "offered something for everyone." Roman Catholicism was declared the official religion, national independence was proclaimed, a constitutional monarchy was announced (preferably Ferdinand VII or some other European), and the persons and property of Spaniards were to be respected. A new Army of the Three Guarantees was created to ensure enforcement of these provisions; in due course it deposed the viceroy, and occupied Mexico City.

Initially, *peninsulares* and criollos tended to see the Plan of Iguala as moderate; the higher clergy supported it because it guaranteed the security of the faith and the property of the Church; and Indians welcomed the possibility of a new leader who would restore autonomy, prosperity, and cultural integrity to their villages.[17] The Plan of Iguala attempted to achieve, at one stroke, what Americans had taken a nearly a decade to accomplish in their own Revolutionary Settlement: the basis of a new, stable political order. It failed. Consensus was superficial at best: what divided Mexicans was stronger than what united them. *Criollo* officers, as much as Indian villagers, looked out for their own interests, seeking to protect their households and neighborhoods first, with only an attenuated loyalty to any larger political community.

Lieutenant Colonel Antonio López de Santa Anna joined Iturbide within a month of the promulgation of the Iguala plan, receiving a quick promotion in return. A colonel at twenty-six, the newly minted Mexican patriot announced that he and his men were "going to put an end to the great work of the reconquest of our liberty and independence." We will, he vowed, "plant the eagle of the Mexican empire" and "cover [our]selves with glory."[18] Hundreds of officers joined Santa Anna in deserting the Royal Army, taking their men, arms, and equipment with them. In August 1821, Iturbide and Spanish officials agreed on the fact of Mexican independence in the Treaty of Córdoba; a constituent congress was formed to erect a permanent government. Santa Anna, less concerned with fashioning political institutions than imposing order, spent the fall subduing the remaining royalist forces in his home province, capturing the city of Veracruz in late October.

Because the officers who created Mexico had devoted the previous decade to subjugating insurgent calls for independence, they chose not to alter the familiar forms of monarchical government, hoping thereby to appeal to people in rural villages. Iturbide intended Mexicans to find unity through personal allegiance and in the spring of 1822 persuaded a segment of delegates to the constituent congress to elect him Emperor Agustín I. When several of Santa Anna's associates disapproved of Iturbide's arrogation of power and attempted to coax the young colonel into the republican party, he remained loyal to Iturbide. Because he had "been reared under a monarchy," he later recalled, he "could not favor such an extreme change and listened to their words with disapproval."[19]

But Santa Anna reversed his course and deserted his emperor within the year. The problem, according to his memoirs, was Agustín I's failure to stabilize Mexico. His unpopularity was leading to "his loss of power and anarchy for the country."[20] Unable to revive the economy (a herculean challenge) or restore political stability, the emperor seemed obsessed with the trappings of royalty and was downright scornful of Congress.

For Santa Anna, instability translated into an unpredictable, dangerous, and unjust world where his status, not to mention his property and his life, was constantly at risk. Agustín I's refusal to reward him with enough power or honors made Santa Anna's fears concrete. The emperor was selling commissions to raise money, and Santa Anna thought he was worth more than a promotion to brigadier general and command of the Veracruz province. He took offense at being awarded a second-degree version of Iturbide's new Order of Guadalupe. Santa Anna's anger over real and perceived snubs found a counterpart in what many other Mexican officers felt when they, too, concluded that the emperor's self-aggrandizement was inimical to their ability to preserve their honor and local authority.

In November 1822, when Agustín I met Santa Anna in Jalapa, the latter's birthplace, to discuss a possible Spanish invasion, the distrust between the two men escalated beyond repair. The emperor complained that Santa Anna was a "scoundrel" who behaved as if he were "the real emperor" in Veracruz. Santa Anna certainly acted the part: escorted to Jalapa by fifty soldiers, he pointedly took a seat in Agustín's presence. When a courtier reminded him that "when the Emperor is standing, no one sits down in his presence," the atmosphere at the conference deteriorated. Ordered to Mexico City, Santa Anna instead returned to Veracruz, protesting so "rude a blow" to his "military pride" and announcing that he had "beheld absolutism in all its power."[21]

Making common cause with remnants of the revolutionary forces of the 1810s, Santa Anna proclaimed the Republic of Mexico in early December 1822. Despite some initial setbacks, the movement, which was more a vote of no-confidence in the emperor than an affirmation of republican political values, attracted the support of other officers. Agustín I abdicated on March 19, 1823. He was later executed after an ill-fated attempt to reclaim his throne.

Independence intensified a debate over the proper relationship between local and national authority that dated from the colonial era. Because Independence revised rather than revolutionized the political order, the gentlemen who wanted to modernize their new nation confronted a formidable challenge. A revolutionary settlement of the kind that emerged in the United States following a protracted war against the forces of the metropolis— a war conceptualized around political ideas that created the potential for a new national identity—was simply impossible in Mexico. The second republic in North America was in fact a congeries of disparate communities in which people thought in concrete local and regional terms rather than abstractions about liberty, communities whose loyalties were to their extended families and villages rather than to the nation.

The *criollo* gentlemen who led Mexico to independence persisted in trying to impose a revolutionary settlement, even though they could not agree among themselves, much less create a national consensus. Arguing for continuity with the late colonial period, conservatives tended to insist on strong institutions (most notably, the Catholic Church) in the interest of maintaining stability. The preeminent conservative was Lucas Alamán. Born in Guanajuato in 1792 to *peninsular* parents, he barely escaped with his life when Hidalgo's followers sacked the city in 1810. Alamán was educated in Mexico City and Europe, where he lived from 1814 to 1820. A man of

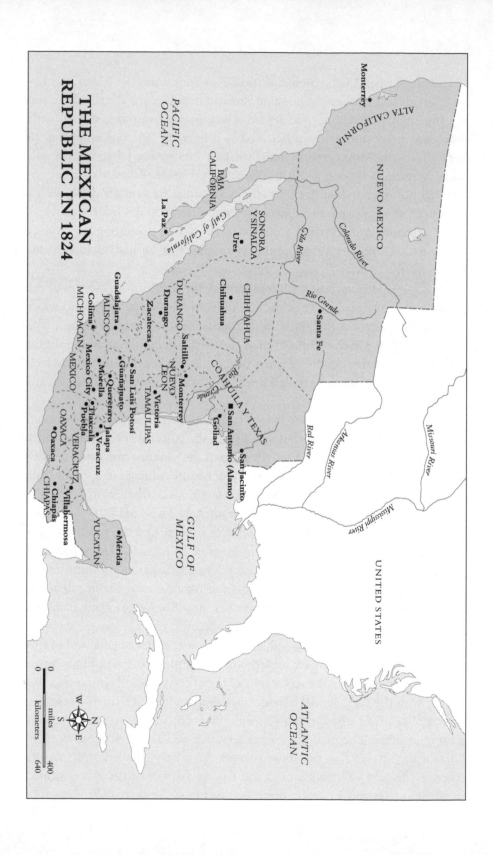

THE MEXICAN
REPUBLIC IN 1824

PACIFIC
OCEAN

Monterrey

ALTA CALIFORNIA

NUEVO MEXICO

BAJA
CALIFORNIA

La Paz

Gulf of California

SONORA
Y SINALOA

Ures

Gila River

Colorado River

Chihuahua

CHIHUAHUA

Rio Grande

Santa Fe

Guadalajara

DURANGO

Durango

Zacatecas

Saltillo

COAHUILA Y TEXAS

Colima

JALISCO

MICHOACAN

Morella

Guanajuato

San Luis Potosí

NUEVO
LEON

Monterrey

Victoria

TAMAULIPAS

San Antonio (Alamo)

San Jacinto

Goliad

Rio Grande

Red River

Arkansas River

Missouri River

UNITED STATES

Mexicó City

MEXICO

Querétaro

Tlaxcala

Puebla

Jalapa

Veracruz

VERACRUZ

OAXACA

Oaxaca

CHIAPAS

Chiapas

Villahermosa

YUCATÁN

Mérida

GULF OF
MEXICO

Mississippi River

ATLANTIC
OCEAN

N
W   E
S

0   miles   400
0   kilometers   640

aristocratic tastes, Aláman believed that the future of Mexico depended on strong leadership from a well-educated elite. Other gentlemen disagreed— to some extent. Among them was Lorenzo de Zavala, who was born near Mérida in 1788 and trained as a physician. His personal antipathy to established authority attracted him to democratic ideals and landed him in jail during the War for Independence. Zavala became a prominent liberal and advocated a federally organized state that left power predominantly in the hands of local officials.[22]

The public debate between such men as Aláman and Zavala climaxed in the constitutional convention of 1824, whose delegates elected Zavala as president. The resulting Constitution was a victory for liberals, creating a federal republic of nineteen states and four territories, whose capital was an autonomous Federal District. There would be an elected president, a bicameral Congress, and an appointed judiciary in a constitutional order similar in conception, if not details, to that of the United States. Mexico City bubbled with intellectual ferment, as leading Mexicans organized themselves into partisan societies and debated public policy in more than two dozen newspapers as well as salons, taverns, and public buildings. Without serious opposition aristocratic titles and symbols were abolished, as was slavery, at least in most states. Congress suggested the use of "ciudadaño" and "madama" rather than "don" and "doña."[23]

The Constitution proclaimed everyone a citizen of Mexico; both it and state constitutions promised equality before the law. Yet the vast majority of Indians and *castas* remained committed to local ways of life and had no interest in adopting liberal notions of private property and individual responsibility, let alone becoming Mexicans. Nor did gentlemen have much interest in treating Indians with respect or in helping them acquire the education and other means to transform their rural worlds. Region and race divided the new nation as they had New Spain. The Republic remained a collection of different groups locked in local systems of patronage, privilege, and personal obedience. There was no central person, institution, or idea around which the various peoples of Mexico wanted to unite. Even the ardent liberal Valentín Gómez Farías supported limited suffrage because "the classes are so varied and diverse and very few of them have people of sufficient aptitude and understanding to be able to carry out the arduous and difficult task which has to be entrusted to their care."[24] Without even a semblance of agreement about the proper way to unite and develop the nation, Mexican dreams of stability disappeared as a series of governments oscillated between liberal and conservative policies.

"Dragged Along by the Insatiable Desire to Acquire Glory"

For decades Antonio López de Santa Anna was, according to Lucas Alamán,
"the leading actor in all of the political events of the country, and the nation's fortunes have become tied to his own, sometimes awarding him the
most absolute power and on others sending him either to prison or into exile."[25] Contemporaries and historians alike have denounced Santa Anna as a
duplicitous creature who cared only about his own personal gratification.
Rumors of insatiable greed, opium addiction, and sexual profligacy suggested narcissism and a complete absence of moral principles. Easily bored,
he seemed more interested in the outcome of cockfights than discussions of
policy. In behavior and attitudes, he had no real parallel among the first two
generations of American leaders.

Santa Anna's vanity, it is true, knew no bounds. He loved pomp and
medals, any visible display of his status. His rhetoric was bombastic, his behavior self-serving and unreliable. In general he lacked self-restraint. On
occasion, his excesses produced farce. A woman whom we know only as
Luisa, unhappy with Santa Anna for refusing her money after she had slept
with him, absconded with the medals from his coat, then took her revenge
by "awarding" the Order of Guadalupe, the Order of Charles III, and the
Cross of Tampico to various unsuspecting poor men in Mexico City. In the
end, Santa Anna had to pay more to recover his medals than the woman had
wanted in the first place.[26]

Santa Anna remained a colonial figure, a man whose aspirations and values reflected an eighteenth-century fascination with gentility and public
performance rather than a nineteenth-century bourgeois obsession with
character and domesticity. He thrived in a culture not unlike those of
eighteenth-century Britain, France, and their colonies in North America,
where the mark of a man was his reputation and what later generations regard as significant moral lapses—adultery, for example—were understood
as private matters and did nothing to discredit a leader whose public virtues
remained unquestioned. But while Santa Anna bore a thoroughgoing resemblance to Washington and most other American revolutionaries in his
concern for reputation, his conviction that deception was a necessary prerequisite of power set him apart from them. The only early American political leader who operated from that conviction to anything like the degree

A romantic portrait of a young Antonio López de Santa Anna, painted by W. H. Dodd
Courtesy of the Prints and Photographs Collection,
Center for American History, University of Texas at Austin

that Santa Anna did was Aaron Burr. For both men, the goal was not to represent a particular ideology or advocate a specific political program but to act the role of a gentleman and win the respect of peers. In this context, Santa Anna's fascination with Napoleon Bonaparte becomes understandable: both were intensely ambitious men from modest provincial backgrounds; both strove more to be fascinating than admirable; both sought fame through public demonstrations of bravery and visible mastery of domestic worlds.

By the mid-1820s, Santa Anna had become a man of power who could make or break politicians; his next step, therefore, was to consolidate his cultural and social standing by constructing the life of a patriarchal gentleman for himself. He bought a hacienda near Jalapa for 25,000 pesos, then set about enlarging it. By 1845, the estate, Manga de Clavo, consisted of 483,000 acres, boasted 40,000 head of cattle and thousands of horses, and extended more than thirty miles along the highway from Jalapa to Veracruz.[27] Manga de Clavo was a private extension of Santa Anna's public reputation. Because his role as patriarch demanded a suitable consort and heirs, Santa Anna married Doña Inés García in 1825. She was Spanish-born, fourteen years old, and an unquestioned virgin whose sons would be legitimate heirs. She bore four, perhaps five, children for Santa Anna before she died in 1844 at the age of thirty-three.

There is no more reason to doubt Santa Anna's affection for his wife than there is to doubt his intimacy with other women. Doña Inés's role was not to be a bourgeois helpmate and romantic lover but the mother of the general's children, manager of his domestic world, and hostess to his many distinguished visitors. Santa Anna's treatment of her fit within a larger insistence on female sexual propriety that "encouraged misogyny while proclaiming worship: all living women, regardless of color-class standing, might be suspected of falling short of the ideal unless strictly monitored by a vigilant patriarch."[28] This requirement of constant vigilance, of course, gave women opportunities to resist patriarchy in many ways, for not even the most ambitious patriarch could also be omnipresent and omniscient. Luisa's distribution of Santa Anna's medals was inspired defiance that publicly mocked his manhood and contested his reputation. The modes of self-assertion open to Doña Inés took other forms; they depended more on accommodation than defiance and were were undoubtedly limited in other ways by the disparity in age between herself and her husband. Nevertheless, Manga de Clavo gave her a unique position from which to exercise a kind of influence available only to the wives of powerful men.

For two decades, Manga de Clavo, like Mount Vernon and the Hermitage, was a physical manifestation of power, a refuge from public life, and a meeting place for leading Mexicans. Beyond the hacienda, the foundation of Santa Anna's immense power was regional and personal. *Santannistas,* loyal followers of the general, participated in an extended network of relationships that were at once economic, social, and political. Whenever he traveled, dozens of men from Veracruz formed Santa Anna's personal entourage. Geography, too, gave him power, for he was the leader of a significant region: the city of Veracruz was the great port of Atlantic Mexico and was surrounded by a rich, well-settled hinterland. Because the road from Veracruz to Mexico City ran through Jalapa, Manga de Clavo lay along the central commercial and strategic artery of the Republic. Merchants, diplomats, and invading armies encountered Antonio López de Santa Anna as they encountered Mexico. If they got the sense that the general and the nation were one and the same, well, so much the better.

There was no mistaking the desire to impress. In December 1839, Frances Calderón de la Barca, her husband (the Spanish minister to Mexico), and their retinue (conveyed in two carriages) stopped at Santa Anna's estate on their way to the capital. She thought the house "pretty, slight-looking, and kept in nice order," but found its minimal furniture and its mistress less appealing. Arriving at six in the morning, the Calderóns were received by a uniformed aide and "several hangers-on" and escorted inside to meet Señora Santa Anna. She impressed them as "a tall, thin, lank, lean, ugly female" dressed in white muslin, silk stockings, and satin shoes and decorated with "very splendid diamond earrings, a magnificent diamond brooch, and a diamond ring the size of a small watch on each finger." Santa Anna, who made his entrance last, appeared to Calderón "a gentlemanly, good-looking, quietly-dressed, rather melancholy-looking person." She was not fooled by his philosophic expression and refinement, for "placid sad-ness" often covered "the countenances of the most cunning, the deepest, most ambitious, most designing and most dangerous statesmen." Calderón reminded herself that the "polished hero" before her with the "air de philosophe" was "perhaps one of the worst men in the world—ambitious of power—greedy of money—and unprincipled—having feathered his nest at the expense of the republic—and waiting in a dignified retreat only till the moment comes for putting himself at the head of another revolution."[29]

Calderón was not alone in observing a tension between Santa Anna's appearance and his character. In the 1820s, Lorenzo de Zavala perceptively observed that Santa Anna's "soul" did "not fit in his body. It lives in perpetual motion." The general was "dragged along by the insatiable desire to acquire glory." His eagerness to achieve "immortal fame" led him to "the summits of recklessness" and to ignore "strategy." Zavala concluded that because Santa Anna "has no fixed principles nor any organized code of public be-havior . . . he always moves to extremes and comes to contradict himself. He does not measure his actions or calculate the results."[30]

Santa Anna nevertheless understood the importance of bravery and loy-alty in a social order based on privilege rather than equality. He took care of the Santannistas. He gave them what he himself craved: respect. And like them he sought social stability and political predictability. Inconsistent in his support of different programs, he was remarkably consistent in his pursuit of a government that would allow him and his followers to enjoy their privi-leges and positions in peace. The means to this end were less important than the end itself. Santa Anna was "a charismatic and energetic general" who many leading Mexicans believed was "the only man whose prestige and resolute nature could prevent Mexico from crumbling in the face of the threat of a social and bloody revolution."[31] Indeed, it was precisely because Santa Anna was committed to a world dominated by gentlemen and cared little about specific policy that leading Mexicans turned to him time and again.

As the caudillo explained to the American envoy Joel Poinsett, "it is very true that I threw up my cap for liberty with great ardor, and perfect sincerity, but very soon found the folly of it. A hundred years to come my people will not be fit for liberty. They do not know what it is, unenlightened as they are, and under the influence of a Catholic clergy, a despotism is the proper government for them, but there is no reason why it should not be a wise and virtuous one." Santa Anna believed in 1834 that "Liberty is the strict observance of the rights of man." His responsibility was to "contain or moderate excessive or precipitate passions of the moment."[32] In other words, Mexico should be governed by benevolent gentlemen such as the patriarch of Manga de Clavo, men whose interests and those of the nation were (at least in their view) one and the same.

The defense of these principles involved Santa Anna in warfare more often than Andrew Jackson, but it was almost exclusively defensive warfare against efforts to destabilize existing political and social structures. Despite forays into Central America in the 1820s, Mexico was not an expansionist power in the manner of the United States. Military operations were mainly directed against rebellions in provinces within the Republic, albeit some as distant as the Yucatán. To the north, the *frontera* was a relatively fixed line of defense rather than an advancing area of settlement.[33] Santa Anna fought mostly against his fellow countrymen and foreign invaders.

A "Frenzy to Usurp and Gain Control of That Which Rightfully Belongs to Its Neighbors"

By the 1830s, the most dangerous threat to Mexico was the United States, which, having conquered eastern North America, was eager to expand trade and acquire land in Texas, New Mexico, and California. Droves of immigrants posed a threat to the security of the Mexican Republic, particularly since only 80,000 people, roughly 1 percent of its population, lived in Alta California, Nuevo Mexico, and the regions of Nuevo Santander, Tejas, and Coahuila that lay north of the Rio Grande. "Instead of attacking California," the French consul Gueroult explained to his minister of foreign affairs in August 1845, the Americans "have peopled it; they have colonized it; they are taking it quietly bit by bit, while Mexico peacefully allows this province to be seized."[34] How did governments uncertain of how to govern Mexico itself deal with the intrusion of Americans into Texas and merchants bearing cheap goods into Santa Fe?

The solution seemed to be to leave matters in local hands. Mexican policy in the 1820s was the opposite of Anglo-American expansion, which required either the transformation of cultural "others" into Americans or their removal. The National Colonization Law of 1824 placed disposition of the national domain to immigrants in the hands of state officials. Aside from a few restrictions on the size and nature of land grants, the act encouraged foreigners to settle within Mexico. The state of Coahuila, which included the region the Mexicans knew as Tejas (Texas), then passed its own colonization act, which was specifically designed to attract Anglos. The religious requirement did not require landholders to be Catholic, only Christian; naturalization was automatic if immigration contracts were fulfilled; colonizers were exempt from taxes for ten years; and restrictions on slavery were notably vague. The last was the crucial issue. Although the Mexican Congress had abolished slavery in 1824, Coahuila, eager to accommodate American immigrants, evasively declared that "no one [was] born a slave" and allowed for the introduction of slaves until six months after the implementation of its constitution. In May 1828, the Coahuila Congress recognized the validity of indentures signed in other countries. Two years later President Vicente Guerrero exempted Texas from his 1830 decree abolishing slavery.[35]

These measures made Texas attractive to large numbers of young white men who were the ideological descendants of Andrew Jackson. Alienated by the presidency of the Massachusetts-born John Quincy Adams (1825–29), many Southern white men believed that Adams, who had lost the popular vote to Jackson, was bent on increasing national power to develop the United States in the image of the Northeast. They worried that Adams's unrealized plans portended future threats to the local worlds of democratic patriarchs. More than a few found Mexican promises of toleration and autonomy as well as the fertile lands of Texas impossible to resist in such a context. There they would be left alone to create and sustain households as they saw fit. That perception flourished until the early 1830s, when the Mexican government shifted sharply toward conservative centralization.[36]

Elected president in 1833, Santa Anna, as always more enamored of the privileges than the responsibilities of power, retired to Manga de Clavo and left Vice President Valentín Gómez Farías to make policy. Gómez Farías, acting on his liberal convictions, proceeded to attack the pillars of the status quo, including the army (which he hoped to replace with state militias) and the Roman Catholic Church. In April 1834, President Santa Anna, the implacable enemy of anything that seemed to destabilize Mexico's social structure, sent Gómez Farías into exile. Outraged liberals immediately rose in rebellion throughout Mexico. Over the next year, Santa Anna suppressed the insurgents with the same determination he had exhibited in the 1810s. The crisis of authority led him to declare himself dictator in May 1835 and to nullify the federal Constitution of 1824. Santa Anna's centralizing tendencies climaxed in the Constitution of 1836, which transformed the largely autonomous states into administrative departments.

By the summer of 1835, the last bastion of serious opposition to this Mexican revolution was Texas, where American émigrés defied Santa Anna in the name of the Constitution of 1824. In December, a group of them forced the surrender of 500 troops under the command of Santa Anna's brother-in-law trapped in the Alamo mission in San Antonio. The Mexican president saw this action as a threat to the honor of the republic he embodied, another episode in the manner of Hidalgo. He understood the Texas rebellion as a local uprising by insurgents intent upon destabilizing the existing order by flaunting the authority of government. The Texas rebels were simply another group of recalcitrant localists to be beaten into submission by direct and, if necessary, brutal means. Moving to quash the Texas rebellion as he would in any other province, Santa Anna gathered an army of more than 6,000 men (including officers from Italy and France) at San Luis Potosí. "If the Americans do not behave themselves I will march across their country and plant the Mexican flag in Washington," he announced to the French ambassador.[37] In keeping with his usual modus operandi, Santa Anna awarded his poorly supplied and inadequately trained conscripts the newly created Legion of Honor (silver crosses for enlisted men, gold for officers, and double colored bands for senior officers) before they set out for Texas.

Americans and Mexicans in Texas organized to defend themselves, justifying their actions in language that echoed that of Andrew Jackson. Among the leaders of the rebellion was Sam Houston, a native of Tennessee and a Jackson protégé. Seriously wounded at the battle of Horseshoe Bend, Houston, along with thousands of other Southerners, had left the United States to make a new home in Texas. In January 1836, he rallied soldiers to a war for independence from Mexico. Would he and his fellow Texans "ever bend our necks as slaves, ever quietly watch the destruction of our property and the annihilation of our guaranteed rights? NO!! Never! . . . The last drop of our blood would flow before we would bow under the yoke of these half-Indians."[38]

Rising originally in defense of the Constitution of 1824, Texans now talked of independence and an alliance with the United States. Immutable cultural differences, they maintained, divided the peoples of the two republics. Santa Anna had deceived them, wrote a resident of Austin. In any case, "The mass of [Mexicans] are ignorant, bigoted, and superstitious; they do not, neither can they understand the true principles of a republican form of government; and consequently a dictatorial form is best suited to their education and habits."[39]

Once again, Americans linked war and liberty in a defense of their households from barbarous tyrants. The acting governor, James Robinson, exhorted Texans to march "with the blessing of your household Gods. . . . Roll back the crimson stream of war to its source, and make the tyrant feel the fiery sun of blazing, burning, consuming war; . . . Let him know how freemen can die, and how free men will live—that one day of virtuous liberty is worth an eternity of slavery." These men construed their rebellion as a principled defense of local authority in the tradition of the American Revolution. Because they were "the sons of the BRAVE PATRIOTS OF '76," they reassured themselves that they would be "invincible in the cause of FREEDOM and the *RIGHTS OF MAN.*" "[A]s fathers, as husbands, as sons, and as brothers," they would not "suffer the *colored* hirelings of a cruel and faithless despot, to feast and revel, in [their] dearly purchased and cherished homes." They would defend white male liberty against people whose race and religion made them unfit for republican citizenship, just as Andrew Jackson had fought for the same cause in the 1810s. On March 2, 1836, they formally declared their independence from Mexico.[40]

Santa Anna marched into Texas determined to reestablish Mexican authority. How could Mexico tolerate the seizure of a valuable department by a "mob of ungrateful adventurers"? "Mexicans, though naturally generous, will not suffer outrages with impunity—injurious and dishonorable to their country—let the perpetrators be whom they may."[41] In late February, Santa Anna's army occupied San Antonio and surrounded the Alamo, behind whose stone walls fewer than 200 Texans bid defiance to the power of the Mexican Republic. To induce them to surrender, the general flew a red flag, meaning that he would execute prisoners taken in arms, standard practice among Mexicans in the War for Independence. But the Texans refused to capitulate. Their twenty-six-year-old South Carolina–born leader, Lieutenant Colonel William Barret Travis, called for reinforcements "in the name of Liberty, of patriotism & every thing dear to the American character." None came. Rather than wait for artillery to subdue the Texans, Santa Anna ordered 1,400 men to storm the mission at one o'clock in the morning of March 6. "The honor of the nation" was in their hands, he told his soldiers, while reminding them that he knew how to "reward . . . distinguished deeds." They finished the job some five and a half hours later. Probably 182 Texans died during the battle, and another 6 were executed on March 7. Seventy-eight Mexicans lost their lives, and 251 were wounded. Santa Anna, as always, had acted boldly and decisively. But his hard-won victory had the unintended consequence of providing the Texans with a rallying cry. The Alamo remembered was far more formidable than the Alamo in reality had ever been, for it seemed to prove every charge against the Mexican leader and his government; this war was truly a fight to the death. Americans would "take courage from this glorious disaster" and move to avenge the deaths of their "bleeding, burning brothers."[42]

Santa Anna dispersed his men to hunt down and kill the rebels, a time-honored strategy in the suppression of previous insurrections and one that met with initial success. Most infamously, Santa Anna ordered the execution of 400 men captured near Goliad. The general, however, was hasty and impatient, and underestimated the determination, organization, and ferocity of his enemy. His forces were divided, and he himself outran other units in the pursuit of the Texans. When Sam Houston laid a trap with 800 men along the San Jacinto River, an overconfident Santa Anna dismissed the possibility of an attack. Assaulting 1,500 Mexicans in the late afternoon of April 21, the Texans defeated them in about eighteen minutes and promptly vented their anger over the Alamo and Goliad on their prisoners. Six hundred and fifty Mexicans were killed while just two Texans met the same fate. Santa Anna escaped, only to be captured the next day, disguised as a common soldier wearing diamond studs in his linen shirt. After some discussion, Santa Anna and Houston negotiated an end to the war and a promise to hear a delegation from Texas in favor of independence. Despite the agreement, which the Mexican government later repudiated because it no longer recognized Santa Anna as president, the victors imprisoned the general. For almost two months, he wore a ball and chain around his leg, later claiming that angry Texans had "fought to get at me and discharged pistols at my prison door."[43]

Santa Anna appealed to the president of the United States, Andrew Jackson, for help. Old Hickory obligingly intervened with a letter to Sam Houston urging clemency. Pragmatism dictated caution in moving ahead with the annexation of Texas. It was not a popular policy in the northeastern United States, where it intersected with growing hostility to slavery and the power of the South. The new Lone Star Republic was a huge territory with a diffuse population and extended borders. Ill and weary, Jackson had also mellowed. Summarily executing Santa Anna would simply alienate Mexicans, at least at the moment. Arguing that "Nothing now could tarnish the character of Texas more than such an act at this late period,"[44] Jackson counseled prudence.

Houston accordingly freed Santa Anna in late 1836 on the condition that he visit his "protector and friend," Jackson. Escorted by two Texans, the general and his aide traveled by steamboat up the Mississippi and Ohio rivers then overland through snowy Kentucky and Virginia. Reveling in the attention paid to him, the Mexican insisted, as always, on being treated like a gentleman. Jackson and Santa Anna met at the White House on January 19. After a public supper attended "by notables of all countries," the two men talked, mainly about the expansion of the United States. Jackson apparently made clear the American desire to acquire Texas and other Mexican territory in some honorable fashion, while Santa Anna was graciously evasive. Because Santa Anna was powerless, nothing was resolved. The humiliated former president was returned to Veracruz by a ship of the U.S. Navy, where an initially chilly reception turned warmer as the *Santannistas* shouted their fealty. On March 3, 1837, his last full day as president of the United States, Andrew Jackson nominated an official representative to the Republic of Texas; he was confirmed by the Senate later the same day.[45]

The loss of Texas was a decisive moment in the development of Mexican attitudes toward the United States. A decade earlier, in the full throes of republican experimentation, some gentlemen had sought to emulate the northern republic in designing Mexican political institutions. The more they learned about Americans, however, the less they liked them. The arrogant South Carolinian Joel R. Poinsett, the American minister to Mexico from 1825 to 1830, became the symbol of an aggressive United States whose citizens insisted on their moral superiority and threatened Mexican territory. "The lives of all Mexicans are at stake," claimed a correspondent of the conservative *El Sol* in 1829. "[F]ree men should gather before the altar of the august god of opinion" and demand the banishment "from the soil of liberty its most terrible enemy [Poinsett]."[46]

The creation of the Republic of Texas transformed apprehension into anger. Mexicans held the United States responsible for both the rebellion and for the increasing influence of American merchants in New Mexico and California. By the late 1830s, newspapers were calling for war against the United States. The manifest design of the northern republic seemed all too clear. Santa Anna's adviser, José María Tornel, later explained that Americans had been united since 1776 in "their desire to extend the limits of the republic to the north, to the south, and to the west," by whatever means necessary. The American "frenzy to usurp and gain control of that which rightfully belongs to its neighbors" resembled the "roving spirit" of "barbarous hordes" from a "far remote north." The United States had been a deceptive "mentor" driven by "boundless ambition" to take advantage of Mexican weakness in a "concealed policy of conquest."

Why should a civilized people respect the Americans? "Nowhere else on the face of the globe is the feeling of the white race stronger against those which, in its pride, it designates as colored." Americans exploited and cheated Indians. Americans enslaved African Americans. Their pompous support for the rights of man rested on tyranny over others. How could Americans, who had "opened a vast market of human flesh in Texas . . . dare to acclaim the sacred name of liberty[?]" Americans' behavior in Texas echoed their behavior in Florida. "[C]laim upon claim of exaggerated or imaginary injuries have been piled up and the opportune moment awaited to present them together." Mexico's "honor," its national rights, its "very political existence," were "at stake." The loss of Texas would inevitably lead to the loss of New Mexico and California. "Our national existence . . . would end like those weak meteors which, from time to time, shine fitfully in the firmament and disappear."[47]

"Who is not familiar with that race of migratory adventurers that exist in the United States," asked Manuel Eduardo de Gorostiza in 1840, drawing on his experience as a special envoy in Washington during the second Jackson administration, "who always live in the unpopulated regions, taking land away from the Indians and then assassinating them? Far removed from civilization, as they condescendingly call it, they are precursors of immorality and pillage." At stake in the dispute over Texas was Mexican "nationality," which required a "war of race, of religion, of language, and of customs."[48]

In 1837 Santa Anna managed to restore his reputation, with his usual flair, by publishing an explanation of his behavior in Texas. He wrote, he said, because "my honor belongs to my country, just as my arm and soul have always been hers." This was a supremely self-serving stance, of course but nonetheless one that clearly indicated the extent to which Santa Anna saw Mexico as an extension of himself and vice versa. Ever the narcissist, he admitted that some people compared his military campaigns to those of Napoleon. Was Texas then his Russia? Santa Anna insisted that the Americans were the aggressors and that he had been forced to fight them without resources or competent subordinates.[49] Although he had behaved well, the perfidious Americans had besmirched his honor and that of the Mexican Republic. In the early 1840s he commissioned a statue of himself with a finger pointing north to Texas, as if to trump his critics by reminding the world of his unfinished business.

More important than words in the reemergence of Santa Anna were deeds. In December 1838, he led a successful defense of Veracruz from a French attack. Grapeshot killed his horse during a charge and so grievously wounded his leg that it had to be amputated below the knee. The pain did not detract from Santa Anna's celebration of his public redemption. "May all Mexicans, forgetting my political mistakes, not deny me the only title I wish to leave my children: that of a good Mexican."[50]

Again elevated to the presidency, Santa Anna crushed a rebellion in Tampico. He also promoted 2,000 men, bought new military uniforms, and had his amputated leg buried in Mexico City in a lavish ceremony. He raised taxes and sold around 12,000 military commissions to raise money to support his extravagant life style. He remained as devoted to cockfights and as indifferent to policy discussions as ever and no less committed to gratifying the needs of the flesh. When Doña Inés died in 1844, he remarried less than two months later. His second wife, Doña María Dolores de Tosta, was fifteen years old. Santa Anna's pattern of relentless self-aggrandizement and self-satisfaction had already alienated Mexicans, and his hasty remarriage in particular hurt his popularity. In 1845, his rivals in the military drove him into exile.

By this point, the problem of the United States loomed over everything in Mexican public affairs. As the disgrace of Texas festered, some Mexicans worried about the impact of a continental war on their unsettled country. The moderate politician Manuel de la Peña, minister of foreign affairs, argued for negotiations with the United States in a long Circular to Departmental Governors in early December 1845. There was no question that the Americans were wrong in their "usurpation of our properties and their rude and shameless violation of our rights." But Peña wondered what was best for Mexico in the long run. "After a period of so many upheavals and

disgraces, we need an era of peace and tranquility, exclusively devoted to re-
pairing our nation's wounds and reviving our economy and sense of national unity." War over Texas was "a hopeless cause, which will consume
both wealth and countless generations and eventually destroy the republic
itself." Still, if "it is necessary to start the war to conserve Mexico's territory
and nationality," the government was willing to do so. The minister of war
agreed. After all, "The United States, which claims to respect justice more
than any other nation, presents itself on the basis of power alone as the most
insolent and shameless usurper in history."[51]

The tentative moderation of Peña and his colleagues could not survive
for long, and they were overthrown at the end of 1845. The movers behind
the coup were conservatives, some of them hoping to exploit the crisis to
create a constitutional monarchy that would finally stabilize Mexico. To this
end, hoping in vain for European intervention on their behalf, they supported a successful rebellion by General Mariano Paredes y Arrillaga. According to an editorial in the conservative newspaper *El Tiempo,* Mexicans
(including some "who are not vulgar") were "dazzled" by the "surprising
prosperity of North America" and "uncritically" admired its republican institutions. They should know that while the United States represented
progress, its commercial spirit would eventually cause its disintegration.
Americans were obsessed with "the search for gold." "Public spirit exists
there only in matters which directly effect pecuniary interests." There was
"no nationality" in the United States because of a plethora of immigrants. In
fact, "there is no morality of any kind, and if good families exist, as some indeed do, their virtue is the more meritorious, since there are no incentives
for good in an environment completely open to evil influences." Mexico
should honor its institutions and wait for the United States to fall apart. But
that was not to be. When the northern republic declared war in May 1846,
Mexico had no choice but to fight. General Mariano Arista, commander of
the Division of the North, explained why in a manifesto addressed to
American soldiers. Mexico had "never given her consent" to their "occupation" of his nation, and they were, therefore, "the blind instruments of . . .
unholy and mad ambition." The United States was using force in the name
of liberty. Its empire rested on coercion rather than consent; conquest and
war were inseparable from the ways in which Americans had come to define
themselves.[52]

To lead the defense of national honor, the leaders of Mexico turned to
the one man with the reputation and experience to rally his countrymen:
Antonio López de Santa Anna. Corrupt, selfish, and volatile, the general

nonetheless commanded the respect of the military. Gentlemen saw him "as the only man whose prestige and resolute nature could prevent Mexico from crumbling in the face of the threat of a social and bloody revolution."[53] Summoned from exile in Havana, the caudillo returned to Veracruz in August and Mexico City in September. In the capital he assumed command of the army and accepted election as provisional president of the Republic. Santa Anna had little time to savor his return to power, however. For he faced the most formidable challenge of his remarkable career in the form of the American troops who had long been poised on the border and were now advancing with impunity onto the sacred soil of Mexico.

CHAPTER SEVEN

Grant's Duty: Imperial War and Its Consequences Redux

S am Houston arrived too late. At six o'clock in the evening of Sunday, June 8, 1845, seventy-eight-year-old Andrew Jackson died in the Hermitage, his mansion outside Nashville. Houston burst into the room, only to find a corpse, on which he collapsed in tears. Regaining control of himself, the hero of San Jacinto turned to his young son and admonished him quietly to "remember that [he] had looked upon the face of Andrew Jackson."[1] Houston need not have worried. Jackson was dead, it was true, but his spirit was alive and well, nowhere more spectacularly than in the thousands of soldiers assembling near the border of the Lone Star Republic of Texas to assert the right of the United States to annex it.

Not all Americans were excited by the prospect of war with Mexico over Texas. Twenty-three-year-old Lieutenant Ulysses S. Grant, a recent graduate of the U.S. Military Academy at West Point stationed with the Fourth U.S. Infantry Regiment at Nachitoches, Louisiana, marveled at the martial enthusiasm of his comrades. "Some of them seem to contemplate with a great deal of pleasure some difficulty where they may be able to gain laurels and *advance a little in rank*." Sam Grant dreamed instead of the domestic life of a professor of mathematics in a college in a town in his home state of Ohio. He was eager to return to Saint Louis and marry Julia Dent, the sister of a West Point friend to whom he had become engaged in April. Julia's sister remarked that the lieutenant approached her father "with the air of a man not to be put aside by anything in the world."[2] Colonel Dent was by no means the last man to give way before a determined U. S. Grant.

In the summer of 1845, however, Sam was a pawn in a contest for continental dominion. Many North Americans shared his suspicion that conflict between Mexico and the United States was all but inevitable. But no one could have guessed that just as imperial war in the 1750s and 1760s unexpectedly transformed North America, producing reform and revolution from New England to Buenos Aires, so the storm of imperial war that was about to break along the Rio Grande would precipitate a new cycle of upheaval and radical change, climaxing in revolutionary civil wars in both the United States and Mexico. Certainly not Sam Grant, going about his duties at a godforsaken post too close to an enemy he did not hate and too far from the woman he loved, dreading a coming war, wanting nothing more than to go home.

"The People of Mexico Are a Very Different Race of People"

Hiram Ulysses Grant was born in Point Pleasant, Ohio, on April 27, 1822, less than a half-century after Lord Dunmore's Virginians had fought an outnumbered force of Shawnees and Mingos to a standstill on that same spot. He changed his name to Ulysses Hiram when he entered West Point in 1839 but accepted the name Ulysses Simpson reported by his congressman. Grant was not the kind to make a fuss over formalities. His family and friends called him Sam. What did it matter what his name was legally? Short and solid, Grant was a quiet boy, a trait he inherited from his mother, Hannah Simpson. He was happiest around animals, especially horses, which he learned to ride expertly. It was his father, Jesse, who pushed Sam toward a life grander than his own existence as a tanner. Insisting that his son attend school, Jesse worked hard to secure him an appointment to the U.S. Military Academy. Sam dutifully graduated in June 1843 without distinguishing himself.[3]

Unlike Jackson, Grant grew up in a region that had developed in little more than a generation into one of the most stable and prosperous sections of the United States. Settled by immigrants from all over eastern North America and northwestern Europe, the states of Ohio, Indiana, and Illinois were remarkably diverse places that thrived on a balance of cities and farms, commerce and agriculture, local autonomy and national direction, and an absence of both slavery and African Americans. Middle-class families prized education, self-discipline, hard work, and a sharp division between public and private lives. Above all, they craved the respect of others, which they sought to earn by being decent, hardworking, reliable people. To be respectable was to succeed in socially acceptable ways, to make a useful life without making oneself conspicuous in the process, to win praise by finding a way to accomplish something you were expected to do.[4] Grant matured in a world with firm borders and rules and always did best in structured situations.

Idling in Louisiana early in the summer of 1845, Grant was about to be swept up in events orchestrated by the new president of the United States, James K. Polk. Polk was an earnest Jackson protégé who has served as Speaker of the House of Representatives and governor of Tennessee. He won the presidency in 1844 by defeating the Whig Henry Clay by 38,000 votes in an election in which 2,700,000 were cast.[5] The major issue at stake in this election was the expansion of the United States. Polk favored both the annexation of the Republic of Texas and the Oregon country, which the United States had occupied jointly with Great Britain since 1827. The Democratic Party crafted a jingoist platform for Polk: one of the slogans of the campaign was "ALL OREGON," a call for the annexation of territory between the Rockies and the Pacific as far north as the present southern border of Alaska (54° 40' north latitude), even if that meant going to war with Britain. Polk was willing to accept war with Mexico over Texas and indeed could not have stopped annexation even if he had wanted to, for Congress voted to annex the Lone Star Republic by joint resolution at the end of February 1845, several days before his inauguration. He was not, however, prepared to fight wars against Mexico and Britain simultaneously. Thus he directed his secretary of state, James Buchanan, to negotiate a treaty with Britain's minister to the United States, Richard Pakenham, that essentially split the difference between American and British interests in the Northwest. The Oregon Treaty (signed June 15, 1846) established the forty-ninth parallel as the border from the United States and Canada from the Continental Divide to the Pacific, and cleared the way for war with Mexico. Polk had ordered 4,000 American troops—about half the strength of the army—to Texas in mid-1845; now all he needed was an excuse to use them.

Sam Grant and the Third and Fourth U.S. Infantry departed from the ironically named Camp Salubrity, near Nachitoches, Louisiana, in late July. His commander was a Virginia-born brevet brigadier general named Zachary Taylor. At sixty-one, Taylor's modest achievements consisted of garrison duty during the War of 1812 and afterward, interrupted by a victory against the Seminoles at Lake Okeechobee in 1837. A model of understatement, "Old Rough and Ready" wore the coat of a civilian and a large palmetto hat and was genuinely democratic in both convictions and demeanor.[6]

Lieutenant Grant's arrival at the new camp at Corpus Christi bordered on farce. While disembarking, he fell into the water and had to be retrieved

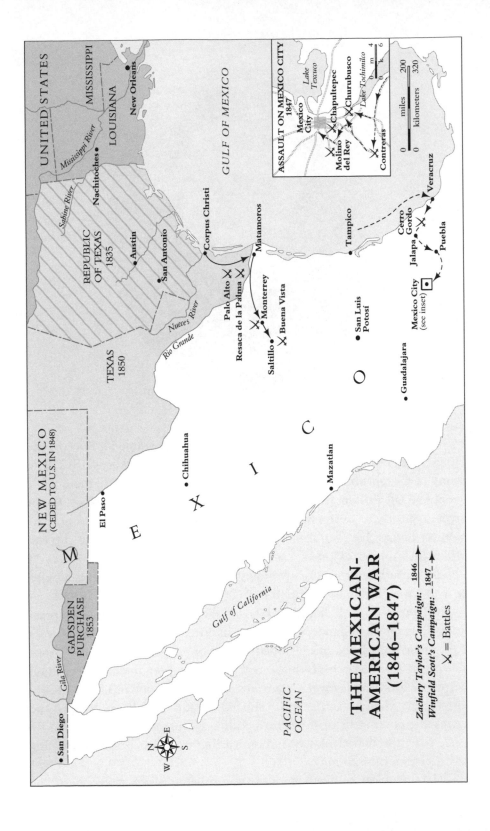

THE MEXICAN-
AMERICAN WAR
(1846–1847)

Zachary Taylor's Campaign: 1846
Winfield Scott's Campaign: 1847
X = Battles

UNITED STATES

MISSISSIPPI

LOUISIANA

New Orleans

Mississippi River

Nachitoches

Sabine River

REPUBLIC
OF TEXAS
1835

Austin

San Antonio

Nueces River

TEXAS
1850

Rio Grande

NEW MEXICO
(CEDED TO U.S. IN 1848)

El Paso

Chihuahua

GADSDEN
PURCHASE
1853

Gila River

San Diego

Gulf of California

PACIFIC
OCEAN

N
W   E
S

M E X I C O

Mazatlan

Guadalajara

San Luis
Potosí

Saltillo

Buena Vista

Monterrey

Resaca de la Palma

Palo Alto

Corpus Christi

Matamoros

GULF OF MEXICO

Tampico

Mexico City
(see inset)

Jalapa

Cerro
Gordo

Veracruz

Puebla

ASSAULT ON MEXICO CITY
1847

Lake
Texcuco

Mexico
City

Chapultepec

Churubusco

Lake
Tochimilco

Molino
del Rey

Contreras

0   m   4
0   k   6

0   200
miles
0   320
kilometers

Lieutenant Ulysses S. Grant, 1849

by his comrades. Grant redeemed himself with determined service in the
largest force put together by the United States since the War of 1812. The
Army of Occupation consisted of three brigades totaling 3,922 men. They
spent the fall drilling, racing horses, and entertaining themselves. Grant
wrote regularly to Julia, pressing for a wedding date. He indulged his passion for horses. He even dabbled briefly in drama, without much success:
when the Americans opened an 800-seat theater with performances of
Othello, the lead actor so strongly protested the casting of Sam as Desdemona
that an actress had to be imported from New Orleans to take his place.[7]

In January 1846, Polk ordered Taylor and his army to establish a presence along the Rio Grande, more than a hundred miles beyond the Nueces
River, which the Mexicans regarded as the border. Marching from Corpus
Christi in early March, Taylor's men in short order fortified a position
across the Rio Grande from Matamoros. This provocation produced the desired result when Mexican cavalry crossed the Rio Grande in late April and
attacked a contingent of Americans, killing eleven and wounding six. By
early May, the two armies were bombarding each other and positioning
themselves for the coming conflict.

The first major engagement of the war came on May 8 at Palo Alto. The battle, Sam's first taste of combat, was a draw. It was an event he never forgot; four decades later, he wrote vividly of the sight of "bayonets and spearheads glisten[ing] in the sunlight formidably."[8] The next day, Taylor's men drove the Mexicans from the field at Resaca de la Palma. Grant led his company through barriers of fallen trees and brush until the "balls commenced to whistle very thick overhead." He later said that the battle "would have been won, just as it was, if I had not been there." Still, he had absorbed in his first engagements the most important lesson that a successful combat commander must learn: although there was "no great sport in having bullets flying about one in direction," there was "less horror when among them than when in anticipation."[9]

On May 9, 1846, upon receiving word of the skirmishing in late April along the Rio Grande, President Polk drafted a message asking Congress to declare war on Mexico. Disavowing responsibility for the conflict, despite massing an army a hundred miles inside what Mexico had always insisted was its border with Texas, Polk denounced the Mexicans for invading "our territory and shed[ding] American blood upon American soil." War resulted from "the act of Mexico herself." Polk demanded "the immediate appearance in arms of a large and overpowering force."[10] Like their president, Southern Democrats generally saw war as "the surest means of fortifying the greatest defenses of liberty, and securing the perpetuity of our glorious institutions." Insisting that they fought as "citizen soldiers" rather than as conscripts in "large standing armies," Americans hoped "to show the Mexicans that a people, without being military, may be *warlike*" and thereby demonstrate that all power rested "in the hearts of the people."[11] A majority in Congress agreed, and Polk signed a formal declaration on May 13.

On May 18, Zachary Taylor became the first American officer since Andrew Jackson in 1818 to lead troops onto foreign soil. South of the Rio Grande, Taylor established headquarters near Matamoros and prepared to assault Monterrey, the capital of the state of Coahuila. Much to his chagrin, Grant found himself appointed quartermaster and commissary officer of the Fourth Infantry. He demanded to share "in the dangers and honors of service with [his] company at the front," but when his request was refused, he set out to become a model quartermaster and to prove that quartermasters, too, could risk their lives. Volunteering at the battle of Monterrey to obtain ammunition for a division that was running dangerously low, Lieutenant Grant rode through enemy fire at a dead run, clinging to the side of his mare, Nelly, whose achievement he seemed to think greater than his own.[12]

Americans were on the offensive throughout the southwestern quadrant of the continent in 1846. The Army of the West, commanded by

Stephen W. Kearny, set out from Fort Leavenworth and occupied Santa Fe, in what is now the state of New Mexico, in August. A month later, some units of Kearny's command proceeded on toward California. By that time the U.S. Navy had already seized the ports of San Francisco and Monterey and, supported by a force of American rebels led by John C. Frémont, had gone on to take Los Angeles on August 13. After the disintegration of Mexican authority in both California and New Mexico, American officers created interim governments.

By late September, with the United States holding much of northern Mexico, the southern republic turned to its indispensable man, Antonio López de Santa Anna. A newspaper promised to forget the past if he would recognize "his errors" and "promote the welfare of the country" by pursuing "a course entirely different from [his] former policy."[13] The U.S. Navy allowed the former president to enter Veracruz on September 12. Within days, Santa Anna was in Mexico City. He then established himself at San Luis Potosí with some 8,000 men. Beyond his predilection for living well and his boredom with detail, Santa Anna faced almost insurmountable problems, including severe shortages of money, equipment, and adequately trained troops.

In January, Santa Anna learned from intercepted American dispatches that the United States was diverting men from Taylor in the north to an army General Winfield Scott was assembling for an assault on Veracruz and Mexico City. He boldly ordered his men to march against Taylor's dwindling force. On February 22, the Mexicans ran into Taylor's men defending a narrow valley. Rather than waiting to deploy his full force of about 14,000 men—roughly three times the number in Taylor's command—Santa Anna attacked immediately. After two days of intense fighting at what came to be known as the battle of Buena Vista, Santa Anna suddenly withdrew, having suffered about 1,800 casualties with hundreds of others captured and thousands missing. The Americans lost from 600 to 700 of the 4,500 engaged. Had Santa Anna's leadership on the battlefield matched his strategic design, he might have scored a decisive victory.

Sam Grant was not at Buena Vista because he was one of thousands transferred to the Army of Invasion under the command of Major General Scott. Landing south of Veracruz, Scott and some 12,000 men captured the port city with remarkably few casualties, then, reenacting the famous campaign of Hernán Cortés against the Aztecs in 1519, left their supply base behind and marched west into the Valley of Mexico. A veteran of the War of 1812, Scott was general in chief of the United States Army, with an ample girth that bespoke the pleasure he took in the finer things in life. He wore elaborate uniforms, earning the nickname "Old Fuss and Feathers," and traveled with servants and furniture. Grant admired Scott's talents but preferred the plainer style of Zachary Taylor. He recalled that while both generals "were pleasant to serve under—Taylor was pleasant to serve with."[14]

Santa Anna rushed to stave off the invasion, melodramatically proclaiming his "duty to sacrifice" himself. He would "die fighting!" he said, calling on Mexicans to rally to his colors and defend their religion, their honor, and their families.[15] And indeed Santa Anna did work bravely to stop the Army of Invasion. His best chance came at Cerro Gordo, a narrow pass between Veracruz and Jalapa some 4,680 feet above sea level. He blocked the main road but neglected to guard an unprotected path on his left flank. Scott sent a detachment to get behind the Mexican force. On April 18, 1847, Scott ordered a general attack, which seized the heights above the pass. As Grant described it in a letter to a friend, seeing the Americans on an elevation that commanded his own position, "Santa Anna Vamoused with a small part of his force leaving about 6000 to be taken prisoners with all their arms supplies &c." "The pursuit was so close upon the retreating few that Santa Anna's carriage and mules were taken and with them his wooden leg and some 20 or 30 thousand dollars in money."[16]

Scott maneuvered into Mexico City in August and early September. Lieutenant Grant fought with distinction at Churubusco, Molino del Rey, and two other engagements, winning citations for bravery and promotion to first lieutenant and brevet captain. He told Julia that the conflicts were "four of the hardest fought battles that the world ever witnessed." The "most astonishing victories [had] crowned the American arms," but they had "dearly . . . paid for it" in the number of dead and wounded. The most spectacular assault by far was on the fort of Chapultepec, home of the Mexican military academy. The young cadets voted unanimously to defend it, only to find themselves overwhelmed along with the fort's other defenders. Watching the flag of the United States wave over Chapultepec, Santa Anna muttered in disgust that "If we were to plant our batteries in Hell, the damned Yankees would take them from us."[17]

The fall of Mexico City on September 14, 1847, brought the war to an end. Scott's brilliant campaign won praise from the Duke of Wellington, the conqueror of Napoleon Bonaparte and the most famous soldier alive. With slightly fewer than 11,000 men, Scott had defeated an entrenched army of more than 30,000.[18] Santa Anna resigned the presidency and fled the city. Forced to give up military command in October, he went into exile in Jamaica in April 1848.

The Army of Invasion had long since settled down to occupy the capital city and await the outcome of peace negotiations. Invariably fascinated by Mexico, "a strange land to us all, and full of novelties," according to Indiana volunteer Lew Wallace, who later wrote the novel *Ben-Hur*, Americans tended to disparage Mexicans. Visits to Aztec ruins and collection of souvenirs led them to reflect on the challenges of extending liberty to people whose race and religion seemed to inhibit their ability to exercise it responsibly. They characterized Mexicans as dirty, ignorant, poor, and degraded, although these attitudes did not prevent them from having sex with Mexican women. Conquest confirmed the soldiers' sense of moral superiority, rooted in education, industry, technology, religion, and free government. "Many, very many years must pass before the common people, the public of this miscalled Republic, will be sufficiently enlightened to enjoy the blessings of independence," lamented Captain Robert Anderson.[19] To become true republicans, Mexicans would have to reject the superstitions of Catholicism and the enormous power of the Church and the army.

Sam Grant was ambivalent about Mexico. It was "a great country." He longed to take Julia on one of his rambles around "the beautiful Valley of Mexico. The whole Valley is spread out to the view covered with numerous lakes, green fields, and little Villages and to all appearance it would be a short ride to go around the whole valley in a day, but you would find that it would take a week." Expressing no such enthusiasm for the people, Grant worried that they were not capable of sustaining a republic. Citizenship was hard work, requiring obedience to law and a willingness to work within commonly accepted legal, political, and cultural borders. Mexicans he saw as too eager to indulge their own pleasure rather than serve the public good. "All gamble Priests & civilians, male & female, and particularly so on Sundays." Echoing Northern middle-class indictments of the South, he argued that the "better class are very proud and tyrinize over the lower and much more numerous class as much as a hard master does over his negroes, and they submit to it quite as humbly. The great majority [of the] inhabitants are either pure or more than half blooded Indians, and show but little more than signs of neatness or comfort in their miserable dwellings than the uncivilized Indian." The "people of Mexico are a very different race of people."[20]

Grant's racism was less virulent than Jackson's. More reflective and less defensive, he implied that the problems with Mexico might be corrected. Above all, Mexicans had to develop national pride and a sense of civic responsibility founded on government by voluntary consent. Nothing indicated the pernicious character of coercion better than the tendency of

Mexican soldiers to give up quickly.[21] Bravery was not the issue. That Americans chose to fight for their country ensured their ultimate victory as much as, if not more than, talent or courage.

Grant was acutely aware of the contradictions inherent in an empire of liberty built on slavery. In July 1846, he condemned some volunteers and "about all the Texans" because they "think it perfectly right to impose upon the people of a conquered City to any extent, and even to murder them where the act can be covered by the dark. And how much they seem to enjoy acts of violence, too!"[22] Grant could hardly have missed the often brutal ways in which white officers treated the black servants who accompanied them into battle (and occasionally took advantage of the situation to run away). To the extent that the citizens of the United States secured their liberty by oppressing other people, whether they were Africans, Indians, or Mexicans, they were sowing the seeds of their own destruction.

In his memoirs, Grant called the American Civil War a direct consequence of the war with Mexico. The United States had invaded Mexico in order to satisfy the ambition of a Southern slave power, which, in its zeal to maintain the liberty of white men, whatever the cost, nearly destroyed the Union a decade and a half later. Grant described the war "as one of the most unjust ever waged by a stronger against a weaker nation. . . . an instance of a republic following the bad example of European monarchies, in not considering justice in their desire to acquire additional territory."[23]

Grant told a journalist in the late 1870s that he had "never altogether forgiven [him]self" for participating in the subjugation of Mexico. Unable to think of "a more wicked war," the conqueror of the Confederacy wondered whether the territory wrested by force from Mexico "might have been obtained by other means." If the Mexicans had chosen to sell Texas and California, Grant would have felt better. Instead, the U.S. Army had compelled them to surrender half their nation. The distinction between an empire constructed on consent and one built on coercion mattered mightily to Grant and many other nineteenth-century Americans. To them, the Mexican-American War was an instance of imperial ambition trumping the cause of human liberty, a moral failure that ultimately required expiation in the form of the more than 600,000 American deaths in the Civil War. Grant observed that "Nations, like individuals, are punished for their transgressions." The "punishment" that the United States merited for its sins in Mexico, he believed, was "the most sanguinary and expensive war of modern times."[24]

Critics of the Mexican-American War worried more about its impact on the conquerors than the conquered. Insisting that Mexicans were incapable of making the informed choices on which democratic government necessarily depended, they supported the idea that "liberty is the lesson, which we are appointed to teach." Nevertheless, they feared the destabilizing impact of war and expansion. A mad rush across the continent would create multitudes of competing interests and identities. It was an "absurd and senseless war" designed to add land "to the boundless wastes we already hold," and reflected "an aggressive spirit and a disposition to tyrannize over the weak, which ought not by any means be fostered in a Republic." A senator repeated Henry Clay's criticism of Jackson in 1819: "Instead of being considered the conservative head of a great system of American republics, we are likely to be looked upon as rapacious, grasping, and unscrupulous conquerors." Congressman Abraham Lincoln, an Illinois Whig, taunted Polk—"a bewildered, confounded, and miserably perplexed man"—about inconsistencies in his earnest rhetoric. Lincoln distrusted Polk's explanation of the origins of the war. The president had deliberately fixed "the public gaze upon the exceeding brightness of military glory—that attractive rainbow, that rises in showers of blood—that serpent's eye, that charms to destroy."[25]

In the end, few Americans were satisfied with the outcome of the war. Under the terms of the Treaty of Guadalupe Hidalgo, which the American emissary Nicholas Trist signed with representatives of the Mexican government on February 12, 1848, Mexico received $15 million and the United States assumed $3 million in claims against Mexico by American citizens. In return, the United States acquired half of Mexico, including the present-day states of California, Nevada, Arizona, New Mexico, Utah, and Colorado, and recognition of the Rio Grande as the border between Texas and Mexico.[26] A bitterly disappointed Polk, who desired even more, contemplated arresting Trist before relenting and asking Congress to ratify the treaty. He declined to run for reelection in 1848 and died shortly after returning to Tennessee. His successor in the White House was Old Rough and Ready, Zachary Taylor, the candidate of the Whig Party.

In percentage terms, the Mexican-American War was the deadliest war in the history of the United States. More than 13,000 American men, or 16.9 percent of those who served, did not return, compared with 16.4 percent of Union troops in the Civil War. (In both conflicts, disease, not wounds, killed the vast majority.) Untold thousands of Mexicans were left dead or maimed. Worse was yet to come for both nations. "The United States will conquer Mexico," the Massachusetts writer Ralph Waldo Emerson confided to his journal in 1846, "but it will be as the man swallows the arsenic, which brings him down in turn. Mexico will poison us."[27]

Before Guadalupe Hidalgo, the African-American abolitionist Thomas Van Rensselaer predicted that the imperial war would produce "evil, and nothing but evil." Bad as it was for the United States, it was "still worse" for Mexico, "because she is poor and ignorant, and compared with us, weak."[28] Prominent Mexicans agreed. Shocked by the extent of their defeat, many despaired of the future. The long-dreaded nightmare of regional and racial conflicts seemed to have arrived. Uprisings in Guanajuato, Queretaro, and San Luis Potosí followed hard on the heels of a rebellion in 1847 in which Mayans nearly gained control of Yucatán before a Mexican counterattack killed 150,000, one-third of the Mayan population.

Imperial war "brought the tensions, strains, and conflicts within Mexican society to the breaking point" and "set in motion a chain of events that altered the course of history." War that originated in "the insatiable ambition of the United States" ended in an American victory made possible by Mexican "weakness." Its legacy was "a feeling of sadness for the evils that it had produced, and in our minds a fruitful lesson of how difficult it is when disorder, asperity, and anarchy prevail, to uphold the defence and salvation of a people."[29] Divisions deepened between conservative nationalists and liberal federalists, between supporters of the army and the Church on the one hand and Indians and mestizos on the other, between Mexico City and the states.

National politics vacillated wildly. In 1853, Santa Anna was once again installed as president. This time, his megalomania knew no bounds. "His Most Serene Highness" auctioned honors and persecuted his enemies, real and imagined. He sold the Mesilla Valley to the United States for $10 million, justifying the Gadsden Purchase (the South Carolinian James Gadsden was the American minister in Mexico City) as a defensive measure designed to keep the United States from cutting "another piece from the body which she had just horribly mutilated."[30] Before Santa Anna could transfer more territory, Mexicans dispatched him into final exile in August 1855. Liberals moved to destroy the bulwarks of the colonial order, eliminating the judicial privileges of the military, clergy, and other corporate bodies and establishing the principle of equality before the law.

Most American citizens paid scant attention to the upheaval in Mexico. The war was over, a horror increasingly construed as a romantic memory. Yet its legacy transformed the world of the victors as much as the world of the vanquished. Working through its consequences polarized the citizens of both republics, led to devastating civil wars, and eventually produced new revolutionary settlements that no one could have imagined in 1848.

"Violence Is the Order of the Day"

Ulysses S. Grant finally married Julia Dent in the parlor of her family's home in Saint Louis on August 22, 1848. Captain Grant took his wife to meet his family in Ohio, and in November they moved to his new posting at Detroit. The birth of a son completed the domestic life they both craved. There was no mistaking the patriarchal dimension of the Grant marriage: the family story was always his story. Indeed, Julia later constructed her life as a narrative of romantic devotion to a great man: loyal wife, devoted mother, and conscientious hostess, she was never the protagonist. Like Andrew and Rachel Jackson, Sam and Julia loved, respected, and depended on each other. But while Sam doted on Julia and patronized her, the Grants understood each other more fully than the Jacksons. They were faithful to each other, sharing a double bed until his final illness, and their partnership, while hardly egalitarian, was genuine. Because the Grants brought out the best in each other, they were always happiest when they were together.[31]

Extended separations therefore made the 1850s a decade of turmoil in the Grant household as much as in the nation at large. In early 1852, the Fourth Infantry Regiment was ordered to the Pacific coast. Sam and Julia decided that mother and son should stay with the Dents rather than brave the rugged life of military posts in the Far West, and the captain went alone to Oregon then California. Without Julia, the lonely Grant fell into depression and found solace in alcohol. Julia later denied the charge that Grant was "slovenly," a code word for an alcoholic. Her Captain Grant "was always perfection, both in manner and person, a cheerful, self-reliant, earnest gentleman . . . [who] was the very nicest and handsomest man I ever saw."[32] No doubt she thought so. But Captain Grant also drank a great deal.

Unhappy in the role of a glorified policeman on the margins of empire, Grant resigned from the army in 1854 and returned to his family. At thirty-two, he was a man without prospects. The world of commerce in the upper Mississippi Valley was a long way from the wide-open world in which Andrew Jackson had flourished. The premium was on patience, hard work, and learning to get along with people. Concern for one's reputation meant establishing reliability rather than personal honor. As Grant told William

Tecumseh Sherman when he ran into him in Saint Louis in August 1857: "West Point and the Regular Army were not good schools for farmers, bankers, merchants, and mechanics."[33]

Grant flailed away at farming without success, notwithstanding the labor of four enslaved African Americans given to Julia by her father and one man he owned himself. Troubled by his complicity in coercion, Grant freed his slave in 1859 despite the precarious state of his family's finances; he lost more than $1,000 in the process. That winter he sold firewood on the streets of Saint Louis. Matters improved in the summer of 1860 when Grant's father persuaded to join him in the leather business in Galena, Illinois. Now within established parameters, Grant functioned better. He loved his four children and enjoyed playing with them. An acquaintance described him as "very domestic . . . and extremely homelike in his ways." He seemed "a sad man" with no other ambition "than to educate his children and take care of his family."[34]

Grant reported in his memoirs that he "was a Whig by education and a great admirer of Mr. [Henry] Clay" who joined the American, or Know-Nothing, Party in the early 1850s when the Whig Party disintegrated. Slavery, he said, had not been a major issue until the annexation of Texas and the Mexican War. Grant voted for the Democrat James Buchanan in 1856 (an act he later justified as an effort to prevent secession) and likely would have voted for Stephen Douglas in 1860 had he lived in Illinois long enough to cast a ballot. Julia's Southern relatives undoubtedly influenced Grant's politics. But his choice to support the laissez-faire attitude of the Democrats rather than the reform-minded zealotry of the new party of Republicans were consistent with his character. Grant preferred the path of least resistance, always seeking stability and accommodation.[35]

Stability, however, was difficult to achieve in the United States in the middle of the nineteenth century. In fact, with rapid population growth fueled by natural increase and the arrival of wave after wave of Irish and German immigrants in the 1840s and 1850s and with their wholehearted embrace of such technological innovations as the railroad and telegraph, Americans seemed to be making a virtue of instability. Many were uncomfortable with, even overwhelmed by, the social transformations that accompanied material change. They were citizens of a huge nation in which the localism that most Americans had prized was becoming increasingly difficult to sustain.

The war with Mexico helped expand the horizons of U.S. citizens. Just as World War II precipitated interest in Asia, the war with Mexico sparked interest in the Spanish and French empires and the imperial history of

North America. New Englanders George Bancroft, Francis Parkman, and William Hickling Prescott chronicled the history of struggles for dominion in North America. Nathaniel Hawthorne sifted through the legacies of the past, and Herman Melville meditated on encounters between peoples of diverse backgrounds.

Most spectacularly, continental war forced sectional tensions and ideological contradictions into the foreground of public life. As Americans thought about why they had fought Mexico and—more critically—what to do with the vast territory they had acquired, they confronted questions that might otherwise have lain dormant. Unlike Britain in the 1760s, the United States emerged from an imperial war without a huge debt. Like Britain, it suddenly had a great deal of new territory to organize and administer, a process that required Americans to define their attitudes toward liberty and empire in ways that tore at the fabric of their political culture.

In August 1846, Congressman David Wilmot, a Democrat from Pennsylvania and an otherwise loyal supporter of President Polk, after expressing his displeasure with a war of conquest against Mexico, proposed an amendment to a military appropriations bill. Borrowing the language of the Northwest Ordinance of 1787, he proposed that "neither slavery nor involuntary servitude shall ever exist in any part" of the territory acquired from Mexico, "except for crime, whereof the party shall be first duly convicted." The House of Representatives passed the amendment by a vote of 83 to 64 then passed the appropriations bill as a whole, 94 to 78. But the Senate failed to vote on the bill before Congress adjourned, so it did not become law. Wilmot had "no morbid sympathy for the slave." Rather he sought to ensure that the new territory, like the Old Northwest, would be a place where "my own race and own color can live without the disgrace" of "association with negro slavery."[36]

The intense reactions to the Wilmot Proviso exposed the fragility of American politics. Since the Missouri Compromise of 1820, American leaders had labored to suppress the issue of slavery because they knew it was so volatile that they could not contain it within normal political borders. Especially after the rise of radical "immediatist" abolitionism in the 1830s, the center would not hold. American politics had long been about the defense of white male liberty against tyrants like George III and Santa Anna. Now American citizens increasingly saw each other as potential tyrants, too, finding strength in sectional coalitions designed to exert dominion over other parts of the nation. They feared that the admission of new states carved out of the Mexican cession would disrupt the balance of power in the Congress.

It would lead to the perpetual dominion of one region over all others.[37] As sectional loyalties trumped partisan identification, Americans were fulfilling Martin Van Buren's 1828 prophecy that in the absence of party conflict, "geographical divisions founded on local interests or, what is worse, prejudices between free & slaveholding states will inevitably take their place."[38]

At midcentury growing numbers of Northerners complained of what they called a Slave Power. As members of the Free-Soil and later Republican parties, they sought to rescue the Republic from aristocrats intent upon expanding slavery and their power into southwestern North America. Many Northerners learned from reading Harriet Beecher Stowe's immensely popular novel, *Uncle Tom's Cabin,* that slavery perverted slaveholders, turning some Southern men into weak, passive creatures unable to follow their consciences and others into angry, violent brutes—caricatures of Andrew Jackson—who exploited both enslaved Africans and women to satisfy their lust for personal independence. "I am jealous of the power of the South," David Wilmot said later, explaining that his proviso was an attempt "to strike an effectual and decisive blow against its domination."[39]

Middle-class Northern men, by contrast, imagined themselves as less violent and more likely to follow the counsel of their wives and consciences than the dictates of personal desire. Ulysses S. Grant was no exception. His devotion to domesticity was part of a larger trend away from celebration of male aggression. No one better embodied the emerging ideal than Abraham Lincoln, the Illinois railroad lawyer who became the successful Republican candidate for president in 1860. Indeed, the Lincoln family was something of a cliché: devoted father, shrewish wife, and rowdy sons. One can scarcely imagine Old Hickory suffering the demands of Mary Todd Lincoln with the patience of Father Abraham—or being celebrated for that forbearance by his followers.

White Southern men took pride in their control of their households. Democratic in their relationships with each other, they were patriarchal in their dealings with everyone else.[40] Easily insulted, they continued to see local autonomy as a foundation of liberty. Supporters of the Wilmot Proviso were saying "in effect to the Southern man, Avaunt! You are not my equal and hence to be excluded." An important part of their identity continued to be wrapped up in projecting themselves into the wider world. If middleclass Northerners like Grant turned mentally and emotionally inward to the family home, many white Southerners continued to look outward and to define themselves through conquest of territory and the domination of racial "others." Whether they were fighting Creeks or Mexicans, many

Southerners validated their honor, defended their liberty, and acquired territory. Without the right to expand with slavery, averred Senator John C. Calhoun, the South would soon be outnumbered by "the nonslaveholding States—overwhelmingly."[41] Southerners feared they would become slaves rather than citizens. No wonder it is hard to think of a time in the decades before the Civil War when considerable numbers of Southern men were not either conquering or contemplating conquest.

Dreams of expansion were especially intense in the 1850s.[42] Southern Democrats eyed the Spanish colony of Cuba as well as the rest of Mexico. President Franklin Pierce, a veteran of the Mexican-American War and a New Hampshire Democrat with an unfortunate fondness for alcohol, made the White House almost as much a center of imperialism as Polk had. Prodded by Secretary of War Jefferson Davis of Mississippi, another veteran who was seriously wounded at Buena Vista, the United States jumped at Santa Anna's proffer of 30,000 square miles for $10 million. In the last year of his administration, Pierce appointed a lawyer and Mexican War veteran, John Forsyth of Alabama, as minister to Mexico to secure Baja California and parts of Sonora and Chihuahua. Forsyth failed in his mission— understandably, given what Mexico had recently lost—and returned to the United States after breaking off relations with the Mexican government.

Earlier, in October 1854, the American ambassadors to Spain, Great Britain, and France convened in Ostend, Belgium, to discuss ways to acquire Cuba. They sent a memorandum (dubbed the Ostend Manifesto) outlining a range of options to Secretary of State William Marcy. The principal author of the letter was the Louisianan Pierre Soulé, the envoy to Madrid and a former senator. His interest in Cuba as a venue for plantation agriculture was as predictable as the bellicose tone he gave the manifesto. Neither expansionism nor bellicosity, however, characterized Soulé's cosigner, the Pennsylvanian James Buchanan, minister to the Court of St. James's and formerly Polk's secretary of state. Buchanan acquiesced because he hoped one day to become president and, like all Northern Democrats with that ambition, he was a prisoner of the Southern votes on which the success of his party depended.

At Ostend the ministers called on Pierce to make an "immediate and earnest effort . . . to purchase Cuba from Spain." The reasons were obvious. Cuba, one of the last of European colonies in the Western Hemisphere, suffered under the "worst of all possible governments, that of absolute despotism." It was close to Florida and astride the channels that linked the Mississippi River and the Atlantic Ocean. The ministers thought Spain likely to sell. If, however, the Spanish declined a generous offer, the United States would have to consider its self-interest, and, by implication, war. "The United States have never acquired a foot of territory except by purchase, or as in the case of Texas, upon the free and voluntary application of the people of that independent State, who desired to blend their destinies with our own." Lest anyone claim that the land acquired from Mexico was an exception, the Americans reminded Pierce that the United States had refused to claim the territory "by right of conquest in a just war"; instead, it purchased it "for what was then considered by both parties a full and ample equivalent."[43] (No one mentioned that an American army occupied Mexico City during the negotiations.) The safety and security of U.S. citizens also demanded action. The Pierce administration would "be unworthy of our gallant forefathers, and commit base treason against our posterity, should we permit Cuba to be Africanized, and become a second St. Domingo, with all its attendant horrors to the white race, and suffer the flames to extend to our own neighboring shores, seriously to endanger or actually to consume the fair fabric of our Union." Secretary Marcy quickly replied to Soulé that while the United States was eager to acquire Cuba, President Pierce was unwilling to obtain the island by any means other than purchase.[44]

The official repudiation of the Ostend Manifesto did not stop Americans from intruding into the nations of the Caribbean basin. The United States, working to beat the British to the punch, signed a treaty with Colombia that permitted American commercial interests to build a canal linking the Atlantic and Pacific oceans. It also negotiated agreements with Honduras and Nicaragua establishing both friendship and the right of the United States to construct a canal across the latter country. Most spectacularly, the filibustering impulse emerged in the person of the "grey-eyed man of destiny," William Walker, who invaded Nicaragua no fewer than four times and actually governed the country from 1855 to 1857. Walker, a native of Nashville, who (after first trying his hand as a doctor, lawyer, and newspaper editor) failed to liberate Sonora and Baja California from Mexico in 1853–54, was one of many American filibusters—freelance imperialists—who worked the Caribbean basin from Cuba to Panama in the 1850s.[45] With the support of the Pierce administration and the Democratic Party, Walker invited Southerners to establish plantations in Nicaragua. Unfortunately for him, his plans conflicted with those of the New York entrepreneur Cornelius Vanderbilt, who intended to build a railroad to transport California-bound Americans from the Atlantic to the Pacific to spare them the tedious and expensive voyage around Cape Horn. Vanderbilt financed Walker's opponents, who overthrew him in 1857 and executed him three years later. Vanderbilt had no interest in governing Nicaragua; he just wanted to develop his railroad. Southerners, on the other hand, needed land in Central America, Cuba, and Mexico to extend their version of American liberty. "I want Cuba," proclaimed Albert Gallatin Brown succinctly. "I want Tamaulipas, Potosí, and one or two other Mexican states; and I want them all for the same reason— for the planting or spreading of slavery."[46]

The largely Southern commitment to expansion primarily through conquest and the largely Northern desire to see the United States develop mainly within its now continental borders were mutually exclusive designs for realizing the nation's "manifest destiny." In 1850 and 1851, political moderates in both regions had sought to finesse the issues raised by victory over Mexico. Congressional decisions to admit California as a free state counterbalancing the slave state of Texas and to leave the fate of slavery in the New Mexico and Arizona territories unresolved was at best a temporary compromise. As Americans continued to move westward in huge numbers, the newly acquired territories had to be organized and states formed, which in turn required a decision for or against slavery. In 1854, when Senator Stephen Douglas, an Illinois Democrat with presidential aspirations who was also eager to foster the construction of a railroad between Chicago and San Francisco, proposed that settlers in the Kansas and Nebraska territories decide whether their states would be slave or free, he unleashed a firestorm of criticism that completed the disintegration of the Whig Party and created the Republican Party, an avowedly sectional organization committed to the containment of slavery and the protection of Northern liberty.

By the late 1850s, many Northern Republicans and Southern Democrats so feared each others' influence and intentions that they could scarcely have a civil conversation. Event after event seemingly confirmed the existence of a determined conspiracy by one side against the liberty of the other. Northerners compared the caning of the Republican senator Charles Sumner of Massachusetts on the floor of the Senate on May 22, 1856, by the South Carolina congressman Preston Brooks to a master whipping a slave; Southerners defended it as a necessary rebuke to an impudent zealot who had insulted the honor of Brooks's kinsman, a South Carolina senator. "Bleeding Sumner" crystallized images of Southerners as aggressive louts intent upon having their way, no matter the cost. "Violence has now found its way into the Senate chamber," editorialized the *New York Evening Post;* "violence is the order of the day; the North is to be pushed to the wall by it, and this [Southern] plot will succeed if the people of the free states are as

apathetic as the slaveholders are insolent." There were similar howls of outrage when a Southern-dominated Supreme Court ruled in the Dred Scott
case in March 1857 that enslaved African Americans were property in the
eyes of the law and therefore that neither state nor federal governments
could restrict owners from transporting them anywhere they wished. Grant
explained later that "the Southern slaveowners believed that, in some way,
the ownership of slaves conferred a sort of patent of nobility—a right to
govern independent of the interest or wishes of those who did not hold
such property. They convinced themselves" that slavery "was not safe in the
hands of any body of legislators but themselves."[47]

For their part, Southerners saw the increasing power of the North and
opposition to the expansion of slavery as threats to their way of life. The
seizure of the U.S. arsenal at Harper's Ferry, Virginia, in October 1859 by
the abolitionist John Brown and a small band of white and black followers
confirmed the widespread belief that pro- and antislavery Americans were
already locked in a war to the death. "It is manifest that the South cannot
possibly consent to dwell in the Union upon sufferance," a Louisiana newspaper editor argued late in 1860. It would be intolerable for the South to exist as "the mere vassal and thrall of a party which aims at her ruin and
degradation."[48]

"No Man Surrenders from Conviction, But from Superior Force"

The Revolutionary Settlement, frayed by the war with Mexico and the tu-
multuous politics of the 1850s, disintegrated completely with the election
of the Republican presidential candidate, Abraham Lincoln, in November
1860. Southern fears that Lincoln would coerce compliance with an antislavery agenda triggered the secession of South Carolina in December and the
creation of the Confederate States of America in February 1861. Two
months later, Confederate troops bombarded Fort Sumter in Charleston
harbor rather than permit U.S. Navy vessels to resupply it. Faced with a
violent assault on federal property and authority, Lincoln declared the secessionist states in rebellion and called for volunteers to restore the integrity
of the Union.

Even as Northern volunteers responded in droves to Lincoln's appeal,
citizens of Virginia, North Carolina, Arkansas, and Tennessee joined their
Deep South brethren in the formation of a new nation. They remained committed to a world fashioned by Andrew Jackson and his peers, a world in

which governments refrained from asserting central power and using military force against its citizens, a world in which, as Thomas Jefferson had promised in 1801, they would be left "free to regulate their own pursuits of industry and improvement."[49] In their view, the debates over territory and slavery provoked by the war with Mexico had exposed not only the fragility of the Revolutionary Settlement but the determination of large numbers of Northerners to redefine it on terms that would destroy the autonomy of white male citizens in managing their own households and communities. Just as the United States' declaration of independence thirteen years after the Treaty of Paris had confirmed a great British imperial victory and triggered unreconcilable controversies over the nature of imperial power and the relationships between colonies and metropolis, subjects and king, so the Confederate States' declaration of independence thirteen years after the Treaty of Guadalupe Hidalgo had sealed an American imperial victory of similar dimensions and sparked equally intractable debates over the nature of imperial power, the relationships between states and the federal government, and the character of citizenship in the Republic.

Not all Southerners were eager to make the break. With many other thoughtful leaders, Mississippi's Senator Jefferson Davis was loath to abandon the American "form of government" and "admirable Constitution." Yet in the end he concluded that he simply had no choice; rather than live "under an Abolition government," he would "appeal to the God of Battles." He had, he believed, been forced into war by Northern Republicans' disdain for the accepted rules of American politics. Explaining the secession of Mississippi, he argued that his state had acted out of "necessity" rather than "choice." "Those who have driven her to this alternative threaten to deprive her of the right to require that her government shall rest on the consent of the governed, to substitute foreign force for domestic support, to reduce a state to the condition from which the colony rose." The threat to liberty now came from within rather than without, said the man who soon became president of the Confederate States of America; it was no longer Indians, British, or Mexicans but Yankees who were intent upon waging war against their fellow citizens.[50]

White Southerners went to war, as they had in 1775, 1812, 1818, 1836, and 1846, to protect their liberty by defending their home and family. "With all my devotion to the Union, and the feeling of loyalty and duty of an American citizen," Colonel Robert E. Lee wrote to his sister when he resigned his commission in the U.S. Army in April 1861, "I have not been able to make up my mind to raise my hand against my relatives, my children, my home." It was as simple as that. A Georgia farmer who owned slaves fought because "our homes our firesides our land and negroes and even the virtue of our fair ones are at stake." Some women understood, much as they disliked watching their sons and lovers go off with no certainty of return. One wife bore her husband's departure by telling herself that he was "gone, gone in the highest exercise of man's highest & holiest duty!"[51]

The war stirred old fears. Taking up arms in the name of Southern liberty threatened to ignite the kind of social revolution that Mexican gentlemen like Santa Anna dreaded. Confederate leaders worried about possible uprisings of African Americans and also resistance from poor whites who had little tangible investment in slavery and more than a few reasons to resent the political domination of their region's great gentry. What if in defending their localist notions of liberty, white Southerners inspired rebellion against their own authority? White women wondered how they were to control slaves made assertive by the possibility of freedom. Southern men who went off to repel Yankees invaders left wives who feared "the blacks more than . . . the Yankees."[52]

Northerners were hardly indifferent to the contradiction inherent in coercing people to embrace liberty. Many Democrats and some Republicans defended secession as an exercise of the right of free men to associate politically with whom they chose. Rutherford B. Hayes, a young Republican lawyer in Cincinnati, had been willing to consider letting the South go until the Confederate attack on Fort Sumter allowed him and many others to view the war as entirely defensive. Once blood had been shed, he saw military service as his civic duty. Like Davis, Hayes believed that he had no choice but to fight. He explained to an old friend from the South that while the use of "force" was generally not "wise," the attack on the federal fort had "forced [war] on us." He would fight to defend the Union, as long as the purpose was not "conquest."[53]

Hayes volunteered to preserve a national political order that strove to balance individual freedom with respect for duly constituted authority. Liberty was not license, the right to do as one saw fit without respect for the rights of others. Obedience to an elected government ensured the greatest degree of freedom for the greatest number of people. Defeating the rebellion was necessary to secure liberty because without respect for law, true liberty could not exist. According to an eager Union volunteer, the war was "not the North against South. It is government against anarchy, law against disorder."[54]

There was no stronger proponent of this idea than William Tecumseh Sherman. Two years older than Grant and also a graduate of West Point, Sherman fought in the Second Seminole War and spent the war with Mexico in California before resigning his commission in 1853 to pursue what turned

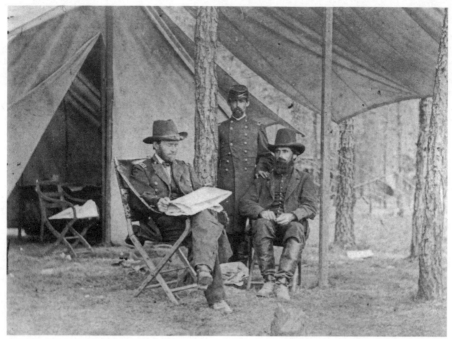

Lieutenant General Ulysses S. Grant in his northern Virginia headquarters, with
Colonel Theodore S. Bowers and Brigadier General John A. Rawlins, 1864

out to be a dismal career in business and law. Wandering from Ohio to California to New York to Kansas, Sherman ended up as the superintendent of the
Louisiana State Seminary and Military Academy in 1859. He considered buying African Americans because he was certain that "the negro . . . must be
subject to the white man, or he must amalgamate or be destroyed."[55]

Yet secession horrified Sherman. Southerners were fools starting down
a path of "confusion & disorder" that would not end until "each state, and
may be each county will claim separate Independence." The problem was
not slavery but "the tendency to anarchy everywhere," against which "our
only hope is in Uncle Sam." The U.S. Army would have to reassert the idea
that "[t]he law is or should be our King, we should obey it, not because it
meets our approval, but because it is the law, and because obedience in some
shape is necessary to every system of civilized government." Sherman resigned his position after Louisiana seceded, returned to Ohio, and accepted
the colonelcy of the Third Regiment of U.S. Infantry, certain that "no man
surrenders from conviction, but from Superior Force, and so with states
and communities."[56]

Ulysses S. Grant agreed. Ambivalent about secession until South Car-

The domestic Grant with his wife, Julia, and son Jesse at City Point, Virginia, 1864

olinians fired on Fort Sumter, Grant committed himself with enthusiasm once the shedding of blood had made the issue clear. He was ready to fight the Southern "aggressors" without interfering with slavery and defend the "integrity of the glorious old *Stars & Stripes,* the Constitution and the Union." Whatever his previous opinions, Grant told his father, "I have but one sentiment now. That is we have a Government, and laws and a flag and they must all be sustained." The Confederate attack on Sumter had simplified matters by reducing all "parties" to two, "Traitors & Patriots." In June, the former captain accepted an appointment as colonel of the Twenty-first Illinois Regiment (he was promoted to brigadier general in August) and went to war in Missouri, suddenly energized after a decade of indolence. His growing "inclination [was] to whip the rebellion into submission, preserving all constitutional rights. If it cannot be whipped in any other way than through a war against slavery, let it come to that legitimately."[57]

Grant liked command. He was at once "silent" and "in control."[58] Beneath his surface calm—stories of his apparent lack of concern in the heat of battle abound—lay determination. Given orders to accomplish a particular task, he found a way to do it. In writing orders he disdained adjectives and adverbs for the verbs that "give his writing its terse, muscular quality." "Move" was a characteristic Grant word.[59] Lacking the fervor of Stonewall Jackson or the mania of William Tecumseh Sherman, he was as stubborn as either of those notoriously tenacious men. He hated to retreat, personally as well as militarily. If he encountered an obstacle, he battered it until it gave way or he found a way around it. People could depend on Grant to do his duty.

Taking territory and killing human beings were merely means to the end of making the enemy surrender. Sherman famously reminded a group of veterans in Columbus, Ohio, in 1880 not to see "war as all glory" because "it is all hell."[60] War did not come easily to Grant or Sherman. Neither was a duelist worried about personal honor. Neither romanticized combat as a test of manly character. Both were professionals who understood that power and fame came more reliably to the patient than the impetuous. Nations should enter into war, they agreed, only after all other possibilities had been exhausted. But once people chose war, they should fight without hesitation.

In early 1862, Grant was in western Kentucky, taking, with the aid of navy gunboats, Fort Henry and Fort Donelson. These victories revived Union morale beaten down by Confederate triumphs in Virginia and made Grant famous. Especially popular was his reply to his friend from West Point, Mexico, and beyond, Simon Bolivar Buckner, the commander of 11,500 men in Fort Donelson, that "No terms except an unconditional and immediate surrender can be received. I propose to move immediately upon your works."[61] Buckner protested the "ungenerous and unchivalrous terms" that Grant dictated but had to accept them. It was, of course, the outcome Grant wished; his business was not to behave in a chivalrous way or even to spare the feelings of an old friend. He understood his mission in the simplest possible terms: to end the fighting as quickly as possible. There would be time enough for generosity when the war was over.

And so he moved against the enemy again and again, maneuvering his way through the politics of command when he had to; depending on close aides to help him fight his tendency to drink when lonely and depressed; traveling upriver into Tennessee; surviving then repulsing a ferocious surprise attack at Shiloh in April 1862, a battle in which the two armies inflicted more casualties in two days than the totals for the War for Independence, the War of 1812, and the war with Mexico combined. When Sherman found Grant standing in the rain smoking a cigar at the end of the first day of the battle, he asked, "Well, Grant, we've had the devil's own day, haven't we?" "Yes," Grant replied. "Yes. Lick 'em tomorrow though."[62]

Repeatedly thwarted in his efforts during the winter of 1862–63 to take

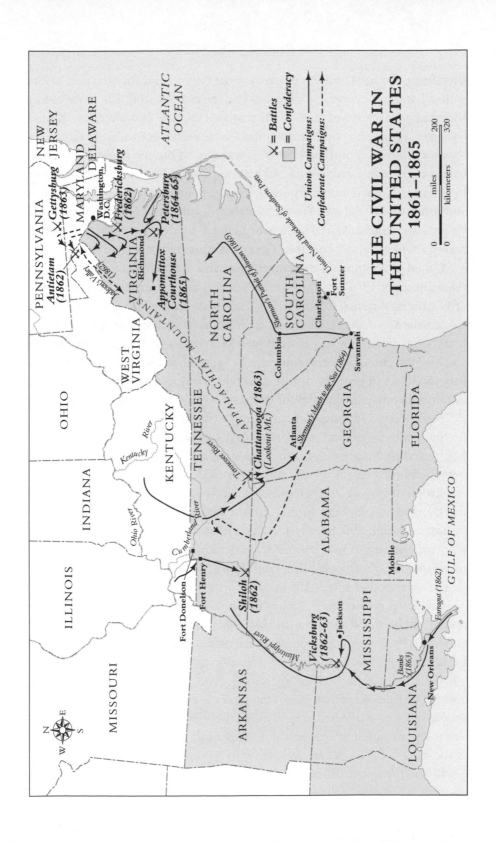

THE CIVIL WAR IN
THE UNITED STATES
1861–1865

X = Battles

☐ = Confederacy

Union Campaigns: →
Confederate Campaigns: ⇢

miles 0 ... 200
kilometers 0 ... 320

ATLANTIC OCEAN

NEW JERSEY

DELAWARE

MARYLAND

PENNSYLVANIA

Gettysburg (1863)

Antietam (1862)

Washington, D.C.

Fredericksburg (1862)

Jackson's Valley (1862)

VIRGINIA

Richmond

Petersburg (1864–65)

Appomattox Courthouse (1865)

WEST VIRGINIA

OHIO

INDIANA

ILLINOIS

MISSOURI

KENTUCKY

Kentucky River

Ohio River

Cumberland River

TENNESSEE

Tennessee River

APPALACHIAN MOUNTAINS

NORTH CAROLINA

SOUTH CAROLINA

Columbia

Charleston

Fort Sumter

Union Naval Blockade of Southern Ports

Sherman's Pursuit of Johnson (1865)

Chattanooga (1863) (Lookout Mt.)

Atlanta

Sherman's March to the Sea (1864)

Savannah

GEORGIA

FLORIDA

ALABAMA

Mobile

GULF OF MEXICO

Fort Donelson

Fort Henry

Shiloh (1862)

MISSISSIPPI

Vicksburg (1862–63)

Jackson

Mississippi River

ARKANSAS

LOUISIANA

New Orleans

Banks (1863)

Farragut (1862)

N
W E
S

Vicksburg, the last Confederate post on the Mississippi River, Grant in late spring hazarded everything on a bold stratagem. Moving his army below Vicksburg, he marched east to Mississippi's capital, Jackson, then turned back toward his objective, drawing the Confederates into a battle they soon lost. Vicksburg fell on July 4, 1863. It was one of the most audacious campaigns of the war. Grant completed his conquest of Tennessee in November by driving a Confederate army out of its entrenched position in Chattanooga and south toward Atlanta. For these accomplishments, Congress confirmed Grant's appointment as a lieutenant general in the Army of the United States, a rank that only one man, George Washington, had held before.

Called to Washington to assume command of all Union forces, Grant in the summer of 1864 launched a massive campaign to grind down the Army of Northern Virginia. Robert E. Lee's celebrated force had successfully defended the Confederate capital of Richmond from larger armies for three years. Only when Lee had taken it into Maryland and Pennsylvania had he and his men tasted defeat, at Antietam in September 1862 and Gettysburg in July 1863. In Virginia, Lee thwarted several commanders of the Army of the Potomac because he was skillful and they were incompetent. Lee also had the considerable advantage of defending strong positions, more often than not the key to victory in Civil War battles. The simple fact was that technology, including longer-range, more accurate, and faster-firing weapons, had outrun infantry tactics, which continued to depend on massed assaults in emulation of Napoleonic practices. Generals on both sides acted like latter-day Bonapartes and Wellingtons, sending tens of thousands of men to their deaths in assaults on heavily fortified defensive positions. Union troops who suffered the consequences at Fredericksburg in December 1862 returned the deadly favor by wrecking George Pickett's troops at Gettysburg on the afternoon of July 3, 1863.

Grant was no innovator. Rather, his considerable genius lay in a combination of stubborn will and a remarkable ability to see battles less as discrete occurrences than as episodes of larger narratives. If something did not work today, he would try something else tomorrow. Assistant Secretary of War Charles Dana described Grant as "sincere, thoughtful, deep and gifted with a courage that never faltered. When the time came to risk all, he went in like a simple-hearted, unaffected, unpretending hero, whom no ill omens could deject and no triumph unduly exalt." A soldier called him "a plain businessman of the republic" going about his work with "no nonsense, no sentiment."[63]

Late in the spring of 1864, Grant relentlessly attacked Lee, concentrating superior manpower and resources on the outnumbered Confederates.

Time and again, the Army of Northern Virginia stymied the assaults of the Army of the Potomac, only to find Grant moving to his left, looking for another place to break through. In June, the Union forces began a siege of the city of Petersburg, south of Richmond, which lasted for ten months. Meanwhile, Sherman was methodically moving against a Confederate army defending northern Georgia. When Atlanta fell in September, Sherman launched an all-out assault on Georgia's economy and society as a whole, cutting a sixty-mile-wide swath through the heart of the state, destroying property and freeing slaves though rarely killing noncombatants. With Savannah in his hands by the end of the year, he turned north toward Grant in Virginia.

Like Grant, Sherman was sure of his mission. Watching fire consume the city of Columbia, South Carolina, in February 1865, he observed that "They have brought it on themselves."[64] Confederates had chosen the path that led to their own destruction. Ironically, it was this attitude that made both Grant and Sherman magnanimous victors. They were policemen, not judges—nor executioners.

By the time the Confederacy disintegrated, the long war had nurtured a second American Revolution that few could have anticipated in 1861, much less in 1846. Using the rebellion as justification, Republicans, prodded by African Americans and whites interested in radical change, fulfilled the predictions of the secessionists that they would transform the United States. For the first time, the federal government developed into a source of power capable of intervening directly in the lives of citizens in the states, overriding at will the authority that the first Revolutionary Settlement had reserved to local jurisdictions. Republican majorities in Congress took advantage of the absence of Southern legislators and the weakness of Northern Democrats to create a national banking system and a national currency, raise tariffs, allocate federal resources in support of public education, and provide for such internal improvements as transcontinental railroads.

This expansion of executive and national power was truly astonishing, amounting to as complete a repudiation of the Revolutionary Settlement as any secessionist could have predicted in 1861. Abraham Lincoln exercised unprecedented authority as commander in chief. In the cause of suppressing rebellion, he suspended the privilege of habeas corpus, jailed and harassed opposition editors and politicians, and enforced a military draft that compelled citizens to fight for their country. After the battle of Antietam in September 1862, he issued an executive order freeing slaves in Confederate-held territory, reversing decades of federal policy that had defended slavery as a species of property right and avoided interference in local and state affairs.[65]

Lincoln justified these extraordinary actions as the means by which the United States might achieve a more generous, inclusive, and positive definition of freedom. The federal government waged the war it did, he said at Gettysburg in November 1863, to preserve a political union forged in the Revolution on principles explained in the Declaration of Independence. But that was not all. Merely to preserve the Union, to defend a Constitution that had been perfectly compatible with a definition of citizenship reserved to white men only, would not suffice. The Civil War had been necessary, Lincoln explained in his Second Inaugural Address, because Americans, failing to live up to the ideals articulated in the Declaration of Independence, had suffered the institution of slavery to survive.

> If we shall suppose that American slavery is one of those offences which, in the providence of God, must needs come, but which, having continued through His appointed time, He now wills to remove, and that He gives to both North and South, this terrible war, as the woe due to those by whom the offence came, shall we discern therein any departure from those divine attributes which the believers in a Living God always ascribe to Him? Fondly do we hope— fervently do we pray—that this mighty scourge of war may speedily pass away. Yet, if God wills that it continue, until all the wealth compiled by the bond-man's two hundred and fifty years of unrequited toil shall be sunk, and until every drop of blood drawn with the lash, shall be paid by another drawn with the sword, as was said three thousand years ago, so still it must be said, "the judgments of the Lord, are true and righteous altogether."[66]

Thus the Civil War, which began as a struggle over power and the perpetuity of a political union, became a moral crusade in the cause of liberty. Union soldiers sang about it in "John Brown's Body," "The Battle Hymn of the Republic," "The Battle Cry of Freedom," and "Marching Through Georgia," even before Lincoln restated it with the eloquence that is still, of all American presidents, uniquely his own.

A considerable number of Northerners dissented from this perspective, of course. Major General George McClellan, commander of the Army of the Potomac from 1861 to 1862 and the Democratic candidate for president in 1864, spoke for hundreds of thousands when he urged Lincoln not to confiscate private property, promote abolition, or subjugate anyone. Nevertheless, many of the soldiers who were risking their lives came to share Lincoln's views. A New Yorker explained that "[e]very soldier [knows] he is fighting not only for his own liberty but [even] more for the liberty of the human race for all time to come." "If I do get hurt," wrote an Ohio corporal to his wife in 1864, "I want you to remember that it will be not only for my Country and my children but for Liberty all over the World that I risked my life, for if Liberty should be crushed here, what hope would there be for the cause of Human Progress anywhere else?"[67] Much to McClellan's surprise, it was the vote of the Union soldiers that did much to defeat him in 1864.

The abolition of slavery by the Thirteenth Amendment was the Constitutional fulfillment of the most radical change since the birth of the Republic. But the most visible manifestation was Lincoln's acquiescence, albeit grudging, in arming black men. Though it did not happen until early 1863, it signaled a remarkable embrace of the universality of freedom. In effect, the government of the United States institutionalized precisely the kind of social revolution that Mexican *criollos* and many white Americans had dedicated their lives to preventing. There could have been no more radical sight in nineteenth-century North America, where visions of the race war in Haiti still haunted the nightmares of whites, than African-American men in uniform carrying rifles on their shoulders. Still, it was not in the heart of the Ohioan James Garfield "to lay a feather's weight in the way of our Black Americans if they choose to strike for what was always their own."[68]

Eventually 180,000 African Americans served in the Union army—10 percent of the whole. G. E. Stephens and more than 600 other black men in the Fifty-fourth Massachusetts Regiment joined the assault on Battery Wagner outside of Charleston, South Carolina, in July 1863; 272 of them died in the attempt. Yet for all the slaughter, Stephens believed the sacrifice had been worthwhile; two months later he wrote that "arming" black men was "the speediest method which could be devised to eradicate that semblance of inferiority of our race, which cruel slavery has created[.]" By embracing citizenship and accepting the ultimate sacrifice it can exact, black men made explicit the importance of war to liberty in the United States. The soldiers of the Union armies "are not contending for a party, not for the spoils of war," said a group of African Americans in Poughkeepsie, New York, in July 1863, "but for Empire—for universal Human Right and Liberty—to maintain intact the heritage bequeathed to the ages by the men of '76; to make this continent in very truth the same refuge for the oppressed of all lands in spite of caste, complexional differences, wealth, poverty, sect, or creed."[69]

"Social Equality Is Not a Policy to Be Legislated Upon"

Early in April 1865, Robert E. Lee reluctantly pulled the Army of Northern
Virginia out of its entrenched positions around Petersburg and left Richmond, the capital of his crumbling nation, open to the forces of the United
States under the command of Ulysses S. Grant. What was left of Lee's
army—some 35,000 hungry and exhausted Confederate troops—dragged
themselves west toward the Appalachian Mountains. By April 9, Palm Sunday, Lee and his men were all but surrounded on the road to Appomattox
Courthouse. Confederates under General John B. Gordon broke through
the ranks of U.S. cavalry only to find two corps of blue-coated infantry
coming up behind them. Gordon sent word to Lee that he could do no
more, and Lee sent word to Grant that he was ready to meet.

Later that day, Lee formally surrendered to Grant in the parlor of a
house owned by Wilmer McLean, who had moved from Manassas, the site
of the war's first great battle, to Appomattox in order to avoid the armies
rampaging through northern Virginia. Grant appeared in the muddy uniform of a private; Lee wore his dress uniform, polished boots, a red silk
sash, and a decorated sword. Grant surprised Lee by granting him and his
men the right to return home and live in peace as long as they observed their
parole and the laws of the United States. Three days later, Major General
Joshua Chamberlain of Maine ordered his men, who had been standing in
formation at "order arms," the position of rest, to "carry arms"—the position of salute—to honor their adversaries as the Confederates gave up their
flags and heavy weapons. Chamberlain wanted the war to end with "mutual
salutation and farewell."[70] Grant, who had refused to accept Lee's sword at
Appomattox, felt the same way. As one Confederate sympathizer wrote two
years later, Grant "spared everything that might wound the feelings or imply the humiliation of a vanquished foe."[71]

The general quietly returned to Washington on Thursday, April 13, with
his usual avoidance of fanfare. At a cabinet meeting the next morning, the
president invited the Grants to join him and Mary Todd Lincoln at Ford's
Theater that night for a performance of Our American Cousin. Grant declined
so that he could accede to Julia's request to leave for New Jersey to visit their
family. It was a decision he regretted, for he always wondered if he might
have stopped John Wilkes Booth from firing a bullet into Lincoln's brain.

Like most Americans, Grant was shocked by the assassination. But he

had little time to mourn the death of Lincoln, let alone celebrate the end of
the Civil War. The demands of a world transformed pressed in from all
sides. His major task as commanding general of the U.S. Army was to ensure the reestablishment of American authority throughout North America. A challenge that went far beyond the borders of the Confederacy, it
involved dealing with freed African Americans, Plains Indians, and Mexicans, as well as former rebels.

Grant was well aware that Benito Juárez, a well-educated Zapotec Indian born in Oaxaca in 1806, had emerged in the 1850s as the leader of the
liberal movement in Mexico. Juárez wanted to build a nation of individual
citizens that transcended Mexico's age-old regional, class, and racial divisions. The "mission of republican government is to protect mankind in the
free development of his moral and physical faculties with the sole limitation
being the rights of other men," proclaimed Juárez, who became president of
Mexico in 1858. "I shall respond with a firm hand to anyone who attempts
to undermine the rights of other men." Juárez tolerated no dissent, let alone
opposition. For outraged conservatives, concentrated in the army, the
Catholic Church, and Mexico City, liberal reform, including assaults on
corporate privilege, was as grave a danger as those presented by Hidalgo or
the Spanish Cortes. Brutal war soon engulfed Mexico. With liberals ascen-
dant in 1861, Napoleon III of France came to the rescue of conservatives by
sending troops to fulfill his own imperial dreams. Napoleon expected no
trouble from the United States, the Monroe Doctrine's warning that the
Republic would resist European intervention in the Americas notwithstanding. The Americans were too busy killing each other to worry about
Mexico. Besides, Napoleon expected a Confederate triumph.[72]

The French invasion began inauspiciously when the Mexicans won a resounding victory on the road from Veracruz to Mexico City on May 5, 1862,
an event now commemorated as the national holiday, Cinco de Mayo. Re-
grouping, the French took the capital in 1863 and established the Austrian
prince Maximilian as emperor in 1864. Marshal Achille-François Bazaine
then led some 40,000 French and conservative troops in a relentless campaign against liberal strongholds. When General Porfirio Díaz surrendered
Oaxaca City in February 1865, Juárez was isolated in the far north. For
years, he had tried to get the United States to help him; now the Americans
seemed ready to oblige.

In June, Grant dispatched General Philip H. Sheridan and 42,000 men to
the Mexican border. From their camp at Brownsville, Texas, the Americans
looked across the Rio Grande at the soldiers of Maximilian stationed in

Matamoros, reenacting the standoff of 1846 in which Grant participated. Grant now described Napoleon's attempt "to establish a Monarchical Government on this continent . . . as an act of hostility against the Government of the United States." Moreover, "large organized and armed bodies of rebels have gone to Mexico to join the imperialists." It would not do to have them "espouse the cause of the Empire." The United States had "a duty . . . to a friendly but downtroden Nation, to send an armed force to capture these recreants who not only threaten the very existence of that Government but the future peace of our own! . . . Let foreign bayonets be withdrawn and we will see how long the Empire, *the choice of the people,* will stand."[73]

The proximate cause of Grant's bellicosity was his desire to eradicate any possibility of further resistance to the U.S. government, but it also reflected a personal commitment to the Mexican liberals.[74] Grant had developed a close friendship with Matías Romero, Juárez's ambassador to the United States, and had come to believe that the liberals were committed to the modernization of Mexico in ways that would encourage political democracy and capitalist development. Sending Sheridan into Mexico was like sending Sherman into Georgia. Grant was attempting to restore a legitimate government that would provide the legal and constitutional order necessary to the flourishing of a liberal society. Perhaps some Southerners would fight with Sheridan in Mexico then stay in the country to transform it. "As our people had saved the Union and meant to keep it, and manage it as we liked, and not as they liked, it seemed to me that the best place for our defeated friends was Mexico."[75]

Because Secretary of State William Henry Seward opposed intervention in Mexico, the American troops remained north of the Rio Grande. In any case, Napoleon III, concerned about growing Prussian hostility toward France, had no stomach for a war with the United States over a distant imperial venture ruled by an incompetent. He decided in January 1866 to pull his army out of Mexico. The last French troops evacuated Veracruz on March 16, 1867. The unfortunate Maximilian was captured in May and executed by a firing squad in the early morning of June 19.

Though the United States did not go to war in Mexico, it was in dealing with the Mexican question that Grant anticipated the central thrust of his post–Civil War policies: to use the power of the national government to encourage democratic governments, political stability, and economic development.[76] Everywhere Grant confronted the dilemma of asserting American authority in ways that demanded serious thinking about American values. He had to deal with unrepentant Confederates in the South who were organizing paramilitary units, such as the Ku Klux Klan, while in the West he confronted Plains Indians who were fighting to defend themselves against American incursions. Resistance to the power of the United States government had not ended at Appomattox. Yet Americans such as Grant were struggling to decide how to proceed in the aftermath of the extraordinary deployment of military force of a nation-state against its own citizens. If anger and resentment over the war at least temporarily fueled support among some Northern whites for the extension of civil rights to freedmen, it was unclear how much they were willing to coerce Southern whites into compliance with nationally directed reform, especially as the war faded into memory and people returned to the concerns of ordinary life.

Of one thing Americans were certain. Even as they fell out with each other over the readmission of Southern states, the definition of citizenship, and the relationship between executive and legislative power (evidenced in the impeachment of President Andrew Johnson), they agreed that the United States did not need a large standing army. Though the Army Act of July 1866 provided for a force larger than had existed in 1860, Congress slashed the military budget and returned almost a million soldiers to civilian life. By 1867, the U.S. Army had fewer than 55,000 men, hardly enough to maintain garrisons, let alone simultaneously intimidate white Southerners into accepting black citizens and the Sioux into accepting white intruders.

Grant was not happy about this reduction because he was keenly sensitive to the dangers to the United States in the South, the West, and Mexico. But he was coming to a more sophisticated understanding of the role of war in American life. The general nicknamed the "butcher" who sent more men to their deaths than any other officer in American history had long believed that force should be used only as a last resort. The United States should engage in warfare only "for a definite cause," most often "the peace that insured security and justice." Once committed, Americans should fight "with vigor" until the enemy acquiesced.[77] Wise policy, however, avoided coercion and supported choice. Conquest through persuasion was preferable to conquest through force. War was a means to establish political stability, not promote social change.

This attitude influenced his policy toward the Plains Indians. Grant had concluded during his service in California and Oregon in the early 1850s that Indians "would be harmless and peaceable if they were not put upon by the whites."[78] His friendship with Ely S. Parker, a Seneca whose Iroquois name was Donehogawa, confirmed this sentiment. Born in 1828 in New York, Parker was a Christian and was formally educated as a civil engineer.

Grant appointed Parker, whom he met in Galena in 1857, to his staff in 1863 and entrusted him with key tasks, including writing the terms of surrender at Appomattox. Grant paternalistically saw Parker, who rose to the rank of brigadier general during the war, as an example of the possibilities of assimilation; he also appointed him the post of commissioner of Indian Affairs during his first term as president.

When Grant and other officers dealt with Indians, they did so in the belief that native peoples would inevitably vanish from North America. However spirited, the resistance of the Sioux and Comanches was doomed to fail. They also believed that the United States government was fundamentally righteous in pursuing the policies that would confine Indians to reservations and subject them to programs intended to turn them from Indians to citizens of the Republic. Because nothing could stop the American triumph, resistance was futile. "We must be masters of the Plains," Sherman told Grant."[79] (More extreme was General Philip Sheridan's alleged remark that "The only good Indian is a dead Indian." The brutal efficiency of Sheridan's campaigns against the Plains nations effectively undercut his denial that he had ever uttered the words.)[80] On the other hand, Grant and Sherman alike held their countrymen largely responsible for the conflict. It was Americans' greed and impatience, their relentless intrusions into Indian territory, that provoked armed resistance and now raised the prospect of the annihilation of Indians altogether. Sherman lamented in 1867 that "the white man's conduct and example, instead of aiding, has been the chief obstacle in the way of the civilization of the Indians."[81] Muddled as their motives and paradoxical as their reasoning may seem in retrospect, the ultimate goal of Grant and his fellow officers in the Plains Indian wars was not extermination but transformation: without any sense of irony, they intended to pacify the Plains not only to make them safe for white settlers but to liberate Indians from the Indianness that prevented them from becoming full participants in the life of the Republic.

Whatever Grant was thinking, many of his fellow citizens thought him the ideal man to restore peace and stability to North America. The most popular of living Americans, the general was the Republican candidate for the presidency in 1868. Less than a decade after he had sold firewood to support his family, he easily won election to the highest office in the government of the United States. Americans had the not unreasonable expectation that Grant would prove as competent a president as he had been a general. They were disappointed. The hero of Vicksburg, so gifted at issuing clear orders in battle, had no talent for articulating policy. What worked well in the military—delegating authority and ignoring public opinion—did not work well in a democracy. Yet Grant was not the blundering fool caricatured by Henry Adams in his autobiography. He became president of a nation whose citizens were sick of war and upheaval and increasingly concerned with economic issues, especially during the hard times of the 1870s. They had little energy for fighting anyone, let alone those recalcitrant Southern white men who carried on what they understood as the fight for personal liberty, local autonomy, and the honor of their wives and families. Indeed, fears of Catholic, Jewish, and southern and eastern European immigrants were merging with distaste for African Americans into prejudice against all peoples whose appearance and cultural norms diverged from those of northern European and Protestant descent.[82]

President Grant tried to steer a middle course by insisting on a distinction between civil rights and social equality. Government should ensure that all citizens enjoyed civil rights, including equality before the law and the protection of persons and property. But blacks, like Indians, would have to earn the economic well-being and moral respectability that were the foundation of social equality. Government, which should oppose all attempts by one group of citizens to tyrannize over another, should not interfere with a democratic society in which individuals chose their own goals and were responsible for their own fates. "Social equality," Grant proclaimed in his second inaugural address, "is not a subject to be legislated upon, nor shall I ask that anything be done to advance the social status of the colored man except to give him a fair chance to develop what there is good in him."[83] The Grant administration upheld federal authority in the South, especially in states still occupied by federal troops. It also acted on occasion to protect blacks from hostile whites. But the president was no more willing to compel white Southerners to accept change than he had been to allow them to hold blacks as slaves. Whites should be "just as free to avoid social intimacy with the blacks as ever they are with white people."[84]

In the same spirit, Grant supported American expansion as long as the acquisition of territory was accomplished by consent. He refused to succumb to popular pressure to intervene in a Cuban rebellion against Spain. He did, however, support the voluntary annexation of Santo Domingo. The U.S. Navy had its eye on a coaling station in the Bay of Samaná. Grant also wanted to make the island an asylum for the thousands of African Americans he hoped would migrate there. Safely segregated from whites, they could perpetuate liberal values, especially by establishing a system of free labor that would undermine slavery in Cuba and attract blacks to migrate from the United States. Grant was adamant that "in all cases the people of a country to be annexed should first show themselves anxious for union with us." Opposition in Congress and the press defeated the scheme. Grant's proposal nevertheless pointed away from conquest and toward the encouragement of liberal governments that with American aid would refashion their countries in the image of the United States.[85]

Grant's "peace policy" toward American Indians, worked out with General Ely Parker at the Office of Indian Affairs, proceeded from the same assumptions that guided his thinking with regard to the South and Santo Domingo. Ever more certain that whites were responsible for conflicts with Indians, Grant wanted to substitute kindness for force. "I do not believe our Creator ever placed the different races on this earth with a view of having the strong exert all his energies in exterminating the weaker." Since wars of extermination were "demoralizing and wicked," Grant pledged to "favor any course . . . which tends to . . . [the] civilization and ultimate citizenship" of "the original occupants of this land."[86] In practice, he favored a liberal policy not dissimilar to those favored by such Mexican leaders as Valentín Gómez Farías, Vicente Guerrero, and Benito Juárez. The United States would insist that Indians were individuals rather than members of communities and benevolently restrict them to reservations until Christian missionaries had through education and religion persuaded them to choose to become Americans culturally as well as politically. Grant would deal with Indians in essentially the same way as with freed African Americans: he would protect them from their enemies until they were well along the path to assimilating Christian culture, and hence fit for citizenship.

However well-intentioned, Grant was advocating conquest without overt coercion—or the possibility of resistance. As racist and naive as he was well-intentioned, the president rarely recognized that rampant discrimination and violence forcibly constrained blacks and Indians from enjoying the benefits of American citizenship. He could not dissuade white Americans from attacking Indians and demanding land, especially after the discovery of gold in the Black Hills of South Dakota in 1874. In Grant's last year as president, 2,000 Sioux and Cheyenne warriors led by Sitting Bull and Crazy Horse, among others, annihilated five companies of the Seventh Cavalry Regiment under the command of George Armstrong Custer near the Little Bighorn River in that part of the Dakota Territory that is now Montana.

Because Custer's Last Stand has acquired mythic status in American memory, the actual mission of the Seventh Cavalry—the forcible removal of several thousand Indian women, children, and men to reservations—is seldom understood as a context for an Indian attack that was in fact defensive in nature. In any case, nothing that happened on June 25, 1876, staved off the hunger and attrition that forced most of the Indians to surrender during the following winter. Sitting Bull went into exile in Canada, and both he and Crazy Horse later died as violently as Custer. Grant, who had seen as many men cut down in a single minute of the battle of Shiloh, understood the battle as unimportant and a needless waste of life by an arrogant, overbold cavalry officer.

When President Grant left the White House in 1877, he had significantly shifted federal policy away from the bellicose expansionism of Jackson and his political heirs to a different reconciliation of American power with American values. The expansion of the United States continued through persuasion rather than coercion. If force were to prove necessary, it should come through temporary interventions (in Mexico, the South, or on the Plains) rather than permanent conquests. The mission of the United States was to use its resources to free other peoples, however different in race and religion, and to provide a stable political order in which they could emulate the values and behavior of Americans.

The controversial election of Grant's successor, Rutherford B. Hayes, his fellow Ohio Republican and a former Civil War general, confirmed the path Grant had chosen. Although Democrat Samuel J. Tilden of New York won the popular vote in 1876, he failed to secure a majority in the Electoral College because of controversy over possible fraud and corruption in three Southern states. A commission appointed by the House of Representatives voted along party lines to award the contested electoral votes (and one in Oregon) to Hayes. Believing that the Republican would support "home rule" and the economic development of the former Confederacy, a sufficient number of Southern Democrats accepted his election as the nineteenth president of the United States. In the words of a prominent Kansas Republican, "the policy of the new administration will be to conciliate the white men of the South. Carpetbaggers to the rear, and niggers take care of yourselves."[87]

The Compromise of 1877 completed the restoration of political power in the former Confederate states to white Democrats, who were free to rule their local worlds and eventually construct new modes of white supremacy. The same administration that refused to send federal troops to compel white Southerners to accept the social revolution of racial equality did not hesitate to use them to suppress labor activism during the Great Strike of 1877. In a fundamental departure from the understandings of local privilege that underlay the first Revolutionary Settlement, which reserved constabulary

Antonio López de Santa Anna in final exile,
painted by Paul L'Ouvier, c. 1858.
Courtesy of the Collection of the New-York Historical Society, 1878. 3

functions within the states to militia, the United States government would now use its army selectively against its own citizens, both to maintain federal authority and to protect the property and interests of such important constituents as the nation's railroad companies.

The ambiguity of this new Revolutionary Settlement extended beyond the borders of the Republic. Three decades after the Treaty of Guadalupe Hidalgo, the United States remained uncertain about how to deal with its southern neighbor, which was itself beginning a new era. Antonio López de Santa Anna, having returned two years earlier to a life of obscurity, died in Mexico City on June 20, 1876. In more ways than one, Santa Anna was a "relic of another epoch."[88] Santa Anna was associated in Mexican memory with political instability and caudillismo. Benito Juárez, who died in 1872, was enshrined as a national hero for his successful resistance to the French and his repudiation of the status quo that Santa Anna embodied.

Several months after Santa Anna's death, General Porfirio Díaz seized power in Mexico. Díaz, a native of Oaxaca, was one of the most effective liberal military leaders in the 1860s. Insulted by Juárez, he became a regional critic. During the presidency of Sebastián Lerdo de Tejada, who allowed public criticism and appeared to be weak, Díaz nurtured opposition that exploded in revolt in early 1876 and elevated him to the presidency in December. As president from 1876 to 1880 and again from 1884 through 1911, he pursued his own version of a Mexican revolutionary settlement in the form of "patriarchal liberalism."[89] Encouraging private enterprise, free trade, and foreign investment, he governed in a personal style that stressed stability over debate, patronage over democracy, private property over social justice, and development over nationalism. Díaz worked to solidify Mexico's political culture, national government, and economy, in no small part by promoting good relations with the United States and American entrepreneurs while ignoring the wishes and needs of millions of Mexicans.

The Hayes administration initially misread the ability of the Díaz regime to control Indians, regulate its borders, and create an environment conducive to capitalist expansion. To make Mexico safe for Americans, the federal government authorized detachments of the army in Texas to pursue Indians and "bandits" across the Rio Grande. Mexicans logically interpreted this order as a prelude to more conquest. Hayes backed down, assuring the world that "the United States does not want any more territory in that direction even if offered as a gift." Official recognition of Díaz's government came in April 1878.[90]

As it became clear that the goals of the two regimes coincided, the histories of the United States and Mexico intersected again in a rapid movement away from public confrontation and toward private cooperation. By the early 1880s, the Hotel Iturbide in Mexico City was packed with American entrepreneurs as eager to invest in Mexico as their countrymen had been to mine the Black Hills in the 1870s. The United States, they believed, could have its way with Mexico simply by encouraging Mexicans to embrace American values and allowing them to enjoy the rewards that would inevitably follow. The U.S. government would use military power only when it had no other choice, and then only to provide stability and liberate people to make informed choices about their future well-being.

Not surprisingly, given his contributions to the evolution of this policy, Ulysses S. Grant was one of the many Americans interested in Mexico. Returning in 1879 from a two-year world tour that had impressed him with the importance of international commerce, Grant was interested in running for a third term as president. Early in 1880, he and Julia traveled to Cuba in the company of Philip Sheridan and his wife, then proceeded to Veracruz and Mexico City. Grant received a warm welcome in the capital he had helped to

conquer in 1847. There were banquets, bullfights, concerts, newspaper ac-
colades, and discussions with Grant's old friend, Matías Romero, and other
prominent Mexicans about improving transportation, both within Mexico
and between it and the United States. Grant publicly promised to support
railroad building. As Grant's political ambitions evaporated, his interest in
economic development in and around Mexico intensified. Named president
of a Nicaragua canal company, he also headed (at least nominally) a New
Mexico gold mining company and a corporation planning to connect the
United States, Cuba, and Mexico by telegraph cable.[91]

Most important, the financier Jay Gould encouraged a scheme by
Romero and Grant to build a railroad in Oaxaca. In March 1881, Grant became president of the Mexican Southern Railroad Company, a corporation
created by a special act of the New York legislature. Romero and Grant departed shortly after to win concessions from the Mexican government. In
Mexico City, Grant declared that further annexation of Mexican territory by
the United States was impossible. "I am sure, even if it could be shown that
all the people in Mexico were in favor of annexation of a portion of their
territory to the United States, it would still be rejected," said Grant. "We
want no more land. We do want to improve what we have, and we want to
see our neighbors improve and grow so strong that the designs of any other
country could not endanger them."[92]

The railroad got the necessary concessions. Two years later, Grant and
Romero negotiated a treaty of commercial reciprocity between the United
States and Mexico, which aroused such a storm of protectionist opposition
that the Senate declined to consider it for ratification. Grant, undeterred by
this setback, continued to promote intracontinental commerce and development in ways that anticipated American policy in the twentieth century.
The former president wanted "to encourage republican government, and
particularly on this continent" through a "new policy" in which ideology,
profit, and nationalism went hand in hand. "We are not so particularly generous as to want to benefit our neighbors at our own expense," Grant told a
Boston audience in 1880. "But when we can benefit ourselves, and them,
too, greatly, we are the most generous people in the world."[93]

In 1883, Porfirio Díaz, out of office but intent upon returning to the
presidency in 1884, spent two months in the United States. He came as
commissioner general of the Mexican delegation to the New Orleans World
Fair to promote Mexico as a stable, modern nation interested in global commerce. The delegation also visited Saint Louis, Chicago, Washington,
Boston, and New York. In Manhattan, Díaz renewed his friendship with

Grant. Saluting the United States, he praised its growth, its material achievements, its system of public education, and its support of many freedoms. "I wish the great American people health and prosperity," Díaz said in his farewell speech, "your country has achieved first place among nations . . . and, through the splendor of its civilization based upon peace, it will eclipse the false sparkle of ancient empires based on war."[94] What he prophesied was in many ways the start of a beautiful friendship for entrepreneurs on both sides of the Rio Grande.

Grant did not share in the bonanza. His investments soured, contributing to his bankruptcy in 1884. Not long after, he developed the cancer of the soft palate and throat that killed him the following year. To secure his family's financial future, he accepted Mark Twain's offer to publish his memoirs under the imprint of his own press with the promise of handsome royalties. Grant took Twain's $10,000 advance and wrote with the same determination he showed at Fort Donelson, Vicksburg, the Wilderness, and Petersburg. As the writing campaign neared completion, he moved his family to the resort community of Mount McGregor, New York, at the foot of the Adirondacks. There, in a modest summer cottage, he spent the last three months of his life, correcting the final proofs in the weeks before his death.

To control the pain and enable him to continue working, Grant's physicians treated him with various combinations of laudanum, morphine, cocaine, and brandy. These made it possible for him to write and revise each day, even to receive visitors. Among the last was his old comrade and enemy, Simon Bolivar Buckner, who came just two weeks before the end. By then Grant could scarcely speak and found it easiest to communicate by handwritten notes. Perhaps the final one was this, an undated message to his doctor:

I do not sleep though I sometimes dose off a little. If up I am talked to and in my efforts to answer cause pain. The fact is I think I am a verb instead of a personal pronoun. A verb is anything that signifies to be; to do; or to suffer. I signify all three.[95]

Grant died, surrounded by his family, on July 23, 1885. His *Memoirs* went on to sell more than 300,000 copies and earn perhaps $450,000 for Julia and their children.

In Mexico City, news of Grant's death inspired President Díaz to lead government officials and private citizens in an elaborate memorial service. One of the many tributes linked the two men as "illustrious generals" who had helped start "a parade of 'bridges, rails, and [railroad] cars' across the Rio Grande."[96] This observation was as profound as it was banal. For the long metamorphosis of young invading officer into railroad promoter heralded a revised relationship between liberty and empire, one that justified the emergence of the United States in the twentieth century as a global power still committed, for better or worse, to the idea that the cause of America was in great measure the cause of all mankind.

CHAPTER EIGHT

MacArthur's Inheritance: Liberty and Empire in the Age of Intervention

On November 25, 1863, a few miles southeast of Chattanooga, Tennessee, four divisions of the Army of the Cumberland disobeyed their orders in full view of their astonished commanding officer, Major General George H. Thomas, and his equally astonished superior, Major General Ulysses S. Grant. Three lines of Confederate trenches defended a long, steep, strategic rise known as Missionary Ridge, which thrust up a thousand feet or more above Moccasin Bend on the Tennessee River. The rebels had been digging in for two months, and their position, Grant thought, looked "impregnable." Nonetheless, he ordered Thomas to launch an assault on the first line of trenches in order to take pressure off Major General William T. Sherman, who had failed to take an adjacent hill. Despite its diversionary character, the plan courted disaster. In order to reach the base of the ridge, Thomas's men would have to cross a broad plain, exposed to artillery and small arms fire.

The behavior of the Army of the Cumberland that November day became the stuff of legend. They overran the first line with apparent ease then headed straight on for the second. "Thomas," Grant demanded through teeth clenched on his cigar, "who ordered those men up the ridge?" "I don't know," Thomas answered; "I did not." As the Confederates' second line broke, the Union lines streamed up the ridge toward the third in what seemed to onlookers like a race to the top of the ridge; they then carried it as well. Watching Confederates flee down the reverse slope, Thomas's men, "frantically drunk with excitement," shouted taunts from the ridge crest, from which dozens of Union regimental flags now waved.[1]

At the center of the Union line as it crossed the field toward the foot of Missionary Ridge was the Twenty-fourth Wisconsin Regiment of Volunteers, and at the center of the regiment was an eighteen-year-old lieutenant, Arthur MacArthur Jr. The son of a Scottish-born judge and a Massachusetts woman who had migrated to Milwaukee, MacArthur picked up the regimental colors when the standard-bearer fell wounded, then led the charge from trench to trench all the way to the summit. It was an act of audacity— or courage, or foolhardiness—of a sort more often found in hyperadrenalized teenage males than any other creature on the planet and uncommon even in them. "On Wisconsin!" MacArthur cried as he reached the top, the first man, he always claimed, to do so.[2]

Of the dozens of standard-bearers who planted flags on the heights that afternoon, it would have been impossible to pick out MacArthur as the one who would serve in the U.S. Army for more than four decades and retire a lieutenant general, the highest-ranking officer of his generation. Even less would it have been possible to foresee the far more illustrious career of his youngest son, Douglas, who entered West Point in 1899 with Ulysses S. Grant III and rose to the rank of General of the Army in World War II. And surely no one could have predicted that father and son would become agents of a new American empire whose dominion rested on intervention rather than conquest.

Arthur MacArthur's career peaked in the imperial war with Spain in 1898 and the Philippine Insurrection of 1899–1902. His legacy and that of his peers who came of age during and after the Civil War was ambiguous at best. Early in the twentieth century, the soldiers, sailors, and marines, whose culture and tactics reflected both the great crusade against slavery and the subjugation of American Indians, intervened militarily in the Caribbean basin, Asia, and eventually even in Europe, always in the interest of American power and always in the defense of liberty as Americans understood it. Unexpected and intense resistance from dark-skinned, non-Christian peoples, however, proved unsettling, troubling, and divisive at home and abroad. Once again military victory forced Americans to confront vexing questions of identity and purpose, as well as the perpetually problematic relationship between war and liberty.[3] In the twentieth century, however, they would have to contend not just with the terms of membership in their continental republic but with the place of the United States in the world as a whole.

Lieutenant Arthur MacArthur

"Martial Virtues Must Be the Enduring Cement"

At the end of the Civil War, Arthur MacArthur took up the study of the law only to abandon it for dreams of further military glory. He returned to active duty in the army as a lieutenant and was shortly promoted to captain. Stationed in New Orleans in 1875, Captain MacArthur met Mary Pinkney Hardy of Norfolk, Virginia, and married her over the objections of her formerly Confederate brothers. Arthur and Pinky, as she was known, had three sons. The oldest, Arthur MacArthur III, became a distinguished naval officer; he died of appendicitis in 1923. Malcolm succumbed to measles when he was five. The MacArthurs' youngest son, Douglas, was born on January 26, 1880, at an army post in Little Rock, Arkansas. The following summer the MacArthurs traveled to Arthur's new assignment in the New Mexico

The MacArthur family, Fort Selden, New Mexico (Douglas is at the far left), c. 1886

Territory, one of a series of moves that took the family to Fort Leavenworth, Kansas, in 1886, Washington, D.C., in 1889, and Fort Sam Houston near San Antonio in 1893.

Nothing Arthur did in the post–Civil War army could rival his moment of glory on Missionary Ridge, and he knew it. By 1880, the army was essentially a national police force, led by men consumed with memories of sacrifice in the Civil War and inhabiting forts across North America. After the defeats of the Sioux, Comanches, and Nez Percés in the 1870s, most Indians were confined to reservations. Bands of Apaches in the southwest continued to fight until the final surrender of Geronimo (Goyathlay) in September 1886. Detained with several hundred others in labor camps in Florida and Alabama, Geronimo was relocated to Fort Sill in what is now Oklahoma in 1892, where he became a Christian and a rancher. He died in 1909, still nominally a prisoner of the United States but in fact a kind of public figure who made personal appearances and had published an autobiography.

The celebrity status of Geronimo—and, for that matter, Sitting Bill (Tatanka Yotanka), a Lakota, or western Sioux, chief who fought at the battle of the Little Bighorn and later took part in Buffalo Bill Cody's Wild West Show—testified to the extent to which Indians had become peripheral in North America. The 156 million acres controlled by Indians in the United States in 1880 fell to 78 million in 1900. At the beginning of the twentieth century, an estimated 400,000 Indians lived in the United States and Canada, the lowest number since the beginning of the Age of Contact.

As events at the Standing Rock Indian Agency in North Dakota demonstrated in December 1890, the position of those few natives was precarious at best. Sitting Bull had become a leader of the Ghost Dance, a revitalization movement that the local Indian agent feared would promote an uprising. The agent ordered him arrested, but when the Indian police tried to do so, the chief's followers fought back. A gunfight broke out, and Sitting Bull was killed. Soon after, his band left Standing Rock to seek refuge at the Pine Ridge Agency in South Dakota. Their intent was peaceful, but the agent construed the very act of leaving Standing Rock as hostile and summoned the army to subdue them. On December 29, 500 troopers from the Seventh Cavalry rounded up the refugees near Wounded Knee Creek, South Dakota. When an attempt to disarm the Indians went badly, the soldiers used four rapid-fire Hotchkiss cannons to obliterate the Lakotas' encampment. At least 146 men, women, and children died in the bombardment; many who were wounded later died in the intense cold.[4] Earlier that same year, the superintendent of the Census had observed that there was no longer an identifiable frontier of white settlement—and hence no longer a contiguous zone that could be thought of as Indian Country—in the continental United States. Four centuries after the founding of the first permanent European colonies, the conquest of North America was complete.

For career officers like MacArthur, the final pacification of the Indians, the end of federal occupation of the former Confederacy, and the rapprochement with Mexico constituted a tragedy of a different sort. Opportunities for advancement on the battlefield were nonexistent. Like his peers, Arthur endured low pay, poor living conditions, and little public respect. But MacArthur was not one to suffer in silence. As his body thickened with age, he became adept at puffing up his accomplishments and cultivating well-connected patrons. He campaigned tirelessly for the Congressional Medal of Honor, which he believed he had earned at Missionary Ridge, finally receiving it in 1889. Yet Arthur MacArthur was more than a relentless self-promoter. His obsession with fame made him a diligent officer who received a law degree as well as the nation's highest military decoration in

1889 and who devoted his free time to reading and self-improvement. Few officers in the history of the army have been more driven to succeed within the confines of a professional military culture. One of them was Arthur's youngest son.

Much as Douglas MacArthur admired his father and sought to emulate his success, he was especially close to his mother. Arthur was too self-absorbed to be much more than a role model to his son. But Mary, like many of her contemporaries, found an acceptable outlet for her ambition by identifying completely with her husband and her sons. She used her considerable social skills to lobby shamelessly for the professional advancement first of Arthur then Douglas.

Mary made her son's career *her* career and never hesitated to do whatever she thought necessary to advance his interests. She dressed him in long hair and skirts until he was eight, then sent him to school in a tie and a tweed suit until he donned the uniform of a cadet at the West Texas Military Academy. Industrious and ambitious, Douglas graduated in 1897 at the top of his class. A year later, mother and son took up residence in Arthur's home town of Milwaukee so Douglas could win an appointment to the U.S. Military Academy at West Point. "Doug, you'll win if you don't lose your nerve," Mary told him in May 1898 on the way to take the entrance examination. "You must believe in yourself, my son, or no one else will believe in you. Be self-confident, self-reliant, and even you don't make it, you will know you have done your best. Now, go to it."[5] Douglas earned the highest score and entered the academy that summer.

Mary MacArthur perfected the craft of subordinating herself to the interests of her husband's and son's careers. Her wheedling and fawning style seems extravagant by today's standards, even offensive; yet Pinky used it to control a situation in which she was allowed no more than a peripheral public role. By the time Douglas went to West Point, there was apparently no border between her identity and that of her son. In a 1901 poem, she wrote

> *Do you know that your soul is of my soul such a part*
> *That you seem to be fiber and core of my heart?*
> *None other can pain me as you, son, can do:*
> *None other can please me or praise me as you.*

Pinky's obsessive desire to live through her son put intense pressure on Douglas, whose "task," she concluded,

shall be
To force this proud world to do homage to me.
Be sure it will say, when its verdict you've won
She reaps as she sowed: "This man is her son!"[6]

Little wonder that Douglas depended so heavily on his mother and she on him that he was unable to sustain a relationship with another woman until she died.

At West Point, Douglas MacArthur joined an army of fewer than 100,000 men. Still suspicious of a standing army, the citizens of the United States were reluctant to support a large military establishment, especially when they felt secure on the continent of North America. Because the defense of national interests and commerce was likely to occur in other parts of the world, a strong navy could accomplish what was militarily necessary, with minimal threat to domestic liberty. Thanks to the prodding of such visionaries as Alfred Thayer Mahan, whose great book, *The Influence of Sea Power Upon History, 1660–1783,* appeared in 1890, the United States modernized its fleet and committed itself to showing the Stars and Stripes throughout the world. Starting in 1883, Congress authorized the construction of steel-hulled, steam-powered cruisers, and, in the 1890s, mixed-battery battleships.[7]

Neglect of the army as an institution did not translate into scorn for the martial spirit, for millions of men who had fought in the Civil War (together with their mothers, fathers, wives, and children) perpetuated the memory of their service in a multitude of ways. This was a departure from previous patterns, for before the Civil War, Americans had done little collectively to remember their wars or their dead. When a group of Massachusetts citizens decided to erect an obelisk to mark the fiftieth anniversary of the 1775 battle of Bunker Hill, it took them eighteen years to bring the project to completion. Veterans rarely organized themselves beyond groups, such as the Society of the Cincinnati and the Aztec Club, that represented only officers. All that began to change at midcentury, when plans took shape for a monument to George Washington on the Mall in the nation's capital. In 1853, Congress authorized the placing of an equestrian statue of Andrew Jackson by the sculptor Clark Mills in Lafayette Park. Following the Mexican War, the United States acquired land for a military cemetery in Mexico City and reinterred the remains of American dead from their original resting place near the city dump.[8]

Memorials to war proliferated following the Civil War. Given the vast number of people directly involved in the conflict, it is hardly surprising that its memory suffused American society for more than a half century after Appomattox. Local efforts by Southern white women and blacks to decorate the graves of the dead in the spring of 1865 quickly became a national phenomenon. Today Americans mark Decoration Day as a national holiday observed toward the end of the May as Memorial Day.

American commemoration of the Civil War was much more than an annual rite of spring. Local communities erected monuments on courthouse squares to those who had served. Citizens addressed prominent men by the rank they held in the Civil War. Republicans campaigned by waving a metaphorical "bloody shirt" and elected a succession of former Union officers to the presidency as well as to Congress and state and local offices. Widows, mothers, sisters, and daughters organized services, cultivated cemeteries, and encouraged historians to honor the dead. Men too young to have seen service sought the kind of emotional connection that the novelist William Faulkner spoke of when he observed that for every Southern boy, it is always noon on July 3, 1863, just south of Gettysburg, where George Pickett's division stands poised for its charge into oblivion.

Americans gradually came to regard battlefields as sacred spaces. In 1883, the state of Texas committed itself to buying the remains of the Alamo, a process that took two decades, and entrusted them to the city of San Antonio then the Daughters of the Republic of Texas. In the last two decades of the nineteenth century, Congress supported the preservation of Civil War battlefields as places worthy of national memory. The first four were Gettysburg, Chickamauga, Shiloh, and Vicksburg. At Gettysburg, the federal government took over the efforts of state and private organizations, incorporating Confederate as well as Union sites. Private and state groups decorated the landscape with almost four hundred monuments to various regiments, individuals, and events. Gettysburg hosted reunions of veterans from both sides, most famously in 1913 on the fiftieth anniversary of the battle.

The perpetuation of the Civil War as a defining moment in American memory owed much to the efforts of the Grand Army of the Republic (GAR). The most prominent of several groups of Union veterans, the GAR was founded in 1866 and grew rapidly under the leadership of John A. Logan of Ohio as what amounted to an auxiliary of the Republican Party. Its membership declined after 1872, but when it transformed itself into a nonpartisan fraternal order in the 1880s its numbers again boomed. By 1890, the GAR boasted over 400,000 members, nearly half of surviving Union veterans.

Logan and his group lobbied hard for the creation of Memorial Day (which Congress recognized as a national holiday in 1887) and the preservation of cemeteries and battlefields. Over time, the GAR followed the example of Grant, emphasizing reconciliation rather than recrimination and stressing the shared experience of war rather than sectional divisions. White men from Alabama and Connecticut finally found common ground in memories of hardship and brotherhood. Battlefield memorials saluted both the blue and the gray. High across the Potomac from Washington, D.C., Robert E. Lee's estate became a national cemetery. Amid the rows of Union dead (and, after 1912, Confederates as well) sat Lee's home, a shrine to the memory of the most famous rebel in American history.

As the commemoration of the Civil War became generic, the contributions of African Americans, who had constituted 10 percent of the Union army, faded from public memory. Memorials to the service of black men or monuments to the end of slavery tended to celebrate the sacrifices of whites, especially Lincoln, who was often depicted as striking the shackles off a passive, supplicant slave. Even the most famous and artistically distinguished memorial to a black regiment, Augustus Saint-Gaudens's bas-relief of the Fifty-fourth Massachusetts Infantry, unveiled near the statehouse in Boston in 1897, was principally a tribute to Colonel Robert Gould Shaw, whose mounted figure dominates the sculpture's foreground. His name and those of the other white officers killed in the attack of July 18, 1863, on Battery Wagner are listed on a stone pedestal; nowhere to be found are the names of the hundreds of black enlisted men who also died that day. So striking was the impulse toward reconciliation between Northern and Southern whites and the exclusion of black veterans that Frederick Douglass wondered in an Memorial Day speech at Arlington National Cemetery in 1871 why Americans were asked to "remember with equal admiration those who struck at the nation's life, and those who struck to save it—those who fought for slavery and those who fought for liberty and justice."[9]

Twenty years after Appomattox, the Civil War had paradoxically become a symbol of unity rather than division in American culture: a tragic but ennobling event that tested American manhood and vindicated a generic national commitment to liberty. Some Americans fretted that their complacent countrymen had forgotten the sacrifices that created their good life and which would inevitably be required to defend it. They needed to remember that war "teaches us to rise above the petty, the unworthy, the selfish. . . . a wholesome war, like one for human liberty and human life, will have its purgatorial effect upon this nation," as a Mississippi senator

insisted in 1898.[10] Young men, raised on their elders' war stories, sought
ways to enact the martial virtues in the absence of war. The growing popularity of team sports, especially football, organized male aggressiveness into
facsimiles of combat. In the dominion of the team, discipline and self-sacrifice equated to patriotism. Similarly, excursions into the "wild" West and
"darkest" Africa allowed men to test their courage by confronting dangerous
game animals and other hazards of the natural world. Theodore Roosevelt,
the charismatic young man who parlayed tenures as New York City police
commissioner, assistant secretary of the navy, and governor of New York
into the Republican vice presidential nomination in 1900 and the presidency after the assassination in 1901 of William McKinley, embodied all
these traits of "the strenuous life": a frail, nearsighted youth, he practiced
rigorous physical culture to toughen himself to the point that he became an
avid player of football at Harvard College, an expert (though never graceful)
horseman, and an accomplished big-game hunter.

Even the pacifist professor William James, who knew the Civil War as the
scourge that had nearly killed one of his brothers and wrecked another's
mind, argued for the necessity of finding a "moral equivalent of war" in order to build a successful world at peace. James envisioned "an army of nature," consisting of young men laboring temporarily in the national interest.
The "martial virtues must be the enduring cement" of such an organization,
he wrote; "intrepidity, contempt of softness, surrender of private interest,
obedience to command, must still remain the rock upon which states are
built." Though war was glorious only in retrospect, said the Civil War veteran and Supreme Court justice Oliver Wendell Holmes Jr., it nevertheless
"touched [hearts] with fire" and taught that "life is a profound and passionate thing."[11]

Douglas MacArthur grew to manhood in an American patrician class
that idolized the manly virtues and a United States in which self-sacrifice in
the cause of liberty was celebrated even as military institutions went begging
for funds and professional soldiers were ignored. The young man had every
reason to believe that fame and meaning lay in war, if he could only find
one. That opportunity arrived late in his father's career but too early for his
own in what Secretary of State John Hay called "a splendid little war." The
United States' first major military conflict since the Civil War, the Spanish-
American War marked a sea-change in the character of American imperialism, and the opening of the Age of Intervention. The United States invaded
the Spanish colonies of Cuba and the Philippines to free people from colonial tyranny only to find itself baffled by the consequences of its noble ges-

ture. Liberating oppressed peoples was heady stuff; the business of helping them reconstruct their societies afterwards was not. For the first time, Americans faced the prospect of fighting for (and against) dark-skinned peoples thousands of miles from their homes. The experience left many embittered and feeling deeply betrayed.

The Spanish-American War initially focused on Cuba, an island Southerners had had their eyes on for a very long time. Decades of Cuban colonial resistance to imperial Spain climaxed in a serious rebellion in the summer of 1895. Some 50,000 men organized into six army corps conducted an effective campaign for independence. The insurrection, in tandem with unrest in the Philippines, provoked Spanish imperial reform and the promise of home rule for Cuba. This sudden shift in policy, however, served mainly to embolden insurgents and demoralize conservatives. It was clear by late 1897 to American critics that Spain was "powerless either to conciliate Cuba or conquer it" and thus that her "sovereignty" over the island was "now extinct."[12]

Americans sympathized with the Cuban independence movement. After all, Americans told themselves, the United States, too, had emerged from a colonial struggle for freedom. The mysterious explosion in February 1898 that destroyed the USS *Maine* while it rode at anchor in the harbor of Havana transformed a rhetorical association into a personal one. War fever swept the United States. Lamenting President McKinley's efforts to find a diplomatic solution, a New York congressman prayed "for one day of an Andrew Jackson in the White House, with his courage, his backbone, his nerve, and his patriotism!" Senator Francis E. Warren of Wyoming experienced "a raising of the blood and temper as well as of shame that we, a civilized people, an enlightened nation, a great republic, born in a revolt against tyranny, should permit such a state of things within less than a hundred miles of our shore as that which exists in Cuba."[13]

Although the war with Spain was manifestly an imperial enterprise, American attitudes toward Cuba and the Philippines in 1898 were not the same as those expressed toward Mexico in 1846. The war with Spain was presented as a new kind of war, an *anti*-imperial war, a war to liberate rather than conquer.[14] On April 11, when McKinley asked Congress to declare war, he condemned Spain for atrocities against Cubans—including the herding of people into what were called concentration camps—and denied that American intervention was a prelude to "forcible annexation, for that cannot be thought of. That, by our code or morality, would be criminal aggression."[15]

Because "the people of the island of Cuba are and of right ought to be free and independent," Congress supported the president's assertion that it was "the duty of the United States to demand" that Spain "relinquish its authority and government." Authorizing McKinley to use military force, Congress proclaimed that the United States had no "disposition or intention to exercise sovereignty, jurisdiction, or control over said island except for the pacification thereof," and would, "when that is accomplished . . . leave the government and control of the island to its people." The last provision, proposed as an amendment to the original resolution by Senator Henry M. Teller of Colorado, was controversial, for some white Southerners still coveted Cuba as their grandfathers had half a century earlier. Most Americans, wanting no part of a war of conquest, construed their government's action more generously. To them, the war with Spain was self-evidently a just war: a military rescue mission for a people whose "suffering had become unbearable to them and to the lookers-on." The United States was modeling behavior "for the rest of the world . . . and for which future generations will bless the name of America."[16]

Combat in Cuba was brief. While the navy blockaded the island, marines seized a base at Guantánamo Bay and the army's Fifth Corps marched on Santiago, the home port of Spain's naval force. On July 1, 1898, roughly 17,000 regulars and volunteers, successfully assaulted Spanish defensive positions on the city's land approaches, including entrenchments on Kettle Hill and San Juan Hill. When American ships destroyed the Spanish naval squadron as it tried to escape to sea, the island's defenders were left with little choice but to surrender, which they did on July 17. The fall of Santiago ended the war in Cuba, but not before some 1,400 Americans were killed or wounded, and nearly as many died from yellow fever, malaria, and other tropical diseases.

Some Americans accepted the deaths and infirmities as the price of ennobling themselves through a war of liberation. They saw the men who fought in Cuba as worthy descendants of the men who fought to end slavery. Citizens of Wooster, Ohio, gathered in their public square on November 16, 1898, to mourn the loss of seventy-two of the town's sons. Military officers and local ministers assured them that the fallen had not died in vain. "It will not do to be too selfish, to keep this higher civilization to ourselves," one speaker remarked. "God has enlarged our borders to bring new blessings to the world with our new duties. No war with higher ambitions, nobler purpose was ever known."[17]

Not all Americans saw it that way. The chairman of the Massachusetts Reform Club, Moorfield Storey, cautioned that victory against Spain would launch the United States "upon a policy of military aggression, of territorial expansion, of standing armies and growing navies . . . inconsistent with the continuance of our institutions."[18] Others wanted Cubans liberated but not independent. At a time when Jim Crow laws were institutionalizing segregation in the American South and middle-class white Protestants in northern cities worried about teeming numbers of Catholic and Jewish immigrants, many white Americans agreed with General William Shafter that the largely African population of Cuba was "no more fit for self-government than gunpowder is for hell." General Samuel Young was even blunter: Cubans were "no more capable of self-government than the savages of Africa."[19] Behind the "beautiful panorama" of white huts and palm trees was "a state only a little advanced beyond barbarism," wrote an Ohio volunteer colonel. The "dusky and shoeless warriors" of the Cuban resistance impressed him not at all: they "seemed to some of us, more like banditti or freebooters than patriots struggling" for freedom.[20]

The "splendid little war" with Spain revealed the United States as a nation at cross-purposes with itself. Some Americans, optimists in the spirit of Jackson's romantic empire, fused an enlightened idea of the Republic as the harbinger of global freedom with the confidence that Americans were uniquely qualified by race and religion to propagate the blessings of liberty. There was no contradiction between liberty and empire; the United States had conquered not to subjugate but to give Spain's former colonists the chance to make something of themselves, something, that is, like Americans. Far from marking the Republic as an empire intent upon its own aggrandizement, the war demonstrated America's benevolence. "What greater liberty, freedom, and independence can be obtained," asked Congressman John B. Corliss in 1901, "than that enjoyed under the protection of our flag?"[21]

Others, less sanguine about the potential of Cubans for self-rule, insisted on the Platt Amendment (1901) as a condition for Cuban nationhood, a measure that severely abridged Cuban sovereignty by requiring Cubans to give up their power to make agreements with other nations, avoid building up a public debt they could not repay, lease land and harbor rights at Guantánamo Bay for a U.S. naval station, and—most important—acknowledge that the United States had "the right to intervene" for the "maintenance of a government adequate for the protection of life, property and individual liberty."[22] Despite vociferous opposition in Cuba, the Platt Amendment became an appendix to the Constitution of 1901. Freed from Spain, Cuba remained at the mercy of the United States until Fidel Castro came to power in 1960.

"Fighting and Civilizing and Educating at the Same Time Doesn't Mix Very Well"

Cuba was only half of the story of the Spanish-American War. The American experience in the Philippines soon made the defeat of Spain in Cuba seem like a cakewalk. It also threw into even starker relief the challenges and contradictions of the Age of Intervention.

The enthusiasm of the American public for war with Spain was largely based on press reports of Spanish atrocities in Cuba. Far fewer Americans knew or cared much about what was going on halfway around the world in the Philippine archipelago. But the McKinley administration, particularly its energetic assistant secretary of the navy, Theodore Roosevelt, was quite aware that American commercial and strategic interests extended in Asia from Japan to the Indian subcontinent and thus understood the need to project American power across the Pacific. The navy's new steel battleships, themselves symbols of the global emergence of the North American republic, required bases stocked with coal, water, and food on such islands as Hawaii and Guam. The Philippines would provide the United States with the greatest foothold of all from which to exert influence in East Asia.

The Philippines had been a Spanish colony since the early sixteenth century. Many Filipinos spoke Spanish; most practiced a syncretic form of Roman Catholicism. Since the Spanish had never really controlled the countryside beyond the city of Manila, they relied on local leaders, or *principales,* to act as intermediaries in a network of patron-client relationships that stretched from peasants up through imperial officials. The Philippines consisted of a collection of loosely related local societies constructed around a dynamic blend of indigenous and imperial practices. Personal ties, especially those within and between extended families, mattered more to the vast majority of people than loyalty to political institutions or abstractions, such as the law. Geography reinforced localism: with 7,000 islands spread across a half-million square miles of ocean, the archipelago supported a bewildering array of languages and cultures, dividing peoples of fiercely independent views and reinforcing an intense suspicion of outsiders. The most

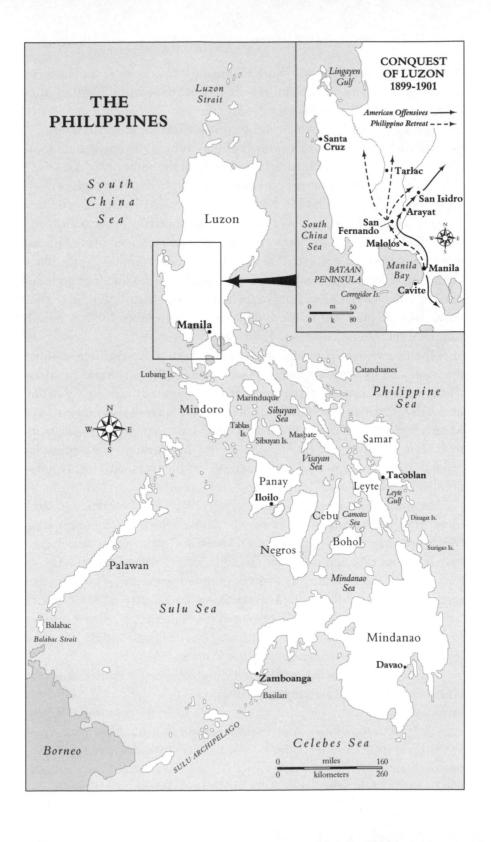

THE PHILIPPINES

Luzon Strait

South China Sea

Luzon

Luzon Strait

Manila

Lubang Is.

Catanduanes

Philippine Sea

Mindoro

Marinduque

Sibuyan Sea

Tablas Is.

Masbate

Sibuyan Is.

Samar

Visayan Sea

Panay

Tacoblan

Leyte

Iloilo

Leyte Gulf

Cebu

Camotes Sea

Dinagat Is.

Negros

Bohol

Surigao Is.

Mindanao Sea

Palawan

Sulu Sea

Balabac
Balabac Strait

Mindanao

Davao

Zamboanga

Basilan

Celebes Sea

SULU ARCHIPELAGO

Borneo

| 0 | miles | 160 |
| 0 | kilometers | 260 |

CONQUEST OF LUZON 1899-1901

American Offensives →
Philippino Retreat --→

Lingayen Gulf

Santa Cruz

Tarlac

San Isidro

Arayat

South China Sea

San Fernando

Malolos

Manila

BATAAN PENINSULA

Manila Bay

Cavite

Corregidor Is.

| 0 | m | 50 |
| 0 | k | 80 |

dramatic examples of this resistance to outside influence were the southern islands of Mindanao and Sulu, which remained defiantly Muslim after three centuries of Spanish Catholic rule.

Spanish officials' late-nineteenth-century efforts at modernization, especially their promotion of commercial agriculture, disrupted traditional economic and social structures and undermined the authority of the *principales,* transforming land into a commodity and displacing thousands of peasants. Meanwhile, middle-class Filipinos, or *ilustrados,* developed a limited sense of nationalism rooted in criticism of the imperial administration and the Catholic Church. Like Mexican *criollos, ilustrados* resented being lumped in with uneducated peasants. Twenty-eight-year-old Emilio Aguinaldo y Famy, son of a *principal* family in Cavite, emerged as the leader of an independence movement. Operating in the hills outside Manila, Aguinaldo declared himself president of the Philippines in November 1897. A month later he went into exile in Hong Kong.

When the United States declared war on Spain, an American fleet under the command of Admiral George Dewey, strategically positioned by Assistant Secretary Roosevelt off the coast of the Philippines, immediately swung into action. On May 1, 1898, Dewey defeated the Spanish ships anchored in Manila Bay. The McKinley administration followed up on the naval victory by rushing troops to the Philippines. Arthur MacArthur, now a brigadier general, arrived in June with 5,000 men, all, he later recalled, "totally ignorant" of the Philippines.[23]

Aguinaldo chose this moment to reassert himself and created a government in July. The Americans besieged Manila, which fell a month later. MacArthur was given command of a division and promoted to major general. It did not take Aguinaldo and his allies long to realize that the Americans planned to substitute one form of empire for another. They declared their independence from the United States on January 21, 1899. With "measureless pride," Aguinaldo lamented, the Americans "treated me as a rebel because I defend the sacred interests of my country, and do not make myself an instrument of their dastardly intentions."[24]

The antagonism between liberators and liberated together with the boredom and cultural contempt that American soldiers felt for the Filipinos created an unstable mixture that soon exploded. On the evening of February 4, 1899, Private William Walter Grayson from Beatrice, Nebraska, was at a guard post in an eastern suburb of Manila when four shadowy figures appeared in the gloom. They did not react as Grayson and his fellow sentry expected them to do when they were challenged. Frightened, thinking his orders had been purposely defied, Grayson leveled his single-shot Spring-field rifle and fired. His comrade followed suit, and soon three Filipinos lay dead. Then Grayson shouted the alarm: "Line up, fellows, the niggers are in here all through these lines."[25] Rifle fire broke out along the ten-mile length of American pickets. Soldiers moved through Manila and beyond with barely a semblance of discipline in an action that more nearly resembled a race riot than a coordinated military operation. Within twenty-four hours, they killed 3,000 Filipinos while suffering losses of fifty-nine dead and close to 300 wounded. The American commander, Major General Elwell S. Otis, ordered one division to the south of the island of Luzon and another to the north in the hope of quelling what promised to become a general revolt against American rule. Arthur MacArthur led the latter group into Aguinaldo's capital at Malolos. The goal, according to an American official in Washington, was to fight "without cessation until the authority of the United States in the Philippines should be, as far as the natives were con-cerned, undisputed."[26]

The fighting proved tough work. Private Edwin Segerstrom of the First Colorado Volunteers complained that the enemy was "a treacherous lot" who would treat other Filipinos as the Spanish had "treated them." He guessed that "our war with them is for the best, no matter what papers far off in the states may say." Another Coloradan, Private Selman Watson, wanted his family to know that reported "skirmishes" were more than that. The insurgents were "getting to shoot straight and close and doing closer shooting every day." Watson had "had all the fighting I care for but I won't quit if a call comes as long as I feel like I do now." Segerstrom agreed; nonetheless, he wrote, despite "frequent drubbings" at the hand of the Americans, the insurgents "'bob up serenely' at different points and it seems to be quite a job to subdue them." Segerstrom had no real idea of what would happen or how long the fighting would continue; he could only hope that "it wont be long now until they give up and behave themselves."[27]

But the Filipinos did not behave themselves, and the American troops soon discovered that no matter how many they killed, how many towns they destroyed, or how much territory they took, they could not sup-press the insurgency. How could they? The invaders were few in number, thousands of miles from home, ignorant of their enemies' cultures and languages, bereft of reliable intelligence. Many, like the Nebraska and Colorado National Guard contingents, had little training and found them-selves under great pressure to perform duties they understood poorly. Sudden and expected calamities beset them, devastating morale. The commander of one of the two American divisions was a fifty-six-year-old major general, Henry Ware Lawton. Brave, hard-drinking, and temperamental, Lawton had enlisted as a private in the Civil War and won the Congressional Medal of Honor for conspicuous bravery in the battle of Atlanta. He cemented his reputation in 1886 when he spent six months tenaciously leading cavalry on the grueling 2,000-mile trek that resulted in the capture of Geronimo. But he did not survive the Philippine Insurrection. In December 1899, the six-foot-four-inch-tall Lawton, garbed in a full-length yellow slicker and a white pith helmet, took a bullet in the chest about eighteen miles northeast of Manila. He died almost immediately.[28] MacArthur, still in command of the other American division, urged General Otis to recognize that they were mired in a guerrilla war similar to ones waged against the Apaches and other Indians and to fight according to proven techniques. Otis took his advice, creating geographical departments policed by autonomous garrisons of soldiers, and attacking the insurgents' bases of support.

The savage counterinsurgency that Otis and MacArthur mounted bore little resemblance to the intentions President McKinley had expressed in justifying intervention the previous year. The "mission of the United States is one of benevolent assimilation," he declared, "substituting the mild sway of justice and right for arbitrary rule." In time, the Filipinos would "come to see our benevolent purpose and recognize that before we can give their people good government our sovereignty must be complete and unquestioned."[29] Meanwhile, back in the United States, the Philippine Insurrection divided Americans even more sharply than Cuba. Thirty thousand members of the Anti-Imperialist League rallied in the Northeast against intervention and attempted to stop the Senate from ratifying the Treaty of Paris, which had been signed on December 10, 1898, surrendering Spanish sovereignty over Cuba, transferring Puerto Rico and Guam to the United States, and selling the Philippines for $20 million. The opponents of ratification almost succeeded, principally because senators recognized that the majority of ordinary white Americans could see no reason to assume responsibility for millions of dark-skinned Spanish- or Tagalog-speaking Catholics who seemed to exhibit little if any promise of self-rule. In the end the Senate approved the treaty by a single vote after adding a provision that stipulated annexation would not imply any claim on American citizenship for Filipinos.[30] Anti-imperialists denounced the conquest of the Philippines as antithetical to American democratic traditions. William James ruefully observed that his countrymen were "now openly engaged in crushing out the sacredest thing in this great human world—the attempt of a people long enslaved to attain to the possession of itself, to organize its laws and government, to be free to follow its internal destinies according to its own ideals." James was certain that supporters of this "war of conquest" were hypocrites who were selling the "ancient soul" of America.[31]

Supporters of the war argued that the United States had always been an imperial power. Linking America's expansion across North America with its involvement in the Caribbean basin and the Philippines, they consciously looked to the past to guide them. "Why," the journalist and peace commissioner Whitelaw Reid asked, should we "mourn over our present course as a departure from the policy of the fathers?" "For over a hundred years the uniform policy which they began and their sons continued has been acquisition, expansion." A writer in *The Atlantic Monthly* agreed that "the question is not whether we shall enter upon a career of colonization or not, but whether we shall shift into other channels the colonization which has lasted as long as our national existence."[32]

Recognizing that they would ultimately succeed in imposing their governance only if they gave the Filipinos reason to trust them, Americans introduced aspects of their legal and tax codes to replace the hated Spanish system, established clinics to treat diseases, built schools, and did their best to demonstrate an interest in the welfare of the populace. The Department of Public Instruction, eventually responsible for a thousand schools and a hundred thousand pupils, expressed an ideal of staged transformation as old as the Northwest Ordinance of 1787: first conquer territory, then create republican institutions, secure basic values, and encourage people to choose do what was clearly best for themselves, abandoning their "savage" ways in favor of "civilization." It was not necessarily a task that soldiers of the occupying army, which ultimately numbered a hundred thousand, particularly relished. One district commander commented that his job was less to fight the enemy than to do all the "duties heretofore performed by civil officials."[33]

Transfixed by the superiority of their own values and institutions, Americans had no interest in understanding Filipino cultural norms or political ideas in their own terms, much less in recognizing them as legitimately different from those of the United States. Beyond the well-educated, Manila-based elite, Filipinos had no desire to make a national government matter more than local authority; nor did they wish to offer children a civic education that insisted on a loyalty to the state (in the form of schools, courts, and military officers) that clearly threatened to displace loyalty to relatives and local patriarchs. The growing importance of public schools in the socialization of children, often celebrated as the great American contribution to the Philippines, came at the expense of the traditional importance of extended families and portended a major transformation in society. Liberation as defined by Americans was conquest as understood by some Filipinos.[34]

Yet the American soldiers were nothing if not persistent. They suffered from tropical diseases and ate "rotten canned beef, canned tomatoes, canned beans." They waded "through rivers and swamps with bullets playing music over" their heads. They improvised a "new method of fighting"—"to fire a few rounds—then advance toward the enemy—firing as we go"—that seemed to yield positive results on the battlefield. Gradually they made gains, but on balance virtually all of them would have preferred to be back home where the rules were clear, dangers came in more or less predictable forms, and they did not have to wonder if they were on a fool's errand that could at any moment turn fatal. Private Walter R. Combs of Bedford, Iowa, put it succinctly: most "of the men doing the fighting out here would rather have the United States establish some form of government for the Filipinos, and let them run it to suit themselves."[35]

Confronted with the challenge of subduing a population of millions spread across thousands of islands, the officers and men of the army did not mince words. Some denounced Filipinos as "niggers" unsuited by race, religion, and history to enjoy liberty. "It may be necessary to kill half of the Filipinos in order that the remaining half of the population may be advanced to a higher plane of life than their present semi-barbarous state affords," remarked General William Shafter. "This business of fighting and civilizing and educating at the same time doesn't mix very well," another soldier observed. Men found themselves quickly hardened by war. The same captain who initially complained that "We come as a Christian people . . . and bear ourselves like barbarians" eventually ordered the destruction of a town after a friend died in an ambush. It was time to "conduct this warfare with the utmost rigour. 'With fire and sword' as it were." One soldier wanted to "blow every nigger into nigger heaven" while another concluded that peace would not come to the Philippines "until the niggers are killed off like the Indians."[36] Such sentiments were not, of course, universal among the troops, but they were surely more nearly the rule than the exception among men who sang as they marched

Damn, damn, damn the Filipinos,
Cut-throat khakiac ladrones!
Underneath the starry flag,

Civilize 'em with a Krag,
And return us to our own beloved homes![37]

Theodore Roosevelt urged army commanders to resort to the tactics used against the Apaches and other Indians. National honor was at stake. To "withdraw from the contest for civilization because of the fact that there are attendant cruelties is . . . utterly unworthy of a great people." Whitelaw Reid agreed; abandoning the Philippines would be the equivalent of leaving Florida in the hands of the Seminoles "instead of sending Andrew Jackson to protect the settlements and subdue the savages[.]"[38] What seemed obvious to one reporter—that "the people of the Philippines do not wish to be governed by us"—was of less immediate concern to the occupation forces than controlling the Filipinos by whatever means could be made to work. The United States, after all, was a civilized nation, and the Philippines seemed to Americans to be neither civilized nor a nation in any recognizable sense. Americans knew what was best for the people whom a successful war had suddenly made their wards.[39]

Arthur MacArthur, promoted to major general, assumed command of the American forces in the Philippines in May 1900. His officers acted under the provisions of General Order 100, which had been issued in 1863 to deal with conquered Confederates. It proclaimed that the mission of the American army was to restore and maintain order by ensuring respect for the authority of the law. All people who cooperated with their efforts were to be treated with dignity and respect, but resistance was deemed a criminal act. Officers were empowered to seize the property of insurgents, imprison them, and, if necessary, execute them.[40] Many did just that. In December, MacArthur announced "a new and more stringent policy" against the rebels and their allies, who seemed able to move in and out of the civilian population at will. The general sanctioned tougher military patrols, purges of municipal governments, harsher treatment of prisoners and civilians, destruction of property, confinement of civilians, and starvation. Filipinos were forcibly "concentrated" in "protected zones," under U.S. military control; those who resisted relocation could be treated as rebels, just as recalcitrant Indians had been. By analogy to Indians who refused to stay on their reservations, Filipinos who tried to escape from their designated zones were presumed to be "hostiles" and shot on sight. MacArthur's troops used torture to extract information, break the will of resisters, and intimidate anyone who happened to fall into their custody. No reliable information exists on the incidence of torture because such practices were not officially sanctioned but left to the discretion of local commanders. The physical coercion of prisoners, however, seems to have been widespread. American soldiers wrote of Filipinos being "kicked and beaten" and hung by their thumbs. Prisoners who proved recalcitrant might be given the "water cure," in which "the victim [was] laid flat on his back and held down by his tormenters. Then a bamboo tube [was] thrust into his mouth and some dirty water, the filthier the better, . . . [was] poured down his unwilling throat."[41] Beyond these abuses, anti-imperialist critics painted lurid pictures of rape and sexual degeneracy to demonstrate their larger point that Americans whose mission had been to defend liberty and the rule of law had themselves become barbarians.[42]

MacArthur proved an effective commander and, as usual, exaggerated his own importance. He quarreled with civilian officials over petty points of protocol and bristled at any suggestion that he should be answerable to non-military authority. When Judge William Howard Taft of Ohio arrived to head the civil commission that would administer the Philippines, MacArthur declined to meet his ship, quartered him in a single room, and refused to surrender the palace he had appropriated for his own residence. (Taft suffered in silence. But he never forgot: later, as president, he denied MacArthur the job he coveted, Army Chief of Staff.) The gloomy Mac-Arthur was as realistic about the challenges of asserting American authority as he was straightforward in his understanding of what it would take to do so successfully: force for the resisters, mercy for those who acquiesced in the rule of the occupation forces, and favorable treatment for active collaborators—a formula Grant would have found familiar—was, he believed, the only way to do the job.

Like his peers, MacArthur believed that Americans were "initiating a stage of progressive social evolution that may reasonably be expected to result in substantial contributions in behalf of the unity of the race and the brotherhood of man." The general later told a Senate committee that Americans, unlike other empire-building "Aryans," were dedicated to planting "imperishable ideas" in their colonies. He thought "the archipelago "a fertile soil upon which to plant republicanism" and "the best characteristics of Americanism." Once Filipinos realized the benefits of association with the United States, they would "follow and support the American flag in whatever contests the future may have in store for it as the symbol of human liberty throughout the world."[43]

On July 4, 1901, MacArthur, proud of the progress he had made against the insurgents, turned over his command to another Civil War veteran, Major General Adna R. Chaffee. Aguinaldo had been captured in March, and other rebel leaders were surrendering; yet the fighting went on and even intensifed in on Samar (which Brigadier General Jacob Smith vowed to turn into "a howling wilderness") and Luzon, where Brigadier General J. Franklin Bell systematically destroyed the food supply and forced large numbers of inhabitants into protected zones. President Roosevelt declared the insurrection at an end on July 4, 1902, but resistance continued among the Moro people, Muslims of the southern islands, until 1913.

The costs were high. At least 20,000 insurgents lost their lives between 1899 and 1902, along with perhaps 180,000 of their countrymen, most of whom succumbed to starvation. The United States spent $400 million—the equivalent of perhaps $30 billion today—to suppress the insurgency. More than a thousand Americans were killed in combat and more than 2,800 were wounded, and roughly 3,000 men died from disease or other causes. Some 125,000 Americans intervened in the Philippines to promote civilization, democracy, and the rule of law as well as to secure the interests of the United States and its citizens. They would exercise dominion over the islands until the people they had liberated proved capable of governing themselves; that is, until a sufficient number of Filipino leaders could overcome what Americans deemed the ignorance and recalcitrance of a primitive race, accept American values and institutions, and rule their society in ways acceptable to the United States.

Senator Thomas MacDonald Patterson of Colorado inquired of MacArthur upon his return whether the "imperishable idea" for which Americans fought in the Philippines was "the right of self-government." The general replied: "Precisely so; self-government regulated by law as we understand it in this Republic." He and his men were "unmistakably the instruments" of American destiny in Asia. "Inspiration and hope," said MacArthur, "go with our flag."[44]

"It Shall Not Lie with the American People to Dictate to Another People What Their Government Shall Be . . ."

Unlike the Seven Years' War and the war with Mexico, the decisive imperial victory over Spain and the suppression of Filipino resistance did not directly destabilize political culture in North America. They did, however, inaugurate two decades of public debate in the United States about the proper relationship between liberty and power. Along with like-minded people in

Europe, a good many middle-class, Protestant, urban Americans were persuaded early in the twentieth century of the power of governments to bring
about social justice. They often thought of themselves as Progressives. The
term, which covers a multitude of diverse peoples and ideas, most basically
constituted a language of "solutions" to problems created by massive urbanization, rapid industrialization, and laissez-faire capitalism.[45] Progressives
tended to see governments as institutional embodiments of the people that
would check the excesses of politicians and plutocrats. Led by educated ex-
perts and analysts, governments could engineer political democracy and
greater economic equality.

Progressives saw their ideas, including municipal control of transportation and utilities, referendums and recalls, direct election of senators, an eq-
uitable system of taxation, the breakup of monopolies, the enforcement of
pure food-and-drug standards, and protection of laborers in the workplace, as
expressions of the democratic potential of the United States. Moreover, they
imagined themselves as participants in conversations about social reform that
transcended national borders. Reformers crisscrossed the Atlantic to attend
conferences and expositions, study urban development and bureaucracies,
and plan new urban landscapes. For perhaps the first time, what happened in
Glasgow's city government was of compelling interest to people concerned
with solving problems in Cleveland. The great nineteenth-century rebuilding
of Paris into an imperial city of broad boulevards and great public spaces inspired planners and architects in Chicago and St. Louis. Germany attracted
Americans interested in its universities, its culture, and its efficiency. Cities in
the Northeast and the Midwest built great public structures of marble and
stone to house government, education, books, art, music, and commerce
and to serve as secular cathedrals of the possibilities of collective knowledge
and action.[46] American soldiers and civilian administrators who engaged in
reconstructing Cuba and the Philippines, in short, represented a nation that
was self-consciously engaged in reconstructing itself.

Having conquered and transformed North America, some Americans
were eager to transform the world as a whole. They confronted the same
quandaries internationally that bedeviled them domestically. Though few
Americans objected on principle to democracy, more than a few objected to
the actual operation of a democracy that incorporated, willy-nilly, the millions
of eastern and southern European immigrants (mainly Catholics and Jews)
who poured annually into the United States. Even more Americans worried
about the prospect of including people of color—from Cuba, the Philippines,
or for that matter the American states—in the American political system.

Mary "Pinky" MacArthur and her son Douglas,
a first-year student at the United States Military Academy
at West Point, 1900

Many distrusted as well the kind of wealthy, sophisticated patricians who sought out and exercised power in the national government: men who seemingly had stronger ties to European intellectuals and politicians than to their countrymen. Such concerned citizens, usually white Protestants of middling economic means or less whose families had lived in the United States for more than a couple of generations, favored immigration restriction, rigid racial segregation, Prohibition, and the homogeneous brand of patriotism called "Americanism" as solutions to the nation's most pressing problems.

Domestic tensions both paralleled and reinforced the tensions that grew out of the new imperial project. Efforts at reconstructing the Philippines and the Caribbean basin in the first two decades of the twentieth century were fraught with contradictions inherent in a process of liberating people whose visions of a satisfactory life did not coincide with the expectations of their paternalistic liberators. To use state power to reform and reconstruct societies inhabited by people whose skin colors and religions made white Americans distinctly uncomfortable was to go to the heart of the American dilemma about the appeals of liberty and empire, choice and coercion, freedom and power, whether the location was Alabama, Manhattan, or Luzon.

Douglas MacArthur embodied many of the self-confident, even cocky, qualities attributed to Americans in the first two decades of the twentieth century. But he was also a work in progress, a dutiful son eager to please his parents still striving to find his way in a world transformed by his father's generation. He thrived at West Point under the watchful eye of his mother, who lived in Craney's Hotel on the edge of the academy grounds while her husband was in the Philippines. Douglas was determined to be "a worthy successor" to his father and to please both of his demanding parents. He worked hard to excel. First in his class for three of his four years at West Point, he accumulated 98.14 percent of available merit points, reputedly the best score since Robert E. Lee had garnered 98.33 percent in 1829. Douglas played baseball and managed the football team in his senior year. On June 11, 1903, General and Mrs. MacArthur beamed with pride as their son graduated at the head of the Long Gray Line of cadets.

The new lieutenant's first posting was in the Philippines. Assigned to the Third Engineer Battalion, Douglas arrived in Manila in October and promptly enacted all the contradictions of the occupation, rebuilding the country in the name of progress while controlling—or crushing—those who resisted American authority. His orders took him to remote parts of the Philippines, where he supervised the construction of wharves and landing areas. Shortly after his arrival at the port of Iloilo, MacArthur took some men to the island of Guimaras to cut timber. Two guerrillas fired at him as he walked through the jungle. He drew his pistol and killed them, suffering no more damage than a hole in his hat.

After two years in the Philippines, Douglas became aide-de-camp to his father, who had been appointed military attaché in Japan. The elder MacArthur was dispatched on a thoroughly Progressive mission: a grand tour of colonial military installations in Asia to gather data about how the British and other powers projected power and protected their interests in global empires. It was a family outing: departing in November 1905, father and son traveled with Mary to India, after visits to Singapore, Java, and Burma. For the next eight weeks, the MacArthurs inspected British posts in the Himalayas and the Khyber Pass before stopping in Bombay and Ceylon. When they returned to Singapore in March, they had traveled nearly 20,000 miles; they added many more later that spring when they visited Siam,

Saigon, and China. The general and his aide had barely settled in Japan when they were both recalled to the United States; on July 17, they boarded a ship in Yokohama bound for San Francisco. Douglas recalled this monumental trip as decisive in his life, a moment of recognition that Asia was "western civilization's last earth frontier." He returned to the United States convinced that "the future, and indeed, the very existence of America, were irrevocably entwined with Asia and its island outposts."[47]

Lieutenant MacArthur reported first to the Engineer School of Application in Washington, D.C., then moved to Fort Leavenworth, Kansas, where he devoted himself to acquiring the education and cultivating the connections required to rise in rank and to coping with his mother's obsessive interest and interference in his professional life. His career prospered even in adversity: following his father's sudden death on September 5, 1912, during an address to a reunion of the Twenty-fourth Wisconsin, the chief of staff of the army, Major General Leonard Wood, an old friend of the family, prevailed upon Secretary of War Henry L. Stimson to support Douglas's appointment to his staff. "In view of the distinguished service of General Arthur MacArthur," Stimson was happy to oblige.[48] Douglas and his mother lived well in Washington; they shared a house on Sixteenth Street Northwest and an African-American chauffeur, who drove them wherever they needed to go in a Cadillac touring car.

Douglas was free to concentrate on a career in a military whose primary activity was to liberate peoples and enhance American strategic interests by means of armed interventions in the Caribbean basin. The Panama Canal, whose construction Theodore Roosevelt facilitated by sending a naval squadron to promote Panama's secession from Colombia in 1903, was the centerpiece of a gunboat diplomacy that both formalized the filibustering schemes of the mid-nineteenth century and sustained the military momentum of the Spanish-American War. "All that this country desires," said Roosevelt in 1905 in describing the operation of the recently announced Roosevelt Corollary to the Monroe Doctrine, "is that the other republics on this continent shall be happy and prosperous; and they cannot be happy and prosperous unless they maintain order within their boundaries and behave with a just regard to their obligations toward outsiders." Thereupon the United States effectively dictated an agreement with the Dominican Republic under which it took over the fiscal operations of the government; for the next several years the United States administered the collection of customs, enforced the timely payment of the republic's foreign debts, and guaranteed its security against the invasion of foreign powers other than itself. When

William Howard Taft assumed the presidency in 1909, he modified this highly direct approach to hemispheric relations by emphasizing economic integration rather than military force; yet Taft's "dollar diplomacy" in no way renounced the right of intervention Roosevelt had claimed. Perhaps so that his intent could not be mistaken, Taft explained the implications of his policy to a Mexican diplomat. All the United States wanted as far as the Central American nations were concerned was "the right to knock their heads together until they should maintain peace between them."[49]

The United States intervened in Honduras in 1911; the following year, 2,600 American troops landed in Nicaragua to insure that the outcome of a civil war there would be favorable to the interests of the United States. They stayed in Nicaragua for two decades. In July 1915 thousands of Marines responded to an uprising in Haiti by occupying the country. Before they finally took their leave in 1934, the Marines had suppressed an armed insurgency, dissolved the Haitian Congress, dictated a new constitution, suppressed a second rebellion, and created a new national government that welcomed foreign investment. The cost in Haitian lives amounted to at least 3,000 (perhaps as many 11,500) killed for resisting the occupation. Intervention in the Dominican Republic followed in 1916, also in the context of a civil war; this occupation lasted until 1924, thereby placing the entire island of Hispaniola under the protection of the United States. When in June 1916, President Woodrow Wilson wrote in a draft of a speech to Congress that "It shall not lie with American people to dictate to another people what their government shall be or what use they shall have or what persons they shall encourage or favor" and gave the text to Secretary of State Robert Lansing to review, Lansing simply wrote "Haiti, S. Domingo, Nicaragua, Panama" in the margin. Wilson took the hint, and gave up on the speech.[50]

Sensitive to charges of imperialism, American soldiers and diplomats insisted that the end justified the means. Military interventions created a temporary dominion that allowed politically immature peoples to become responsible citizens. But there was no gainsaying the racist paternalism of the Americans. According to General Smedley Butler, who did not particularly like his role in strong-arming the Haitians, his men considered the black citizens of Haiti their "wards"; the Marines were "endeavoring to make for them a rich and productive property, to be turned over to them at such a time as our government saw fit." In rhetoric as well as in tactics, Haiti seemed to be a small-scale reprise of the Philippine adventure: not the conquest of a people but their liberation from the tyrants and wicked men who would otherwise have kept them uncivilized and backward, the better to subjugate them.[51]

Mexicans, who had already lost half their territory to the United States, had good reason to resent the American troops who repeatedly invaded their territory in the 1910s. American leaders happy with the government of Porfirio Díaz were deeply troubled when Francisco Madero led a revolution that forced the aging dictator into exile in 1911. Madero promised more democracy and more restraints on foreign investors. With the tacit support of the Taft administration's ambassador, General Victoriano Huerta overthrew Madero in February 1913 and had him shot. The coup infuriated Woodrow Wilson, who became president of the United States in March. Appalled by Huerta, he denounced the general's brutality, immorality, and opposition to democratic reform. "I am going to teach the South American republics to elect good men," Wilson declared.[52] He needed only an excuse to do so.

That came soon enough. When a Mexican officer briefly detained seven American sailors at Tampico in April 1914, the United States responded by seizing the port of Veracruz. By the end of the month, 7,000 Americans under the command of General Leonard Wood occupied the city, taking charge of its customhouse (and hence a substantial proportion of Mexico's public revenues). Among the American troops was Wood's protégé, Captain Douglas MacArthur, who lost no time in conducting a daring—and utterly unauthorized—nighttime reconnaissance mission to Alvarado, forty miles southeast of Veracruz, in search of railroad locomotives. MacArthur returned unscathed, although exchanges of gunfire with Mexican soldiers left him with several bullet holes in his clothing and one slightly wounded companion. The adventuresome captain concluded that he deserved the Congressional Medal of Honor. (The army disagreed. The same officers who admired the captain's initiative worried about his tendency toward grandstanding; it was not a good idea to hand out medals to officers who ignored their direct commanders.[53]) In the end, the occupation of Veracruz accomplished little beyond improving conditions in the city's red-light district. United States casualties totaled ninety (nineteen dead) while the Mexicans lost 321 (126 dead). Huerta's government collapsed for domestic reasons, and the Americans evacuated Veracruz in November.

The Wilson administration was not yet finished with Mexico. In March 1916, President Wilson sent 7,000 men under the command of General John J. Pershing on a 350-mile "punitive expedition" through northern Mexico in search of Francisco "Pancho" Villa, a caudillo who had executed sixteen American engineers and sacked Columbus, New Mexico, with the loss of nineteen American lives. Villa proved elusive, however, and Pershing requested reinforcements. By the end of April, 12,000 American soldiers were involved in the chase; that summer, 150,000 National Guardsmen from a variety of states were stationed along the border. On at least two occasions, Pershing's forces exchanged gunfire with Mexican soldiers, resulting in the deaths of at least fourteen Americans and forty Mexicans. Only the growing prospect of a European war led Wilson to withdraw Pershing's force in February 1917, leaving Villa as a symbol of resistance to imperialism.

Wilson, the Virginia-born former history professor and president of Princeton University, consistently turned to coercion when conciliation failed. Like Theodore Roosevelt, his more personally bellicose rival, Wilson had a keen sense of history, a deep regard for the righteousness of American democracy, and the best of intentions. But Wilson at his most idealistic was Wilson at his most problematic: his genuine devotion to the cause of liberty as Americans understood it made him an imperialist who understood himself as a democrat, a combination of traits that made him the quintessential spokesman for the American empire in the Age of Intervention. The United States, he told the graduating midshipmen at the Naval Academy on June 5, 1914, used "her navy and her army . . . as the instruments of civilization, not as the instruments of aggression. The idea of America is to serve humanity, and every time you let the Stars and Stripes free to the wind you ought to realize that that is in itself a message that you are on an errand which other navies have sometimes forgotten; not an errand of conquest, but an errand of service. . . . When I look at that flag it seems to me as if the white stripes were stripes of parchment upon which are written the rights of man, and the red stripes the streams of blood by which those rights have been made good."[54] The test of this idealism in determining the degree to which American power could and should be deployed for the greater good of mankind proved to be the war that engulfed Europe just two months after Wilson delivered his commencement address at Annapolis.

"We Desire No Conquest, No Dominion . . ."

The assassination of the Austrian-Hungarian archduke Franz Ferdinand and his wife, Sophie, in Sarajevo, Bosnia, on June 28, 1914, triggered a series of diplomatic and military moves under the terms of various alliances that resulted in a general war in Europe in August. By the spring of 1915, Germany, Austria-Hungary, and the Ottoman Empire were pitted against Russia in the east and France, Great Britain, and Italy in the west. Germans confronted the British and French in what quickly evolved into a sanguinary deadlock between millions of troops occupying entrenchments that ran without interruption from the Belgian coast across northeastern France to the Swiss border. Over 65 million men worldwide were mobilized before the armistice of November 11, 1918. More than 8 million of them died, and another 21 million suffered wounds: on average, in other words, the war inflicted nearly 20,000 casualties a day.[55]

Sensational stories of savage barbarism against women and children by evil "Huns" outraged Americans. But it took more than tales of horrors inflicted on Belgians to persuade the citizens of the United States to participate in the Great War. The United States had deliberately avoided alliances with European powers since the Convention of 1800 ended the revolutionary era alliance between the United States and France. Unembroiled in Europe's affairs, Americans demanded that Europeans stay out of the Americas, a position formally enunciated in the Monroe Doctrine of 1823 and subsequently reiterated by the Polk and Lincoln administrations. To be sure, the United States had, in the half century after its Civil War, grown into a global industrial power. Still, people in Mississippi and Nebraska wondered, why should Americans die to save Europeans from themselves? Only a direct threat to the security of the United States would persuade them to break with tradition and fight in Europe. The sinking of British commercial and passenger ships with Americans on board (most famously, the *Lusitania*) by German submarines was critical to this shift. So, too, was the threat of an alliance between Germany and Mexico.[56]

Early in 1917, the British passed on to the Americans an intercepted telegram dated February 24 from the German foreign minister, Arthur Zimmermann, to the German minister to Mexico. If the United States entered the war in Europe, Germany and Mexico should "make war together, make peace together," with "generous [German] financial support and an understanding on our part that Mexico is to reconquer the lost territory in Texas, New Mexico, and Arizona."[57] The possibility of Mexico's retaking land lost in 1848 was sufficiently ludicrous that the Wilson administration did not take the threat seriously. Nonetheless, release of the telegram on March 1, 1917, galvanized public opinion because it detailed what seemed a clear and present danger to the United States.

On April 2, in the wake of more attacks on American shipping, Wilson asked Congress to declare war on Germany, or rather he asked Congress to "formally accept the status of belligerent which has thus been thrust upon it." "The world," Wilson declared, "must be safe for democracy. Its peace must be planted upon the tested foundations of political liberty. We have no selfish ends to serve. We desire no conquest, no dominion. . . . We are but one of the champions of the rights of mankind. We shall be satisfied when those rights have been made as secure as the faith and the freedom of nations can make them."[58] Speaking for "the silent mass of mankind everywhere," a president whose military occupied portions of Mexico, Haiti, the Dominican Republic, Panama, Nicaragua, Cuba, and the Philippines, affirmed his belief that all nations should be free to evolve as their peoples saw fit.[59] Congress passed the war resolution by wide majorities in both houses four days later.

Though comparatively few American Progressives disagreed with Wilson's sentiment, many were troubled by the idea that war might be a means to that end. Some worried that the European war heralded a return to barbarism and the destruction of progress through cooperation. Jane Addams, the founder of Hull-House in Chicago and arguably the leading voice of Progressive reform in the United States, vocally opposed war as a solution to the world's problems. Born in Illinois in 1860, Addams had attended the first congress of the Women's International League for Peace and Freedom in The Hague in 1915. No isolationist, she argued in June 1917 that the United States "should lead the nations of the world into a wider life of co-ordinated political activity" that transcended national interests and "the creation of an international government able to make the necessary political and economic changes when they are due." But she also believed that "the aim of this government of ours and of similar types of government the world over [was] to replace coercion by the full consent of the governed, to educate and strengthen the free will of the people through the use of democratic institutions and to safeguard even the rights of minorities." Pacifists strove "for social and political justice with a fervor perhaps equal to that employed by the advocates of force." They simply did not think "a finely tempered sense of justice" could be "secured in the storm and stress of war."[60]

Other Progressives, untroubled by pacifist scruples, took comfort in the hope that the war would ultimately hasten the triumphs of democracy over aristocracy and equality over monopoly. The United States had to do something. "It is the genius of our people to live in peace," wrote the Kansas journalist William Allen White. "We care little for glory and conquest." But, noted one periodical, because "much has been given us; much will be required in return." Ray Stannard Baker, a journalist who later was an adviser to Wilson and his biographer, asked: "Is there no social gospel for nations? . . . America: servant of humanity. America: world leader." Precisely because the United States was a model for all nations of democracy, tolerance, and the rule of law, it could not shirk its responsibility.[61] Despite considerable contention over the value of intervention, most Progressive Americans tended to support Wilson's quest for "peace without victory."

Their support was severely tested by the administration's strenuous efforts to manage news through the Committee on Public Information and to repress dissent through the vague provisions of the Espionage Act of 1917 and the Sedition Act of 1918. The arrests of over fifteen hundred Americans, only a handful of whom were engaged in anything more dangerous than open dissent, seemed as blatant a contradiction of democratic principles as had similar actions by the Lincoln administration. Speaking out against such abuses in 1918, Senator Robert La Follette of Wisconsin charged that ordinary citizens were "being terrorized and outraged in their rights by those sworn to uphold the laws and protect the rights of the people."[62] His status as a senator protected him from arrest for voicing such views. Less well protected and less fortunate was the Socialist orator and five-time presidential candidate Eugene V. Debs. He was arrested in the summer of 1918 for an antiwar speech in Canton, Ohio, and sentenced to ten years in prison and the revocation of his citizenship.

Popular intolerance and repression also flourished. Many Americans, willing to restrict traditional rights as necessary wartime measures, attacked Germans and their descendants in the United States and sought to eradicate names, symbols, and customs with German origins. Most famously, sauerkraut became liberty cabbage. Recently admired as a model of efficiency, culture, and social progress, Germany became a symbol of barbarism and tyranny, even in Midwestern states with large populations of German-Americans.[63] Still, though Americans thought Germans were behaving barbarously, they did not believe them to be inherently barbaric. Liberating Europe was different from liberating the Philippines—or Haiti, or Mexico— because the nobility of the cause was seemingly untarnished by questions of race and ambitions for empire. White Americans would return to the continent of their ancestors and, like Union soldiers marching through Georgia, free Europeans from the power of those who would obstruct the progress of democracy and freedom.

In truth, American sons, brothers, and husbands went to Europe with mixed emotions. Like soldiers in other wars, their motives ran the gamut from pure idealism to the hunger for adventure, from the absence of employment opportunities to the coercion of conscription. Patriotism, while a consideration for the vast majority of American recruits, was a decisive factor for only a minority, probably a small one. Years later, one participant vividly recalled "the eagerness of the men to get to France and above all to reach the front." Why? "Perhaps we already felt that, in the American interest, Western democracy must not be allowed to go under. But I doubt it. I can hardly remember a single instance of serious discussion of American policy or of larger war issues. We men, most of us, were simply fascinated by the prospect of adventure and heroism."[64]

An officer as ambitious as Douglas MacArthur did not have to explain why he was eager to get to Europe. Promoted to major in December 1915, MacArthur ached to fight a worthy enemy. Shooting at Mexicans in the dark was nothing compared with a struggle against the armies of the kaiser. In Europe alone lay the potential to achieve the kind of immortality that the great captains of history—Caesar, Marlborough, Wellington, Napoleon— had attained, men whose exploits were the stuff of drama and poetry as well as dispassionate analysis by the faculties and impassioned debate by the cadets of military academies around the world.

MacArthur, however, had to be patient. The National Defense Act of 1916 called for an increase in the size of the regular army from 108,000 to 175,000 in peace and 286,000 in war and for more federal control of the 400,000 men in the National Guard. Major MacArthur, assigned to the general staff in Washington, helped prepare the legislation. He also worked on improving motor transportation and handled press relations, including making a case for the Selective Service Act of May 1917. His agility in completing such varied and critical assignments added to his growing reputation for competence and contributed to the willingness of Secretary of War Newton D. Baker in the summer of 1917 to accept the major's idea to form a division comprised of National Guard units from all over the United States. MacArthur gave the division its nickname when he remarked that it would cover the United States like a rainbow.

Promoted to colonel in August, he was assigned to the new Forty-second ("Rainbow") Division of the American Expeditionary Forces in France. Given a choice of assignments between the infantry and engineers (the branch in which he had originally been commissioned), MacArthur chose the former, later claiming that he "could think only of the old Twenty-fourth Wisconsin Infantry."[65]

As chief of staff of the Forty-second, Colonel MacArthur supervised its organization and training. When the division joined the exhausted allies in northeastern France in late February 1918, MacArthur flung himself into the thick of preparations to prepare men for deployment to the front, a process prolonged by the insistence of General Pershing, the AEF commander, that American troops operate under American authority rather than being integrated piecemeal into other Allied commands. It was May before American soldiers and marines engaged German troops, at Cantigny and Château-Thierry. Members of the American Expeditionary Forces fought at Saint-Mihiel in September and participated in the Meuse-Argonne offensive from late September until early November, gaining some thirty-four miles over a six-week period.

MacArthur's activity, courage, and calm demeanor over the 110 days that Americans were involved in combat earned him the Distinguished Service Cross; a whiff of poison gas won him a Purple Heart. Wearing his signature outfit of turtleneck sweater, muffler, puttees, and crushed cap, he was rarely seen without a riding crop and almost never wore a helmet. He seldom, if ever, carried a sidearm. Ordinary infantrymen wondered what anyone attired like MacArthur could possibly be doing on the front lines. When one of them learned who the officer was whom he and his friends had been calling "The Dude," "you could have knocked him over with a feather."[66]

Knowing that the war was creating a vast demand for general officers, Mary MacArthur lost no opportunity to lobby General Pershing to make her son a brigadier general, but he earned the promotion, which came in late June, himself. According to the commanding officer of the Forty-second, Colonel MacArthur was "the bloodiest fighting man in this army. I'm afraid we're going to lose him sometime, for there's no risk of battle that any soldier is called upon to take that he is not liable to look up and see MacArthur at his side."[67] By the time of the armistice in November 1918, MacArthur's command of the Eighty-fourth Brigade had marked him as one of the ablest combat officers in the army.

Most of the 1.39 million Americans who served on the Western Front in Europe cut a far less dashing and romantic figure than Douglas MacArthur. The experience of modern warfare in which machine guns, gas, grenades, tanks, artillery, and planes mauled and maimed human bodies into unrecognizable pieces soon tempered the eagerness for combat that most claimed to feel before arriving at the front lines. A lieutenant calmly described the explosion of a grenade that "tore off the right foot about six inches below the knee, the leather of my shoe holding the foot on." Another officer recalled how shellings began with "a faraway moan that grows to a scream, then a roar like a train, followed by a ground-shaking smash and a diabolical red light. . . . There is nothing to do. Whether you get through or not is just sheer chance and nothing more. You may and you may not. *C'est la guerre.*" The positive images men carried away were "beautiful memories of loyalty and comradeship" of "a sort of tenderness and love for their fellows fightin' with" them.[68]

Moments of American cultural imperialism occurred regularly among Yanks whose previous experience with the wider world was frequently limited to the state of their birth and the location of their training camp. One English woman, perhaps in amusement, remembered a Texan who called on her several times a week. He regaled her with "talk about our limited ideas, out-of-date traditions, laziness." He had been in England for only four weeks but that was long enough to make him certain that British "civilization" was "on its way out."[69] The paradoxes of American culture were never more evident than when African Americans praised American ideals, if only to contrast them with the reality of racial discrimination. Two black women with the Young Men's Christian Association were thrilled to be going to Europe as "crusaders on a quest for Democracy!" Their language was subversive, however. They noted that black men liked to guard German prisoners because it was a "refreshing . . . change . . . from a country where it seemed everybody's business to guard them." Though the war did not completely remove "the shackles" from the body of the black man who went to Europe, it had "in some measure removed the fetters from his soul."[70]

Members of the triumphant if battered Rainbow Division occupied the Rhineland for several months after the Armistice, returning to the United States in April 1919. Before leaving Europe, they voted to forgo pomp and pageantry in order to fulfill "their desire to promptly return to their homes." They need not have worried. No crowds greeted their ship when it arrived in New York City. "One little urchin asked us who we were," MacArthur reported to a friend, "and when we said—we are the famous Forty-second—he asked if we had been to France. Amid a silence that hurt . . . we marched off the dock, to be scattered to the four winds—a sad, gloomy end of the Rainbow."[71]

"They Must Settle It for Themselves."

Woodrow Wilson and many others throughout the Atlantic world persisted in their hope that "peace without victory" would mean a new era of social justice and democracy. The Great War, according to Felix Adler, the Jewish intellectual and founder of the Ethical Culture movement, "had been a war of liberation" and "the effects of it must be the liberation of the disadvantaged people of the world."[72] The most visible manifestation in the United States was the ratification in 1920 of the Nineteenth Amendment to the Constitution, by which women acquired the right to vote. While the amendment was largely a tribute to the tireless efforts of such women as Susan B. Anthony, Alice Paul, and Carrie Chapman Catt, it was the manifest contributions of ordinary women to the war effort and their commitment to patriotic principles that carried the day in Congress and state legislatures. The Great War served as a catalyst for a more inclusive definition of citizenship, as had the American Revolution and the Civil War.

While Wilson, like Lincoln, had done more than his share to suppress dissent during wartime, he hoped that his administration would do for people throughout Europe what Lincoln's had done for enslaved African Americans. Thus he embarked on a policy of international reconstruction aimed at ensuring political democracy, social justice, and economic opportunity in the postwar era. Not a moment was to be lost in demonstrating that American power would make the world a safer place. The signature of Wilson's policy was the fourteen points he outlined in a speech in January 1918 to Congress; they included commitments to free trade, free seas, self-determination, arms reduction, and the creation of "a general association of nations . . . under specific covenants for the purpose of affording mutual guarantees of political independence and territorial integrity to great and small states alike."[73]

Wilson's mission was complicated by the emergence of a new revolutionary and imperial rival. The Soviet Union put the United States on the ideological defensive for the first time in its history. The expensive and ineffective Russian participation in the Great War had undermined the already fragile power of Tsar Nicholas II. In March 1917, when the army refused to support the tsar against his increasingly militant critics, Nicholas abdicated in favor of a liberal government modeled on European democracies. That regime lasted barely half a year before it collapsed. In November, V. I. Lenin led the Bolsheviks to control of Russia in "ten days that shook the world."

Now in putative control of a huge nation, the Bolsheviks saw themselves as leaders of a global movement to liberate people everywhere from bonds forged in the American and French Revolutions of the late eighteenth century and fastened on the limbs of workers in particular during the Industrial Revolution of the nineteenth.[74] Lenin defined imperialism as "the monopoly stage of capitalism" and "a colonial policy of monopolistic possessions of the territory of the world which has been completely divided up.[75]

The Bolshevik government made a separate peace with the Central Powers but was unable to prevent Japan from seizing Vladivostok in an apparent prelude to an annexation of Russia's Pacific northeast. In the midst of the general upheaval, the United States joined Great Britain and France in dispatching troops to Murmansk and Archangel in the west and a somewhat larger independent force to Vladivostok. As American interventions went, it was a small commitment, amounting to only about three reinforced regiments, with no clear aim beyond encouraging resistance "through propaganda campaigns, moral encouragement of patriotic Russians, financial support for anti-Bolshevik groups, limited military expeditions to Russian ports, weapons shipments to White armies, and 'humanitarian' assistance to forces fighting against the Red Army." In effect, Wilson was pioneering the use of "indirect and covert forms of intervention." "[A]ny people is entitled to any kind of government it damn pleases," Wilson told the Democratic National Committee in February 1919. "It is none of our business to suggest or influence the kind that it is going to have." Nevertheless, national security, ideology, and morality demanded that he support democracy (or at least anticommunism) against the "intolerable tyranny" of the Bolshevik regime.[76]

Though few Americans became Communists, more than a few American radicals thrilled at the dynamism and possibilities inherent in the Bolshevik Revolution. The "soul" of Russia's "real people," said Eugene Debs, "throbs with international solidarity and appeals with infinite compassion to the spirit of worldwide brotherhood." According to members of the Amalgamated Clothing Workers of America and the International Ladies Garment Workers Union, "the fate of the first great working class republic in the world cannot but be matter of prime concern to organized and progressive workers of all countries."[77]

Whether as supporters or critics, Americans paid close attention to Russia because it seemed to exemplify a new revolutionary spirit detached from their own largely liberal, middle-class tradition; indeed, it seemed rooted in an attack on middle-class capitalism and democracy as enslaving rather than liberating forces. Tensions ran high in the United States because the revolution in Russia implied that a communist revolution might be possible anywhere; and that, depending on one's perspective, might herald either the millennium or Armageddon. Overwhelmed by returning servicemen competing for jobs, buffeted by inflation, and shocked by the growing number of black faces appearing in the cities of the Northeast and Midwest, Americans took to the streets. Over 4 million workers participated in some 3,600 strikes in 1919, including major ones in the steel and coal industries and in the cities of Seattle and Boston. Though the strikers were concerned with immediate economic issues, the public debates over their behavior raised familiar questions about coercion and choice, liberty and power.

In Cleveland, Socialists celebrated May Day 1919 with a large parade; they carried red flags, demanded freedom for Eugene Debs and assistance for people without jobs, and rallied their red-ribboned supporters along the way. Mockery and denunciations followed them and eventually turned into full-scale assaults. Veterans were prominent among the members of the crowds that attacked the Socialists and their headquarters. Only the deployment of army tanks restored order to Cleveland. In the aftermath of the melee, Socialists were forbidden to hold public meetings or carry red flags, and the city ordered more tanks.[78]

Worried about the consequences of revolutionary radicalism at home and abroad, white middle-class Protestants and businessmen winked at mobs that attacked radicals and African Americans. They supported government intervention to stamp out the "red menace," fulfilling Jane Addams's fear that war would strengthen nationalism and repression rather than enhance internationalism and freedom. The Red Scare preoccupied Americans in 1919 and 1920. Attorney General A. Mitchell Palmer justified his department's arrests of thousands of suspected radicals as a defense of a way of life against "seditious societies" and "the blaze of revolution." Communists were not a political party, Palmer maintained, but an international criminal ring whose goals were "to overthrow the decencies of private life, to usurp property that they have not earned, to disrupt the present order of life regardless of health, sex or religious rights."[79]

A great war and its outcome, once again, forced Americans to confront the boundaries of power and liberty, without as well as within the United States. The American intervention in Russia, limited as it was, provoked considerable controversy because it exposed the tensions embedded in military interventions undertaken in the name of liberation. Did the United States intend to use its power all over the world, whether that power was welcome or not?

How much would Americans have to pay in lives lost and treasure spent to free the oppressed if, as in the Philippines and Mexico, the beneficiaries of liberation rejected America's well-intentioned efforts? The Treaty of Versailles, negotiated between January and June 1919, focused the larger issue of postwar international reconstruction. Beyond punishing Germany and calling for self-determination, the treaty contained in its first section the Covenant of a League of Nations, which would "promote international co-operation" and "international peace and security" by avoiding war, encouraging fair dealing among nations, and respecting international law.

Critics, of whom there were multitudes, stubbornly resisted the idea that the United States was now a leading member of a larger world community with economic and strategic interests that could not be divorced from global considerations. They were also genuinely committed to self-determination. Senator William E. Borah of Idaho wanted no part of the League of Nations or intervention in Russia. If "there is anything that is settled beyond peradventure in the American mind it is that every people have a right to set up their own form of government and to establish their own system and method of living. If they see fit to have a soviet government, it is their business. They must settle it for themselves." The fact "[t]hat we do not like the government of a country," exclaimed Senator Robert La Follette of Wisconsin, "is no reason for making war upon it." Senator Hiram Johnson of California was more succinct: "We're getting too terribly militaristic."[80] The popularity of these notions, as well as the collapse of Woodrow Wilson's health following a stroke in the fall of 1919, curtailed the Russian intervention. The United States withdrew its last troops from Russia in the spring of 1920, having lost several hundred men. In the meantime, prodded by the "irreconcilables" Borah, La Follette, and Johnson, the Senate had refused to ratify the Treaty of Versailles because it included the Covenant of the League of Nations.[81]

In essence, Americans entered the third decade of the twentieth century with an addendum to their nineteenth-century Revolutionary Settlement: the United States government would stay out of the affairs of other nations and it would use force only when absolutely necessary to protect liberty from tyranny. "America's present need is not heroics, but healing," proclaimed the Republican presidential candidate Warren G. Harding in May 1920, "not nostrums, but normalcy; not revolution, but restoration; not agitation, but adjustment; not surgery, but serenity; not the dramatic, but the dispassionate; not experiment, but equipoise; not submergence in internationality, but sustainment in triumphant nationality. It is one thing to battle successfully against world domination by military autocracy . . . but it is quite another thing to revise human nature."[82]

Elected in November 1920, Harding oversaw the reduction of the army and navy to fewer than 250,000 men and called the Washington Conference of 1921–22, at which the United States, Japan, Great Britain, France, and Italy agreed to limit the size of their navies. Six years later, Republican president Calvin Coolidge's secretary of state, Frank B. Kellogg, helped French foreign minister Aristide Briand work out a treaty, eventually signed by over sixty nations, promising never to resort to war.[83] Coolidge's successor, Republican Herbert Hoover, was a Quaker and pacifist whose unstinting organization of efforts to feed starving people after World War I gained him the gratitude—and vote—of Jane Addams.

In the 1920s, many white Protestant Americans focused on creating a prosperous life at home. They wanted to protect and preserve the status quo, to emphasize what worked in North America rather than to undertake the liberation and reform of diverse and often ungrateful peoples throughout the globe. Many sought to draw sharp cultural boundaries by means of a federally mandated Prohibition, and some participated in a revival of the Ku Klux Klan, whose targets were often Catholics and Jews as well as African Americans. In 1924, Congress reversed more than a century of immigration policy by passing the National Origins Act. Quotas were established for European and Asian immigrants; no more than 2 percent of the population of any national group counted in the 1890 census (a year chosen because it preceded the heavy influx of southern and eastern European immigrants) could enter the United States in a given year. University and school curricula now emphasized American history, Western civilization, and civics. Patriotism furnished a public identity that trumped personal identities rooted in religion, ethnicity, or gender. In the Midwest, where diverse cultural commemorations—parades, festivals, names, and clothes—had testified to a robust ethnic consciousness before the World War, national consumer-driven models of generic Americanism became the norm. Cities that had once stressed the multicultural dimensions of their populations now promoted racial and ethnic homogeneity.[84]

Former Progressives were disappointed by the return to politics as usual. Not necessarily devotees of Wilson, they nonetheless saw the Great War and its immediate aftermath as an opportunity lost. Senators criticized Wilson, the California newspaper editor Chester Rowell observed, because he had "failed to live down to . . . purely selfish nationalism," not because he had "failed to live up to his ostensible idealism." Ray Stannard Baker was more fatalistic. "The fundamental difficulty, after all, is that only a very small minority of people in the world—small also in America—*really* believe in the principles laid down in the Fourteen Points."[85]

It was evident to nearly everyone that the Great War had demonstrated the awesome power that a modern nation-state could bring to bear against its enemies and indeed its own citizens. Machine guns, poison gas, and airplanes exemplified the technological development that allowed governments to express the will of those who controlled them with devastating efficiency. War could result in liberation, as in the creation of the United States or the abolition of slavery, but it could as easily produce tyranny and unparalleled destruction. Power flowing from the same entity and with the same impulse could liberate Europe and subjugate the Philippines; power could defend human rights or destroy human beings. No matter how well-intentioned the motivation, the concentrated use of state power in warfare inevitably led to unexpected outcomes, new challenges, and a world transformed in ways unforeseeable when war began. Once unleashed, war seemed to become a force unto itself, a tempest that drove people and nations in directions they would never have wished, or imagined.

In October 1921, the remains of an unidentifiable American soldier who had fallen on the Western Front were carried on board the USS *Olympia,* Admiral George Dewey's flagship at Manila Bay in 1898. Transported with great dignity to Washington, the Unknown Soldier lay in state in the rotunda of the Capitol, where the leaders of all branches of government, the diplomatic corps, and over 90,000 citizens came to pay their respects. On Armistice Day, November 11, the casket was loaded on a caisson to be borne to Arlington National Cemetery, escorted by a military honor guard, the president and cabinet, members of Congress, the justices of the Supreme Court, representatives of the services, diplomats, governors, the Daughters of the American Revolution, the Knights of Columbus, the National Catholic War Council, the Jewish Veterans of the World War, the Red Cross, and a delegation of African-American citizens. President Harding spoke, then awarded the Unknown the Congressional Medal of Honor and the Distinguished Service Cross; diplomats from other nations followed suit with the Victoria Cross, the Croix de Guerre, and a host of comparable honors. The solemn celebration of generic patriotism was above all a tribute to the importance of peace, "the central theme of the ceremonies." Over the next few years, some Americans mourned the Unknown Soldier as a martyr in the cause of world peace, a lost soul for whom "militarism [was] his continued crucifixion."[86]

Among the dignitaries in the crowd on November 11 was former president Woodrow Wilson, making one of the last public appearances of his life. Wilson rode out in his carriage and briefly joined the procession as it moved slowly down the Mall, across the Potomac, and up the steep Arlington bluff to the Tomb of the Unknowns. He did not speak at the ceremony, merely acknowledging Harding and returning home. A lonely and bitter invalid convinced that his dream of a global democratic transformation led by the United States had become a nightmare of nationalism, isolationism, and indifference, he died a little over two years later, on February 3, 1924.

Douglas MacArthur did not share Wilson's disillusionment. He deeply believed it the duty of the United States to bear witness to the values of democracy and Christianity before the world. To MacArthur the Unknown Soldier was no martyr in the cause of peace, no victim of militarism, but the exemplar of the American fighting man as a heroic type. He made his position clear in an address to the annual reunion of the Rainbow Division veterans in 1935, "The Spirit of the Unknown Soldier." The American fighting man, said MacArthur, "needs no eulogy from me or from any other man; he has written his own history, and written it in red on his enemy's breast." He belonged to "posterity as the instructor of future generations in the principles of liberty and right." Now Americans, citizens of "a pre-eminently Christian and conservative nation," "far less militaristic than most," "not especially open to the charge of imperialism," must keep faith with the Unknown and his fallen comrades. To do so, Americans had to overcome the emotional and seductive appeals of pacifism, with its rejection of war as an unmitigated evil. If they did not, MacArthur warned, the United States would suffer the fate of all great empires. "Once each was strong and militant. Each rose by military prowess. Each fell through degeneracy of military capacity because of unpreparedness. The battlefield was the bed upon which they were born into this world, and the battlefield became the couch upon which their worn-out bodies finally expired. Let us be prepared, lest we, too, perish."[87]

The veneration of heroic sacrifice, the affirmation of war as a glorious and necessary endeavor, the belief that the United States had a special destiny in the history of the world: these were MacArthur's faith, his shield, his inheritance. He was fifty-five years old when he gave his address, had served in the army for more than three decades and had been its chief of staff for the previous five years. Yet with no higher rank left to attain and at an age at which most modern general officers retire, MacArthur devoted most of the remainder of his life to defending the United States and its ideals of liberty against adversaries who he believed were gathering strength in Europe, Asia, and at home. The challenges to America and its mission, as he understood them, were grave; the confrontation toward which they were building, however, was one that he welcomed as an opportunity to prove himself worthy of his father's example and to fulfill the destiny that he was convinced awaited him.

CHAPTER NINE

MacArthur's Valedictory:
Lessons Learned, Lessons Forgotten

Like many of the great captains he strove to emulate, Douglas MacArthur loved to read history. Starting with books collected by his father, he had amassed a personal library of 7,000 to 8,000 volumes by the late 1930s. He was particularly keen on the lives of military officers. His second wife, Jean Faircloth, fed this appetite with Christmas presents that included biographies of such notable generals as Robert E. Lee, Thomas Jonathan "Stonewall" Jackson, and Nathan Bedford Forrest. MacArthur read avidly, sometimes consuming three books in a day.[1] He laced his public speeches with historical references and used them in conversation with a frequency that intimidated visitors and acquaintances alike. Late in life, MacArthur wrote his own history in the form of autobiography. In recording his "participation in our great struggles for national existence, human liberty, and political equality," he confessed (in a line that must have evoked a smile from readers who knew him) that his "greatest difficulty" lay in "recounting my share in the many vital events involved without giving my acts an unwarranted prominence."[2]

In character and implications, MacArthur's *Reminiscences* differed sharply from Grant's *Memoirs*. Grant's narrative gathered power from the forward movement of simple, direct statements; MacArthur constructed his as a leisurely and orotund scrapbook of personal memories, supported by excerpts from letters and speeches. Readers have judged Grant equally brilliant as memoirist and general because he reported with such clarity the decisions he made and the actions he took and then assessed with such candor the consequences of those acts, for his men, his mission, and himself. By contrast, MacArthur never passed up an opportunity to instruct the reader on the importance of the things he had accomplished, unless he could quote other authorities to the same effect. Above all, Grant conveyed the drama and tragedy of the Civil War while doing justice to the ambiguities of its origins and outcomes. MacArthur, on the other hand, concentrated on conveying the excitement and nobility of wars about which he felt no ambivalence at all: wars fought in the defense of freedom, democracy, and Christianity, conducted by officers whose devotion to duty, honor, and country offered a motive sufficient to justify the sacrifice of their own lives, and the lives of the soldiers they led.

MacArthur's fascination with history was a transparent effort to locate himself within a tradition of military glory. But it was more than that. He was also driven to situate the modern United States in a larger narrative conceived around what he believed to be the necessary relationship between war and freedom. It was an essentially conservative impulse, for it was predicated on the assumption that the mission of twentieth-century Americans was to preserve and extend values established in the eighteenth and nineteenth centuries. Denying the radicalism of the American Revolution and the Civil War as well as the imperialism of the Seven Years' War and the Mexican War, MacArthur and others championed a passive-voice history that stressed consensus and continuity. American wars were always just wars: they occurred only when citizens had to defend themselves against those who, out of lust for power or devotion to ideology or even a simple affinity for evil, sought to enslave them.

Looking "back through the history of English-speaking peoples," MacArthur found that "in every instance . . . the most sacred principles of free government have been acquired, protected, and perpetuated through the embodied, armed strength of the peoples concerned." In the twilight of his life, he held up the United States as a beacon of freedom against the tyranny of communism. He railed against the growing size of the federal government, particularly its power to tax. For MacArthur, the Cold War was a continuation of a long struggle to uphold the idea that "free men can successfully manage their own affairs" against a "reckless faith in political power" that had animated empires from "ancient Babylon, ancient Greece and ancient Rome" to the fascist and communist regimes of the twentieth century.[3]

Douglas MacArthur conjoined autobiography and national history in an almost touching effort to wrestle his own demons into submission. Emulating his image of his father, he took up the banner of Christianity and American democracy and carried it all over the world, living to bring the story of the United States to a fitting climax. In trying to embody the triumphant spirit of the Republic, however, he also embodied its tragedy. Understanding American wars as variations of the charge up Missionary Ridge by free men who had chosen to risk their lives in freedom's cause, Douglas MacArthur never comprehended how or why other people could have notions about the meanings of freedom that differed from his own. The irony of MacArthur's life, as well as of his *Reminiscences,* was that for all the keenness of his mind and the greatness of his military accomplishments, he never understood that liberty and the United States—and indeed the United States and Douglas MacArthur—were not necessarily one and the same.

"The Air Was Charged with Renewed Vitality"

Americans in the 1920s found common ground in a culture of consumption. Following the advice of newspaper and magazine advertisements, billboards, brochures, and radio commercials, they bought automobiles and appliances by the million and attended motion pictures and theatrical shows in droves. They also indulged a seemingly insatiable appetite for celebrity. Learning about well-known human beings—or, more accurately, learning about popular images of them—became a major pastime. Prominent men had of course fascinated Americans since the days of George Washington, but the proliferation of cheap daily newspapers in the nineteenth century had altered the terms of fascination by creating torrents of gossip about infamous figures and news about upstanding ones. Scandals involving sex or money proved to be immensely popular, especially when they revealed the foibles of the great. The huge upsurge in celebrity journalism during the 1920s, therefore, reflected less an intensification of demand than an increase in supply. The burgeoning media offered reams of information about people celebrated (often temporarily) for their looks, their personalities, or their participation in notable events. Whether the acts of the celebrities in question were commendable or reprehensible mattered a good deal less than the fact that stories about celebrities sold newspapers and magazines.

This new world of constructed appearances nurtured an insatiable hunger for public figures who combined an appealing, modest, and preferably mysterious charm with remarkable accomplishments that they had achieved, at least in the telling, by dint of determination and sheer grit. The most popular combined mastery of twentieth-century technology with attributes of nineteenth-century character. The quintessential figure was the Lone Eagle, Charles A. Lindbergh, whose flight in 1927 from Long Island to Paris in the *Spirit of St. Louis* captured the attention and admiration of the world. But there were others, too: war heroes like Eddie Rickenbacker and Alvin York, movie stars like Rudolph Valentino and Douglas Fairbanks, sports heroes like Babe Ruth and Jack Dempsey.[4]

Only a few of the celebrities who emerged in the 1920s held the public imagination for as long as Douglas MacArthur. A dashing figure in an army dominated by older men, he was even more flamboyant in demeanor and dress than he had been in France. The journalist William Allen White said MacArthur had "the grace and charm of a stage hero." He was a "vivid," "captivating," and "magnetic" man, "all that [the actors John] Barrymore and John Drew hoped to be. And how he could talk!" The artist Joseph C. Case noted his "quick . . . movements, physical and mental" and his "changing moods"—how he "knits his brow or laughs heartily with equal facility, and often during the same sentence." When MacArthur married the wealthy divorcée Louise Cromwell Brooks in 1922—a woman whose military tastes had led her into a previous affair with General John J. Pershing— a newspaper reported it under the headline "MARS MARRIES MILLIONS."[5]

Like many celebrity marriages, this one ended in divorce when husband and wife grew bored with each other and—more important—when Louise refused to accept a subordinate role in the story of Douglas MacArthur. He liked strong women well enough but not independent ones: he needed a wife willing to emulate Pinky and devote herself to his career, his fame. For MacArthur unashamedly imagined himself as the model American, the strong right arm of a benevolent empire whose mission was to liberate the rest of the world from tyranny and superstition. General Enoch Chamberlain reportedly remarked that "Arthur MacArthur was the most flamboyantly egotistic man I had ever seen, until I met his son."[6]

MacArthur's relentless ambition and love of attention set him apart from most of his contemporaries in the officer corps. The leaders of "the brown shoe army" were generally conservative men who quietly acquiesced in budget cuts and tried to keep low profiles until they arrived safe in the haven of retirement. Younger officers endured low pay, slow promotion, boredom, obscurity, and stagnation. More than a few devoted themselves to alcohol, cards, and sports. Some left for more promising opportunities in business. What man of real ambition, after all, would want to invest time and energy in an army George C. Marshall later joked would barely fill Yan-

kee Stadium, an army not much larger than the one Germany was allowed
to keep by the Treaty of Versailles?[7]

A group of bright young West Point graduates nonetheless chose to remain in the army, despite their frustrations. Indeed, they did more; they made
it their mission to reform it. Dwight D. Eisenhower, George S. Patton, and
Omar Bradley, among others, assumed the inevitability of another major war
and committed themselves to building an army that could fight it effectively.
The lessons of the Great War weighed heavily in their thinking. In company
with a pair of older officers who had not attended West Point, Brigadier General William "Billy" Mitchell and Colonel George C. Marshall, they advocated rearming with modern weapons, including tanks and airplanes, in the
hope of making the ghastly trench warfare they witnessed in France obsolete.
They also understood that although modern officers still had to possess the
traditional characteristics of probity, courage, decisiveness, and calmness under pressure, they now required skills more nearly akin to those of executives
in large corporations, men who could efficiently direct complex organizations
and manage huge numbers of men, machines, and supplies.

Although MacArthur was in many ways sympathetic to the goals of
these reform-minded officers, he was too senior in rank and too eager for
future promotion to make common cause with them. Even more significant, perhaps, was a brush with reform that made him wary. In 1919, the
army's rigorous, effective chief of staff, General Peyton March, appointed
the thirty-nine-year-old Brigadier General MacArthur as superintendent of
the U.S. Military Academy at West Point. MacArthur set out to update the
training of cadets. He attacked the brutal system of hazing, devised an honor
code, emphasized sports, replaced the study of the Civil War with an examination of the Great War, and broadened an engineering curriculum that had
been essentially unchanged for a century by creating a history department
and instituting instruction in government and economics. He began to send
cadets to Fort Dix, New Jersey, every summer to participate in training with
active-duty units. He insisted on the value of intramural athletic competition in bringing out "the qualities of leadership, quickness of decision,
promptness of action, mental and muscular coordination, aggressiveness,
and courage." "Improvisation will be the watchword" in modern wars, and
officers needed both "an intimate understanding of the mechanics of human feelings, [and] a comprehensive grasp of world and national affairs."
Their education must respond to those demands.[8]

West Point's faculty deeply resented these efforts at reform. Many

disliked MacArthur personally, but it would also be fair to say that the vigorous young superintendent never really warmed to them, either. Living
with his mother on the grounds of the academy, MacArthur was reserved at
best and struck more than a few as arrogant. Few, however, doubted his
earnestness or his industry. One cadet remembered that with MacArthur's
arrival "the air was charged with renewed vitality." Another claimed that the
superintendent was "the only man in the world who could walk into a room
full of drunks and all would be stone sober within five minutes."[9] Still, senior officers in Washington, including March's successor as chief of staff,
General of the Army John Pershing, were not pleased. Pershing replaced
MacArthur in 1922 with Brigadier General Fred W. Sladen, who set out to
return West Point to what it had been in 1919. Coolly characterizing
MacArthur's tenure as superintendent as "above average," Pershing observed that MacArthur had "an exalted opinion of himself."[10]

Dispatched from the academy to virtual exile in the Philippines, where
he supervised a few hundred men in Manila, MacArthur took several years
to rebound professionally from the West Point experience. Pinky continued
to campaign on her son's behalf with oleaginous letters to the chief of staff,
whose reactions can best be left to the imagination. "Won't you be real good
and sweet—The 'Dear Old Jack' of long ago," she wrote to Pershing, "and
give me some assurance that you will give my Boy his well earned promotion before you leave the Army?"[11] Her "Boy" finally became the youngest
major general in the service, but not until January 1925, four months after
Pershing retired.

While two stars were better than one, they were by no means enough to
satisfy the ambitions of the insatiable MacArthurs. Neither mother nor son
could persuade the army decoration board to grant him a Distinguished Service Medal for his freelance reconnaissance at Veracruz. MacArthur's patience
for those who snubbed him remained low. Given command of the Fourth
Corps in Atlanta in May 1925, he demanded a new assignment almost immediately because of an incident at an Episcopal church. When the general and
his staff attended Sunday services, more than half of the congregation walked
out rather than worship with the son of a Yankee invader.[12] The army accom-
modated MacArthur's request. He was entrusted with the Third Corps in
Baltimore, a more ecclesiastically hospitable post where he could expect to be
treated with the respect he believed he and his uniform deserved.

However little his temperament may have altered, MacArthur had nevertheless learned important lessons from his West Point tenure. He was cautious when necessary, as his conduct in the celebrated court-martial of

General Billy Mitchell demonstrated between late October and mid-December 1925. Mitchell, an outspoken advocate of air power who vigorously promoted an independent air force over the objections of the army and navy leadership, had called senior military officers criminally negligent for refusing to replace dangerously obsolescent aircraft with safer, more modern machines. The court-martial that tried Mitchell for insubordination was second in publicity only to the Scopes Monkey trial of the previous summer; after seven weeks the judges found Mitchell guilty of conduct prejudicial to good discipline and suspended him from the service for five years. He resigned from the army six weeks later. MacArthur, a judge on the court-martial panel, kept uncharacteristically quiet during the proceedings. He later claimed to have voted to find Mitchell not guilty. At the time, his silence seemed to mark a politic recognition that Mitchell was doomed anyway and that there was no point in damaging his own career by seeming to favor acquittal.

MacArthur's post–West Point sojourn in the Philippines had given him other lessons to ponder following his rehabilitation in the mid-1920s. Specifically, what MacArthur had come to understand was the importance of cultivating important Filipinos; even if they were only colonial subjects, they could still be remarkably useful. As a rule MacArthur liked members of the Philippine elite, and liked the way they deferred to him as a powerful patron. When he returned to the islands in 1928, to assume command of the U.S. Army there, he made a special point of renewing his friendship with Senator Manuel Luis Quezon y Molina. Born in 1878, Quezon was a *mestizo* who had fought as a nationalist in the insurrection of 1899–1902. He emerged from six months in jail to become a lawyer and a favorite of American officials. Quezon served as a territorial delegate in the House of Representatives from 1909 to 1916 then became an important member of the newly created Philippine National Assembly, where he was a strong proponent of home rule. In 1935, when the Philippines were made a commonwealth of the United States, he defeated Emiliano Aguinaldo to become president.

Quezon invoked the values of democracy, but he understood his loyalty to the United States in traditional terms, more specifically, in terms of his personal connection to Douglas MacArthur.[13] MacArthur developed another Philippine attachment at this same time, in the form of a mistress, Isabel Rosario Cooper. "Dimples," as she was known, was more than twenty years his junior and was the daughter of a Scottish businessman and a Chinese *mestizo*. She was a movie actress, so the liaison therefore contributed not only to the general's connection to Filipino high society but to his no-toriety. The couple's affection for each other was genuine; he brought her back with him to the United States, installed her in a Washington hotel (he was still sharing a house with his mother), visited her when he could, and wrote her frequent florid love letters.

MacArthur returned to the United States in 1930 when President Her-bert Hoover summoned him to assume the position that had eluded Arthur MacArthur, chief of staff of the army. It was a moment of fulfillment for the general and perhaps even more so for Pinky. At fifty, her son was the youngest man ever to occupy the post, and his appointment vindicated her hope that he would force "the proud world" to do her homage as the mother of a great man. MacArthur's tenure, which lasted until 1935, was controversial. One of his greatest assets was his ability to identify talented officers and put them to work on ambitious tasks, giving them free rein to do so. Able majors and lieutenant colonels found the chief of staff a rewarding officer to serve *under,* but no one ever mistook him for a pleasant general to serve *with.* He was prickly, aloof even in dealing with his closest aides, and always insisted on seeing himself as the leading man in the unfolding drama of his destiny. Yet he recognized ability where he found it and consistently rewarded loyalty with loyalty. As long as men did their jobs well, MacArthur left them alone. Prominent among his protégés was Major Dwight D. Eisenhower, a West Point graduate (class of 1915) who had distinguished himself in various as-signments. Appointed as an assistant to the secretary of war in 1929, Eisen-hower soon caught MacArthur's eye, and found himself drafting major speeches and annual reports for the general as early as 1931. He became MacArthur's aide in February 1933. It is unclear that he would have regarded an even closer relationship with much pleasure; from the time he began working on MacArthur's speeches through 1934, he was so busy that he took no more than six days' leave.

Eisenhower was indefatigable, but more than his industry made him in-dispensable to the chief of staff. He was an effective advocate of moderniza-tion who disdained President Herbert Hoover's Quakerish reluctance to intervene militarily in a troubled world. He was also disturbed by the even greater financial restrictions on the military made necessary by the Great Depression. The 1932 annual report of the War Department, which Eisen-hower wrote, warned that the 125,000-man army, the sixteenth-largest in the world, was inadequate and inefficient. Eisenhower called attention to the need for motorized vehicles, including tanks. Future conflicts should not be reprises of the deadly massed infantry assaults of the Great War. The army needed to "mechanize" to be able to "move swiftly" and "concentrate . . . at critical points." Tanks would allow it to "strike with the maximum power of fire and shock" and "exploit rapidly and fearlessly" all the advantages of the offensive. Eisenhower recommended that American industry produce tanks and airplanes while the military worked out ways to coordinate responses to future threats.[14]

Politicians overwhelmed by the impact of the Great Depression ignored the major's pleas, but MacArthur, Eisenhower, and other officers did not cease to nurture a vision of the Republic's global mission. Well-intentioned people might dream of peace, might even plan for peace, but sooner or later Americans would find themselves embroiled in conflict, and then they would need an effective military to defend them and preserve their liberty. MacArthur could claim to have foreseen it all. "With the Red menace in Russia, Poland in disorder, Rumania threatened with secession, France fighting in Morocco, Nicaragua in revolution, Mexico in confusion, and civil war raging in China," he predicted in 1927, "it does not seem unlikely that our streets will again be filled with marching men and our country again have need of our services."[15]

The Depression intensified fears of domestic unrest, even social revolution in the United States. MacAthur knew it was his duty to resist radicalism, and in the summer of 1932, he ordered 800 soldiers to use bayonets, tear gas, horses, and tanks to disperse 2,000 or so members of the Bonus Army, impoverished veterans of the Great War who marched on Washington to demand early payment of compensation that Congress had agreed to in 1924 but deferred until 1945. MacArthur denounced the veterans as criminals. To "defy existing law [was] to recognize a state of anarchy and the collapse of properly constituted authority." Governments and armies—and organized religion—existed because imperfect human beings needed to be controlled. If the United States stood firm against subversives and those they seduced, MacArthur was confident "that a red-blooded and virile humanity which loves peace devotedly, but is willing to die in the defense of the right, is Christian from center to circumference, . . . will continue to be dominant in the future as in the past."[16] American rhetoric about universal liberty had become a defense of national power and the status quo.

The lack of financial support for the military in the midst of the Great Depression outraged MacArthur, who conflated his reputation with those of the army and the nation. In a heated discussion with Hoover's successor, Franklin Delano Roosevelt, over his plan to cut the army budget, MacArthur "spoke recklessly . . . to the general effect that when we lost the next war, and an American boy, lying in the mud with an enemy bayonet through his belly and an enemy foot on his dying throat spat out his last curse, [he] wanted the name not to be MacArthur but Roosevelt." The president angrily reminded the general to address his commander in chief with respect. MacArthur apologized and resigned, but Roosevelt declined to accept his resignation.[17] Both the substance and style of the general endeared him to Republican opponents of the New Deal; they saw him as staunchly committed to traditional American values. Roosevelt clearly had his doubts about MacArthur, whose tendency to disdain civilian supremacy over the armed forces led the president to privately call him one of the most dangerous men in America, yet in the end the two worked well enough—if warily—together during the last half of his tenure as chief of staff.

The Depression was above all a time of adjustment to new limits for MacArthur and his fellow officers. The Hoover and Roosevelt administrations, perilously short of money, continued to face the perennial problem of political stability in the Western Hemisphere. The older pattern of frequent interventions and prolonged occupations to enforce American hegemony was prohibitively expensive and did nothing to endear the United States to the republics of Latin America. Roosevelt formally announced a new approach to hemispheric relations, the Good Neighbor policy, in his inaugural address of 1933, and the United States officially renounced armed intervention at the Montevideo Conference later that year. The new policy was actually older than its name and marked a shift in, rather than an abandonment of, a model of American engagement with the nations to its south that was undertaken by the Hoover administration.

The United States had intervened in Nicaragua in 1927 during the Coolidge administration to support a conservative leader threatened by a radical insurrection led by General Augustino Sandino. Hoover's State Department took a step back from the (Theodore) Roosevelt Corollary in 1928 by issuing a memorandum that specified that the United States would henceforth construe the Monroe Doctrine as applying to European, not Latin American, nations. Thereafter the Marines in Nicaragua continued to conduct operations when they had to but concentrated on training Nicaraguan National Guardsmen to the point that they, not the Marines, would be able to stabilize the country on a footing acceptable to the United States. As a result, in 1933 the lame-duck Hoover administration felt sufficiently secure to entrust power to the commander of the National Guard, General Anastasio Somoza, a longtime friend of the United States who had lived in Philadelphia, preferred English to Spanish, and loved baseball. In 1934, Somoza ordered the assassination of Sandino, who had become a folk hero for resisting American occupation. An eight-day civil war in 1936 ended with Somoza in control of Nicaragua. His family remained in power until 1979.

In the Pacific, the Philippines made the transition to commonwealth status in 1935 with the promise of complete independence a decade later. Congress approved this plan less out of idealism than as a result of exhaustion brought on by the expensive and contradictory imperial policy America had pursued since 1898. Isolationist Americans wanted to be rid of problems far from home. Affluent Filipinos were generally content with autonomy and the promise of independence, even if the bright, charismatic, self-important Quezon governed more like a patriarch than a democrat and ignored widespread economic problems that fueled social unrest.

Worried about Japan, which was lengthening its imperial reach with growing confidence throughout East Asia, Quezon sought the advice of his old friend, Douglas MacArthur. It was a propitious moment to do so. The fifty-five-year-old general was frustrated with tight budgets and New Deal politics and had become embroiled in what promised to be a deeply embarrassing scandal. The columnist Drew Pearson wrote about the general and Dimples as their affair decayed, and MacArthur sued Pearson for libel. Dimples, who had MacArthur's love letters to offer in evidence, let it be known that she was prepared to testify on Pearson's behalf if the case came to court. The general paid her $15,000 to return his love letters and dropped the suit. William Leahy, a friend who later became an admiral, noted that MacArthur was a fool. "All he had to do was look everybody in the face and say: 'So what?'"[18] But Douglas MacArthur preferred being a fool to looking like one. His story was more than the story of an ordinary individual, something Dimples had clearly forgotten.

Thus when President Quezon offered to make MacArthur his chief military adviser with an annual salary of $33,000 and a package of benefits that included a spacious air-conditioned penthouse apartment atop the Manila Hotel, the chief of staff seized the opportunity. Tolerant when it came to issues of race, MacArthur was someone to whom class and status were everything. In the Philippines, he could play the role of a benevolent patriarch with little competition and expect to be treated like a great man in return. With his octogenarian mother at his side, MacArthur made the move to Manila in the fall of 1935. Pinky died shortly after their arrival. He had her body heavily embalmed against the day her remains could be reinterred alongside her husband's in Arlington National Cemetery.

Pinky's death came as a heavy blow to the son from who she had rarely been parted, but it also opened a new chapter in his life. When he returned to the United States to bury her in 1937, he retired from the army and married the woman who took Pinky's place in his life, a thirty-seven-year-old Tennessean, Jean Marie Faircloth. He called her "Ma'am"; she called him "General" or (playfully) "Sir Boss." Their only child, a son, was born in February 1938. They named him Arthur.

Louise MacArthur had mocked her husband's vanity and refused to subordinate herself to her husband's career. Jean MacArthur made no such demands, accepting her place as a key supporting character in a narrative that was all about her general. Nineteen years younger than he, she readily accepted the role of household manager to the great man. The journalist John Gunther and his wife, who lunched with the MacArthurs many years later, thought her a perfect hostess. She made guests comfortable, took care to learn of their interests, and facilitated her husband's grand entrances. Not one to put on airs, Jean did little "to differentiate herself from other officers' wives." Her only perceptible challenge to her husband was mild and designed to serve his image: she helped give her "guests voice, in case they [were] too timid to talk, or in the event that the General's eloquence [was] in full majestic flow, by interrupting gently" and suggesting that someone else had something to say.[19]

Now fully retired from the U.S. army, MacArthur accepted the rank of field marshal from President Quezon and undertook the task of creating the Philippine Army. He and Jean and young Arthur lived like aristocrats. Their penthouse offered breathtaking views of Manila; his position put him in an equally commanding position at the center of the most important networks of power and status in the commonwealth. MacArthur was, moreover, happy in a job that seemed likely to cause him far less irritation than serving a chief executive who expected some degree of deference from his chief of staff. He planned to use the Philippine Constabulary—a national paramilitary police force that had been used to suppress guerrilla activities since 1901 and had been commanded by Filipino officers since 1917—as the nucleus of an 11,000-man force of regular soldiers. They would in turn direct the training of the Philippine Army, a militialike organization with a projected strength of 400,000. The task of the Philippine Army would be to cooperate with the comparatively small U.S. Army garrison in the islands in holding Japanese invaders at bay—for there was no other likely enemy—until the United States could come to the rescue with reinforcements. Major Eisenhower, who had dutifully accompanied MacArthur to the Philippines and stayed on his staff there until 1940, found the whole scheme dubious. But the field marshal was confident, and President Quezon insisted.

MacArthur saw the Philippine Defense System as an extension of the American tradition of citizen soldiers. In 1936 he celebrated the inculcation in the people of the Philippines of the "[t]hree controlling precepts in the American doctrine"—"personal liberty, religious freedom, and the maintenance of democratic institutions that insure to every citizen a voice in his own government"—that had transformed the archipelago into "an outpost of democratic civilization in the Far East." The defense system "reposes responsibility . . . not in a costly professional force that could conceivably be made the instrument of autocracy, but in the people themselves, the final repository of power in a democracy."[20] MacArthur, in short, asserted that the American mission in the Philippines, from the military origins in which his father had played so great a role to its ideological fulfillment under his own tutelage, had been a success.

"War, War, War, All You Boys Ever Talk About Is War"

Neither his accomplishments nor his elegant life in Manila fully satisfied Douglas MacArthur. Without an opportunity to bestride the world stage and assume the leading role be believed to be his destiny, his career would be nothing more than a footnote in the history of the U.S. Army. In that sense, MacArthur needed a war, and he also needed to find a convergence between his personal story and what he took to be the story of the United States as a whole. Most of all he wanted his fellow citizens to see America's role as he did, to understand the global struggles of the twentieth century as part of the great narrative of American freedom begun in the Revolutionary War. Then they, too, could embrace the part that they must play in the coming defense of freedom, even, perhaps, understand the significance of a man like Douglas MacArthur, whose life had been a long preparation to lead them in the struggle.

But Americans frustrated MacArthur. Safe (as they thought) inside the vast moat of the oceans, most of his fellow citizens cared little about the growth of militarism in Japan and fascism in Germany and Italy. What held their attention were the economic and social issues of the Great Depression and the New Deal. Most seemed to have lost their faith in the association between the United States with the self-sacrifice and idealism that had so long sustained its greatness. Few now seemed willing to lay down their lives in the defense of freedom; the personal price was too high. Ernest Hemingway's portrait of a physically and psychically maimed former soldier in *The Sun Also Rises* (1926), a man incapable of making the connections with others necessary for a full human life, was widely understood by contemporaries as a metaphor for the impact of modern wars on human beings and the specific effects of the Great War on a generation of disillusioned veterans. White middle-class Americans, the very ones who MacArthur saw as the backbone of the nation, seemed less committed to the old verities of patriotism than impatient with them, less willing to trust in Christian values than in stoicism and personal loyalty.

But his obsessive fear that cynicism and the desire to retreat from war would undermine the moral fortitude of the Republic blinded MacArthur to another dimension of American popular culture, one that coalesced in the 1930s into a kind of national script with a starring role tailor-made for a character like himself. While MacArthur viewed American life from across the Pacific, lamenting the decline of old certainties, entrepreneurs and artists in the United States, catering to the desires of consumers, were busy creating a new kind of public culture. They did it in the name of no higher ideals than amusement and profit.

Even in the Depression, ordinary citizens spent money on diversions that combined entertainment with edification. The perfect holiday often involved a relatively inexpensive family trip by car to a festival, pageant, or historical site. Both governments and businesses encouraged tourism with advertisements, brochures, and guidebooks. Less complicated and expensive but perhaps more important were regular trips to local theaters to see a movie. Thanks to a largely visual popular culture at both public sites and the movies, history was becoming personal and concrete. As a result, more Americans knew more about their collective past (or, more properly, *thought* they knew more about their past) than ever before. Where once most people had imagined American history with their own families or communities squarely in the foreground, now they could see where those familiar individual stories fit into a larger pattern.

As we have seen, nineteenth-century Americans had developed a narrative of the progress of the United States as the progress of human liberty. Though they contested its meanings, especially the extent to which liberty was limited to white men, the Civil War had affirmed the general idea, laid out most eloquently and succinctly by Abraham Lincoln at Gettysburg in November 1863, that the United States was a unique experiment in self-rule, political democracy, and equality before the law. Progressive school reformers, venerating Lincoln as a martyr in the cause of human freedom, sought to embed patriotism and Lincolnian ideas in civic education and history instruction, both during and after the Great War. At the same time, popular cynicism grew among those who went to war believing in its high purpose then came home to find that those who avoided service were leading lives of comfort and that war profiteers were luxuriating in fortunes built on the sufferings of millions of men like themselves.

In this context of disillusionment, a new mode of historical writing, critical of the patriotic myths that had structured so much of the received schoolbook narrative, emphasized the fallible and self-interested side of men who had always been seen as heroes. These "debunkers" offered a near inversion of the familiar story, stressing (for example) George Washington's land-speculating interests and Benjamin Franklin's infidelities instead of more familiar stories of their honesty, heroism, and dedication to the principles of liberty.

The debunkers were, for the most part, popularizers rather than professional historians, and they never made up more than a small minority of those who wrote on America's past; they enjoyed little respect among historians who considered themselves scholars. What the vogue of the debunkers signaled most clearly was a new diversity in possible tellings of the American story and hence the emergence of new possibilities for contestation. On the great majority of Americans, however, neither the cynicism of the debunkers nor the scientific empiricism and cultural relativism of academic historians had much effect. They embraced (with a dash of skepticism absent before the war) a general narrative of their history as a tale of the inexorable progress of liberty-loving European peoples blessed by a benevolent Christian god with the pursuit of the good life in America. It was a tale in which people of color, Indians, and people outside the expanding borders of the Republic had few or no roles. As broadly understood, it was a tale of episodic conflicts between freedom and slavery, North and South, broad constructionists versus defenders of states' rights, but at its heart it was a story that emphasized what Americans had in common. It was a tale that avoided questions of power by presenting the United States as a union of dispersed and democratic citizens. In this narrative, Americans acted boldly as individuals, whether they were pioneers, inventors, warriors, or reformers;

taken collectively, however, they were reactive. American citizens *made* history, but history *happened* to the United States.

Sesquicentennial celebrations of the American Revolution unleashed a tidal wave of memorials, pageants, and monuments. The congressionally appointed George Washington Bicentennial Commission marked the "father of the country's" two-hundredth birthday in 1932 with over 16,000 activities a day (for a total in excess of 4.7 million) and 3.5 million school programs. The purpose was to encourage "emotional loyalty" to the United States. Congressman Sol Bloom, who supervised the commemoration, announced that he wanted to "defend that flag, to honor that flag, and to preserve that flag as long as time shall be."[21] There was little interest in explaining the contingent path of Washington from British colonist to American citizen. Washington's choices, insofar as he was required by this narrative to make any, were straightforward and unproblematic. An American from the beginning, his identity as a British subject and soldier of empire in the Seven Years' War amounted to little more than prelude to the American Revolution. There was more than a little irony in these efforts. The creation of colonial Williamsburg in Virginia with the generous financial support of John D. Rockefeller celebrated the nation's founding fathers by scrupulously, if inaccurately, reconstructing an orderly, antiseptic version of an eighteenth-century British colonial capital inhabited almost exclusively by white gentry.[22]

In 1933 the Roosevelt administration consolidated all federally owned national parks, monuments, battlefields, cemeteries, and capital parks under the auspices of the National Park Service. In so doing, "the federal government intervened in the discussion over public memory in a very substantial way and created a national forum for the expression of interests on the subject."[23] The National Park Service sought to bring unity to the whole of the American past. Its official historian insisted that "key sites" illustrate a "pageant" and tell a "story." While the federal government did not control local and private efforts to remember the past, its "insistence on national significance and major themes forced individuals and localities into exaggerated attempts to distort their past, to make their own memories part of the national record, and, by implication, to discard or reconfigure whatever appeared inappropriate."[24] Citizen consumers visited sites, read plaques, and heard speeches that emphasized a bland history designed to inspire as many people as possible and offend none.

The Mall in Washington, D.C., became a mecca for secular pilgrims. In addition to touring marble public buildings, including the Capitol rotunda with its huge canvasses and murals representing major moments in American history, visitors saw the Declaration of Independence, the Constitution, and the Bill of Rights; viewed artifacts in the Smithsonian's Museum of American History; paid homage to a trinity of presidents associated with the expansion of liberty. Opened to the public in 1888, the Washington Monument was joined in 1922 by the Lincoln Memorial and in 1943 by the Jefferson Memorial. The latter two featured larger-than-life statues flanked by quotations from two of the most eloquent political figures in the history of the United States. Yet they were excerpts without context, powerful but generic truisms. (Who, for example, could argue with Jefferson's "eternal hostility to every form of tyranny over the mind of man"?)

Military sites and celebrations throughout the country highlighted individual sacrifices, the national quest for peace, and the endurance of the Union and the values it represented. Rarely did they address the origins of wars or try to assess their consequences; almost always the message was a variation on the theme of "all's well that ends well." The tone had been established on June 24–26, 1926, when more than 20,000 cars brought over 70,000 people to commemorate the fiftieth anniversary of the battle of the Little Bighorn. The event was the "largest and most elaborate commemoration ever staged at the Little Big Horn," celebrating the triumph of civilization over savagery and the assimilation of American Indians, including their supposed adoption of "a life with new rights and new opportunities which the relentless march of civilization demand that [they] assume." On June 25, white Americans in cavalry uniforms, representing Custer and his men, met a contingent of "Sioux and Cheyenne warriors, garbed in their war regalia," at the Custer Monument. There they solemnly "exchanged peace signs and clasped hands in token of friendship."[25]

It was a curious moment, elaborately marking the anniversary of an episode of negligible consequence in a centuries-long struggle between American natives and newcomers, one made all the more extraordinary by the fact that the United States' victories over Indian people and, for that matter, other, more costly defeats that Indians inflicted on American troops received no such ceremonial treatment. Horseshoe Bend, the site of Jackson's defeat of the Creeks, for example, did not become a national military park until 1959. Tippecanoe, where Governor William Henry Harrison fought the Indians of the Great Lakes to a draw in 1811, never did; the site is now administered by the Tippecanoe County Historical Association.

Even more to the point, the place where the Ohio Indians defeated General Arthur St. Clair in November 1791, a battle in which more than three times the number of American soldiers died than were killed at the Little Bighorn, attracted almost no public attention.[26]

While this pattern resulted from a host of factors, it embodied a tendency to commemorate military events that portrayed white Americans as innocent victims of others' aggression. The sanctification of various sites in the 1930s participated in an older pattern of commemoration in which outnumbered, ill-led, poorly trained, or otherwise unprepared American men, caught off guard by a militarily superior enemy, demonstrated their *moral* superiority by laying down their lives in "last full measure of devotion" of which Lincoln spoke so movingly in the Gettysburg Address. No matter what actually took place at those sites and regardless of the complicated contexts in which the events occurred, places like Lexington and Concord, Bunker Hill, the Alamo, Fort Sumter, and the Little Bighorn could all be made to function as examples of how individual Americans defended what was dear to them against invaders or usurpers or savages. Against this backdrop of self-sacrifice, enemy commanders, from Tecumseh to Santa Anna to Crazy Horse, appeared as talented leaders, even geniuses, at the head of overwhelming numbers of fanatical, well-disciplined, well-armed fighting men. It was crucial to the emotional appeal of this narrative that the doomed American heroes not be more numerous, or acting as obvious invaders. Hence St. Clair's defeat was never a feasible occasion for commemoration even though American troops suffered nearly 900 casualties in the battle. The worst defeat that the U.S. Army ever suffered at the hands of native warriors, by the logic of commemoration, was the army's own fault. St. Clair was the aggressor, had the better-equipped force, and outnumbered the Indians. While St. Clair's defeat was a great sacrifice of life, it was not a sacrifice worthy of remembrance.

The national pageant laid out in the 1930s was a story built around sites of American defiance to those who sought to hinder the peaceful, progressive advance of democracy, capitalism, and Protestant moral values. Though not particularly sophisticated, it was an emotionally powerful scheme and undeniably effective in creating a national narrative consistent with the central tenets of American political culture. What the story, common to school textbooks of the day as well as to public sites, left out was as important as what it celebrated. It was not merely that this version of the American story drained diversity and dissent from the records of the past (although it did indeed do that) or that it ignored African Americans, Indians, women, and indeed any group that was not white and male (although it did that, too). The most significant omission was the recognition that national power had played any consequential role in the founding, expansion, and preservation of the United States. The American Revolution and Civil War, milestones in the defense of liberty, were the central events; everything else either anticipated or resulted from them. The Seven Years' War, the Mexican War, and the Spanish-American War were minor conflicts, usually subsumed under the vague, bloodless heading of expansion. There was no mention of empire anywhere as a fundamental impulse in American development.

Biographies of the kind MacArthur had in his library located exemplary American lives within this narrative. Pulitzer juries in the 1930s and early 1940s awarded prizes to studies of Sam Houston, Theodore Roosevelt, Robert E. Lee, Andrew Jackson, and Woodrow Wilson. General John J. Pershing won the history Pulitzer in 1932 for *My Experiences in the World War.* The most successful was Carl Sandburg's multivolume life of Abraham Lincoln, which won the history prize in 1940. Like the other authors, Sandburg's deeply admiring work held up Lincoln as the embodiment of the individualistic, patriotic American spirit. The glory of the United States lay in its parts, not its whole, in the dispersion of power rather than its concentration. The vast influence of the historian Frederick Jackson Turner, who received the 1933 history Pulitzer for a collection of his essays, made this perspective received wisdom. Turner's "frontier thesis" traced the roots of American democracy and hence of American national character to the experience of settling (not conquering) open (not previously inhabited) land. National expansion had not entailed conquest so much as it had liberated individuals, enabling them to realize their potential for personal and political growth in ways that never would have been possible in the hierarchically structured societies of the Old World. Now the mission of the United States, Turner argued, was to preserve the work of Jackson, Grant, Lincoln, and others like them. "The problem of the United States is not to create democracy, but to conserve democratic institutions and ideals."[27]

Arguably more important than books in propagating this emerging narrative of American history was the enormously popular medium of film. Movies shaped the sensibilities of Douglas MacArthur and millions of his fellow citizens. The general loved going to the movies, especially westerns with "fast-moving action, dramatic moments, clearly defined issues, noble heroes, and unmistakably wicked villains."[28] Hours spent watching flickering images on theater screens taught audiences that war was a storm that suddenly engulfed individuals and families in trial and tragedy and left them shaken but also tougher, wiser, more sure of themselves, more aware of what was truly important in life. Why people fought with each other or with enemies beyond their borders was easily summarized in a handful of platitudes centered on the protection of happy, homogeneous local communities.

On screen, Americans went to war not to change the world and certainly not to conquer but to restore peace and justice. The brilliantly executed D. W. Griffith film *The Birth of a Nation* (1915) set the pattern by chronicling the rise of Ku Klux Klan freedom fighters who make it their mission to save whites, especially white women, from freed black savages and Northern intruders in the aftermath of the Civil War. Two decades later, *Drums Along the Mohawk* (1939) personalized the efforts of the peaceful residents of western New York during the War of Independence to defend themselves against the incursions of brutal Indians and their British allies.

The dramatic personalization of war and its impact reached a kind of apogee in *Gone With the Wind* (1939), which told the story of wartime upheaval from a female point of view. The significance of the Civil War in this hugely popular film seemed largely to lie in its capacity to disrupt the marriage plans of its heroine, Scarlett O'Hara. "War, war, war," she chides the doomed Tarleton twins at the beginning of the film, "all you boys ever talk about is war." Scarlett understands little or nothing of why the Confederacy must fight; even the cynical blockade-runner Rhett Butler ultimately proves more susceptible to the cause of the South. The amazing appeal of the film lay in its evocation (surprisingly, since it was made by MGM when the patriarchal studio system was at the height of its power) of a protofeminist narrative of American war. Here there was no prattling about liberty; apart from the burning of Atlanta, nothing approaching a battle scene. Rather, Scarlett's war was personal, nasty, and destructive, evoked primarily through scenes like those that showed a crowd snatching the freshly printed list of casualties at Gettysburg, the ruin of the Twelve Oaks plantation, and the lack of food and clothing.

Notwithstanding its racism and melodrama, *Gone With the Wind* derived great power from its defiance of conventional masculine narratives of war. In this movie, white men could not preserve a familiar world, much less restore it; Southern men, such as the ineffectual Ashley Wilkes, often proved weaker than their womenfolk. War, not men, shaped the world: war brought Yankee soldiers to plunder and rape; war brought carpetbaggers intent on stealing from the South in a more systematic and sustained way and determined to force Southerners to accept a humiliating new political order, unwanted (according to the film) as much by blacks as by whites.

The historical films of the 1930s also encouraged Americans to identify with the English as the carriers of the torch of freedom against tyranny until the United States was ready to assume the responsibility. In part this reflected a pervasive Anglophilia among Hollywood's studio heads, and in part it was a product of eagerness to exploit the talents of English actors and actresses. But there was undeniably a tendency to draw parallels between the American narrative of freedom and its defense and the British record of opposition to tyranny. *Fire over England* (1937), *The Adventures of Robin Hood* (1938), and *That Hamilton Woman* (1941) portrayed Englishmen confronting sudden, inexplicable terror from power-mad Spaniards, their own tyrannical King John and his henchman the sheriff of Nottingham, and Frenchmen with no discernible motivation beyond simple evil.[29] Who knew why tyrants loved tyranny or even what tyranny was beyond high taxes, brutality, and the general mistreatment of the hero and heroine? Who cared? So long as Errol Flynn could vanquish his villainous enemies, restore peace and justice, and marry Olivia de Havilland before the end of the last reel, all was well.

True matinee idols like Flynn could win even in defeat. At the climax of *They Died With Their Boots On* (1942), the widow (de Havilland) of the recently deceased George Armstrong Custer (Flynn) reads a letter from her husband to General Philip Sheridan asking that Indians "be protected in their right to an existence in their own country." As if that were not astonishment enough, Sheridan replies by repeating a promise from President Grant to make it so and ends the film with an even more astonishing line: "Come, my dear, your soldier won his last fight after all."[30]

While Douglas MacArthur and his fellow officers did what they could to prepare for a new global war despite inadequate manpower, starvation budgets, and obsolescent armaments, popular culture primed millions of Americans for what was coming. Monuments and movies, of course, did not hurl the United States into the maelstrom of World War II, but they did help Americans situate Pearl Harbor in a larger context when it happened. In the 1940 presidential campaign, the Republican nominee Wendell Wilkie proclaimed that "The American people do not want war. . . . They are determined to keep America at peace." The incumbent president rushed to tell "mothers and fathers . . . again and again and again[:] Your boys are not going to be sent into any foreign wars. . . . The purpose of our own defense is defense."[31] Like the happy and contented guests at the Wilkes family's barbecue at Twelve Oaks in the spring of 1861, Americans in the autumn of 1940 believed themselves to be committed to peace and justice, reluctant to fight but willing to do so if they had no alternative. What they did not know was how much and in what ways their world would change over the next few years or how much they would be called on to sacrifice and endure in the process.

"An Army of Freedom Dedicated . . . to the Cause of Human Freedom"

In the movie *Casablanca* (1942), the expatriate American saloon keeper Rick (Humphrey Bogart) spends his time in a corrupt French North African city, selling liquor and running an illegal casino while polishing a hard-bitten persona and a sardonic manner. He wants only to shield himself from the memory of the pain he suffered when his lover, Ilsa (Ingrid Bergman), deserted him as the Germans prepared to occupy Paris. The film instructed its audience in the ways that war wrecks private lives by preventing people from enjoying love and happiness. But its enduring appeal lay in the transformation of the alienated Rick, a latter-day Rhett Butler, into a complex champion of freedom. Full of national (or at least local) pride—there are, he tells a haughty Nazi officer, certain parts of New York City he would advise the Germans not to invade—he comes to renounce personal happiness for a cause larger than himself. In the end, Rick sends off the woman he loves and could now have kept and joins forces with Casablanca's Vichy police captain Louis (Claude Rains) to volunteer for service with the Free French garrison at Brazzaville. The foundation of the "beautiful friendship" between the once-cynical American and the once-corrupt Frenchman is their belated realization that there are more important things in the world than the private problems of individuals: specifically, the defense of freedom against a tyranny that will otherwise consume the world.

Viewers learned that, too, accepting Rick's decision in the closing moments of the film to put Ilsa on board an airplane out of Casablanca along with her husband, Victor Laszlo (Paul Henried), simply because Rick knows that Laszlo is worthy of her. He is neither a phony nor a fanatic but a true freedom fighter who has given over his life to the cause of resisting Nazism. In the absence of the Nazi threat, Laszlo might seem insufferably self-righteous, but the brutal realities of tyranny overwhelm all other considerations. When Laszlo silences a party of overbearing German officers in Rick's café by rallying the band to play the "Marseillaise," it is a glorious moment, totaling lacking in irony, that taught those who saw the film an unmistakable lesson: ordinary people must fight for their freedom if they are to live lives of dignity and honor. The Nazis, in short, embodied evil with such clarity that even Americans as suspicious of idealism as Rick could dedicate themselves once more to the defense of liberty.

The Japanese attack on Pearl Harbor on the morning of December 7, 1941, made that case in cordite and TNT with a kind of persuasiveness that celluloid alone could never manage. Sinking or disabling nineteen ships, killing 2,335 servicemen and 68 civilians, and wounding 1,178 more, the Japanese Imperial Fleet very effectively reanimated American resolve to defend of liberty at all costs. And it did not stop at Pearl Harbor. By the end of the day, Japanese military forces had also launched closely coordinated, highly effective air attacks on Wake Island, Guam, and the Philippines and also British-held Hong Kong and Malaya. Much to the surprise of Japanese leaders, who reasoned that the citizens of the United States lacked the will to defend possessions and interests across the Pacific, Americans took up the protection of liberty and democracy with a unanimity that all but obliterated the familiar, hitherto popular arguments of isolationists. Japan's long-term prospects in a war with the United States were not good.

Pearl Harbor fit into the popular narrative of American history that emerged in the 1930s like a key into the lock for which it had been cut. The USS *Arizona* was barely underwater before it became a shrine sacred to the memory of the men entombed within its hull, victims of a savage foe that had appeared in the sky on an otherwise beautiful Sunday morning to kill them. Yet Americans, especially their leaders, had for years followed global events, including the militant expansionism of Germany and Japan, two dynamic, relatively new nation-states eager to assert themselves and to gain access to such indispensable strategic resources as oil and rubber. Japan had occupied Manchuria in 1932 and had been at war with China since 1937. When Hitler ordered the invasion of Poland on September 1, 1939, and Great Britain and France declared war on Germany, few Americans expressed sympathy or support for the German aggressor. But the rapid fall of the Netherlands, Belgium, and France in the summer of 1940 and the subsequent Battle of Britain produced only loans and supplies from the United States.

Though concerned about Japan, Douglas MacArthur assumed (like most of his contemporaries) that the island empire would continue its expansion in China with possible incursions into Southeast Asia in search of strategic resources. More worried about Europe, the Roosevelt administration and the army chief of staff George C. Marshall nevertheless took the precaution of creating a regional command for the western Pacific, U.S. Army Forces in the Far East, recalling MacArthur to active duty in the summer of 1941, promoting him to lieutenant general, and placing him in charge. Despite strong doubts in Washington about the advisability of defending the Philippines, MacArthur spent the fall preparing for a Japanese attack, which he publicly suggested could not occur before April.

No one was fully prepared, however, for the attack on Pearl Harbor or the aerial assault on Clark Field in the Philippines later that day, in which the Japanese destroyed more than 100 of the 125 combat planes in MacArthur's U.S. Far East Air Force. Cool in the crisis, MacArthur was later severely criticized for the loss of aircraft, but there was only so much he could do.[32] The 22,000 U.S. regulars (including 12,000 Philippine Scouts), 3,000 members of the Philippine Constabulary, and 107,000 men of the Philippine Army were in no way prepared for the Japanese invasion that began in earnest on December 22. Some 43,000 Japanese troops landed at the south end of Lingayen Gulf on the island of Luzon and overwhelmed the Philippine Army units that opposed them, soldiers who lacked both the training and resources to mount a successful resistance. From his headquarters on Corregidor Island in Manila Bay, MacArthur, now promoted to general, initially dispersed his troops, but the futility of this strategy became clear as Philippine Army units collapsed everywhere they came under attack. In response, MacArthur opted not to defend Manila, instead ordering some 80,000 Filipinos and Americans to withdraw to the mountainous Bataan peninsula on the opposite side of Manila Bay from the capital. His idea was to continue resistance from jungle strongholds there while holding on as long as possible to the harbor defenses of Corregidor Island and its satellite forts. Unfortunately, in the withdrawal from Manila large amounts of supplies and equipment had to be abandoned. Thus while the rugged terrain and the determination of the besieged Americans and Filipinos together held off the Japanese for five months, disease, starvation, and the waning of hope that relief would ever come ultimately destroyed the will and the ability of the defenders to resist.

In addition to dealing with the exigencies of a world war, chief of staff George C. Marshall now had to deal with the problem of Douglas MacArthur. The general had few friends in Washington. The Boston lawyer Harvey Bundy, who worked in the War Department, summarized the general sentiment when he declared that MacArthur "was an opera star and everything had to be his way."[33] Marshall had known MacArthur for twenty years and did not much like him.[34] But MacArthur's Republican supporters fancied him a presidential candidate in 1944, and the news media identified the American struggle in the Philippines with the general. MacArthur facilitated his apotheosis, according to Secretary of War Henry Stimson, with "magniloquent communiques" studded with references to himself. The celebrity image of "the Lion of Luzon" disgusted Marshall's chief of war planning, Brigadier General Dwight Eisenhower. "The public has built itself a hero out of its own imagination," he wrote in his diary, but in truth, he thought, his former boss was "as big a baby as ever." He was refusing "to look facts in the face, an old trait of his." Nevertheless, the pragmatic Eisenhower concluded, "we've got to keep him fighting."[35]

MacArthur in fact wanted to stay and fight and demanded more troops to do so. That was impossible, and on March 11, 1942, he acceded to a direct order from President Roosevelt to place Lieutenant General Jonathan Mayhew Wainwright in command on Corregidor and relocate himself, his family, and his principal staff officers to Australia. Once there in April, he assumed the supreme command of the Southwest Pacific and Pacific Area. Awarded the Congressional Medal of Honor for his well-publicized defense of the Philippines, MacArthur pledged that he would personally return to liberate the islands. The beleaguered defenders of Bataan would have welcomed relief, but they were not necessarily anxious to have him back again. Some announced trips to the latrine with the refrain: *"I shall return!"* They also sang new lyrics to "The Battle Hymn of the Republic":

> *Dugout Doug's not timid, he's just cautious, not afraid,*
> *He's protecting carefully the stars that Franklin made.*
> *Four-star generals are as rare as good food on Bataan.*
> *And his troops go starving on.*[36]

Trapped and exhausted, Major General Edward P. King surrendered Bataan to the Japanese on April 9 and Wainwright turned over what remained of the island fortress of Corregidor a month later. "With broken heart and head bowed in sadness but not in shame," Wainwright capitulated in order "to end this useless effusion of blood and human sacrifice." The surrender marked the worst defeat in the history of the U.S. military, and the sacrifices of the Filipino and American captives were only beginning. Forced to travel on foot to Camp O'Connell in north-central Luzon in what became known as a "death march," the 75,000 men suffered from disease and starvation and also the cruelty of Japanese soldiers dealing with more prisoners than they could handle. By midsummer 1942, close to 2,000 Americans and roughly 25,000 Filipinos had perished.[37]

Fulfilling his pledge to return consumed MacArthur, who felt that his honor was at stake. Surprising no one who knew him, he took the fall of the Philippines personally, even to the point of blaming the victims. He refused to recommend a Medal of Honor for Wainwright after the surrender, saying that others had done more. His fellow officers knew otherwise. Eisenhower noted that Wainwright had done the fighting while "another got such glory as the public could find in the operation."[38] (In 1945, on the recommendation of George Marshall, Harry S. Truman finally directed that Wainwright receive the medal.) MacArthur singlemindedly concentrated on getting Washington to commit to a strategy that would take him back to the Philippines as a way-station to the invasion of Japan. As usual, he acted imperiously, forcing Roosevelt to remind him of who, in fact, was the commander in chief.[39]

Regardless, a speedy return to the Philippines was a pipe dream. The Japanese continued to press the advantage they had gained by surprise in New Guinea and Burma. On the other side of the world, Adolf Hitler and Nazi Germany declared war on the United States on December 10, 1941. The United States, already shipping massive amounts of matériel to Britain and the Soviet Union under lend-lease, now engaged in building up its strength in Britain to mount a cross-Channel invasion (planned for 1943) and in preparing to launch a North African offensive, Operation Torch, in late 1942. Russia was under terrible pressure on the Eastern Front; Allied strategic bombing had not yet markedly reduced Germany's war-making capacity. Roosevelt was desperate for a morale-boosting victory, but it was slow to arrive.

The Americans' focus in the Pacific theater was, in contrast to the massive buildup in Europe, primarily defensive, an attempt to check the Japanese advance and shore up the Nationalist Chinese. On May 7–8, 1942, American and Japanese fleets fought to a draw in the battle of the Coral Sea, the first naval battle in history conducted entirely by air, one in which the crews of the opposing ships never saw each other. Stopped in their southward expansion, the Japanese doggedly resisted Allied offensives in New Guinea and the Solomon Islands begun in the last months of 1942. Meanwhile, in the central Pacific, one of the great naval engagements of the war, the battle of Midway, delivered a decisive blow to Japanese air and naval power on June 4–6. The U.S. Navy surprised a Japanese fleet steaming toward Midway Island to finish what it had begun in December. American pilots sank four aircraft carriers and destroyed 253 airplanes, devastating the Japanese, who lacked the industrial capacity and manpower to recover quickly.

Good news from North Africa followed in the fall of 1942. The British under General Bernard Law Montgomery defeated Rommel's Afrika Korps at El Alamein in October and with the arrival of American reinforcements pushed the Germans toward Tunisia. In the South Pacific, the Americans counterattacked on New Guinea and held Guadalcanal Island despite fierce Japanese resistance. The most critical blow against the Axis powers was struck on the Russian front, where the siege of Stalingrad bled the overextended German Army white and exposed it to a powerful Soviet counteroffensive in November 1942. The remnants of the German Sixth Army surrendered at Stalingrad in February.

In the summer of 1943 the Russians inflicted a catastrophic defeat on German armored forces at Kursk, in the biggest tank battle in history. Meanwhile, British and American forces compelled a complete German surrender in North Africa in May. Two months later, the Allies invaded Sicily, precipitating the overthrow of Benito Mussolini in July and prompting an Italian attempt to withdraw from the war. Throughout 1943, thousands of aircraft poured out of American factories while American aircrews engaged the Luftwaffe in a deadly war of attrition for control of the skies over western Europe. By October 1943 American and British units had taken control of the Italian boot as far north as Naples. In January 1944, Allied forces landed further up the peninsula at Anzio and in spite of bitter German resistance captured Rome on June 4.

Two days later General Dwight D. Eisenhower presided over the largest amphibious assault in history when American, British, and Canadian troops stormed the windswept beaches of Normandy. The fighting that summer across France was grim and deadly, but by autumn the Allies had broken through to positions within striking distance of Germany itself. A massive German counterattack in the Ardennes on December 16—the beginning of the Battle of the Bulge—surprised American and British forces but failed to break through. The offensive stalled, then failed, at Bastogne at the turn of the year. On January 3 the Allies counterattacked, eliminating the Ardennes salient in a matter of days. That spring they pressed eastward to the Rhine.

The Germans were now under tremendous pressure in the east, where the Russians had launched a great offensive in January, as well as on the Western Front, where American, French, and British troops crossed the Rhine between March 22 and 26. German forces in northern Italy still held the Gothic Line, but everywhere else their resistance was collapsing in a general retreat toward Berlin. Hitler committed suicide on April 30, just under three weeks after Roosevelt's death in Warm Springs, Georgia. When

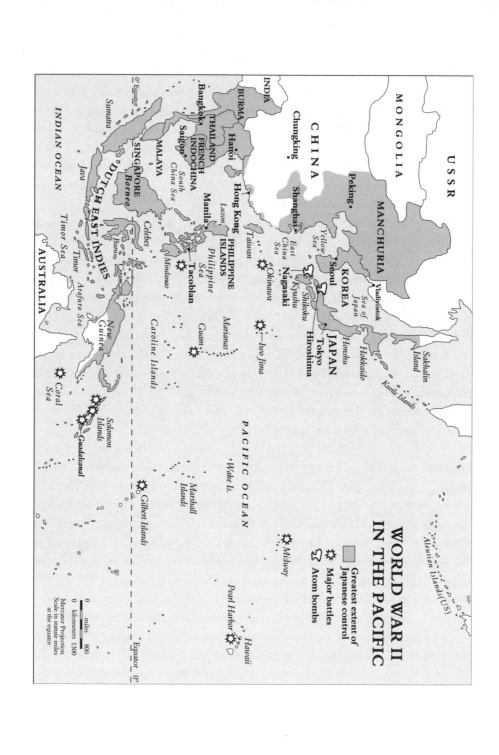

WORLD WAR II
IN THE PACIFIC

Greatest extent of
Japanese control

Major battles

Atom bombs

USSR

MONGOLIA

MANCHURIA

Vladivostok

Sakhalin
Island

Kurile Islands

Aleutian Islands (US)

165°

CHINA

Peking

Sea of
Japan

Hokkaido

KOREA

Seoul

Honshu

Tokyo

Hiroshima

JAPAN

Shikoku

Nagasaki

Kyushu

Yellow
Sea

East
China
Sea

Shanghai

Chungking

INDIA

BURMA

Hanoi

THAILAND

Bangkok

FRENCH
INDOCHINA

Saigon

Taiwan

Hong Kong

Manila

Luzon

PHILIPPINE
ISLANDS

Philippine
Sea

Okinawa

Iwo Jima

Marianas

Guam

Mariana

Tacloban

Mindanao

Caroline Islands

PACIFIC OCEAN

Wake Is.

Midway

Pearl Harbor

Hawaii

Marshall
Islands

Gilbert Islands

Solomon
Islands

Guadalcanal

Coral
Sea

New
Guinea

Ceram

Buru

Celebes

Borneo

SINGAPORE

MALAYA

DUTCH EAST INDIES

Sumatra

Java

INDIAN OCEAN

Timor Sea

Timor

Arafura Sea

AUSTRALIA

South
China
Sea

0° Equator

Mercator Projection
Scale in statute miles
at the equator

0   miles   800

0   kilometers   1300

Equator   0°

the German high command surrendered unconditionally on May 7–8, the war in Europe was over.

The Pacific war, meanwhile, had progressed at a different tempo, according to different demands. MacArthur concentrated on getting back to Manila, despite serious doubts in Washington about the wisdom of attacking the Philippines rather than strategic targets closer to Japan. A series of leapfrogging operations in 1942 and 1943 allowed the Americans to flank the Japanese on New Guinea and adjacent islands. Simultaneously, American forces commanded by Admiral Chester Nimitz moved from Hawaii toward Japan with victories in the Gilbert Islands. The next year, Nimitz's men were in the Marshall Islands and the Marianas.

Major Weldon E. "Dusty" Rhoades, the pilot of MacArthur's B-17, code-named Bataan, recalled MacArthur's adamant obsession with the Philippines and his opposition to alternative plans, such as an assault on Formosa. The general allowed Republicans to court him as a possible presidential candidate in 1944 before formally withdrawing his name from consideration. (Roosevelt, seemingly unconcerned about MacArthur's political ambitions, approved his promotion to General of the Army that same year.) In July, Rhoades piloted MacArthur to Honolulu to meet with Roosevelt. Uncertain of the purpose of the meeting, MacArthur was full of "guarded resentment and obvious apprehension." He "blew his top" when ordered to delay his arrival so that Admiral Nimitz could meet him personally. "To have a commander whom he considered junior to himself even try to tell him *how* to make a trip was a bit too much," Rhoades wrote, but there was clearly more to it than that. MacArthur knew that Nimitz was in favor of bypassing the Philippines in favor of a direct invasion of Formosa and had no intention of letting MacArthur speak to Roosevelt before he could. When the meeting made it clear that Roosevelt had decided in favor of the Philippines, MacArthur's spirits rose. On the return, Rhoades noted, he was in fine form, "like a child with new toys." "[I]f you reach for the stars you may never quite grasp them," he told his pilot, "but you'll never come up with a handful of mud."[40]

Like most of the men in MacArthur's inner circle, Rhoades deeply admired the general, forgiving his temperamental perfectionism and egotism because he drove himself as hard as he drove his men. It seemed clear to Rhoades that MacArthur "had some feeling that he was a man of destiny," a conviction that led him to take great risks in the belief that "he was especially protected so that he could fulfill a mission." Rhoades did not take these attitudes as evidence of megalomania but rather saw them as proof

General Douglas MacArthur and his staff wade ashore on
Leyte Island, Philippines, October 20, 1944

that MacArthur "believed in himself" and in the ideals for which he—and
America—stood: principles of loyalty and honor that required him, as he
promised, to liberate the Philippines and restore American dominion in the
western Pacific. That MacArthur believed so strongly in his destiny made it
possible for Rhoades to believe in it, too.[41]

American forces invaded the Philippines on October 20, 1944, from
Leyte Gulf, landing near Tacoblan, where MacArthur had worked as a lieutenant of engineers in October 1904. The general went ashore together with
his staff at 2:30 P.M. on a beach where, he was informed, the hardest fighting
was taking place. The much anticipated moment was surprisingly under-
stated though well-choreographed for the benefit of the photographers who
recorded it. The five-star general waded through the waves in unadorned
khakis, wearing aviator sunglasses and the crushed hat of a field marshal in
the Philippine Army, then announced to a small group on the beach: "I have
returned." Conscious that he was constructing a narrative of the reconquest
of the Philippines as personal history, he made a radio address an hour later
to repeat his comment to a vastly larger audience. "I have returned," he said
again; "Rally to me." Together, the forces of the United States and the

Philippines were "dedicated and committed" to "destroying every vestige of enemy control over [their] daily lives, and of restoring, upon a foundation of indestructible strength, the liberties of your people."[42] Uncharacteristically for a man who had made it a point to carry only a riding crop on the front lines of France in World War I and who disliked being photographed with a weapon, MacArthur came ashore armed on October 20. In his pocket he carried his father's two-barreled derringer pistol. Leyte Gulf was by no means Missionary Ridge, but it would do.

The Japanese put up a stout defense. The battle of Leyte Gulf (October 23–25) that accompanied the landing was the largest naval engagement in the history of the world and the last with exchanges of gunfire by battleships. The Japanese exploitation of a division in American command structure and the embarrassment of Admiral William "Bull" Halsey was no more than a temporary setback; in the end, the Japanese lost most of their Third Fleet, including four aircraft carriers. Without air power to deploy against the invaders, the Japanese defense of the Philippines became a prolonged, agonizing holding action. Manila fell on March 4 after a month-long battle from street to street and house to house. The Japanese defenders of the rebuilt harbor fortifications, Corregidor and Fort Drum, held out virtually to the last man and were not cleared until mid-April. Other Japanese units withdrew to the mountains north and east of Manila and resisted the Americans and Filipinos until the end of the war, some far longer. Nonetheless, MacArthur addressed the Filipinos after the fall of Manila as if everything had been decided. It had been the victory, he said, of "an army of freedom dedicated, with your people, to the cause of human liberty" and the restoration "under democracy's banner" of churches, schools, industry, and personal freedom.[43]

The Japanese surrendered unconditionally on August 14 after the dropping of atomic bombs on Hiroshima and Nagasaki, ordered by President Harry S. Truman. MacArthur arrived in devastated Tokyo and Yokohama on August 30 and held an emotional reunion with General Wainwright. Foreign Minister Mamoru Shigemetsu and other Japanese officials boarded the USS *Missouri* in Tokyo Bay on September 2 and formally capitulated to the Allies. General of the Army Douglas MacArthur, now Supreme Allied Commander in Chief, Allied Forces in Japan, threw up in the captain's cabin before the ceremony. After he recovered his composure, he emerged to give a brief speech and participate in the signing of the documents in a ceremony that took all of twelve minutes. When it was over, MacArthur's most evident concern was to retrieve the six pens that were used for the signatures. Later in that same month, Emperor Hirohito paid an unprecedented visit to the U.S. Embassy to pay a half-hour call on MacArthur. The Japanese monarch, Major Rhoades observed, seemed "properly humiliated."[44]

World War II holds a place of pride in American military history along-side the Civil War as a conflict of supreme significance. Both were colossal in scale. The numbers of citizens mobilized and the numbers of military personnel killed, wounded, or captured far exceeded those of all other American wars combined. More than 16 million men and women served in the armed forces during World War II; of these, 400,000 died, a number far larger than the entire strength of the army (270,000 officers and men) in 1941. The government spent $318 billion in prosecuting the war, more than all previous American wars combined and the equivalent, adjusted for inflation, of over 6 trillion dollars today. Equally important, the Second World War, like the Civil War, defined the worlds of the people who lived through them. No one forgot December 7, 1941. Indeed, the lessons of that day—to be prepared for an attack anywhere, to trust no one—dominated American thinking for the rest of the twentieth century.

Few argue against the necessity (or the fundamental justice) of a war fought to defeat the dictatorial, militarist regimes of Germany, Italy, and Japan, headed by tyrants who terrorized their own citizens, subjugated weaker nations, and used murder as an instrument of policy. In no other war has the American mission to extend the empire of liberty been less controversial; in no other has the American rhetoric of liberation seemed more perfectly suited to circumstances. The Nazis' assertion of racial superiority and their methodical extermination of Jews, homosexuals, and gypsies, like the Japanese campaign of terror in China in the late 1930s and the brutal Japanese treatment of prisoners of war, gave the Second War World a clarity of purpose—in retrospect, an unmistakable clarity—that most military conflicts never have. It was impossible to imagine that the young Americans who laid down their lives at Anzio, Normandy, Guadalcanal, and Iwo Jima had done anything less than give the last full measure of their devotion to the cause of freedom throughout the world.

The daily reality of war for those who served was, of course, far from glorious. African-American soldiers were eager to point out that they were "fighting for something called 'Democracy' which in general we will never receive." "As long as I am a soldier," wrote "A Loyal Negro Soldier" in 1943, "I fight for a mock Democracy." Another asked: "Isn't it true we are fighting for the same cause as the white man—for democracy—which is not prac-ticed in the land in which we serve? . . . Whites are treated as human beings [in the army] and we are treated as slaves."[45] The hypocrisy of denying freedom to people of color in the United States while fighting to free others outside gave enormous impetus to the civil rights movement in the postwar period. It was no accident that President Truman desegregated the armed forces in 1948; as in the Union army of the Civil War, blacks who served during World War II had established an unassailable moral claim to equal treatment as citizens by sharing equally in the defense of the nation and its ideals. Similarly, the long shadow of Auschwitz, Dachau, and Bergen-Belsen made clear the ultimate implications of racism as a basis for policy and the exercise of state power.

White Americans continued to engage in casual racism, even in the midst of devastation. A Red Cross worker in the Philippines in the summer of 1945 was appalled by the "low class" natives and the primitive conditions in a Filipino town. "The soldiers were really doing the town—there, the natives 'associate' with both white and colored Americans." Meanwhile, the results of a Pacific war in which both sides defined their enemy heavily in terms of racial inferiority were evident everywhere. Manila was utterly in ruins, "there is nothing but rubble left."[46] The cities of Japan had similarly been pulverized and burned with a thoroughness even greater than those of Europe. When the journalist Ernie Pyle observed upon his arrival in the Pacific in early 1945 that "In Europe we felt our enemies, horrible and deadly as they were, were still people. But out here I've already gathered the feeling that the Japanese are looked upon as something inhuman and squirmy—like some people feel about cockroaches or mice." Pyle himself thought the Japanese "thoroughly inconsistent in what they do, and very often illogical" but "a very nasty people while the shooting's going on." It was nothing like the war in Europe, where the average GI had had "a sense of being near civilization that is like his own."[47]

Born in rural Indiana in 1900, Pyle was an unpretentious, shy man who listened well and wrote in an engagingly conversational style. War in his dispatches had little to do with glory or high principles; war was death and fear and endurance and exhaustion. Returning from the invasion of Sicily, Pyle admitted that he "had come to despise and be revolted by war clear out of any logical proportions. [I] couldn't find the Four Freedoms among the dead men." Yet he could, and manifestly did, admire their tenacity and fortitude. They had to contend with "perpetual dust," "snatched food," heat, flies, noise, and everything that eventually "works itself into an emotional tapestry of one dull, dead pattern— . . . We've drained our emotions until they cringe from being called out from hiding." Pyle met a soldier named

Frank "Buck" Eversole in Italy in early 1944. Born in Iowa, Sergeant Eversole was a twenty-eight-year-old cowboy with a Purple Heat and two Silver Stars. He was a "practical" man who killed Germans in order to stay alive. Somebody had to do the job. Like many others, he found meaning in a fraternity forged in the face of death, in the shadows of "the unnatural sight of cold dead men scattered over the hillsides and in the ditches along the high rows of hedge throughout the world."[48] Forty-four-year-old Ernie Pyle joined their ranks when he was shot in the head on the island of Ie Shima off Okinawa on April 18, 1945.

Ernie Pyle's writings offer unmistakable evidence that not all Americans shared MacArthur's model of the future of their nation, let alone the world. For many, the war was a difficult time full of trials and pain and discrimination, a time that acquired luster only in memory.[49] But even before the era of retrospectives and commemorations, World War II evaded, if it did not erase, the ambiguities that had been so evident to Americans earlier in the Age of Intervention. MacArthur was not the only one to see it as an unfolding of a larger plan that involved the destiny of the United States. What had been for Thomas Paine a cry of hope uttered amid doubt and darkness became a statement of self-evident fact: the cause of America was, without question, the cause of mankind. MacArthur stood before the Philippine Congress on July 9, 1945, to proclaim without irony the American "passion for liberty," to quote without hesitation the Declaration of Independence on the equality of men, and to reaffirm the American commitment to "our basic concept of human freedom, in defense of which we have fought and still continue to fight on the battlefields of the world." The war had vindicated the freedom-loving character of the Filipino people and certified their capacity for self-government. "[The] sacrifice of lives is a flaming torch to light the will and steel the hearts of free men to resist likewise if need be unto death all efforts, however devious the means, to compromise that freedom for which they died."[50]

MacArthur's pilot, Dusty Rhoades, was less optimistic. In fact, he was depressed. In October 1945, he reflected on "the stupid way in which" the United States seemed "to be attempting to solve" "the problems of the world." The atomic bomb meant that old ways of fighting and thinking about the "meaning of individual safety and security" were suddenly obsolescent. "Either we get along with the world or we build a force ready for the *immediate offensive* and so powerful that none can challenge us with any hopes of success." A few weeks in Japan persuaded Rhoades that "the making of a democracy out of an autocracy is an almost imperceptible, tedious process. Perhaps General MacArthur can detect some progress, but most of us cannot."[51]

"We Must Assist Free People to Work Out
Their Own Destinies in Their Own Way"

Audiences sitting in darkened theaters watching the 1946 film *The Best Years of Our Lives* no doubt found postwar America as topsy-turvy as the fictional characters in that Academy Award–winning film. Worried about readjustments and a revival of the Depression, no one could have imagined how much the United States would change over the course of the next quarter century. Suburbs and interstate highways, rock and roll and television, civil rights and feminism transformed an America that for the next half-century was governed largely by veterans of World War II. The images of hundreds of suddenly obsolete aircraft in *The Best Years of Our Lives* seemed to herald a major rollback in the size of the military, as happened after the Civil War and World War I.

Many citizens, especially those in small towns and rural areas who tended to vote for Republicans or conservative Democrats, remained suspicious of standing armies and wary of alliances that entangled American interests with those of European and Asian nations. Distrusting foreign influence and susceptible to rumors of plots against their autonomy, they worried that the creation of "a garrison state" with a large permanent army would destroy "the very qualities and virtues and principles we originally set out to save." Such conservative Americans were committed to protecting themselves from a nation-state, created by the New Deal and World War II, that they saw as bent on intrusions into local communities within as well as without the nation. Their spokesman, more than any other, was Senator Robert Taft of Ohio, who in 1951 defined the mission of the United States as "to maintain the liberty of our people" and not to "reform the entire world." Wars encouraged "dictatorship and totalitarian government." The nation should go only "as far toward preparing for war as we can go in time of peace without weakening ourselves . . . and destroying forever the very liberty which war is designed to protect."[52]

But urban and suburban Americans with growing interests both in international trade and culture and in the reform of American society thought differently. Fighting the dangers posed by the Soviet Union and the People's Republic of China, they believed, was essential to the progress of both the

United States and the world. Liberal Democrats such as Senator Hubert H. Humphrey of Minnesota, who had risen to national prominence as an ardent advocate of civil rights for African Americans, argued that it could be "hard to tell . . . where war begins and where it ends." Engaged in a crusade to defend liberty wherever it seemed threatened and mindful of the extent to which the United States had ignored the emergence of Japanese militarism and German fascism, a new generation of leaders urged constant vigilance to ensure that the United States would not repeat that pattern with respect to the threat of international communism. In 1950, a subcommittee of the National Security Council produced NSC-68, "the Bible of American national security." The document, whose contents were soon an open secret, pledged the United States to massive defense spending to be prepared for war at a moment's notice. It assumed that the struggle against international communism permeated all aspects of American life.[53]

The Pentagon, built during World War II to integrate previously scattered offices of the War Department, became the home of the newly created Department of Defense in 1947. With more than 5 million square feet—about 115 acres—of floor space, the Pentagon was not only the largest office building in the world but a symbol of vast power and influence in American culture and politics. The army, navy, air force, and Marine Corps now consolidated in the Department of Defense were unimaginably large and complex in comparison with the armed forces as they had existed only a decade earlier. The expansion fueled the growth of Washington, D.C., as tens of thousands of people streamed into the once sleepy city to work for the mushrooming federal bureaucracy.

Defense spending stimulated the growth of the electronics, engineering, aviation, computer, and nuclear industries. Government contracts became the lifeblood of industries now largely manned and managed by veterans of World War II. In 1950, manufacturing and activities related to the armed forces accounted for roughly 10 percent of the goods and services produced in the United States. The indirect benefits were immeasurable and muted the criticism of skeptics. So tightly interwoven were the military and the economy that Dwight D. Eisenhower's comment in January 1961 about a growing "military-industrial complex" that carried the risk of a "disastrous rise of misplaced power" seemed to some less a warning than a description of a system already in place. The good life enjoyed by many Americans was linked, one way or the other, to the sprawling business of national defense.[54]

The alliance between the Soviet Union and the United States had frayed long before the end of World War II. Rival powers, they saw themselves as defenders of antithetical ideologies. The United States stood for free markets and free elections against the collective tyranny of communism while the Soviet Union represented the interests of workers and other peoples who felt misused by capitalism, who understood what the Americans celebrated as "the Free World" as one that exploited the mass of mankind for the benefit of a small group of mostly American industrialists and financiers. The distrust between the two nations, only slightly assuaged by the United States' recognition of the Union of Soviet Socialist Republics in the 1930s and the alliance of the war years, exploded over the future of Eastern European countries, such as Poland, in which communist regimes under Moscow's direct influence gained power after the return of peace.

In March 1947, Harry Truman, who became president upon the death of Franklin Roosevelt in April 1945, enunciated what was soon termed "the Truman Doctrine," the major statement of American policy during the Cold War. "I believe that it must be the policy of the United States to support free peoples who are resisting attempted subjugation by armed minorities or by outside pressures," Truman told Congress. "I believe that we must assist free peoples to work out their own destinies in their own way." He hoped to accomplish his goal through economic assistance to Greece and Turkey, where the threat of communist subversion seemed strong. There was something unmistakably militant in his stark juxtaposition of the American "way of life . . . based upon the will of the majority, and . . . distinguished by free institutions, representative government, free elections, guarantees of individual liberty, freedom of speech and religion, and freedom from political oppression" with the communist "way of life . . . based upon the will of the minority forcibly imposed upon the majority. It relies on terror and oppression, a controlled press and radio, fixed elections, and the suppression of personal freedoms."[55] Although articulated in the narrow context of aid for two countries threatened by political instability, the Truman Doctrine hinted at something much broader: an open-ended global campaign against communism, the archenemy of freedom.

These were familiar themes. World War II revived rather than created the Age of Intervention. The Soviet Union was a new and menacing addition to a long line of adversaries—Indian, British, Mexican, Spanish, German, Japanese, and others—that had threatened liberty and therefore the United States. To intervene in the cause of freedom, to overturn evil men and institutions, was nothing new to Americans; they had been doing it since at least the late 1700s, advancing across North America then around the world as a whole, seeking ways to conquer without war whenever possible, fighting when opponents would not yield. They had let down their guard in the 1920s and the 1930s. Now they were back in the forefront of the crusade for freedom. And yet old ghosts haunted them. Forced to confront the hypocrisies of racial segregation and white supremacist rule at home—the legacies of the second Revolutionary Settlement—Americans once again had to deal with the ambiguities and contradictions of an imperialism sustained by the rhetoric of benevolence but often perceived outside the borders of the United States as a peculiar mixture of self-righteousness, self-interest, hypocrisy, and coercion.

At the end of the war, the United States was determined not only to rebuild devastated nations but to ensure that they would become bastions of economic freedom and political democracy, allies in the contest with the Soviet Union. Winning the peace required the expansion of American hegemony. Of primary interest was Europe, in part because of the danger of Russian expansion to the west and in part because the great majority of Americans identified culturally with the European nations from which their ancestors had come. The Marshall Plan, passed by Congress in 1948, allocated some 13 billion dollars for grants and loans to reconstruct war-ravaged countries in Western Europe. France, Great Britain, Italy, West Germany, and a dozen other nations benefited enormously from this generosity. The United States, of course, recouped its investment many times over in the form of thriving capitalist economies and democratic polities in a stable Western Europe.

Race made Asia different. Supervision of Japan's transformation from monarchy to democracy fell into the confident hands of the Supreme Commander of Allied Powers in Japan, General of the Army Douglas MacArthur, who explained at the surrender ceremonies in Tokyo Bay that "Freedom of expression, freedom of action, even freedom of thought were denied [under the previous regime] through suppression of liberal education, through appeal to superstition, and through the application of force. We are committed . . . to see that the Japanese people are liberated from this condition of slavery." What MacArthur envisioned for Japan was a version of the Philippine experience, which, he believed, ended successfully when the United States granted the commonwealth its independence on July 4, 1946. The U.S. Army of Occupation in Japan—as in the Philippines—was an "Army of freemen" whose "role has never been to rule, never been to subjugate, never been to oppress." Philippine independence, achieved with the benevolent support of the United States, was a fulfillment of the American Revolution, an "event in the sweep of democracy through the earth as foretelling the end of mastery over peoples by power of force alone—the end of empire as the political chain which binds the unwilling weak to the unyielding strong."[56] Japan's ascent to membership of the community of democratic nations would follow the same pattern.

The "demilitarization and democratization" of Japan was conducted under the tutelage of MacArthur and his fellow American military officers between 1945 and 1952. Their policy, MacArthur announced, was "to avoid oppressive or arbitrary action, and to infuse into the hearts and minds of the Japanese people principles of liberty and right heretofore unknown to them." "However high-minded they may have been," concludes historian John W. Dower, General MacArthur and his command ruled their new domain as neocolonial overlords, beyond challenge or criticism, as inviolate as the emperor and his officials had ever been. They epitomized hierarchy—not merely vis-à-vis the defeated enemy, but within their own rigidly layered ranks as well as by their white-men's rule."[57]

MacArthur's fusion of personal and national narratives was now complete. He was, in the words of the journalist John Gunther, the "Caesar of the Pacific," operating with a confidence born of "his unalterable conviction that he is a man of destiny." He left Tokyo and its immediate environs only twice between 1945 and 1950 and rarely met with Japanese or, for that matter, Americans. "God," remarked Gunther, "does not choose often to expose himself." So, remote and aloof, MacArthur imposed "democracy—like a dictator." Interested as ever in his public reputation, the general saw himself as embodying American patriotism and Christian values in the transformation of the Far East. According to Gunther, he thought "of himself and the Pope as the two leading representatives of Christianity. . . . The Pope fights on the spiritual front . . . while he tackles communism on the ground."[58]

American liberty thus came to Japan from the hands of proconsuls—of whom, of course, MacArthur was chief—who had at their command all the coercive power of an occupying army. MacArthur and his colleagues wanted to remake their enemy in their image of themselves, a simple enough process in the basic outlines of a redefinition of subjects as citizens. But as ever, it was critical to the Americans that the Japanese *choose* democracy. The twin goals of the military government—"[t]o insure that Japan will not again become a menace to the United States or to the peace and security of the world" and "[t]o bring about the eventual establishment of a peaceful and responsible government"—were not necessarily compatible, but MacArthur and his fellow officers believed they were ultimately reconcilable. That faith rested on the efficacy of "revolution from above," the assumption that the

eradication of Japanese militarism and imperialism would allow the people
of Japan to choose freely the ideals and values of their conqueror and thus
become the supporters of a postwar order that would, in effect, be an American imperium. "The United States desires that this government should
conform as closely as may be to principles of democratic self-government
but it is not the responsibility of the Allied Powers to impose upon Japan
any form of government not supported by the freely expressed will of
the people."[59]

One does not have to doubt the sincerity of this statement to wonder
whether the United States would have accepted a free decision by the Japanese people to form a socialist government and ally themselves with the
Soviet Union. Throughout the occupation, especially as the Cold War intensified, the Americans imposed a "censored democracy" and evidenced a "reflexive animosity" toward "those who disagreed with them." There could be
no public criticism of MacArthur, American policy, or the handling of the
occupation. "This [policy] was not a screen for weeding out threats to
democracy (as official justifications claimed), but rather a new chapter in an
old book of lessons about acquiescing to overweening power and conform-
ing to a dictated consensus concerning permissible behavior."[60]

The Americans had not come to conquer like Romans sowing the fields
of Carthage with salt; their policy was successful and, by the standards of
most victorious empires in world history, benevolent. Within a quarter century of their defeats, Japan and West Germany had become reliable allies of
the United States and two of the most powerful capitalist democracies in
the world, evidence of the failures of the more brutal and less effective imperialism of the Soviet Union in Eastern Europe. There was no widespread
sense among the Germans or Japanese who came to maturity in the postwar
era that prosperity and freedom had been forced upon them. That alone was
enough to reassure most citizens of the United States that Japan and West
Germany were symbols of the success of the American system and American values and to reassure the political leaders of the United States that the
policy of intervention, born at the turn of the century and revived in the
1940s, could be a powerful instrument for good in a disorderly and dangerous world. Imperialism in the service of liberty was no vice.

Yet means do matter. The American insistence on denying that they
were practicing coercion, that their power was not in any sense truly imperial or militaristic in character, obscured the extent to which they reinforced
authority to achieve their goals. MacArthur quickly recognized the importance of Emperor Hirohito in establishing his own legitimacy as the de facto

absolute ruler of conquered Japan. Rather than remove Hirohito or place him on trial for his role in Japan's war policies, MacArthur used him as a tool with which to create a constitutional monarchy. Early in 1946, when the general dictated the basic principles to be followed in drafting a constitution for Japan, he took care to stipulate that the "Emperor is at the head of the State" and his "succession is dynastic." "His duties and powers will be exercised in accordance with the Constitution and responsible to the basic will of the people as provided therein." MacArthur wanted an end to war, emperor worship, and the remnants of feudal nobility, but he left the monarchy, though weakened and demystified, intact. The reason was clear: at a time when voices of Japanese democratic reform were calling for an end to the monarchy, MacArthur needed the emperor as much as Hirohito needed him. The two men legitimized each other.[61]

In the United States, the public mood reflected little of the certainty about America's future that MacArthur felt about Japan's. Preoccupied by the communist menace, sobered by the memory of Pearl Harbor, and nostalgic for the unanimity of purpose that had characterized public life during the war, many Americans feared the reappearance of political dissent, imagining that subversive elements and infiltrators would rob the United States of the resolve to stand up for liberty in Asia and Europe. The stifling of dissent associated with Senator Joe McCarthy and other red-hunting politicians seemed to many Americans no more than appropriate in perilous times. Americans were now geared to act swiftly whenever their leaders perceived a danger to the intertwined interests of the United States and liberty. American opinion-makers in the late 1940s and in the 1950s played fortissimo the theme of the Republic's cause as the cause of all mankind, a theme stated, qualified, and developed for more than a century and a half, a theme that now overwhelmed all underlying notes of anxiety.

So it was once again when the United States rose to the defense of beleaguered Korea in the fall of 1950. Colonized by Japan for most of the century, the residents of the peninsula found themselves caught between the great powers of the world when the Japanese empire disintegrated in 1945; their homeland stood at a point of contact between the rival blocs of the Cold War. At the end of World War II, the United States and the Soviet Union had agreed to divide Korea temporarily, like Germany, into zones of influence with a border at the thirty-eighth parallel. Like Germany, the peninsula soon had rival governments: the pro-American Republic of Korea in the South under the control of Syngman Rhee and the pro-Soviet Democratic People's Republic in the North, headed by Premier Kim Il Sung.

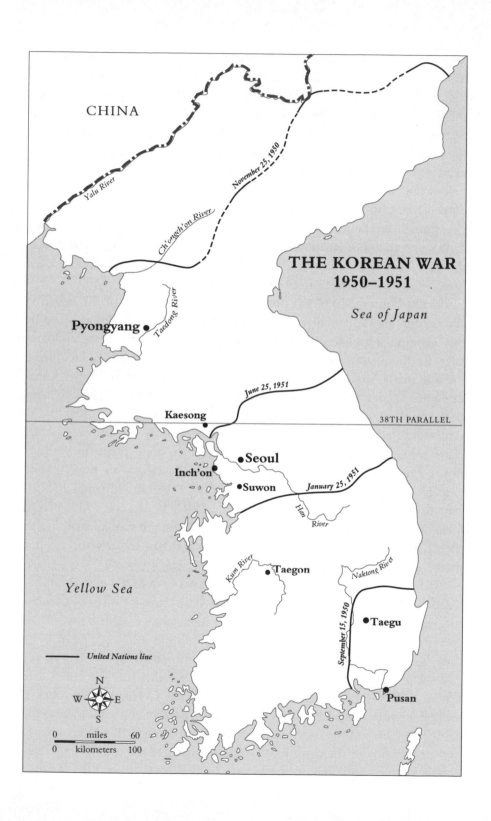

CHINA

Yalu River

November 25, 1950

Ch'ongch'on River

Taedong River

Pyongyang •

THE KOREAN WAR
1950–1951

Sea of Japan

June 25, 1951

Kaesong •

38TH PARALLEL

• **Seoul**

Inch'on •

• Suwon

January 25, 1951

Han
River

Kum River

• **Taegon**

Naktong River

Yellow Sea

September 15, 1950

• **Taegu**

—— *United Nations line*

N
W ✸ E
S

0   miles   60
0   kilometers   100

• **Pusan**

The United States withdrew its occupation forces in June 1949, leaving the defense of the Republic of Korea in the hands of a 100,000-man army that was at best an ill-trained and lightly armed national constabulary. The North Korean army, by contrast, was a third larger, was throughly trained by Soviet advisers, and boasted an armored brigade equipped with Russian T-34 tanks.

In June 1950, Kim ordered the North Korean army to cross the border and reunify the peninsula under his rule. The Truman administration, shaken by the communist takeover of China in 1949 led by Mao Zedong and suspicious that the Soviet Union had ordered the North Korean invasion, responded by sending American military forces to the rescue under the aegis of United Nations resolutions denouncing North Korean aggression and authorizing a military response. Over the next couple of years, sixteen nations contributed to the United Nations' cause in Korea; four out of five UN troops were Americans.

The UN commander in 1950 was Douglas MacArthur, America's indispensable man in the Far East and already on the scene at his headquarters in Japan. After reinforcing the battered remnant of South Koreans holding out in the southeastern quadrant of the peninsula around Pusan, MacArthur on September 15 staged a bold, brilliantly executed amphibious assault well behind enemy lines at Inchon. The Inchon landing was followed in short order by the breakout of forces from the Pusan perimeter, forcing the North Koreans to retreat in disarray toward the thirty-eighth parallel. It was a strategic masterstroke, and it was entirely MacArthur's. By the end of the month Seoul was under UN control.

The conflict might have ended there, but Truman, acting on advice from the Joint Chiefs of Staff, shifted the war aims of the United States and the United Nations from the restoration of the status quo to the reunification of the peninsula under the control of the Republic of Korea. The new communist government of China warned the UN command against moving beyond the parallel, but on October 7, with the support of a UN resolution authorizing the reunification of Korea, MacArthur ordered his forces north. On October 19, the North Korean capital of Pyongyang fell, and allied forces moved on toward the border with China—the Yalu River—against evidently failing resistance. Then they paused to reorganize and resupply themselves for what MacArthur expected to be the final triumphant offensive in November.

Unbeknownst to MacArthur, October 19 was also the day that Mao Zedong and the People's Republic of China intervened by sending a quarter of

President Harry S. Truman and General Douglas MacArthur at
their October 1950 meeting on Wake Island

a million "volunteers" across the Yalu to reinforce the North Koreans. When MacArthur ordered the forces of the U.S. Eighth Army to advance on November 24—he did so after promising the troops they would be home by Christmas—they almost immediately encountered heavy, unexpected attacks by Chinese forces, which pushed the allies back down the Korean peninsula. By Christmas, the allied forces had retreated to the thirty-eighth parallel; on January 3, they abandoned Seoul.[62]

In the midst of crisis, MacArthur blustered, blaming the White House and Joint Chiefs of Staff for his reverses by making him fight a limited war. He talked bleakly of dire outcomes unless he was given authority to use every means to wage war against the Chinese, even including the use of nuclear weapons. Truman's own military experience was limited to his service in World War I as a captain commanding a Missouri National Guard artillery battery in France, but his convictions on civilian supremacy over the military were deeply rooted in his knowledge of American history and government. He found MacArthur's self-aggrandizement and penchant for issuing his own statements without consulting his superiors to be increasingly intolerable. Truman had reevaluated the situation, abandoned the idea that the peninsula could be reunified, and decided to seek a negotiated settlement as soon as the military situation of the allied forces could be stabilized and the Chinese rolled back to some reasonable position, preferably the thirty-eighth parallel. The risk that bombing and invading China would trigger a third world war were simply too great.[63]

In fact, the military position of the UN forces improved in late December when Lieutenant General Matthew Ridgway took command of the Eighth Army. A tough West Pointer (Class of 1917), Ridgway was a paratrooper who always wore hand grenades on his web gear and who had jumped into France in June 1944 as commanding general of the Eighty-second Airborne Division. He quickly mounted counterattacks in January and February, retook Seoul on March 15, and launched another offensive that pushed the Chinese and North Koreans back across the parallel in April. This, Truman thought, was the perfect opportunity to offer a cease-fire and negotiate a peace settlement that would once more stabilize the peninsula along its prewar dividing line. But MacArthur, who had devoted himself to commenting on political issues while Ridgway slugged it out with the Chinese, disagreed, making it clear that he thought the Truman administration was weak and that the war should be carried into China with a view to destroying the communist regime of Mao Zedong and reinstalling the refugee Nationalist government of Chiang Kai-shek. Learning of Truman's offer of a cease-fire, MacArthur issued a bombastic, highly public ultimatum to his enemy counterpart, deliberately sabotaging the president's plan and dashing hopes for a negotiated settlement.

Truman concluded that MacArthur "thought he was the proconsul for the government of the United States and could do as he damned pleased." He was long past the end of his patience when, on April 5, 1951, Congressman Joseph W. Martin Jr. of Massachusetts, the Republican leader in the House of Representatives, made public a letter from MacArthur advocating American backing for a Nationalist Chinese attack on the mainland to be launched from Taiwan. "There is no substitute for victory," MacArthur had written.[64] He may have thought that it went without saying there was also no substitute for Douglas MacArthur. If he did the illusion did not last much longer. On April 11, Truman summarily relieved him of all his commands on the grounds of insubordination. Ridgway, now elevated to the rank of general, replaced MacArthur as supreme commander in the Far East; Lieutenant General James Van Fleet was rushed from the United States to assume Ridgway's position as commander of the UN forces on the ground in Korea.

Removing MacArthur ignited a political firestorm. Republicans had done well in the midterm elections in November 1950 by focusing on the rise of communism around the globe and holding the Truman administration responsible for the "loss" of China. By March 1951, 57,120 Americans were dead, wounded, or missing in a Korean war that seemed no closer to resolution than it had been nine months before. The *Chicago Tribune* demanded Truman's impeachment. Republican senators, including Richard Nixon and Robert Taft, denounced Truman's policies as giving aid and comfort to the enemy. MacArthur's conservative political convictions were well known, as was the fact that he had flirted in the past with the idea of running as the Republican Party's candidate for president. For Truman, however, the issue went beyond politics to the bedrock conviction that "civilian control of the military is one of the strongest foundations of our system of free government." The intrinsic superiority of civilian over military rule rested on perspective: an "elected official," he later wrote, "will never forget—unless he is a fool—that others as well or better qualified might have been chosen and that millions remain unconvinced that the last choice made was the best one possible." Military officers, on the other hand, thought in terms of "obedience" and "command." Truman believed that "the military definitions of these words are not definitions for use in a republic."[65]

Douglas MacArthur saw himself as a modern Caesar, a man who merited the obedience of lesser men, a man who deserved to lead. He merged his career and the history of his nation into a seamless whole; like Andrew Jackson, he imagined himself as the tribune of democratic imperialism. Having saved the Philippines and transformed Japan, MacArthur envisioned completing the arc of his personal destiny by conquering communist China and instituting free government there as well. Though that was not to be, Americans greeted MacArthur as a hero upon his return to the United States, his first time on the mainland since 1937. An estimated 7.5 million people lined the streets of New York City to shower him with ticker tape. He addressed a joint session of Congress on April 19 in a speech broadcast throughout the nation. "The communist threat is a global one," he asserted. "You cannot appease or otherwise surrender to communism in Asia without simultaneously undermining our efforts to halt its advance in Europe." The United States must rally to the support of the courageous Koreans who were standing up to the communists. "They have chosen to risk death rather than slavery."[66]

For Douglas MacArthur, a similar impulse united all the wars of the United States into a coherent whole. In his mind, selfless American citizen soldiers were forever defending Concord, the Alamo, and Bataan, or charging up Missionary Ridge, going over the top from the trenches of northeastern France, and storming the beaches of Normandy and Luzon. He could no more associate the United States with the exercise of naked power than he could conceive that Indians, Mexicans, Cubans, Haitians, and the Japanese might construe Americans as anything other than liberators. But by 1952 what MacArthur thought mattered less and less. With the election to the presidency of his congenial, pragmatic former protégé, Dwight D. Eisenhower, MacArthur finally did, in his own famous phrase, "fade away." He died in New York City on April 5, 1964, and was buried after an elaborate state funeral in his mother's birthplace of Norfolk, Virginia.

MacArthur rarely stepped out of the seclusion that marked the last years of his retirement; when he did, it was primarily to take part in ceremonial occasions. His last major appearance came two years before his death when he traveled with Jean to West Point to accept the Sylvanus Thayer Award for outstanding service to the United States. (He went to the Philippines the previous year to commemorate both the fifteenth anniversary of the independence of the islands and the twentieth anniversary of the fall of Bataan and Corregidor.)[67] His speech to the cadets was a compendium of previous public statements, its baroque style and unashamed sentimentality relics of an era long past. The cadets, MacArthur said, faced "a new world—a world of change. The thrust into outer space of the satellite, spheres and missiles" was opening "another epoch in the long story of mankind—the chapter of the space age."[68]

He might just as easily have mentioned social movements that had brought African Americans and women into the corps of cadets. Or he might have referred to the mission that the cadets' commander in chief, John F. Kennedy, a man little more than half MacArthur's age who had experienced war as a naval lieutenant in the South Pacific, proclaimed on assuming the presidency:

The torch has been passed to a new generation of Americans, born in this century, tempered by war, disciplined by a hard and bitter peace, proud of our ancient heritage, and unwilling to witness or permit the slow undoing of those human rights to which this nation has always been committed, and to which we are committed today at home and around the world. Let every nation know, whether it wishes us well or ill, that we shall pay any price, bear any burden, meet any hardship, support any friend, oppose any foe to assure the survival and the success of liberty.[69]

But he made no reference to any of these. Instead, MacArthur himself, symbol with his father of a century's service to a republic not yet two centuries old, held the torch aloft one last time.

He spent close to an hour urging the cadets, many of whom later led men into battle in Vietnam, to hold fast to their ideals and to keep faith with previous generations of American soldiers. Whatever happened, their "mission remains fixed, determined, inviolable—it is to win our wars. . . . For a century and a half, you have defended, guarded, and protected [the Republic's] hallowed traditions of liberty and freedom, of right and justice." As he approached the end, MacArthur admitted that the cadets would move forward without him; his long devotion to the creed of the corps of cadets—Duty, Honor, Country—was nearing an end. "The shadows are lengthening for me," he said; "the twilight is here." Still, he longed for more, for a return to the glory and comradeship of his youth, and he summoned every reserve of pathos and grandiloquence to evoke it in his peroration:

> I listen vainly, but with thirsty ear, for the witching melody of faint bugles blowing reveille, of far drums beating the long roll. In my dreams I hear again the crash of guns, the rattle of musketry, the strange mournful mutter of the battlefield.
>
> But in the evening of my memory, always I come back to West Point. Always there echoes and reechoes Duty—Honor—Country.
>
> Today marks my final roll call with you, but I want you to know that when I cross the river my last conscious thoughts will be of the corps, and the corps, and the corps.
>
> I bid you farewell.[70]

As some in the crowd wept at what they knew was his valedictory, the frail old soldier blew a kiss to Jean and stepped away from the lectern. The determined son whose life was above all else a relentless crusade to fuse the story of Douglas MacArthur and the story of the United States into one grand narrative of the defense of freedom had taken his final bow.

Powell's Promise

I remember a soldier, while I was still battalion exec, who had stepped on a mine. One leg hung by a shred, and his chest had been punctured. We loaded him onto a slick and headed for the nearest evac hospital at Duc Pho, about fifteen minutes away. He was just a kid, and I can never forget the expression on his face, a mixture of astonishment, fear, curiosity, and, most of all, incomprehension. He kept trying to speak, but the words would not come out. His eyes seemed to be saying, why? I did not have an answer, then or now. He died in my arms before we could reach Duc Pho.[1]

Soldiers always die in war, and those who survive must somehow make sense of those deaths and of their own survival. Telling stories helps them do it. Whether the result is the *Iliad* or a soliloquy delivered from a barstool, the underlying impulse is the same and as powerful as any in history or literature. The war story above recounts, in scarcely more than a hundred words, the last minutes in the life of a GI whose name appears somewhere on the section of the Vietnam Memorial that records the deaths of 1968. Every name carved on that wall has such a story behind it, each unique in its details, all identical in their outcome. What invests this particular scene with a significance beyond its private poignancy is that the man who held the dying soldier in his arms went on to become the highest-ranking officer in the military establishment of the United States and eventually to serve as the nation's sixty-fourth secretary of state.

Colin Powell published *My American Journey,* the autobiography in which this passage appears, in 1995, when he was fifty-eight years old. Most of the book concerns the remarkable military career that began in 1954 when he enrolled as a cadet in the Army Reserve Officers' Training Corps at the City College of New York and concluded in 1993 when he retired as a four-star general and the chairman of the Joint Chiefs of Staff. But as its title implies, his memoir is more than a retrospective assessment of Powell's professional accomplishments. Instead, it participates in a classic American genre, the success story. In Powell's case it is a tale, told with considerable modesty, of how the son of immigrant parents rose from a South Bronx childhood to extraordinary heights of power and responsibility in the nation's capital by virtue of talent, hard work, luck, and the help of influential patrons. Perhaps with less conscious intent, *My American Journey* relates a classic story of another sort, too, for it shows how war influenced the life of a general who, like Washington, Jackson, Grant, and MacArthur went on to play a crucial part in the governance of the Republic.

In retrospect, Powell saw the moment when he cradled a dying soldier in the din of a helicopter's open passenger bay as emblematic of a turning point in his life and that of his country. In the middle of his second tour in Vietnam, he was losing faith in America's ability to win the war that he and a half-million of his countrymen had been sent halfway around the world to fight. Powell's efforts to answer the question he saw in the dying soldier's eyes shaped the rest of his career, in and out of the army. In a larger sense, America's struggle to deal with the experience of defeat in Vietnam—the first war the United States ever, unequivocally, lost—profoundly influenced the nation's approach to the rest of the world for more than a generation.

"War Should Be the Politics of Last Resort"

Colin Powell, the son of Luther and Arie Powell, both Jamaican immigrants, was born in Harlem in 1937. Growing up in the Hunts Point section of the South Bronx, he was a well-behaved but unfocused child in a close-knit, hardworking family, a boy with few visible academic or athletic gifts and little evident ambition. By his own reckoning he was "a black kid of no early promise" who was mainly content to drift through life.[2] Only after he matriculated at the City College of New York in the fall of 1954 and joined the Army Reserve Officers Training Corps did Powell find a sense of purpose. Once he put on the uniform he felt "something I had never experienced all the while I was growing up; I felt distinctive."[3] In the Pershing Rifles—a student society made up of cadets willing to undertake extra training, particularly in close-order drill—he experienced "the discipline, the structure, the camaraderie, the sense of belonging" he "craved."

> I became a leader almost immediately. I found a selflessness within our ranks that reminded me of the caring atmosphere within my family. Race, color, background, income meant nothing. The P[ershing] R[ifle]s would go the limit for each other and for the group. If this was what soldiering was all about, then maybe I wanted to be a soldier.[4]

Having found his niche, Powell excelled—in drill and military subjects if not in academics generally—and at graduation was offered his second lieutenant's commission in the regular army rather than the army reserve. The offer was a mark of distinction, the greatest recognition that an ROTC graduate could attain, for it was, in effect, the army's invitation to make his career as a professional officer. Powell embraced it with all his heart.[5]

The U.S. Army had been racially integrated for less than a decade when Lieutenant Powell entered active service in 1958. As an institution it was still rife with racial prejudice, but it had come a great distance from the Jim Crow army that Harry Truman ordered desegregated in 1948. The genocidal consequences of Nazi "scientific" racism and the drive for Aryan racial purity had been only too clear at the end of World War II. The horror of the Holocaust and the centrality of America's claims to have fought in defense of freedom and equality made it impossible to sustain an official policy that discriminated against nonwhite soldiers on the basis of race. While Truman was unquestionably eager to secure the support of African-American voters at the polls, he also believed that desegregating the armed forces, by Executive Order 9981, was simply the right thing to do. To resist the communist bloc in the Cold War, Truman reasoned, the United States had to be as good as its best principles. In a worldwide contest for the hearts and minds of the "desperate populations of battle-ravaged countries," he wrote, the United States "can no longer afford the luxury of a leisurely attack upon prejudice and discrimination."[6] If the communists were to be beaten back from the advances they were making on every front, the United States could not afford to cede them the high ground of commitment to racial equality.

Of course, practicality had as much to do with the integration of the armed forces as principle. All-black units persisted in the army and Marines until the intense personnel demands of the Korean War forcibly ended segregation in 1951. Seven years later, when Powell entered the Infantry

Officers' Basic Course at Fort Benning, Georgia, the army officer corps was
still more than 95 percent white. Affirmative action as a concept lay well in
the future, and racial integration in the South remained unheard-of outside
the gates of the region's many military bases.

It was therefore a genuine testimony to his strength of character as well
as his drive to succeed and his love of things military—uniforms, ceremonies, rituals, decorations, discipline, camaraderie, and the culture of
self-sacrifice—that Colin Powell excelled as a junior officer. Powell stood
out as the kind of diligent, smart, earnest, and easy-to-like lieutenant who
impresses both his troops and his superior officers as a natural leader. Pro-
gressing from assignment to assignment and excelling at each, he acquired
patrons who helped make sure that he was in the right place to prove himself when the time came to do so. Powell's loyalties were never oriented exclusively upward, however. In assignments in Germany and Fort Devens,
Massachusetts, he sought to learn what made ordinary GIs "tick": He found
that

> American soldiers love to win. They want to be part of a successful
> team. They respect a leader who holds them to a high standard and
> pushes them to the limit, as long as they see a worthwhile objective.[7]

A worthwhile objective: that was the key. Soldiers needed to understand not
only what they were expected to do but *why* they should do it, why it was
worth doing, why ultimately it might be worth the sacrifice of their lives.[8]

Powell needed to understand his mission as much as his men did, but as
a company-grade professional officer he was less inclined to ask questions of
his superiors than to accept the tasks they set before him and seek to excel
as he accomplished them. During his first tour in Vietnam, as a captain advising a battalion in the Army of the Republic of Vietnam (ARVN) in 1963,
he suppressed any private doubts. Shortly after his arrival in Saigon, a major
general from MAAG—the Military Assistance Advisory Group, which
became the much larger MACV, the Military Assistance Command, Vietnam—briefed Powell and his fellow advisers on what they were supposed to
accomplish. At that point Powell had been married just four months to the
woman who was carrying their first child; he had left her to await his return
in Birmingham, Alabama, when that city was the ground zero of racial confrontation in the United States. Despite his training, his ambitions, and his
eagerness to please, these circumstances left him feeling equivocal, unsure
of whether the path ahead could possibly justify what he had left behind.

General Colin Powell, chairman of the Joint Chiefs of Staff,
on a tour of military facilities in Saudi Arabia, 1990

Then the general asked the assembled officers, evidently with a rhetorical
flourish,

> Why had we left our loved ones behind? Why had we come here to
> fight halfway around the world? To stop the spread of Marxism; to
> help the South Vietnamese save their country from a communist
> takeover. That was the finest thing we could do for our families, our
> country, and freedom-loving people everywhere.

It was as much a pep talk as a briefing, and—for the moment, at least—it
worked. When it ended, Powell recalled, "I was fired up all over again."[9]

The captain's uneasiness resurfaced, however, once he arrived at A
Shau, a fortified outpost in the old French style ("*Beau Geste* without the
sand") near the Laotian border, where he was assigned to help an ARVN infantry battalion stem the flow of supplies from North to South Vietnam
down the A Shau Valley over the Ho Chi Minh Trail.[10] Several things
seemed seriously wrong to him at A Shau. No one could explain why the
base camp had been located in the vulnerable position it occupied, nor

could anyone tell him how the endless patrols he undertook with the ARVN troops were expected to accomplish anything more than subjecting them to ambush after ambush. Most of all, no one could explain how burning peasant huts and crops would be more effective in discouraging guerrilla warfare than in simply breeding new generations of Viet Cong recruits and sympathizers. Still, Powell obeyed his orders and did his best:

> [A]s a young officer, I had been conditioned to believe in the wisdom of my superiors. . . . I had no qualms about what we were doing. This was counterinsurgency at the cutting edge. Hack down the peasants' crops, thus denying food to the Viet Cong, who were supported by the North Vietnamese, who, in turn, were backed by Moscow and Beijing, who were our mortal enemies in the global struggle between freedom and communism. It all made sense in those days.[11]

And, indeed, when he left the country in November 1963 after eleven months of duty in combat and on the staff, he remained "a true believer. I had experienced disappointment, not disillusionment. I remained convinced that it was right to help South Vietnam remain independent, and right to draw the line against communism anywhere in the world. The ends were justified, even if the means were flawed." The job was simply bigger than everyone had thought.[12]

When Powell came back to Vietnam four and a half years later, he had passed through advanced infantry training at Fort Benning and the command and general staff school at Fort Leavenworth with distinction and had earned an early promotion to major. He was on his way up the hierarchy of command, and this second tour should have been the one by which (as the phrase went) Powell "got his ticket punched" for further promotion. Indeed, he did continue to advance thereafter and at an accelerated pace; but his second Vietnamese tour was no mere ticket-punching experience for Major Powell.

Conditions had changed dramatically in his absence. In late 1963, the United States had committed only about 16,000 troops to the war effort, and they still acted (at least ostensibly) in an advisory capacity to the ARVN. By the time he returned in 1968, President Lyndon Johnson had used the authority Congress had granted in the Gulf of Tonkin Resolution (August 1964) to build up the American force commitment to more than a half-million men. By 1968 American forces had effectively taken over the fight.

Yet the enemy, though rocked by strategic bombing in the North and ham-
mered by airmobile infantry assaults in the South, fought on. At home,
racial strife and an antiwar movement were growing apace in a volatile, increasingly violent political climate. What most alarmed Powell, however,
was the state in which he found his new unit, the Twenty-third Infantry
(Americal) Division. Race relations were tense in the base camps although
still reasonably well-contained in the field; the draft was operating in-
equitably, filling the ranks with men from the poorest, least well educated
strata of American society; the quality of junior officers and sergeants was radically uneven; drug abuse was reaching alarming heights; officers and sergeants
the troops deemed untrustworthy were being fragged—assassinated—by
their men. Hundreds of American soldiers were dying every week, yet no
one seemed able to explain what this seemingly endless blood sacrifice
would accomplish.

Powell was appalled. "These were good men," he believed, "the same
kind of young Americans who had fought, bled, and died winning victory
after victory throughout our country's history. They were no less brave or
skilled, but by this time in the war, they lacked inspiration and a sense of
purpose." The emptiness at the heart of the war effort had exacerbated racial
conflict, especially as blacks became increasingly numerous in the infantry
units that invariably took the heaviest casualties, but the universal demoral-
ization seemed to Powell even worse than racial hostility. "Both blacks and
whites were increasingly resentful of the authority that kept them here for a
dangerous and unclear purpose. The number one goal was to do your time
and get home alive." Powell was a popular officer, but even he began to
make it a practice to sleep every night in a new location, at least in part for
fear that some disaffected soldier might decide to roll a fragmentation
grenade under his cot.[13]

Major Powell did his duty as battalion executive officer and later as the
division G-3 (operations officer), collecting two medals and some exemplary performance reports, getting his ticket punched along with his fellow
career officers. But the medals meant little to him, because the army handed
out so many of them as a means of padding the promotion files of officers
and noncoms. The inflation in medal-giving was but one symptom of an in-
sidious careerism that, as Powell saw it, had corrupted the army and indeed
the whole enterprise of the war. Even more corrosive to the soul of the army
were the routine lies embodied in reports of progress against the enemy.
Worst of all was the cynicism of making soldiers from poor and minority
backgrounds bear the brunt of the fighting while the sons of wealthy and

middle-class families dodged the draft or served without risk in reserve or National Guard units. The lives of American citizens were being wasted, Powell believed, in a war that had nothing to do with the defense of freedom. Senior officers who knew that the war was unwinnable merely went along with the pretense that it could indeed be won because to do so would earn them continued promotions, whereas to tell the truth and say openly what everyone knew would end their careers on the spot.[14]

When Powell left Vietnam in July 1969 he knew that something had gone badly wrong in the war and that the institution he served—and loved— was in deep trouble. A fundamental principle he had learned a decade earlier in the infantry officers' basic course had been forgotten.

> We were taught at Fort Benning . . . that American soldiers must know the reason for their sacrifices. Our GIs are not vassals or mercenaries. They are the nation's sons and daughters. We put their lives at risk only for worthy objectives. If the duty of the soldier is to risk his life, the responsibility of his leaders is not to spend that life in vain.[15]

He was not alone in that view. Thousands of other professional officers, his near contemporaries, had had the same training, heard the same lessons, and drawn the same inferences. "Many of my generation," Powell later wrote,

> the career captains, majors, and lieutenant colonels seasoned in that war, vowed that when our turn came to call the shots, we would not quietly acquiesce in halfhearted warfare for half-baked reasons that the American people could not understand or support. If we could make good on that promise to ourselves, to the civilian leadership, and to the country, then the sacrifices of Vietnam would not have been in vain.[16]

If there was a tendency to judge Vietnam by the standards of World War II rather than by those of (say) the Indian wars or the Philippine Insurrection it was at least understandable, given the universalistic terms in which Americans had invariably justified their wars since the Age of Revolutions and Empires began. Powell's disgust at the disparity between the rhetoric of freedom as a justification for war and the reality of coercion for coercion's sake was not materially different from the disgust that Ulysses Grant felt as he contemplated the character and consequences of the Mexican-American War. Nurtured in the afterglow of World War II and stirred by the pervasive cultural memory of the Revolution and the Civil War, Colin Powell and his contemporaries believed that American wars of the past had been justified. Only in Vietnam, it seemed, had the Republic prostituted its ideals. The resolve of the farmers who gathered in the mist of an April morning on Lexington common in April 1775; the fierce determination of the men of the Fifty-fourth Massachusetts Infantry Regiment as they formed ranks to advance on Battery Wagner in July 1863; the stoicism and courage of soldiers huddled in landing craft off the Normandy beaches in June 1944: all of these indelible images reflected the very real determination of Americans who were willing to forgo the individual pursuit of happiness and hazard their lives in the defense of freedom. Amid the ironies of Vietnam, these images and ideals retained the power of conviction.

Powell's promise, and that of his generation in the armed forces, was that once they were in a position to determine policy, there would be never be another Vietnam. In the first half of the 1970s, as the nation gradually extricated itself from Southeast Asia and the army made its tortured transition from the last demoralized days of conscription to its present form as a volunteer force, Powell and his contemporaries were still years away from defining policy, so the promise remained only a hopeful pledge. For Powell himself, the idea of what precisely would be necessary to avoid future Vietnams emerged fully formed only in 1975, when as a student in the National War College he read Carl von Clausewitz's nineteenth-century treatise, *On War*. It was for him "like a beam of light from the past, still illuminating present-day military quandaries."

"No one starts a war, or rather no one in his senses should do so," Clausewitz wrote, "without first being clear in his mind what he intends to achieve by that war and how he intends to achieve it." Mistake number one in Vietnam. Which led to Clausewitz's rule number two. Political leaders must set a war's objectives, while armies achieve them. In Vietnam, one seemed to be looking to the other for the answers that never came. Finally, the people must support a war. Since they supply the treasure and the sons, and today the daughters too, they must be convinced that the sacrifice is justified. That essential pillar had crumbled as the Vietnam War ground on. Clausewitz's greatest lesson for my profession was that the soldier, for all his patriotism, valor, and skill, forms just one leg in a triad. Without all three legs engaged, the military, the government, and the people, the enterprise cannot stand.[17]

Clausewitz thus provided the intellectual scaffolding for what had been more a disposition than a plan; now it became the beginnings of a policy he hoped one day to implement.

At the moment of his epiphany, Powell was thirty-nine years old and already a colonel, having received an "accelerated promotion" to the rank after only eighteen years of active duty. It was yet another mark of distinction in a steep upward career trajectory that testified both to his talents and to his mentors' faith that he could continue to develop at the highest levels of command. In another three years he became a brigadier general, the youngest in the army. That promotion, which might have capped a distinguished career, was in fact only the threshold to an astonishing continued rise, as Powell went on to become national security adviser to President Ronald Reagan and, finally, chairman of the Joint Chiefs of Staff. When President George H. W. Bush appointed him to that post in 1989, Powell was both the youngest man and the first African American to hold the job. He was also positioned to become the most powerful chairman in the forty-year history of the office.

Originally, the chairman of the JCS had been the first among equals on a board consisting of the service chiefs; he acted as their official spokesman but could not vote on issues that divided them. The Goldwater-Nichols Act of 1986 changed that by reforming the Joint Chiefs' structure, making the chairman the president's principal adviser on military matters and enabling him to speak not merely as a representative of the body but as its leader. Powell was the first chairman to serve his entire term under this new structure, and he used his power to revise and reorient the military strategy of the United States at the end of the Cold War. Most of all, his position enabled him to make good on the promise he had never forgotten, in the form that has come to be known as the Powell Doctrine: "War should be the politics of last resort. And when we go to war, we should have a purpose that our people understand and support; we should mobilize our country's resources to fulfill that mission and then go in to win."[18]

Powell used these principles at the midpoint of his term as chairman of the Joint Chiefs of Staff to advise President Bush on the military measures necessary to eject the forces of Iraq from Kuwait. Saddam Hussein invaded the small, oil-rich nation in August 1990 then annexed it as the nineteenth province of Iraq. This move effectively doubled the oil reserves under the dictator's control—indeed, it left him in command of approximately one-fifth of the world's oil supply—and created a situation intolerable for the United States. It was not, however, on the basis of that powerful geopolitical and strategic fact and its potential threat to the welfare of the petroleum-dependent American economy that the Bush administration ultimately justified going to war against Saddam. Rather, the formal U.S. justification for assembling a massive international coalition to support the half-million American soldiers, sailors, and airmen in their effort to eject the Iraqi forces from Kuwait was the historically familiar one of the defense of freedom. A small and defenseless country had been overrun by the forces of a tyrant, just as the forces of Nazi Germany had annexed Austria and the Czech Sudetenland in 1938. Saddam Hussein was by analogy another Hitler, one whose aggression could not be appeased without results similar to those of 1938, which plunged the whole world into war. It was necessary to liberate Kuwait not because its oil was critical to America's national interest but because freedom had to be defended against tyranny.

This argument convinced large numbers of the American people in a way that no rationale based solely on protecting American access to Middle Eastern petroleum could ever have done. On that basis the United States carried out the first Persian Gulf war with great popular support and a clear goal in view. The third condition of the Powell Doctrine—overwhelming force to accomplish the mission—fell quickly into place with the opening of Operation Desert Storm. A weeklong air campaign destroyed Iraq's air force and air defenses; the ground operations that followed were over, to all intents and purposes, in two days. If it was possible to conceive a war utterly unlike Vietnam, this was it, and it could only have given the greatest gratification to the man whose strategic vision structured it.[19]

But the story of American military involvement in the Persian Gulf and in the Middle East and South Asia generally did not end in 1991. What had seemed a clear-cut victory over Iraq proved instead to be an overture to a somber drama that has thus far produced an invasion of Afghanistan (2002), a second Gulf war (2003), and the military occupation of Iraq. These large, ambitious interventions were undertaken to remove two regimes obnoxious to the United States: the Taliban ruling party in Afghanistan because it was sheltering elements of al-Qaeda, the organization responsible for the terrorist attacks of September 11, 2001, and the Ba'athist dictatorship of Saddam Hussein in Iraq, which was thought to be prepared to offer weapons of mass destruction to al-Qaeda and other terrorist groups for use against the United States. Congress approved both interventions as aspects of a general war on terrorism that President George W. Bush announced with the backing of a cabinet that included, as secretary of state, Colin Powell.

How Secretary Powell understood these conflicts in light of his Vietnam experience, the Powell Doctrine, and his earlier strategic direction of the first Gulf war, was not fully clear when we wrote these words in mid-2004.[20] The larger implications of the Bush administration's decision to launch a preemptive attack on Iraq remain equally uncertain. As historians, of course, we cannot comment on the potential significance of this latest chapter in the long nation's narrative of war and freedom until events have reached some kind of conclusion, and that cannot possibly happen for some years to come. What we can say, however, is that now, as with World War I and World War II, a war fought in the name of freedom created the conditions that led to another; now, as with the Seven Years' War, a decisive military victory failed to produce a definitive peace; and now, as with the Spanish-American War and the Philippine Insurrection, substantial numbers of the people American forces believed they were liberating find it impossible to regard their liberators as anything but a new species of oppressor. It seems clear that once again an American war that was fought in the name of freedom and in the hope of stabilizing a situation thought to portend great threat to the nation has produced unpredictable outcomes, created a new set of contingencies, and altered the world in ways that Americans will have to reckon with for years to come.

On Memorial Day weekend in 2004, a vast concourse of people, many of them in their late seventies or eighties, gathered on the Mall in Washington, D.C., to witness the dedication of the newest monument to an American war, the World War II Memorial. The dedication fell very nearly on the sixtieth anniversary of D-Day, the interval that separated the dedication of the Lincoln Memorial (1922) from the Emancipation Proclamation (1862). The identical length of time is surely no accident; in both, the passing of the generation that fought the war was crucial to the impulse to commemorate it and the similar impulse to situate it in the larger contexts of American history. The 1920s and 1930s, as we have seen, were a crucial period for defining the meaning of the Civil War, in forms as diverse as the chiseled inscriptions of the Lincoln Memorial and the flickering images on movie screens. It was then, just as the event itself was passing out of living memory, that the connections Lincoln had so eloquently drawn between the ideals of the Revolution and the ordeal of the Civil War became firmly fixed in public memory as dominant events in the grand narrative of American history. Just so now, as the memory of the Second World War passes through a similar romantic metamorphosis, it may be worthwhile to return to the point where we began and to reflect not only on the significance of the wars recalled by the three great monuments that dominate the Mall's central axis but also the wars whose monuments haunt its margins and the wars to which no monuments will likely ever be raised.

In many ways, our purpose in writing this book was to rearrange the landscape of historical memory and meaning by emphasizing the importance of the wars Americans have fought less to preserve liberty than to extend the power of the United States *in the name of* liberty. We have sought to complicate the self-image of Americans as a free people who marshal their collective power most conclusively only in crises and then only to protect themselves and other freedom-loving peoples from tyranny. To see the imperialist military adventures of 1812, 1846, and 1898 and the wars of liberation begun in 1775, 1861, and 1941 as related—indeed, as enmeshed in a larger contingent narrative of a continent's development through half a millennium—is to view the American past from an unfamiliar perspective.

That vantage point encourages us to read the majestic phrases chiseled into the Lincoln Memorial's walls in a more ambiguous context. We would not wish to diminish the force of Lincoln's words even if we could. Yet we also believe that the present is a peculiarly fitting time for Americans to understand those words in the broadest possible frame: not as the product (as Lincoln thought) of a history that began in 1776 but rather as the remarkable result of more than three centuries of North America's development in the context of imperial competition, imperial ambition. Now, we think, is a proper occasion to contemplate the possibility that the United States was conceived in empire as well as in liberty and dedicated not only to the proposition that all men are created equal but to the corollary that any nation so conceived and so dedicated bears the obligation to use its power to preserve and extend freedom's realm.

When Abraham Lincoln composed the Gettysburg Address, the history of the United States was only four-score-and-seven-years long. He wrote in the hope that this brief story would not conclude in violence but rather continue until the great sin of slavery was expiated and the nation's original commitment to freedom was reborn. His narrative began with a sharp break from the colonial past and the birth of a new nation, independent and free. With its movement from empire through revolution to empire, our story has no such dramatic discontinuity but rather a war-driven transformation and a great irony at its center.

For two and a half centuries after Europeans arrived in North America, empire was a fact of life on a continent where relations between peoples were continually shaped and reshaped by warfare. Native attempts to survive and prosper by manipulating the colonizers and maneuvering between powers seeking to extend their imperial sway knit together the story of those centuries and their forgotten wars. They are of enormous importance if we wish to understand why Lincoln could say the things he did and why modern Americans still can find those words so deeply meaningful. Through that first half of North America's history it remained unclear that any one empire would dominate the continent or that Indians were doomed to subordination. Two of the three European colonial regimes that survived to the middle of the eighteenth century depended on native peoples for their survival; the Indians themselves demonstrated extraordinary resourcefulness and skill in adapting to the demands of life in an imperial world. At the close of the Age of Colonization and Conflict, Britain's American subjects were unique among European colonists in that only they cared less about trading with the Indians, exploiting their labor, or saving their souls than about appropriating their lands. No one—not even the British—yet imagined that English-speaking peoples would one day achieve hegemony in North America.

The highly contingent events and unprecedented outcomes of the Seven Years' War at the outset of the Age of Empires and Revolutions altered forever the equations of power on the continent. The war produced a decisive result in the competition between empires, then heightened tensions between the British metropolis and colonies until the victorious empire tore itself apart. The great disintegration came about because Britain's rulers and Britain's colonists could no longer agree on the rules by which their transatlantic political community would function. Indeed, the concepts of liberty and equality of rights that the colonists emphasized in their resistance to Parliament and the crown were attempts to define acceptable terms of allegiance *and thus to save* the empire. Only after Independence did that same ideology inspire the creation of new governments and define a new constitutional logic for the legitimate exercise of power in the public sphere. But none of the republican ideas that animated the Revolution diminished the Americans' determination to impose order on what they perceived as a dangerously disorderly periphery.

The desire to impose order is, of course, a fundamental impulse behind the creation of empires throughout history. Those driven by a rage for order need not actually *intend* to expand territorially or acquire greater resources or transform the lives of the peoples they conquer as a primary goal; imperialism can easily arise from isolationist motives and need not be accompanied by any ideological justification at all. It was, therefore, a profoundly ironic accident of the revolutionary origins of the United States that the power-abhorring ideology of resistance, republicanism, formed the basis of political culture in what soon proved one of the most dynamically expansionist territorial empires in world history.

The rhetoric of liberty by which Americans justified war in 1775 and Independence in 1776 adapted remarkably well to changing circumstances as the United States consolidated its control in eastern North America and then passed through a second cycle of imperial overextension, revolution, and consolidation in the last half of the nineteenth century. The wars of the first half of the nineteenth century contributed mightily to the conviction shared by most white Protestant Americans that liberty came naturally only to those who shared their race, religion, and cultural traditions. Victory over Indians and Mexicans and what became, in a purely contingent way, a revolutionary war against human slavery affirmed the notion that the United States was something new under the sun, the very model of a society of independent individuals who accepted the responsibility to liberate other peoples so that they, too, could choose to embrace a superior way of life. Americans, in short, constructed their conquest of North America as a collective sacrifice in the service of human liberty. Their romantic linking of the cause of the United States with the cause of freedom led the citizens of the world's greatest imperial republic to understand any rejection of their nation as a rejection of liberty itself. They thus freed themselves from any obligation to understand other peoples and places on their own terms and in their own contexts.

Perhaps as a consequence, Americans found it difficult to accept, let alone confront, the extent of their national power, especially as expressed in military form. Born in a revolution against empire, the United States seemed to nineteenth- and twentieth-century Americans a benign vessel of liberty, constructed to resist the exertion of power over human beings. To understand the United States as a nation with interests that diverged sharply from those of other peoples and that centered on perpetuating itself and extending its dominion—that is, seeing it as an empire—was to challenge the central dimensions of American identity.

This equation of freedom with the nation—this image of the United States as liberator rather than conqueror—justified interventionism without losing any of its racist, ethnocentric edge when twentieth-century Americans abandoned empire-building by territorial acquisition in favor of hegemonic imperialism. To this day the tendency persists (albeit in a form shorn of overt racism) to justify war as an altruistic determination to rid the world of tyrannies that would crush the human spirit. Distinguished by sincerity rather than hypocrisy, Americans' faith in freedom's vindicating power has enabled the United States to undertake wars and interventions with great regularity, even as it has diverted attention from the radically unpredictable, often destabilizing, effects that those conflicts have had on the development of the nation, the continent, the hemisphere, and the world.

The constraints of the accustomed grand narrative, centering on wars of liberation and marginalizing the rest, make it difficult if not impossible to appreciate the degree to which American notions of rights and liberty are culture-bound products of specific, contingent historical circumstances. We hope, therefore, that this alternative telling may encourage our fellow citizens to consider past events and present values in light of what seems to us the distinctly American dilemma: how to exercise power legitimately and productively in a world made up of peoples who do not universally embrace individual freedom or affirm the desirability of egalitarian democratic governance.

The need to protect American freedom by the direct exertion of power has always coexisted uneasily with the American faith that other peoples if offered the chance will voluntarily adopt political systems and values consistent with those of the United States. Whether justified by promises of liberation or not, coercion and conquest foster fear, resentment, and a desire for revenge much more reliably than they promote understanding and respect in the conquered for the values of the conqueror. Because the values of liberty and individual rights cannot be imposed by force, only embraced voluntarily, military power wielded in the name of liberty can all too easily work at cross-purposes with the goal of creating worldwide acceptance of the values that Americans cherish.

At what point do the contradictions between the advocacy of liberty and the use of coercive means become overwhelming? We have no sure or ready answer. We do believe, however, that the question can best be addressed in light of a pattern of development in which the values of republicanism and empire have consistently complemented one another, a history in which war and freedom have long intertwined. Whatever the answer may be, historical processes are so contingent in character that it will be fully known only in retrospect. As our narrative of North America's past suggests, there are no easily predictable results in history and no resolutions free of irony, least of all when the most important outcomes are decided in the unpredictable dominion of war.

NOTES

Introduction: A View in Winter

1. "Grand narrative," a coinage of Jean-François Lyotard, has become a term of art that historians use to describe the overarching story of humanity within whose bounds specific narratives are constructed to describe some aspect of the larger story. Allan Megill, in his essay "'Grand Narrative' and the Discipline of History," in *A New Philosophy of History,* Frank Ankersmit and Hans Kellner, eds. (Chicago: University of Chicago Press, 1995), distinguishes between a universal "grand narrative" and the "master narratives" of individual nations or groups. We use the term as adapted by Dorothy Ross, in "Grand Narrative in American Historical Writing: From Romance to Uncertainty," *American Historical Review* 100 (1995), 3:651–77, to describe national history as well as the history of humanity. "In practice," Ross writes, ". . . the master narratives of the United States and Europe . . . are integrally related to grand narratives of the progress of humanity and generally imply their existence" (651 n. 2).

   Grand narrative, in the sense we use it here, refers to a broad set of understandings in American popular and political culture, *not* to any specific argument or interpretative scheme constructed by American historians. Although some scholarly writers share the assumptions that undergird the commonly accepted grand narrative, many more are explicitly critical of it and passionately contest its very premises. In the absence of those critical scholarly histories, we could not have hoped to create the counter-narrative that follows, which we could attempt only because we were standing on the shoulders of giants. We hope our colleagues will understand us as having scrambled to that lofty perch in the hope of surveying the historical landscape from a new perspective, not with the intention of boxing them about the ears.

2. Address to the New York Provincial Congress, June 26, 1775, in W. W. Abbot, et al., eds., *The Papers of George Washington, Revolutionary War Series,* vol. 1, *June–September 1775* (Charlottesville: University Press of Virginia, 1985), 41.

3. Anthony Pagden, *Peoples and Empires: A Short History of European Migration, Exploration, and Conquest, from Greece to the Present* (New York: Modern Library, 2001), xxi.

4. Fred Anderson and Andrew R. L. Cayton, "The Problem of Fragmentation and the Prospects for Synthesis in Early American Social History," *William and Mary Quarterly,* 3rd Ser., 50 (1993), 299–310; Andrew R. L. Cayton, "Insufficient Woe: Sense and Sensibility in Writing Nineteenth-Century History," *Reviews in American History,* 31 (2003) 3: 331–41.

One: Champlain's Legacy

1. Samuel de Champlain, "The Voyages to the Great River Saint Lawrence by the Sieur de Champlain, Captain in the Royal Navy, from the year 1608 until 1612, Book Second," in H. P. Biggar, gen. ed., *The Works of Samuel de Champlain,* vol. 2, *1608–1613,* trans. John Squair (Toronto: The Champlain Society, 1925), 95.

2. Biographical information: Marcel Trudel, "Champlain, Samuel de," *Dictionary of Canadian Biography,* vol. 1, *1000 to 1700* (Toronto: University of Toronto Press, 1966), 186–99, and Samuel Eliot Morison, *Samuel de Champlain: Father of New France* (Boston: Little, Brown, 1972), 16–18. On the Eighth War of Religion and its contexts: Ernest R. Dupuy and Trevor N. Dupuy, *The Harper Encyclopedia of Military History* (New York: HarperCollins, 1993), 524–25; Garrett Mattingly, *Renaissance Diplomacy* (Boston: Houghton Mifflin, 1955), 191–208; Geoffrey Parker, *The Military Revolution: Military Innovation and the Rise of the West, 1500–1800* (New York: Cambridge University Press, 1996), 41–43. On the *Saint-Julien* and its voyage: Champlain, "Brief Narrative of the Most Remarkable Things that Samuel Champlain of Brouage Observed in the West Indies," in H. P. Biggar, ed., *The Works of Samuel de Champlain,* vol. 1, *1599–1607,* trans. H. H. Langton and W. F. Ganong (Toronto: The Champlain Society, 1922), 3–7; quotation at 6–7.

3. Champlain, "Brief Narrative," *Works of Champlain,* 1:38–41, 44–45.

4. Ibid., 61–65.

5. Ross Hassig, *Mexico and the Spanish Conquest* (London: Longman, 1994), passim; Mark A. Burkholder and Lyman L. Johnson, *Colonial Latin America* (New York: Oxford University Press, 1994), 36–43; Ian K. Steele, *Warpaths: Invasions of North America* (New York: Oxford University Press, 1994), 9; John Keegan, *A History of Warfare* (New York: Knopf, 1993), 108–14; Alan Taylor, *American Colonies* (New York: Viking, 2001), 52–54. The most recent interpretation of the conquest places renewed emphasis on technological factors and discounts the notion that

the Aztecs were made culturally vulnerable to conquest by a prophecy that identified the Spanish with the returning god Quetzalcoatl; see Camilla Townsend, "Burying the White Gods: New Perspectives on the Conquest of Mexico," *American Historical Review* 108 (June 2003), 3:659–87.

6. Within two years after he founded Saint Augustine, Menéndez de Avilés established strategic bases at Tampa Bay and Charlotte Harbor on the west coast of the peninsula and at five locations on the east coast and to the north, from Biscayne Bay (near modern Miami) to Santa Elena (now Parris Island, in Port Royal Sound, South Carolina). By 1574, only the forts at Saint Augustine and Santa Elena remained. The Spaniards abandoned Santa Elena as indefensible in 1586, withdrawing all colonists and soldiers to Saint Augustine. See David J. Weber, *The Spanish Frontier in North America* (New Haven, Conn.: Yale University Press, 1992), 70–75; Taylor, *American Colonies,* 77–79; and Steele, *Warpaths,* 25–30.

7. Steele, *Warpaths,* 25–36; quotations are from page 31. The later experience of Spain's colonization in New Mexico in many ways paralleled the history of Florida. Once again, the motivation in founding the colony was strategic. At the end of the sixteenth century the Spanish crown worried that Francis Drake's circumnavigation of the world (1578–80) indicated that he had discovered the strait of Anián, connecting the Atlantic and Pacific oceans, and might therefore threaten the rich new silver mines of Chihuahua in northern Mexico. The Spanish therefore planned to found a colony near what they supposed the location of the strait to be, in what is now northern New Mexico. The Pueblos, a sedentary agricultural people along the upper Rio Grande, lived in the area. They were numerous—perhaps 50,000 in all—and prosperous and had a serious problem with the nomadic Navajos and Apaches who raided them for provisions and captives. Initially the Spanish looked like potential allies, just as they had to the Tlaxcalans and the Timucuas, and the Pueblos welcomed Governor and Captain-General Juan de Oñate when he arrived in 1598 with 400 or so soldiers, settlers, and Franciscan friars. Tribute soon became a disruptive issue, however, and when resistance emerged at Acoma Pueblo, where the Indians killed a dozen soldiers, Oñate responded by cannonading the town, killing or mutilating its men, and enslaving its women and children. The remainder of the Pueblo villages submitted quietly, receiving missionaries and paying tribute in foodstuffs and forced labor as they were commanded.

Only in 1680 did the Spanish realize how thoroughly the Pueblos, who resented forced labor for the *encomenderos* and chafed at the missionaries' interference in their culture, had come to hate them. In that year a shaman of Tewa Pueblo named Popé succeeded in organizing an alliance of several pueblos to kill the missionaries in their villages and attack the principal Spanish settlement at Santa Fe. The uprising was phenomenally successful. Pueblo warriors killed 400 colonists and expelled the remainder together with numerous Indian converts. The refugees abandoned everything and fled 250 miles down the Rio Grande to El Paso del Norte. They did not return for twelve years; when they did, it was hardly the *reconquista* they claimed.

In the interim, the Apaches acquired horses from the herds the Spanish abandoned, learned to ride them, and began raiding the pueblos with greater ferocity and to greater effect than ever. Several pueblos had to be abandoned and their populations relocated to Santa Fe. At the same time, Popé had proved a better war leader than political unifier and the interpueblo alliance broke down. In weakness and isolation, some of the pueblos actually sought alliances with Apache groups, leaving the Pueblo people vulnerable even to civil war. Thus when a new governor-general, Diego de Vargas, tentatively returned at the head of 200 troops in 1692, the Pueblos made no effort to resist. They needed an ally with access to trade goods, weapons to help protect them from their newly formidable enemies, and a mediator to settle their internal disputes. Vargas was in reality all three of those and a conqueror only in name.

That the Pueblos could have resisted, had they chosen to do so, seems clear from the experience of the Zuñi and Hopi pueblos further west, which refused to reaccept Spanish missions and remained independent for more than a century and a half thereafter. That the Spanish realized they had "reconquered" New Mexico on sufferance from the Pueblos themselves seems clear from Vargas's refusal to reinstitute forced labor under the *encomienda* system, his hesitance to use arms to coerce the rebels, and his promotion of trade on terms as favorable as could be managed in a colony so distant from sources of supply. Missionary fathers in the postrevolt era no longer interfered so aggressively in Pueblo cultural life, tolerating the sub rosa survival of indigenous religious beliefs in return for external adherence to Catholic ritual. Most significantly, Spanish settlers participated as allies in the Pueblos' wars against Navajo, Apache, Comanche, and other enemies. The New Mexico colony became secure only when the Spanish at length controlled their desire to act as overlords and integrated themselves into an indigenous system of warfare and trade.

The wars the Pueblos and their Spanish allies fought against the Apaches, Navajos, Comanches, and other nomadic peoples became increasingly intense. In the eighteenth century, the mutual raiding for captives, livestock, and goods occasionally became severe enough to depopulate whole areas of the New Mexican frontier. To help pay the expenses of these wars, the Spanish began sending captives to Havana for sale as slaves. The Spanish crown prohibited the sale of Apache men, who were regarded as excessively dangerous, in 1800; but Apache women, and presumably other captives, continued to be sold at Havana until 1821. Thus the integration of the Spanish into the Pueblo complex of trade and war stabilized Pueblo-Spanish relations. In doing so, however, it transmuted the mutual raiding of indigenous warfare into a much more deadly and destructive form and eventually commercialized the taking of captives, transforming what had once functioned as a mechanism of demographic replacement into a procurement tool of the international slave trade.

(This account is derived from Weber, *Spanish Frontier,* 77–100, 122–41,

195–96, 204–35 passim; Robert Silverberg, *The Pueblo Revolt* [Lincoln: University of Nebraska Press, 1994], 52–204; Herman J. Viola, *After Columbus* [Washington, D.C.: Smithsonian Books, 1990], 47–51, 76–83. See also Oakah L. Jones Jr., *Pueblo Warriors and Spanish Conquest* [Norman: University of Oklahoma Press, 1966]; Andrew L. Knaut, *The Pueblo Revolt of 1680: Conquest and Resistance in Seventeenth-Century New Mexico* [Norman: University of Oklahoma Press, 1995]; Elizabeth A. H. John, *Storms Brewed in Other Men's Worlds: The Confrontation of Indians, Spanish, and French in the Southwest, 1540–1795* [College Station: Texas A&M University Press, 1975]; Ramon Gutiérrez, *When Jesus Came, the Corn Mothers Went Away* [Stanford, Calif.: Stanford University Press, 1991]; Jack D. Forbes, *Apache, Navaho, and Spaniard* [Norman: University of Oklahoma Press, 1960]; Henry Warren Bowden, *American Indians and Christian Missions: Studies in Cultural Conflict* [Chicago: University of Chicago Press, 1981], 53–55; Charles Hackett, ed., *Revolt of the Pueblo Indians*, 2 vols. [Albuquerque: University of New Mexico Press, 1942]; Thomas H. Naylor and Charles W. Polzer, eds., *The Presidio and Militia on the Northern Frontier of New Spain*, vol. 1: *1570–1700* [Tucson: University of Arizona Press, 1986]. A good recent synthesis can be found in Taylor, *American Colonies*, 79–90. The larger context of war-making, cross-cultural adoption, and enslavement in the southwestern borderlands has been most brilliantly delineated in James F. Brooks, *Captives and Cousins: Slavery, Kinship, and Community in the Southwest Borderlands* [Chapel Hill: University of North Carolina Press, 2002]; for this period, see esp. chaps. 1 and 2.)

8. Bruce G. Trigger and William R. Swagerty, "Entertaining Strangers: North America in the Sixteenth Century," in Bruce G. Trigger and Wilcomb E. Washburn, eds., *The Cambridge History of the Native Peoples of the Americas*, vol. 1, *North America, Part 1* (Cambridge, U.K.: Cambridge University Press, 1996), 349–54.

9. Arthur J. Ray, "The Northern Interior, 1600 to Modern Times," in Bruce Trigger and Wilcomb Washburn, eds., *The Cambridge History of the Native Peoples of the Americas*, vol. 1, *North America, Part Two* (Cambridge, U.K.: Cambridge University Press, 1996), 267–69; Morison, *Champlain*, 25–27; Champlain, "Of Savages, or Voyage of the Sieur De Champlain Made in the Year 1603," *Works of Champlain*, 1:91.

10. Champlain and his French contemporaries distinguished the seminomadic native peoples of northern woodlands, *les sauvages* (the uncivilized), from the sedentary native inhabitants of the Spanish possessions (the Spanish Indies), whom they called *indiens*, on the basis of their modes of living. (The Spanish observed a similar distinction between *indios* and *indios bárbaros*). The habit of conflating of all native groups into a single category, Indians, was characteristic of Anglophones, who, as we shall see, saw less reason to distinguish one kind of native from another.

11. Champlain, "Of Savages," *Works of Champlain*, 1:98–109; quotations at 107–09. A note on names: the Algonquins were one of the native nations of Canada with whom Champlain had repeated dealings. Other Indian peoples, below, will be

referred to as "Algonquians"—linguistically and culturally related nations including the Algonquins, Mi'kmaqs, Malecites, Abenakis, Mahicans, Narragansetts, Delawares (Unami and Munsee), Shawnees, Fox, Ojibwas, Potawotomis, and others. Confusing as it may seem, it is necessary for narrative purposes to distinguish between the specific Algon*quins* of whom Champlain wrote and the Algon*quians* who will become important later in our story.

12. Ibid., 178–80.

13. Ibid., 110–20; quotations at 118 ("agile"), 110 ("cheerful"), 119 ("rackets" [snowshoes]), 118 ("visions"), 119–20 (sexual mores), and 111 ("revenge"); dialogue with Anadabijou, 111–17 ("approved what I had said" and "brought to be good Christians," 117). The last quotation is not H. H. Langton's translation but our own of *"ils seroient reduicts bon Chrestiens si l'on habitoit leur terres, ce qu'ils desireroient la plus part."*

14. Champlain, "The Voyages of the Sieur de Champlain of Saintonge, Captain in Ordinary for the King in the Navy," 1613, Book 1, *Works of Champlain,* 1:203–469.

15. Ibid., 384, 392–94; Morison, *Champlain,* 72, 78.

16. Champlain, "Voyages" (1613, Book 1), *Works of Champlain,* 1:394.

17. Ibid., 395–96.

18. Ibid., 398.

19. Ibid., 399–401. On previous amicable relations with the Cape Ann Pawtuckets, see ibid., 334–42. On the identity of this group, which Champlain identified merely as Almouchiquois, see Bert Salwen, "Indians of Southern New England and Long Island: Early Period," in Bruce G. Trigger, ed., *Handbook of North American Indians,* vol. 15, *Northeast* (Washington, D.C.: Smithsonian Institution Press, 1978), 169–70.

20. For the identity of the Stage Harbor attackers, see Salwen, "Indians of Southern New England," 171–72. Hostile encounters with the Indians: Champlain, "Voyages" (1613, Book 1), *Works of Champlain,* 1:400–01 (Gloucester), 416–32 (Stage Harbor).

21. Ibid., 428–29 n. 1; quotation, 431.

22. Ibid., 443, 457–58.

23. The inimical quality of competition became unmistakable on the next voyage. Champlain reached Tadoussac on June 3, 1608, trailing the fur monopoly partner François Gravé du Pont by a week. Upon arriving he learned that Gravé du Pont had tried to inform the Basques who were trading there they had no right to do so and that they had replied with violence. Gravé du Pont was wounded and one of his men was killed by a Basque crew that boarded their vessel and forcibly seized its cannon and ammunition. Asserting that "they would barter in spite of the king's orders," the Basques refused to give back the company's armaments unless Gravé du Pont returned to France. Champlain ultimately negotiated a peaceful settlement to the crisis but not without difficulty. Champlain, "Voyages" (1613, Book 2), *Works of Champlain,* 2:11–12.

24. Champlain, "Of Savages," *Works of Champlain,* 1:129.
25. Morison, *Champlain,* 106–08; Champlain, "Voyages," (1613, Book 2), *Works of Champlain,* 2:44–58. Unlike Tadoussac, where the Montagnais population was comparatively large and sophisticated in the ways of trade, the Montagnais band at Quebec was small and poor and had probably inhabited the region for only a short time. When Cartier explored the area in 1535–36 and 1541–42, the area was home to a sizable population of Iroquoian-speaking "Stadaconans." These and the rest of the Saint Lawrence Valley's Iroquoian peoples vanished in the late sixteenth century, perhaps dispersed as a consequence of attacks by the Five Nations Iroquois. The Montagnais who lived near Quebec in 1608 were still subject to repeated Five Nations raiding, as were the Algonquins and Hurons who lived upriver. See Bruce Trigger, "Early Iroquoian Contacts with Europeans," in Trigger, ed., *Handbook,* 15:346; Daniel K. Richter, *Facing East from Indian Country: A Native History of Early America* (Cambridge, Mass.: Harvard University Press, 2001), 26–40.
26. Champlain, "Voyages" (1613, Book 2), 2:67–68. The "league" that Champlain used was *la petite lieue marine,* equivalent to approximately 2.5 nautical miles (i.e., 3.75 statute miles or 4.6 kilometers); see Morison, *Champlain,* xiii. Champlain's party met the Huron and Algonquin party opposite the island of Saint-Eloi, a little over twenty leagues (about eighty miles) from Quebec.
27. Champlain, "Voyages" (1613, Book 2), 2:69–70.
28. Ibid., 71.
29. Ibid., 76.
30. Ibid., 79.
31. Ibid.
32. Ibid., 85.
33. Ibid., 83–85.
34. Ibid., 86.
35. Ibid., 88–89. Our translation varies here from that of John Squair; we thank Professor Matthew Gerber for helping us to verify its accuracy.
36. Ibid., 86.
37. Ibid., 94, 95.
38. Ibid., 96.
39. Ibid., 98.
40. Ibid., 99–100. Our wording varies from that of John Squair; again, we are grateful to Matthew Gerber for his advice on the translation.
41. Ibid., 101–03.
42. Ibid., 104–05.
43. Ibid., 106.
44. Ibid., 107.
45. Ibid., 109, 110.
46. Ibid., 120–21.

47. Ibid., 121–22.

48. Ibid., 124–44.

49. Ibid., 135.

50. The foregoing list of wars was compiled from William L. Langer, *An Encyclopedia of World History* (Boston: Houghton Mifflin, 1968), and Dupuy and Dupuy, *Harper Encyclopedia of Military History.* For a comprehensive treatment of the impact of American silver on Spain and the European economic and state systems generally, see Stanley J. Stein and Barbara H. Stein, *Silver, Trade, and War: Spain and America in the Making of Early Modern Europe* (Baltimore, Md.: Johns Hopkins University Press, 2000), 3–56.

51. Parker, *Military Revolution,* chap. 1, esp. 43–44; David Kaiser, *Politics and War: European Conflict from Philip II to Hitler* (Cambridge, Mass.: Harvard University Press, 1990), chap. 1.

52. Philip II had some idea that a naval attack on England would prove decisive but no sense of whether that would occur by naval victory in the Channel or the seizure of Ireland; nor is it clear whether he expected the result to be Elizabeth's withdrawal of support for the Dutch, the establishment of toleration for English Catholics, or the cessation of English attacks on Spanish shipping. Rather than the emergence full-blown of an integrated naval and military strategy, then, the Armada itself must be seen as a forerunner of later developments. See Kaiser, *Politics and War,* 38; Felipe Fernández-Armesto, *The Spanish Armada: The Experience of War in 1588* (Oxford, U.K.: Oxford University Press, 1988), 72–134.

53. Garrett Mattingly, *The Defeat of the Spanish Armada* (Boston: Houghton Mifflin, 1984), 354.

54. This is of course the famous formulation of the post-Napoleonic Prussian theorist of war, Carl von Clausewitz. (The quotation is from *On War,* ed. Michael Howard and Peter Paret [Princeton N.J.: Princeton University Press, 1989], 87.) From this dictum strategic thinkers have derived a distinction between power and force on which rests the syllogism of contemporary realpolitik: that national power depends upon the ability of a state to make other states do what it wishes; that military force furnishes the ultimate means of coercion but making war diminishes a nation's capacity to continue using force; and that the prudent national leader must, therefore, resort to war sparingly as a means of achieving political goals. This understanding of policy and warfare, power and force, is extraordinarily useful in historical analysis if carefully employed, as Edward Luttwak does in *The Grand Strategy of the Roman Empire: From the First Century B.C. to the Third* (Baltimore Md.: Johns Hopkins University Press, 1976), and as we try to do in the remainder of this book. We will argue, however, that its uncritical application can distort one's vision of prestate warfare systems.

It is also worth noting that Clausewitz's insight has been more frequently invoked than carefully examined and thus has become a kind of shibboleth in strategic thinking. John Keegan has observed, for example, that the usual translation of Clausewitz's German misses much of his intended meaning: that "policy" inadequately reflects the subtler *politischen Verkehrs* ("political intercourse"), and that "by other means" similarly distorts Clausewitz's *mit Einmischung anderer Mittel* ("with the intervention of other means"). See *A History of Warfare*, 3. Keegan goes on to argue that accepting Clausewitz's definition as normative rather than as the product of specific historical circumstances has led strategic thinkers and military historians to misunderstand the character of warfare and to misconstrue its meaning in human history.

55. William H. McNeill, *The Pursuit of Power* (Chicago: Chicago University Press, 1982), discusses the interaction between the expansion of market behavior and values and the expansion of European power. In the eighteenth century, the money economy and the operation of market incentives made possible the mobilization of manpower and other resources at a previously unimaginable level; see esp. "The Market Asserts Control," 102–16. This development was not uncontested: "The European public, as much as European rulers of the early modern centuries, disliked and distrusted the handful of monied men who enriched themselves by constraining rulers and their subjects to conform to the dictates of the market" (116). Mercantilism thus emerged from the need to harness the energies and values of the marketplace to governmental ends. See chaps. 4 and 5 and esp. 150–51.

56. By this we mean "in the fifteenth century." Earlier on, the Mississippian cultures—invaders, perhaps conquerors, probably from Mesoamerica—had evidently fielded armies, but the decline of the Mississippian culture complex and the dispersal of its urban populations into small settlements ended this phase of development more than a century before European contact. See Richter, *Facing East*, 2–7; Neal Salisbury, "The Indians' Old World: Native Americans and the Coming of Europeans," *William and Mary Quarterly*, 3d ser., 53 (1996), 435–58; also Francis Jennings, *The Founders of America* (New York: W.W. Norton, 1993), and two volumes edited by Bruce D. Smith, *Mississippian Settlement Patterns* (New York: Academic Press, 1978) and *The Mississippian Emergence* (Washington, D.C.: Smithsonian Institution Press, 1990).

57. The following is based largely on Daniel K. Richter, *Ordeal of the Longhouse: The Peoples of the Iroquois League in the Era of European Colonization* (Chapel Hill: University of North Carolina Press, 1992), chaps. 1 and 2; Richter, *Facing East*, 62–67; Richard White, *The Middle Ground: Indians, Empires, and Republics in the Great Lakes Region, 1650–1815* (New York: Cambridge University Press, 1991); Marian W. Smith, "American Indian Warfare," New York Academy of Sciences, *Transactions*, 2d Ser., 13 (June 1951), 348–65; Jonathan Haas, ed., *The Anthropology of War* (Cambridge, U.K.: Cambridge University Press, 1990); Keith F. Otterbein, *Feuding and Warfare* (Langhorne, Pa.: Gordon and Breach, 1994), xvii–xxxii, 1–23, 33–73, 195–200; S. P. Reyna and R. E. Downs, eds., *Studying War: Anthropological Perspectives* (Langhorne, Pa.: Gordon and Breach, 1994), chaps. 1 and 2;

R. Brian Ferguson and Neil L. Whitehead, eds., *War in the Tribal Zone: Expanding States and Indigenous Warfare* (Santa Fe, N.M.: School of American Research Press, 1992), chaps. 1 and 7; R. Brian Ferguson, ed., *Warfare, Culture, and Environment* (Orlando, Fla.: Academic Press, 1984), chaps. 1, 4, and 8. Anthropologists of war currently seem to divide into two broad camps: materialists, who argue that the motives for war are rooted in competition for resources and that the result of warfare is cultural selection to magnify the values that lead to success; and socio-biologists, who agree that wars begin in competition for resources but argue for considering their effects in biological evolution and selection for aggressive traits rather than cultural selection alone. An older interpretation, which holds that warfare represents a kind of cultural imperative similar to competitive play, seems now to have fewer adherents, although both materialists and sociobiologists agree that war, once begun, depends on cultural factors for its perpetuation. This seems to grant that wars can result from previous wars, in a contingent and historically based sense that we still find persuasive.

There were two great exceptions to the generalization we make here: the Aztecs and other state or statelike systems that evolved in Mexico where armies existed and warfare took on a form extraordinarily prodigal of human life; and took on those groups in which war was either attenuated or absent: the Coast Salish, the Indians of the Columbia Plateau (the Nez Percé, Spokane, and others), the peoples of the upper Northwest Coast among whom the potlatch system prevailed (the Kwakiutl and related groups), and the Eskimos. The Aztecs and their system are discussed above. The Northwest Coast, Columbia Plateau, and Arctic peoples tended to display open aggression only at a personal level—where it could assume extreme, even "berserk" forms, especially among Eskimos—and to channel intergroup competition into ritualized forms. Eskimo song contests, Coast Salish ceremonial gamble and challenge rites, and the potlatch competitions of the northern Northwest Coast all involved groups and kin networks in supporting the contestants, and were rituals used to settle disputes that offered opportunities to gain prestige and provided a means of transferring allegiance from one leader to another. In these respects, the contests provided an alternative way to manage issues that elsewhere might trigger wars. At least in part the groups that avoided war did so by utilizing exchange relationships to channel competition into nonviolent forms. However, in settings where these otherwise pacific groups encountered warlike competitors—on the eastern edge of the Columbia Plateau where Great Plains tribes contacted plateau peoples, at fishing sites claimed by both the Coast Salish and the Nootka, or in the Subarctic zone where Eskimos and Crees came in contact—they could show a ferocity as great as any group in North America. For a description of this predominantly nonwarlike culture complex, which she identifies as "shame-aggression" to distinguish it from the "mourning-war" complex of the rest of North America north of Mexico, see

Smith, "American Indian War," esp. 350–51, 359–60, and 363–64; for a more modern interpretation, which gives larger scope to warfare even among the Kwakiutl but does not in every respect supersede Smith's general account, see R. Brian Ferguson, "A Reexamination of the Causes of Northwest Coast Warfare," in Ferguson, ed., *Warfare, Culture, and Environment,* 267–328.

58. Mourning warfare was, in cultural terms, a means of coming to terms with grief; it typically began when bereaved mothers or wives appealed to warriors to provide them with substitutes for deceased sons or husbands: captives who, at the discretion of the women, might be ritually tortured to death or tortured as a prelude to adoption. Wars allowed adolescent males to practice skills and demonstrate virtues central to their cultures, and enabled the ritual attainment of manhood; they gave grown men opportunities to gain prestige by displaying courage and distinguishing themselves with feats of arms.

59. Richter, *Ordeal of the Longhouse,* 35, 54; also Smith, "American Indian Warfare," 349.

60. Richter, *Ordeal of the Longhouse,* 29. Richter quotes an eighteenth-century Iroquois sachem: "The trade and the peace we take to be one thing" (ibid.). Compare Daniel Usner's treatment of the relationship between peace and trade in *Indians, Settlers, and Slaves in a Frontier Exchange Economy: The Lower Mississippi Valley Before 1783* (Chapel Hill: University of North Carolina Press, 1992); and see esp. Richard White's extended analysis of trading relations, "The Fur Trade," chap. 3 of *The Middle Ground,* 94–141. White quotes the anthropologist George Dalton in analyzing an instance of exchange between Ottawas and Crees in the 1660s: "Gifts created 'peace and a sort of conditional friendship between potentially hostile persons of groups.' And precisely because 'to break off the gift giving [was] to break off the peaceful relationships,' the exchange was consciously and purposefully uneven. After giving the [beaver robes] for the European goods, the Crees made a further gift of furs to induce, or perhaps, obligate the Ottawas to return." (98–99; quoted passages are from George Dalton, "The Impact of Colonization on Aboriginal Economies in Stateless Societies," *Research in Economic Anthropology,* 1:138.)

61. Christopher L. Miller and George R. Hamell, "A New Perspective on Indian-White Contact: Cultural Symbols and Colonial Trade," *Journal of American History* 73 (1986), 2:322: Richter, *Ordeal of the Longhouse,* 28.

62. Smith, "American Indian Warfare," 349.

63. Champlain, "Voyages" (1613, Book 1), *Works of Champlain,* 1:458 n. 1.

64. The reason for the disappearance of the Saint Lawrence Iroquoians remains obscure. Cartier traded with them and lived among them at Stadacona (Quebec) in 1535–36 and 1541–43. Their disappearance may well have had something to do with those unhappy sojourns, perhaps by occasioning an intensification of war with other groups, by disease, or crop failure. For an inventive, persuasive

approach to the mystery of the Stadaconans and the Iroquoians of Hochelaga (Montreal), see Richter, *Facing East,* 28–40 passim.

65. Victor Hugo Paltsits, "Henry Hudson," *Dictionary of American Biography on CD-ROM* (New York, 1997; originally published New York: Charles Scribner's Sons, 1932); Allen W. Trelease, *Indian Affairs in Colonial New York: The Seventeenth Century* (Ithaca, N.Y.: Cornell University Press, 1960), 25–28; quotation at 27.

66. Ibid., 30–35.

67. The following account of Mohawk-French-Mahican-Dutch relations in the 1620s follows Richter, *Ordeal of the Longhouse,* 87–90, and Bruce G. Trigger, "The Mohawk-Mahican War (1624–28): The Establishment of a Pattern," *Canadian Historical Review* 52 (1971), 276–86.

68. The turning point in the Mohawk-Mahican war came in 1626, when in a reprise of Champlain's sorties against the Mohawks, the Fort Orange commissary Daniel van Krieckenbeeck and six musketeers agreed to accompany a Mahican war party in a raid against a Mohawk fort. Rather than effecting the wholesale slaughter Champlain and his allies had achieved in 1610, however, van Krieckenbeeck blundered into a Mohawk ambush. Taken wholly by surprise, he and three of his men were slain in a hail of arrows; one was roasted and eaten in a ritual feast and the body parts of others became trophies of war. Within days the Dutch sent an emissary to the Mohawks to make peace and to promise their neutrality in a contest that thereafter ran ever more decisively against the Mahicans. On van Krieckenbeeck's expedition, see Trelease, *Indian Affairs,* 46–48.

69. Seamus Heaney, trans., *Beowulf: A New Verse Translation* (New York: Farrar, Straus and Giroux, 2000), line 3009.

70. Steele, *Warpaths,* 67–68; Eccles, *France in America,* 27–29.

71. Kirke to Champlain, July 8, 1628, in Champlain, "Second Part of the Voyages of the Sieur de Champlain," Book II (1632); in H. P. Biggar, ed., *The Works of Samuel de Champlain,* vol. 5, *1620–1629,* trans. W. D. LeSueur (Toronto: The Champlain Society, 1933), 280–91.

72. Champlain to Kirke, n.d., ibid., 283–85.

73. Ibid., 240.

74. Ibid., 297–301; quotations at 299 and 301. The French did not try to hunt for themselves, evidently because the Indians would not permit it. On the one occasion that Chomina allowed Frenchmen to accompany his hunters on snowshoes, Champlain gladly furnished powder and match from his tiny stock, but the effort yielded less meat than discord. The musketeers succeeded in taking "a moose of great size" but then "devour[ed] it like ravenous wolves, without giving us any share beyond about twenty pounds." Realizing that a repeat performance of this episode might further undermine his authority and perhaps tear the French community apart altogether, Champlain "reproach[ed] them for their gluttony" and "did not send them out again, but employed them in other ways" (301).

75. Ibid., 239–65.

76. Ibid., 285–86.

77. "Second Part of the Voyages of the Sieur de Champlain," Book III, in H. P. Biggar, ed., *The Works of Samuel de Champlain*, vol. 6, *1629–1632*, trans. W. D. LeSueur and H. H. Langton (Toronto, 1936), 8–25 (quotation at 25). Diet at Quebec in June: Morison, *Champlain*, 194.

78. Morison, *Champlain*, 199, reports the value of the 1629 exports as 300,000 *livres*, a sum equivalent to £28,846 at the average rate of exchange for *livres Tournois* on sterling in that year (John J. McCusker, *Money and Exchange in Europe and America, 1600–1775: A Handbook* [Chapel Hill, N.C., 1978], 88 [Table 2.23]); Steele, *Warpaths*, 68, notes that the 30,000 pelts shipped in 1630 was "a record." There were apparently two reasons that the Kirkes extracted furs with greater success than Champlain. First was simply that the war, a deficit of trade goods at Quebec, and the unwillingness of the Montagnais to trade with Champlain while he held hostages had allowed a large supply to accumulate in the Indians' hands. The second factor was that, unlike Champlain, the Kirkes were willing to provide liquor to the Indians virtually without limit and hence accelerated the rate of exchange as well as increasing as the level of social disorder among natives in the vicinity of Quebec.

79. Morison, *Champlain*, 211–17; quotation at 217.

80. Ibid., 217–18; Bruce G. Trigger, "Champlain Judged by His Indian Policy: A Different View of Early Canadian History," *Anthropologica*, N.S. 13 (1971), Special Issue [*Pilot Not Commander: Essays in Memory of Diamond Jenness*]: 108; Trigger, *The Children of Aataentsic: A History of the Huron People to 1660* (Montreal and London, 1976), 2:456–57.

81. For the best explanation of Iroquois beliefs and their significance, see Richter, *Ordeal of the Longhouse*, 30–49.

82. Richter, *Ordeal of the Longhouse*, 58–59; *Looking East*, 60.

83. Steele, *Warpaths*, 115; Richter, *Ordeal of the Longhouse*, 62, 64, 93–95; Brian J. Given, "The Iroquois Wars and Native Arms," in Bruce A. Cox, ed., *Native People, Native Lands* (Ottawa: Carleton University Press, 1988), 3–13; George T. Hunt, *The Wars of the Iroquois: A Study in Intertribal Trade Relations* (Madison: University of Wisconsin Press, 1967), 165–75 (prices quoted at 170); José António Brandão, *"Your Fyre Shall Burn No More": Iroquois Policy toward New France and Its Native Allies to 1701* (Lincoln: University of Nebraska Press, 1997), 100. Iroquois—especially Mohawk—warriors had acquired as many as 300 muskets before the trade was officially sanctioned. Between 1643 and 1645, they acquired another 400 with the approval of the governor of New Netherland. This made them incomparably the best-armed native people of the eastern woodlands. All official vestiges of the ban on the firearms trade were lifted in New Netherland in 1648.

84. See esp. Brandão, *"Your Fyre Shall Burn No More,"* 6–18.

85. Ibid., 63, and Appendix D, "The Statistics of War: Iroquois Hostilities to 1701."

86. Ibid., 92–93; about half of the French in Canada were killed during the Beaver

Wars. Note that Brandão would not agree with the inference we draw here, which follows Richter, *Ordeal of the Longhouse,* 64.

87. Richter, *Ordeal of the Longhouse,* 62 (quotation), 60–64 (dates of conquests); Steele, *Warpaths,* 117. For detailed summaries and numbers of casualties, see Brandão, *"Your Fyre Shall Burn No More,"* 72–116 and Appendix D.

88. See esp. White, *Middle Ground,* chap. 1.

89. Richter, *Facing East,* 60; Neal Salisbury, *Manitou and Providence: Indians, Europeans, and the Making of New England, 1500–1643* (New York: Oxford University Press, 1982), 105–6, 114–16.

90. John O'Beirne Ranelagh, *A Short History of Ireland,* 2d ed. (Cambridge, U.K.: Cambridge University Press, 1994), 43–65; also Nicholas Canny, "The Origins of Empire: An Introduction" and "England's New World and the Old, 1480s–1630s," in Canny, ed., *The Origins of Empire: British Overseas Enterprise to the Close of the Seventeenth Century,* in Wm. Roger Louis, gen. ed., *The Oxford History of the British Empire* (Oxford: Oxford University Press, 1998), 1–33, 148–69; and Jane H. Ohlmeyer, "'Civilizinge of those Rude Partes': Colonization within Britain and Ireland, 1580s–1640s," ibid., 124–47.

91. On the importance of livestock husbandry and its unanticipated consequences for intercultural relations in the seventeenth-century Chesapeake and New England, see esp. Virginia DeJohn Anderson, *Creatures of Empire: How Domestic Animals Transformed Early America* (New York: Oxford University Press, 2004).

92. The analogy to the South African system is Ian Steele's; see *Warpaths,* 49.

93. The main exception to this rule can be found in Connecticut's durable alliance with the Mohegan chief Uncas; on which see Harold Selesky, *War and Society in Colonial Connecticut* (New Haven, Conn.: Yale University Press, 1990), 3–12. This connection lasted only until the opportunistic Uncas died, in 1683 or 1684; his sons lost all freedom of action and became outright clients of the Connecticut colony. It is arguable that Uncas—who initially allied himself with the Connecticut Puritans to gain advantage over the Pequots, rivals of the Mohegans for trade with the Dutch and English—himself became an English client rather than an ally as a result of the Pequot War. In 1640 he ceded the lands on which the Mohegans' tributary peoples lived to Connecticut, in return for the colony's guarantee of his own people's land and a favored position in the wampum trade. This put the Mohegans at odds with the Narragansetts of Rhode Island, a more numerous and still-powerful people, and forced Uncas into closer, perhaps more subservient relations with the Puritans. Nevertheless, by means of accommodation he managed the considerable feat of maintaining the autonomy of his people on their lands until after King Philip's War. See Steele, *Warpaths,* 93–94; Salisbury, *Manitou and Providence,* 210–35 passim; and Michael Leroy Oberg, *Uncas: First of the Mohegans* (Ithaca, N.Y.: Cornell University Press, 2003).

94. W. J. Eccles, "The Social, Economic, and Political Significance of the Military Establishment in New France," in Eccles, ed., *Essays on New France* (Toronto: Ox-

ford University Press, 1987), 110–24. Although the Spanish experience was typically more mixed and less successful in Florida and Texas, Santa Fe and the surrounding New Mexican settlements in the eighteenth century were principally defended by young Hispanic settlers who joined Pueblo warriors in raids against their common enemy, *los indios bárbaros:* the Navajo, Apache, and Comanche nomads whose acquisition of horses and European weapons made them ever more formidable enemies. By contrast, the regular troops who had been sent to defend the frontiers meanwhile tended to remain in their *presidios.* Insofar as they contributed to the defense of the Spanish settlements, it was because individual commanders were willing to avoid confrontations and turn their forts into trading posts. See Weber, *Spanish Frontier,* 186–98, 204–15.

95. Salisbury, *Manitou and Providence,* 13 (quotation), 231–32.

96. A classic expression of mercantilism, the Navigation Act of 1651 was arguably the first English attempt to impose an imperial framework on its colonies. Following English victories at the Downs (May 1652), Portland (February 1653), North Foreland (June 1653), and Texel (July 1653), the United Provinces agreed to recognize the Navigation Act at the Treaty of Westminster, 1654, and to indemnify England for the costs of the fighting.

97. For the most perceptive available account of Kieft's War, see Evan Haefli, "Kieft's War and the Cultures of Violence in Colonial America," in Michael Bellesiles, ed., *Lethal Imagination: Violence and Brutality in American History* (New York: New York University Press, 1999), 17–40.

98. On Dutch relations with the Indians of the lower Hudson Valley, see esp. Steele, *Warpaths,* 115–19; also Trelease, *Indian Affairs,* 138–74.

99. Steele, *Warpaths,* 72–75; Richter, *Ordeal of the Longhouse,* 105–254. Also see Francis Jennings, *The Ambiguous Iroquois Empire* (New York: W. W. Norton, 1984), and Stephen Saunders Webb, *1676: The End of American Independence* (New York: Knopf, 1984).

100. Steele, *Warpaths,* 137–40.

101. Richter, *Ordeal of the Longhouse,* 173.

102. Ibid., 188; Steele, *Warpaths,* 147–48.

103. Richter, *Ordeal of the Longhouse,* 210–13.

Two: Penn's Bargain

1. On the painting, its reception, and its relationship to *The Death of General Wolfe,* see Robert C. Alberts, *Benjamin West: A Biography* (Boston: Houghton Mifflin, 1978), 106–12; Allen Staley, *Benjamin West: American Painter at the English Court* (Baltimore: Baltimore Museum of Art, 1989), 59–62; Ann Uhry Abrams, *The Valiant Hero: Benjamin West and Grand-Style History Painting* (Washington, D.C.: Smithsonian Institution Press, 1985), 191–95; Helmut von Erffa and Allen

Staley, *The Paintings of Benjamin West* (New Haven, Conn.: Yale University Press, 1986), 67–69, 206–08. Much of contemporary familiarity with this image of Penn and the Indians derives from Edward Hicks's inclusion of a version of the scene as part of the background in his many versions of *The Peaceable Kingdom.*

2. Franklin dined frequently with West and his wife, Elizabeth; they got along so well that in August of 1772 he stood up as godfather at the christening of the Wests' second son, yet another Benjamin. Alberts, *West,* 112.

3. West to William Darton, February 2, 1805, quoted in von Erffa and Staley, *Paintings of West,* 207. (Spelling as in the original.)

4. From his initial appointment as commander of the twenty-eight-gun frigate *Fellowship* in 1644, the admiral's career trajectory was remarkably steep; by 1655 he had risen to the rank of General-at-Sea, the highest rank in the Commonwealth Navy. Because admirals were entitled to a substantial share in all commercial and naval prizes taken at sea, Penn's rank made him a rich man as well as a powerful one. By 1656 he held estates in England and Ireland amounting to more than 12,000 acres. On his distinguished career, see Mary Maples Dunn, "The Personality of William Penn," in Richard S. Dunn and Mary Maples Dunn, eds., *The World of William Penn* (Philadelphia: University of Pennsylvania Press, 1986), 4–5; and Catherine Owens Peare, *William Penn: A Biography* (Ann Arbor: University of Michigan Press, 1966), 9–20 passim. On the extent of his Irish holdings, granted him outright following the suppression of the Irish rebellion of 1649–50, see "Penn's Lands and Tenants in Ireland, 1667–70," in Mary Maples Dunn and Richard S. Dunn, eds., *The Papers of William Penn,* vol. 1, *1644–1679* (Philadelphia: University of Pennsylvania Press, 1981), 570–73. Penn's English estates were principally acquired by purchase, evidently with at least part of his prize money for 1652. In that year his share amounted to at least 67,000 pieces of eight, or approximately £15,400 (ibid., 569).

5. Christopher Hill, *God's Englishman: Oliver Cromwell and the English Revolution* (New York: Dial Press, 1970), 158–59; Derek Hirst, *Authority and Conflict: England, 1603–1658* (Cambridge, Mass.: Harvard University Press, 1986), 330, 339–40; Peare, *Penn,* 21.

6. Penn to Mary Pennyman, November 22, 1673, *Papers of Penn,* 1:265. Cf. Penn's later comment, "The Lord first appeared unto me . . . about the 12th year of my age, Anno 1656." ("An Account of My Journey into Holland & Germany," ibid., 476.)

7. Peare, *Penn,* 23–24; Penn to Gulielma Springett, October 7, 1668, *Papers of Penn,* 1:68.

8. He evidently felt little of the sympathy for the Irish that he later manifested toward Pennsylvania's Indians. In later writings he mentioned the Irish who still lived on the family's lands almost exclusively in terms of their status as tenants. See, e.g., "My Irish Journal [1669–70]," his most extensive account of life in Ireland, which makes no direct mention of the circumstances of the Irish in the countryside; *Papers of Penn,* 1:101–43. See also Nicholas Canny, "The Irish Background to Penn's Experiment," *World of Penn,* 139–56.

9. Peare, *Penn,* 24–26; J. R. Jones, *Country and Court: England, 1658–1714* (Cambridge, Mass.: Harvard University Press, 1978), 118–36.

10. Penn to Robert Turner, Anthony Sharp, and Roger Roberts, April 12, 1681, in Mary Maples Dunn and Richard S. Dunn, eds., *The Papers of William Penn,* vol. 2, *1680–1684* (Philadelphia: University of Pennsylvania Press, 1982), 89.

11. Penn, "An Account of My Journey into Holland and Germany," *Papers of Penn,* 1:476.

12. Peare, *Penn,* 40–44 (quotation, from Samuel Pepys's diary, at 43).

13. Ibid., 46–47, 51; Jones, *Country and Court,* 99–100; John Miller, *James II* (New Haven, Conn.: Yale University Press, 2000), 50; R. Ernest Dupuy and Trevor N. Dupuy, *The Harper Encyclopedia of Military History* (New York: HarperCollins, 1993), 607–09.

14. The younger William in fact needed substantial legal training to protect the family's Irish holdings. With the Restoration, Irish royalists petitioned for the return of confiscated estates, one of which was Macroom. The admiral surrendered it to the crown and received in compensation a tract near Kinsale and other lands. This exchange required William to adjust titles, execute new leases, and perform many other legal tasks in addition to the routine business of collecting rents (Peare, *Penn,* 52).

15. Peare, *Penn,* 55–61; Harry Emerson Wildes, *William Penn* (New York: Macmillan, 1974), 40–42.

16. "Account of My Life Since Convincement," in Mary Maples Dunn and Richard S. Dunn, eds., *The Papers of William Penn,* vol. 3, *1685–1700* (Philadelphia: University of Pennsylvania Press, 1986), 366–37, and Peare, *Penn,* 83; quotation ibid., 88.

17. "Penn's Lands and Tenants in Ireland, 1667–70," *Papers of Penn,* 1:570.

18. Richard S. Dunn, "Penny Wise and Pound Foolish: Penn as a Businessman," *World of Penn,* 38–40, 51. See the summary of the Ford-Penn controversy in Peare, *Penn,* 383–404, and the documents and commentary in Mary Maples Dunn and Richard S. Dunn, eds., *The Papers of William Penn,* vol. 4, *1701–1718* (Philadelphia, 1987), 399–652 passim.

19. Peare, *Penn,* 89–126; Wildes, *Penn,* 54–68.

20. Mary Maples Dunn, *William Penn: Politics and Conscience* (Princeton, N.J.: Princeton University Press, 1967), 47. His most notable works of this period were *The Great Case of Liberty of Conscience, Once More Briefly Debated and Defended by the Authority of Reason, Scripture, and Antiquity* (1670); *Truth Rescued from Imposture* (1670); *A Seasonable Caveat Against Popery* (1670); *The Proposed Comprehension Soberly and not Unseasonably Considered* (1672); *A Discourse of the General Rule of Faith and Practice, and Judge of Controversie* (1673); *The Christian Quaker* (1674); *Christian Liberty As it was Soberly Desired in a Letter, To Certain Forreign States* (1674); *England's Present Interest Discovered with Honour to the Prince, and Safety to the People* (1675); *The Continued Cry of the Oppressed for Justice* (1675); *One Project for the Good of England; That is, Our Civil Union Is Our Civil Safety* (1679); *An Address to Protestants of All*

Persuasions, More Especially the Magistracy and Clergy, for the Promotion of Virtue and Charity (1679); and *A Brief Examination and State of Liberty Spiritual* (1681).

Dunn treats these with admirable clarity in Chapter II of *Politics and Conscience.* Because it casts so bright a light on the principles he later followed in creating the government of Pennsylvania, a brief summary of her argument may be useful here. In general, Penn maintained that any attempt to reduce religious liberty threatened all other natural rights, even including rights of property. Since God had given human beings the ability to believe, only God could judge the fitness of beliefs; for the state and its established church to intervene between the believer and the Creator infringed on God's sovereignty and invited God's just punishment. Religious persecution, such as that visited on Quakers—or for that matter, other English dissenters—could not possibly serve God's will in the world. It only invited the strong to abuse their power and tempted the weak to practice the arts of dissimulation, and neither tyranny nor hypocrisy could be counted as traits desirable in English subjects. God himself had ordained governments to impose order on society; to enlist religion in that cause only corrupted state and church alike.

Instead of religious conformity, Penn argued, rulers should require *moral* uniformity of their subjects: adherence to just laws, constructed in such a way as to promote behavior according to the Golden Rule and protect the natural rights with which God had endowed his creatures. Governments existed (and in this Penn followed many other contemporary writers) by virtue of an original contract made among men when humanity was still in a state of nature to protect their lives and property and to secure justice. No government deriving its powers from such a contract could justly pursue a course inimical to the welfare of the people or their rights. Thus, because of the manifest ills that accompanied religious persecution, all links between church and state should be severed. Inasmuch as religious organizations needed to preserve moral discipline within their membership, they could do so by excommunicating everyone who refused to conform to their doctrines; but the state's intervention to punish peaceable dissent by fines or imprisonment could only be inequitable and unjust. It was altogether appropriate to resist such laws by peaceable means, because no civil authority—not the king, not Parliament—could legitimately destroy the liberties of property and person that came from God and were protected by the original contract of government.

21. Penn, *England's Present Interest Discovered,* quoted ibid., 67.
22. Penn, "Account of My Life Since Convincement," *Papers of Penn,* 3:338–39.
23. "Resolved to withdraw": ibid. On the virulent politics of the Exclusion Crisis, see Jones, *Country and Court,* 197–216.
24. Peare, *Penn,* 169–74; Alan Taylor, *American Colonies* (New York: Viking Penguin, 2001), 262–64.
25. Dunn, "Penny Wise and Pound Foolish," *World of Penn,* 40.
26. "The Charter of Pennsylvania," March 4, 1681, Jean R. Soderlund, ed., *William Penn and the Founding of Pennsylvania, 1680–1684: A Documentary History* (Philadel-

phia: University of Pennsylvania Press, 1983), 41. The Privy Council, a medieval institution of government that originally consisted of the private advisers of the monarch, had by the seventeenth century become the chief administrative body of government in England, performing many of the functions that are now vested in the Cabinet. At this point in English history, the Privy Council consisted not only of courtiers but of the princes of the blood, the two archbishops, the principal secretaries of state, the chief law officers of the crown, and other high ministers of government. These dignitaries, who varied in number but usually amounted to thirty or more, did the Council's business in committees, e.g., the Board of Trade and the Judicial Committee, which employed clerks (proto–civil servants) to do the actual work.

27. Dunn, "Penny Wise and Pound Foolish," *World of Penn,* 42.

28. On the proprietary colonies and their systems of government, see Charles M. Andrews, *The Colonial Period of American History: The Settlements,* vol. 3 (New Haven, Conn.: Yale University Press, 1937; rpt. 1977), 70–328. An excellent brief treatment of the same provinces is in John M. Murrin et al., *Liberty, Equality, Power: A History of the American People* (New York: Harcourt Brace, 1996), 64–66, 88–99. Gary B. Nash, *Quakers and Politics: Pennsylvania, 1681–1726* (Princeton, N.J.: Princeton University Press, 1968), 28–47, discusses the shape and operation of the Frame of Government.

29. On these and subsequent tracts promoting Pennsylvania, see Edwin B. Bronner and David Fraser, eds., *The Papers of William Penn,* vol. 5, *William Penn's Published Writings, 1660–1726: An Interpretive Bibliography* (Philadelphia: University of Pennsylvania Press, 1986), 264–69: [*Some Account of Pennsylvania,* first printed in London in 1681, translated into Dutch and printed in Amsterdam and Rotterdam, 1681, and translated into German and printed at Frankfurt, 1683]; 270–76 [*Brief Account of Pennsylvania,* London editions of 1681 and 1682, with German translation in 1683]; 298–303 [*Letter to the Free Society of Traders,* printed in London, 1683, reprinted in Dutch at Amsterdam and in German at Hamburg, 1684]; 304–07 [*Map of the Improved Part of the Province of Pennsilvania in America. A General Description of Pennsylvania,* London editions in 1687 and 1697, reprinted in German in Frankfurt and Leipzig, 1700]; 308–09 [*Recueil de Diverses Pieces, Concernant la Pennsylvanie,* a French translation of *Some Account* and *A Letter to the Free Society of Traders,* published in La Haye, 1684]; 320–23 [*A Further Account of the Province of Pennsylvania,* published in London, 1685, and in Dutch translation in Amsterdam, 1685]; 327–29 [*Information and Direction to Such Persons as are inclined to America, More Especially Those related to the Province of Pennsylvania,* published in London and Amsterdam, 1686]; and 367–69 [*Some Proposals for a Second Settlement in the Province of Pennsylvania,* published in London, 1690].

30. Penn, "Some Account of the Province of Pennsylvania," *Penn and the Founding of Pennsylvania,* 60–62 (quotation at 60).

31. Ibid., 62–63.

32. Ibid., 65 (*"inconveniences . . . plenty"*), 64.

33. Ibid., 62.

34. Penn estimated that he spent nearly £12,000 in the first two years of his colonial venture; see Nash, *Quakers and Politics,* 11. This was a vast sum, equivalent in purchasing power to considerably more than £1,000,000 today. (On conversion to modern values, see John J. McCusker, *How Much Is That in Real Money? A Historical Price Index for use as a Deflator of Money Values in the Economy of the United States* [Worcester, Mass.: American Antiquarian Society, 1992], 37–350: Table B-1, "Consumer Price Indexes, Great Britain, 1600–1991.")

35. Nash, Quakers and Politics, 18–28.

36. Penn to the kings of the Indians, October 18, 1681, *Papers of Penn,* 2:128–29.

37. "Conditions or Concessions to the First Purchasers," *Penn and the Founding of Pennsylvania,* 74.

38. Peare, *Penn,* 224–38; "Business Agreements with Philip Ford," *Papers of Penn,* 2:290–95.

39. *Penn and the Founding of Pennsylvania,* 155–62; James H. Merrell, *Into the American Woods: Negotiators on the Pennsylvania Frontier* (New York: W. W. Norton, 1999), 190.

40. Penn to the Free Society of Traders, August 16, 1683, *Papers of Penn,* 2:452–53.

41. Anthony F. C. Wallace, "Woman, Land, and Society: Three Aspects of Aboriginal Delaware Life," *Pennsylvania Archaeologist* 17 (1947), 1:1–35.

42. Francis Jennings, "Glory, Death, and Transfiguration: The Susquehannock Indians in the Seventeenth Century," *Proceedings of the American Philosophical Society* 112 (1968), 1:20.

43. Ibid., 39–40.

44. A bill in 1682 for the services of the province's interpreter, Lasse Cocke, indicates twenty "guns" (muskets) given to Indians as diplomatic presents, along with twenty pounds of powder and forty pounds of lead; the account of goods paid to Indians for lands on the Delaware below the falls, August 1682, includes forty muskets, fifteen pistols, 150 pounds of powder, 300 "small bars" of lead, and fifty pounds of duck shot. The preamble to the latter agreement also acknowledges receipt by the Indians of "ten guns more than are mentioned in the within deed." *Penn and the Founding of Pennsylvania,* 145, 158, 161.

45. William Markham, Memorandum [conditions of sale, c. August 1, 1682], ibid., 160.

46. Eric Hinderaker, *Elusive Empires: Constructing Colonialism in the Ohio Valley, 1673–1800* (New York: Cambridge University Press, 1997), 18–20, 25–26; Merrell, *Woods,* 21, 36; Francis Jennings, "Iroquois Alliances in American History," in Jennings et al., eds., *The History and Culture of Iroquois Diplomacy* (Syracuse, N.Y.: Syracuse University Press, 1985), 41.

47. Penn's patent stipulated that the boundary between Pennsylvania and Maryland would be fixed at 40 degrees north latitude, a position Calvert rightly believed infringed on his own, much older patent. Before Penn's arrival, William Markham was slow to begin surveying the line, and Calvert was convinced that a letter

Penn wrote to settlers on the northern edge of Maryland advising them that their lands might fall within his new patent, was "not neighborlike." (Baltimore to William Markham, June 5, 1682, in *Penn and the Founding of Pennsylvania,* 154.)

48. Ibid., 276–83.

49. Penn, "A History of My Life from 1684," *Papers of Penn,* 3:341.

50. Penn was further hindered by the oversight of his secretary, Philip Theodore Lehnmann, who left behind in Philadelphia papers that Penn had gathered regarding Dutch colonization of the Delaware that he believed would prove his case before the Privy Council. Furious, immediately after his arrival in England, he wrote to his steward in America, James Harrison, to send the papers, for "I am now here w[i]th my finger in my mouth. he [Lehnmann] could not have done me a wors[e] injury nor balti[more] a greater service, if he had had the bribe of 10000 [pounds] to do it." Eventually he sacked Lehnmann, replacing him with William Markham. Penn to Harrison, October 7, 1684, *Papers of Penn,* 2:601, 603n.

51. Order in Privy Council, November 13, 1685, *Papers of Penn,* 3:68.

52. Penn to Lloyd, August 15, 1685, ibid., 50.

53. Peare, *Penn,* 296–97.

54. Ibid., 297–302.

55. Quitrents were a feudal relic, small annual fees that manorial lords were entitled to collect from freeholders and copyholders in lieu of service. Penn as lord proprietor of Pennsylvania was entitled to collect quitrents of one shilling per every hundred acres from the property holders of his province as a means of securing their land titles. Penn in turn owed the king a quitrent of two beaver pelts per year for the possession of his province, in recognition of the king's prior right to the land as sovereign. Despite the small size of quitrents, freeholders greatly resented them as an archaic intrusion on their rights of absolute property ownership and frequently refused to pay. For a discussion of quitrents and opposition in Pennsylvania, see Peare, *Penn,* 219–20; Nash, *Quakers and Politics,* 92–97 and passim. (Despite their modest individual size, if Penn had been able to collect what was due him, the quitrents from Pennsylvania by this time would have amounted to something like £350 a year, not an insigificant sum.)

56. Dunn, "Penny Wise and Pound Foolish," *World of Penn,* 50–51; quotation at 50.

57. "Calendar of Legal Transactions Between William Penn and Philip Ford, 1685–1699," *Papers of Penn,* 3:658 (documents A and B).

58. Peare, *Penn,* 306–13; Nash, *Quakers and Politics,* 114–27.

59. "Calendar of Legal Transactions," *Papers of Penn,* 3:659 (documents D and E). The legal process by which Penn transferred the province to Ford's ownership was complex. He previously mortgaged Pennsylvania and Delaware to the steward in the form of a 5,000-year lease in April 1687 to cover his debt of £6,000; this made Ford the mortgagee, not the owner, of the province. On August 30, 1690, apparently in the belief that he would be attainted as a traitor and have all his estates forfeited to the crown, Penn "relinquished to Philip Ford all the equity of redemption

in the foregoing mortgage; on September first Ford assigned over to Thomas Ell-wood the same mortgage 'in trust to attend the freehold and inheritance of the premises.'" Penn then, on September 3, made a secret "absolute conveyance" of ownership to Ford, "without defeasance ([that is, Penn renounced the] right to have the deed defeated or rendered void)." Peare, *Penn,* 315.

60. Peare, *Penn,* 317; "Lying Low," *Papers of Penn,* 3:275.

61. On the Lower Counties/Upper Counties division, see Nash, *Quakers and Politics,* 67–83, 131–34. The politics of Pennsylvania's Quakers were considerably com-plicated in these matters by the Keithian schism, a controversy over the divinity of Christ that evolved into riotous political factionalism. Ibid., 145–61, 179–80. Taylor, *American Colonies,* 269–71, provides an excellent summary.

62. Peare, *Penn,* 331–51; Penn to Arthur Cook and others, November 5–9, 1695, *Papers of Penn,* 3:416.

63. Peare, *Penn,* 353–54; Dunn, "Penny Wise and Pound Foolish," *World of Penn,* 51. The £630 rent was equal to the interest on the total debt, at 6 percent, com-pounded annually; paying it did not in any way reduce the principal sum Penn owed to Ford. The agreement was finalized in April 1697.

64. Peare, *Penn,* 354–58; *Papers of Penn,* 3:21.

65. He had already tried to make those arguments, which failed, by writing privately to the province's most influential political leaders. Quakers in England pay their taxes in wartime, he wrote, even though they know what the money will be used for; in Pennsylvania the Friends in the legislature at least have the liberty to ap-propriate the funds with acts "under the Style off Peace & Safety, or to defray the exegencies of the Gover[n]m[en]t." To scruple at supporting the crown under those comparatively lenient conditions, he suggested, would "Contradict fr[ien]ds here, who pay much more barefacedly." Besides, to pay the crown this modest sum was the only way to preserve "the Country from such Complaints as may oversett the Governm[en]t again," a risk that Pennsylvanians woud surely prefer not to run. The leaders' lack of receptiveness to such rationalization led him to conclude that he would have no success at all if he were to make the same points publicly. See Penn to Arthur Cook and others, November 5–9, 1695, *Papers of Penn,* 3:416.

66. Nash, *Quakers and Politics,* 49–66, 208–09; Thomas M. Doerflinger, *A Vigorous Spirit of Enterprise: Merchants and Economic Development in Revolutionary Philadelphia* (Chapel Hill: University of North Carolina Press, 1986), 70–164; John J. Mc-Cusker and Russell R. Menard, *The Economy of British America, 1607–1789* (Chapel Hill: University of North Carolina Press, 1985), 193–208 and passim.

67. Nash, *Quakers and Politics,* passim; Nash, "The Early Merchants of Philadelphia: The Formation and Disintegration of a Founding Elite," *World of Penn,* 337–53.

68. Penn to Charlwood Lawton, December 10, 1700, *Papers of Penn,* 3:624.

69. Nash, *Quakers and Politics,* 224–26; Peare, *Penn,* 375–77.

70. In 1696, as part of the agreement to return the province to Penn as proprietor, the

Assembly agreed to provide the Exchequer with £300 annually, the equivalent to the cost of a company of infantry. In return, the Assembly insisted on amending the Frame of Government to give itself—the lower house—the power to initiate legislation and fix its dates of adjournment. At the time Penn had no choice but to acquiesce; even after the passage of five years he had not ceased to resent the Assembly's presumptuousness.

71. Nash, *Quakers and Politics,* 227–36.

72. Penn to James Logan, November 3, 1701, *Papers of Penn,* 4:119. The rights that Penn instructed Logan to enforce in this passage by their archaic and attenuated quality testify to his desperation: "escheats" were estates that reverted to a feudal lord when no heirs survived to claim the property; "deodands" were personal chattel that had caused the death of a human being (e.g., a horse that had kicked its master to death or a house that had fallen in on its occupants) and were forfeit to the crown's representative; and "strays" were animals that had escaped the control of their owners, been taken up by colony authorities, and remained unclaimed.

73. Penn initially conceived the Susquehanna project in 1690–91 when, though he was effectively in hiding, he wrote a prospectus, *Some Proposals for a Second Settlement in Pennsylvania.* He actually solicited subscriptions from leading Friends, offering 3,000-acre lots for sale at £100 each, before the scheme collapsed. He reused the prospectus in 1696 when he revived the project. See Penn to Friends in Ireland, January 8, 1691, in *Papers of Penn,* 3:291–92.

74. See the headnote and document, "The Subscribers to a Susquehanna Settlement, 1696," in *Papers of Penn,* 3:671–78.

75. Susquehanna deed, September 13, 1700, quoted in Peare, *Penn,* 373.

76. Articles of Agreement with the Susquehanna Indians, April 23, 1701, *Papers of Penn,* 4:49–55; quotation at 52. See esp. commentary on the episode by Francis Jennings in *The Ambiguous Iroquois Empire: The Covenant Chain Confederation of Indian Tribes with the English Colonies* (New York: W. W. Norton, 1984), 236–37.

77. Jennings, *Ambiguous Empire,* 239.

78. Penn to Lt. Gov. John Nanfan, July 2, 1701, quoted in Peare, *Penn,* 378.

79. Address of the Indian kings, c. October 7, 1701, quoted in Jennings, *Ambiguous Empire,* 238; see also Peare, *Penn,* 381, and Merrell, *Woods,* 122–23.

80. Peare, *Penn,* 382–95; Frederick B. Tolles, *James Logan and the Culture of Provincial America* (Boston: Little, Brown, 1957), 40–43, 55–57.

81. "At Law: Ford v. Penn, October 1705–July 1708," *Papers of Penn,* 4:399–402; Peare, *Penn,* 397–404.

82. Penn to Friends in Pennsylvania, June 29, 1710, *Papers of Penn,* 4:676.

83. Penn to Logan, October 4, 1712, ibid., 727.

84. Peare, *Penn,* 413–14.

85. Nash, *Quakers and Politics,* 319–20; Taylor, *American Colonies,* 314–323.

86. For a discussion of the term and its meanings, see James T. Lemon, *The Best Poor Man's Country: A Geographical Study of Early Southeastern Pennsylvania* (Baltimore:

Johns Hopkins University Press, 1972); and esp. the introduction to Barbara De Wolfe, *Discoveries of America: Personal Accounts of British Emigrants to North America during the Revolutionary Era* (New York: Cambridge University Press, 1997).

87. On the significance of Penn as a symbol susceptible to manipulation by Indians and colonists alike and hence a crucial part of the symbolic armamentarium of intercultural politics, see Merrell, *Woods,* 122–27.

88. Ibid.; Daniel K. Richter, *Facing East from Indian Country: A Native History of Early America* (Cambridge, Mass.: Harvard University Press, 2001), 151–88.

89. Merrell, *Woods,* 106–27.

90. On go-betweens, the prevention of wars before 1755, and the limitations of the system of cultural mediation, ibid., 128–224.

91. Ian K. Steele, *Warpaths: Invasions of North America* (New York: Oxford University Press, 1994), 99–109, 151–62; Daniel K. Richter, "Native Peoples of North America and the Eighteenth-Century British Empire," in Wm. Roger Louis, gen. ed., *The Oxford History of the British Empire,* vol. 2, *The Eighteenth Century,* ed. P. J. Marshall (Oxford, U.K.: Oxford University Press, 1998), 350–51. (Maine was a district of Massachusetts Bay Colony, and a part of the state of Massachusetts from 1776 to 1820.)

92. Steele, *Warpaths,* 53–58.

93. On the origins of Chesapeake slavery see esp. Edmund S. Morgan, *American Slavery, American Freedom: The Ordeal of Colonial Virginia* (New York: W.W. Norton, 1975); Gloria L. Main, *Tobacco Colony: Life in Early Maryland, 1650–1720* (Princeton, N.J.: Princeton University Press, 1982); and Philip D. Morgan, *Slave Counterpoint: Black Culture in the Eighteenth-Century Chesapeake and Lowcountry* (Chapel Hill: University of North Carolina Press, 1998). On slavery in the Carolina lowcountry, in addition to Morgan, see Peter H. Wood, *Black Majority: Negroes in Colonial South Carolina from 1670 through the Stono Rebellion* (New York: Knopf, 1974). A striking new treatment of the interactions between Indian wars and the creation of a functioning slave system in the American South is Alan Gallay, *The Indian Slave Trade: The Rise of the English Empire in the American South, 1670–1717* (New Haven, Conn.: Yale University Press, 2002).

94. Gallay, *Indian Slave Trade,* passim; Richter, *Facing East,* 162–63.

95. Ibid.; Taylor, *American Colonies,* 231–35; Steele, *Warpaths,* 159–60; Gallay, *Indian Slave Trade,* 259–87. Casualty and prisoner estimates follow Steele; Richter estimates that 1,000 were killed and about 700 enslaved.

96. Richter, "Native Peoples," 352; Taylor, *American Colonies,* 234–36; Gallay, *Indian Slave Trade,* 327–54. As Ian Steele observes, this was a complex conflict in which the Cherokees initially sided with the Yamassees, Catawbas, and Creeks, withdrawing only from the alliance in 1716 "when it became clear that the Virginians would not trade arms or ammunition to be used against their fellow English in the Carolinas." At the same time the Catawbas also withdrew from hostilities. The Creeks abandoned the Yamassees in 1717 and moved west to Alabama, from which they attacked the Cherokees, whom they regarded as their most danger-

ous enemies, for another decade. South Carolina suffered heavy casualties (over 7 percent of the white settler population was killed) and was so disordered by the end of the war that the settlers overthrew the proprietary government and asked the crown to take direct control of the colony. The Yamassees, most of whom withdrew to Florida by 1718, entered into an alliance with the Spanish, their old enemies, and raided the Carolina frontier until 1727 (*Warpaths,* 165–66).

97. The following discussion of the eighteenth-century geography of European power and Indian autonomy derives from Richter's analysis in "Native Peoples," 356–63, and *Facing East,* 165–79.

98. Richter, "Native Peoples," 357. In the original, the passage quoted reads "seven clusters of autonomous local communities"; we have said six because we speak here of the period around 1725–30, whereas Richter refers to the situation c. 1750, when a new cluster, the Ohio Indians, emerged to take part in the politics of the play-off system.

99. Ibid., 357–58; quotation: Colin Calloway, *The Western Abenakis of Vermont, 1600–1800: War, Migration, and the Survival of an Indian People* (Norman: University of Oklahoma Press, 1990), 240.

100. Richter, *Facing East,* 167–68; Richard White, *The Middle Ground: Indians, Empires, and Republics in the Great Lakes Region, 1650–1815* (New York: Cambridge University Press, 1991), passim.

101. Richter, *Facing East,* 169.

102. Ibid., 169–70; Kathryn E. Holland Braund, *Deerskins and Duffels: Creek Indian Trade with Anglo-America, 1685–1815* (Lincoln: University of Nebraska Press, 1993), 6–10, 26–80.

103. Richter, *Facing East,* 170; Daniel H. Usner Jr., *Indians, Settlers, and Slaves in a Frontier Exchange Economy: The Lower Mississippi Valley before 1783* (Chapel Hill: University of North Carolina Press, 1992), passim.

104. Richter, *Facing East,* 171.

105. Tolles, *Logan,* 6–14, 196–214, and passim; Jeffrey B. Webb, "Logan, James," in John A. Garraty and Mark C. Carnes, gen. eds., *American National Biography,* vol. 13 (New York: Oxford University Press, 1999), 835–36.

106. Tolles, *Logan,* 86–87; Francis Jennings, "The Indian Trade of the Susquehanna Valley," *Proceedings of the American Philosophical Society,* 110 (1966) 6:406–24.

107. Tolles, *Logan,* 89–91; quotation at 91.

108. As we have seen, Penn reserved the lands west of the river as well as other parts of the valley to the Indians in the treaty of 1701 and confirmed the agreement before his final departure from the province.

109. Jennings, "Indian Trade," 415; Hinderaker, *Elusive Empires,* 105–06. When Logan began his adventures in the skin trade in 1712, his net worth stood at £2,250; by 1720 it approximated £12,000. Moreover, the latter sum did not count his real estate holdings as assets. Had it done so, his net worth would have been far higher.

110. Lorett Treese, *The Storm Gathering: The Penn Family and the American Revolution* (University Park: Pennsylvania State University Press, 1992), 7–8.

111. Hinderaker, *Elusive Empires,* 109–10.

112. Logan to the Penn heirs, November 16, 1729, quoted ibid., 110.

113. Civility to Logan, "late summer" 1727, quoted in Tolles, *Logan,* 160.

114. Merrell, *Woods,* 158–67; Hinderaker, *Elusive Empires,* 124–26.

115. Logan to the Penn heirs, "autumn" 1729, quoted in Tolles, *Logan,* 167.

116. Jennings, *Ambiguous Empire,* 278–81; Tolles, *Logan,* 103–09. The ostensible intention of this division of responsibilities for Indian affairs was to stabilize the frontier by separating the Iroquois from the Cherokees and other southern nations they raided; at least that was how Logan and Keith represented it to Spotswood. It seems clear, however, that Logan also understood it as an opportunity to use the Iroquois to strengthen Pennsylvania's Indian shield to the north.

117. Ibid., 111; Jennings, *Ambiguous Empire,* 281–82; Hinderaker, *Elusive Empires,* 122–23.

118. Tolles, *Logan,* 103–09.

119. Tolles, *Logan,* 110–12; Jennings, *Ambiguous Empire,* 289–98; Hinderaker, *Elusive Empires,* 123–24.

120. Hinderaker, *Elusive Empires,* 121; Merrell, *Woods,* 167–68, 204.

121. Hinderaker, *Elusive Empires,* 28–32.

122. An edited version of the Memorial can be found in Joseph E. Johnson, ed., "A Quaker Imperialist's View of the British Colonies in America: 1732," *Pennsylvania Magazine of History and Biography* 60 (1936), 2:97–130; the following summary is based on that edition. See also the summary in Tolles, *Logan,* 164–65.

123. "Imperialist's View," 118.

124. Ibid., 120, 123, 124.

125. Ibid., 125.

126. Ibid., 126.

127. Ibid., 127.

128. Ibid., 130.

129. Tolles, *Logan,* 155–57.

130. Jennings, *Ambiguous Empire,* 314–16.

131. Ibid., 322–24.

132. Ibid., 309–14; Francis Jennings, "Incident at Tulpehocken," *Pennsylvania History* 35 (1968), 4:335–355.

133. Jennings, *Ambiguous Empire,* 320–22.

134. Hinderaker, *Elusive Empires,* 127; Jennings, *Ambiguous Empire,* 330–42, 388–97; Francis Jennings, "The Scandalous Indian Policy of William Penn's Sons: Deeds and Documents of the Walking Purchase," *Pennsylvania History* 37 (1970), 1:19–39.

135. Quoted in Jennings, *Ambiguous Empire,* 344.

136. He was not the last. A young Philadelphia printer with whom Logan dealt in his official capacity as secretary of the province first became a student of empire by

conversing with him. Logan found the intellectual ambitions of the printer impressive, even if he did not particularly care for the antiproprietary cast of his political opinions. Logan lent him books and even allowed him to examine his own unpublished writings on various topics, such as the "Memorial" on the state of the empire in 1732 that he sent, fruitlessly, to Sir Robert Walpole. The printer, Benjamin Franklin, thought enough of the analysis in that document to make himself a copy of it; indeed, the only complete version that survives is in Franklin's own precise hand. There can be no question that it formed the point of departure for his own thinking about the character of empire and what is necessary for its success; it contained the seeds that ultimately germinated in the Franklin's draft of the Albany Plan of Union of 1754.

Three: Washington's Apprenticeship

1. John Adams to Abigail Adams, May 26, 1775, in L. H. Butterfield, ed., *The Adams Papers,* Ser. II, *Adams Family Correspondence,* vol. 1, *December 1761–May 1776* (Cambridge, Mass.: Harvard University Press, 1963), 206. The First Continental Congress met at Philadelphia from September 5 through October 26, 1774.
2. John Adams to Abigail Adams, May 29, 1775, ibid., 207.
3. Adams did not specify the appearance of the uniform, so it is possible, as Douglas Southall Freeman argued in *George Washington: A Biography,* vol. 3, *Planter and Patriot* (New York: Charles Scribner's Sons, 1951), 426 n. 40, that Washington was wearing the old blue-and-red uniform from the First Virginia Regiment. Washington, however, had ordered his indentured tailor, Andrew Judge, to make him up "1 Suite Regimentals" in November 1774 at about the time he agreed to act as the field commander of five Virginia Independent Companies of volunteers (those of Fairfax, Prince William, Fauquier, Spotsylvania, and Richmond counties), should those units ever be required to act together. According to W. W. Abbot et al., eds., *The Papers of George Washington, Colonial Series,* vol. 10, *March 1774–June 1775* (Charlottesville: University Press of Virginia, 1995), 174, this was "almost certainly the uniform GW wore at the Second Continental Congress." Because Charles Willson Peale depicted Washington in the blue-and-buff uniform of the Fairfax Independents in 1776 and because Washington ordered his next known uniform in 1777, it seems at least highly likely that he also wore it at the meetings of Congress in the spring of 1775. (Private electronic communication, Robert Scott Stephenson to Fred Anderson, c. April 15, 2004.)
4. This seems to be a common assumption; see, e.g., John Ferling, *The First of Men: A Life of George Washington* (Knoxville: University of Tennessee Press, 1988), 113; Paul Longmore, *The Invention of George Washington* (Berkeley: University of California Press, 1988), 170.
5. The sash dated from 1709 and originally belonged to Braddock's father; Braddock

gave it to Washington along with a pair of pistols as a memento before his death. The sash is now at Mount Vernon. An image showing the date of manufacture woven into the mesh can be found in Fred Anderson, ed., *George Washington Remembers: Reflections on the French and Indian War* (Lanham, Md.: Rowman and Littlefield, 2004), 55.

6. Freeman, *Washington,* 3:292–93. Given Washington's boredom and irritation at his forced immobility while Peale worked, he may well have intended never to have another made; see Washington to Jonathan Boucher, May 21, 1772, in W. W. Abbot et al., eds, *The Papers of George Washington, Colonial Series,* vol. 9, *January 1772–March 1774* (Charlottesville: University Press of Virginia, 1994), 49.

7. Agreement of the gentlemen and freeholders of Fairfax County, September 21, 1774, quoted in *Papers of Washington, Col. Ser.,* 10:173–74.

8. Douglas Southall Freeman, *George Washington: A Biography,* vol. 1: *Young Washington* (New York: Charles Scribner's Sons, 1948), 31. Then, as now, the size of a successful householder's estate grew as he aged. Optimally, it was at its largest when it was passed along to the heir (or heirs) who would build upon that foundation for the benefit of future generations of heirs. Premature death, particularly if repeated over a series of generations, restrained the intergenerational accumulation of wealth. Its effects in colonial British America have been most systematically studied in a region characterized by partible inheritance practices and a distribution of wealth far less unequal than that of the Chesapeake, but the conclusions of John J. Waters regarding preindustrial inheritance strategies are instructive for understanding even areas (like the Chesapeake) where probate practices strongly favored eldest sons. See his two articles, "Patrimony, Succession, and Social Stability: Guilford, Connecticut in the Eighteenth Century," *Perspectives in American History* 10 (1976), 131–62, and "Family, Inheritance, and Migration in Colonial New England: The Evidence from Guilford, Connecticut," *William and Mary Quarterly,* 3d Ser., 39 (1982), 1:64–86.

9. Ferling, *First of Men,* 8; Freeman, *Washington,* 1:74.

10. Dorothy Twohig, "The Making of George Washington," in Warren Hofstra, ed., *George Washington and the Virginia Backcountry* (Madison, Wisc.: Madison House, 1998), 6–8; Philander D. Chase, "A Stake in the West: George Washington as Backcountry Surveyor and Landholder," ibid., 162–63.

11. On Lawrence Washington's accomplishments and George's admiration, see Freeman, *Washington,* 1:57–58, 70–71, 76–77; Ferling, *First of Men,* 8.

12. A circumferentor was the eighteenth-century ancestor of the modern transit instrument. It consisted of a tripod-mounted compass set within a rotating brass ring to which open sights had been fitted. By sighting on an object, surveyors could measure the bearing in degrees and (approximate) minutes of a line. The two-pole surveyor's chain consisted of fifty iron links that fully extended measured thirty-three feet, or two perches (or rods or poles) in length. Virginia surveyors preferred the two-pole chain, half the length of the standard hundred-link English surveying chain because of its handiness in running lines over rough or

wooded ground. See Chase, "A Stake in the West," 163–65. On the most precise application of eighteenth-century surveying techniques and measures, see Edwin Danson, *Drawing the Line: How Mason and Dixon Surveyed the Most Famous Border in America* (New York: John Wiley, 2001), 67–69, 98–99.

13. There were two ways to acquire land from the province. One was to identify a tract, ascertain with the help of a surveyor that it was under no prior claim, then register the official plat with the secretary of the colony at Williamsburg, who in turn issued the patent, or title, to the land. The other approach, favored by the great speculators, was to petition the governor and Council for a grant of a certain size (say fifty thousand or sixty thousand acres) in a specified region. If the Council approved, it would order the county surveyor to lay off the acreage in one or more tracts. Upon the payment of certain fees, these would then be patented to the petitioner, subject to certain conditions; usually the patentee was required to "seat" one settler family for each thousand acres of the grant within a specified period of time (typically two or more years). For the operation of the system, see Turk McCleskey, "Rich Land, Poor Prospects: Real Estate and the Formation of a Social Elite in Augusta County, Virginia, 1738–1770," *Virginia Magazine of History and Biography* 98 (1990), 3:460–62; also Warren R. Hofstra, "'A Parcel of Barbarian's and an Uncooth Set of People': Settlers and the Settlement of the Shenandoah Valley," in Hofstra, ed., *Washington and the Virginia Backcountry,* 93–94.

14. McCleskey, "Rich Land, Poor Prospects," 449–86. The effectiveness of gentry control over frontier counties was probably the largest single factor in explaining the absence in Virginia of "regulator" (vigilante) movements such as those that appeared in backcountry regions of North and South Carolina in the 1760s and 1770s.

15. Chase, "Stake in the West," 160–61.

16. That the Northern Neck was ready for development in the 1740s reflected the growth of British power over the previous century. In 1649 Charles II had granted the Northern Neck to a Fairfax ancestor and six other courtiers. The area remained Indian country until the Susquehannock War of 1675–76. That conflict enabled Colonel John Washington—George's great-grandfather—to join with his fellow militia officers in evicting the Doeg people (who had been Virginia's allies during the war) from the Neck and claim the best of its lands for themselves. In 1735 Gus Washington sited a small house on a bluff bounded by the curving Potomac River and a creek, Dogue Run, whose name was now the sole reminder of the land's previous inhabitants. Eight years later Lawrence Washington replaced the original structure with a larger one. Eventually he named it Mount Vernon. Robert F. Dalzell Jr. and Lee Baldwin Dalzell, *George Washington's Mount Vernon: At Home in Revolutionary America* (New York: Oxford University Press, 1998), 20–31. On the Susquehannock War and Colonel John Washington's military activities, which may have included the massacre of several chiefs, see ibid., 22–25; Wilcomb E. Washburn, *The Governor and the Rebel: A History of Bacon's Rebellion in Virginia* (Chapel Hill: University of North Carolina

Press, 1957), 20–23; and J. Frederick Fausz, "'Engaged in Enterprises Pregnant with Terror': George Washington's Formative Years among the Indians," *Washington and the Virginia Backcountry,* 117–18.

17. On the vague definition and tangled history of the Fairfax grant, see "The Northern Neck Proprietary to 1745," Freeman, *Washington,* 1:447–513. The charter granted the original proprietors the lands between the rivers, from the mouths to their "heads," a term that could be construed in one of two ways. "The heads of navigation" occurred at the first falls, a few miles upstream from their mouths, beyond which seagoing vessels could not pass; that would have limited the grant to the Tidewater. On the other hand, the "head springs" or "headwaters" were located high in the Appalachians, so far to the West that no one knew where they were until well into the eighteenth century. For obvious reasons Lord Fairfax favored the latter definition and successfully argued for it in *Fairfax v. Virginia,* which the Privy Council decided on April 6, 1745, thereby granting him the largest possible amount of territory.

18. Chase, "Stake in the West," 170–77.

19. Twohig, "Making of Washington," 8.

20. Cf. George Meredith, *The Ordeal of Richard Feverel* (1859), ch. 34; in *The Oxford Dictionary of Quotations,* 3rd ed. (Oxford, U.K.: Oxford University Press, 1994), 338.

21. Twohig, "Making of Washington," 9–11.

22. Washington, "A Journal of my Journey over the Mountains," entry of March 23, 1748, in Donald Jackson, ed., *The Diaries of George Washington,* vol. 1, *1748–65* (Charlottesville: University Press of Virginia, 1976), 13.

23. Ibid., 18 (entry of April 4, 1748).

24. His reward, he continued, made it worthwhile: "Dubbleloon is my constant gain every day that the Weather will permit my going out and sometime Six Pistoles." Washington to Richard ———, n.d. [fall, 1749 or 1750], in W. W. Abbot, ed., *The Papers of George Washington, Colonial Series,* vol. 1, *1748–August 1755* (Charlottesville: University Press of Virginia, 1983), 44. A doubloon (*doblon*) was a Spanish gold coin, another name for which was the pistole. It was worth approximately £0.83 (sixteen shillings, seven pence) in 1750, a sum that a laborer would count himself fortunate to earn in a week. A day's earnings of six pistoles (£5) was roughly equivalent to a month's wages for a skilled artisan. John J. McCusker, *Money and Exchange in Europe and America, 1600–1775: A Handbook* (Chapel Hill: University of North Carolina Press, 1978), 5–11.

25. See, among many other examples, William Byrd II, *The Secret History of the Dividing Line* (c. 1729; a useful edition is William K. Boyd, ed., *William Byrd's Histories of the Dividing Line betwixt Virginia and North Carolina* [1929]), and the Reverend Charles Woodmason's diary of 1766–68, published as Richard J. Hooker, ed., *The Carolina Backcountry on the Eve of the Revolution: The Journal and Other Writings of Charles Woodmason, Anglican Itinerant* (Chapel Hill: University of North Carolina

Press, 1953). The most comprehensive, elegant statement of the view that back-woods settlers were culturally and physically retrograde can be found in the essay "What is an American," by J. Hector St. John de Crèvecœur; see *Letters from an American Farmer* (1782; rpt. New York: Penguin, 1981), Letter III.

26. Washington, "Journal of my Journey over the Mountains," entry of March 13, 1748, *Diaries of Washington,* 1:7.

27. The following spring, Washington laid out another 760 acres for himself on the same creek as his initial purchase, Bullskin Run. He patented that tract in March 1752 and added another 552 acres by purchase. This gave him at age 20 a total holding in the Shenandoah Valley of over 2,300 acres, some 1,862 forming a single block on the South Fork of the Bullskin. He added more Shenandoah territory to his holdings over the next two decades. Washington began by using his own slaves to work Bullskin Farm before 1755; by the mid-1760s he was leasing it and his other Shenandoah Valley holdings to tenant farmers. Tenant labor added greatly to their value by expanding the amount of "improved" land, but Washington continued to lease them through the 1790s. In 1797 he remarked that he had bought these tracts "at five pounds per hundred acres, and [at] the highest (on account of small improvements) at twenty five pounds per hund[re]d[acres.] I could now sell [them], very readily at five pounds an *acre.*" See Chase, "Stake in the West," 175–77; quotation (Washington to Daniel McCarty, November 3, 1797) at 177.

28. Francis Jennings, *The Ambiguous Iroquois Empire: The Covenant Chain Confederation of Indian Tribes with the English Colonies from Its Beginnings to the Lancaster Treaty of 1744* (New York: W. W. Norton, 1984), 356–60.

29. Freeman, *Washington,* 1:236–37; Kenneth P. Bailey, *The Ohio Company of Virginia and the Westward Movement, 1748–1792: A Chapter in the History of the Colonial Frontier* (Glendale, Calif.: Arthur H. Clark, 1939), 30–31, 59–60.

30. Washington, Memorandum [1749–1750], *Papers of Washington, Col. Ser.,* 1:45.

31. Fred Anderson, *Crucible of War: The Seven Years' War and the Fate of Empire in British North America, 1754–1766* (New York: Knopf, 2000), 36–41.

32. "Express Messenger": Commission from Robert Dinwiddie, October 30, 1753, *Papers of Washington, Col. Ser.,* 1:58. Other quotations: Instructions from Robert Dinwiddie, October 30, 1753, ibid., 60–61.

33. Anderson, *Crucible of War,* 44–45.

34. Francis Jennings, *Empire of Fortune: Crowns, Colonies, and Tribes in the Seven Years War in America* (New York: W. W. Norton, 1988), 60–64; Richard White, *The Middle Ground: Indians, Empires, and Republics in the Great Lakes Region, 1650–1815* (New York: Cambridge University Press, 1991), 237–40; Michael N. McConnell, *A Country Between: The Upper Ohio Valley and Its Peoples, 1724–1774* (Lincoln: University of Nebraska Press, 1992), 107–08.

35. Freeman, *Washington,* 1:329–50.

36. In fact there were about five hundred men in the French force; Ensign Edward Ward perhaps overestimated their number because he had so few men—about

forty—to defend the newly named Fort Prince George (named for the sixteen-year-old heir apparent). Washington to James Hamilton, c. April 24, 1754, *Papers of Washington, Col. Ser.*, 1:82–84; Freeman, *Washington*, 1:345–50.

37. McConnell, *A Country Between*, 22–23. To put this number in perspective, it seems that at the time the entire population of the Iroquois League could not have far exceeded 6,000, with approximately 1,100 warriors.

38. McConnell, *A Country Between*, 19.

39. Eric Hinderaker, *Elusive Empires: Constructing Colonialism in the Ohio Valley, 1673–1800* (New York: Cambridge University Press, 1997), 40–45; Nicholas B. Wainwright, *George Croghan: Wilderness Diplomat* (Chapel Hill: University of North Carolina Press, 1959), 10–14.

40. Hinderaker, *Elusive Empires*, 43.

41. Anderson, *Crucible of War*, 26–32.

42. Ibid., 128–29, 169–72.

43. The Fort William Henry episode was the basis for James Fenimore Cooper's novel *The Last of the Mohicans* (1826). The definitive historical treatment of the incident is Ian K. Steele, *Betrayals: Fort William Henry and the "Massacre"* (New York: Oxford University Press, 1990); see also, and generally, his superb synthesis *Warpaths: Invasions of North America* (New York: Oxford University Press, 1994).

44. Frank L. Brecher, *Losing a Continent: France's North American Policy, 1753–1763* (Westport, Conn.: Greenwood Press, 1998), 140–42.

45. Washington to Dinwiddie, undated [c. June 10, 1754], *Papers of Washington, Col. Ser.*, 1:129.

46. For an extended narrative of the episode and an examination of the evidence for this interpretation, see Anderson, *Crucible of War*, 5–59.

47. Dinwiddie to Washington, June 4, 1754, *Papers of Washington, Col. Ser.*, 1:126–28; Freeman, *Washington*, 1:339, 381.

48. Speech at Aughwick, quoted in Jennings, *Empire of Fortune*, 67.

49. Anderson, *Crucible of War*, 60–64.

50. Don Higginbotham, *George Washington and the American Military Tradition* (Athens: University of Georgia Press, 1985), 7–38.

51. See Washington to Loudoun, January 10, 1757, in W. W. Abbot, et al., eds., *The Papers of George Washington, Colonial Series*, vol. 4, *November 1756–October 1757* (Charlottesville: University Press of Virginia, 1984), 79–93; note esp. the character of his narrative of the war's coming and progress before 1757 and the alterations, additions, and omissions he later made in his letter-book copy.

52. "Chimney Corner Politicians," from his petition to Loudoun, is also quoted in Higginbotham, *Washington and Tradition*, 36; Higginbotham is especially insightful in his analysis of Washington's deference to civilian authority, and the difficulty that Washington initially had in grasping the importance of the principle.

53. Ibid., 27–31.

54. James R. W. Titus, *The Old Dominion at War: Society, Politics, and Warfare in Late*

Colonial Virginia (Columbia: University of South Carolina Press, 1991), 41–49 and passim.

55. Titus, *Old Dominion*, 67–68, 91–92, 105, 136–40; Higginbotham, *Washington and Tradition*, 14–15; John Morgan Dederer, *War in America to 1775: Before Yankee Doodle* (New York: New York University Press, 1990), 138–40.

56. Washington to Dinwiddie, September 17, 1757, *Papers of Washington, Col. Ser.*, 4:411.

57. Hofstra, "'A Parcel of Barbarian's,'" 104.

58. On Washington's distaste for frontier settlers, frustration with the militia, and concentration on cultivating gentlemanliness in his officers, see Twohig, "Making of Washington," 14–16; Hofstra, "'A Parcel of Barbarian's,'" 88–90, 103–9; John Ferling, "School for Command: Young George Washington and the Virginia Regiment," 211–15; Don Higginbotham, "George Washington and Revolutionary Asceticism: The Localist as Nationalist," 228–30; all in Hofstra, ed., *Washington and the Virginia Backcountry*. See also Titus, *Old Dominion at War*, 137–38, and Higginbotham, *Washington and Tradition*, 16–17.

59. Titus, *Old Dominion at War*, 135–40; Ferling, "School for Command," 213.

60. Address from the officers of the Virginia Regiment, December 31, 1758, in W. W. Abbot et al., eds., *The Papers of George Washington, Colonial Series*, vol. 6, *September 1758–December 1760* (Charlottesville: University Press of Virginia, 1988), 178–81.

61. Washington to the Officers of the Virginia Regiment, January 10, 1759, *Papers of Washington, Col. Ser.*, 6:186–87.

62. Twohig, "Making of Washington," 15–16; J. Frederick Fausz, "'Engaged in Enterprises Pregnant with Terror,'" 132–36. Quotation: Washington to Dinwiddie, May 24, 1757, *Papers of Washington, Col. Ser.*, 4:163.

63. Robert D. Mitchell, "'Over the Hills and Far Away': George Washington and the Changing Virginia Backcountry," in Hofstra, ed., *Washington and the Virginia Backcountry*, 74–78; Robert D. Mitchell, *Commercialism and Frontier: Perspectives on the Early Shenandoah Valley* (Charlottesville: University Press of Virginia, 1977), 93–97, 156–60 and passim.

64. On Washington's lack of churchgoing in the late colonial period, see Paul F. Boller Jr., *George Washington and Religion* (Dallas: Southern Methodist University Press, 1963), 28–30; on his fundamentally theistic and providentialist beliefs, ibid., 92–115; on his rare pre-Revolutionary attendance at the Masonic Lodge he joined in 1752 and his increasing frequency of participation while serving as commander in chief of the Continental Army, see Steven C. Bullock, *Revolutionary Brotherhood: Freemasonry and the Transformation of the American Social Order, 1730–1840* (Chapel Hill: University of North Carolina Press, 1996), 104, 121–33.

65. James C. Riley, *The Seven Years War and the Old Regime in France: The Economic and Financial Toll* (Princeton, N.J.: Princeton University Press, 1986), 3–37, 104–31, 224–26; see esp. Table 4.1 and Chart 4.2, with commentary, 109–11; quotation at 226.

66. Ibid., 184, 190–91.

67. William H. McNeill, *The Pursuit of Power: Technology, Armed Force, and Society since A.D. 1000* (Chicago: University of Chicago Press, 1982), 179.

68. Ibid., 163–64, 166–74; Lee Kennett, *The French Armies in the Seven Years' War: A Study in Military Organization and Administration* (Durham, N.C.: Duke University Press, 1967), 139–40; Alfred Cobban, *A History of Modern France* (New York: Braziller, 1965), 94.

69. R. R. Palmer, *The Age of Democratic Revolution: A Political History of Europe and America, 1760–1800,* vol. 1, *The Challenge* (Princeton, N.J.: Princeton University Press, 1959), 86–99.

70. Quoted in C. B. A. Behrens, *The Ancien Régime* (New York: Harcourt Brace, 1967), 158–59.

71. E. N. Williams, *The Ancien Régime in Europe* (New York: Harper & Row, 1970), 114–33.

72. Steve J. Stern, *The Secret History of Gender: Women, Men, and Power in Late Colonial Mexico* (Chapel Hill: University of North Carolina Press, 1995).

73. Mark A. Burkholder and Lyman L. Johnson, *Colonial Latin America,* 2nd ed. (New York: Oxford University Press, 1994), 194–97.

74. D. A. Brading, *Miners and Merchants in Bourbon Mexico, 1763–1810* (Cambridge, U.K.: Cambridge University Press, 1971); Susan Deans-Smith, *Bureaucrats, Planters, and Workers: The Making of the Tobacco Monopoly in Bourbon Mexico* (Austin: University of Texas Press, 1992).

75. Christon I. Archer, *The Army in Bourbon Mexico, 1760–1810* (Albuquerque: University of New Mexico Press, 1977); Lyle N. McAlister, *The "Fuero Militar" in New Spain, 1764–1800* (Gainesville: University of Florida Press, 1957).

76. The best account of Pontiac's War is Gregory Evans Dowd, *War under Heaven: Pontiac, the Indian Nations, and the British Empire* (Baltimore, Md.: Johns Hopkins University Press, 2002); the previous standard account, Howard H. Peckham, *Pontiac and the Indian Uprising* (Princeton, N.J.: Princeton University Press, 1947), still has value. See also White, *Middle Ground,* 269–314; Richter, *Facing East,* 193–201; Steele, *Warpaths,* 234–47; and Anderson, *Crucible of War,* 535–53, 617–37.

77. John Brewer, *The Sinews of Power: War, Money, and the English State, 1688–1783* (New York: Knopf, 1989), xvii–xxi, 140–43, 191–217.

78. In *Britons: Forging the Nation, 1707–1837* (New Haven: Yale University Press, 1992), Linda Colley identifies Protestantism as the most important factor in unifying Britain after 1707 but only after admitting that "War played a vital part in the invention of the British nation after 1707" (367). See her general discussion, 364–75. Relevant here, too, are her comments on page 53: "Self-evidently, the Protestant construction of British identity involved the unprivileging of minorities who would not conform: the Catholic community, most Highland Scots before 1745, and the supporters of the exiled Stuart dynasty, those men and women who were not allowed to be British so that others could be. Self-evidently, too,

this way of viewing the world fostered and relied on war. There are few more effective ways of bonding together a highly disparate people than by encouraging it to unite against its own and other outsiders."

Our argument about war in North America has been influenced by John Brewer's call, in *The Sinews of Power,* for seeing war in the broadest possible context, especially with regard to ideological and economic change. His strictures on the way we look at the liberal state have been particularly influential: "The liberal focus on the British state has resolutely concentrated its gaze on relations with the domestic polity. I want to draw attention to the state's international role, to its actions as a military and diplomatic power." "The British government was able to act effectively against its international enemies but was weak in dealings with its own subjects." This very "lightness of touch" in governing at home increased its ability to exert force beyond the limits of the realm: "The heavy-handedness of British rule increased the farther it extended beyond the metropolis" (xviii–xix).

Our characterization of Anglicization as war-driven ultimately derives from John Murrin's 1966 Yale Ph.D. thesis, "Anglicizing an American Colony: The Transformation of Provincial Massachusetts"; for a concise statement of the argument, see his article, "The Legal Transformation: The Bench and Bar of Eighteenth-Century Massachusetts," in Stanley N. Katz, ed., *Colonial America: Essays in Politics and Social Development* (Boston: Little, Brown, 1976), 415–49. We draw attention to this quality because some of the current literature on consumption patterns in British America suggests that Anglicization was largely a commercial process. The most powerful recent statement of this position is T. H. Breen, *The Marketplace of Revolution: How Consumer Politics Shaped American Independence* (New York: Oxford University Press, 2004). He moves beyond the concept to discuss the political implications of a growing consumer culture; see esp. chapter 5. See also his essay, "Ideology and Nationalism on the Eve of the American Revolution: Revisions *Once* More in Need of Revising," *Journal of American History* 84 (1997), 1:13–40. We acknowledge that commerce played a central role but believe that it needs to be seen as only one component of a larger set of processes.

79. On tobacco and planter indebtedness, see T. H. Breen, *Tobacco Culture: The Mentality of the Great Tidewater Planters on the Eve of Revolution* (Princeton, N.J.: Princeton University Press, 1985), 125–32, 147–50, 208–09, and passim; also Freeman, *Washington,* 3:71–118.

80. Charles Royster, *The Fabulous History of the Dismal Swamp Company: A Story of George Washington's Times* (New York: Knopf, 1999), offers the most complete treatment of Washington's postwar speculative endeavors; see also Anderson, *Crucible of War,* 593–94, 738–41.

81. Daniel M. Friedenberg, *Life, Liberty, and the Pursuit of Land: The Plunder of Early America* (Buffalo, N.Y.: Prometheus Books, 1992), 173–74; Bernhard Knollenberg, *George Washington: The Virginia Period, 1732–1775* (Durham, N.C.: Duke University Press, 1964), 90–95.

82. Anderson, *Crucible of War,* 740.

83. Washington to Crawford, September 17, 1767, in W. W. Abbot et al., eds., *The Papers of George Washington, Colonial Series,* vol. 8, *June 1767–December 1771* (Charlottesville: University Press of Virginia, 1993), 26–29 (quotation at 28).

84. Freeman, *Washington,* 3:239–40, 245–48, 252–53.

85. The most convenient source to follow Washington's activities on this trip and his other visits to the West from 1753 through 1784 and his engagements in trans-Appalachian land speculation, is Hugh Cleland, ed., *George Washington in the Ohio Valley* (Pittsburgh: University of Pittsburgh Press, 1955); his diary of the 1770 trip is at 240–69. Cf. the more heavily annotated version in Donald Jackson and Dorothy Twohig, eds., *The Diaries of George Washington,* vol. 2, *1766–70* (Charlottesville: University Press of Virginia, 1976), 276–328.

86. Washington to Croghan, November 24, 1770, *Papers of Washington, Col. Ser.,* 8:403–4. Croghan evidently offered to sell the land at five shillings per acre, so it seems clear that Washington's far lower offer was based on his estimate of the risks involved in dealing with a flawed title; see Wainwright, *George Croghan,* 276.

87. Washington to Johnson, July 20, 1770, *Papers of Washington, Col. Ser.,* 8:360. Unfortunately, Joel Achenbach's study, *The Grand Idea: George Washington's Potomac and the Race to the West* (New York: Simon & Schuster, 2004), came to hand too late to influence our interpretation, which seems to be broadly consistent with his.

88. Longmore, *Invention of Washington,* 91–99.

89. Washington dined with Dunmore on October 31, 1771, and March 3, 1772; spent the evening with him on March 4, 1772; breakfasted, dined, and supped with him on November 3, 1772; dined with him again on March 7, 1773. (Donald Jackson and Dorothy Twohig, eds., *The Diaries of George Washington,* vol. 3, *1771–75, 1780–81* [Charlottesville: University Press of Virginia, 1978], 65, 94–95, 141, 165.)

90. Washington to Dunmore, April 13, 1773, in W. W. Abbot et al., eds., *The Papers of George Washington, Col. Ser.,* vol. 9, *January 1772–March 1774* (Charlottesville: University Press of Virginia, 1994), 55–57.

91. Washington described her death as "this Sudden, and unexpected blow," which "has almost reduced my poor Wife to the lowest ebb of Misery." (To Burwell Bassett, June 20, 1773, *Papers of Washington, Col. Ser.,* 9:243.) Since marrying Martha in 1759, Washington had acted as guardian to both her children by Daniel Parke Custis, John ("Jack") and Martha ("Patsy"), and as such assumed responsibility for managing their inheritance until they reached legal majority. With Patsy's death, her £16,000 portion passed by halves to her brother and mother. Washington used Martha's £8,000 share to pay off the family's debts to London creditors and thus in 1774 finally achieved the financial independence he had worked toward for the previous fifteen years. See Freeman, *Washington,* 3: 325–6.

92. Washington to Lord Dunmore and the council, c. November 3, 1773, *Papers of Washington, Col. Ser.,* 9:358–66.

93. John Connolly to Washington, June 29, 1773, *Papers of Washington, Col. Ser.,* 9:250–51 and 251 n. 6; Connolly to Washington, September 12, 1773, ibid., 314–15. Connolly was a natural philosopher by inclination as well as a physician by training and a trader/speculator by preference. On more than one occasion he sent Washington descriptions of such Ohio Valley curiosities as mammoth teeth and Indian mounds. He was also—or so Washington believed—a nephew of George Croghan. (Ibid., 9:98 n. 1.)

94. Washington to Crawford, September 25, 1773 (two letters of the same date), *Papers of Washington, Col. Ser.,* 9:328–32. Quotation at 332.

95. George Morgan, quoted in Eric Hinderaker and Peter C. Mancall, *At the Edge of Empire: The Backcountry in British North America* (Baltimore, Md.: Johns Hopkins University Press, 2003), 155.

96. Dunmore to the Earl of Dartmouth (secretary of state for America), March 18, 1774, in K. G. Davies, ed., *Documents of the American Revolution, 1770–1783 (Colonial Office Series),* vol. 8, *Transcripts, 1774* (Shannon: Irish University Press, 1975), 65.

97. Hinderaker, *Elusive Empires,* 189–90; Wainwright, *Croghan,* 287.

98. Hinderaker, *Elusive Empires,* 190–91; Hinderaker and Mancall, *Edge of Empire,* 157–58.

99. For a fine overview, see P. J. Marshall, "The British in Asia: Trade to Dominion, 1700–1765," in Wm. Roger Louis, gen. ed., *The Oxford History of the British Empire,* vol. 2, *The Eighteenth Century,* ed. P. J. Marshall (Oxford: Oxford University Press, 1998), 487–507. On the effects of involvement in Indian governance on the company and on British politics of the period, see esp. H. V. Bowen, "British India, 1765–1813: The Metropolitan Context," ibid., 530–51, and also Bowen's monograph *Revenue and Reform: The Indian Problem in British Politics, 1757–1773* (Cambridge, U.K.: Cambridge University Press, 1991).

100. Washington's moderation was such that he took no apparent note of the Tea Act or the destruction of the tea until after the Coercive Acts were passed. According to Freeman, *Washington* 3:341, Washington learned of the destruction of the tea around the beginning of January 1774, but the first mention of it in his correspondence came on a letter written between June 10 and 15 to George William Fairfax, in which he noted "the oppressive and arbitrary Act of Parliament for stopping up the Port & commerce of Boston." (W. W. Abbot et al., eds., *The Papers of George Washington, Colonial Series,* vol. 10, *March 1774–June 1775* [Charlottesville: University Press of Virginia, 1995], 94–101; quotation at 95.) Interestingly enough, although the Quebec Act had the effect of invalidating all of Virginia's land claims north of the Ohio River, he mentioned it only once in his correspondence, in a brief addendum ("P.S. Pray what do you think of the Canada Bill?") to a letter to Bryan Fairfax on August 24, 1774, in which he expressed outrage at the draconian measures directed against Boston. (Ibid., 154–56; quotation at 156.) While it is impossible to say with certainty, Washington's apparent lack of reaction to the Quebec Act may have stemmed from the

fact that all of his speculative properties in the Ohio country lay on the south side of the river, and hence were unaffected by the new measure.

101. *Diaries of Washington,* 3:251.

102. Resolution of the Convention, May 30, 1774, in Robert L. Scribner, ed., *Revolutionary Virginia: The Road to Independence,* vol. 1, *Forming Thunderclouds and the First Convention, 1763–1774* (Charlottesville: University Press of Virginia, 1973), 99–100.

103. In lieu of wages, the governor promised the provincials plunder (Hinderaker, *Elusive Empires,* 193). Such a sizable and rapid completion of two regiments despite the lack of pay suggests that enlistment was driven both by fear of Indian attacks on the frontier and by the desire to gain access to western lands; most of the men who enlisted were from frontier districts.

104. Hinderaker, *Elusive Empires,* 194.

105. James Parker to Charles Steuart, January 27, 1775, quoted in Woody Holton, *Forced Founders: Indians, Debtors, Slaves, and the Making of the American Revolution in Virginia* (Chapel Hill: University of North Carolina Press, 1999), 144.

106. Resolution of March 25, 1775, quoted ibid. Even after the Second Continental Congress had created the Continental Army, in the summer of 1775 the Virginia convention met the demand for defense by issuing £350,000 in paper currency to create Virginia's new regiments *and* to pay the bills still outstanding from Dunmore's War. (Ibid., 176.)

107. Quotation: Washington to Bryan Fairfax, August 24, 1774, *Papers of Washington, Col. Ser.,* 10:155.

108. Washington to Dunmore, April 3, 1775, *Papers of Washington, Col. Ser.,* 10:320–22. Quotation at 320.

109. Dunmore to Washington, April 18, 1775, ibid., 337–38. Dunmore's letter read, in its entirety:

> Sir
>
> I have reveived [*sic*] your letter dated the 3d Instant. The Information you have received that the Patents granted for the Lands under the Proclamation of 1754 would be declared Null and Void, is founded on a report that the Surveyor who Surveyed those Lands did not qualify agreeable to the Act of Assembly directing the duty and qualification of Surveyors, if this is the Case the Patents will of Consequence be declared Null and void. I am Sir Your Most Obedient humble Servant
>
> Dunmore

Washington could hardly have failed to recall that the surveyor who laid out his plots on the Ohio was Captain William Crawford, whom the governor himself recently employed to survey lands near Pittsburgh.

110. Dunmore to the Earl of Dartmouth, May 1, 1775, in K. G. Davies, ed., *Documents*

of the American Revolution, 1770–1783, vol. 9, *Transcripts 1775, January to June* (Shannon: Irish University Press, 1975), 107–10.

111. On the fear of a slave uprising, see Holton, *Forced Founders,* 140–43; "would declare freedom" is from the "Deposition of Dr. William Pasteur," quoted ibid., 145.

112. Arrival of news: Freeman, *Washington,* 3:412–13, nn. 84, 85.

113. Longmore, *Invention of Washington,* 146–52.

114. Holton, *Forced Founders,* 146–48; Stuart Leibiger, *Founding Friendship: George Washington, James Madison, and the Creation of the American Republic* (Charlottesville: University Press of Virginia, 1999), 12–13; Freeman, *Washington,* 3:410–12; *Diaries of Washington,* 3:323, 325. One company did not disband: Patrick Henry, also appointed a delegate to the Continental Congress, led his men from Hanover County toward Williamsburg on May 2. Dunmore reissued his threat in the lightly veiled form of a proclamation reminding Virginians of their "internal weakness" and pledging to use all necessary means of maintaining his authority. With that he armed his own slaves and also the Shawnee chiefs who were staying as guests—and hostages, against fulfillment of the promise to treat for peace—at his mansion. This gesture, unmistakably serious, evidently persuaded Henry to accept a proposal made by two prominent planters acting as emissaries of the governor who intercepted his force on the march and offered to pay for the powder. Thus the episode ended with governor not following through on his threat to summon the slaves to his standard, Henry saving face, and the fifteen half-barrels remaining in the custody of the Royal Navy.

115. Address to the Continental Congress, in W. W. Abbot, et al., eds., *The Papers of George Washington, Revolutionary War Series,* vol. 1, *June–September 1775* (Charlottesville: University Press of Virginia, 1985), 1.

Four: Washington's Mission

1. Unless otherwise noted, the treatment of New England military culture and institutions in the following paragraphs draws on Fred Anderson, *A People's Army: Massachusetts Soldiers and Society in the Seven Years' War* (Chapel Hill: University of North Carolina Press, 1984), and Anderson, "The Hinge of Revolution: George Washington Confronts a People's Army, July 3, 1775," *Massachusetts Historical Review,* 1 (1999): 21–48. A different, though broadly comparable, perspective on the New England military system and culture can be found in Harold E. Selesky, *War and Society in Colonial Connecticut* (New Haven, Conn.: Yale University Press, 1984).

2. Douglas Southall Freeman, *George Washington: A Biography,* vol. 3, *Planter and Patriot* (New York: Charles Scribner's Sons, 1951), 477–80.

3. Ibid., 480–83; Anderson, "Hinge of Revolution," 21–31 passim.

4. Washington to Lieutenant Colonel Joseph Reed, February 1, 1776, in W. W.

Abbot, et al, eds., *The Papers of George Washington, Revolutionary War Series,* vol. 3, *January–March 1776* (Charlottesville: University Press of Virginia, 1988), 238.

5. The phrases are from a paragraph in Washington's General Orders of July 4, 1775, which anticipates the nationalism that ultimately sustained both Washington and his army throughout the war. It is worth quoting in full:

> The Continental Congress having now taken all the Troops of the several Colonies, which have been raised, or which may be hereafter raised, for the support and defence of the Liberties of America; into their Pay and Service: They are now the Troops of the United Provinces of North America; and it is hoped that all Distinctions of Colonies will be laid aside; so that one and the same spirit may animate the whole, and the only Contest be, who shall render, on this great and trying occasion, the most essential service to the great and common cause in which we are all engaged.

(W. W. Abbot et al., eds., *The Papers of George Washington, Revolutionary War Series.,* vol. 1, *June–September 1775* [Charlottesville: University Press of Virginia, 1985], 54.)

6. Charles Royster, *A Revolutionary People at War: The Continental Army and American Character, 1775–1783* (Chapel Hill: University of North Carolina Press, 1979), 114–18 and passim.

7. Washington, as we have seen, read what classical military history he could find in translation, but it is almost impossible to believe that the approach he adopted after the retreat across the Jerseys in late 1776 was inspired by familiarity with the generalship of Quintus Fabius Maximus, who opposed Hannibal in Italy during the Second Punic War (219–20 B.C.). Commentators who were deeply familiar with the classics, such as John Adams, were conscious of the parallels, but Washington himself was far more motivated by the lack of manpower and an adequate system of supply than the desire to imitate a classical model. In fact, he detested the strategy of retreat, harassment, and force conservation he practiced with such consummate skill; as Charles Royster has observed, "he never adopted [Fabian strategy] fully or preferred it. He wanted a regular, eighteenth-century army that could defend the capital, meet the enemy on the plain, or take New York back by siege and assault." (*Revolutionary People,* 116.)

8. Mark V. Kwasny, *Washington's Partisan War, 1775–1783* (Kent, Ohio: Kent State University Press, 1996), 273–75 and passim. See also David Hackett Fischer's excellent narrative of the period from early 1776 through early 1777, *Washington's Crossing* (New York: Oxford University Press, 2004), for a careful assessment of Washington's ability to exploit the complementary qualities of militia and continental troops; esp. 179–225, 263–76, 346–62.

9. Nathanael Greene to Jacob Greene, January 3, 1778, quoted in Royster, *Revolutionary People,* 116.

10. For the most eloquent statement of this theme, see John Shy, "The Military Conflict Considered as a Revolutionary War," in Shy, *A People Numerous and Armed: Reflections on the Military Struggle for American Independence* (New York: Oxford University Press, 1976), 193–224, esp. 209–14.

11. Neal Salisbury, "Native People and European Settlers in Eastern North America, 1600–1783," in Bruce G. Trigger and Wilcomb E. Washburn, eds., *The Cambridge History of the Native Peoples of the Americas,* vol. 1, *North America, Part One* (Cambridge, U.K.: Cambridge University Press, 1996), 450–51. "Family quarrel" is from the Continental Congress's speech to the Six Nations, July 1775, quoted in Christopher Ward, *The War of the Revolution,* vol. 1 (New York: Macmillan, 1952), 143.

12. The most systematic exposition of the practice of total war in British North America and the early United States, and a work of considerable influence on this analysis, is John Edward Grenier, "The Other American Way of War: Unlimited and Irregular Warfare in the Colonial Military Tradition" (Ph.D. dissertation, University of Colorado at Boulder, 1999).

13. James H. O'Donnell III, *Southern Indians in the American Revolution* (Knoxville: University of Tennessee Press, 1973), 34–61; Tom Hatley, *The Dividing Paths: Cherokees and South Carolinians through the Era of the Revolution* (New York: Oxford University Press, 1993), 191–228; Daniel K. Richter, *Facing East from Indian Country: A Native History of Early America* (Cambridge, Mass.: Harvard University Press, 2001), 451.

14. Ammunition: Hatley, *Dividing Paths,* 218. Quotation: David Ramsay, *The History of the Revolution in South Carolina from a British Province to an Independent State* (1785), in J. Russell Snapp, *John Stuart and the Struggle for Empire on the Southern Frontier* (Baton Rouge: Louisiana State University Press, 1996), 178.

15. Hatley, *Dividing Paths,* 229–41. Also in general see William G. McLoughlin, *Cherokee Renascence in the New Republic* (Princeton, N.J.: Princeton University Press, 1986), for an account of the cultural dimensions of Cherokee resistance.

16. Eric Hinderaker, *Elusive Empires: Constructing Colonialism in the Ohio Valley, 1673–1800* (New York: Cambridge University Press, 1997), 210.

17. Richard White, *The Middle Ground: Indians, Empires, and Republics in the Great Lakes Region, 1650–1815* (New York: Cambridge University Press, 1991), 380–86; Hinderaker, *Elusive Empires,* 210–12; Richter, *Facing East,* 221.

18. George Rogers Clark to Governor Patrick Henry, n.d. (summer or fall, 1777), in Henry Steele Commager and Richard B. Morris, eds., *The Spirit of 'Seventy-Six: The Story of the American Revolution as Told by Participants* (New York: Harper & Row, 1975), 1037.

19. Willard M. Wallace, *Appeal to Arms: A Military History of the American Revolution* (New York: Harper & Row, 1951), 201–03; Ward, *War of the Revolution,* 2:850–61.

20. White, *Middle Ground,* 366–86.

21. The Oneida and Tuscarora peoples, who had been evangelized by Protestant missionaries in the aftermath of the Seven Years' War, were pro-American and did not participate. The Onondaga, traditionally the "firekeepers" of the Great League,

remained the only nation that tried consistently to remain faithful to the old policies of neutrality. The standard account of the Six Nations' experience in the Revolutionary era is Barbara Graymont, *The Iroquois in the American Revolution* (Syracuse, N.Y.: Syracuse University Press, 1972). A more recent account, which treats the experiences of several native peoples, is Colin G. Calloway, *The American Revolution in Indian Country: Crisis and Diversity in Native American Communities* (New York: Cambridge University Press, 1995); on the Iroquois see esp. 46–64.

22. Ward, *War of the Revolution,* 2:629–37.

23. Instructions to Major General John Sullivan, May 31, 1779, in John C. Fitzpatrick, ed., *The Writings of George Washington,* vol. 15, *May 6, 1779–July 28, 1779* (Washington, D.C.: U.S. Government Printing Office, 1936), 189, 190.

24. Ibid., 192.

25. Sullivan to John Jay (President of Congress), October 15, 1779, quoted in Ward, *War of the Revolution,* 2:644.

26. Ibid., 645; Wallace, *Appeal to Arms,* 200.

27. Douglas Southall Freeman, *George Washington: A Biography,* vol. 5, *Victory with the Help of France* (New York: Charles Scribner's Sons, 1952), 450.

28. Washington to the chevalier de Chastellux, October 12, 1783, in John C. Fitzpatrick, ed., *The Writings of George Washington,* vol. 27, *June 11, 1783–November 28, 1784* (Washington, D.C.: U.S. Government Printing Office, 1938), 188. That his imagination had indeed been fired by what he had seen was evident in a letter to the marquis de Lafayette, dated the same day. Washington proposed that the two of them together make "A great tour": "thro' all the Eastern States, thence into Canada; then up the St. Lawrence, and thro' the Lakes to Detroit; thence to lake Michigan by Land or water; thence thro' the Western Country by the river Illinois, to the river Mississippi, and down the same to New Orleans; thence into Georgia by the way of Pensacola; and then thro' the two Carolina's home." This was no mere daydream; he proposed that they depart at "the latter end of April" 1784. Ibid., 187.

29. Washington to Governor George Clinton, November 25, 1784, *Writings of Washington,* 27:500–03.

30. Garry Wills, *Cincinnatus: George Washington and the Enlightenment* (Garden City, NY: Doubleday, 1984), esp. 133–48; H. Trevor Colbourn, *The Lamp of Experience* (Chapel Hill: University of North Carolina Press, 1965), 22–25; Douglass Adair, "Fame and the Founding Fathers," in Trevor Colbourn, ed., *Fame and the Founding Fathers: Essays by Douglass Adair* (Chapel Hill: University of North Carolina Press, 1974), 3–25. See also "A Note on Certain of Hamilton's Pseudonyms," ibid., 284–85.

31. On the suspicion of standing armies and its effect on congressional support for the army, see esp. Royster, *Revolutionary People,* 35–43, 66–69, 262–68, and passim. E. Wayne Carp, *To Starve the Army at Pleasure: Continental Army Administration and American Political Culture, 1775–1783* (Chapel Hill: University of North Carolina Press, 1984), describes in detail how congressional suspicion of the army

inhibited the tasks of the supply officers charged with providing clothing, provisions, and equipment.

32. For a particularly eloquent and extensive exploration of this theme, see Royster, *Revolutionary People,* passim.

33. For the best account of the Newburgh conspiracy and Washington's role in defeating it, see Richard H. Kohn, *Eagle and Sword: The Beginnings of the Military Establishment in America,1783–1802* (New York: Free Press, 1975), 17–39; also Royster, *Revolutionary People,* 333–41, and Don Higginbotham, *George Washington and the American Military Tradition* (Athens: University of Georgia Press, 1985), 96–100.

34. On the larger issue of Anglo-American provincialism as the basis of American political culture, see esp. Bernard Bailyn, "Politics and the Creative Imagination," in Bailyn, *To Begin the World Anew: The Genius and Ambiguities of the American Founders* (New York: Knopf, 2003), 3–36.

35. The best description of Washington's emotional leave-taking from Congress is still Douglas Southall Freeman's; see *Washington,* 5:475–77.

36. Washington to the Earl of Tankerville, January 20, 1784, *Writings of Washington,* 27:309.

37. Douglas Southall Freeman, *George Washington: A Biography,* vol. 6, *Patriot and President* (New York: Charles Scribner's Sons, 1954), 4, 14; Memorandum Given to George McCormick, July 12, 1784, *Writings of Washington,* 27:443–44; Robert F. Dalzell Jr. and Lee Baldwin Dalzell, *George Washington's Mount Vernon: At Home in Revolutionary America* (New York: Oxford University Press, 1998), 181–87. The Dalzells note that Lund Washington was personally ill at ease with slavery; he freed his own slaves by will when he died in 1797 (ibid., 187).

38. Washington to John Augustine Washington, June 6, 1780, in John C. Fitzpatrick, ed., *The Writings of George Washington,* vol. 19, *June 12, 1780–September 5, 1780* (Washington, D.C.: U.S. Government Printing Office, 1937), 135.

39. Washington to Jefferson, March 29, 1784, *Writings of Washington,* 27:375. Washington *knew* that the Yorkers would not delay, of course, because he was partners with one of them, Governor George Clinton. The 6,000 acres the two bought at Oriskany were strategically located to take advantage of the portage from the upper Mohawk to the Wood Creek–Lake Oswego–Oswego River–Lake Ontario drainage.

40. Memorandum following diary entry of October 4, 1784, in Dorothy Twohig, ed., *George Washington's Dairies: An Abridgement* (Charlottesville: University Press of Virginia, 1999), 262. This extended essay of approximately 2,500 words on his journey became the basis of Washington's further thoughts and actions on the navigation of the Potomac and the development of the western country.

41. Ibid.; quotations at 264 ("Hitherto . . .") and 265 ("see how astonishingly . . ." through "political point of view").

42. Ibid., 265–66.

43. Washington to Thomas Jefferson, March 29, 1784, *Writings of Washington,* 27:374.

44. For a fine explication of Washington's views and activities as archetypal in the

larger movement for public funding of transportation and other projects, see John Lauritz Larson, *Internal Improvement: National Public Works and the Promise of Popular Government in the Early United States* (Chapel Hill: University of North Carolina Press, 2001), 10–20.

45. Ibid., 15; Freeman, *Washington,* 6:28–30. The Virginia assembly also chartered the James River Company for the same purposes at the same time. It ordered 100 shares of the Potomac Company and 50 shares of the James River Company purchased with public funds and vested in Washington as originator of the projects and president of the Potomac Company (he declined the presidency of the James Company). This gift embarrassed Washington, who declined to make the shares a source of "personal emolument" but ultimately accepted with the understanding that any profits arising from the stock would be directed "to objects of a public nature." The House of Delegates respected his wishes and passed an amendment to the act authorizing Washington to choose the beneficiaries of the income. (Washington to Governor Patrick Henry, October 29, 1785, in W. W. Abbot, et al., eds., *The Papers of George Washington, Confederation Series,* vol. 3, *May 1785–March 1786* [Charlottesville: University Press of Virginia, 1994], 326 and 327 n. 1.)

46. Washington to Jefferson, August 1, 1786, in W. W. Abbot, et al., eds., *The Papers of George Washington, Confederation Series,* vol. 4, *April 1786–January 1787* (Charlottesville: University Press of Virginia, 1995), 184.

47. On this episode, which might better be called the Massachusetts Regulation of 1786–87, see Leonard L. Richards, *Shays's Rebellion: The American Revolution's Final Battle* (Philadelphia: University of Pennsylvania Press, 2002); Robert A. Gross, ed., *In Debt to Shays: The Bicentennial of an Agrarian Rebellion* (Charlottesville: University Press of Virginia, 1993); and David P. Szatmary, *Shays's Rebellion: The Making of an Agrarian Insurrection* (Amherst: University of Massachusetts Press, 1980).

48. Freeman, *Washington,* 6:68–75.

49. On the creative genius of the delegates, see esp. Gordon S. Wood, *The Creation of the American Republic, 1776–1787* (Chapel Hill: University of North Carolina Press, 1969), 530–32, 544–47, 598–600, and passim; and Bernard Bailyn, "The Ideological Fulfillment of the American Revolution," in Bailyn, *Faces of Revolution: Personalities and Themes in the Struggle for American Independence* (New York: Knopf, 1990), 225–78, esp. 251–53, 266.

50. This discussion derives from our understanding of Gordon S. Wood, *The Radicalism of the American Revolution* (New York: Knopf, 1991); Peter S. Onuf, *The Origins of the Federal Republic: Jurisdictional Controversies in the United States, 1775–1787* (Philadelphia: University of Pennsylvania Press, 1983); *Beyond Confederation: Origins of the Constitution and American National Identity,* ed. Richard Beeman, Stephen Botein, and Edward C. Carter II (Chapel Hill: University of North Carolina Press, 1987); Joyce Appleby, *Capitalism and a New Social Order: The Republican Vision of the 1790s* (New York: New York University Press, 1984); John M. Murrin, "The Great Inversion, or Court versus Country: A Comparison of the Revolution

Settlements in England (1688–1721) and America (1776–1816)," in J. G. A. Pocock, ed., *Three British Revolutions: 1641, 1688, 1776* (Princeton, N.J.: Princeton University Press, 1980), 368–453; James H. Kettner, *The Development of American Citizenship, 1608–1870* (Chapel Hill: University of North Carolina Press, 1978); J. G. A. Pocock, "States, Republics, and Empires: The American Founding in Early Modern Perspective," in Terence Ball and Pocock, eds., *Conceptual Change and the Constitution* (Lawrence: University Press of Kansas, 1988), 55–77; and Carroll Smith-Rosenberg, "Dis-Covering the Subject of the 'Great Constitutional Discussion,' 1787–1789," *Journal of American History* 79 (1992), 841–73.

51. Saul Cornell, *The Other Founders: Anti-Federalism and the Dissenting Tradition in America, 1788–1828* (Chapel Hill: University of North Carolina Press, 1999), provides the most complete and nuanced treatment of the Anti-Federalists as critics of the Constitution; see also the classic treatments of Anti-Federalism in Jackson Turner Main, *The Anti-Federalists: Critics of the Constitution, 1781–1788* (Chapel Hill: University of North Carolina Press, 1961), and Cecilia Kenyon, "Men of Little Faith: The Anti-Federalists on the Nature of Representative Government," *William and Mary Quarterly,* 3rd Ser., 12 (1955), 3–43.

52. The basic works on the military in the early republic include Lawrence Delbert Cress, *Citizens in Arms: The Army and the Militia in American Society to the War of 1812* (Chapel Hill: University of North Carolina Press, 1982); Kohn, *Eagle and Sword;* Edward M. Coffman, *The Old Army: A Portrait of the American Army in Peacetime, 1784–1898* (New York: Oxford University Press, 1986); Francis Paul Prucha, *The Sword of the Republic: The United States Army on the Frontier, 1783–1846* (New York: Macmillan, 1969); William B. Skelton, *An American Profession of Arms: The Army Officer Corps, 1784–1861* (Lawrence: University Press of Kansas, 1992). Eliga H. Gould, *The Persistence of Empire: British Political Culture in the Age of the American Revolution* (Chapel Hill: University of North Carolina Press, 2000), describes the ways in which military service and war defined the obligations of British subjects and American citizens in the era of the Seven Years' War and American Revolution, and thus adds a significant degree of depth and context to this distinguished literature.

53. See Peter S. Onuf, *Statehood and Union: A History of the Northwest Ordinance* (Bloomington: Indiana University Press, 1987).

54. Andrew R. L. Cayton, *The Frontier Republic: Ideology and Politics in the Ohio Country, 1780–1825* (Kent, Ohio: Kent State University Press, 1986), 1–50.

55. Andrew R. L. Cayton, *Frontier Indiana* (Bloomington: Indiana University Press, 1996), 98–166; Cayton, "'Separate Interests' and the Nation-State: The Washington Administration and Origins of Regionalism in the Trans-Appalachian West," *Journal of American History* 79 (1992), 39–67; Cayton, "'When Shall We Cease to Have Judases?': The Blount Conspiracy and the Limits of the 'Extended Republic,'" in Ronald Hoffman and Peter J. Albert, eds., *Launching the "Extended Republic": The Federalist Era* (Charlottesville: University Press of Virginia, 1996); and Cayton, "Radicals in the 'Western World': The Federalist

Conquest of Trans-Appalachian North America," in Doron Ben-Atar and Barbara Oberg, eds., *Federalists Reconsidered* (Charlottesville: University Press of Virginia, 1998), 77–96. Professor John Murrin has suggested another important dimension of the Northwest Ordinance's significance and practicality: the prohibition of slavery in the territory may well have been intended as a defensive measure to protect slavery to the south of the Ohio River. By promoting the growth of a free, white, smallholder population between the growing numbers of slaves in Kentucky and western Virginia and British-controlled territories to the north, the ordinance in effect created a buffer that would discourage slaves from seeking their freedom by flight to Upper Canada. At the same time, the sturdy farmers of the Northwest, if properly armed and trained as militiamen, would reduce the likelihood of successful British intrigues with Indians on the frontier. Reasoning similar to this lay behind the decision to create the colony of Georgia, in 1732, as a strategic barrier to Spanish influence on the vulnerable slave society of South Carolina. It is entirely possible that Thomas Jefferson, who first proposed the exclusion of slaves from the area north of the Ohio in the Land Ordinance of 1784 (the direct ancestor of the Northwest Ordinance), was aware of the Georgia precedent. (Private communication, December 16, 2000.)

56. See, e.g., Edmund S. Morgan, "George Washington," in Morgan, *The Meaning of Independence* (Charlottesville: University Press of Virginia, 1975), 29–55; and Marcus Cunliffe, *George Washington: Man and Monument* (Boston: Little, Brown, 1958), 16–24, 129–213.
57. White, *Middle Ground,* 416.
58. The most notable of these was an American army officer, Brigadier General James Wilkinson. He remained on the Spanish payroll as a secret agent while he continued to rise in command responsibility; eventually he served as commanding general of the United States Army.
59. Richter, *Facing East,* 224–25; Cayton, "Radicals," 86. The settlers migrating westward were encouraged by theoretically large cessions gained at the treaties of Fort Stanwix (1784), Fort McIntosh (1785), and Fort Finney (1786), all of which asserted American claims by right of conquest in the Revolutionary War. All, according to Richard White, were "the products of American illusions" and did not represent the interests (or the cooperation) of the nations of the Western Confederacy. They might have been renegotiated into a viable form in 1788, but the Confederation Congress dissolved in the fall of that year in preparation for the beginning of the new government under the Constitution in 1789 (*Middle Ground,* 417).
60. Knox, "Report," July 10, 1787, quoted in Cayton, "Radicals," 87.
61. Wiley Sword, *President Washington's Indian War: The Struggle for the Old Northwest, 1790–1795* (Norman: University of Oklahoma Press, 1985), 101–21.
62. Sword, *Washington's Indian War,* 150–95. St. Clair's casualty rate was almost identical to that of General Braddock in 1755 at the Battle of the Monongahela. The number of dead, 627, exceeded the highest number of Continentals killed in any

battle of the Revolutionary War except possibly Camden, August 16, 1780, where from 600 to 650 men died.

63. Kohn, *Eagle and Sword,* 124–27. Unlike the army, which had a regimental structure that organized its units by function as infantry, artillery, and cavalry, the legion integrated all three types of units into what today would be called a combined arms organization. Its four sublegions were "in effect four little armies of about 1,200 men each," with a high level of flexibility and the capacity for rapid deployment (124).

64. Report of the secretary of war to Congress, July 10, 1787, quoted in White, *Middle Ground,* 416.

65. Washington to Congressman James Duane, September 7, 1783, *Writings of Washington,* 27:140.

66. White, *Middle Ground,* 455–66.

67. Kohn, *Eagle and Sword,* 155–57; White, *Middle Ground,*466–68; Richter, *Facing East,* 225; Cayton, "Radicals," 88; Paul David Nelson, *Anthony Wayne: Soldier of the Early Republic* (Bloomington: Indiana University Press, 1985), 249–72.

68. Andrew R. L. Cayton, "'Noble Actors' upon 'the Theatre of Honour': Power and Civility in the Treaty of Greenville," in Andrew R. L. Cayton and Fredrika Teute, eds., *Contact Points: American Frontiers from the Mohawk Valley to the Mississippi, 1750–1830* (Chapel Hill: University of North Carolina Press, 1998), 235–69.

69. Cayton, "Radicals," 90–91.

70. On excise taxes in Britain, see John Brewer, *The Sinews of Power: War, Money, and the English State, 1688–1783* (New York: Knopf, 1989); on the whiskey excise, Thomas P. Slaughter, *The Whiskey Rebellion: Frontier Epilogue to the American Revolution* (New York: Oxford University Press, 1986); on Hamilton and the excise, Forrest McDonald, *Alexander Hamilton: A Biography* (New York: W.W. Norton, 1979), 149–52, 190–97.

71. Slaughter, *Whiskey Rebellion,* 114–15, 119–24; quotation: Washington to the secretary of state (Thomas Jefferson), September 15, 1792, in John C. Fitzpatrick, ed., *The Writings of George Washington,* vol. 32, *March 10, 1792–June 30, 1793* (Washington, D.C.: U.S. Government Printing Office, 1939), 149.

72. Proclamation, September 15, 1792, *Writings of Washington,* 32:151.

73. Slaughter, *Whiskey Rebellion,* 179–80, 186–88.

74. Proclamation, August 7, 1794, in John C. Fitzpatrick, ed., *Writings of Washington,* vol. 33, *July 1, 1793–October 9, 1794* (Washington, D.C.: U.S. Government Printing Office, 1940), 460–61.

75. Kohn, *Eagle and Sword,* 164–65.

76. Proclamation, September 25, 1794, *Writings of Washington,* 33:507–09.

77. John Alexander Carroll and Mary Wells Ashworth, *George Washington,* vol. 7, *First in Peace* (New York: Charles Scribner's Sons, 1957), 199. This news heartened Washington, who was relieved to see evidence of thoroughness and deliberation in the report. Wayne, he knew, was "vain," "easily imposed upon," possibly "addicted to the bottle," and not necessarily the sort of commander who would

consolidate control effectively after a victory. Indeed, Washington initially consented to his appointment only because no more qualified candidate was available (Washington's "Opinion of the General Officers," March 9, 1792, quoted in Kohn, *Eagle and Sword,* 125).

78. Diary entries of October 5–20, 1794, in Twohig, ed., *Washington's Diaries,* 396–401; Carroll and Ashworth, *Washington,* 7:200–13. Hamilton accompanied the army to Pittsburgh as Washington's proxy and remained until November 19 (McDonald, *Hamilton,* 302).

79. *Washington's Diaries,* 401.

80. Slaughter, *Whiskey Rebellion,* 219–20.

81. Carroll and Ashworth, *Washington,* 7:229.

82. Ibid., 221–35 passim.

83. Washington to Hamilton, May 15, 1795, in John C. Fitzpatrick, ed., *The Writings of George Washington,* vol. 35, *March 30, 1796–July 31, 1797* (Washington, D.C.: U.S. Government Printing Office, 1940), 50. The draft Washington sent was largely based on a farewell address that James Madison wrote for him in 1792 when he contemplated retiring from office at the end of his first administration.

84. Farewell Address (First Draft), May 15, 1796, *Writings of Washington,* 35:51–61; quotations at 54 ("children"), 58 ("Constitutional purity," "Union"), 56 ("Intreigues"), 57 ("prepared for War," "bid defiance").

85. Joseph J. Ellis, *Founding Brothers: The Revolutionary Generation* (New York: Knopf, 2000), 129.

86. Circular to the States, June 8, 1783, in John C. Fitzpatrick, ed., *The Writings of George Washington,* vol. 26, *January 1, 1783–June 10, 1783* (Washington, D.C.: U.S. Government Printing Office, 1938), 484.

87. Ellis, *Founding Brothers,* 160. The reference to his own vine and fig tree, a favorite phrase of Washington's, is from Micah 4:3–4: "And [the Lord] shall judge among many people, and rebuke strong nations afar off; and they shall beat their swords into plowshares, and their spears into pruninghooks: nation shall not lift up a sword against nation, neither shall they learn war any more. But they shall sit every man under his vine and under his fig tree; and none shall make *them* afraid; for the mouth of the Lord of hosts has spoken it."

88. Following the election of John Adams as Washington's successor in 1796, relations with Revolutionary France deteriorated to the point that French naval officers and privateers seized American shipping bound for British ports. In May 1797 Adams requested appropriations of funds for defense and dispatched a three-man delegation (Charles Cotesworth Pinckney, John Marshall, and Elbridge Gerry) to Paris to demand reparations for ships and cargoes seized and to ask for release from certain provisions of the Treaty of Alliance of 1778. In return the commissioners were authorized to offer concessions on neutral rights and trade comparable to those granted to Britain in Jay's Treaty. When Pinckney, Marshall, and Gerry arrived, they found that the French foreign minister, Charles-Maurice de Talleyrand, re-

fused to meet with them; three intermediaries soon explained that he would be willing to do so only if they first provided a direct payment of $250,000 and a large loan to France. The American ministers refused to submit to the terms proposed (Pinckney, memorably, replied to the demand for a bribe, "No! No! Not a six-pence!"), and Pinckney and Marshall returned to the United States to report to the president. In April 1798 Adams asked Congress for further appropriations for defense, submitting documents to substantiate the ministers' story, with the letters X, Y, and Z substituted for the names of Talleyrand's go-betweens. Congress instituted sanctions against France and approved of a major naval buildup; at the same time, divisions between the Republicans and Federalists grew ever deeper and more bitter. Although hostilities were never formally declared by either power, French and American naval vessels engaged on the high seas from 1798 until 1800 in what is known as the Quasi-War. See Alexander DeConde, *The Quasi-War: The Politics and Diplomacy of the Undeclared War with France (1797–1801)* (New York: Scribner, 1966); and William Stinchcombe, *The XYZ Affair* (Westport, Conn.: Greenwood Press, 1980).

89. Washington to John Adams, July 4, 1798, in W. W. Abbot, et al., eds., *The Papers of George Washington, Retirement Series,* vol. 2, *January–September 1798* (Charlottesville: University Press of Virginia, 1998), 369.

90. Washington to John Quincy Adams, January 20, 1799, in W. W. Abbot et al., eds., *The Papers of George Washington, Retirement Series,* vol. 3, *September 1798–April 1799* (Charlottesville: University Press of Virginia, 1999), 321.

91. Washington to James McHenry, November 17, 1799, in W. W. Abbot et al., eds., *The Papers of George Washington, Retirement Series,* vol. 4, *April–December 1799* (Charlottesville: University Press of Virginia, 1999), 410.

92. Washington to James Anderson, December 13, 1799, *Papers of Washington, Retirement Ser.,* 4:455.

93. For accounts of Washington's death see esp. Carroll and Ashworth, *Washington,* 7:617–25, and Peter R. Henriques, *The Death of George Washington: He Died as He Lived* (Mount Vernon, Va.: Mount Vernon Ladies' Association, 2002). Tobias Lear, Washington's personal secretary, wrote a pair of touching narratives; see *Papers of Washington, Retirement Ser.,* 4:542–555. The quotations "made light of it," "remarkably chearful," and "diverting or interesting" are from Lear's journal account, ibid., 542–43. Washington's final diary entry is in Dorothy Twohig, ed., *George Washington's Diaries: An Abridgement* (Charlottesville: University Press of Virginia, 1999), 428.

Five: Jackson's Vision

1. Tobias Lear, "The Journal Account," December 15, 1799, in W. W. Abbot et al., eds., *The Papers of George Washington, Retirement Series,* vol. 4, *April–December 1799*

(Charlottesville: University Press of Virginia, 1999), 542–46; quotations at 543 ("ague"), 544 ("blood ran slowly"), and 545 (*I feel myself going,*" and "without a struggle").

2. Quoted in Charles Royster, *Light-Horse Harry Lee and the Legacy of the American Revolution* (New York: Knopf, 1981), 202, 201.

3. S. Robert Teitelman, *Two Hundredth Anniversary Edition [of] Birch's Views of Philadelphia, A reduced Facsimile of The City of Philadelphia . . . as it appeared in the year 1800* (Philadelphia: Free Library of Philadelphia, 2000).

4. Quoted in Robert V. Remini, *Andrew Jackson and the Course of American Empire, 1767–1821* (New York: Harper and Row, 1977), 109. Remini is Jackson's most thorough biographer and energetic champion. See Remini, *Andrew Jackson and the Course of American Freedom, 1822–1832* (New York: Harper and Row, 1981), and *Andrew Jackson and the Course of American Democracy, 1833–1845* (New York: Harper and Row, 1984). James C. Curtis, *Andrew Jackson and the Search for Vindication* (Boston: Little, Brown, 1976), is a useful brief biography. Michael Paul Rogin, *Fathers and Children: Andrew Jackson and the Subjugation of the American Indian* (New York: Knopf, 1975), is a critical and suggestive study. We benefited from reading Andrew Burstein, *The Passions of Andrew Jackson* (New York: Knopf, 2003), after initially drafting this chapter.

5. "Speech Before the House of Representatives," December 29, 1796, in Sam B. Smith and Harriet Chappell Owsley, eds., *The Papers of Andrew Jackson, Volume 1: 1770–1803,* 6 vols. (Knoxville: University of Tennessee Press, 1980–), 106–07.

6. Hendrick Booraem, *Young Hickory: The Making of Andrew Jackson* (Dallas: Taylor Trade Pub., 2001).

7. "Jackson's Description of His Experiences During and Immediately Following the Revolutionary War," in Smith and Owsley, eds., *Papers of Jackson,* 1:7.

8. Roger G. Kennedy, *Mr. Jefferson's Lost Cause: Land, Farmers, Slavery, and the Louisiana Purchase* (New York: Oxford University Press, 2003); David J. Weber, *The Spanish Frontier in North America* (New Haven, Conn.: Yale University Press, 1992), 229, 230.

9. Daniel K. Richter, *Facing East from Indian Country: A Native History of Early America* (Cambridge, Mass.: Harvard University Press, 2001), 223–36.

10. The most recent history is Jon Kukla, *A Wilderness So Immense: The Louisiana Purchase and the Destiny of America* (New York: Knopf, 2003).

11. Jefferson, "First Inaugural Address," March 4, 1801, in Merrill D. Peterson, ed., *Thomas Jefferson, Writings* (New York: Library of America, 1984), 493, 494. See Peter S. Onuf, *Jefferson's Empire: The Language of American Nationhood* (Charlottesville: University Press of Virginia, 2000).

12. Jackson to John Sevier, February 24, 1797, in Smith and Owsley, eds., *Papers of Jackson,* 1:126.

13. Stephanie McCurry, *Masters of Small Worlds: Yeoman Households, Gender Relations, and the Political Culture of the Antebellum South Carolina Low Country* (New York:

Oxford University Press, 1995), 304. Among the many virtues of Elizabeth A. Perkins, *Border Life: Experience and Memory in the Revolutionary Ohio Valley* (Chapel Hill: University of North Carolina Press, 1998), is its astute discussion of masculinity, power, and status.

14. Quoted in Remini, *Andrew Jackson and the Course of American Empire,* 62. We have followed Burstein, *The Passions of Andrew Jackson,* 29–32, 241–48, in our account of the Jackson marriage.

15. Quoted in Burstein, *The Passions of Andrew Jackson,* 159, 124, 170; "wife" quoted in Remini, *Andrew Jackson and the Course of American Empire,* 67.

16. See Perkins, *Border Life,* 117–49.

17. Quoted in Remini, *Andrew Jackson and the Course of American Empire,* 121.

18. We follow the account in ibid., 113–43 (quotations at 136).

19. Quoted in ibid., 186. See Joanne B. Freeman, *Affairs of Honor: National Politics in the New Republic* (New Haven, Conn.: Yale University Press, 2001), and Joseph J. Ellis, *Founding Brothers: The Revolutionary Generation* (New York: Knopf, 2000).

20. "Order to Brigadier Generals of the 2nd Division," October 4, 1806, in Smith and Owsley, eds., *Papers of Andrew Jackson,* 2:112.

21. Jackson to James Winchester, January 1, 1807; "To the 2nd Division [Jan. 10, 1807], in ibid., 130, 143.

22. "To the Officers of the 2nd Division," April 20, 1808, in ibid., 191. For more on warfare against Indians as a source of unity among Americans in the early republic, see John Mack Faragher, "'More Motley than Mackinaw': From Ethnic Mixing to Ethnic Cleansing on the Frontier of the Lower Missouri, 1783–1833," in Andrew R. L. Cayton and Fredrika J. Teute, eds., *Contact Points: American Frontiers from the Mohawk Valley to the Mississippi, 1750–1830* (Chapel Hill: University of North Carolina Press for the Omohundro Institute of Early American History and Culture, 1998), 304–26; Eric Hinderaker, "Liberating Contrivances: Narrative and Identity in Midwestern Histories," in Andrew R. L. Cayton and Susan E. Gray, eds., *The American Midwest: Essays on Regional History* (Bloomington: Indiana University Press, 2001), 48–67; Perkins, *Border Life,* 151–76; and Richter, *Facing East from Indian Country,* 189–236.

23. Jefferson, "Eighth Annual Message," November 8, 1808, and "Sixth Annual Message," December 2, 1806, in Peterson, ed., *Jefferson, Writings,* 547, 530.

24. Robert J. Allison, *The Crescent Obscured: The United States and the Muslim World, 1776–1815* (New York: Oxford University Press, 1995), esp. 3–34.

25. Jefferson to William Henry Harrison, February 27, 1803, in Peterson ed., *Jefferson, Writings,* 1118, 1119. See Anthony F. C. Wallace, *Jefferson and the Indians: The Tragic Fate of the First Americans* (Cambridge, Mass: Harvard University Press, 1999).

26. Quoted in William G. McLoughlin, *Cherokee Renascence in the New Republic* (Princeton, N.J.: Princeton University Press, 1986), 37.

27. McLoughlin, *Cherokee Renascence,* 163. Bernard W. Sheehan, *Seeds of Extinction: Jeffersonian Philanthropy and the American Indian* (Chapel Hill: University of North

Carolina Press for the Institute of Early American History and Culture, 1973), 141–43.

28. Joel W. Martin, "Cultural Contact and Crises in the Early Republic: Native American Religious Renewal, Resistance and Accommodation," in Frederick E. Hoxie, Ronald Hoffman, and Peter J. Albert, eds., *Native Americans and the Early Republic* (Charlottesville: University Press of Virginia, 1999), 231. See also Gregory Evans Dowd, *A Spirited Resistance: The North American Indian Struggle for Unity, 1745–1815* (Baltimore: Johns Hopkins University Press, 1992).

29. Claudio Saunt, *A New Order of Things: Property, Power, and the Transformation of the Creek Indians, 1733–1816* (Cambridge: Cambridge University Press, 1999), 164–204.

30. Quoted in Martin, "Cultural Contact and Crises," 252–53.

31. "Address to the Citizens of Nashville," January 16, 1809, in Smith and Owsley, eds., *Papers of Jackson,* 2:210. Michael Paul Rogin offers a sharp critique in *Fathers and Children;* Robert V. Remini, *Andrew Jackson and His Indian Wars* (New York: Viking, 2001), is a staunch defense.

32. Jackson to the Second Division, March 7, 1812, in ibid., 291, 292.

33. Jackson to Willie Blount, June 4, 1812, in ibid., 300; Jackson, "The Massacre at Duck Creek," July 7, 1812, in ibid., 310, 311.

34. Jackson to the Tennessee Volunteers, July 31, 1812; Jackson to the Second Division, September 8, 1812; Jackson to Pathkiller, October 23, 1813, in ibid., 317, 321, 440–41.

35. Our discussion of the significance of the War of 1812 is indebted to Steven Watts, *The Republic Reborn: War and the Making of Liberal America, 1790–1820* (Baltimore: Johns Hopkins University Press, 1987). J. C. A. Stagg, *Mr. Madison's War: Politics, Diplomacy, and Warfare in the Early American Republic, 1783–1830* (Princeton, N.J.: Princeton University Press, 1983), is an expert narrative.

36. Speech on "the Bill to Raise an Additional Military Force," December 31, 1811, in James F. Hopkins, ed., *The Papers of Henry Clay,* 11 vols. (Lexington: University of Kentucky Press, 1959–92), *1: The Rising Statesman, 1797–1814,* 606.

37. Madison, "Second Inaugural Address," in Jack N. Rakove, ed., *James Madison, Writings* (New York: Library of America, 1999), 693, 695; Monroe, "Newspaper Editorial," April 14, 1812, in Hopkins, ed., *Papers of Henry Clay,* 1:645.

38. Robert V. Remini, *Henry Clay: Statesman for the Union* (New York: Norton, 1991); Stephen Aron, *How the West Was Lost: The Transformation of Kentucky from Daniel Boone to Henry Clay* (Baltimore: Johns Hopkins University Press, 1996).

39. Irving H. Bartlett, *John C. Calhoun: A Biography* (New York: Norton, 1993); John Niven, *John C. Calhoun and the Price of Union* (Baton Rouge: Louisiana State University Press, 1988).

40. Calhoun, "Report on Relations with Great Britain," November 29, 1811; "Speech on the Report of the Foreign Relations Committee," December 12, 1811; "Speech on the Albany Petition for Repeal of the Embargo," May 6, 1812,

"Report on the Causes and Reasons for War," June 3, 1812, in Robert L. Meriwether, ed., *The Papers of John C. Calhoun,* 28 vols. (Columbia: University of South Carolina Press, 1959–), 1:67, 76, 77, 82, 83, 107, 110, 122.

41. Clay, "Speech Supporting Bill to Raise Volunteers," January 11, 1812; "Speech on the Bill to Raise an Additional Military Force," January 9, 1813, in Hopkins, ed., *Papers of Clay,* 1:615, 769, 773; Calhoun, "Speech on the Dangers of 'Factious opposition,'" January 15, 1814, in Meriwether, ed., *Papers of Calhoun,* 1:190.

42. "The American to the British Commissioners," October 13, 1814, in Hopkins, ed., *Papers of Clay,* 1:92.

43. Quoted in Linda K. Kerber, *Federalists in Dissent: Imagery and Ideology in Jeffersonian America* (Ithaca, N.Y.: Cornell University Press, 1970), 164.

44. Quoted in James M. Banner, Jr., *To the Hartford Convention: The Federalists and the Origins of Party Politics in Massachusetts, 1789–1815* (New York: Knopf, 1970), 307, 308.

45. Jefferson, "First Inaugural Address," in Peterson, ed., *Jefferson, Writings,* 495. See Lawrence Delbert Cress, *Citizens in Arms: The Army and the Militia in American Society to the War of 1812* (Chapel Hill: University of North Carolina Press, 1982).

46. Clay, "Speech on the Bill to Raise an Additional Military Force," December 31, 1811; "After Dinner Remarks," July 27, 1812; "Speech on Bill to Raise an Additional Military Force," January 8–9, 1813, in Hopkins, ed., *Papers of Clay,* 1:603, 605, 606, 697, 769.

47. Calhoun, "Speech on the Report of the Foreign Relations Committee," December 12, 1811; "Speech on the Results of the War," February 27, 1815, in Meriwether, ed., *Papers of Calhoun,* 1:79, 91, 282; Clay, "Speech on the Bill to Raise an Additional Military Force," January 8–9, 1813, in Hopkins, ed., *Papers of Clay,* 1:760.

48. Dowd, *Spirited Resistance,* 123–90, and David Curtis Skaggs and Larry L. Nelson, eds., *Sixty Years' War for the Great Lakes, 1754–1814* (East Lansing: Michigan State University Press, 2001). A reliable narrative is Donald R. Hickey, *The War of 1812: A Forgotten Conflict* (Urbana: University of Illinois Press, 1989).

49. Quoted in Sheehan, *Seeds of Extinction,* 211–12.

50. Thomas Kanon, "'A Slow, Laborious Slaughter': The Battle of Horseshoe Bend," *Tennessee Historical Quarterly* 58 (1999), 2–15.

51. Jackson to Willie Blount, January 2 [1814]; Jackson to Rachel Jackson, February 21, 1814, in Smith and Owsley, eds., *Papers of Andrew Jackson, 3: 1814–1815* (Knoxville: University of Tennessee Press, 1991), 5, 34.

52. Jackson to Rachel Jackson, April 1, 1814; Jackson to Tennessee Troops in Mississippi Territory, April 2, 1814; Jackson to Tennessee Troops in Mississippi Territory, April 28, 1814, in ibid., 55, 57–58, 65.

53. Jackson to John Williams, May 18, 1814, in ibid., 74, 75.

54. "Treaty of Fort Jackson," August 9, 1814, in Wilcomb E. Washburn, ed., *The American Indian and the United States: A Documentary History* (4 vols., New York: Random House, 1973), 4:2348.

55. Robert V. Remini, *The Battle of New Orleans* (New York: Viking, 1999). American

casualties for the entire New Orleans campaign amounted to 333, of whom 57 were killed; British losses came to 2,444 (378 killed).

56. Jackson to James Winchester, January 19, 1815, in Smith and Owsley, eds., *Papers of Jackson,* 3:252.

57. James W. Covington, *The Seminoles of Florida* (Gainesville: University Press of Florida, 1993), 3–27.

58. Quoted in Saunt, *A New Order of Things,* 245. See David S. Heidler and Jeanne T. Heidler, *Old Hickory's War: Andrew Jackson and the Quest for Empire* (Mechanicsburg, Pa.,: Stackpole Books, 1996).

59. Quoted in ibid., 278.

60. Quoted in ibid., 284.

61. Quoted in ibid., 287–88.

62. Jackson to Monroe, March 4, 1817, in Smith and Owsley, eds., *Papers of Andrew Jackson,* 4:93, 95.

63. Jackson to Francisco Caso de Luengo, April 6, 1818; Jackson to Calhoun, May 5, 1818, in ibid., 186, 187, 197, 199.

64. James E. Lewis Jr., *The American Union and the Problem of Neighborhood: The United States and the Collapse of the Spanish Empire, 1783–1829* (Chapel Hill: University of North Carolina Press, 1998), 96–125.

65. Law quoted in Catherine Allgor, *Parlor Politics: In Which the Ladies of Washington Help Build a City and a Government* (Charlottesville: University Press of Virginia, 2000), 104. See Fredrika J. Teute, "Roman Matron on the Banks of the Tiber Creek: Margaret Bayard Smith and the Politicization of Spheres in the Nation's Capital," in Donald R. Kennon, ed., *A Republic for the Ages: The United States Capitol and the Political Culture of the Early Republic* (Charlottesville: University Press of Virginia for the United States Capitol Historical Society, 1999), 89–121.

66. Smith quoted in Allgor, *Parlor Politics,* 104–05.

67. Jan Lewis, "Politics and the Ambivalence of the Private Sphere: Women in Early Washington, D.C.," in Kennon, *A Republic for the Ages,* 138–39.

68. William B. Skelton, *An American Profession of Arms: The Army Officer Corps, 1784–1861* (Lawrence: University Press of Kansas, 1992), 3–11.

69. Report of Committee on Military Affairs, January 12, 1819, in *Debates and Proceedings in the Congress of the United States . . . Fifteenth Congress, Second Session* (Washington, D.C.: Gales and Seaton, 1855), 517.

70. Speech of Richard M. Johnson, January 12, 1819, in ibid., 522, 525–26.

71. Speech of Thomas W. Cobb, January 18, 1819, in ibid., 590, 591.

72. Speeches of John Holmes, January 19, 1819; John Floyd, February 8, 1819, in ibid., 613, 615, 1120.

73. Speech of Henry Clay, January 20, 1819, in ibid., 634, 635, 637, 639, 640, 643.

74. Ibid., 654.

75. Remini, *Andrew Jackson and the Course of American Empire,* 370–77 (quotation at 371).

76. "Second Annual Message," December 6, 1830, in James D. Richardson, ed., *A*

Compilation of the Messages and Papers of the Presidents, 1789–1902, 10 vols. (Washington, D.C.: Bureau of National Literature and Art, 1903), 2:522.

77. John F. Marszalek, *The Petticoat Affair: Manners, Mutiny, and Sex in Andrew Jackson's White House* (Baton Rouge: Louisiana State University Press, 2000); Allgor, *Parlor Politics*, 190–238 (quotations at 200).

78. Quoted in Allgor, *Parlor Politics*, 208.

79. "First Inaugural Address," March 4, 1829, in Richardson, ed., *Messages and Papers*, 2:438.

Six: Santa Anna's Honor

1. Ann Fears Crawford, ed., *The Eagle: The Autobiography of Santa Anna* (Austin: Pemberton Press, 1967), 7, 245, 7. As we have seen in Chapter 3, Mexican society was arranged according to a hierarchy of blood purity, at the top of which were *los peninsulares*—those born in Iberia—and the *criollos* (creoles)—colonists born in New Spain of unmixed Spanish ancestry. Free persons of mixed blood belonged to a variety of *castas* (castes); the most numerous and important of these were *mestizos*, the offspring of Spanish-Indian unions. Purebloods also occupied the bottom of the social scale: the numerous Indians and the smaller number of enslaved Africans.

2. Ramón Eduardo Ruiz, *Triumphs and Tragedy: A History of the Mexican People* (New York: Norton, 1992), 133–43; Colin M. MacLachlan and Jaime E. Rodriguez O., *The Forging of the Cosmic Race: A Reinterpretation of Colonial Mexico* (Berkeley: University of California Press, 1980), 251–93; Stanley J. Stein and Barbara H. Stein, *The Colonial Heritage of Latin America: Essays on Economic Dependence in Perspective* (New York: Oxford University Press, 1970); Brian R. Hamnett, *Roots of Insurgency: Mexican Regions, 1750–1824* (Cambridge, U.K.: Cambridge University Press, 1986); D. A. Brading, *The First America: The Spanish Monarchy, Creole Patriots, and the Liberal State, 1492–1867* (New York: Cambridge University Press, 1991).

3. William B. Taylor, *Drinking, Homicide, and Rebellion in Colonial Mexican Villages* (Stanford, Calif.: Stanford University Press, 1979), 169. See also Eric Van Young, *The Other Rebellion: Popular Violence, Ideology, and the Mexican Struggle for Independence, 1810–1821* (Stanford, Calif.: Stanford University Press, 2001).

4. Eric Van Young, "In the Gloomy Caverns of Paganism: Popular Culture, Insurgency, and Nation-Building in Mexico, 1800–1821," in Christon I. Archer, ed., *The Birth of Modern Mexico, 1780–1824* (Wilmington, Del.: SR Books, 2003), 49.

5. Francisco Primo Verdad y Ramos, September 12, 1808, quoted in Hugh M. Hamill, "An 'Absurd Insurrection'?: Creole Insecurity, Pro-Spanish Propaganda, and the Hidalgo Revolt," in Archer, ed., *Birth of Modern Mexico*, 71.

6. We follow the account of Hidalgo's life in Hugh M. Hamill Jr., *The Hidalgo Revolt: Prelude to Mexican Independence* (Gainesville: University of Florida Press, 1966), 53–88.

7. Quoted in ibid., 131.

8. Quoted in Ruiz, *Triumphs and Tragedy,* 155. In 1810, the roughly one million people who were either *peninsulares* or criollos constituted slightly less than 20 percent of Mexicans as a whole; Indians numbered approximately 3 million, and mestizos and other *castas* about 1.3 million.

9. Van Young, "In the Gloomy Caverns of Paganism," 46.

10. Hamnett, *Roots of Insurgency,* 46–73, 125–49.

11. Jaime E. Rodriguez O., "Mexico in the Age of Democratic Revolutions," in Rodriguez O., ed., *Mexico in the Age of Democratic Revolutions, 1750–1850* (Boulder, Colo., 1994), 15–90; Mark Wasserman, *Everyday Life and Politics in Nineteenth Century Mexico: Men, Women, and War* (Albuquerque: University of New Mexico Press, 2000), 61–63.

12. Christon I. Archer, "Years of Decision: Félix Calleja and the Strategy to End the Revolution of New Spain," in Archer, ed., *Birth of Modern Mexico,* 143.

13. Will Fowler, "The Repeated Rise of General Antonio López de Santa Anna in the so-called 'Age of Chaos' (Mexico, 1821–55)," in Fowler, ed., *Authoritarianism in Latin America Since Independence* (Westport, Conn.: Greenwood Press, 1996); 1–30; Fowler, *Tornel and Santa Anna: The Writer and the Caudillo, Mexico, 1795–1853* (Westport, Conn.: Greenwood Press, 2000); John Lynch, "Antonio López de Santa Anna: Mexico, 1821–1855," in Lynch, *Caudillos in Spanish America, 1800–1850* (Oxford: Clarendon Press, 1992), 316–64. See also Brian Loveman and Thomas M. Davies Jr., *The Politics of Antipolitics: The Military in Latin America* (Lincoln: University of Nebraska Press, 1978).

14. Crawford, ed., *The Eagle,* 8.

15. Christon I. Archer, "The Young Antonio López de Santa Anna: Veracruz Counter-insurgent and Incipient Caudillo," in Judith Ewell and William H. Beezley, eds., *The Human Tradition in Latin America* (Wilmington, Del.: SR Books, 1992), 3–16.

16. Timothy E. Anna, *The Fall of the Royal Government in Mexico City* (Lincoln: University of Nebraska Press, 1978).

17. Timothy E. Anna, *The Mexican Empire of Iturbide* (Lincoln: University of Nebraska Press, 1990), 1–26 (quotation at 4).

18. Quoted in Oakah L. Jones, *Santa Anna* (New York: Twayne Publishers, 1968), 28.

19. Crawford, ed., *The Eagle,* 15.

20. Ibid.

21. Quoted in Jones, *Santa Anna,* 33; quoted in Robert L. Scheina, *Santa Anna: A Curse Upon Mexico* (Washington, D.C.: Brassey's, 2002), 12.

22. On constitutional questions, we have relied heavily on Stanley C. Green, *The Mexican Republic: The First Decade, 1823–1832* (Pittsburgh: University of Pittsburgh Press, 1987).

23. Doris M. Ladd, *The Mexican Nobility at Independence, 1780–1826* (Austin: Institute of Latin American Studies, University of Texas, 1976).

24. Quoted in Wasserman, *Everyday Life and Politics,* 51. See Timothy E. Anna, "Iturbide, Congress, and Constitutional Monarchy in Mexico," in Kenneth J. Andrien and Lyman L. Johnson, eds., *The Political Economy of Spanish America in the Age of Revolution, 1750–1850* (Albuquerque: University of New Mexico Press, 1994), 17–38; Michael P. Costeloe, "*Hombres de Bien* in the Age of Santa Anna," in Rodriguez O., ed. *Mexico in the Age of Democratic Revolutions,* 247–48; Costeloe, *The Central Republic in Mexico, 1835–1846:* Hombres de Bien *in the Age of Santa Anna* (Cambridge: Cambridge University Press, 1993); Will Fowler, *Mexico in the Age of Proposals, 1821–1853* (Westport, Conn: Greenwood Press, 1998); and Torcuato di Tella, *National Popular Politics in Early Independent Mexico, 1820–1847* (Albuquerque: University of New Mexico Press, 1996).
25. Quoted in Fowler, "Repeated Rise," 5.
26. Crawford, ed., *The Eagle,* xii.
27. Scheina, *Santa Anna,* 17.
28. Steve J. Stern, *The Secret History of Gender: Women, Men, and Power in Late Colonial Mexico* (Chapel Hill: University of North Carolina Press, 1995), 15. See also, Florencia E. Mallon, *Peasant and Nation: The Making of Postcolonial Mexico and Peru* (Berkeley: University of California Press, 1994), 74–88.
29. Howard T. Fisher and Marion Hall Fisher, ed., *Life in Mexico: The Letters of Fanny Calderón de la Barca* (Garden City, N.Y.: Doubleday, 1966), 64, 65, 66.
30. Quoted in Jones, *Santa Anna,* 4; quoted in Scheina, *Santa Anna,* 87.
31. Fowler, "Repeated Rise," 26.
32. Crawford, ed., *The Eagle,* xiv; quoted in Jones, *Santa Anna,* 59.
33. David J. Weber, *The Spanish Frontier in North America* (New Haven, Conn.: Yale University Press, 1992), 229, 230.
34. Gueroult to the French Minister of Foreign Affairs, August 13, 1845, in Ward McAfee and J. Cordell Robinson, eds., *Origins of the Mexican War: A Documentary Source Book* (Salisbury, N.C.: Documentary Publications, 1982), 1:66.
35. Andrés Tijerina, *Tejanos and Texas Under the Mexican Flag, 1821–1836* (College Station: Texas A & M University Press, 1994), 111, 118–19, 120.
36. Andrew R. L. Cayton, "Continental Politics: Liberalism, Nationalism, and the Appeal of Texas in the 1820s," in Jeffrey L. Pasley, Andrew W. Robertson, and David Waldstreicher, eds., *Beyond the Founders: New Approaches to the Political History of the Early American Republic* (Chapel Hill: University of North Carolina Press, 2004).
37. Quoted in Scheina, *Santa Anna,* 26.
38. Sam Houston to "Soldiers, Citizens of Texas!" January 15, 1836, in John H. Jenkins, ed., *The Papers of the Texas Revolution, 1835–1836,* 10 vols. (Austin: Presidial Press, 1973) 4:30.
39. Thomas H. Borden to "The Voters of the Municipality of Austin," January 19, 1836, in ibid., 71.

40. James W. Robinson, Proclamation, January 19, 1836; D. C. Barrett, et al., to the PEOPLE of Texas, February 13, 1836; John W. Hall to the Public, [February 1836?]; Texas Declaration of Independence, March 2, 1836, in ibid., 76, 319, 470, 493–97.

41. Santa Anna to the army, February 17, 1836, in ibid., 373, 374.

42. William Barret Travis to the public, February 24, 1836; Santa Anna to the generals, et al., March 5, 1836, in ibid., 423, 519; David Burnet, Inaugural Address, March 17, 1836, in Jenkins, ed., *Papers of the Texas Revolution,* 5:103.

43. Crawford, ed., *The Eagle,* 56.

44. Quoted in Robert V. Remini, *Andrew Jackson and the Course of American Democracy, 1833–1845* (New York: Harper and Row, 1984), 361.

45. Crawford, ed., *The Eagle,* 57; Remini, *Andrew Jackson and the Course of American Democracy,* 364–68, and Jones, *Santa Anna,* 73–75.

46. Quoted in Gene M. Brack, *Mexico Views Manifest Destiny, 1821–1846: An Essay on the Origins of the Mexican War* (Albuquerque: University of New Mexico Press, 1975), 35. See Brian Hamnett, *Juárez* (London: Longman, 1994), 8–9.

47. José María Tornel, *Relations between Texas, the United States of America, and Mexico* [1837], in Carlos E. Castañeda, ed., *The Mexican Side of the Texas Revolution* (Austin, Tex: Graphic Ideas, 1970, 1956), 287, 288, 294, 325, 326, 328, 343, 367, 369, 370.

48. Quoted in Brack, *Mexico Views Manifest Destiny,* 96, 97.

49. Antonio López de Santa Anna, *Manifesto Relative to His Operations in the Texas Campaign and His Capture,* in Castañeda, ed., *Mexican Side,* 6, 7.

50. Quoted in Scheina, *Santa Anna,* 39.

51. Manuel de la Peña, December 11, 1845; Peña to Tomás Murphy, Mexican minister to Great Britain, October 27, 1845; Pedro María Anaya to Manuel de la Peña, in McAfee and Robinson, eds., *Origins of the Mexican War,* 1:135, 144, 152, 153.

52. [Lucas Alamán?], February 5, 1846, proclamation of Mariano Arista, April 20, 1846, in McAfee and Robinson, eds., *Origins of the Mexican War,* 2:53–55, 122, 123. See Miguel E. Soto, "The Monarchist Conspiracy and the Mexican War," in Douglas W. Richmond, ed., *Essays on the Mexican War* (College Station: Texas A & M University Press, 1986), 66–84.

53. Quoted in Fowler, "Repeated Rise," 26.

Seven: Grant's Duty

1. Quoted in Robert V. Remini, *Andrew Jackson and the Course of American Democracy, 1833–1845* (New York: Harper and Row, 1984), 525. See Lorman A. Ratner, "Sam Houston: The Prodigal Son," in Ratner, *Andrew Jackson and His Tennessee Lieutenants: A Study in Political Culture* (Westport, Conn.,: Greenwood Press, 1987), 99–108.

2. Grant to Julia Dent, May 6, 1845, in John Y. Simon, ed., *The Papers of Ulysses S. Grant: Volume 1, 1837–1861,* 26 vols. to date (Carbondale: Southern Illinois University Press, 1967–), 43; quoted in Jean Edward Smith, *Grant* (New York: Simon & Schuster, 2001), 38.

3. Grant has been blessed with several excellent recent biographies, including William S. McFeely, *Grant* (New York: Norton, 1981); Geoffrey Perret, *Ulysses S. Grant, Soldier and President* (New York: Random House, 1997); Brooks D. Simpson, *Ulysses S. Grant: Triumph over Adversity, 1822–1865* (Boston: Houghton Mifflin, 2000); and Smith, *Grant.* See also John Keegan's astute assessment of Grant in *The Mask of Command* (New York: Viking, 1987).

4. Andrew R. L. Cayton, *Ohio: The History of a People* (Columbus: The Ohio State University Press, 2002), 13–105.

5. Michael F. Holt, *The Rise and Fall of the American Whig Party: Jacksonian Politics and the Onset of the Civil War* (New York: Oxford University Press, 1999), 162–207. For a fascinating exploration of the significance of this election, see Gary Kornblith, "Rethinking the Coming of the Civil War: A Counterfactual Exercise," *Journal of American History* 90 (2003), 1:76–105.

6. K. Jack Bauer, *Zachary Taylor: Soldier, Planter, Statesman of the Old Southwest* (Baton Rouge: Louisiana State University Press, 1985).

7. Darwin Payne, "Camp Life in the Army of Occupation: Corpus Christi, July 1845 to March 1846," *Southwestern Historical Quarterly* 73 (January 1970), 326–42.

8. Ulysses S. Grant, *Personal Memoirs* (New York: Penguin, 1999 [1885, 1886]), 48.

9. Ibid., 50, 51; Grant to Julia Dent, May 11, 1846, in Simon, ed., *Papers of Grant,* 1:86.

10. "President James K. Polk's War Message to Congress, May 11, 1846," in Ward McAfee and J. Cordell Robinson, eds., *Origins of the Mexican War: A Documentary Source Book,* 2 vols. (Salisbury, N.C.: Documentary Publications, 1982), 2:149, 150. The Mexicans were slow to respond to American provocation, which consisted not only of the stationing of Taylor's force on the Rio Grande but the dispatch of an emissary, John Slidell, to demand that Mexico sell New Mexico and California to the United States for $30 million, the ordering of a U.S. naval squadron to patrol the Gulf coast of Mexico, and secret orders sent to the American consul in Monterey, Alta California, to stir up annexationist sentiment among expatriate Americans there. Frustrated, Polk had actually begun to draft his war message to Congress on May 9 without reference to hostilities merely on the grounds that Mexico had refused to cooperate with American demands. The arrival of news on the evening of the ninth that Mexican troops had crossed the Rio Grande and killed American soldiers on land claimed by the United States gave Polk the chance to revise his war message on the basis of invasion. Had the dispatches not arrived in such a timely way, the doctrine of preemption as a justification for undertaking war might have entered the political lexicon of the United States more than a century and a half before it did.

11. Quoted in Michael A. Morrison, *Slavery and the American West: The Eclipse of*

Manifest Destiny and the Coming of the Civil War (Chapel Hill: University of North Carolina Press, 1997), 19, 29; quoted in Robert W. Johannsen, *To the Halls of the Montezumas: The Mexican War in the American Imagination* (New York: Oxford University Press, 1985), 39, 25.

12. Smith, *Grant,* 56–60 (quotation at 52).

13. Quoted in Robert L. Scheina, *Santa Anna: A Curse Upon Mexico* (Washington, D.C.: Brassey's, 2002), 49.

14. Grant, *Personal Memoirs,* 72. See John S. D. Eisenhower, *Agent of Destiny: The Life and Times of General Winfield Scott* (New York: Free Press, 1997); Timothy D. Johnson, *Winfield Scott: The Quest for Military Glory* (Lawrence: University Press of Kansas, 1998).

15. Quoted in Oakah L. Jones, Jr., *Santa Anna* (New York: Twayne Publishers, 1968), 113.

16. Grant to John W. Lowe, May 3, 1857, in Mary Drake McFeely and William S. McFeely, eds., *Ulysses S. Grant: Memoirs and Selected Letters* (New York: Library of America, 1990), 924.

17. Grant to Julia Dent, September 1847, in Simon, ed., *Papers of Grant,* 1:146–48; Santa Anna quoted in Smith, *Grant,* 67.

18. K. Jack Bauer, *The Mexican War, 1846–1848* (New York: Macmillan, 1974), 322.

19. Quoted in Richard Bruce Winders, *Mr. Polk's Army: The American Military Experience in the Mexican War* (College Station: Texas A & M University Press, 1997), 167, 183.

20. Grant to Julia Dent, March 22, 1848; Grant to Julia Dent, January 9, 1848; Grant to Julia Dent, June 26, 1846; in Simon, ed., *Papers of Grant,* 1:153, 149, 150, 97.

21. Grant to unknown [August 22, 1847], in ibid., 144.

22. Grant to Julia Dent, July 25, 1846, in ibid., 102. See Robert E. May, "Invisible Men: Blacks and the U.S. Army in the Mexican War," in Darlene Clark Hine and Earnestine Jenkins, eds., *A Question of Manhood: A Reader in U.S. Black Men's History and Masculinity. 1: "Manhood Rights": The Construction of Black Male History and Manhood, 1750–1870* (Bloomington: Indiana University Press, 1999), 473–85.

23. Grant, *Personal Memoirs,* 25.

24. Quoted in John Russell Young, *Around the World with General Grant,* 2 vols. (New York: American News Co., 1879), 2:448; Grant, *Personal Memoirs,* 27.

25. Quoted in Morrison, *Slavery and the American West,* 21, 23, 73, 74. "Speech in the U.S. House of Representatives on the War with Mexico," in Don Fehrenbacher, ed., *Abraham Lincoln, Speeches and Writings* (New York: Vintage, 1992), 65, 63. See John H. Schroeder, *Mr. Polk's War: American Opposition and Dissent, 1846–1848* (Madison: University of Wisconsin Press, 1973).

26. See Trist's opinion quoted in Josefina Zoraida Vásquez, "Causes of the War with the United States," in Richard V. Francaviglia and Douglas W. Richmond, eds., *Dueling Eagles: Reinterpreting the U.S. Mexican War, 1846–1848* (Fort Worth: Texas Christian University Press, 2000), 60, 61.

27. Smith, *Grant*, 36, 631 n. 6; William H. Gilman and others, eds., *The Journals and Miscellaneous Notebooks of Ralph Waldo Emerson*, 16 vols. (Cambridge, Mass.: Belknap Press of Harvard University Press, 1960–82), 9:430–431.

28. Thomas Van Rensselaer, November 28, 1847, in C. Peter Ripley, ed., *The Black Abolitionist Papers*, 5 vols. (Chapel Hill: University of North Carolina Press, 1991), *4: The United States, 1847–1858*, 16, 17.

29. Richard N. Sinkin, *The Mexican Reform, 1855–1876: A Study in Liberal Nation-Building* (Austin: Institute of Latin American Studies, University of Texas, 1979), 23; Ramón Alcaraz, *The Other Side: Or Notes for the History of the War Between Mexico and the United States*, ed. Albert C. Ramsay (New York: B. Franklin, 1970 [1850]), 456.

30. Quoted in Scheina, *Santa Anna*, 81.

31. William S. McFeely, *Ulysses S. Grant, An Album* (New York: Norton, 2003), 29–46.

32. Julia Dent Grant, *The Personal Memoirs of Julia Dent Grant*, ed., John Y. Simon (New York: Putnam, 1975), 75.

33. Quoted in Smith, *Grant*, 92.

34. Quoted in ibid., 93.

35. Grant, *Personal Memoirs*, 112; McFeely, *Grant*, 41–66.

36. Wilmot quoted in Momson, *Slavery and the American West*, 41; and in William W. Freehling, *The Road to Disunion: Secessionists at Bay, 1776–1824* (New York: Oxford University Press, 1990), 458–59.

37. Morrison, *Slavery and the American West*, 39–45.

38. Quoted in Michael F. Holt, *The Political Crisis of the 1850s* (New York: John Wiley, 1978), 20.

39. Quoted in ibid., 51.

40. Stephanie McCurry, *Masters of Small Worlds: Yeoman Households, Gender Relations, and the Political Culture of the Antebellum South Carolina Low Country* (New York: Oxford University Press, 1995); J. Mills Thornton III, *Politics and Power in a Slave Society, Alabama, 1800–1860* (Baton Rouge: Louisiana State University Press, 1978). See Nicole Etcheson, *Bleeding Kansas: Contested Liberty in the Civil War Era* (Lawrence: University Press of Kansas, 2004).

41. Peter Daniel and Calhoun, quoted in Freehling, *Road to Disunion*, 461, 462.

42. Robert E. May, *The Southern Dream of a Caribbean Empire, 1854–1861* (Baton Rouge: Louisana State University Press, 1973).

43. James Buchanan, J. Y. Mason, and Pierre Soulé to William L. Marcy, October 18, 1854, in *Executive Documents . . . [of] the House of Representatives, Thirty-third Congress, Second Session* (Washington, D.C.: Gales and Seaton, 1855), 127, 128, 131.

44. Ibid., 131; William Marcy to Pierre Soulé, November 13, 1854, in ibid., 134–36.

45. Robert E. May, *Manifest Destiny's Underworld: Filibustering in Antebellum America* (Chapel Hill: University of North Carolina Press, 2002).

46. Quoted in Eugene D. Genovese, *The Political Economy of Slavery: Studies in the*

Economy and Society of the Slave South (New York: Pantheon, 1965), 257, 258.

47. Quoted in William E. Gienapp, *The Origins of the Republic Party, 1852–1856* (New York: Oxford University Press, 1987), 301; Grant, *Personal Memoirs,* 119.

48. Quoted in Holt, *Political Crisis of the 1850s,* 253.

49. Thomas Jefferson, "First Inaugural Address," March 4, 1801, in Merrill D. Peterson, ed., *Thomas Jefferson, Writings* (New York: Library of America, 1984), 494.

50. Jefferson Davis, "Speech at Vicksburg," November 27, 1858, in Lynda Lasswell Crist, ed., *Papers of Jefferson Davis,* 10 vols. to date (Baton Rouge: Louisiana State University Press, 1971–), 6:228; Davis to Franklin Pierce, January 20, 1861, Davis, "Farewell Address," January 21, 1861; "Speech at Atlanta," February 16, 1861; in Crist, ed., *Papers of Davis,* 7:17, 20, 44.

51. R. E. Lee to Mrs. Anne Marshall, April 20, 1861, in Clifford Dowdey, ed., *The Wartime Papers of R. E. Lee* (Boston: Little, Brown, 1961), 10; quoted in James M. McPherson, *For Cause and Comrades: Why Men Fought in the Civil War* (New York: Oxford University Press, 1997), 19; quoted in Drew Gilpin Faust, *Mothers of Invention: Women of the Slaveholding South in the American Civil War* (Chapel Hill: University of North Carolina Press, 1996), 16.

52. Quoted in Faust, *Mothers of Invention,* 59. See George C. Rable, *The Confederate Republic: A Revolution Against Politics* (Chapel Hill: University of North Carolina Press, 1994).

53. Hayes to Guy, May 8, 1861, in Charles Richard Williams, ed., *Diary and Letters of Rutherford Birchard Hayes,* 5 vols. (Columbus: Ohio State Archaeological and Historical Society, 1922–26), 2:13, 14.

54. Quoted in McPherson, *For Cause and Comrades,* 18.

55. Quoted in Brooks D. Simpson and Jean V. Berlin, eds., *Sherman's Civil War: Selected Correspondence of William T. Sherman, 1860–1865* (Chapel Hill: University of North Carolina Press, 1999), 3. See Michael Fellman, *Citizen Sherman: A Life of William Tecumseh Sherman* (New York: Random House, 1995); Lee B. Kennett, *Sherman, A Soldier's Life* (New York: HarperCollins, 2001); John F. Marszalek, *Sherman: A Soldier's Passion for Order* (New York: Free Press, 1993); and Charles Royster, *The Destructive War: William Tecumseh Sherman, Stonewall Jackson, and the Americans* (New York: Knopf, 1991), 79–143.

56. Sherman to Ellen Ewing Sherman, November 23, 1860; Sherman to George Mason Graham, Christmas, 1860; Sherman to Graham, January 5, 1861; Sherman to Thomas Ewing Jr., February 3, 1861, in ibid., 8, 27, 30, 54.

57. Grant to Frederick Dent, April 19, 1861; Grant to Jesse Root Grant, April 21, 1861, in Simon, ed., *Papers of Ulysses S. Grant, 2: April–September 1861,* 3, 7; quoted in McFeely, *Grant,* 96.

58. McFeely, *Grant,* 67.

59. McPherson, "Introduction," Grant, *Personal Memoirs,* xviii, ix.

60. Quoted in Royster, *Destructive War,* 253.

61. Quoted in McFeely, *Grant,* 101.

62. Quoted in Smith, *Grant,* 201.

63. Quoted in ibid., 233.

64. Quoted in Royster, *Destructive War,* 26.

65. James M. McPherson, *Battle Cry of Freedom: The Civil War Era* (New York: Oxford University Press, 1988); Garry Wills, *Lincoln at Gettysburg: The Words that Remade America* (New York: Simon & Schuster, 1992).

66. Lincoln, "Second Inaugural Address," in Fehrebacher, ed., *Lincoln: Selected Speeches and Writings,* 450.

67. James M. McPherson, *What They Fought For, 1861–1865* (Baton Rouge: Louisiana State University Press, 1994), 6, 31.

68. Quoted in Allan Peskin, *Garfield, A Biography* (Kent, Ohio: Kent State University Press, 1978), 177.

69. G. E. Stephens, September 19, 1863, "Manifesto of the Colored Citizens of the State of New York," July 16, 1862, in Ripley, ed., *Black Abolitionist Papers, 5: The United States, 1859–1865,* 242, 227.

70. Quoted in McPherson, *Battle Cry of Freedom,* 850. We have followed McPherson's account of the last days of Lee's army, 844–50, supplemented with Smith, *Grant,* 369–407.

71. Edward Pollard, *The Lost Cause* (1867), quoted in Smith, *Grant,* 409.

72. Quoted in Brian R. Hamnett, *Juárez* (New York: Longman, 1994), 77, 93, 94; quoted in Sinkin, *Mexican Reform,* 148. See Hamnett, *Juárez,* and Mark Wasserman, *Everyday Life and Politics in Nineteenth Century Mexico: Men, Women, and War* (Albuquerque: University of New Mexico Press, 2000), 91–157.

73. Grant to Andrew Johnson, June 19, 1865; Grant to E. M. Stanton, June 20, 1865, in Simon, ed., *Papers of Grant,* 15:156, 157, 158, 205, 206.

74. Grant to Major General Philip H. Sheridan, July 25, 1865, in ibid., 286.

75. Young, *Around the World with General Grant,* 2:164.

76. Eric Foner, *Reconstruction: America's Unfinished Revolution, 1863–1877* (New York: Harper and Row, 1988).

77. Quoted in Scott L. Stabler, "Ulysses S. Grant and the 'Indian Problem,'" *Journal of Illinois History* 6 (2003), 313–14, 313.

78. Grant to Julia Grant, March 19, 1853, in Simon, ed., *Papers of Grant,* 1:296.

79. Quoted in Stabler, "Ulysses S. Grant and the Indian Problem," 302.

80. Ibid., 304.

81. Quoted in ibid., 303.

82. David W. Blight, *Race and Reunion: The Civil War in American Memory* (Cambridge, Mass.: Harvard University Press, 2001); David R. Roediger, *The Wages of Whiteness: Race and the Making of the American Working Class* (rev. ed., New York: Verso, 1999).

83. Heather Cox Richardson, *The Death of Reconstruction: Race, Labor and Politics in the*

Post–Civil War North, 1865–1901 (Cambridge, Mass.: Belknap Press of Harvard University Press, 2001), 122–24 (quotation at 128).

84. Grant, *Personal Memoirs*, 113.

85. Quoted in Smith, *Grant*, 689, n. 30. See McFeely, *Grant*, 336–52, and Brooks D. Simpson, *The Reconstruction Presidents* (Lawrence: University Press of Kansas, 1998). Also see in particular an excellent book that came to hand too late to influence our interpretation directly but which we believe to be highly consistent with it: Eric T. L. Love, *Race Over Empire: Racism and United States Imperialism, 1865–1900* (Chapel Hill: University of North Carolina Press, 2004).

86. Grant to George H. Stuart, October 26, 1872, in Simon, ed., *Papers of Grant*, 23:270; quoted in McFeely, *Grant*, 305.

87. See Foner, *Reconstruction*, 564–601 (quotation at 581).

88. Quoted in Scheina, *Santa Anna*, 151. See Charles A. Hale, *The Transformation of Liberalism in Late Nineteenth-Century Mexico* (Princeton, N.J.: Princeton University Press, 1989); Sinkin, *Mexican Reform*.

89. Paul H. Garner, *Porfirio Díaz* (Harlow, U.K.,: Longman, 2001), 94. Garner's first chapter is an interesting overview of Díaz's role in Mexican historiography and memory.

90. Quoted in Kenneth E. Davison, *The Presidency of Rutherford B. Hayes* (Westport, Conn.: Greenwood Press, 1972), 200.

91. Our discussion follows closely David M. Pletcher's narrative of Grant in *Rails, Mines, and Progress: Seven American Promoters in Mexico, 1867–1911* (Ithaca, N.Y.: Cornell University Press, 1958), 149–81.

92. Quoted in ibid., 166.

93. Quoted in ibid., 165, 168.

94. Quoted in Garner, *Porfirio Díaz*, 144.

95. "Message to his doctor," in McFeely and McFeely, eds., *Grant: Memoirs and Selected Letters*, 1120. On Grant's final days, see McFeely, *Grant*, 495–517.

96. Pletcher, *Rails, Mines, and Progress*, 180.

Eight: MacArthur's Inheritance

1. Quoted in James M. McPherson, *Battle Cry of Freedom: The Civil War Era* (New York: Oxford University Press, 1988), 680.

2. Geoffrey Perret, *Old Soldiers Never Die: The Life of Douglas MacArthur* (New York: Random House, 1996), 7, 64–65.

3. Paul A. Kramer, "Empires, Exceptions, and Anglo-Saxons: Race and Rule between the British and United States Empires, 1880–1910," *Journal of American History* 88 (2002), 1315–53.

4. Angie Debo, *Geronimo: The Man, His Time, His Place* (Norman: University of

Oklahoma Press, 1976). Population statistics and information on Wounded Knee are in Frederick E. Hoxie, ed., *Encyclopedia of North American Indians* (Boston: Houghton Mifflin, 1996), 500–02, 694–96.

5. Quoted in D. Clayton James, *The Years of MacArthur,* 3 vols. (Boston: Houghton Mifflin, 1970–85), *I: 1880–1941,* 65.

6. Pinky's poem may be found at http://www.pbs.org/wgbh/amex/macarthur/filmmore/reference/primary/pinky01.html.

7. "Mixed-battery" battleships were initially intended to be used for coastal defense and were characterized by heavy guns (typically four twelve-inch and eight eight-inch rifles), heavy armor, and slow speed (around eighteen knots maximum); the first were constructed in 1888, the last in 1908. The *Maine* was a good example of this class of vessel; it was one of the most advanced warships of its day. They were superseded by the new, more heavily armed, faster dreadnought class battleships built beginning in 1910; examples include both the *Arizona* and *Oklahoma,* sunk at Pearl Harbor in 1941. The dreadnoughts were ancestors of the fast battleships of the *Iowa* class, which were most identified with service in World War II; two, the *Missouri* and the *Wisconsin,* remained in service through the first Gulf war of 1991 and were formally retired only in 1995. See John C. Reilly Jr. and Robert L. Scheina, *American Battleships 1886–1923: Predreadnought Design and Construction* (Annapolis: Naval Institute Press, 1980); Malcolm Muir Jr., *The Iowa Class Battleships: Iowa, New Jersey, Missouri, and Wisconsin* (Poole: Blandford, 1987); William H. Garzke Jr. and Robert O. Dulin Jr., *Battleships: United States Battleships, 1935–1992* (Annapolis: Naval Institute Press, 1995).

8. This and succeeding paragraphs on commemorations follow G. Kurt Piehler, *Remembering War the American Way* (Washington, D.C.: Smithsonian Institution Press, 1995), 10–91. We are also deeply in debt to David W. Blight, *Race and Reunion: The Civil War in American Memory* (Cambridge, Mass.: Belknap Press of Harvard University Press, 2001), and Kenneth E. Foote, *Shadowed Ground: America's Landscapes of Violence and Tragedy* (Austin: University of Texas Press, 1997).

9. Quoted in Blight, *Race and Reunion,* 106.

10. Quoted in Kristin L. Hoganson, *Fighting for American Manhood: How Gender Politics Provoked the Spanish-American and Philippine-American Wars* (New Haven: Yale University Press, 1998), 73.

11. Quoted in ibid., 235, 236, 219.

12. Quoted in Louis A. Perez Jr., *The War of 1898: The United States and Cuba in History and Historiography* (Chapel Hill: University of North Carolina Press, 1998), 11.

13. Quoted in Hoganson, *Fighting for American Manhood,* 93; quoted in Lewis L. Gould, *The Spanish-American War and President McKinley* (Lawrence: University Press of Kansas, 1980), 40.

14. Here we happily acknowledge our immense debt to several scholars who have

490NOTES (Pages 327–332)

long insisted on the importance of empire in American history, albeit with the caveat that we do not necessarily agree with all their conclusions. See, among many others, William Appleman Williams, "The Frontier Thesis and American Foreign Policy," *Pacific Historical Review* 24 (1955), 39–95; Williams, *The Tragedy of American Diplomacy,* Revised Edition (New York: Dell, 1972 [1962]); Walter LaFeber, *The New Empire: An Interpretation of American Expansion, 1860–1898* (Ithaca, N.Y.: Cornell University Press for the American Historical Association, 1963); Williams, *America Confronts a Revolutionary World, 1776–1976* (New York: Morrow, 1976); Richard Drinnon, *Facing West: The Metaphysics of Indian-Hating and Empire Building* (Minneapolis: University of Minnesota Press, 1980); E. J. Hobsbawm, *The Age of Empire* (New York: Pantheon, 1987); Amy Kaplan and Donald E. Pease, eds., *Cultures of United States Imperialism* (Durham, N.C.: Duke University Press, 1993); Matthew Frye Jacobson, *Barbarian Virtues: The United States Encounters Foreign Peoples at Home and Abroad, 1876–1917* (New York: Hill and Wang, 2000); and Amy Kaplan, *The Anarchy of Empire in the Making of U.S. Culture* (Cambridge, Mass.: Harvard University Press, 2002).

It is worth noting the particular influence of William Appleman Williams. While we accept the economic dimension of American imperialism as part of the general context in which our story unfolds, we also stress the ideological and cultural dimensions as something far more than propaganda or empty platitudes designed to hide unsavory motives.

15. William McKinley to the Congress of the United States, April 11, 1898, in James D. Richardson, ed., *A Compilation of the Messages and Papers of the Presidents, 1789–1908,* 10 vols. (Washington, D.C.: Bureau of National Literature and Art, 1908), 10:61.

16. Joint Resolution of Congress, April 20, 1898, in ibid., 72, 73; quoted in Perez, *The War of 1898,* 41.

17. *Wooster Daily Republican,* November 17, 1898, in Robert H. Ferrell, ed., *Banners in the Air: The Eighth Ohio Volunteers and the Spanish-American War* (Kent, Ohio: Kent State University Press, 1988), 89.

18. Quoted in Daniel B. Schirmer, *Republic or Empire: American Resistance to the Philippine War* (Cambridge, Mass.: Schenkman, 1972), 54.

19. Quoted in Perez, *The War of 1898,* 29.

20. Ferrell, ed., *Banners in the Air,* 39, 40.

21. Quoted in Perez, *The War of 1898,* 35.

22. Quoted in ibid., 33.

23. "Testimony of Arthur MacArthur," in Henry F. Graff, ed., *American Imperialism and the Philippine Insurrection: Testimony taken from Hearings on Affairs in the Philippine Islands before the Senate Committee on the Philippines—1902* (Boston: Little, Brown, 1969), 135.

24. Emiliano Aguinaldo, "To the Philippine People," February 5, 1899, in Daniel B. Schirmer and Stephen Rosskamm Shalom, eds. *The Philippines Reader: A History*

of Colonialism, Neocolonialism, Dictatorship, and Resistance (Boston: South End Press, 1987), 20. See Michael Salman, *The Embarrassment of Slavery: Controversies over Bondage and Nationalism in the American Colonial Philippines* (Berkeley: University of California Press, 2001).

25. Quoted in Stanley Karnow, *In Our Image: America's Empire in the Philippines* (New York: Random House, 1898), 140.

26. Quoted in ibid., 146.

27. Edwin Segerstrom to Mother and Sister, March 7, 1899; Selman Watson to Sister, April 24, 1899; Segerstrom to Mother and Sister, April 25, 1899, in Frank Harper, ed., *Just Outside of Manila: Letters from Members of the First Colorado Regiment in the Spanish-American and Philippine-American Wars* (Denver: Colorado Historical Society, 1991), 65, 89, 90.

28. Karnow, *In Our Image,* 148–49, 159.

29. Quoted in Gould, *The Spanish-American War and President McKinley,* 116. See Stuart Creighton Miller, *"Benevolent Assimilation": The American Conquest of the Philippines, 1899–1903* (New Haven, Conn.: Yale University Press, 1982).

30. For a subtle and important analysis of racism as a limiting factor in nineteenth-century imperialism generally and the annexation debates specifically and for an account that stresses the narrowness of the margin by which the Senate ratified the Treaty of Paris, see Eric T. L. Love, *Race Over Empire: Racism and United States Imperialism, 1865–1900* (Chapel Hill: University of North Carolina Press, 2004), chap. 5.

31. William James, "Letter to Boston Evening Transcript," March 1, 1899, in Schirmer and Shalom, eds., *The Philippines Reader,* 28, 29. See Richard E. Welch Jr., *Response to Imperialism: The United States and the Philippine-American War, 1899–1902* (Chapel Hill: University of North Carolina Press, 1979).

32. Quoted in Walter L. Williams, "United States Indian Policy and the Debate over Philippine Annexation: Implications for the Origins of American Imperialism," *Journal of American History* 66 (1980), 817.

33. Quoted in Brian McAllister Linn, *The Philippine War, 1899–1902* (Lawrence: University Press of Kansas, 2000), 199, 201.

34. Karnow, *In Our Image,* 106–226.

35. Walter R. Combs to his parents, May 2, 1899, in A. B. Feuer, *America at War: The Philippines, 1898–1913* (Westport, Conn.: Praeger, 2002), 140.

36. Shafter quoted in Luzviminda Francisco, "The Philippine-American War," in Schirmer and Shalom, eds., *Philippines Reader,* 11; quoted in *Philippine War,* 211 ("this business"); quoted in Stuart Creighton Miller, "The American Soldier and the Conquest of the Philippines," in Peter W. Stanley, ed., *Reappraising an Empire: New Perspectives on Philippine-American History* (Cambridge, Mass.: Committee on American–East Asian Relations of the Department of History in Collaboration with the Council on East Asian Studies, Harvard University, 1984), 22, 20.

37. The words to this song, evidently sung to the tune of "Tramp, Tramp, Tramp, the

Boys Are Marching," have been widely reprinted in various forms; this one follows the version in Warren Zimmerman, *First Great Triumph: How Five Americans Made Their Country a World Power* (New York: Farrar, Straus and Giroux, 2002), 406. The term "khakiac ladrones" in the second line equates roughly to "crazy yellow bandits": "khakiac" seem to combine "khaki", the yellowish-brown color of army uniforms, with "maniac," while "ladrones" is an old term for highwaymen (in Scots usage) or thieves (in Spanish and southwestern U.S. English). Spanish colonizers also used it to refer to rural brigands in the Philippines. The "Krag" of the fourth line refers to the Model 1892 Krag-Jorgensen rifle, a .30-caliber, bolt-action repeater issued to regular army and (more sporadically) National Guard units, not a particularly popular weapon but much preferred by the soldiers to the heavy .45-caliber, single-shot model 1873 Springfield rifle it replaced. We are grateful to Geoffrey Hunt for reminding us of the significance of the song and sharing his knowledge of the small arms used in the Philippines by various army and National Guard regiments.

38. Quoted in Williams, "United States Indian Policy and the Debate over Philippine Annexation," 826, 827.

39. John Bass, June 1899, quoted in Karnow, *In Our Image,* 155.

40. Linn, *The Philippine War,* 9.

41. Glenn A. May, "Private Presher and Sergeant Vergara: The Underside of the Philippine-American War," in Stanley, ed., *Reappraising an Empire,* 43.

42. Quoted in ibid., 213, 214, 213–17; quoted in Williams, "United States Indian Policy and the Debate over Philippine Annexation," 828. Contrast Linn, *The Philippine War,* who sees reports of torture as exaggerated and scattered, with Miller, *"Benevolent Assimilation."*

43. "Testimony of Arthur MacArthur," in Graff, ed., *American Imperialism,* 136, 137.

44. Ibid., 138, 139.

45. Daniel T. Rodgers, "In Search of Progressivism," *Reviews in American History* 10 (1982), 113–32. We have relied heavily on Daniel T. Rodgers, *Atlantic Crossings: Social Politics in a Progressive Age* (Cambridge, Mass.: Belknap Press of Harvard University Press, 1998), and John A. Thompson, *Reformers and War: American Progressive Publicists and the First World War* (Cambridge, U.K.: Cambridge University Press, 1987).

46. Rodgers, *Atlantic Crossings.*

47. Douglas MacArthur, *Reminiscences* (Annapolis: Naval Institute Press, 2001 [1964]), 32.

48. Quoted in James, *Years of MacArthur,* 1:109.

49. Quoted in Walter LaFeber, *Inevitable Revolutions: The United States in Central America* (New York: Norton, 1983), 37, 38.

50. Quoted in ibid., 54.

51. Quoted in Mary A. Renda, *Taking Haiti: Military Occupation and the Culture of U.S.*

Imperialism, 1915–1940 (Chapel Hill: University of North Carolina Press, 2001), 13. See Hans Schmidt, *Maverick Marine: General Smedley Butler and the Contradictions of American Military History* (Lexington: University Press of Kentucky, 1987), Schmidt, *The United States Occupation of Haiti, 1915–1934* (New Brunswick, N.J.: Rutgers University Press, 1971); and Renda, *Taking Haiti,* 185–300.

52. Quoted in Howard Jones, *Crucible of Power: A History of American Foreign Relations from 1897* (Wilmington, Del.: SR Books, 2001), 60.

53. MacArthur, *Reminiscences,* 42–43.

54. "A Commencement Address," June 5, 1914, in Arthur S. Link, ed., *Papers of Woodrow Wilson* (Princeton, N.J.: Princeton University Press, 1966–1994), *vol. 30: May 6–September 5, 1914,* 145, 146, 147, 148. Our discussion of Wilson is particularly indebted to Frederick S. Calhoun, *Uses of Force and Wilsonian Foreign Policy* (Kent, Ohio: Kent State University Press, 1993); Lloyd C. Gardner, *Wilson and Revolutions, 1913–1921* (Philadelphia: Lippincott, 1976); and the essays in Arthur S. Link, ed., *Woodrow Wilson and A Revolutionary World, 1913–1921* (Chapel Hill: University of North Carolina Press, 1982).

55. R. Ernest Dupuy and Trevor N. Dupuy, eds., *The Harper Encyclopedia of Military History: From 3500 B.C. to the Present,* 4th ed. (New York: HarperCollins, 1993), 1083.

56. The literature on American entry into the Great War is immense. We have found elements of the following particularly helpful: William E. Leuchtenburg, "Progressivism and Imperialism: The Progressive Movement and American Foreign Policy, 1896–1916," *Mississippi Valley Historical Review* 39 (1952), 483–504; Gerald E. Markowitz, "Progressivism and Imperialism: A Return to First Principles," *The Historian* 37 (1975), 257–75; Williams, *Tragedy of American Diplomacy*; Arthur S. Link, *Wilson: Campaigns for Progressivism and Peace, 1916–1917* (Princeton, N.J.: Princeton University Press, 1965; Robert H. Ferrell, *Woodrow Wilson and World War I, 1917–1921* (New York: Harper and Row, 1985); and Thomas J. Knock, *To End All Wars: Woodrow Wilson and the Quest for a New World Order* (New York: Oxford University Press, 1992).

57. Quoted in Walter Hines Page to Woodrow Wilson, February 24, 1917, in Arthur S. Link, ed., *Papers of Woodrow Wilson, vol. 41: January 24–April 6, 1917,* 281.

58. "An Address to a Joint Session of Congress," April 2, 1917, in Link, ed., *Papers of Woodrow Wilson, vol. 41,* 523, 525.

59. "Address to the Senate," January 22, 1917, in Arthur S. Link, ed., *Papers of Woodrow Wilson, vol. 40: November 20, 1916–January 23, 1917,* 534, 536–37, 538, 539.

60. Jane Addams, "Patriotism and Pacifists in Wartime," June 18, 1917, in Jean Bethke Elshtain, ed., *The Jane Addams Reader* (New York: Basic Books, 2002), 357, 354, 362, 364.

61. Quoted in Thompson, *Reformers and War,* 121, 123.

62. Quoted in David P. Thelen, *Robert M. La Follette and the Insurgent Spirit* (Boston: Little, Brown, 1976), 142.

63. Jon Gjerde, *The Minds of the West: Ethnocultural Evolution in the Rural Middle West, 1830–1917* (Chapel Hill: University of North Carolina Press, 1997).

64. Quoted in James H. Hallas, *Doughboy War: The American Expeditionary Force in World War I* (Boulder, Colo., and London: Lynne Rienner Publishers, 2000), 9.

65. MacArthur, *Reminiscences,* 46.

66. James, *MacArthur,* 1:158.

67. Quoted in ibid., 181.

68. Quoted in Hallas, *Doughboy War,* 70, 174–75, 178, 329.

69. Storm Jameson in Joyce Marlow, ed., *The Virago Book of Women and the Great War, 1914–1918* (London: Virago, 1998), 295, 296.

70. Addie W. Hunton and Kathryn M. Johnson, *Two Colored Women with the America Expeditionary Force* (New York: Brooklyn Eagle Press, 1971 [1920]), 11–12, 15, 253.

71. James, *MacArthur,* 1:256; MacArthur, May 13, 1919, quoted in MacArthur, *Reminiscences,* 72.

72. Quoted in Thompson, *Reformers and War,* 250.

73. "An Address to a Joint Session of Congress," January 8, 1918, in Arthur S. Link, ed., *The Papers of Woodrow Wilson, vol. 45: November 11, 1917–January 15, 1918,* 538.

74. R. Craig Nation, *War on War: Lenin, the Zimmerwald Left, and the Origins of Communist Internationalism* (Durham, N.C.,: Duke University Press, 1989), 222–36.

75. V. I. Lenin, *Imperialism: The Highest Stage of Capitalism* (1917), quoted in Michael W. Doyle, *Ways of War and Peace: Realism, Liberalism, and Socialism* (New York: Norton, 1997), 346, 347.

76. Quoted in David S. Foglesong, *America's Secret War Against Bolshevism: U.S. Intervention in the Russian Civil War, 1917–1920* (Chapel Hill: University of North Carolina Press, 1995), 296, 293.

77. Eugene V. Debs, "The Soul of the Russian Revolution" and "Resolution of the Amalgamated Clothing Workers, 1918," in Philip S. Foner, ed., *The Bolshevik Revolution: Its Impact on American Radicals, Liberals, and Labor: A Documentary Study* (New York: International Publishers, 1967), 91, 98.

78. John Bodnar, *Remaking America: Public Memory, Commemoration, and Patriotism in the Twentieth Century* (Princeton, N.J.: Princeton University Press, 1992), 96–97.

79. A. Mitchell Palmer, "The Case Against the 'Reds,'" *Forum* (1920), 63, 173–85, in David F. Trask, ed., *World War I At Home* (New York: Wiley, 1970), 185, 188, 189.

80. Borah, September 5, 1919; La Follette, January 7, 1919; and Felix Morley, "Johnson Breaks with GOP on Russia," *New York Call,* January 8, 1919, quoted in Foner, ed., *Bolshevik Revolution,* 200, 157, 159.

81. Helpful on this topic are Lloyd E. Ambrosius, *Woodrow Wilson and the American Diplomatic Tradition: The Treaty Fight in Perspective* (Cambridge, U.K.: Cambridge University Press, 1987); John Milton Cooper, *Breaking the Heart of the World: Woodrow Wilson and the Fight for the League of Nations* (Cambridge, U.K.: Cambridge University Press, 2001); Knock, *To End All Wars*; and Margot Louria, *Triumph and*

Downfall: America's Pursuit of Peace and Prosperity, 1921–1933 (Westport, Conn.: Greenwood Press, 2001).

82. Warren G. Harding, Speech in Boston, May 14, 1920, http://www.pbs.org/great-speeches/timeline/. See Randolph C. Downes, *The Rise of Warren Gamaliel Harding, 1865–1920* (Columbus: Ohio State University Press, 1970), 410–11.

83. Ronald E. Powaski, *The Cold War: The United States and the Soviet Union, 1917–1991* (New York: Oxford University Press, 1998), 29–34.

84. Gjerde, *Minds of the West*; Bodnar, *Remaking America*; Matthew Frye Jacobson, *Whiteness of a Different Color: European Immigrants and the Alchemy of Race* (Cambridge, Mass.: Harvard University Press, 1998). On the 1920s, see Lynn Dumenil, *The Modern Temper: American Culture and Society in the 1920s* (New York: Hill and Wang, 1995).

85. Quoted in Thompson, *Reformers and War*, 246, 247.

86. Piehler, *Remembering War the American Way*, 116–125 (quotations at 121 and 122). A copy of George Rothwell Brown's very detailed *Washington Post* article on the event, dated November 12, 1921, can be found at http://www.arlingtoncemetery.net/unk-wwi.htm.

87. "Let Us Remember [Address before the annual reunion of the Veterans of the Rainbow (Forty-second) Infantry Division, July 14, 1935]," in Vorin E. Whan Jr., ed., *A Soldier Speaks: Public Papers and Speeches of General of the Army Douglas MacArthur* (New York: Praeger, 1965), 69, 71, 74.

Nine: MacArthur's Valedictory

1. D. Clayton James, *The Years of MacArthur: vol. I: 1880–1941* (New York: Houghton Mifflin, 1970), 557–58.

2. Douglas MacArthur, *Reminiscences* (Annapolis: Naval Institute Press, 2001 [1964], v.

3. "Let Us Remember [Address before the annual reunion of the Veterans of the Rainbow (Forty-second) Infantry Division, July 14, 1935]," in Vorin E. Whan Jr., ed., *A Soldier Speaks: Public Papers and Speeches of General of the Army Douglas MacArthur* (New York: Praeger, 1965), 71; MacArthur, *Reminscences*, 414–18 (quotations at 418).

4. John William Ward, "The Meaning of Lindbergh's Flight," *American Quarterly* 10 (1958), 3–26; and Elliott J. Gorn, "The Manassa Mauler and the Fighting Marine: An Interpretation of the Dempsey-Tunney Fights," *Journal of American Studies* 9 (April 1985), 27–47.

5. White and Chase quoted in James, *Years of MacArthur*, 1:254; Geoffrey Perret, *Old Soldiers Never Die: The Life of Douglas MacArthur* (New York: Random House, 1996), 127. James's multivolume biography is exhaustive while Perret offers more nuanced interpretations. See also William Manchester, *American Caesar:*

Douglas MacArthur, 1880–1964 (Boston: Little, Brown, 1978); Frazier Hunt, *The Untold Story of Douglas MacArthur* (New York: Devin-Adair, 1954); Gavin Long, *MacArthur as Military Commander* (London: Batsford, 1969); and Courtney Whitney, *MacArthur: His Rendezvous with History* (New York: Knopf, 1964).

6. Quoted in John Gunther, *The Riddle of MacArthur: Japan, Korea, and the Far East* (New York: Harper, 1951), 24. See Weldon E. "Dusty" Rhoades, *Flying MacArthur to Victory* (College Station: Texas A & M University Press, 1987), 287 and passim, and Gunther, *Riddle of MacArthur,* 27, for MacArthur's love of talking about himself.

7. Matthew F. Holland, *Eisenhower Between the Wars: The Making of a General and Statesman* (Westport, Conn.: Praeger, 2001), 42.

8. "A Look at the New West Point [*Annual Report of the Superintendent of the U.S. Military Academy,* June 20, 1922]," in Whan., ed., *A Soldier Speaks,* 18, 21; "A New Look at West Point [*Annual Report of the Superintendent of the U.S. Military Academy,* June 30, 1920]," in Whan, ed., *A Soldier Speaks,* 10, 11, 12 (quotations at 21, 12).

9. Earl Balik quoted in James, *The Years of MacArthur,* 1:266; quoted in Gunther, *Riddle of MacArthur,* 26.

10. Quoted in Perret, *Old Soldiers Never Die,* 128.

11. Quoted in James, *Years of MacArthur,* 1:304.

12. Rhoades, *Flying MacArthur to Victory,* 287.

13. Stanley Karnow, *In Our Image: America's Empire in the Philippines* (New York: Random House, 1989), 232–35, 270–72, 267–68.

14. Quoted in Holland, *Eisenhower Between the Wars,* 85.

15. Quoted in James, *MacArthur,* 1:317–18.

16. "Privilege Without Responsibility" [Letter to the editor of *The World Tomorrow*], June 2, 1931, in Whan, ed., *A Soldier Speaks,* 37, 40.

17. Quoted in Robert Dallek, *Franklin D. Roosevelt and American Foreign Policy, 1932–1945* (New York: Oxford University Press, 1979), 36.

18. Quoted in Karnow, *In Our Image,* 269.

19. Gunther, *Riddle of MacArthur,* 44–46 (quotation at 46).

20. "The Keystone of Philippine Defense [Excerpts from a report on national defense by the Military Advisor to the President of the Philippines, April 27, 1936]," in Whan, ed., *A Soldier Speaks,* 85, 86, 89.

21. John Bodnar, *Remaking America: Public Memory, Commemoration, and Patriotism in the Twentieth Century* (Princeton, N.J.: Princeton University Press, 1992), 172–74 (Bloom quotation at 174).

22. Mike Wallace, *Mickey Mouse History and Other Essays in American Memory* (Philadelphia: Temple University Press, 1996), 13–15.

23. Bodnar, *Remaking America,* 170, and more generally, 169–205.

24. Ibid., 182.

25. Edward Tabor Linenthal, *Sacred Ground: Americans and Their Battlefields* (Urbana: University of Illinois Press, 1991), 135, 137, 136.

26. See Andrew R. L. Cayton, "The Meanings of the Wars for the Great Lakes," in

David Curtis Skaggs and Larry L. Nelson, eds., *The Sixty Years' War for the Great Lakes, 1754–1814* (East Lansing: Michigan State University Press, 2001), 373–390.

27. Frederick Jackson Turner, "Contributions of the West to American Democracy" [1905], in Ray Allen Billington, ed., *Frontier and Section: Selected Essays of Frederick Jackson Turner* (Englewood Cliffs, N.J.: Prentice-Hall, 1961), 95.

28. James, *Years of MacArthur,* 1:559.

29. Gore Vidal, *Screening History* (Cambridge, Mass.: Harvard University Press, 1990), 31–63. Through "ear and eye," writes Vidal, "we are both defined and manipulated by fictions of such potency that they are able to replace our own experience, often becoming our *sole* experience of a reality" (32).

30. Leon F. Litwack, "The Birth of a Nation"; Anthony F. C. Wallace, "Drums Along the Mohawk"; Catherine Clinton, "Gone With the Wind"; and Alvin M. Josephy Jr., "They Died With Their Boots On," in Mark C. Carnes, ed., *Past Imperfect: History According to the Movies* (New York: H. Holt, 1995), 136–41; 94–97; 132–35; 146–49.

31. It is interesting that these quotations appear in a popular textbook published during World War II, Charles A. Beard and Mary R. Beard, *A Basic History of the United States* (New York: Doubleday Doran, 1944), 466.

32. Our account of the defense of the Philippines and MacArthur's behavior follows Perret, *Old Soldiers Never Die,* 226–75. Also very useful were R. M. Connaughton, *MacArthur and Defeat in the Philippines* (Woodstock, N.Y.: Overlook Press, 2001), and Michael Schaller, *Douglas MacArthur: The Far Eastern General* (New York: Oxford University Press, 1989).

33. Quoted in Ed Cray, *General of the Army: George C. Marshall, Soldier and Statesman, 1939–1942* (New York: Norton, 1990), 230.

34. Marshall thought MacArthur vain and excessively prone to grand gestures, so much so that when in 1942 he saw a portrait of himself that he did not much like, he complained that it represented "more of a MacArthur personality than my own less colorful characteristics." Quoted in Forrest C. Pogue, *George C. Marshall: Ordeal and Hope* (New York: Viking, 1966), 185.

35. Quoted in Cray, *General of the Army,* 298, 297, 298, 297.

36. Quoted in Kenneth S. Davis, *FDR: The War President, 1940–1943* (New York: Random House, 2000), 409n. A personal memoir is Damon Gause, *The War Journal of Major Damon "Rocky" Gause* (New York: Hyperion, 1999).

37. Karnow, *In Our Image,* 299–305. The Wainwright quotation is on page 301.

38. Quoted in Cray, *General of the Army,* 303. See also, Pogue, *George C. Marshall,* 258–59.

39. See Francis L. Loewenheim, Harold D. Langley, and Manfred Jonas, eds., *Roosevelt and Churchill: Their Secret Wartime Correspondence* (New York: Saturday Review Press, 1975), 212–14.

40. Rhoades, *Flying MacArthur to Victory,* 257, 260, 261.

41. Ibid., 524, 523.

42. "I Have Returned [Proclamation to the people of the Philippines, October 17, 1944]," in Whan, ed., *A Soldier Speaks,* 132, 133. See Perret, *Old Soldiers Never Die,* 417–23

43. "Manila Liberated," Address, February 26, 1945, in Whan, ed., *A Soldier Speaks,* 135.

44. Rhoades, *Flying MacArthur to Victory,* 444–455 (quotation at 469).

45. "A Negro Soldier" to Mr. Carl Murphy, March 21, 1943; "A Loyal Negro Soldier" to Truman K. Gibson Jr., November 5, 1943; "A Soldier" to *The Chicago Defender,* January 9, 1944; in Phillip McGuire, ed., *Taps for a Jim Crow Army: Letters from Black Soldiers in World War II* (Santa Barbara, Calif.: ABC-Clio, 1983), 82, 86, 88.

46. Jacqueline Haring to "Mother and Dad," August 6, 1945, in Judy Barrett Litoff and David C. Smith, eds., *We're In This War, Too: World War II Letters from American Women in Uniform* (New York: Oxford University Press, 1994), 239, 240.

47. David Nichols, ed., *Ernie's War: The Best of Ernie Pyle's World War II Dispatches* (New York: Random House, 1986), 367, 372, 373, 384.

48. Ibid., 166, 153, 154, 212–13, 419.

49. Michael C. C. Adams, *The Best War Ever: America and World War II* (Baltimore: Johns Hopkins University Press, 1994). See also Clayton D. Laurie, *The Propaganda Warriors: America's Crusade Against Nazi Germany* (Lawrence: University Press of Kansas, 1996).

50. "Philippine Freedom Restored [Address to the Philippine Congress, July 9, 1945]," in Whan, ed., A *Soldier Speaks,* 140, 141, 143, 144.

51. Rhoades, *Flying MacArthur to Victory,* 482, 474.

52. Hanson Baldwin, 1947 and Taft, January 5, 1951, quoted in Michael J. Hogan, *A Cross of Iron: Harry S. Truman and the Origins of the National Security State, 1945–1954* (Cambridge, U.K.: Cambridge University Press, 1998), 1, 329.

53. Humphrey, 1951, quoted in Hogan, *A Cross of Iron,* 330; Hogan, *A Cross of Iron,* 12 and passim. See also Lisle A. Rose, *The Cold War Comes to Main Street: America in 1950* (Lawrence: University Press of Kansas, 1999).

54. Michael S. Sherry, *In the Shadow of War: The United States Since the 1930s* (New Haven, Conn.: Yale University Press, 1995); the Eisenhower quotation is in John Whiteclay Chambers II, ed., *The Oxford Companion to American Military History* (New York: Oxford University Press, 1999), 439.

55. Harry S. Truman, Speech to Congress, March 12, 1947, quoted in David McCullough, *Truman* (New York: Simon & Schuster, 1992), 548, 547.

56. "Today the Guns Are Silent," September 2, 1945; "Speech at the Independence Ceremonies of the Philippine Islands," July 4, 1946, in Whan, ed., *A Soldier Speaks,* 151–52, 171, 173.

57. "Address to the Members of the Allied Council for Japan, April 5, 1946," in Whan, ed., *A Soldier Speaks,* 165; John W. Dower, *Embracing Defeat: Japan in the*

Wake of World War II (New York: Norton/New Press, 1999), 27. See also Richard B. Finn, *Winners in Peace: MacArthur, Yoshida, and Postwar Japan* (Berkeley: University of California Press, 1992).

58. Gunther, *Riddle of MacArthur,* 3, 8, 9, 75.
59. "Initial Postsurrender Policy," quoted in Dower, *Embracing Defeat,* 76–77.
60. Ibid., 438, 439.
61. Quoted in ibid., 360; Message to the War Department, February 20, 1947, in Whan, ed., *A Soldier Speaks,* 182. See Herbert P. Bix, *Hirohito and the Making of Modern Japan* (New York: HarperCollins, 2000), 533–646, for a compelling case that Hirohito could indeed have been placed on trial for giving sanction to war crimes in the 1930s and 1940s.
62. Steven Hugh Lee, *The Korean War* (Harlow, U.K.: Longman, 2001), 39–59.
63. William Stueck, *Rethinking the Korean War: A New Diplomatic and Strategic History* (Princeton, N.J.: Princeton University Press, 2002), 213–39.
64. Truman quoted in McCullough, *Truman,* 836–37; MacArthur quoted in Alonzo L. Hamby, *Man of the People: A Life of Harry S. Truman* (New York: Oxford University Press, 1995), 555. See also Dennis Wainstock, *Truman, MacArthur, and the Korean War* (Westport, Conn.: Greenwood Press, 1999), and Stanley Weintraub, *MacArthur's War: Korea and the Undoing of an American Hero* (New York: Free Press, 2000).
65. Harry S. Truman, *Memoirs,* 2 vols. (Garden City, N.Y.: Doubleday, 1955–1956), 2:444, 445.
66. MacArthur, "Old Soldiers Never Die," Speech delivered to a joint session of the U.S. Congress, April 19, 1951, in Whan, ed., *A Soldier Speaks,* 244, 251.
67. MacArthur's appearance at West Point is described in Perret, *Old Soldiers Never Die,* 584–585.
68. MacArthur, *Reminiscences,* 425.
69. John F. Kennedy, "Inaugural Address," in Houston Peterson, ed., *A Treasury of the World's Great Speeches* (New York: Simon & Schuster, 1965), 832.
70. MacArthur, *Reminiscences,* 425, 426.

Conclusion: Powell's Promise

1. Colin L. Powell, with Joseph E. Persico, *My American Journey* (New York: Random House, 1995), 147.
2. Ibid., viii.
3. Ibid., 26.
4. Ibid., 28.
5. Ibid., 37.
6. Quoted in Michael S. Sherry, *In the Shadow of War: The United States since the 1930s* (New Haven, Conn.: Yale University Press, 1995), 146.

7. Powell, *Journey*, 51–52.

8. This insight into the qualities of American soldiers was hardly original with Powell. Baron Friedrich Wilhelm von Steuben, the German soldier of fortune Washington first employed as drillmaster at Valley Forge and later made inspector general of the Continental Army, said something very much like it during the Revolutionary War. "The genius of this nation," he wrote to his friend, the baron von Gaudy, "is not in the least to be compared with that of the Prussians, Austrians or French. You say to your soldier 'Do this' and he doeth it; but I am obliged to say 'This is the reason why you ought to do that'; and then he does it." In the end it came down, Steuben realized, to the mutual respect of leaders and led, the essential precondition under which citizens who pride themselves on equality will voluntarily acquiesce in the inherently unequal power relations of military society. (Steuben, as quoted in Christopher Ward, *The War of the Revolution,* ed. John Richard Allen, 2 vols. [New York: Macmillan, 1952], 2:554.)

9. Powell, *Journey*, 80.

10. Ibid.

11. Ibid., 87.

12. Ibid., 103.

13. Ibid., 132–33. That the Americal division was troubled in many ways became clear to Powell only with time. Three months before he joined the unit, on March 16, 1968, First Lieutenant William Calley led a platoon of soldiers from the Americal division's Eleventh Brigade in the slaughter of 347 women, children, and old men at the hamlet of My Lai 4. Before Ron Ridenhour and Seymour Hersh investigated and reported the atrocity, the only evidence that anything out of the ordinary had happened was the unusually high body count for March 16, the occasion of a special commendation given to the division for the numbers of enemy killed in action. Powell first suspected that something had gone wrong only a year afterward, in March 1969, when he was serving as assistant G-3 and had to respond to a series of questions from an investigator from the inspector general's office who showed an unusual interest in the division's operations log for the previous year. Powell learned of what had happened—"an appalling example of much that had gone wrong in Vietnam"—only in the fall of 1969. (Ibid., 142–46; quotation at 144.)

14. Ibid., 148–49. For the most damning indictment of the army's high command in this regard, one that argues that the mendacious, careerist culture of the Pentagon both antedated Vietnam and enabled the decisions that made it an unwinnable war, see H. R. McMaster, *Dereliction of Duty: Lyndon Johnson, Robert McNamara, the Joint Chiefs of Staff, and the Lies That Led to Vietnam* (New York: HarperCollins, 1997).

15. Ibid., 42.

16. Ibid., 149.

17. Ibid., 207–08.

18. Ibid., 148.
19. On the first Persian Gulf war, in addition to Powell's own account, ibid., 456–542, see Rick Atkinson, *Crusade: The Untold Story of the Persian Gulf War* (New York: Houghton Mifflin, 1993), and Michael R. Gordon and Bernard E. Trainor, *The Generals' War: The Inside Story of the Conflict in the Gulf* (Boston: Little, Brown, 1995).
20. As of early June 2004 there were indications, none of them conclusive, that Powell was consulted too late about the Iraq invasion to have exercised significant influence on the decision to commit troops; the Department of State, furthermore, seems to have been allowed to play only a marginal role in planning the postwar occupation. Bob Woodward, *Plan of Attack* (New York: Simon & Schuster, 2004).

ACKNOWLEDGMENTS

The idea that became *The Dominion of War* crystallized in an accidental conversation late in the afternoon of March 21, 1993. After picking up Drew at Logan Airport, Fred took a wrong turn and then spent an impossibly long time groping his way back to Cambridge through a maze of Chelsea, Revere, Malden, Medford, and Somerville streets. Meanwhile, we found ourselves equally (if more happily) lost in rethinking the history of the continent. Why *not* think big? we asked. Why not try to reconceive North American history outside the usual periodization, over a long period of time, as historians have done in writing about Europe or Asia or Africa? What great themes, playing out over centuries, could organize such a large narrative?

Not surprisingly given our previous work, we turned to questions of war and empire. Soon we were exchanging drafts of an essay setting out the basic terms of interpretation that grew into a long academic paper that we presented at the annual meeting of the Institute of Early American History and Culture (IEAHC) in the summer of 1996. Although it was only later, at the annual meeting of the American Historical Association in January 2000, that we hit upon the idea of organizing our narrative around the lives of individuals, the IEAHC conference gave us the faith that we actually could write this book.

John Murrin is in many ways the intellectual godfather of the project. Little in this volume will surprise John because he has known most of it for years. At the 1996 IEAHC conference, he offered helpful (and, as always with him, hilarious) comments on the outline of our argument. We drew on that advice for years after, and indeed continue to do so; as we did on his later suggestion that we include a chapter on Penn—a suggestion for which we continue to be grateful, notwithstanding the extra work it caused. Pauline Maier, who was unable to attend the conference but provided an invaluable written critique of the paper, may be surprised to learn that in chiding us for having slighted the contingency and human drama of history in our paper, she started us on the path toward the narrative strategy that structures this book. Again, much more work resulted; but we hope she will think the effort has not been altogether wasted. The third IEAHC panelist, Daniel Richter, gave a brilliant comment that helped us see how much our narrative would benefit from more systematic attention to both Canada and Mexico. Later, when he became the director of the McNeil Center at the University of Pennsylvania, he did us the enormous favor of inviting us to present our work to a helpful and sympathetic audience. Dan's friendship has been indispensable to us, both personally and professionally, and it is a pleasure to acknowledge it here.

Two other historians were critical in the gestation of *The Dominion of War*. Reid Mitchell suggested that a book we had once imagined ending in 1917 might benefit from being extended to the end of the twentieth century. It was his view that the Spanish-American War could be taken as the beginning of an age of intervention. We hope that he will regard it as indicative of our very real gratitude when he finds how shamelessly we incorporated his idea in our scheme. John Shy, one of the few historians who has taken war's effects on American development seriously, would have been an inspiration to us even if his scholarship had not deeply influenced our understanding of war and its consequences. We appreciate John's generosity of spirit and continuing interest in this project more than we can say.

In May 2002, we were blessed with a month at the Rockefeller Foundation's Study Center in Bellagio, Italy. This made it possible for us to write, exchange drafts, and talk about the project at length. As anyone who has experienced the beauty of Villa Serbelloni, the friendship and hospitality of Gianna Celli, and the attentive care of her expert staff will attest, a month like the one we had on the lovely banks of Lake Como can be the experience of an academic lifetime. To our delight, our fellow inmates—especially Ellen and Fran Voigt, Jim and Lyra Cobb, Ibrahim Ado-Kurawa, Prathibha Karanth, Ruth Macklin, Rebecca West, Bill Tait, Joseph Harris, Monika Totten, Sharon and Elie Shenhav, Karen Press, Kristin Jones, Andrew Ginzel, Lou Mallozzi, Sandra Binion, Antonia Contro, and Gordon and Susan Conway—became friends of this book as well as its authors. We, in turn, gained enormous benefit from the opportunity to learn about their disciplines, cultures, and passions.

At the March 2004 meeting of the Organization of American Historians in Boston, Eric Foner, Kathleen Brown, David Montejano, and Michael Sherry paid us the compliment of taking our work seriously. Their comments were so helpful that we spent the next six weeks doing our best to respond to them in our final revisions. We deeply appreciate the rigor and candor of their responses, and the care they took in reading a forbiddingly large manuscript. We also took heart from the questions of an overflow audience of historians who seemed eager to engage the arguments we were trying to make.

Lisa Adams, our indefatigable agent and friend (who, together with her equally wonderful partner David Miller, comprises one-half of the Garamond Agency) has been steadfast in her enthusiasm for our project and in support of its authors. She has so often gone so much more than the extra mile for this book that we can safely say no one could have done more for it, or for us. Our editor at Viking, Jane Von Mehren, enthusiastically supported our work from her initial encounter with it in the form of a proposal through the final stages of writing and revision, despite a change in position and heavy increases in her professional and family responsibilities. Jennifer Ehmann helped guide the book to completion, and Brett Kelly did all that was needful to speed it on its way. Senior Development Editor Beena Kamlani and copyeditor David Hawkins did us any number of good turns. We are similarly grateful for the thoughtful attention the design of the book received from Ellen Cipriano and its cover received from Paul Buckley and Jon Gray.

Fred Anderson would like to thank colleagues and friends at the University of Colorado, Boulder, including Gloria Lund Main, Robert Ferry, Mark Pittenger, Robert and Martha Hanna, Matthew Gerber, Ralph Mann, Susan Kingsley Kent, Julia Greene, and Jeffrey Cox. The denizens of other institutions, as well—John Grenier at the U.S. Air Force Academy; Steven Epstein at the University of Kansas; Philip Deloria at the University of Michigan; Kevin Keane, Bill Griswold, and Arthur Worrall of Colorado State University; Eric Hinderaker at the University of Utah; Brian DeLay at Harvard; Don Higginbotham at the University of North Carolina, Chapel Hill; and Ian Steele of the University of Western Ontario—have all added in their own ways (some more direct than others) to this project. Fred is also grateful to the institutions that have provided financial support, particularly the University of Colorado, where Provost Philip DiStefano and Dean Todd Gleason have been of great aid; to the Charles Warren Center at Harvard University; and to the John Simon Guggenheim Memorial Foundation.

Drew Cayton happily acknowledges the advice, encouragement, and doubts of P. Renée Baernstein, Wietse de Boer, Curt Ellison, Dan Goffman, Carolyn Goffman, Charlotte Newman Goldy, Matthew Gordon, Susan Gray, Jack Kirby, Stephen Norris, Carla Pestana, Bradley Schrager, Peggy Shaffer, Fredrika Teute, Bob Thurston, Allan Winkler, and Peter Williams. Jeri Schaner once again demonstrated why the History Department at Miami University is lucky to have the most efficient administrative assistant in the world. Dozens of students at Miami University, especially those enrolled in "The Conquest of Mexico City" and "The Early American Republic" during the Spring 2004 semester, wrestled with the issues addressed in *The Dominion of War* and offered useful suggestions—and warnings. Irene Kleiman and Marj Nadler helped Drew think about narrative while making sure he did not take himself *too* seriously. And without Jenny Jennings, *The Dominion of War* would have concluded with the death of George Washington.

Over the past decade, we have become proficient at answering our colleagues' most common question, "What is it like to collaborate?" We answer that it has proven a source of both pleasure and enlightenment and that our friendship has deepened as our collaboration has progressed. While Fred drafted the first four chapters, Drew the last five, and both of us together wrote the introduction and epilogue, we have revised them all so many times we cannot begin to tell where one's ideas or one's prose ends and the other's begins. As we have been delighted to learn, collaboration on such terms allows us to divide equally the blame for whatever errors of fact and argument this book may contain.

No one (except perhaps the authors) is happier to see this book completed than Virginia DeJohn Anderson and Mary Kupiec Cayton. For too many years, they have tolerated our long phone calls, extended walks in the Rocky Mountains, endless suppers at conferences, and impromptu seminars on whatever aspect of the project was agitating us at the moment—even in such unlikely settings as Siena, where our preoccupation threatened to interrupt the rather more important enterprise of finding the head of Saint Catherine. More important, their questions and comments have decisively influenced the arguments and structure of this book. Of all the people who have advised us on how to proceed, none has been wiser than Virginia and Mary.

Samuel Anderson, Elizabeth Cayton, and Hannah Cayton know us more as fathers than as historians, which is on balance a good thing. No doubt they will not want to know that a considerable portion of the conversations that produced the *The Dominion of War* were actually about them. But it is true nevertheless. So it is entirely fitting that their names should appear at the beginning of a volume that grew while they grew, creating in us a hope for the future that all the books in the world could not give. This book is theirs, with love.

Index

Page numbers in *italics* refer to illustrations.